YOWAMUSHI PEDAL

WATARU WATANABE

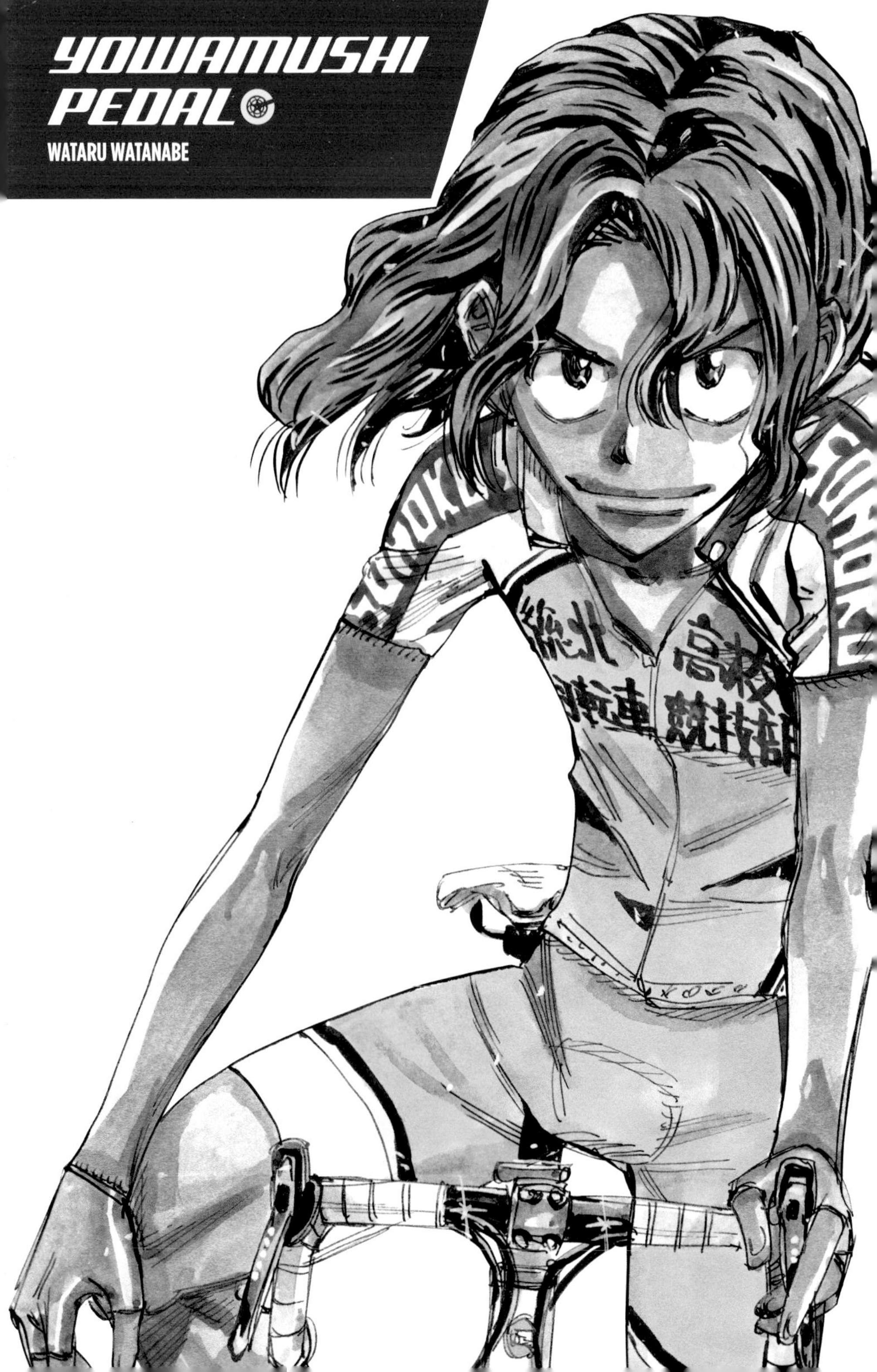

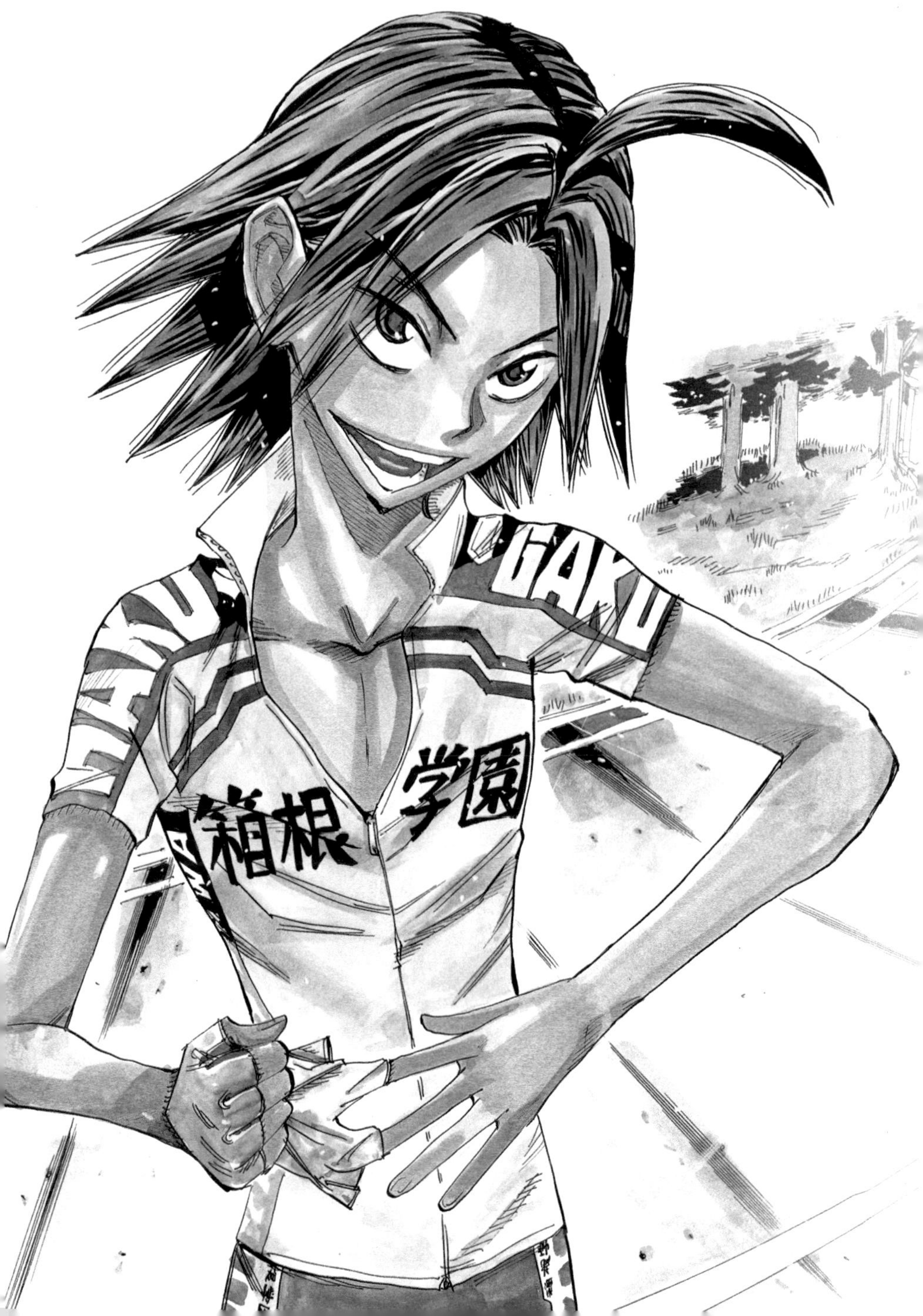
GAKU
箱根学園

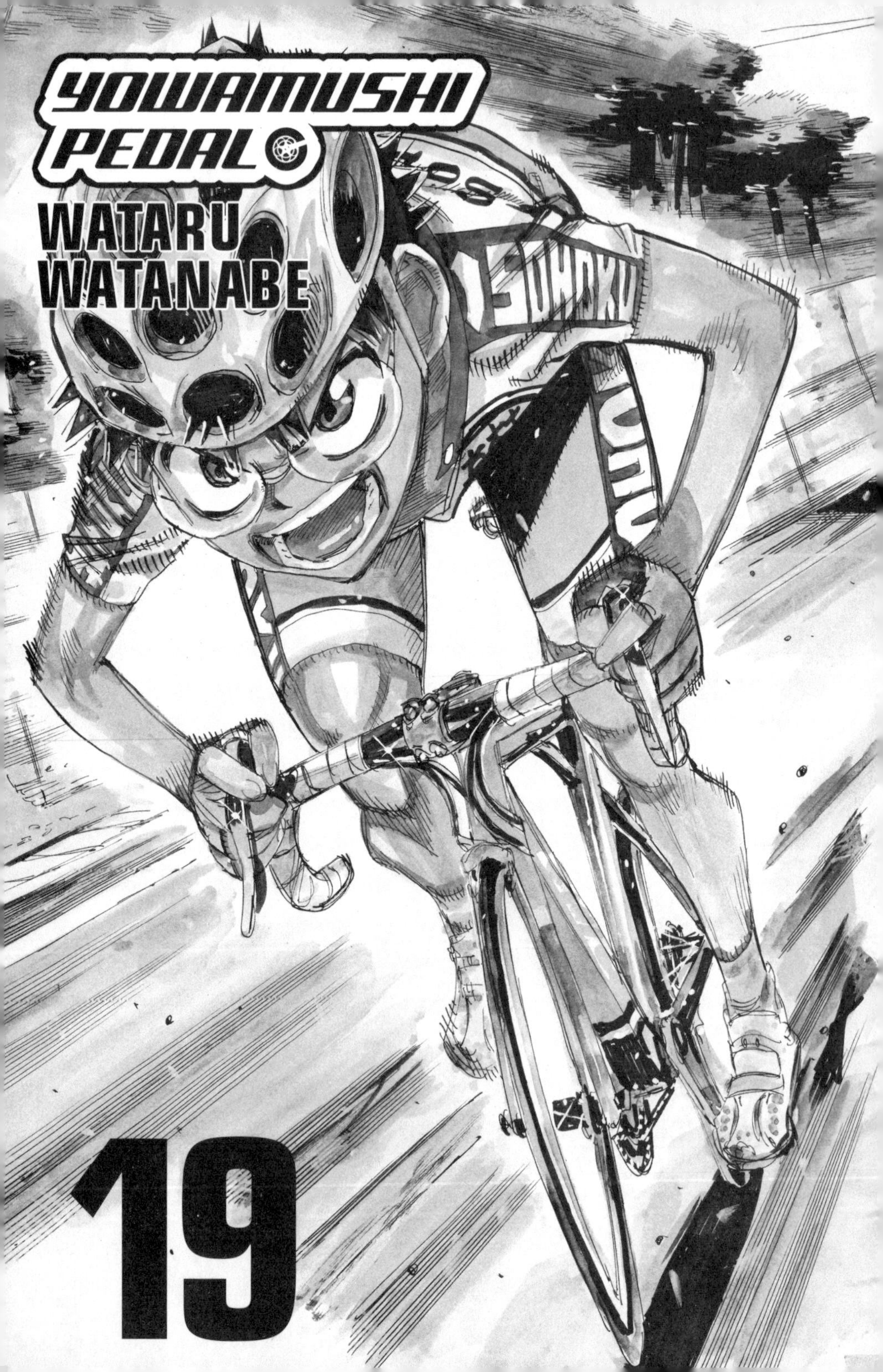
YOWAMUSHI PEDAL
WATARU WATANABE
19

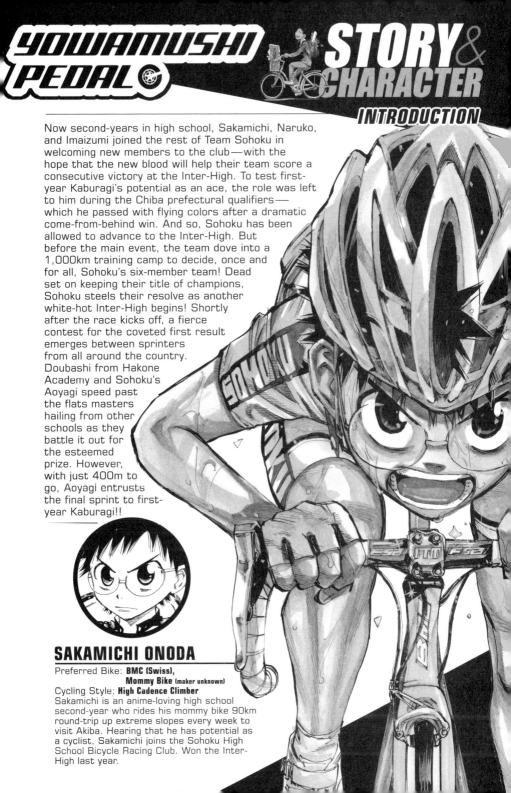

YOWAMUSHI PEDAL

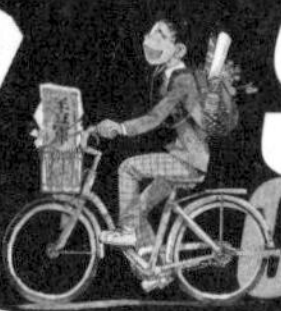

STORY & CHARACTER INTRODUCTION

Now second-years in high school, Sakamichi, Naruko, and Imaizumi joined the rest of Team Sohoku in welcoming new members to the club—with the hope that the new blood will help their team score a consecutive victory at the Inter-High. To test first-year Kaburagi's potential as an ace, the role was left to him during the Chiba prefectural qualifiers—which he passed with flying colors after a dramatic come-from-behind win. And so, Sohoku has been allowed to advance to the Inter-High. But before the main event, the team dove into a 1,000km training camp to decide, once and for all, Sohoku's six-member team! Dead set on keeping their title of champions, Sohoku steels their resolve as another white-hot Inter-High begins! Shortly after the race kicks off, a fierce contest for the coveted first result emerges between sprinters from all around the country. Doubashi from Hakone Academy and Sohoku's Aoyagi speed past the flats masters hailing from other schools as they battle it out for the esteemed prize. However, with just 400m to go, Aoyagi entrusts the final sprint to first-year Kaburagi!!

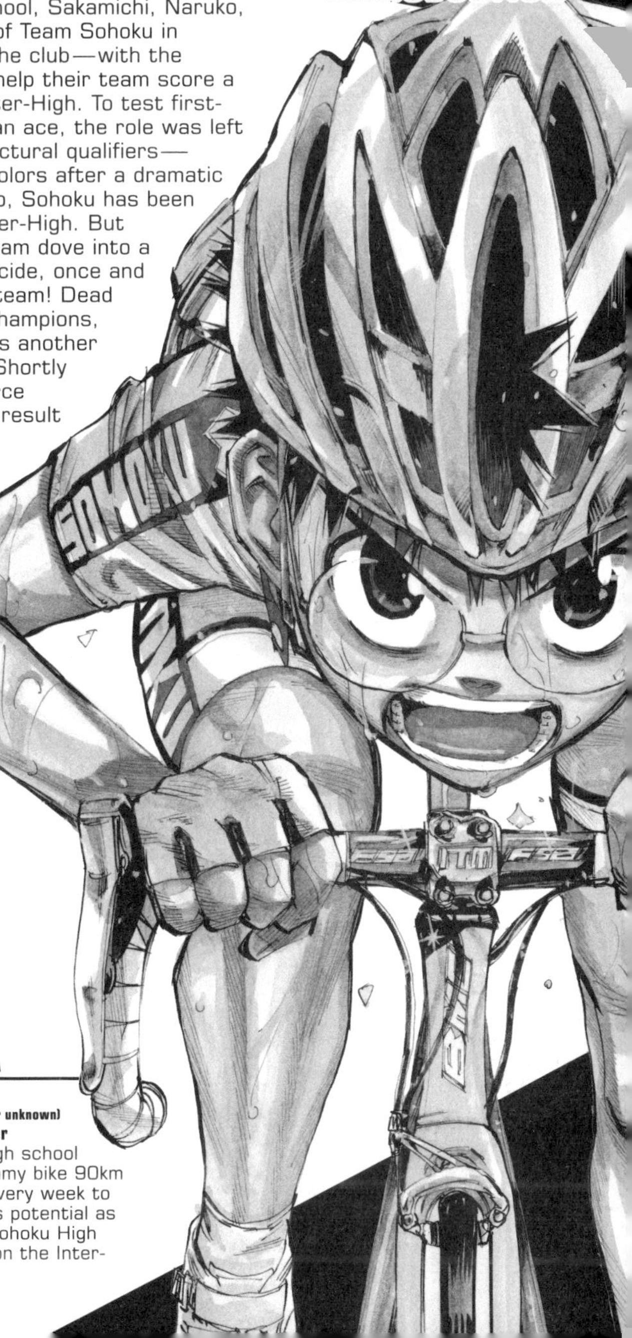
SOHOKU

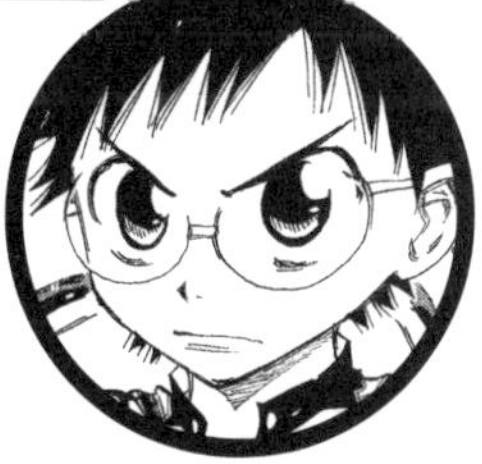

SAKAMICHI ONODA

Preferred Bike: **BMC (Swiss), Mommy Bike** (maker unknown)

Cycling Style: **High Cadence Climber**

Sakamichi is an anime-loving high school second-year who rides his mommy bike 90km round-trip up extreme slopes every week to visit Akiba. Hearing that he has potential as a cyclist, Sakamichi joins the Sohoku High School Bicycle Racing Club. Won the Inter-High last year.

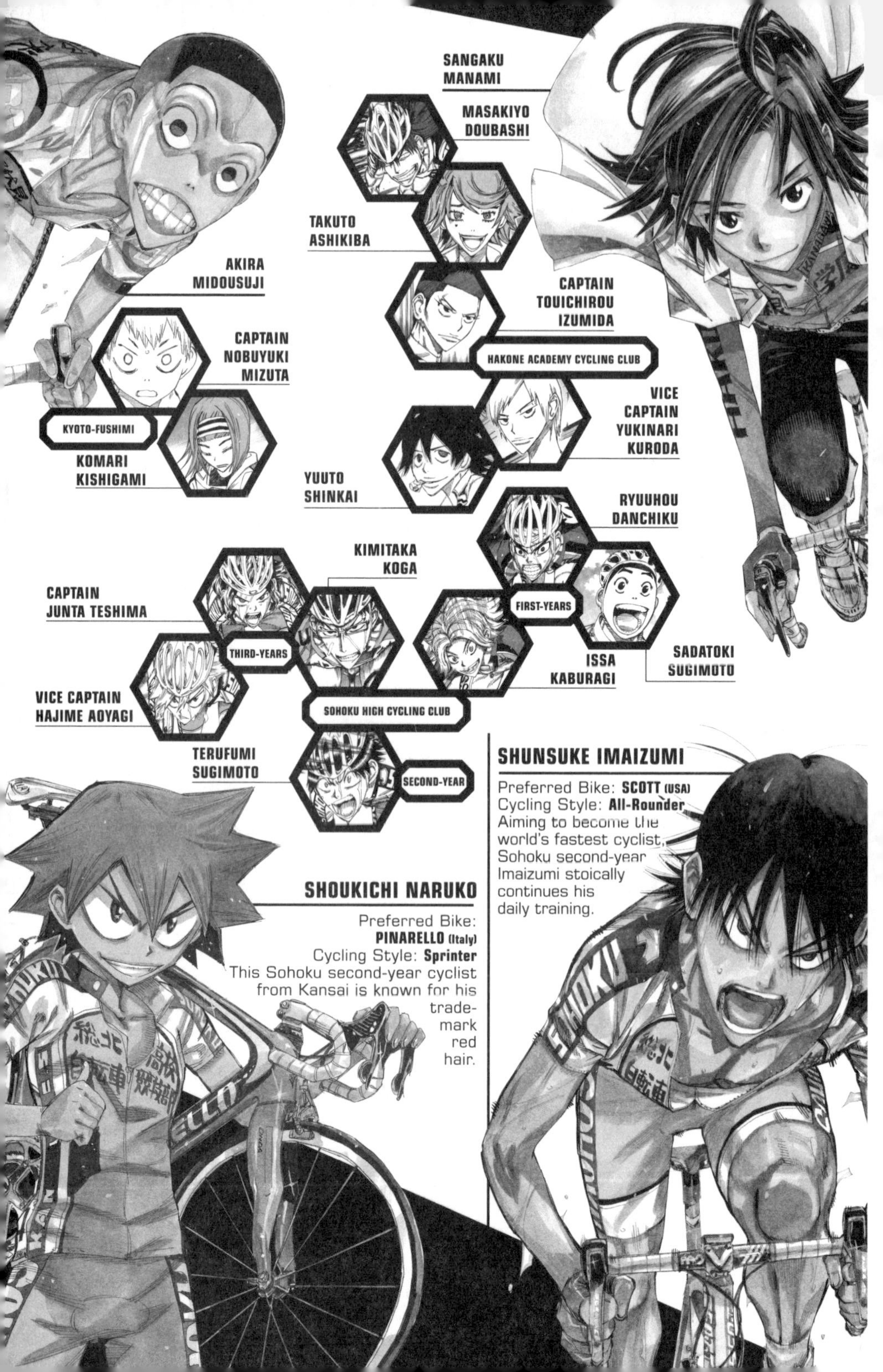
SANGAKU MANAMI
MASAKIYO DOUBASHI
TAKUTO ASHIKIBA
CAPTAIN TOUICHIROU IZUMIDA
HAKONE ACADEMY CYCLING CLUB
VICE CAPTAIN YUKINARI KURODA
YUUTO SHINKAI
AKIRA MIDOUSUJI
CAPTAIN NOBUYUKI MIZUTA
KYOTO-FUSHIMI
KOMARI KISHIGAMI
RYUUHOU DANCHIKU
FIRST-YEARS
SADATOKI SUGIMOTO
ISSA KABURAGI
KIMITAKA KOGA
CAPTAIN JUNTA TESHIMA
THIRD-YEARS
VICE CAPTAIN HAJIME AOYAGI
SOHOKU HIGH CYCLING CLUB
TERUFUMI SUGIMOTO
SECOND-YEAR
SHUNSUKE IMAIZUMI
Preferred Bike: SCOTT (USA)
Cycling Style: All-Rounder
Aiming to become the world's fastest cyclist, Sohoku second-year Imaizumi stoically continues his daily training.
SHOUKICHI NARUKO
Preferred Bike: PINARELLO (Italy)
Cycling Style: Sprinter
This Sohoku second-year cyclist from Kansai is known for his trade-mark red hair.

VOL.19 YOWAMUSHI PEDAL CONTENTS

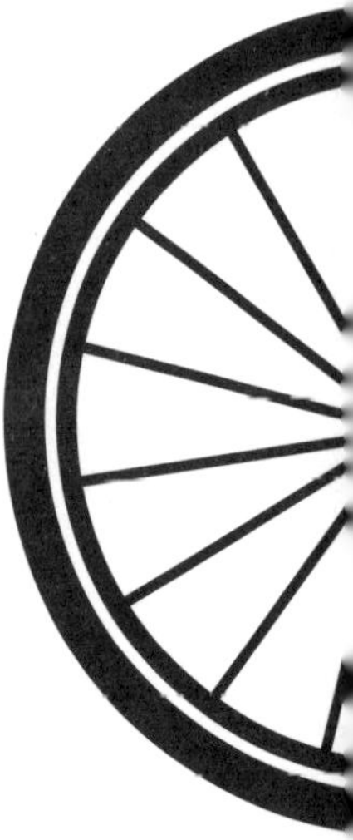

YOWAMUSHI PEDAL

RIDE.312 THE TWO SPRINTERS

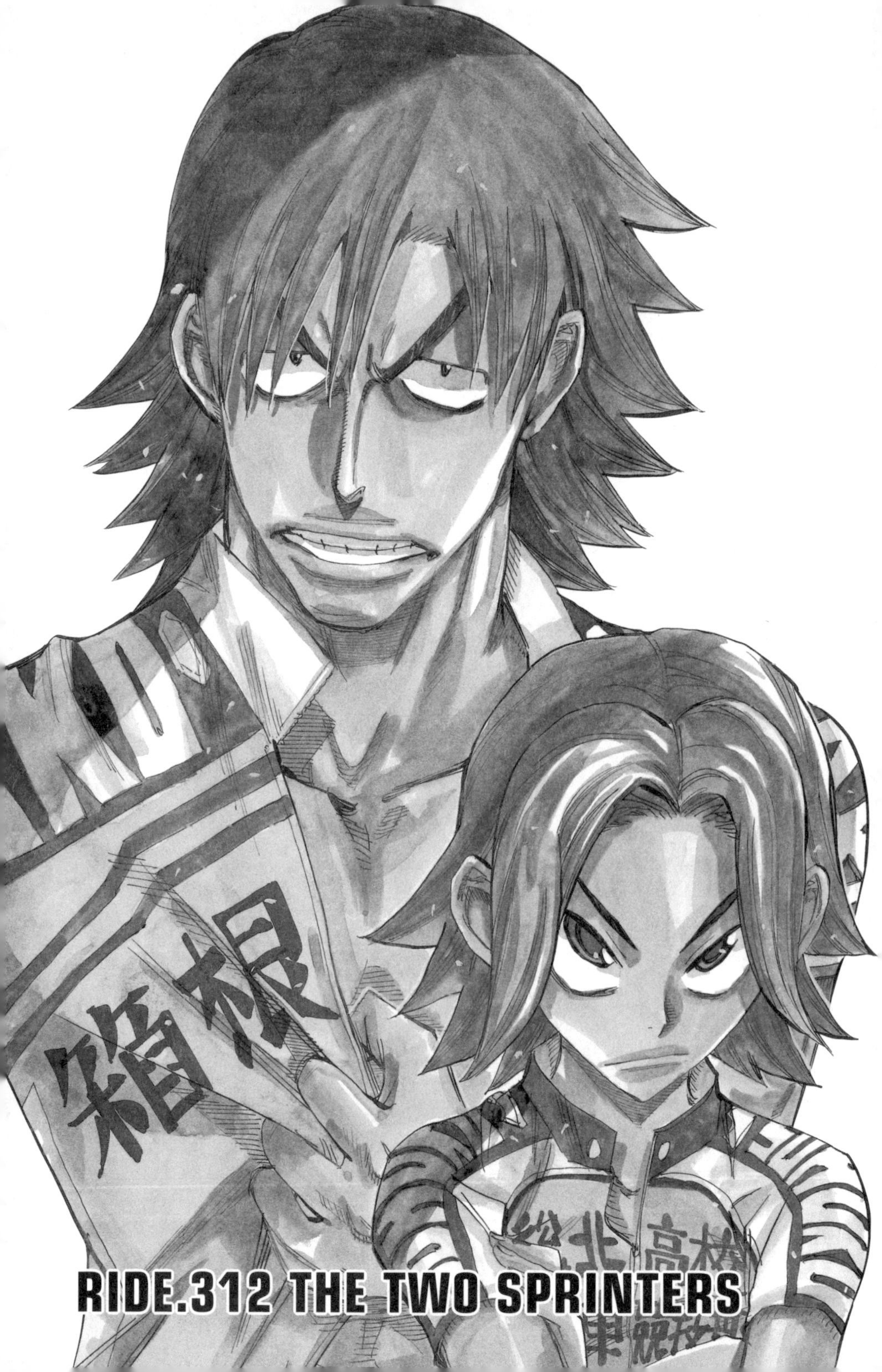
箱根
総北高校

MESSAGE

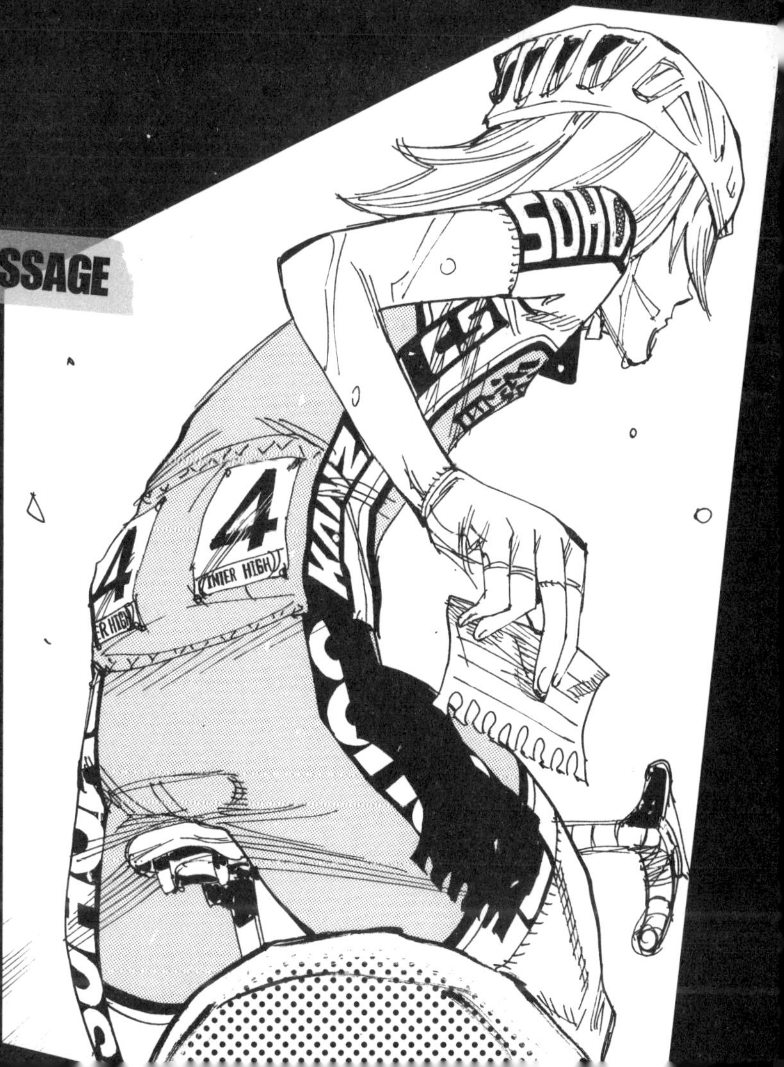
4
INTER HIGH

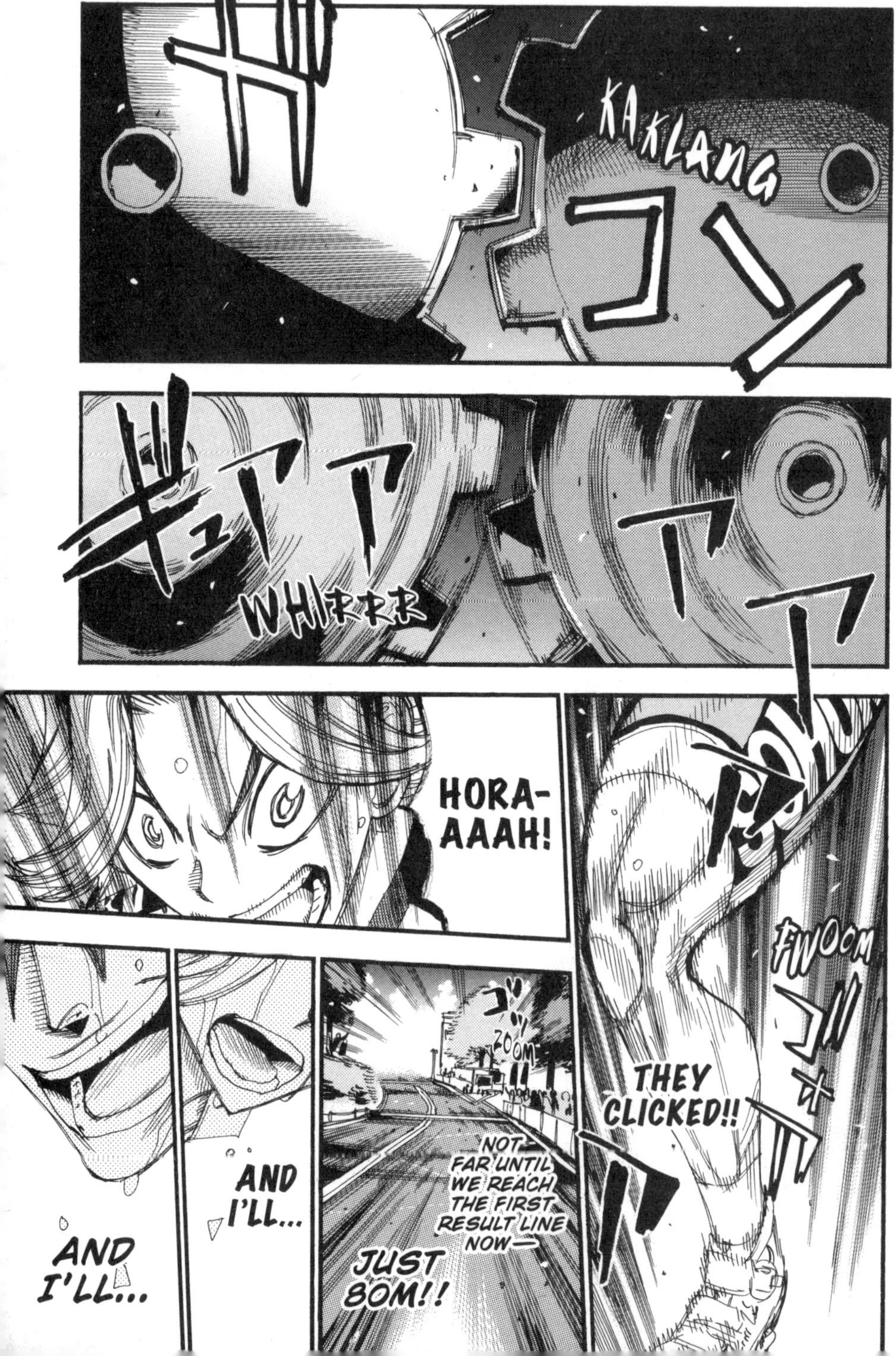

KAKLANG
コン
ガ
アア
ギュア
WHIRRR
FWOOM
ゴッ
THEY CLICKED!!
HORA-AAAH!
ゴッ
ZOOM
NOT FAR UNTIL WE REACH THE FIRST RESULT LINE NOW—
JUST 80M!!
AND I'LL...
AND I'LL...

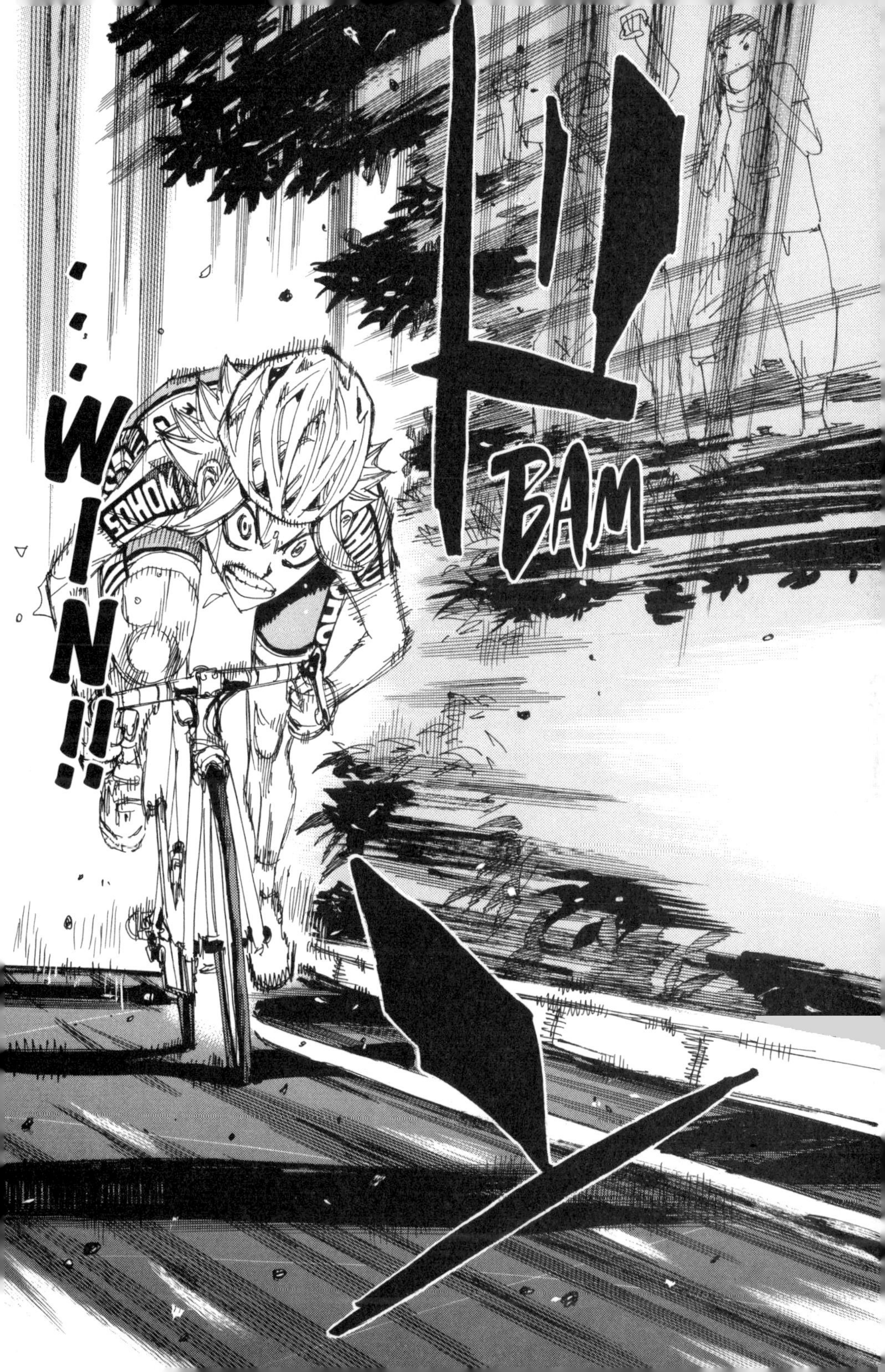
...WIN!!
BAM

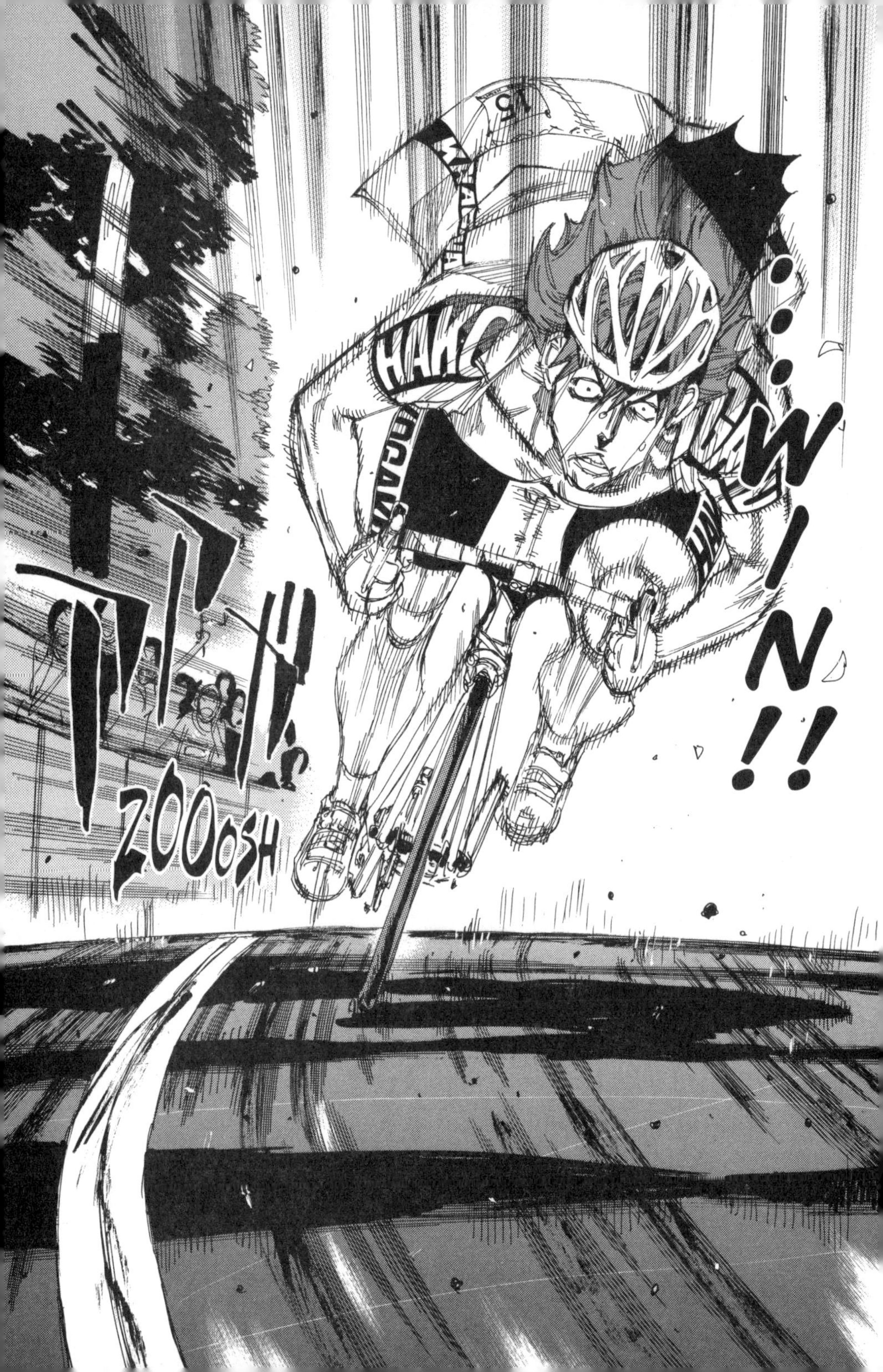
...WIN!!
ZOOOSH

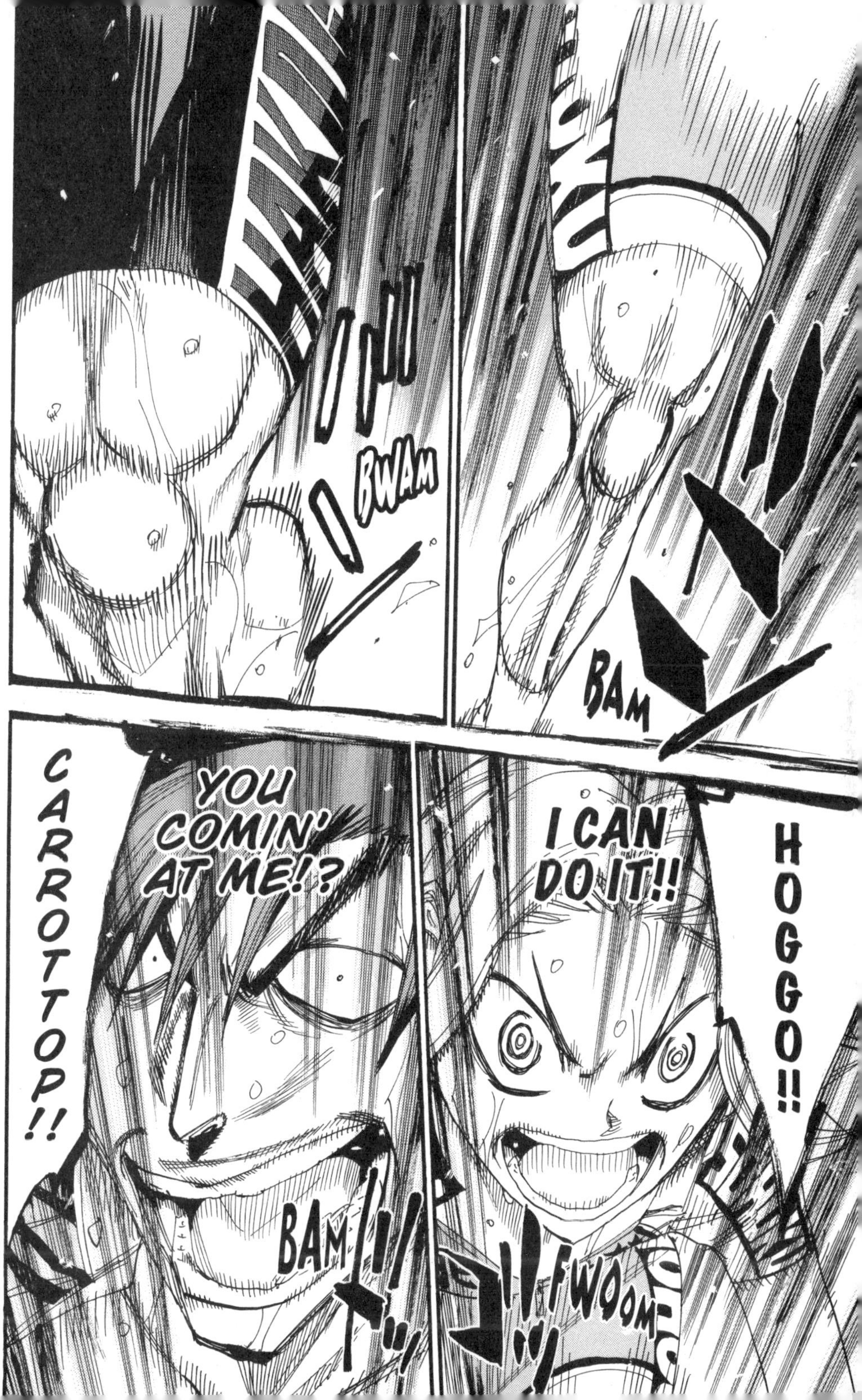
BAM
BWAM
HOGGO!!
I CAN DO IT!!
FWOOM
CARROTTOP!!
YOU COMIN' AT ME!?
BAM

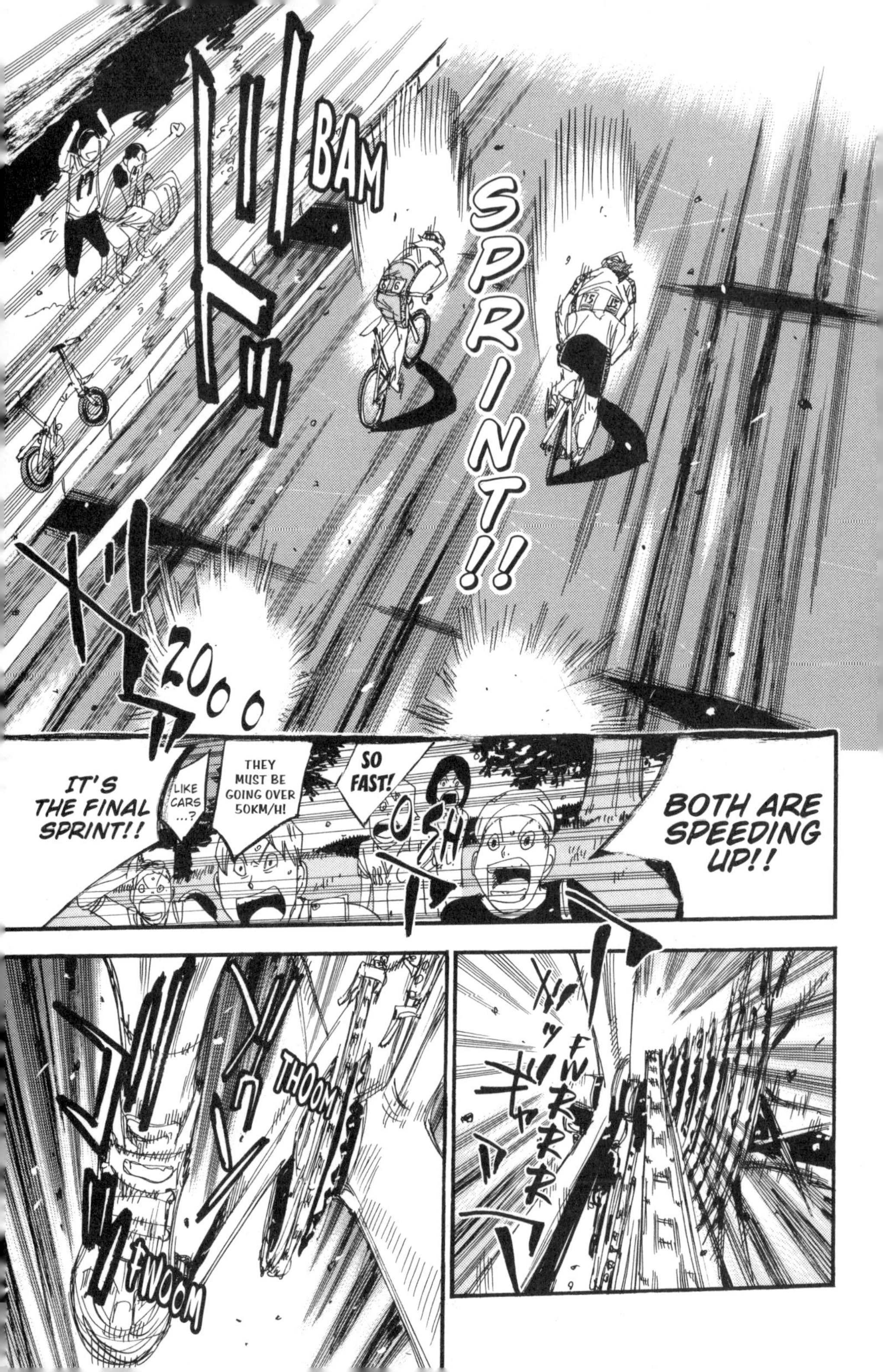
BAM
SPRINT!!
ZOOO
BOTH ARE SPEEDING UP!!
SO FAST!
THEY MUST BE GOING OVER 50KM/H!
LIKE CARS ...?
IT'S THE FINAL SPRINT!!
FWRRRR
THOOM
FWOOM

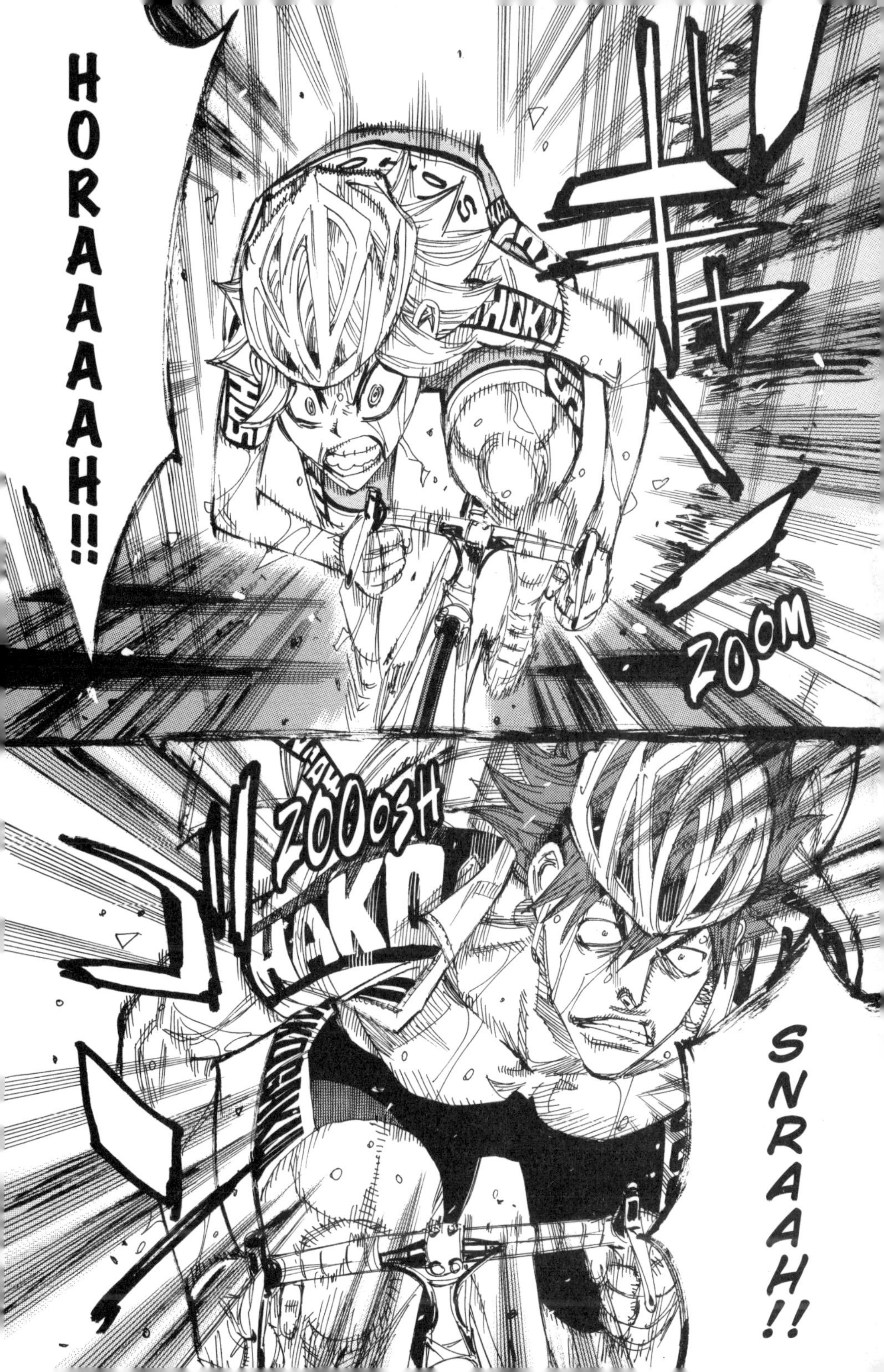
ZOOM
HORAAAAAH!!
ZOOOSH
SNRAAAH!!

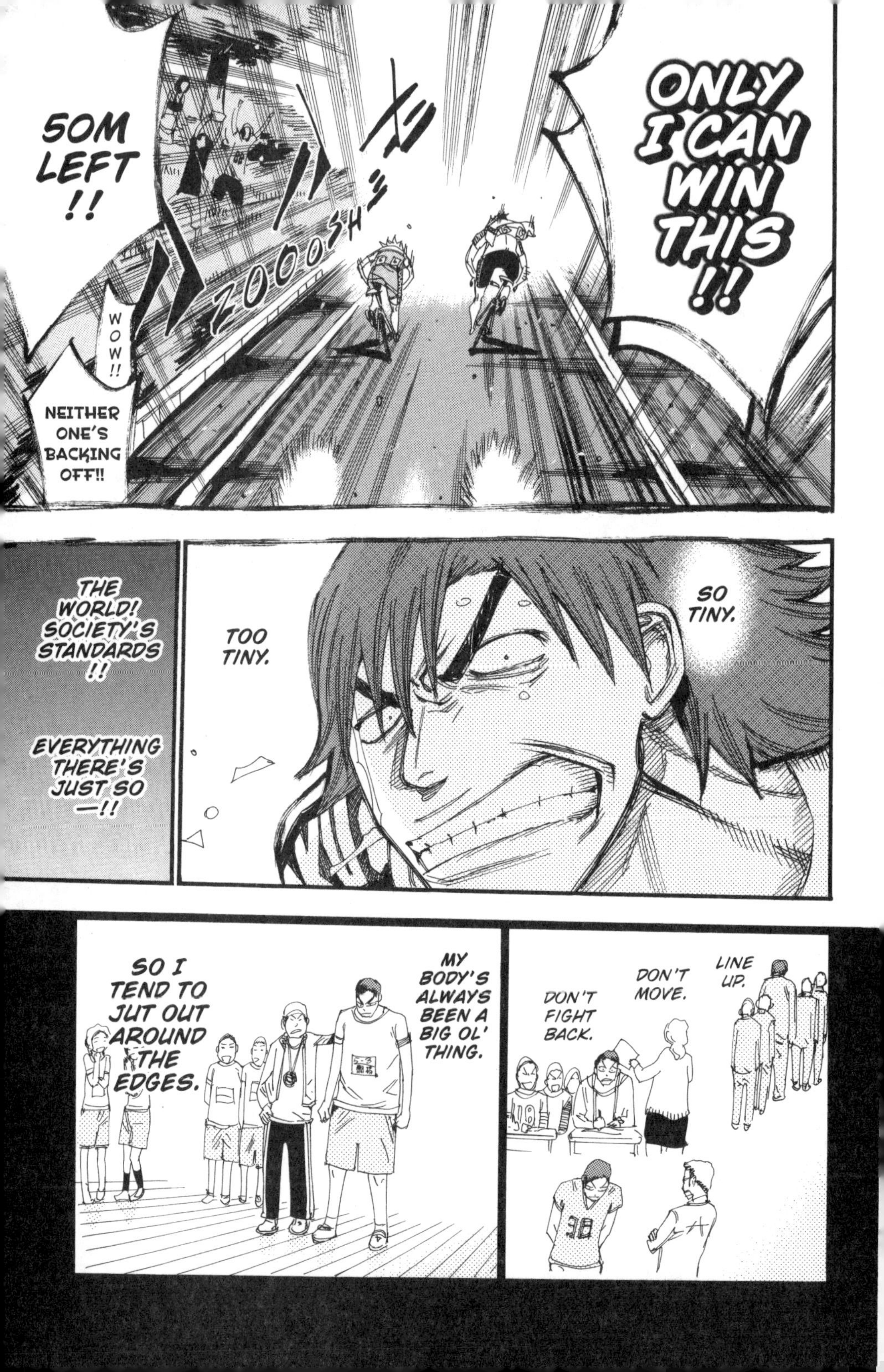
ONLY I CAN WIN THIS!!
50M LEFT!!
ZOOOOSH
WOW!!
NEITHER ONE'S BACKING OFF!!
SO TINY.
TOO TINY.
THE WORLD! SOCIETY'S STANDARDS!!
EVERYTHING THERE'S JUST SO—!!
LINE UP.
DON'T MOVE.
DON'T FIGHT BACK.
MY BODY'S ALWAYS BEEN A BIG OL' THING.
SO I TEND TO JUT OUT AROUND THE EDGES.

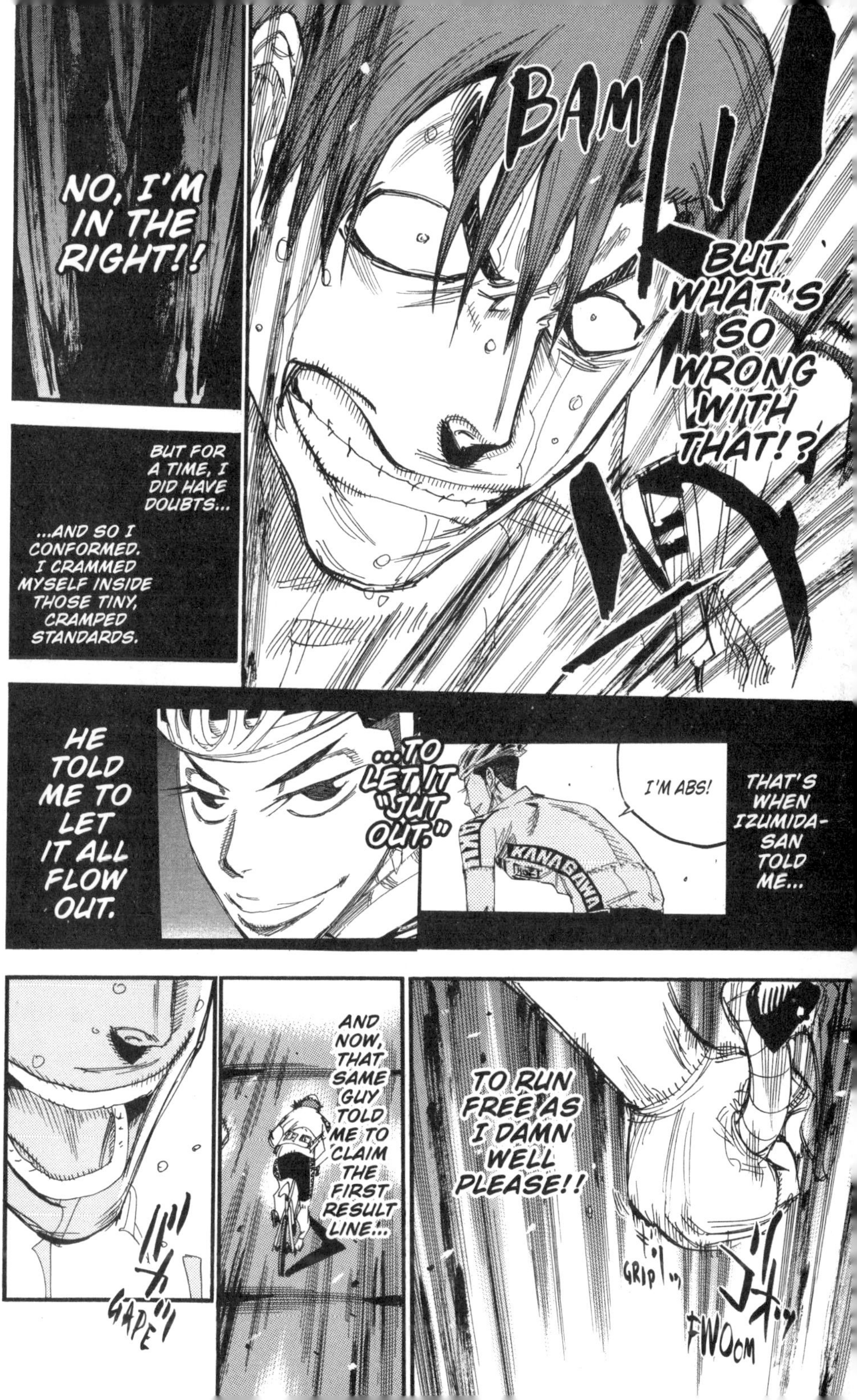
BAM
BUT WHAT'S SO WRONG WITH THAT!?
NO, I'M IN THE RIGHT!!
BUT FOR A TIME, I DID HAVE DOUBTS...
...AND SO I CONFORMED. I CRAMMED MYSELF INSIDE THOSE TINY, CRAMPED STANDARDS.
THAT'S WHEN IZUMIDA-SAN TOLD ME...
I'M ABS!
KANAGAWA
...TO LET IT "JUT OUT."
HE TOLD ME TO LET IT ALL FLOW OUT.
TO RUN FREE AS I DAMN WELL PLEASE!!
GRIP
FWOOM
AND NOW, THAT SAME GUY TOLD ME TO CLAIM THE FIRST RESULT LINE...
GAPE

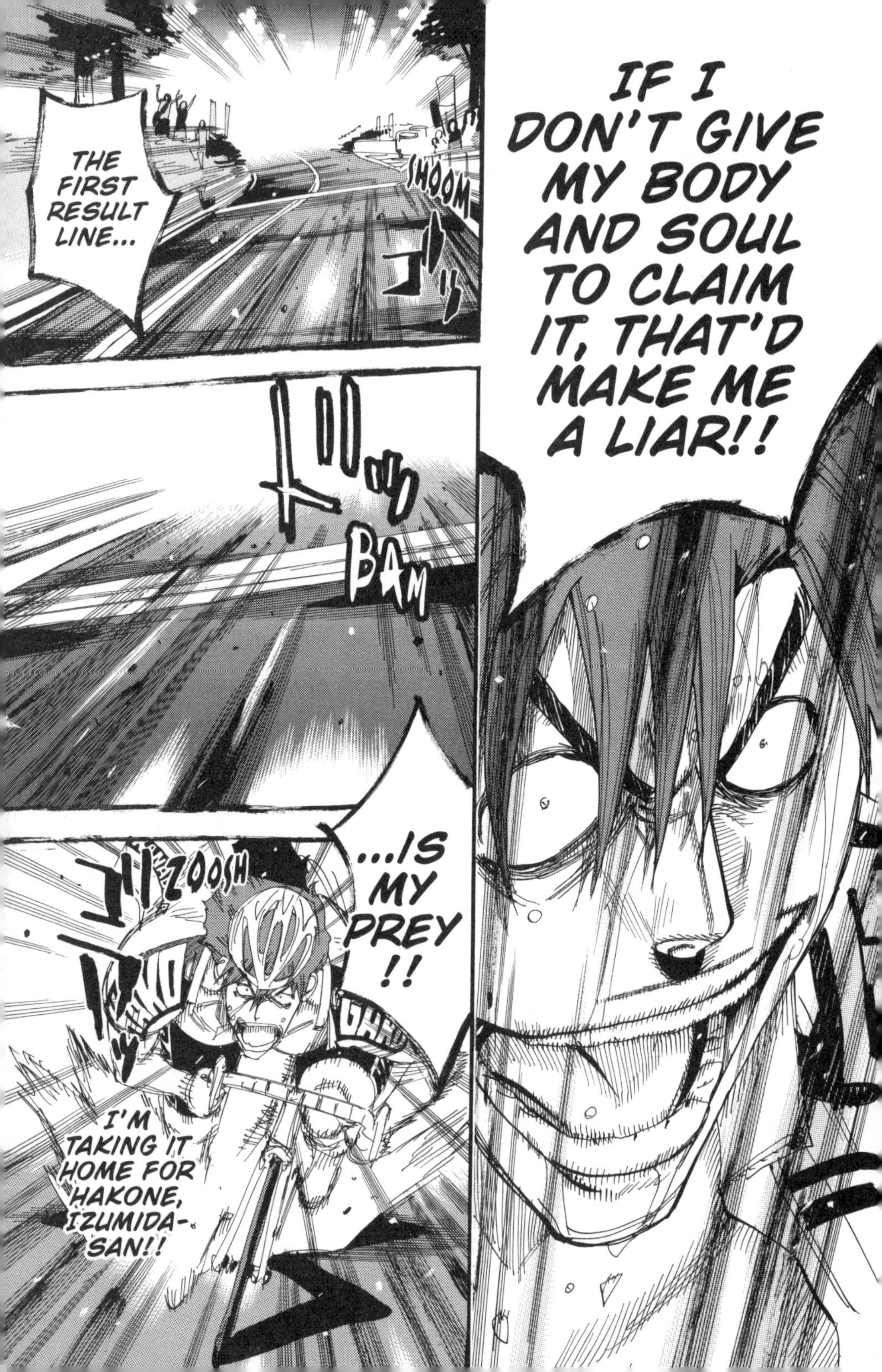
IF I DON'T GIVE MY BODY AND SOUL TO CLAIM IT, THAT'D MAKE ME A LIAR!!
SHOOM
THE FIRST RESULT LINE...
BAM
...IS MY PREY!!
ZOOSH
I'M TAKING IT HOME FOR HAKONE, IZUMIDA-SAN!!

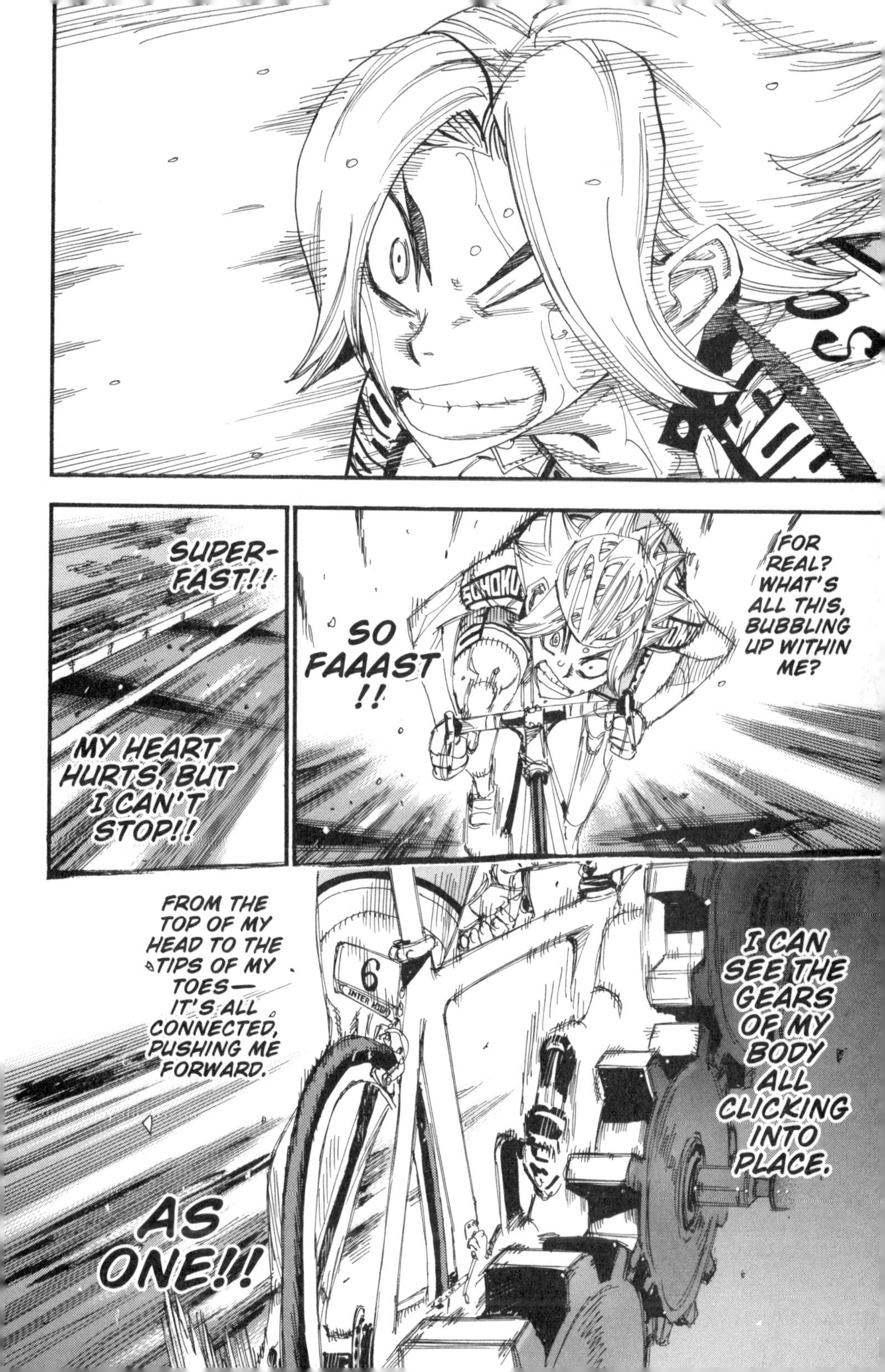
FOR REAL? WHAT'S ALL THIS, BUBBLING UP WITHIN ME?
SO FAAAST!!
SUPER-FAST!!
MY HEART HURTS, BUT I CAN'T STOP!!
I CAN SEE THE GEARS OF MY BODY ALL CLICKING INTO PLACE.
FROM THE TOP OF MY HEAD TO THE TIPS OF MY TOES— IT'S ALL CONNECTED, PUSHING ME FORWARD.
AS ONE!!!

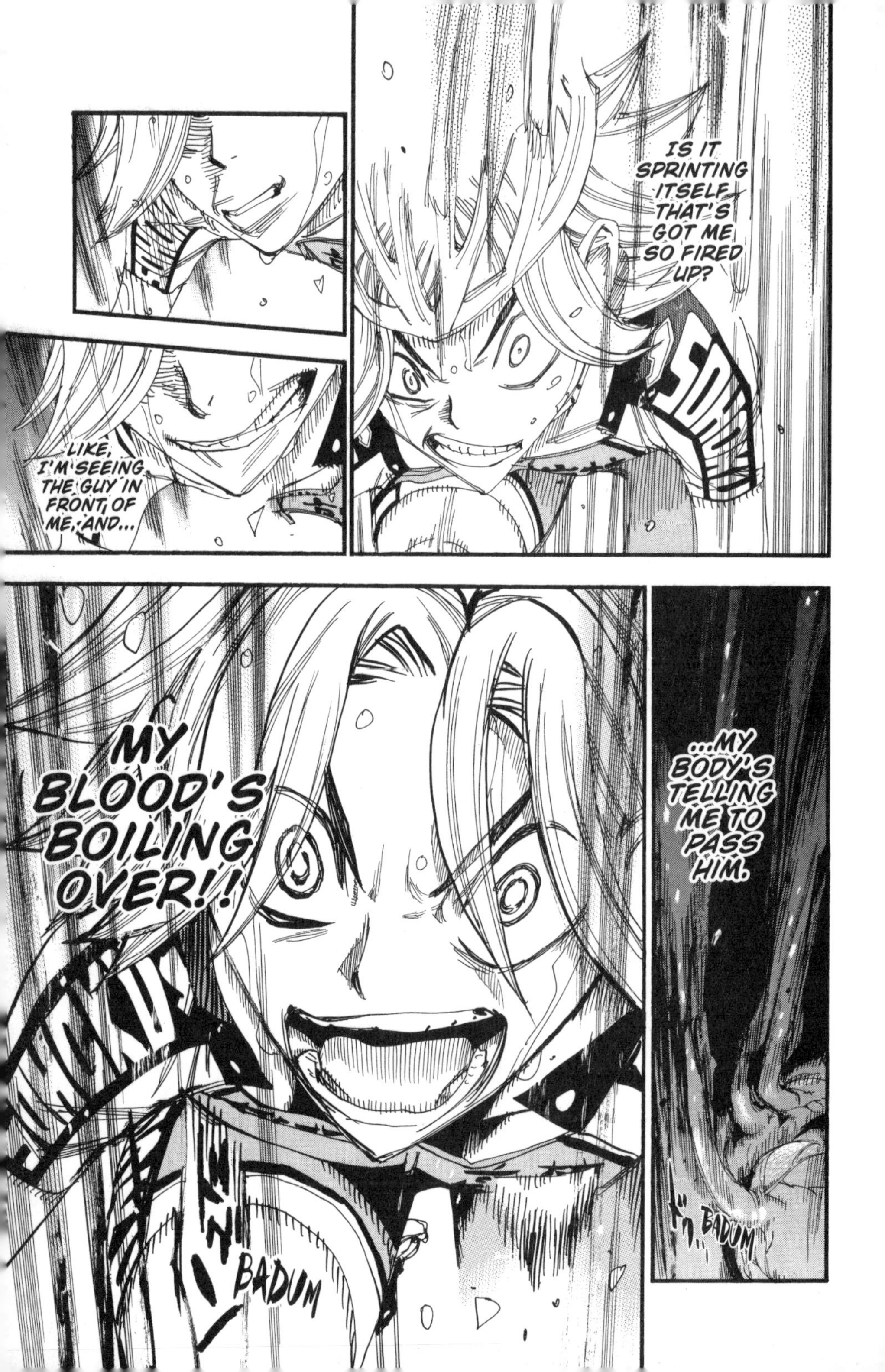
IS IT SPRINTING ITSELF THAT'S GOT ME SO FIRED UP?
LIKE, I'M SEEING THE GUY IN FRONT OF ME, AND...
...MY BODY'S TELLING ME TO PASS HIM.
BADUM
MY BLOOD'S BOILING OVER!!
BADUM

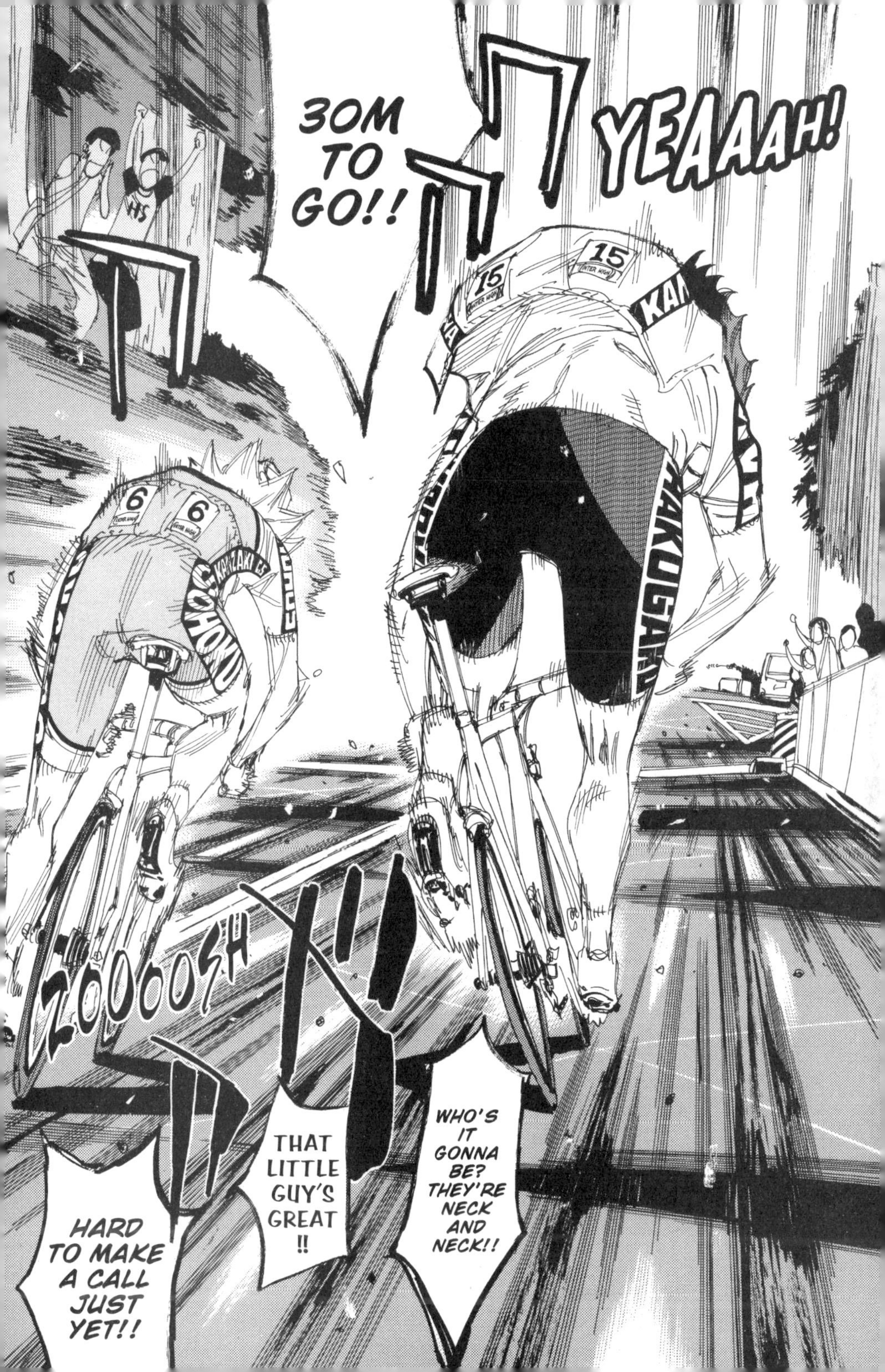
YEAAAH!
30M TO GO!!
ZOOOOSH
WHO'S IT GONNA BE? THEY'RE NECK AND NECK!!
THAT LITTLE GUY'S GREAT!!
HARD TO MAKE A CALL JUST YET!!

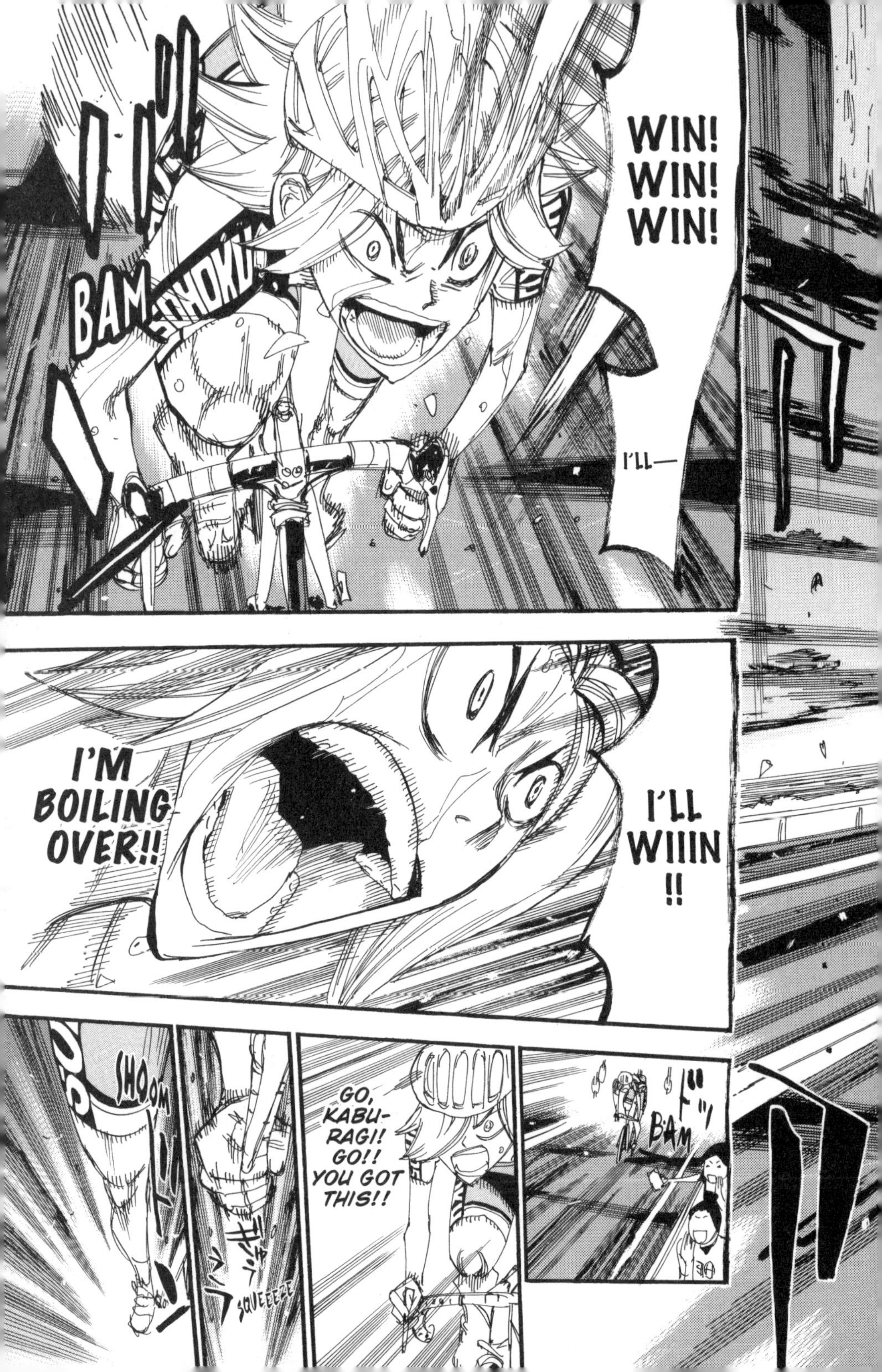

WIN! WIN! WIN!
I'LL—
BAM
I'LL WIIIN!!
I'M BOILING OVER!!
BAM
GO, KABURAGI! GO!! YOU GOT THIS!!
SQUEEEZE
SHOOM

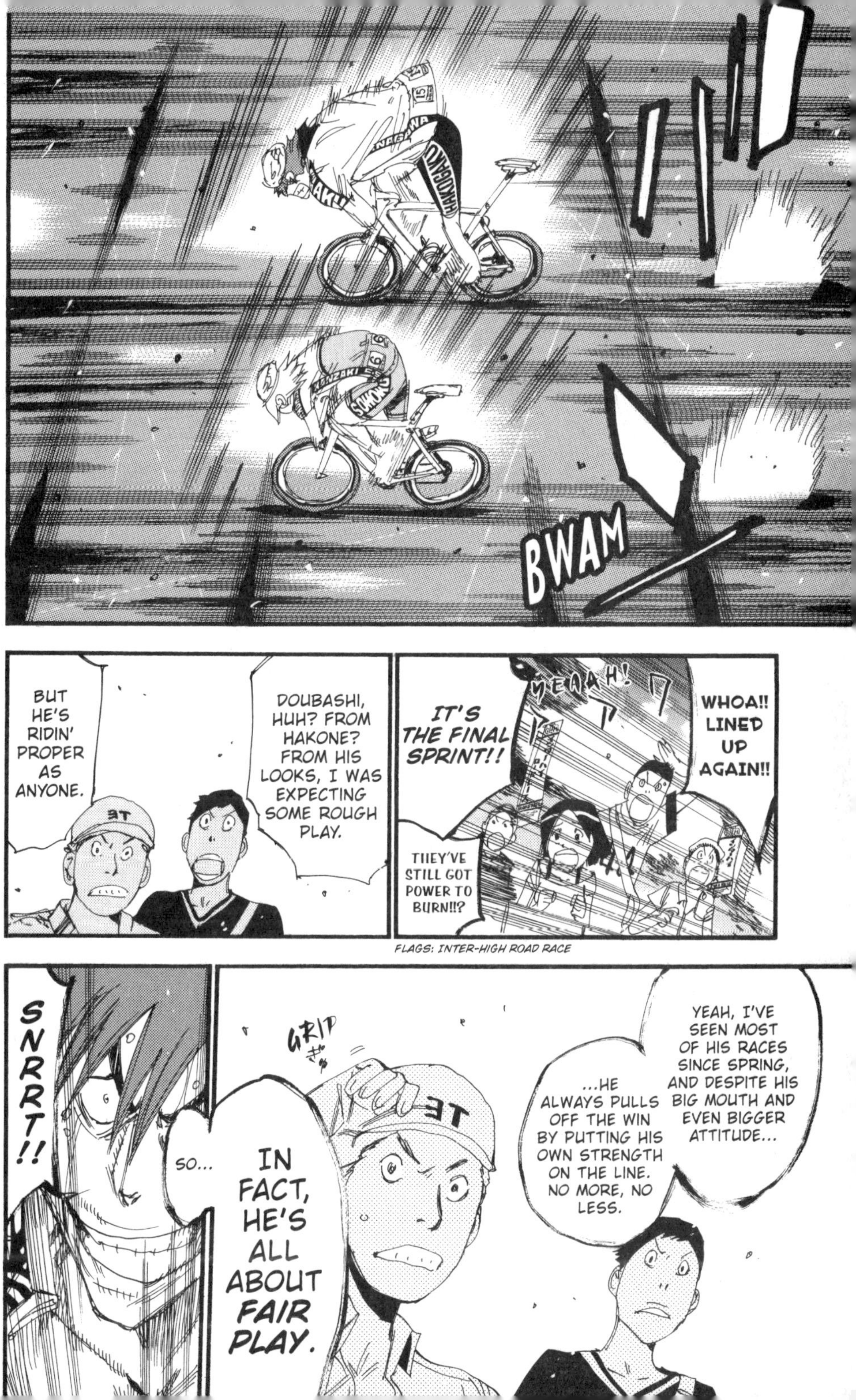
BWAM
WHOA!! LINED UP AGAIN!!
YEAAH!
IT'S THE FINAL SPRINT!!
THEY'VE STILL GOT POWER TO BURN!!?
DOUBASHI, HUH? FROM HAKONE? FROM HIS LOOKS, I WAS EXPECTING SOME ROUGH PLAY.
BUT HE'S RIDIN' PROPER AS ANYONE.
FLAGS: INTER-HIGH ROAD RACE
YEAH, I'VE SEEN MOST OF HIS RACES SINCE SPRING, AND DESPITE HIS BIG MOUTH AND EVEN BIGGER ATTITUDE...
...HE ALWAYS PULLS OFF THE WIN BY PUTTING HIS OWN STRENGTH ON THE LINE. NO MORE, NO LESS.
GRIP
IN FACT, HE'S ALL ABOUT FAIR PLAY.
SO...
SNRRT!!

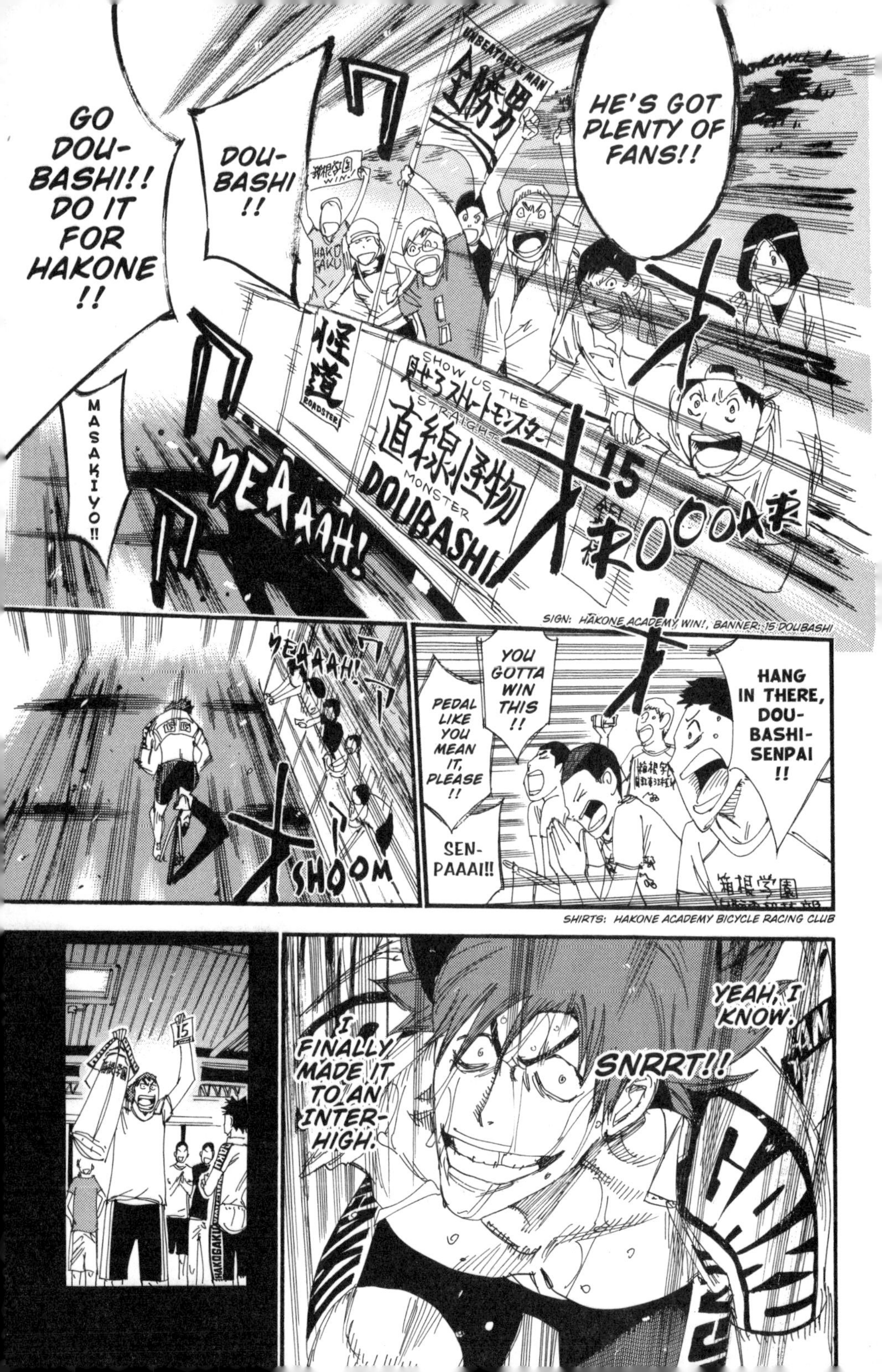
HE'S GOT PLENTY OF FANS!!
UNBEATABLE MAN
DOU-BASHI!!
GO DOU-BASHI!! DO IT FOR HAKONE!!
WIN!
HAKO GAKU
ROADSTER
SHOW US THE STRAIGHT MONSTER DOUBASHI
15
ROOOOAR
YEAAAAH!
MASAKIYO!!
SIGN: HAKONE ACADEMY, WIN!, BANNER: 15 DOUBASHI
HANG IN THERE, DOU-BASHI-SENPAI!!
YOU GOTTA WIN THIS!!
PEDAL LIKE YOU MEAN IT, PLEASE!!
SEN-PAAAI!!
YEAAAAH!
SHOOM
SHIRTS: HAKONE ACADEMY BICYCLE RACING CLUB
YEAH, I KNOW.
SNRRT!!
I FINALLY MADE IT TO AN INTER-HIGH.

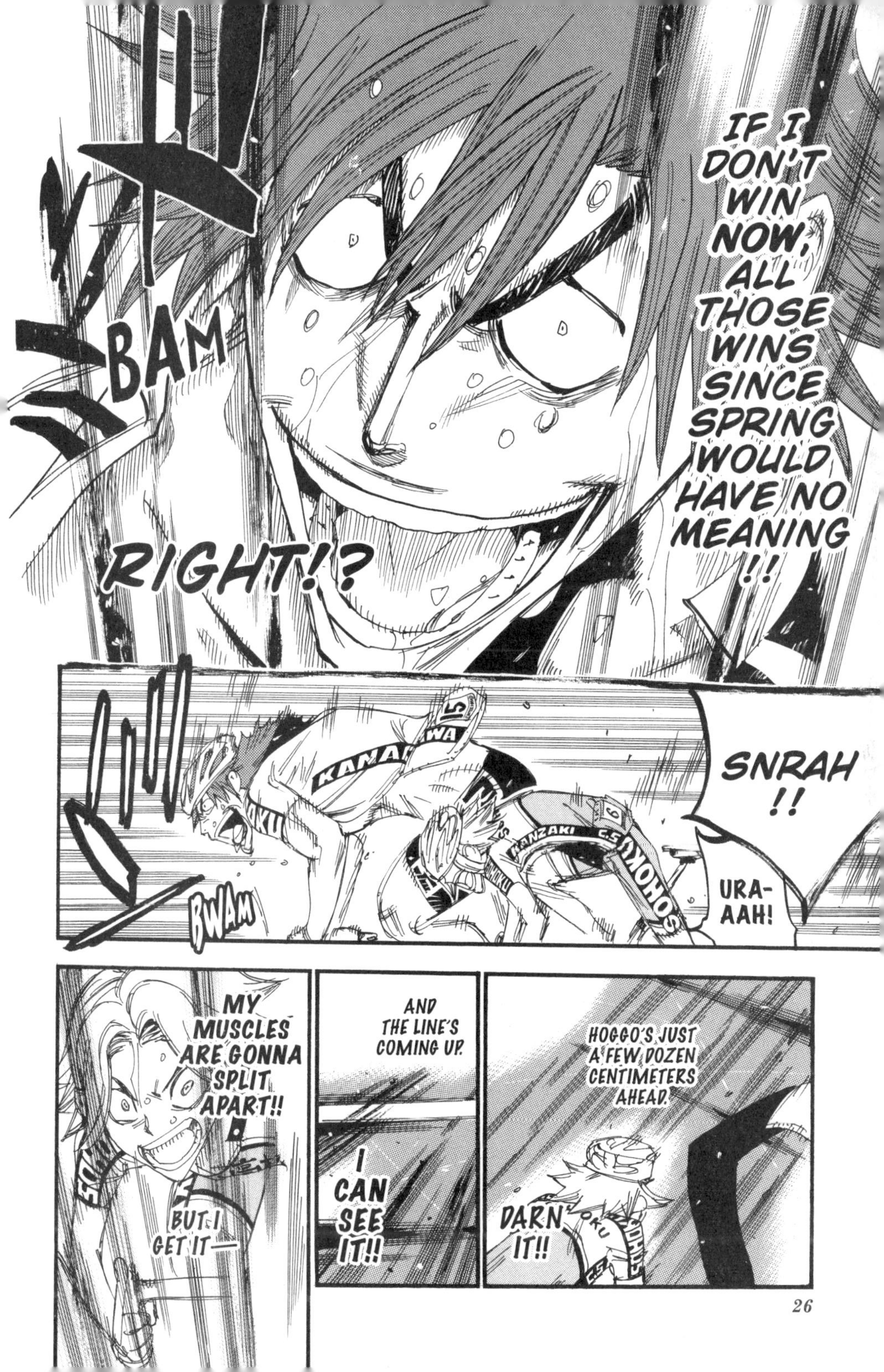
IF I DON'T WIN NOW, ALL THOSE WINS SINCE SPRING WOULD HAVE NO MEANING!!
BAM
RIGHT!?
SNRAH!!
URA-AAH!
BWAM
HOGGO'S JUST A FEW DOZEN CENTIMETERS AHEAD.
DARN IT!!
AND THE LINE'S COMING UP.
I CAN SEE IT!!
MY MUSCLES ARE GONNA SPLIT APART!!
BUT I GET IT—

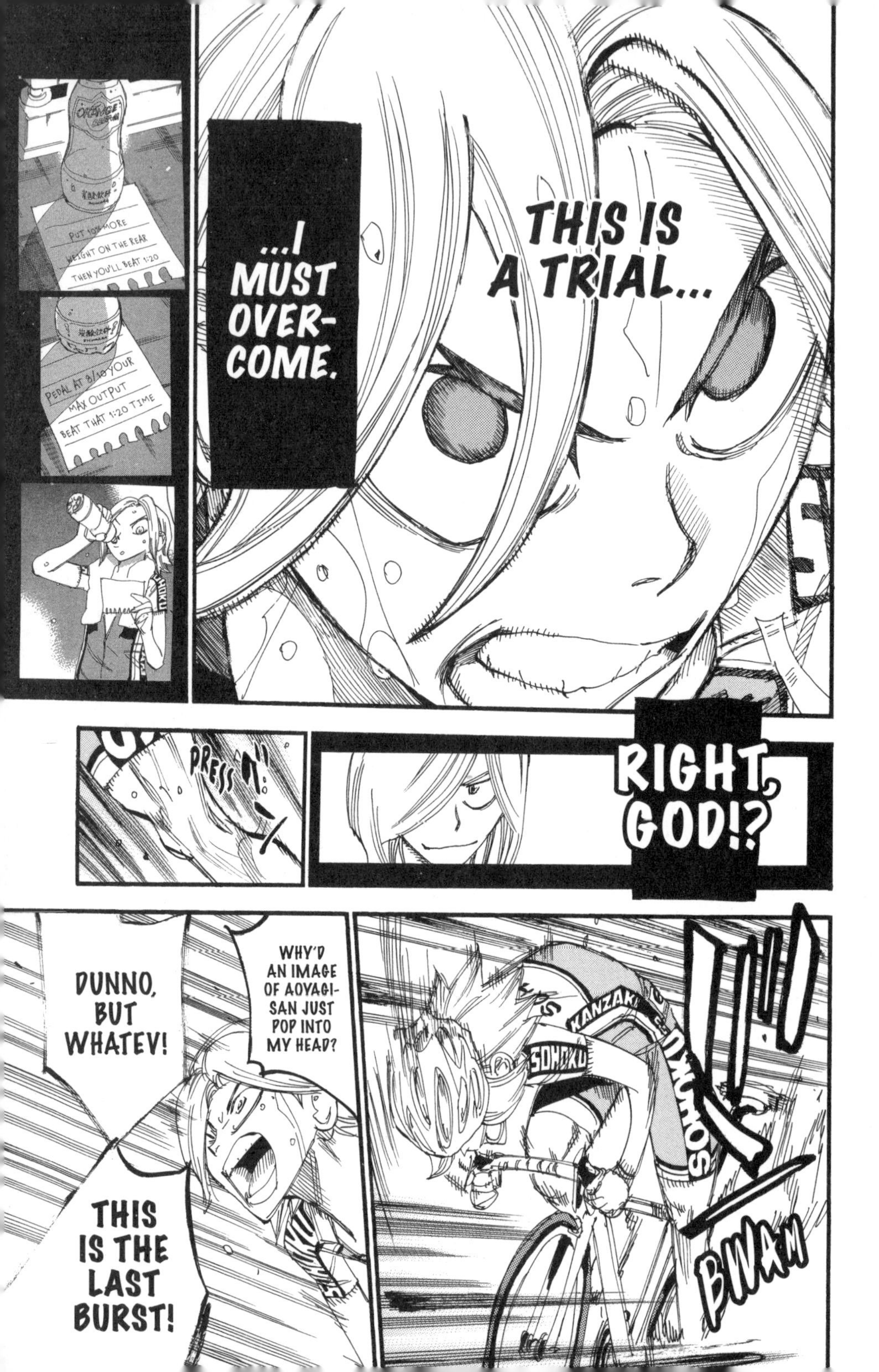
THIS IS A TRIAL...
...I MUST OVERCOME.
PUT 10% MORE WEIGHT ON THE REAR THEN YOU'LL BEAT 1:20
PEDAL AT 8/10 YOUR MAX OUTPUT BEAT THAT 1:20 TIME
RIGHT, GOD!?
PRESS
KANZAKI
SOHOKU
BWAM
WHY'D AN IMAGE OF AOYAGI-SAN JUST POP INTO MY HEAD?
DUNNO, BUT WHATEV!
THIS IS THE LAST BURST!

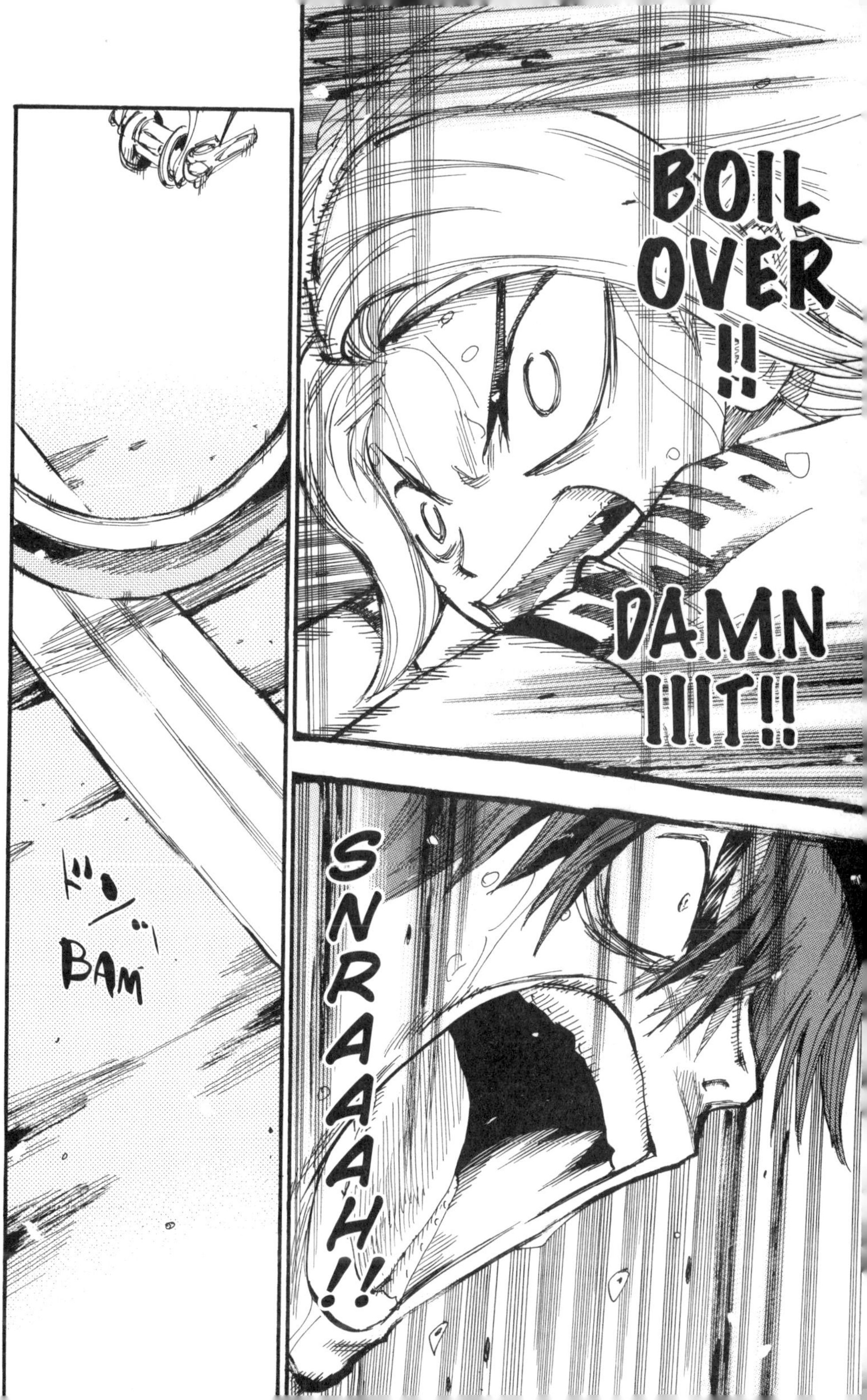
BOIL OVER!!
DAMN IIIT!!
SNRAAAH!!
BAM

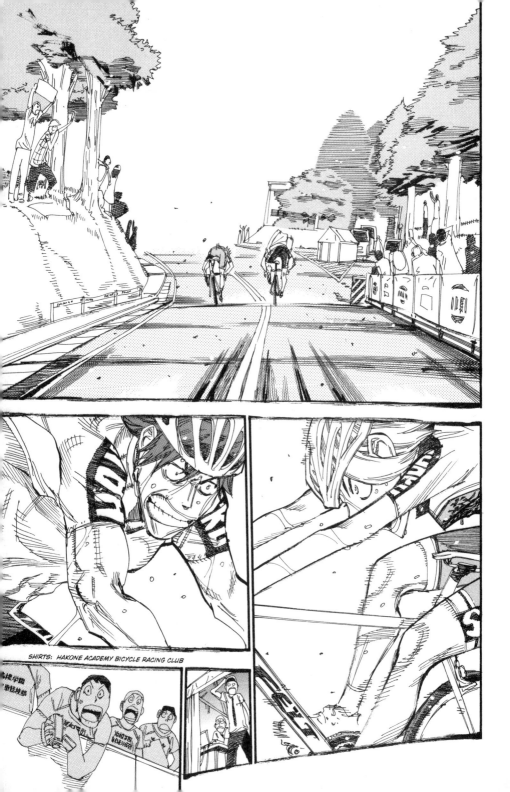

SHIRTS: HAKONE ACADEMY BICYCLE RACING CLUB

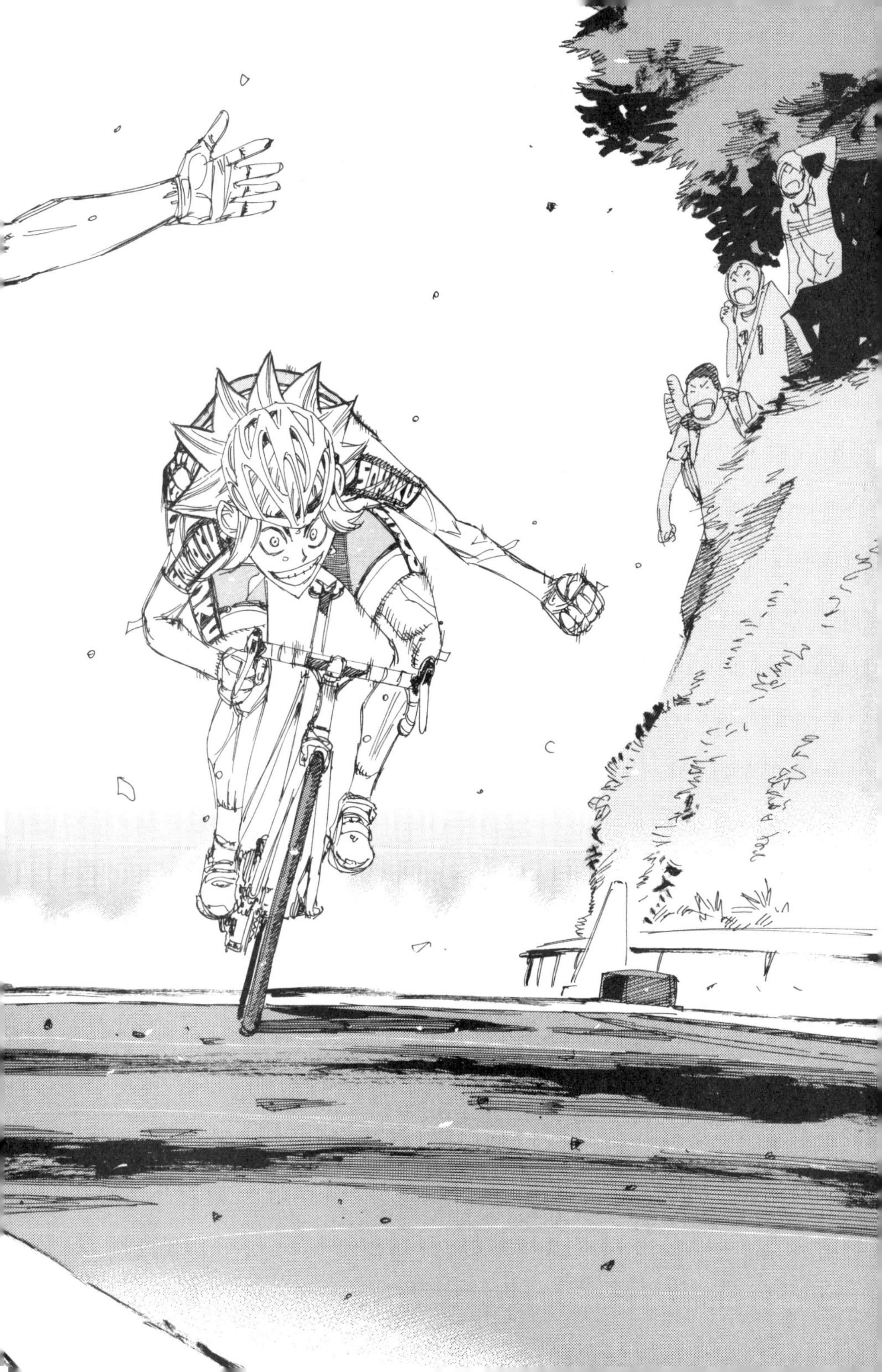

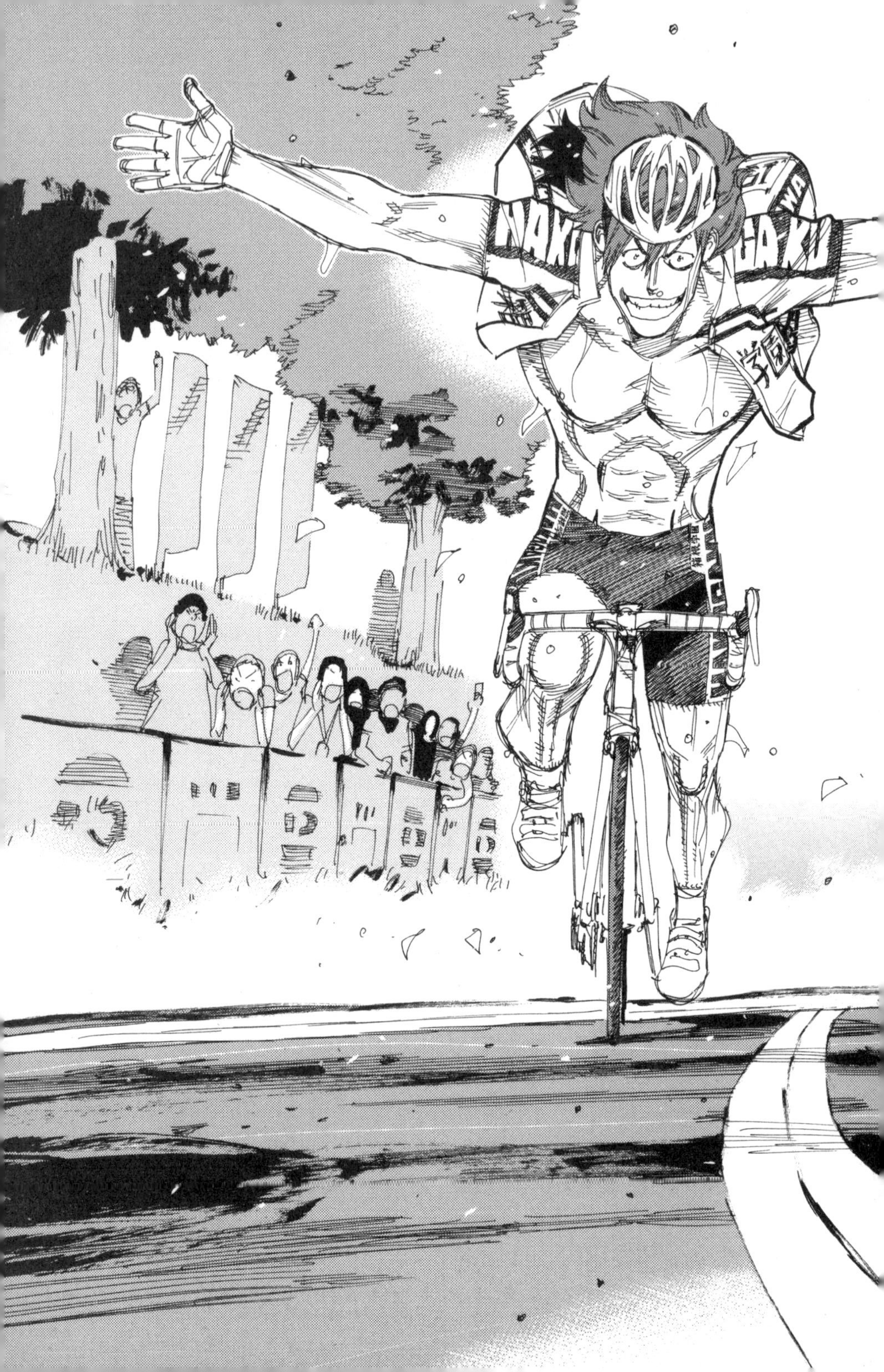

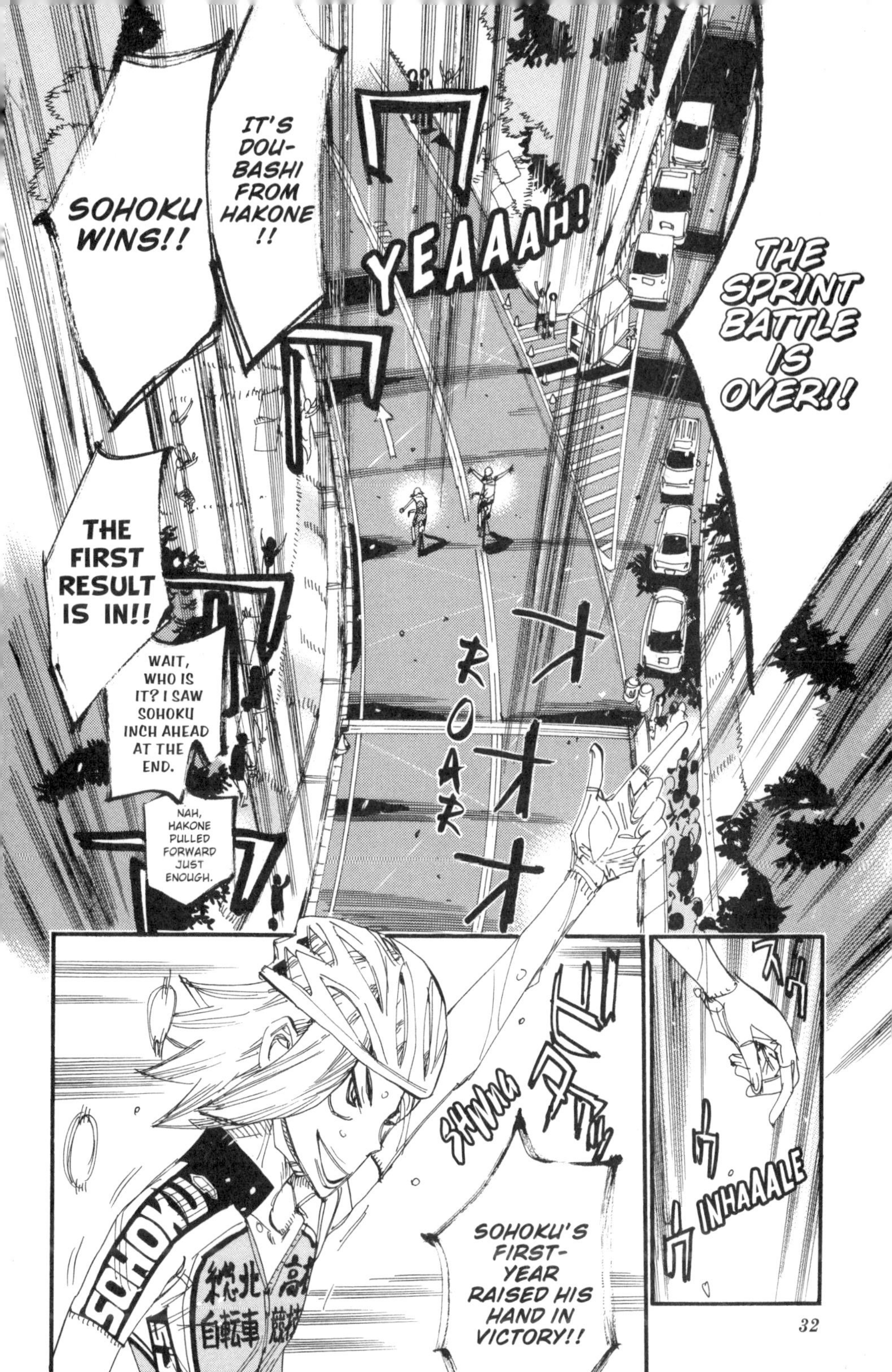
THE SPRINT BATTLE IS OVER!!
IT'S DOU-BASHI FROM HAKONE!!
SOHOKU WINS!!
YEAAAAH!
THE FIRST RESULT IS IN!!
WAIT, WHO IS IT? I SAW SOHOKU INCH AHEAD AT THE END.
NAH, HAKONE PULLED FORWARD JUST ENOUGH.
ROAR
INHAAALE
SHWING
SOHOKU
SOHOKU'S FIRST-YEAR RAISED HIS HAND IN VICTORY!!

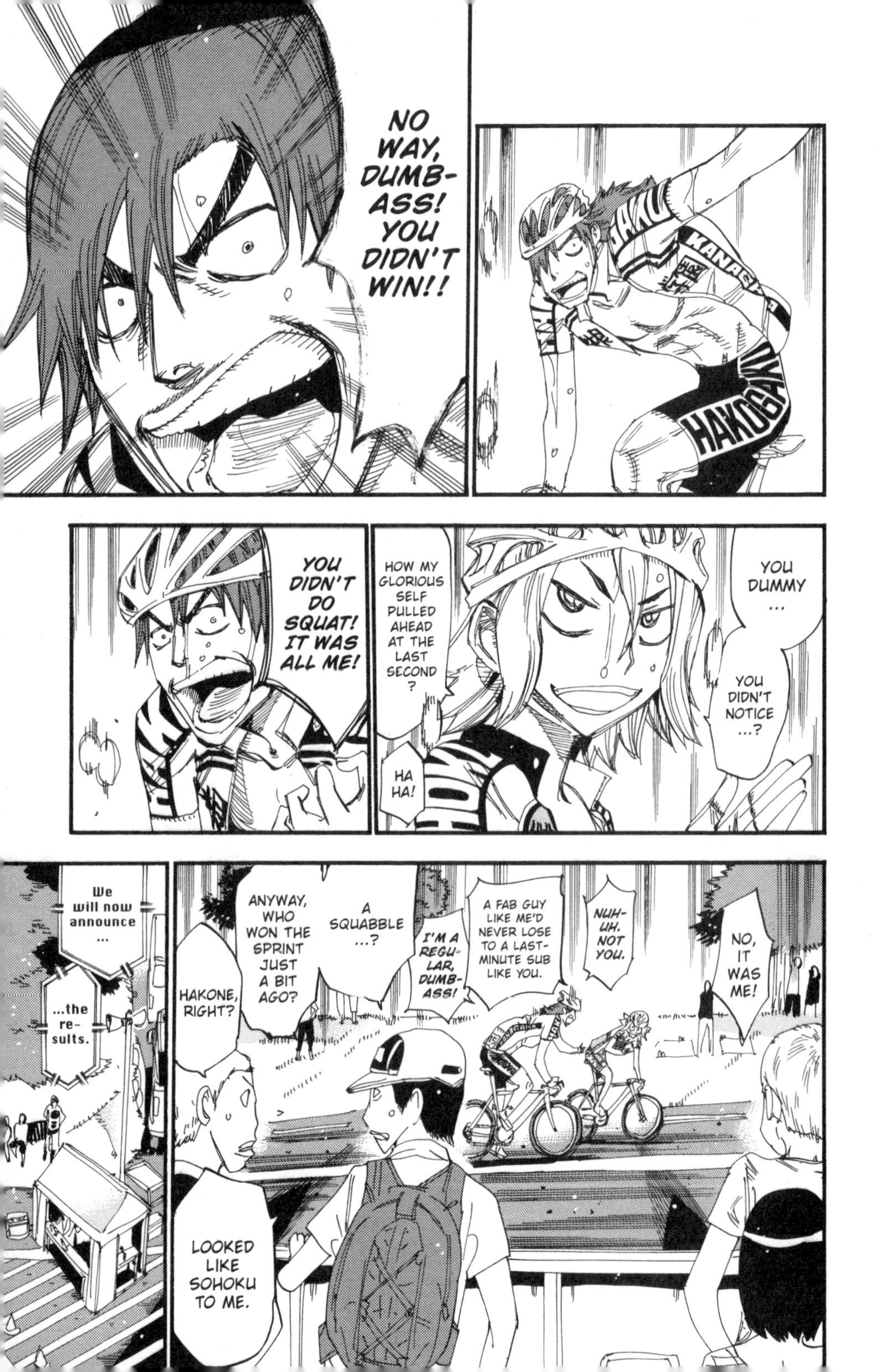
NO WAY, DUMB-ASS! YOU DIDN'T WIN!!
YOU DUMMY ...
YOU DIDN'T NOTICE ...?
HOW MY GLORIOUS SELF PULLED AHEAD AT THE LAST SECOND?
HA HA!
YOU DIDN'T DO SQUAT! IT WAS ALL ME!
NO, IT WAS ME!
NUH-UH. NOT YOU.
A FAB GUY LIKE ME'D NEVER LOSE TO A LAST-MINUTE SUB LIKE YOU.
I'M A REGU-LAR, DUMB-ASS!
A SQUABBLE ...?
ANYWAY, WHO WON THE SPRINT JUST A BIT AGO?
HAKONE, RIGHT?
LOOKED LIKE SOHOKU TO ME.
We will now announce ...
...the re-sults.

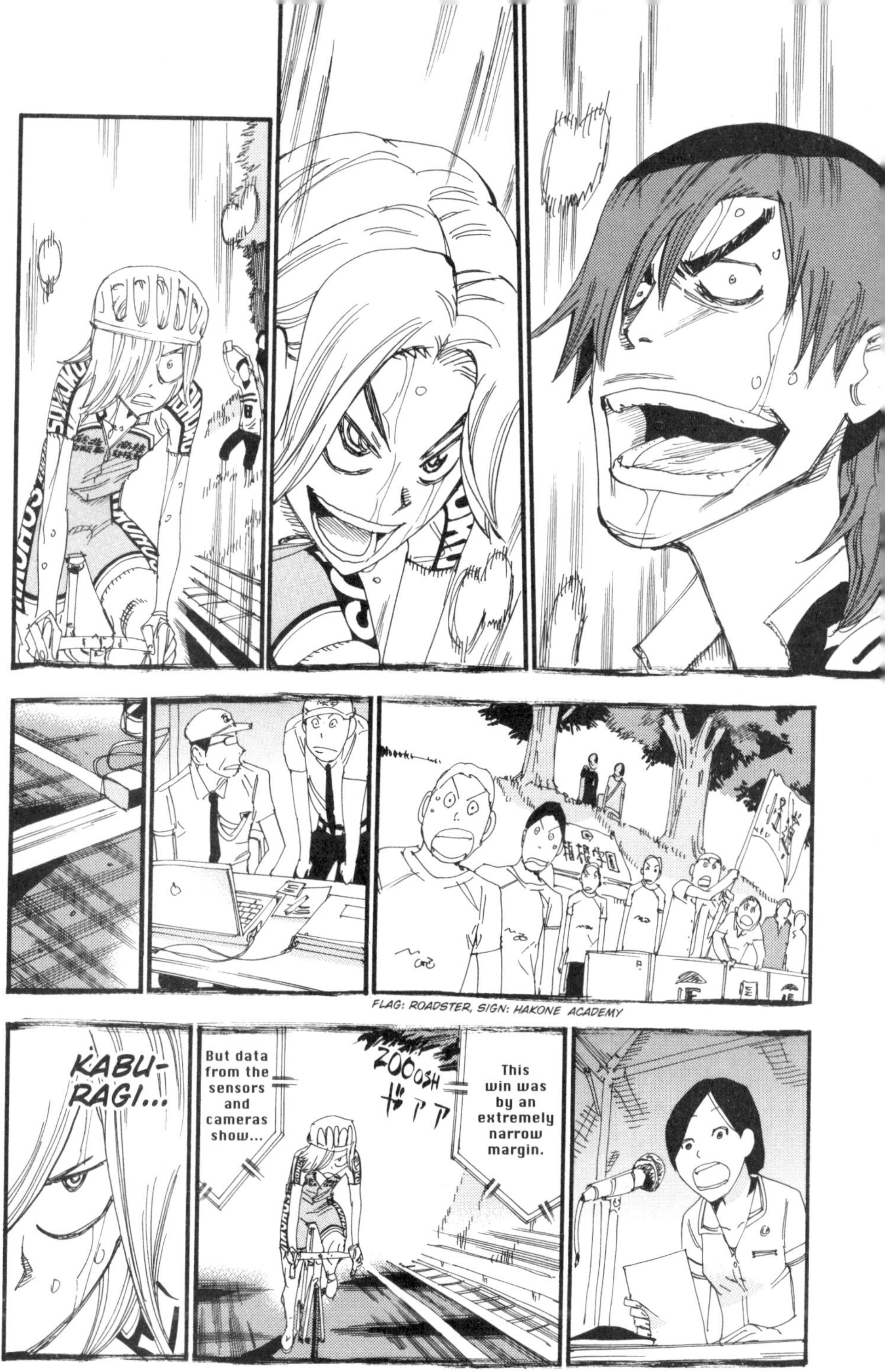
FLAG: ROADSTER, SIGN: HAKONE ACADEMY
This win was by an extremely narrow margin.
ZOOOSH
But data from the sensors and cameras show...
KABU-RAGI...

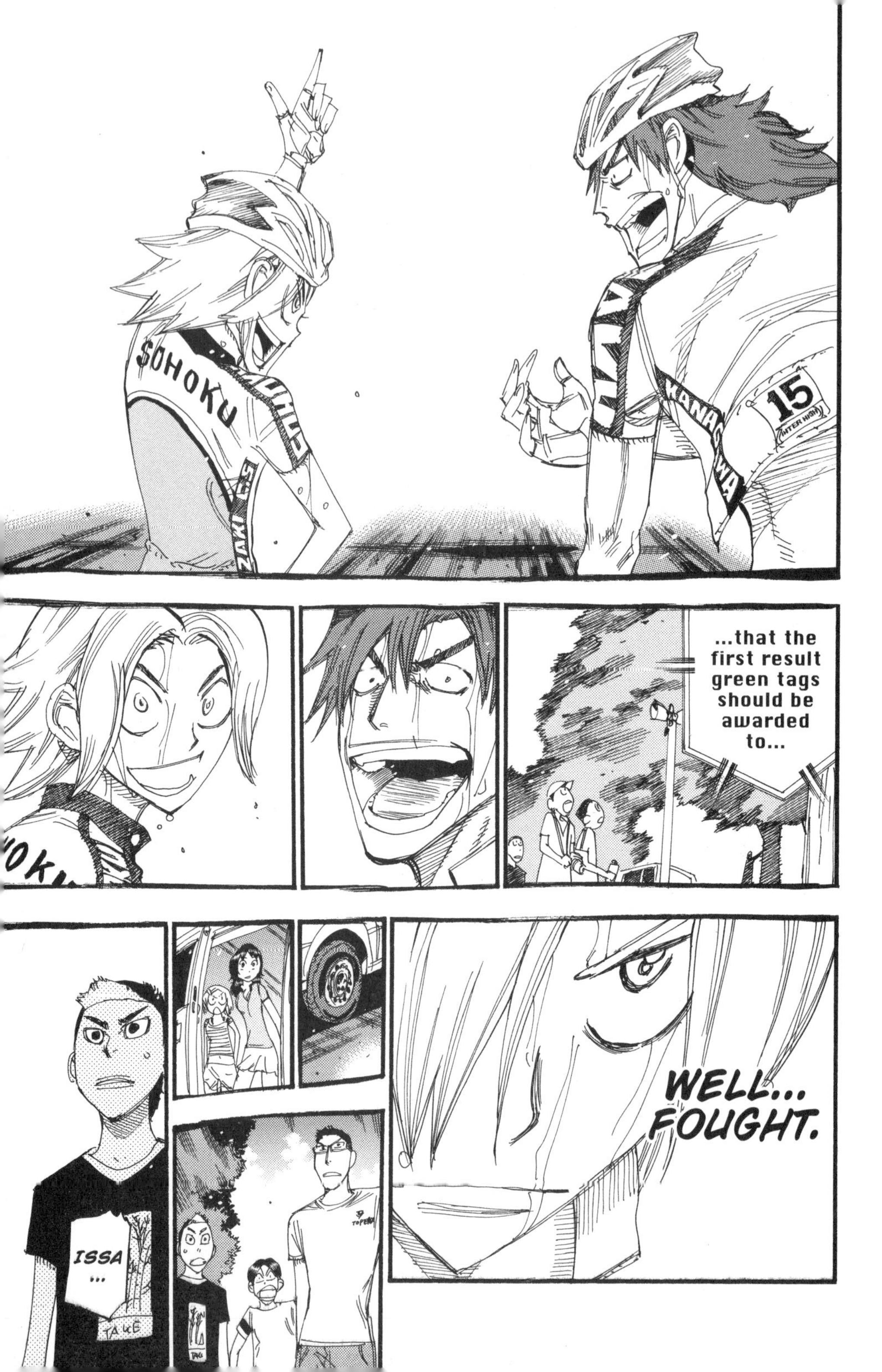
SOHOKU
KANAGAWA
15
INTER HIGH
...that the first result green tags should be awarded to...
WELL... FOUGHT.
TOPEAK
ISSA ...
TAKE

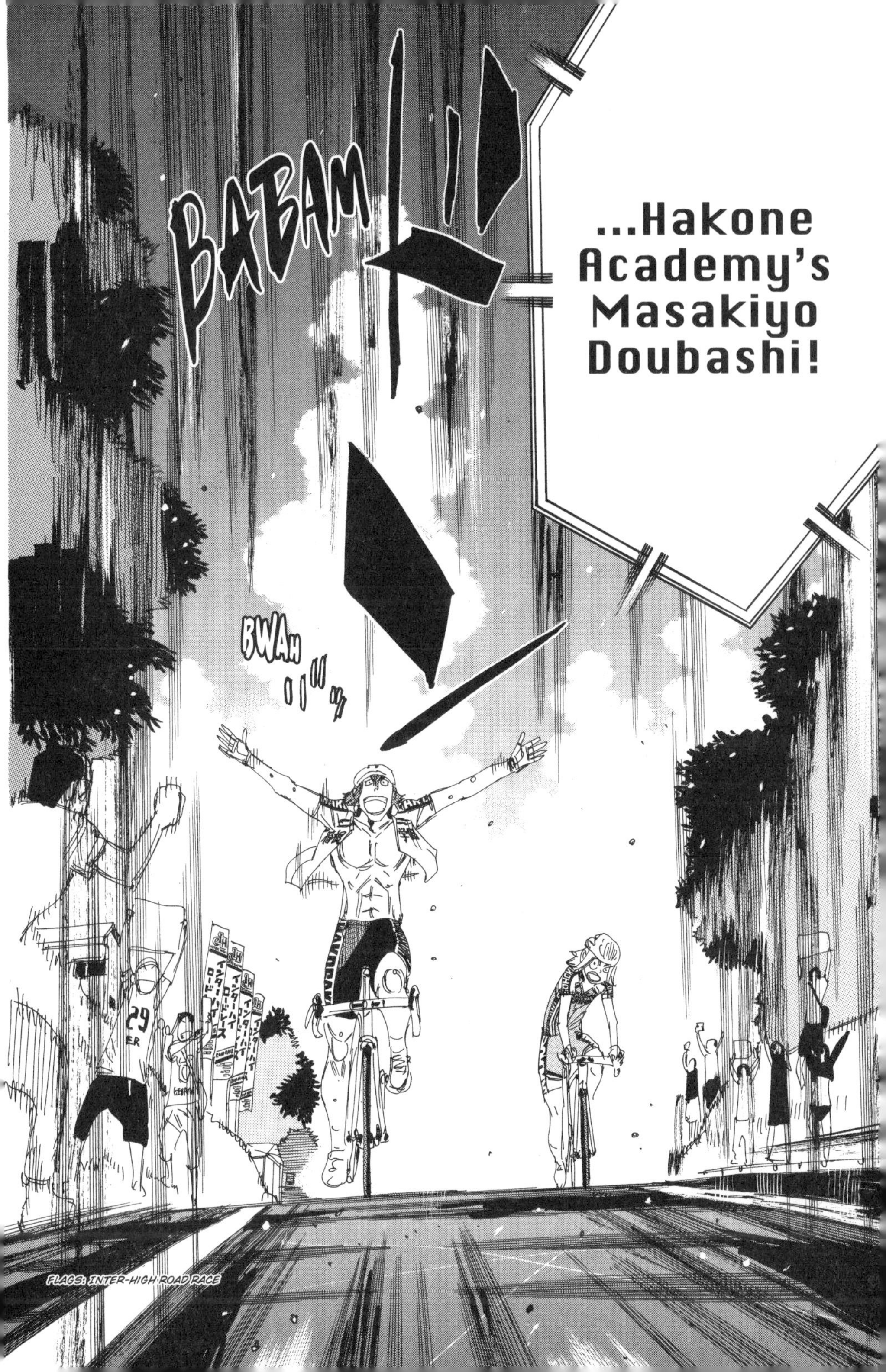
...Hakone Academy's Masakiyo Doubashi!
BABAM!!
BWAH
FLAGS: INTER-HIGH ROAD RACE

RIDE.313 HAKONE DEPLOYS!

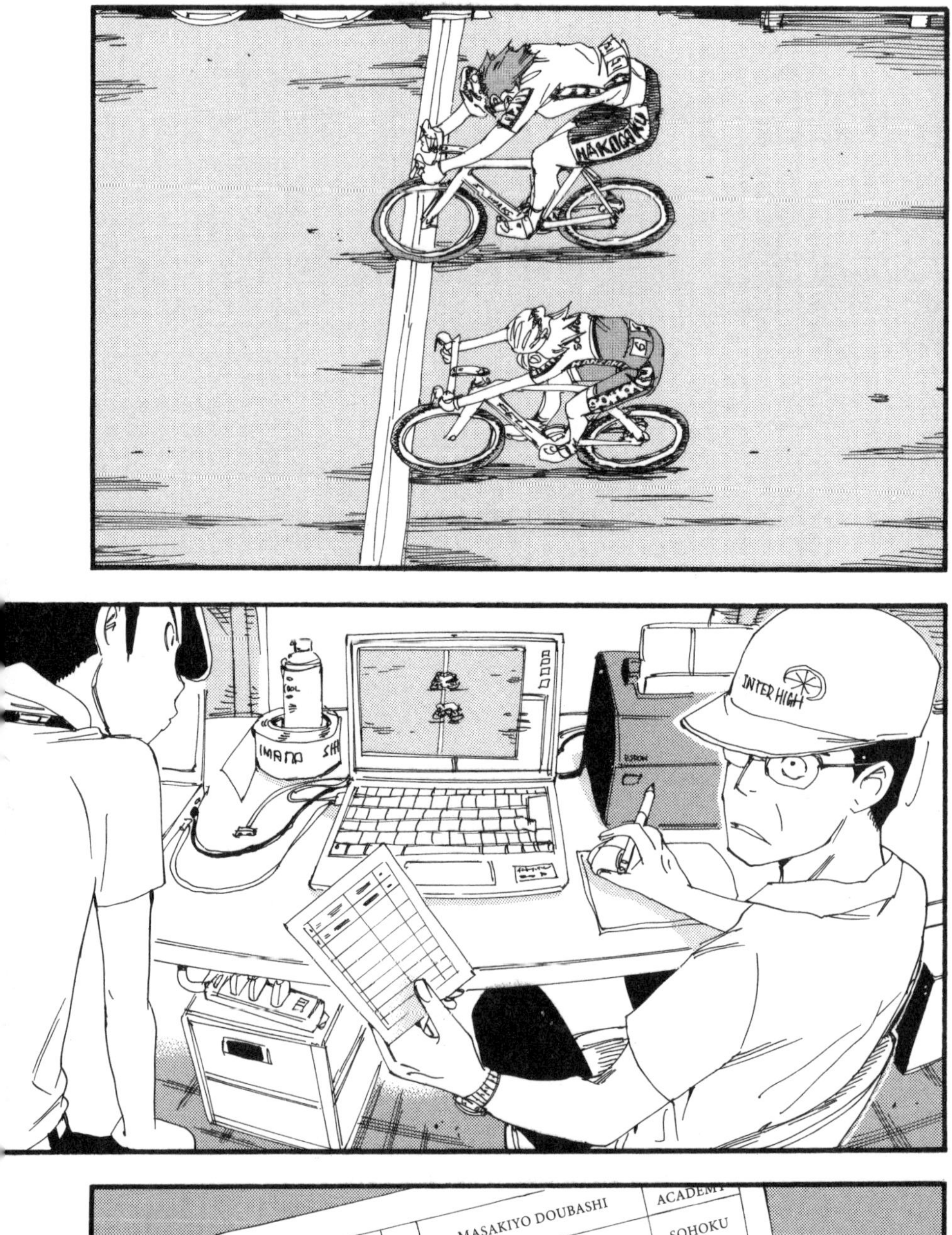
HAKOGAKU
INTER HIGH
1 KANAGAWA 15 MASAKIYO DOUBASHI ACADEMY
2 CHIBA 6 ISSA KABURAGI SOHOKU

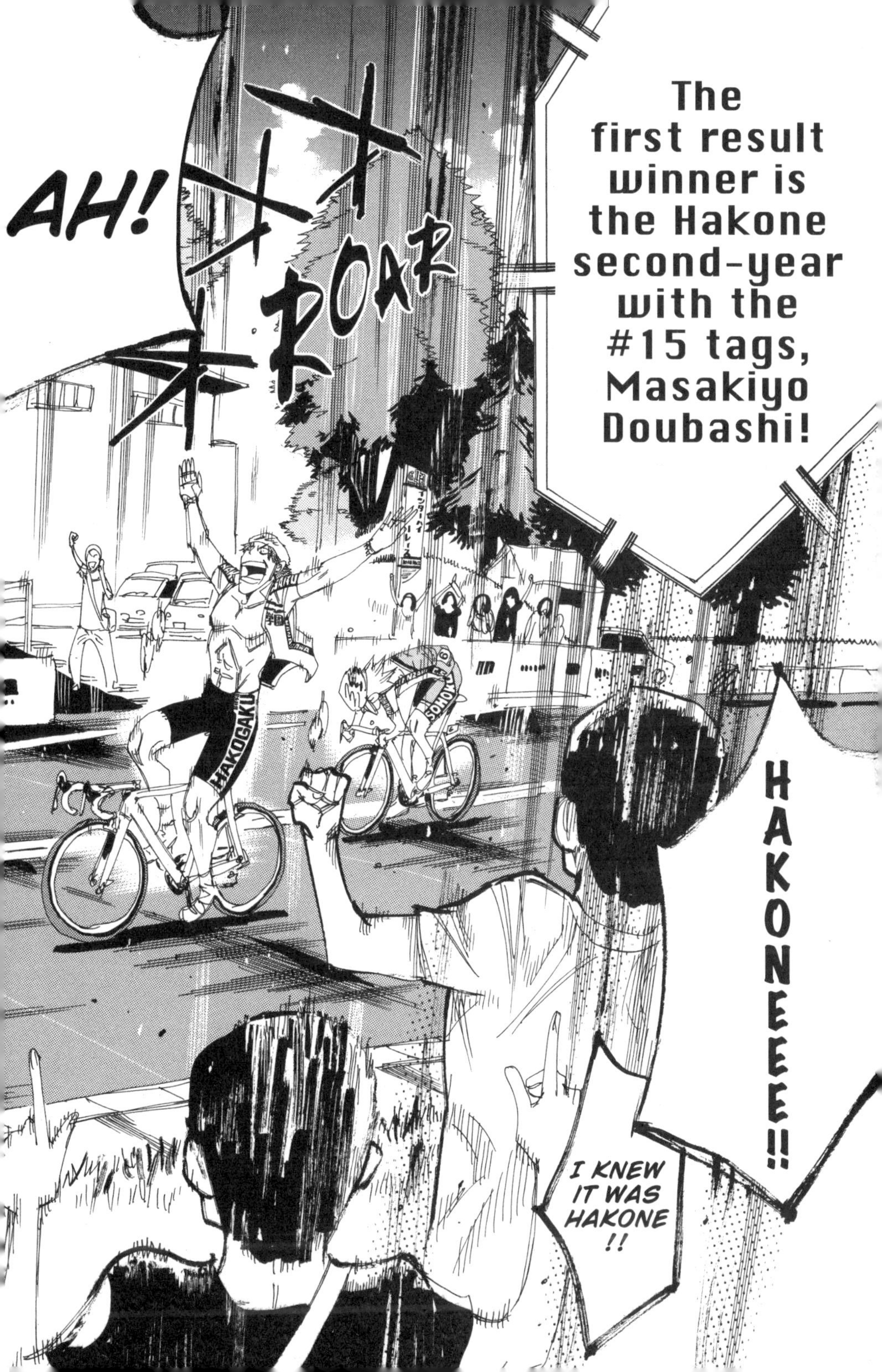
The first result winner is the Hakone second-year with the #15 tags, Masakiyo Doubashi!
AH!
ROAR
HAKONEEEE!!
I KNEW IT WAS HAKONE!!

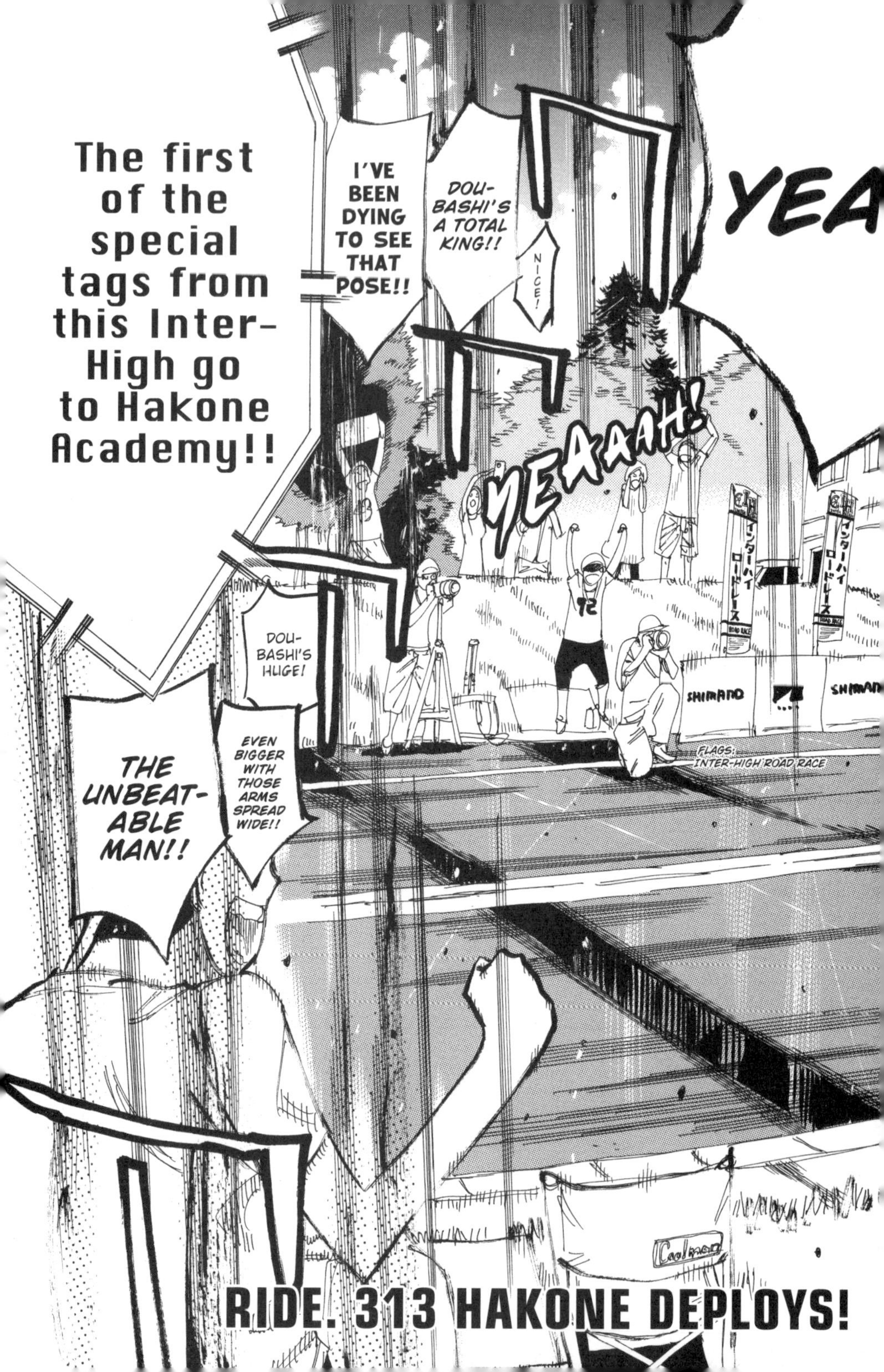
YEA
DOU-BASHI'S A TOTAL KING!!
NICE!
I'VE BEEN DYING TO SEE THAT POSE!!
The first of the special tags from this Inter-High go to Hakone Academy!!
YEAAAH!
DOU-BASHI'S HUGE!
EVEN BIGGER WITH THOSE ARMS SPREAD WIDE!!
THE UNBEAT-ABLE MAN!!
FLAGS: INTER-HIGH ROAD RACE
RIDE. 313 HAKONE DEPLOYS!

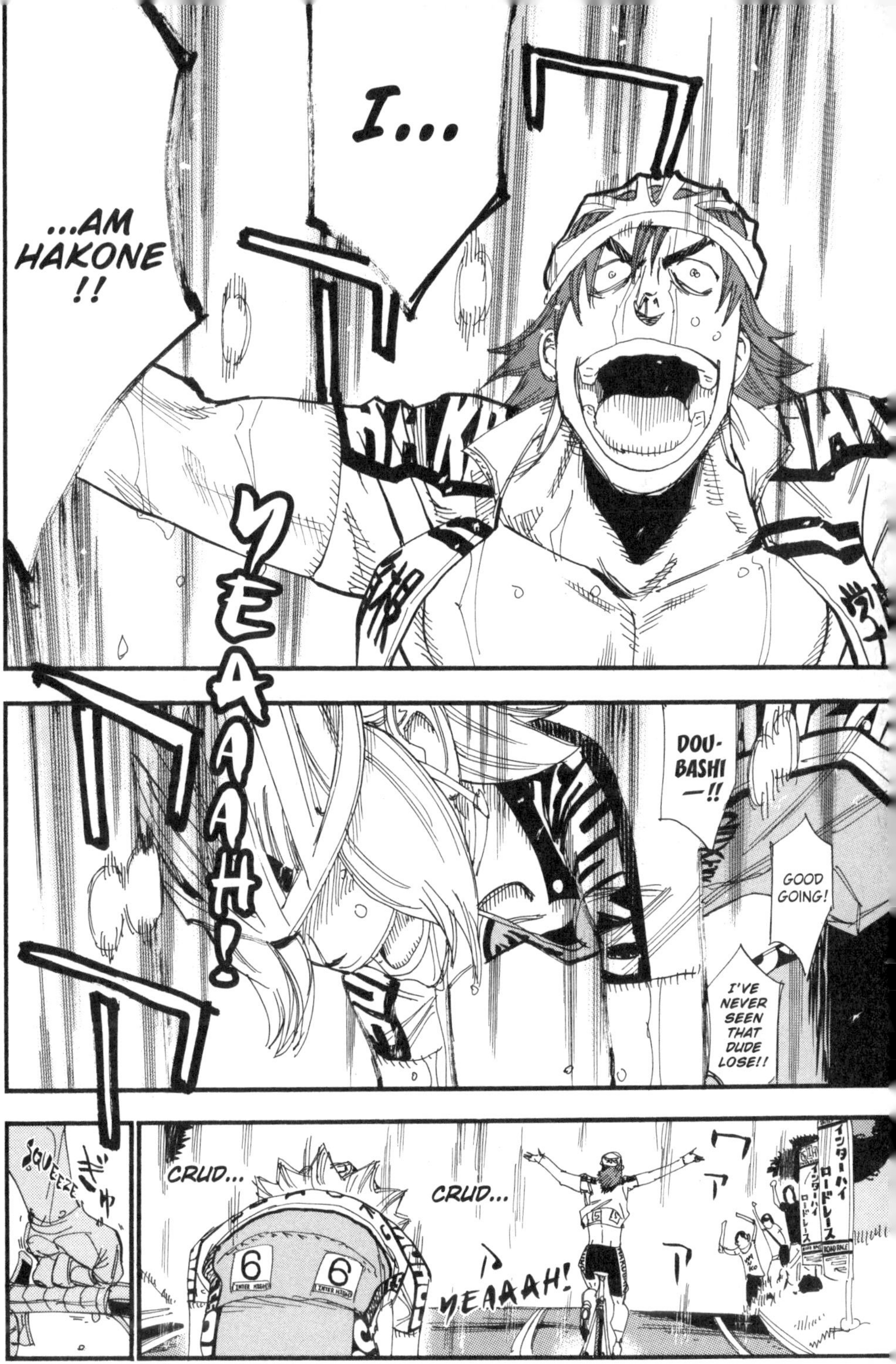

I...
...AM HAKONE!!
YEAAAAAH!
DOU-BASHI—!!
GOOD GOING!
I'VE NEVER SEEN THAT DUDE LOSE!!
インターハイ ロードレース
ワァ
ア
YEAAAH!
CRUD...
CRUD...
SQUEEZE
ぎゅ

FLAGS:INTER-HIGH ROAD RACE

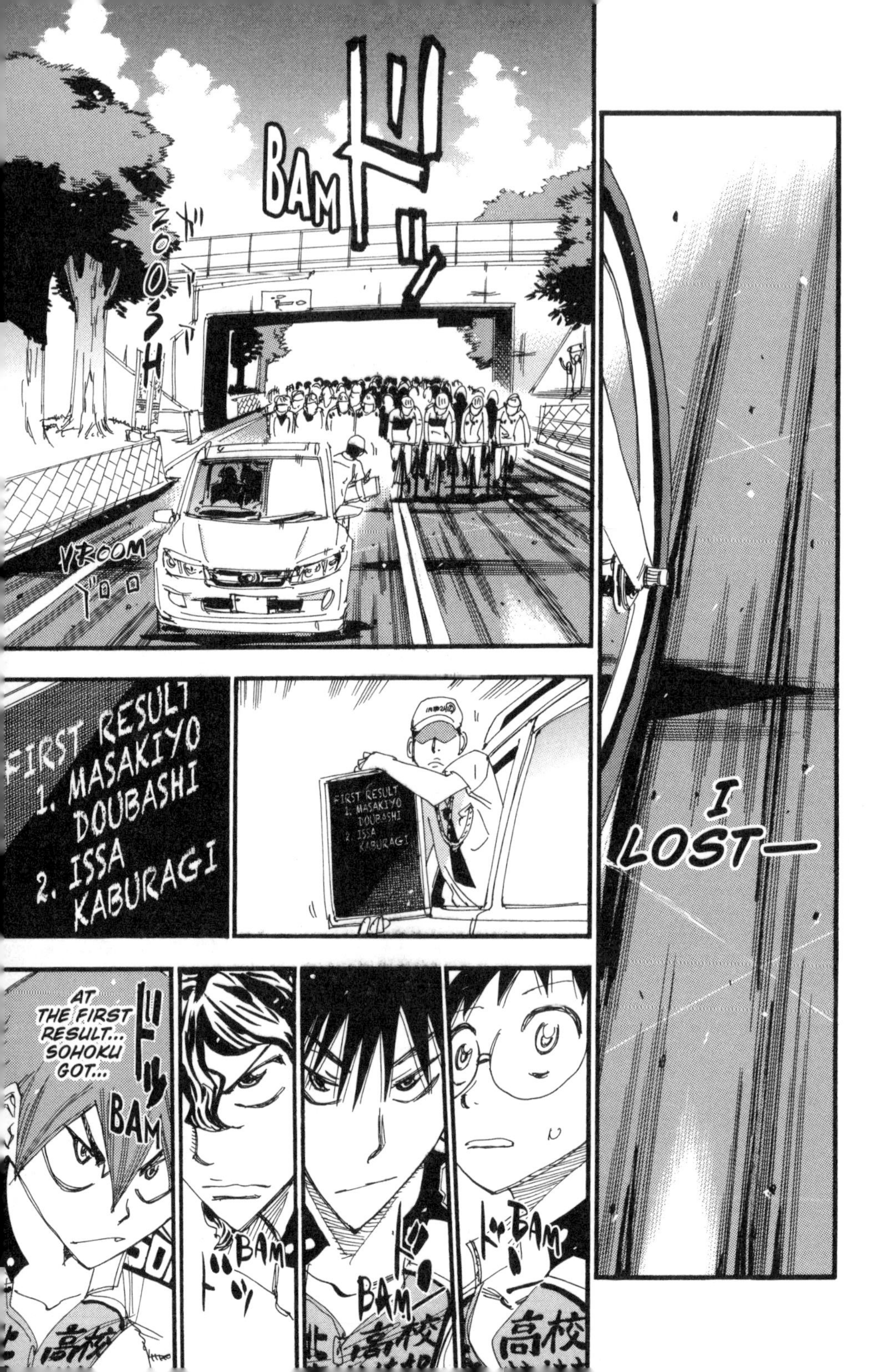
I LOST—
BAM
ZOOOSH
VROOM
FIRST RESULT
1. MASAKIYO DOUBASHI
2. ISSA KABURAGI
FIRST RESULT
1. MASAKIYO DOUBASHI
2. ISSA KABURAGI
BAM
BAM
BAM
BAM
AT THE FIRST RESULT... SOHOKU GOT...
BAM

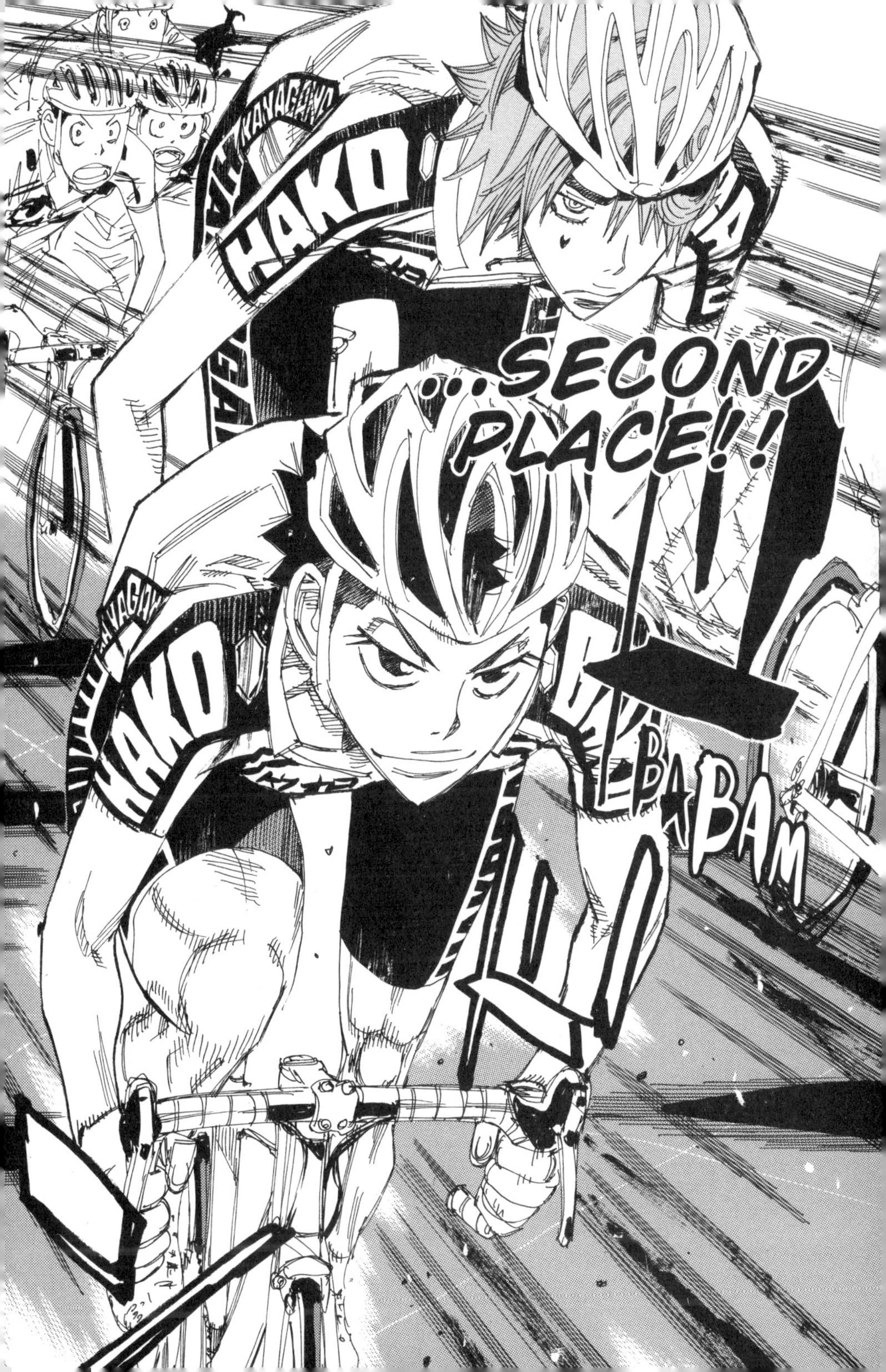
...SECOND PLACE!!
BA BAM

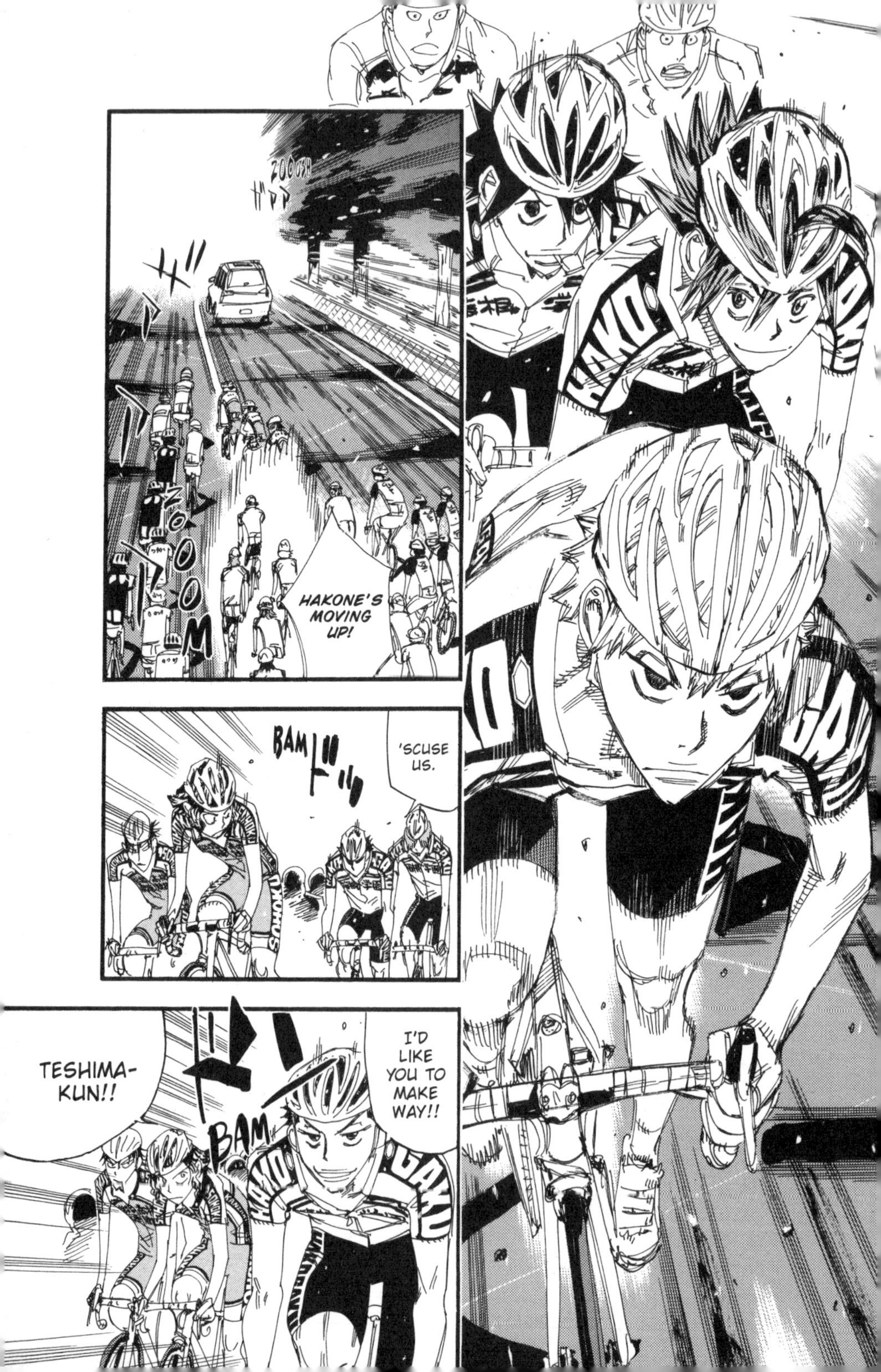
ZOOOSH
ZOOOOM
HAKONE'S MOVING UP!
BAM
'SCUSE US.
I'D LIKE YOU TO MAKE WAY!!
BAM
TESHIMA-KUN!!

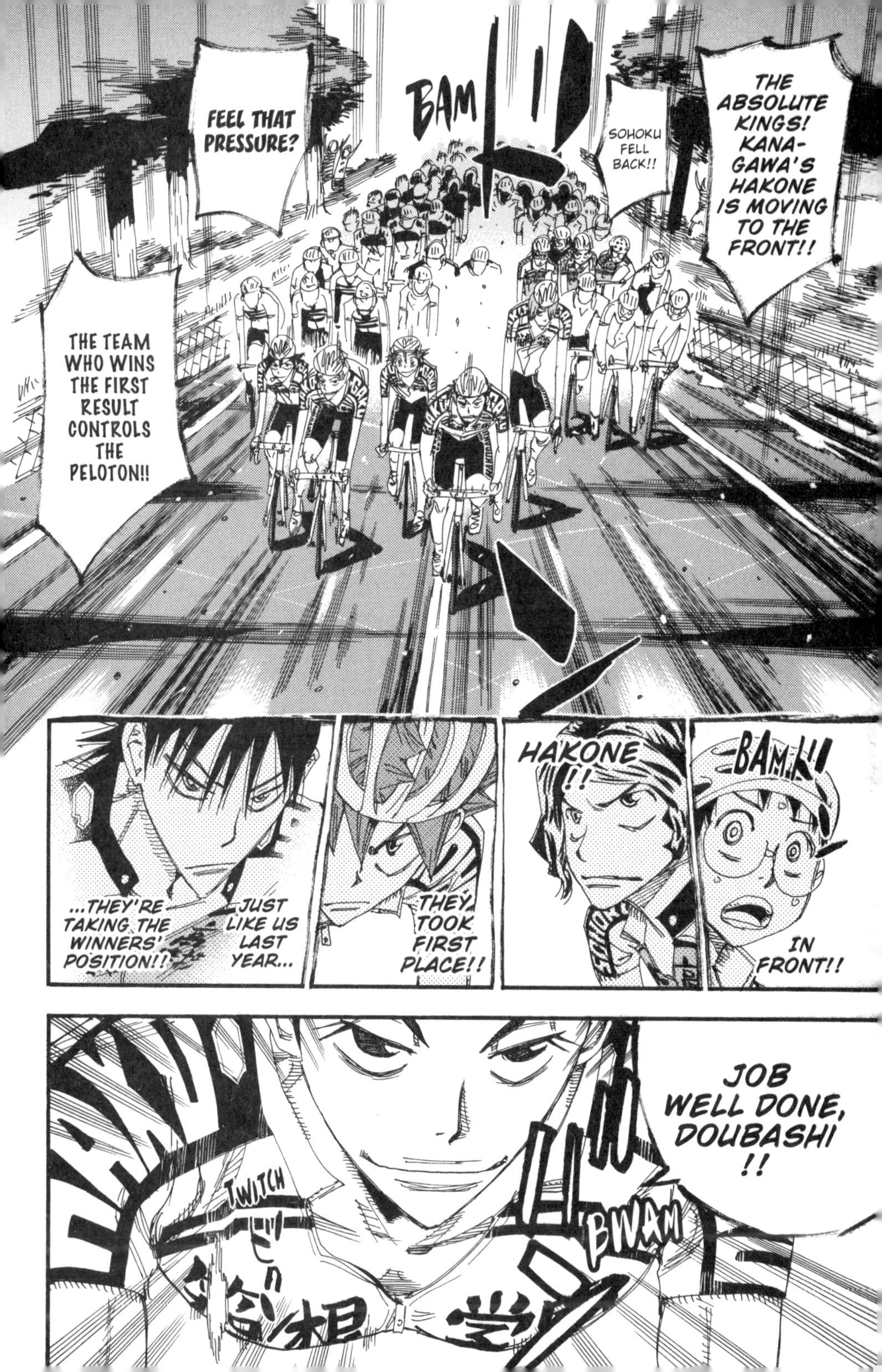
THE ABSOLUTE KINGS! KANAGAWA'S HAKONE IS MOVING TO THE FRONT!!
SOHOKU FELL BACK!!
BAM
FEEL THAT PRESSURE?
THE TEAM WHO WINS THE FIRST RESULT CONTROLS THE PELOTON!!
BAM!!
IN FRONT!!
HAKONE!!
THEY TOOK FIRST PLACE!!
JUST LIKE US LAST YEAR...
...THEY'RE TAKING THE WINNERS' POSITION!!
JOB WELL DONE, DOUBASHI!!
BWAM
TWITCH

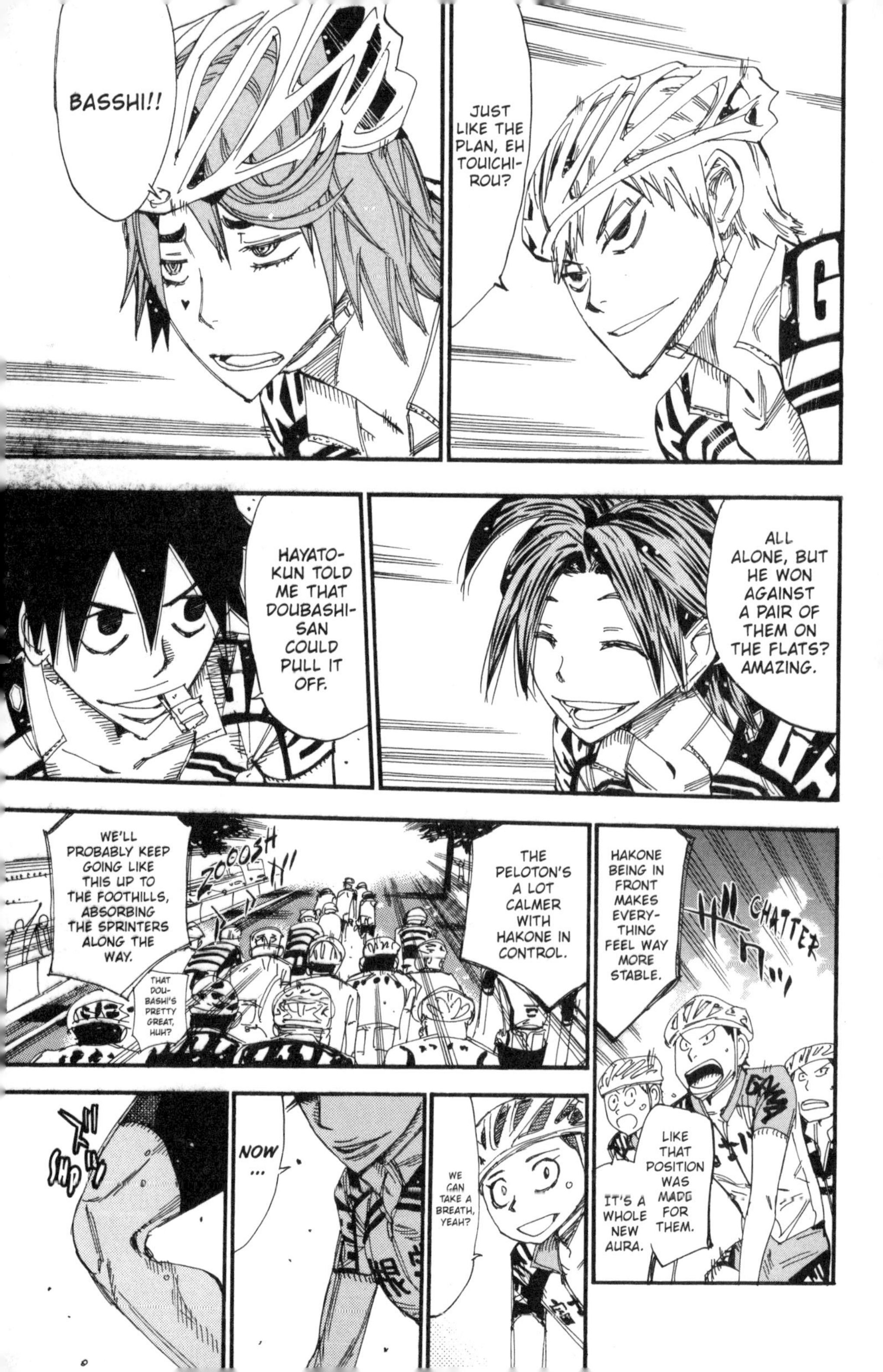
JUST LIKE THE PLAN, EH TOUICHI-ROU?
BASSHI!!
ALL ALONE, BUT HE WON AGAINST A PAIR OF THEM ON THE FLATS? AMAZING.
HAYATO-KUN TOLD ME THAT DOUBASHI-SAN COULD PULL IT OFF.
HAKONE BEING IN FRONT MAKES EVERY-THING FEEL WAY MORE STABLE.
CHATTER
LIKE THAT POSITION WAS MADE FOR THEM.
IT'S A WHOLE NEW AURA.
THE PELOTON'S A LOT CALMER WITH HAKONE IN CONTROL.
ZOOOSH
WE'LL PROBABLY KEEP GOING LIKE THIS UP TO THE FOOTHILLS, ABSORBING THE SPRINTERS ALONG THE WAY.
THAT DOU-BASHI'S PRETTY GREAT, HUH?
WE CAN TAKE A BREATH, YEAH?
NOW ...
SHP

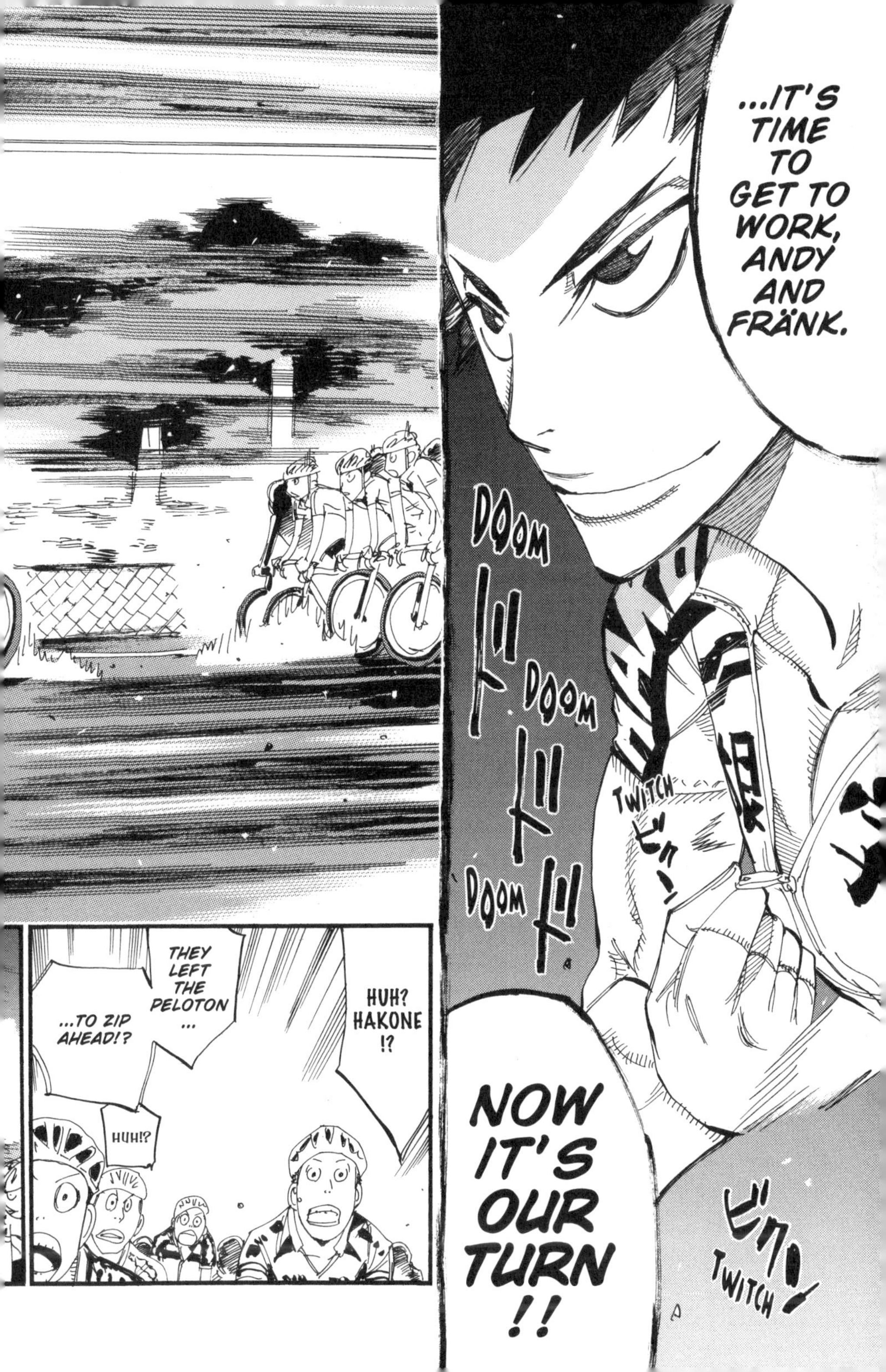
...IT'S TIME TO GET TO WORK, ANDY AND FRÄNK.
DOOM
DOOM
DOOM
TWITCH
NOW IT'S OUR TURN!!
TWITCH
HUH? HAKONE!?
THEY LEFT THE PELOTON...
...TO ZIP AHEAD!?
HUH!?

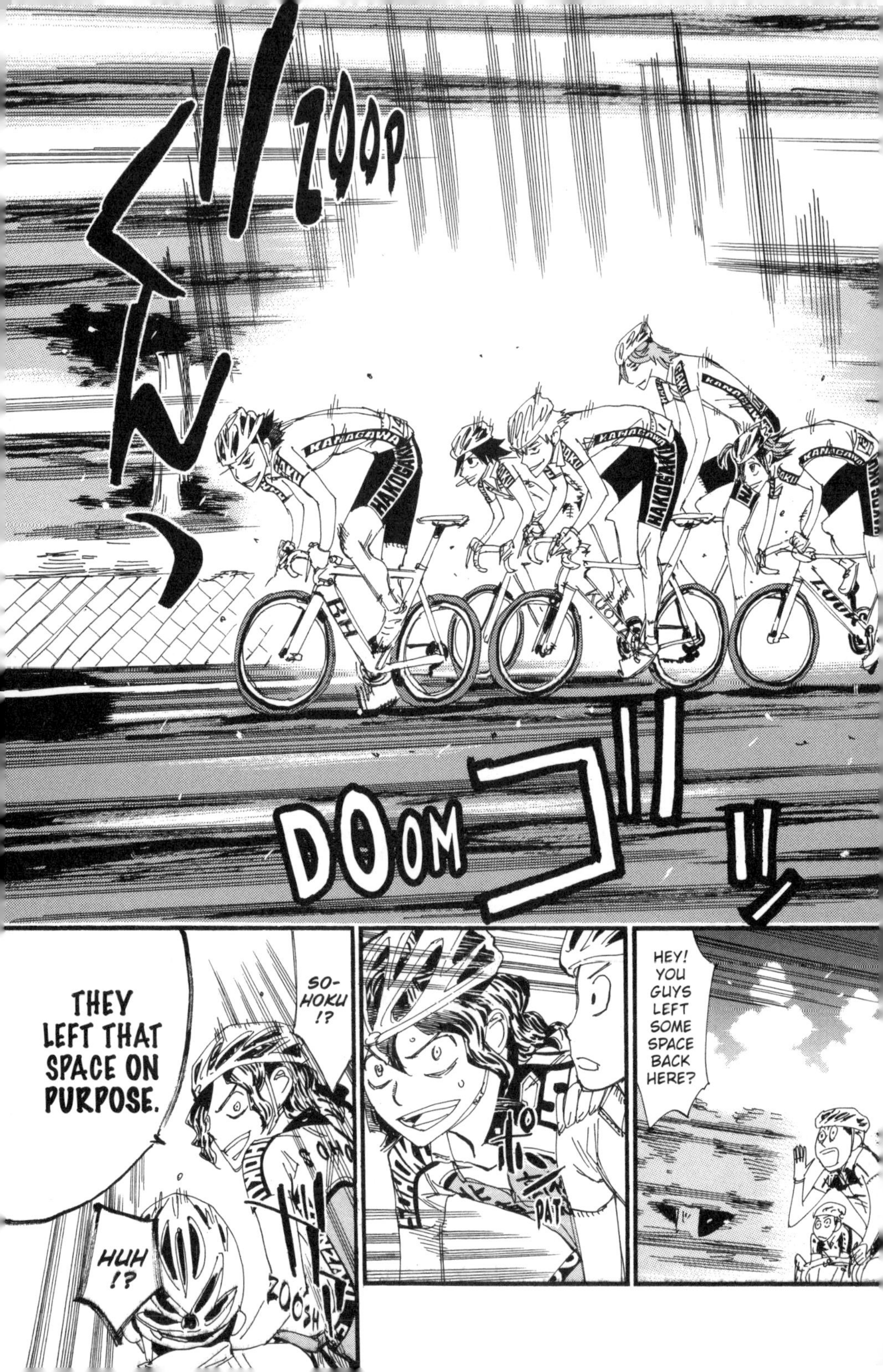
ZOOP
DOOM
HEY! YOU GUYS LEFT SOME SPACE BACK HERE?
SO-HOKU!?
PAT
THEY LEFT THAT SPACE ON PURPOSE.
HUH!?
ZOOSH

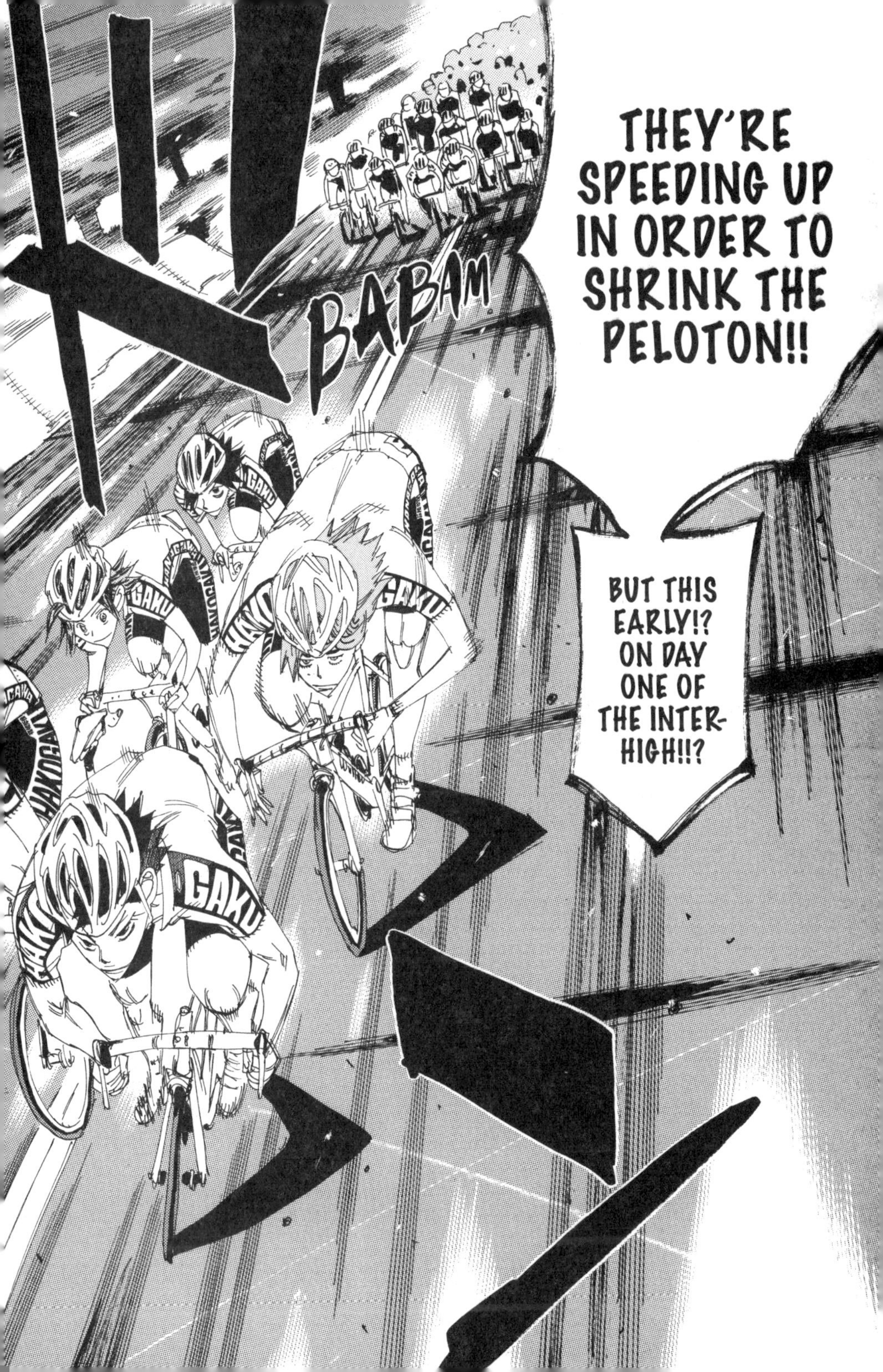
THEY'RE SPEEDING UP IN ORDER TO SHRINK THE PELOTON!!
BABAM
BUT THIS EARLY!? ON DAY ONE OF THE INTER-HIGH!!?

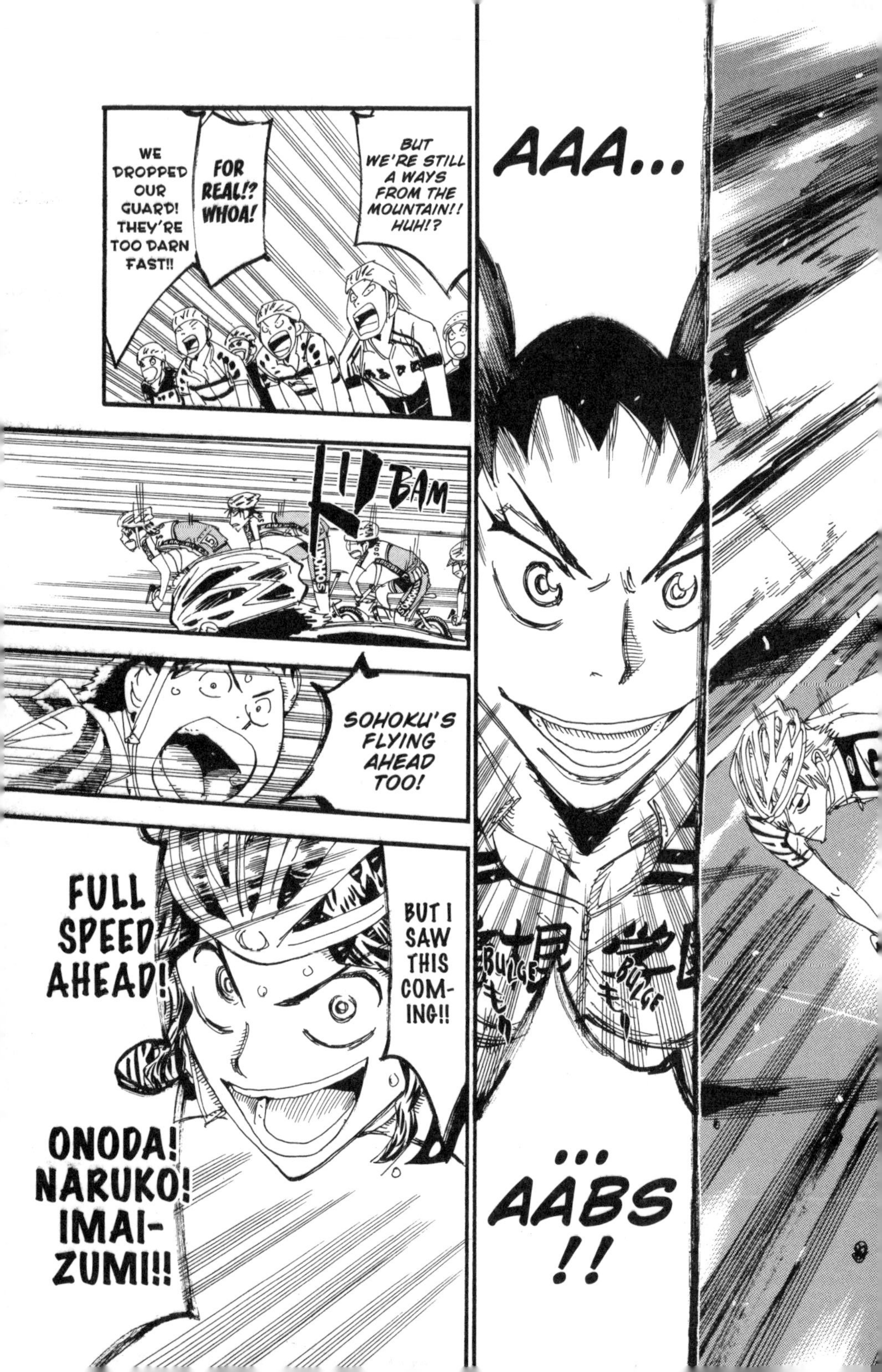
AAA...
...AABS!!
BULGE
BULGE
BUT WE'RE STILL A WAYS FROM THE MOUNTAIN!! HUH!?
FOR REAL!? WHOA!
WE DROPPED OUR GUARD! THEY'RE TOO DARN FAST!!
BAM
SOHOKU'S FLYING AHEAD TOO!
BUT I SAW THIS COMING!!
FULL SPEED AHEAD!
ONODA! NARUKO! IMAIZUMI!!

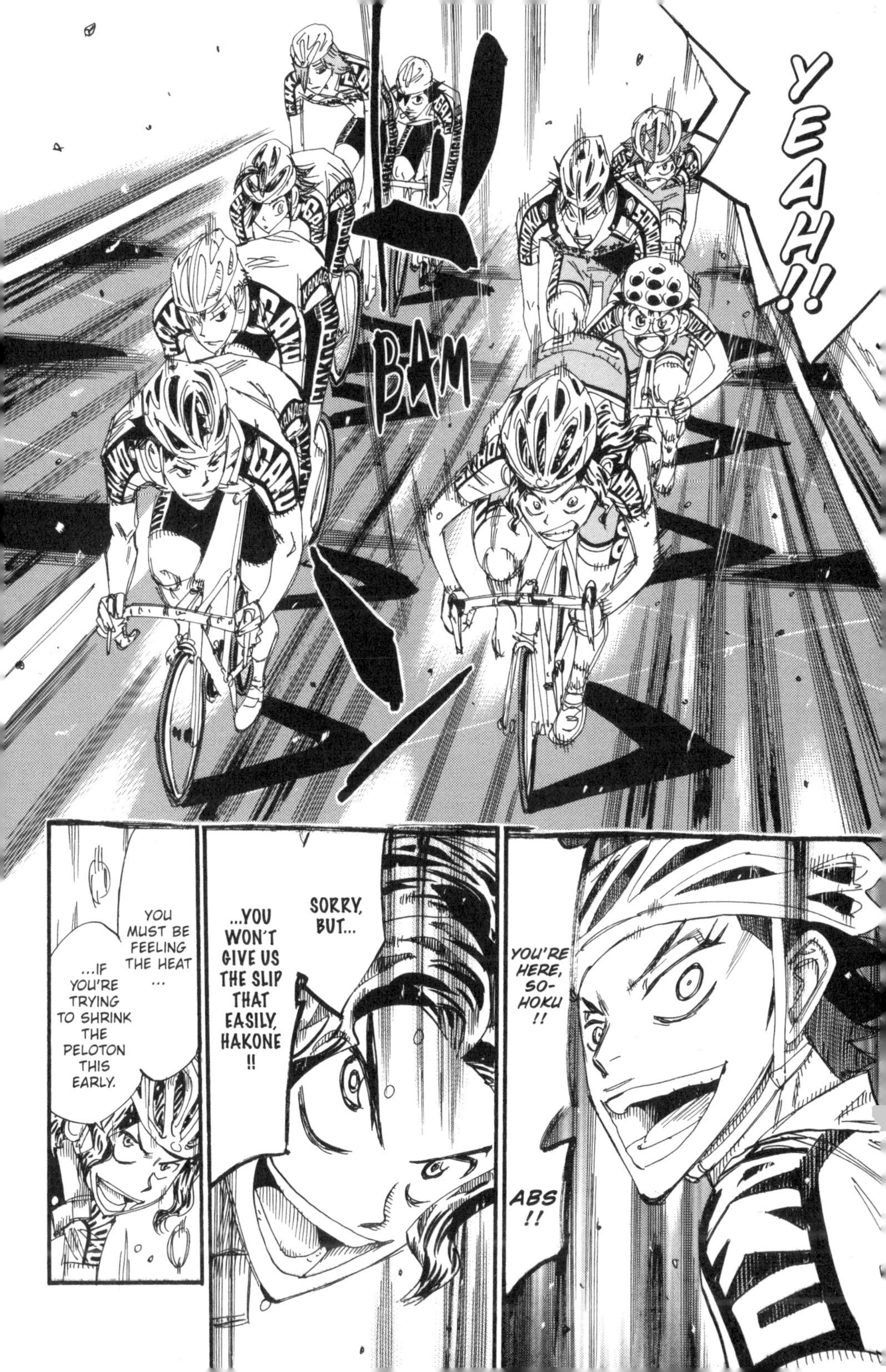
YEAH!!
BAM
YOU'RE HERE, SO-HOKU!!
ABS!!
SORRY, BUT...
...YOU WON'T GIVE US THE SLIP THAT EASILY, HAKONE!!
YOU MUST BE FEELING THE HEAT...
...IF YOU'RE TRYING TO SHRINK THE PELOTON THIS EARLY.

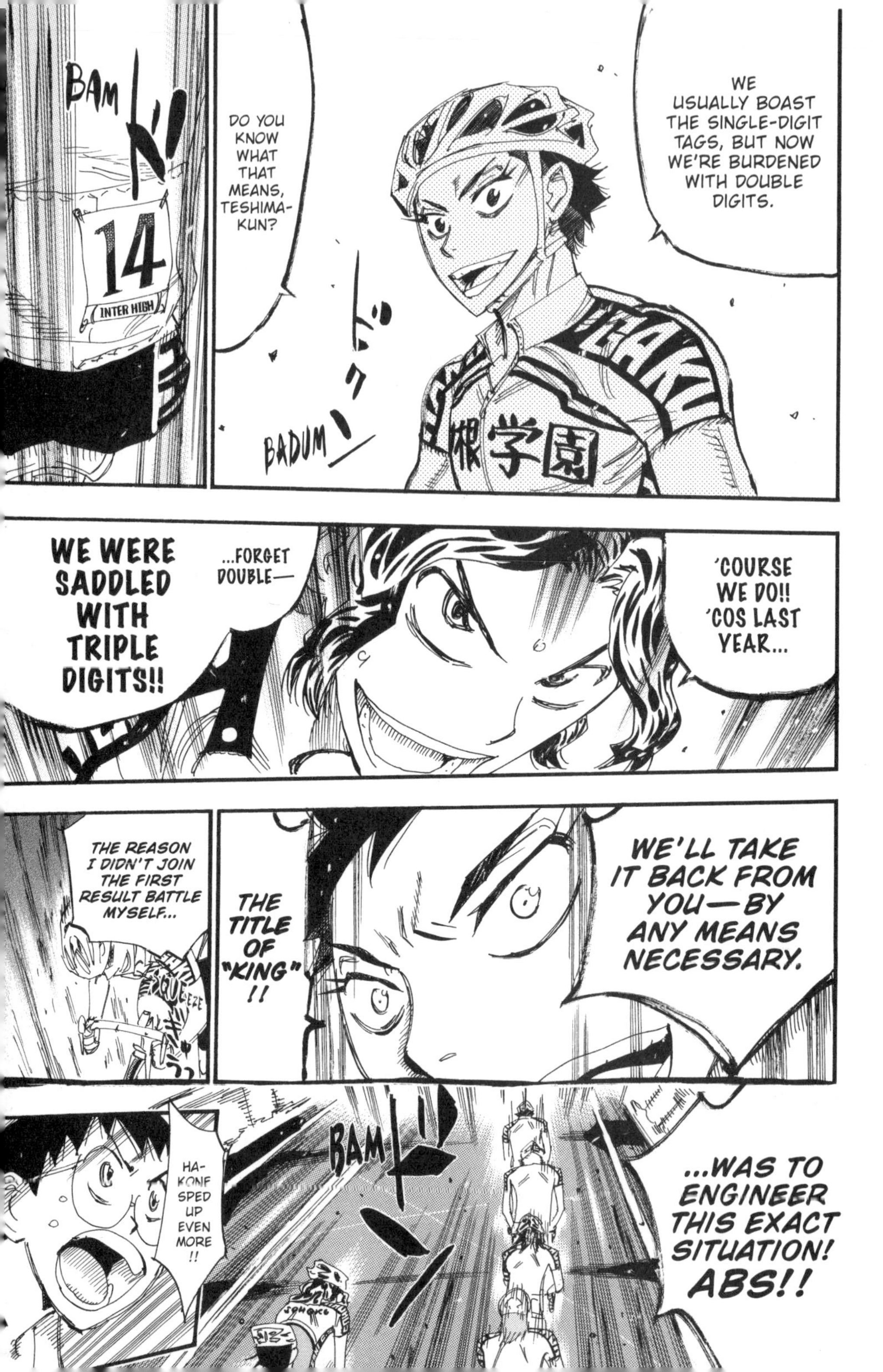
WE USUALLY BOAST THE SINGLE-DIGIT TAGS, BUT NOW WE'RE BURDENED WITH DOUBLE DIGITS.
DO YOU KNOW WHAT THAT MEANS, TESHIMA-KUN?
BADUM
BAM
14
INTER HIGH
'COURSE WE DO!! 'COS LAST YEAR...
...FORGET DOUBLE—
WE WERE SADDLED WITH TRIPLE DIGITS!!
WE'LL TAKE IT BACK FROM YOU—BY ANY MEANS NECESSARY.
THE TITLE OF "KING" !!
THE REASON I DIDN'T JOIN THE FIRST RESULT BATTLE MYSELF...
SQUEEZE
...WAS TO ENGINEER THIS EXACT SITUATION! ABS!!
BAM
HA-KONE SPED UP EVEN MORE !!

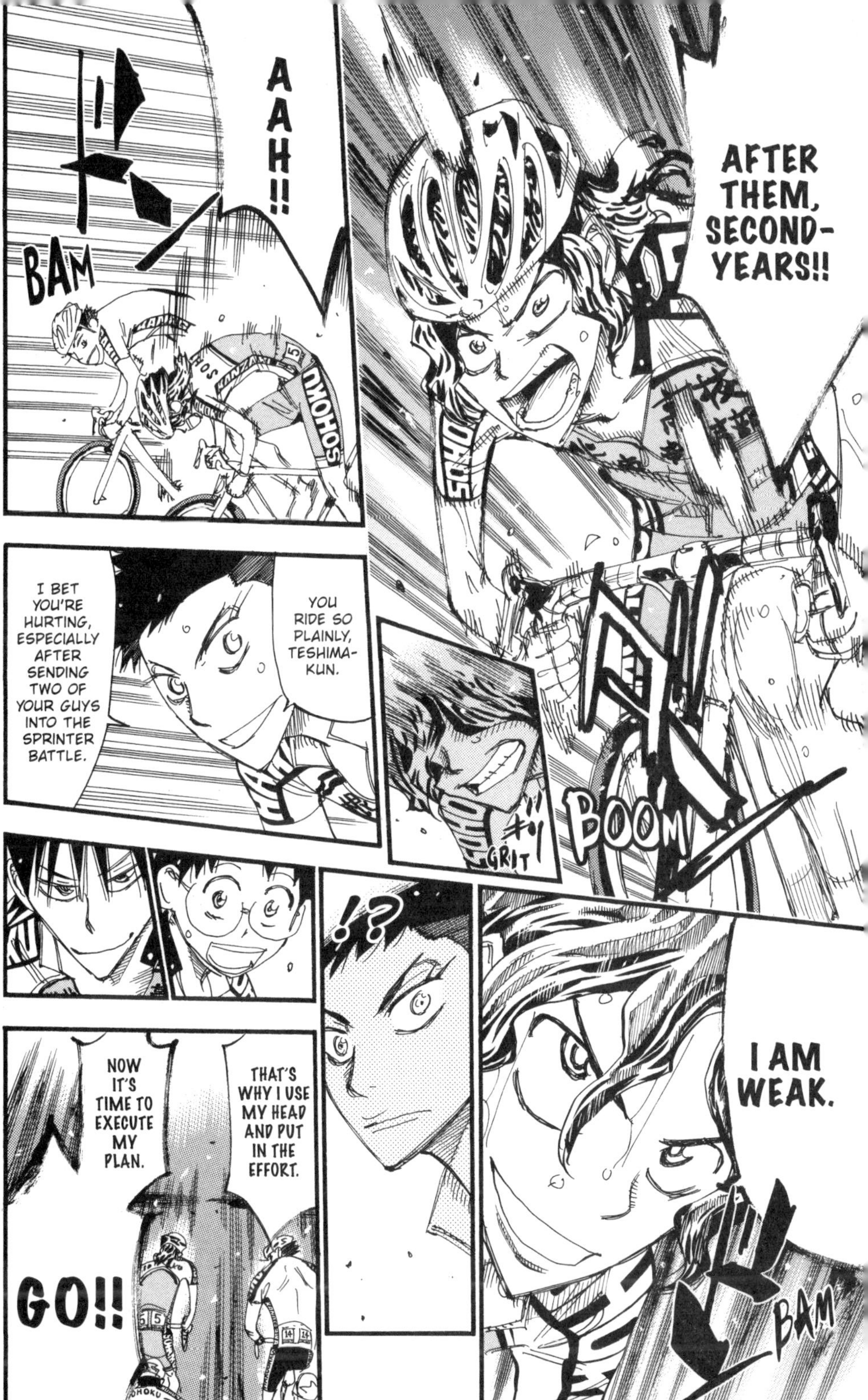
AFTER THEM, SECOND-YEARS!!
BOOM
AAH!!
BAM
GRIT
YOU RIDE SO PLAINLY, TESHIMA-KUN.
I BET YOU'RE HURTING, ESPECIALLY AFTER SENDING TWO OF YOUR GUYS INTO THE SPRINTER BATTLE.
I AM WEAK.
BAM
!?
THAT'S WHY I USE MY HEAD AND PUT IN THE EFFORT.
NOW IT'S TIME TO EXECUTE MY PLAN.
GO!!

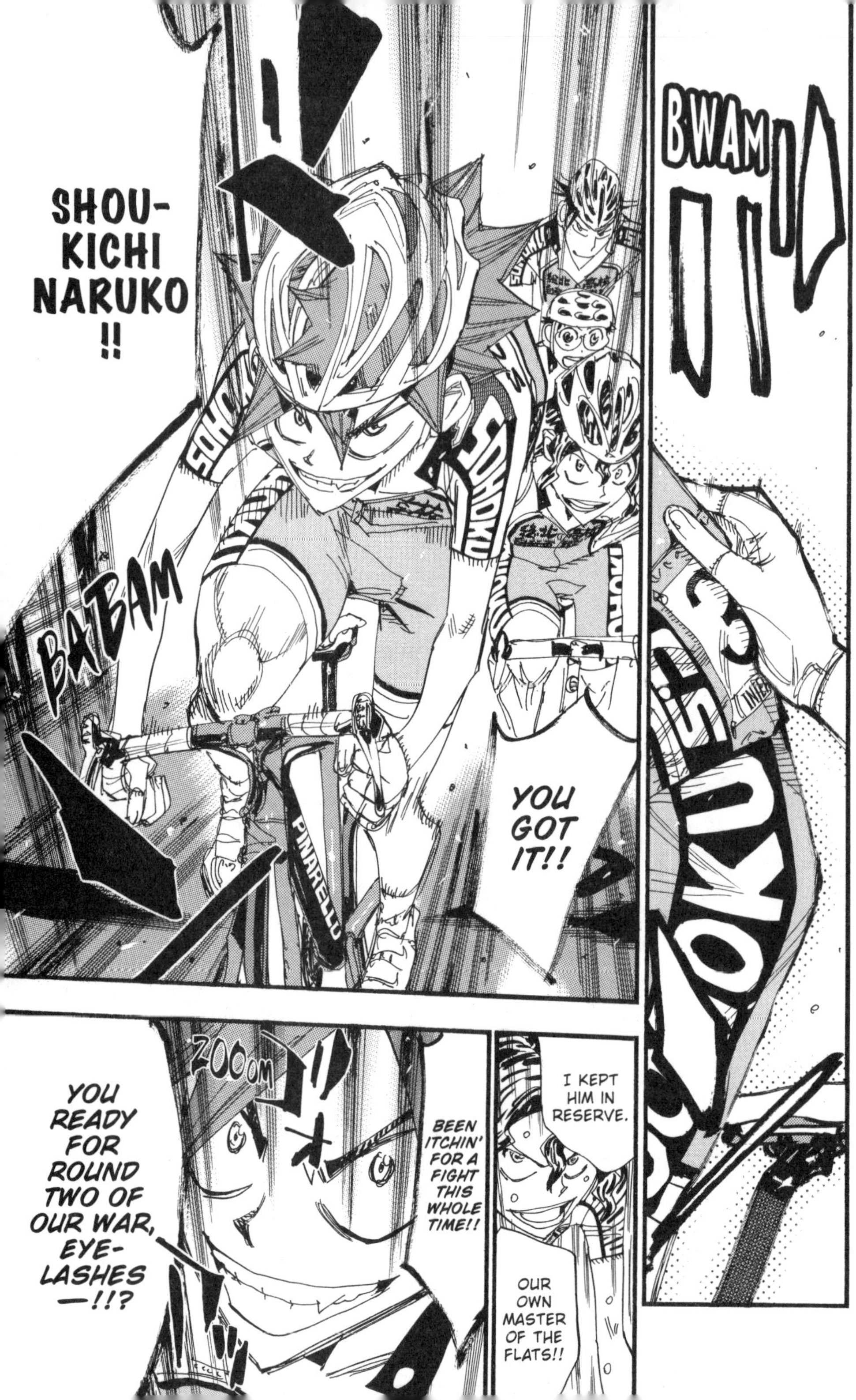
BWAM
SHOU-KICHI NARUKO!!
BABAM
YOU GOT IT!!
I KEPT HIM IN RESERVE.
BEEN ITCHIN' FOR A FIGHT THIS WHOLE TIME!!
OUR OWN MASTER OF THE FLATS!!
ZOOOM
YOU READY FOR ROUND TWO OF OUR WAR, EYE-LASHES—!!?

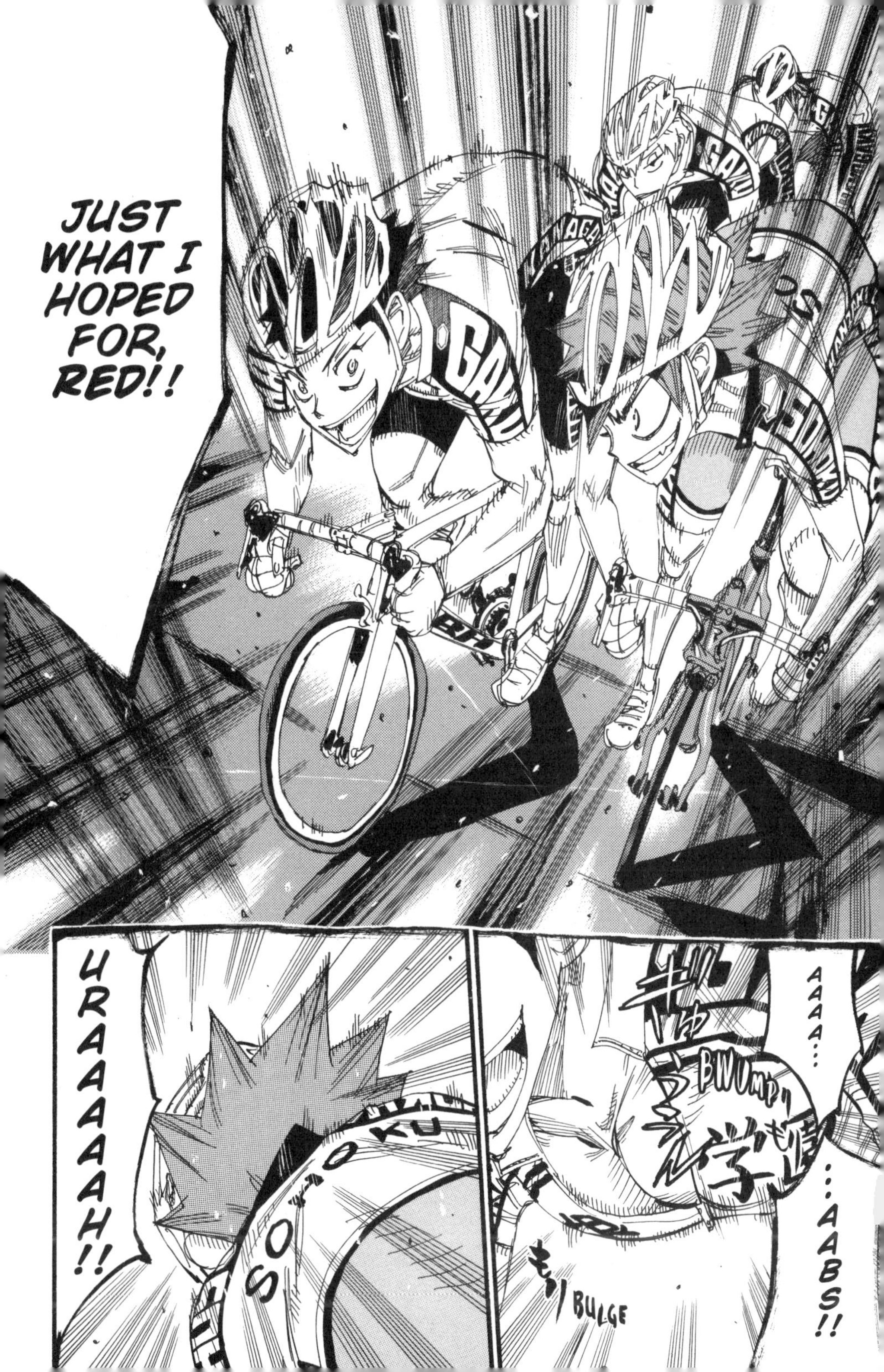
JUST WHAT I HOPED FOR, RED!!
AAAA...
BWUMP
BULGE
...AAABS!!
URAAAAAAAH!!

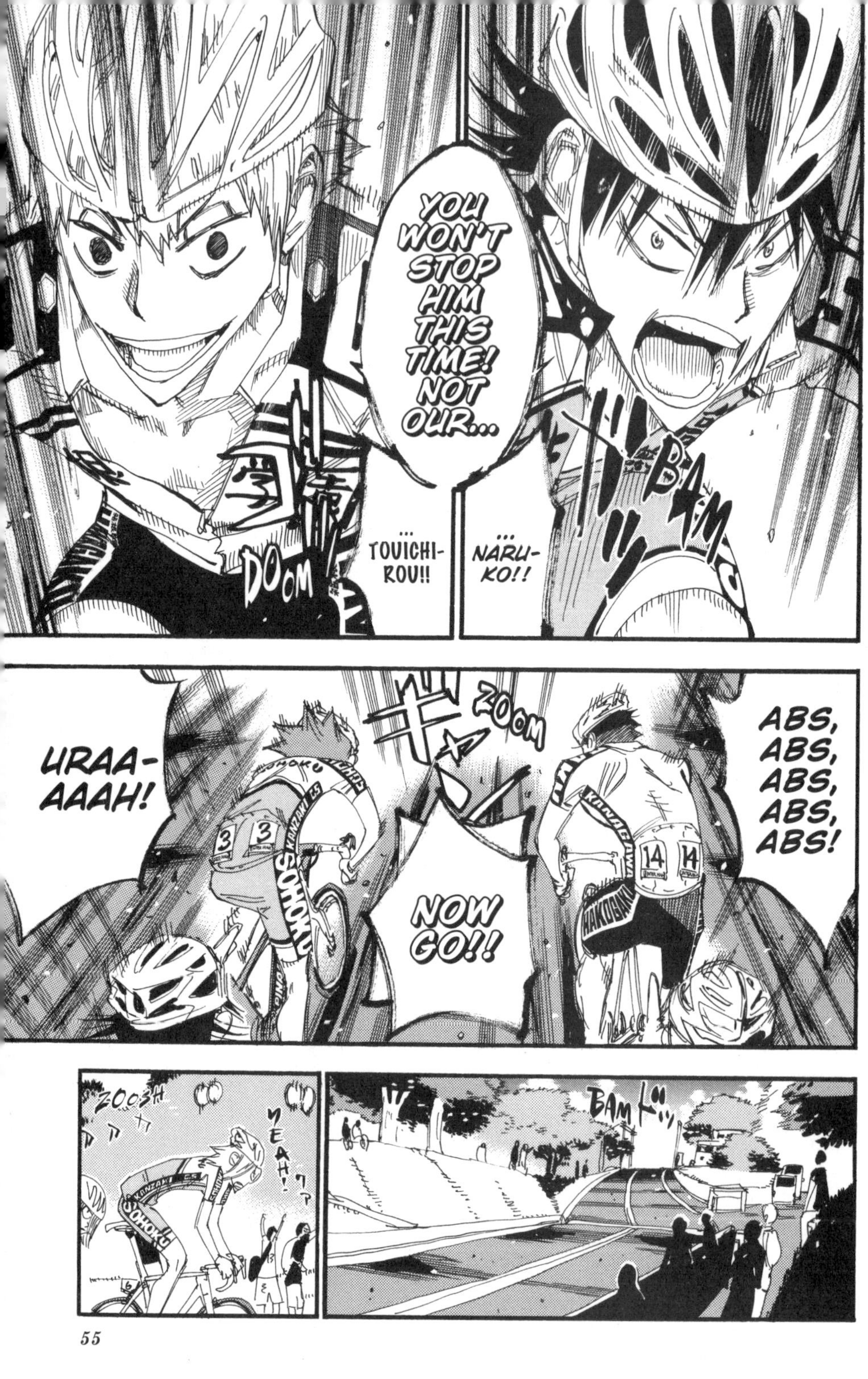
YOU WON'T STOP HIM THIS TIME! NOT OUR...
BAM
...NARU-KO!!
...TOUICHI-ROU!!
DOOM
ABS, ABS, ABS, ABS, ABS!
ZOOM
NOW GO!!
URAA-AAAH!
BAM
ZOOSH
YEAH!

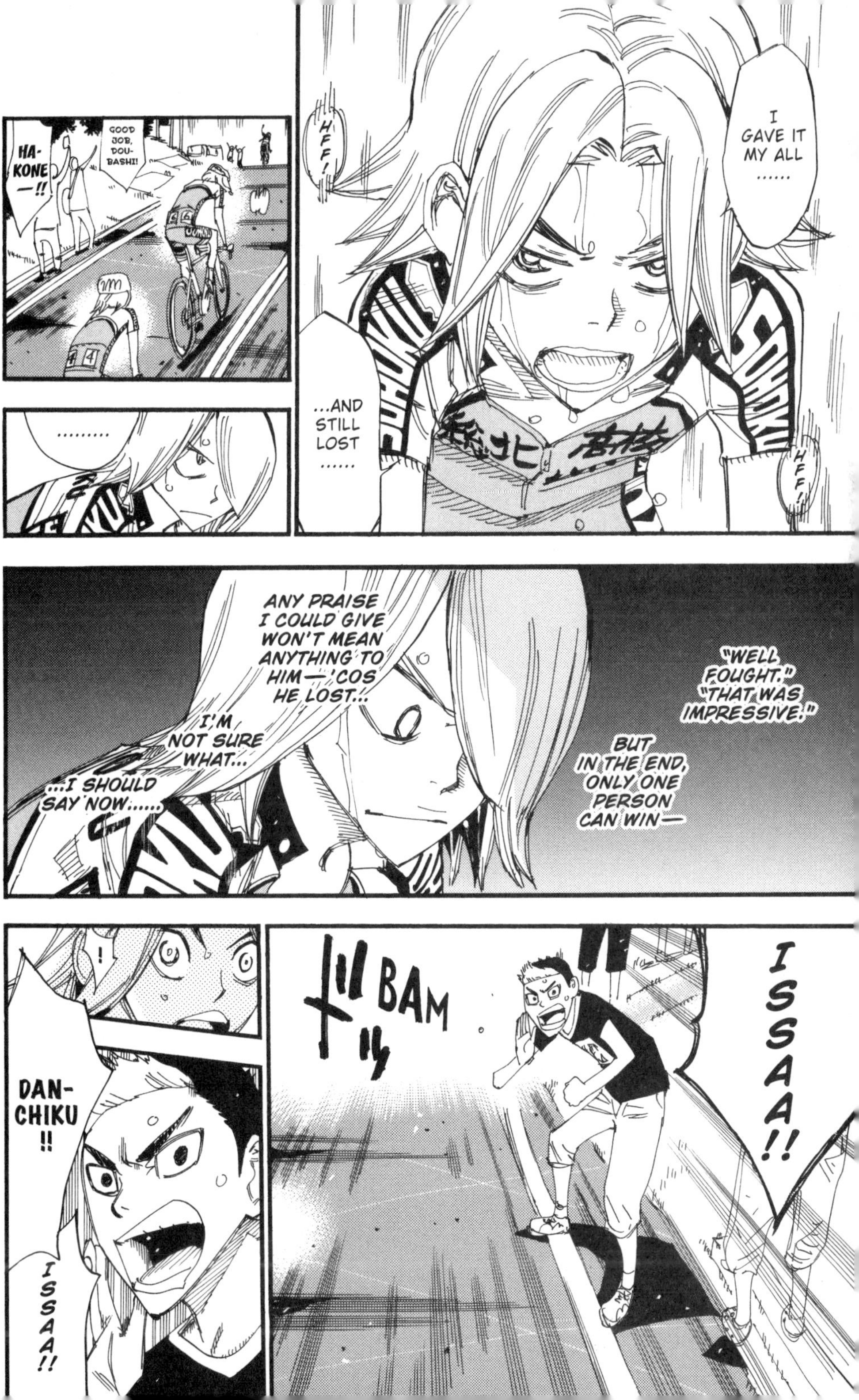
I GAVE IT MY ALL ......
HFF!
...AND STILL LOST ......
HFF!
HA-KONE—!!
GOOD JOB, DOU-BASHI!
....
"WELL FOUGHT." "THAT WAS IMPRESSIVE."
BUT IN THE END, ONLY ONE PERSON CAN WIN—
ANY PRAISE I COULD GIVE WON'T MEAN ANYTHING TO HIM—'COS HE LOST...
I'M NOT SURE WHAT...
...I SHOULD SAY NOW......
ISSAA!!
BAM
!
DAN-CHIKU!!
ISSAA!!

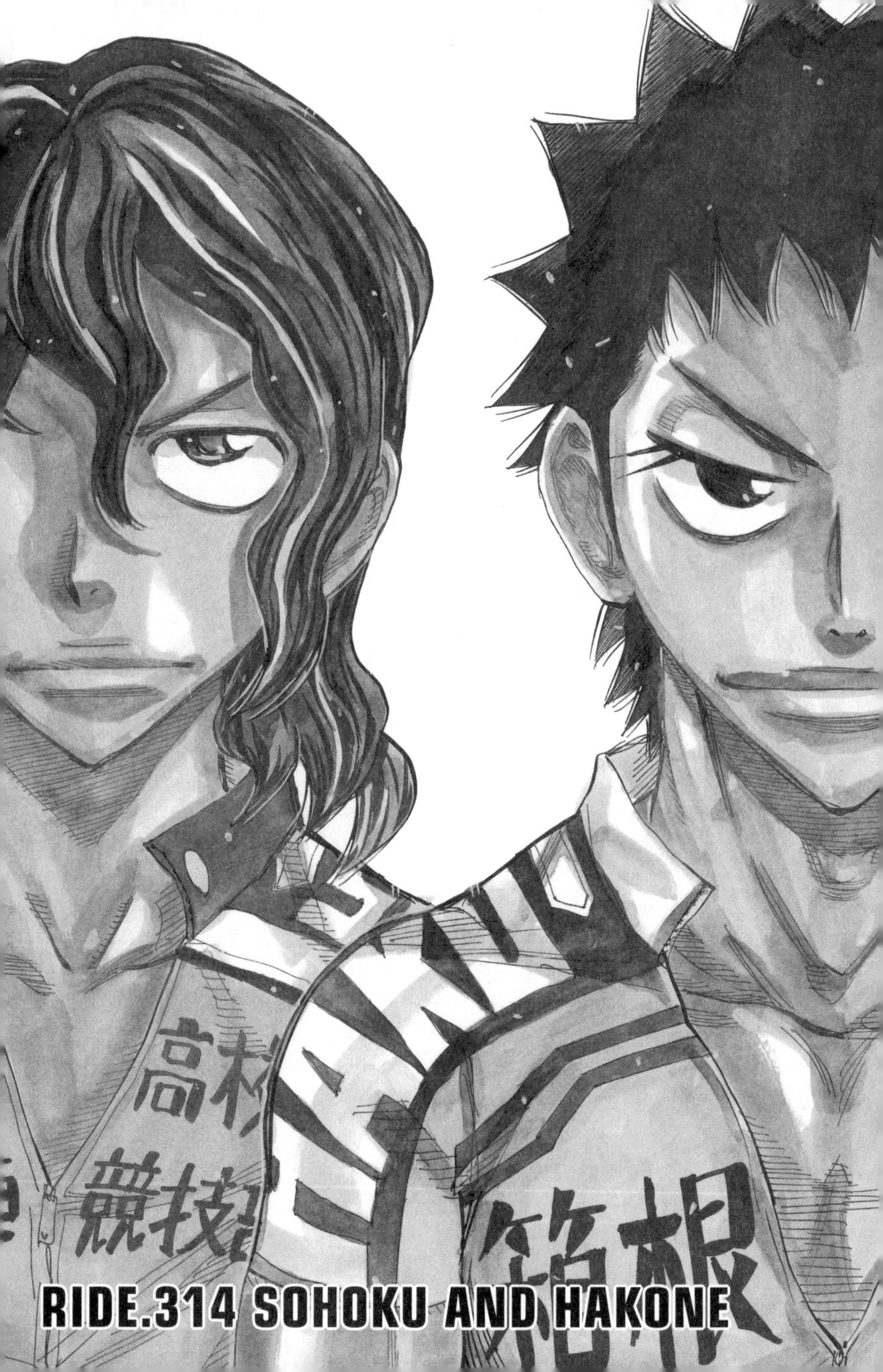
箱根

RIDE.314 SOHOKU AND HAKONE

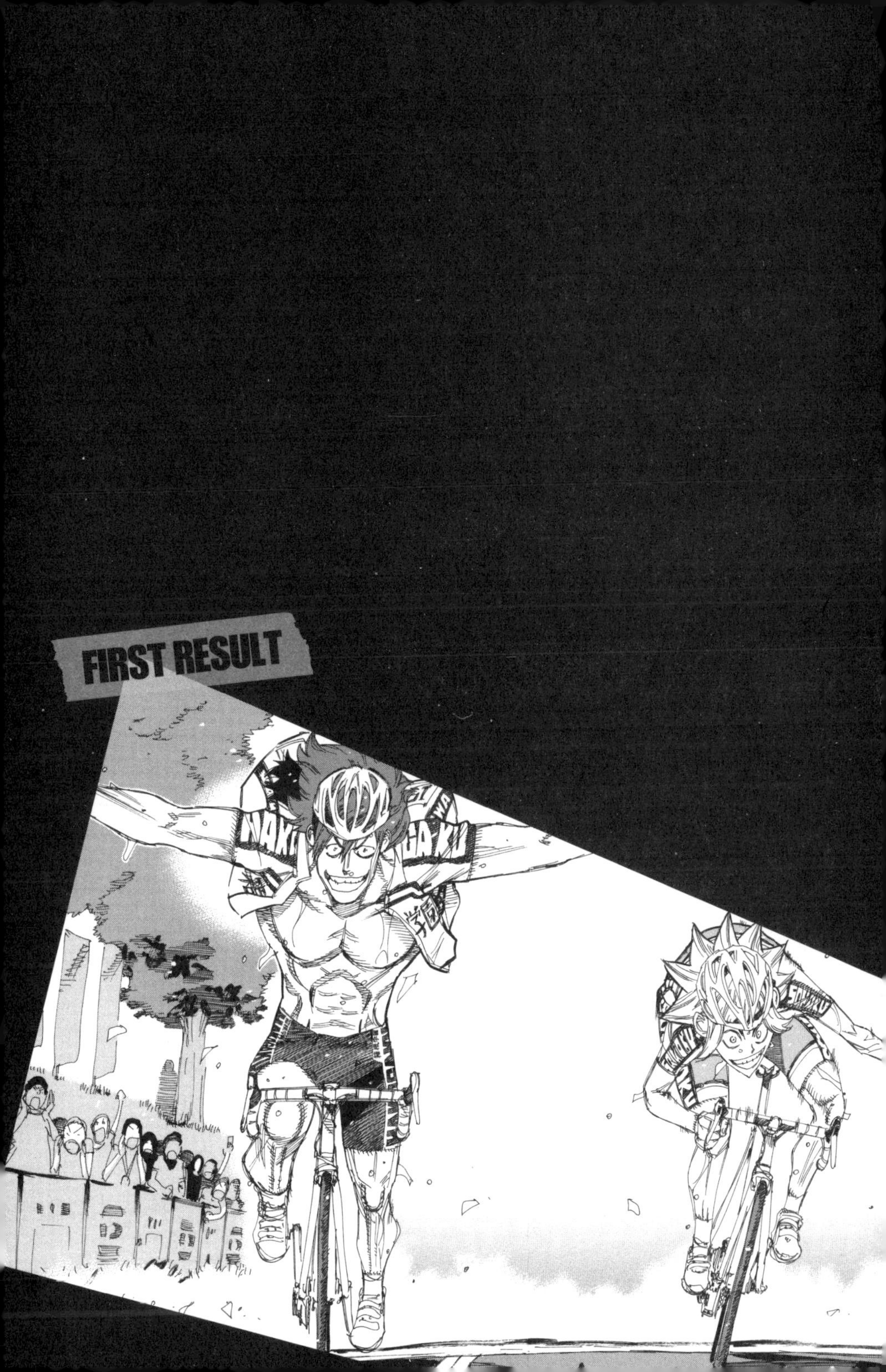
FIRST RESULT

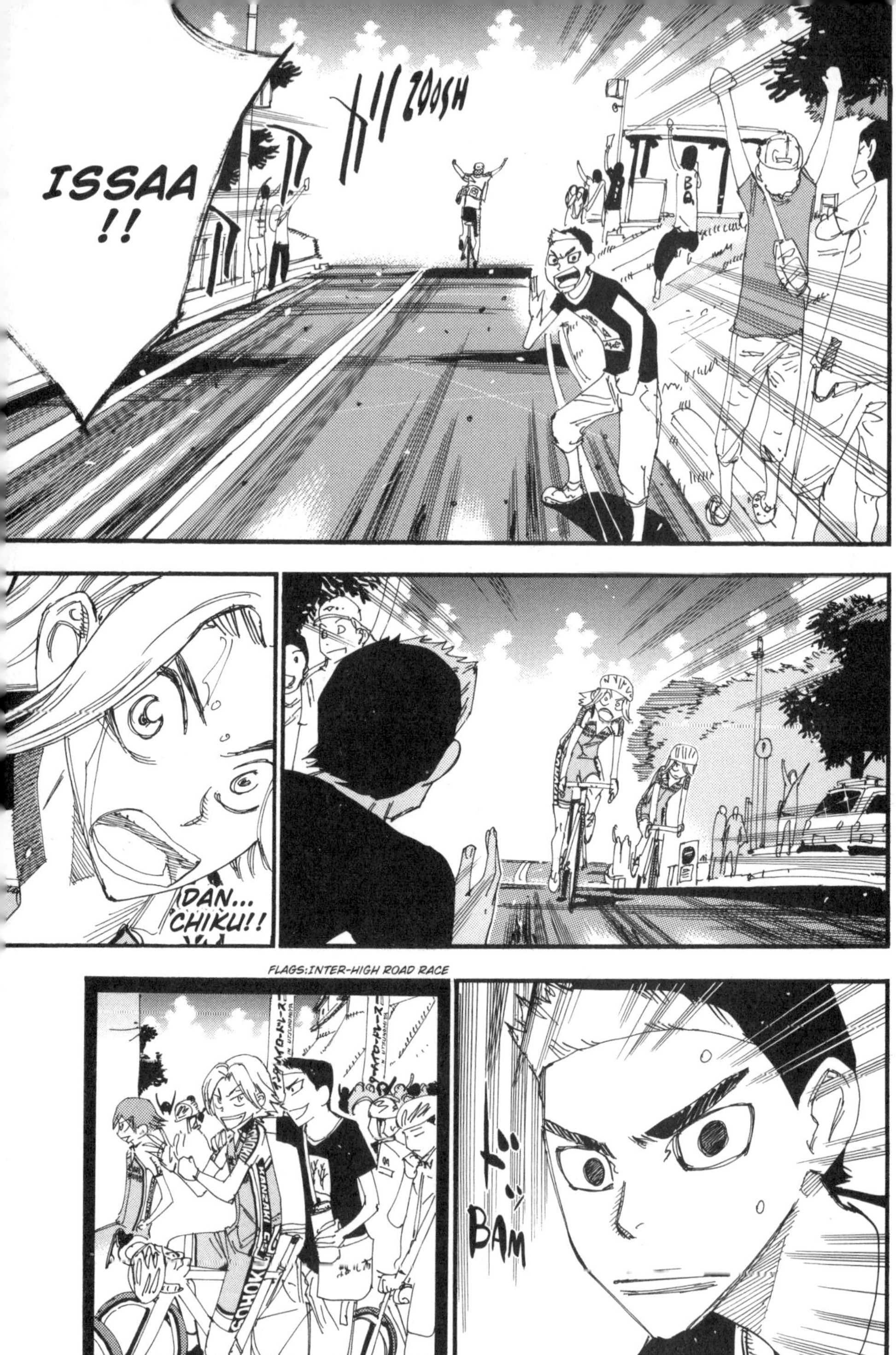
ZOOSH
ISSAA!!
DAN... CHIKU!!
BAM
FLAGS: INTER-HIGH ROAD RACE

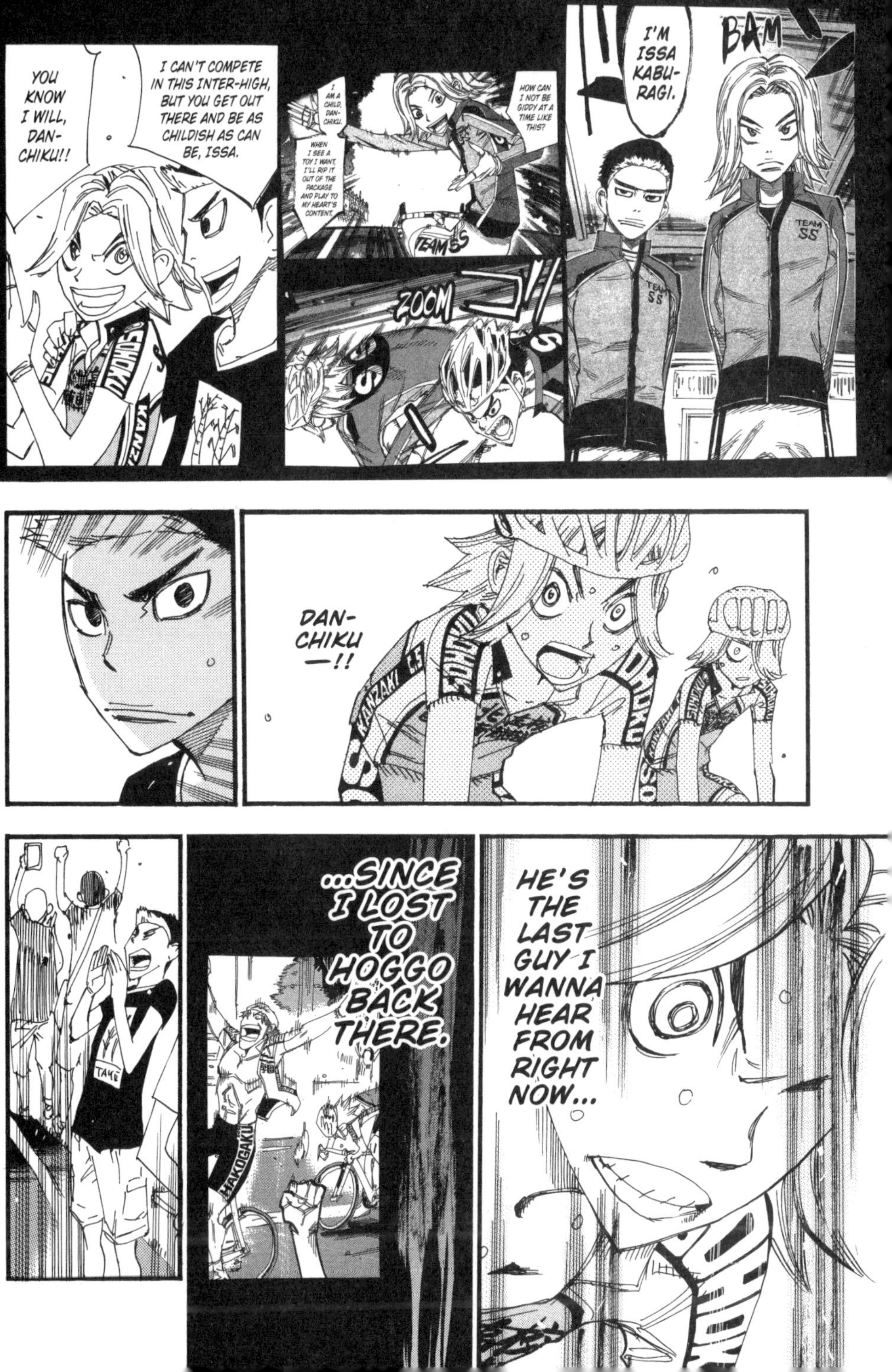

BAM
I'M ISSA KABURAGI.
HOW CAN I NOT BE GIDDY AT A TIME LIKE THIS?
I AM A CHILD, DAN-CHIKU.
WHEN I SEE A TOY I WANT, I'LL RIP IT OUT OF THE PACKAGE AND PLAY TO MY HEART'S CONTENT.
ZOOM
I CAN'T COMPETE IN THIS INTER-HIGH, BUT YOU GET OUT THERE AND BE AS CHILDISH AS CAN BE, ISSA.
YOU KNOW I WILL, DAN-CHIKU!!
DAN-CHIKU—!!
HE'S THE LAST GUY I WANNA HEAR FROM RIGHT NOW...
...SINCE I LOST TO HOGGO BACK THERE.

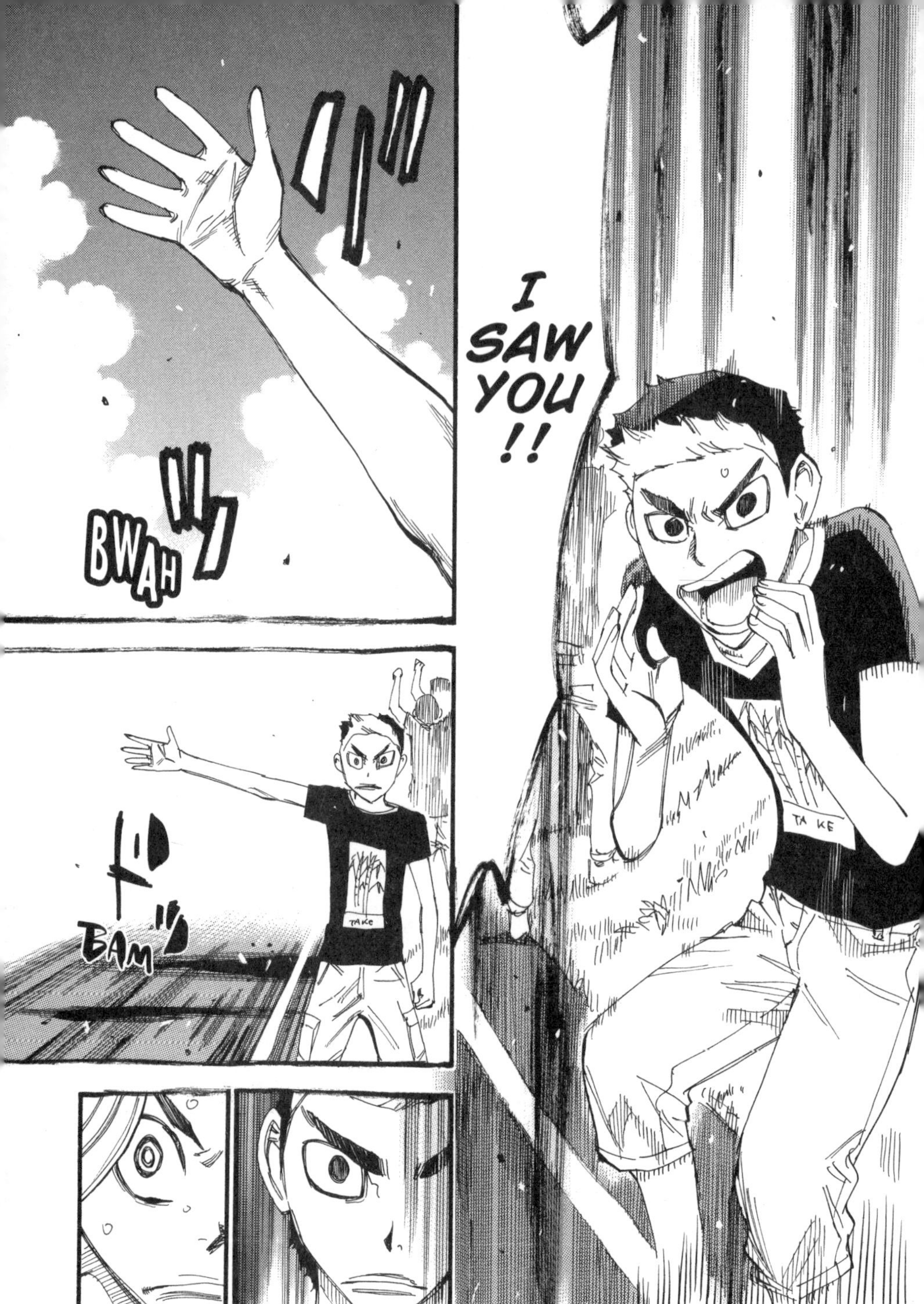
I SAW YOU !!
TAKE
BWAH
TAKE
BAM

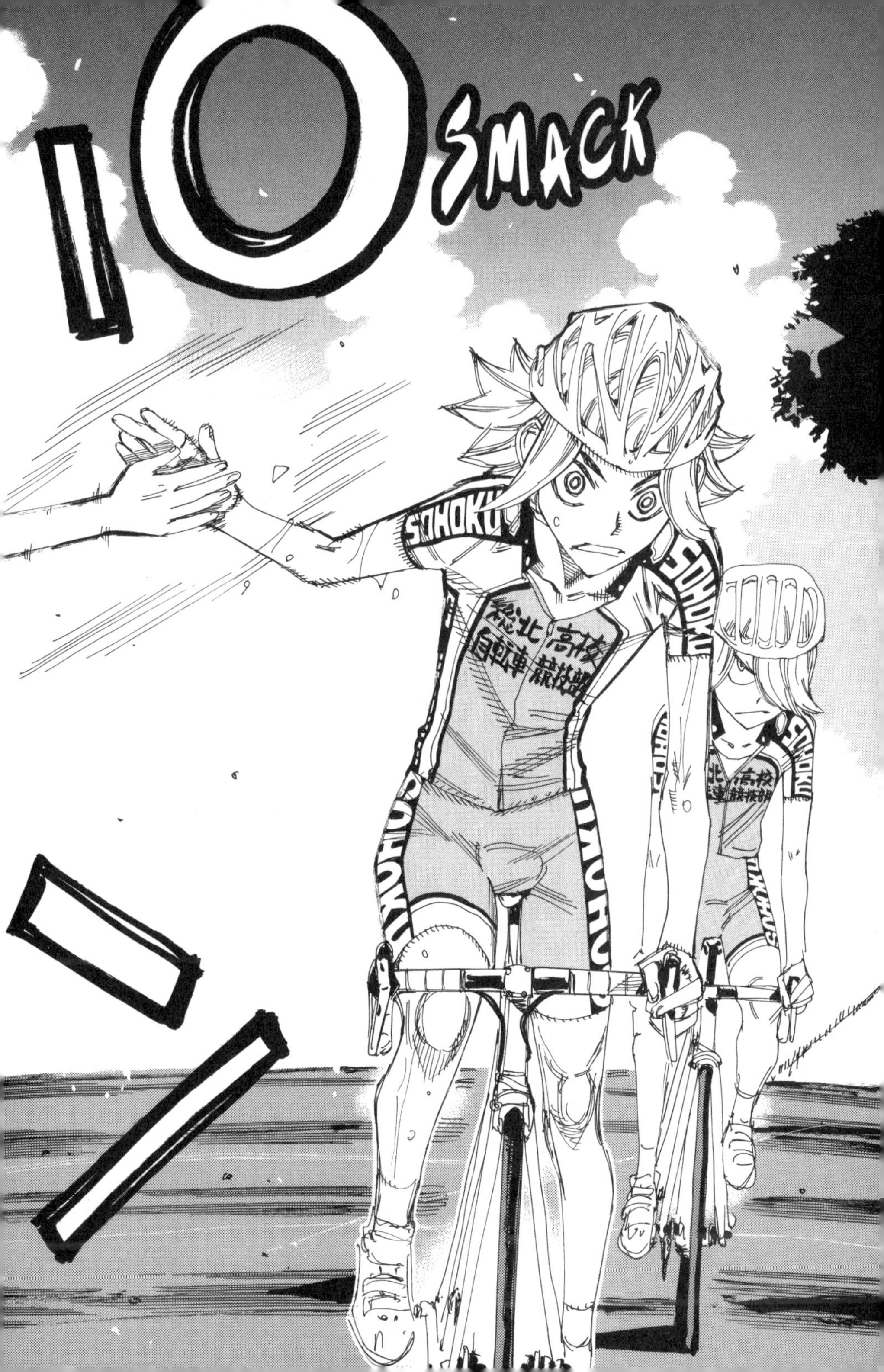
SMACK
SOHOKU
総北高校
自転車競技部

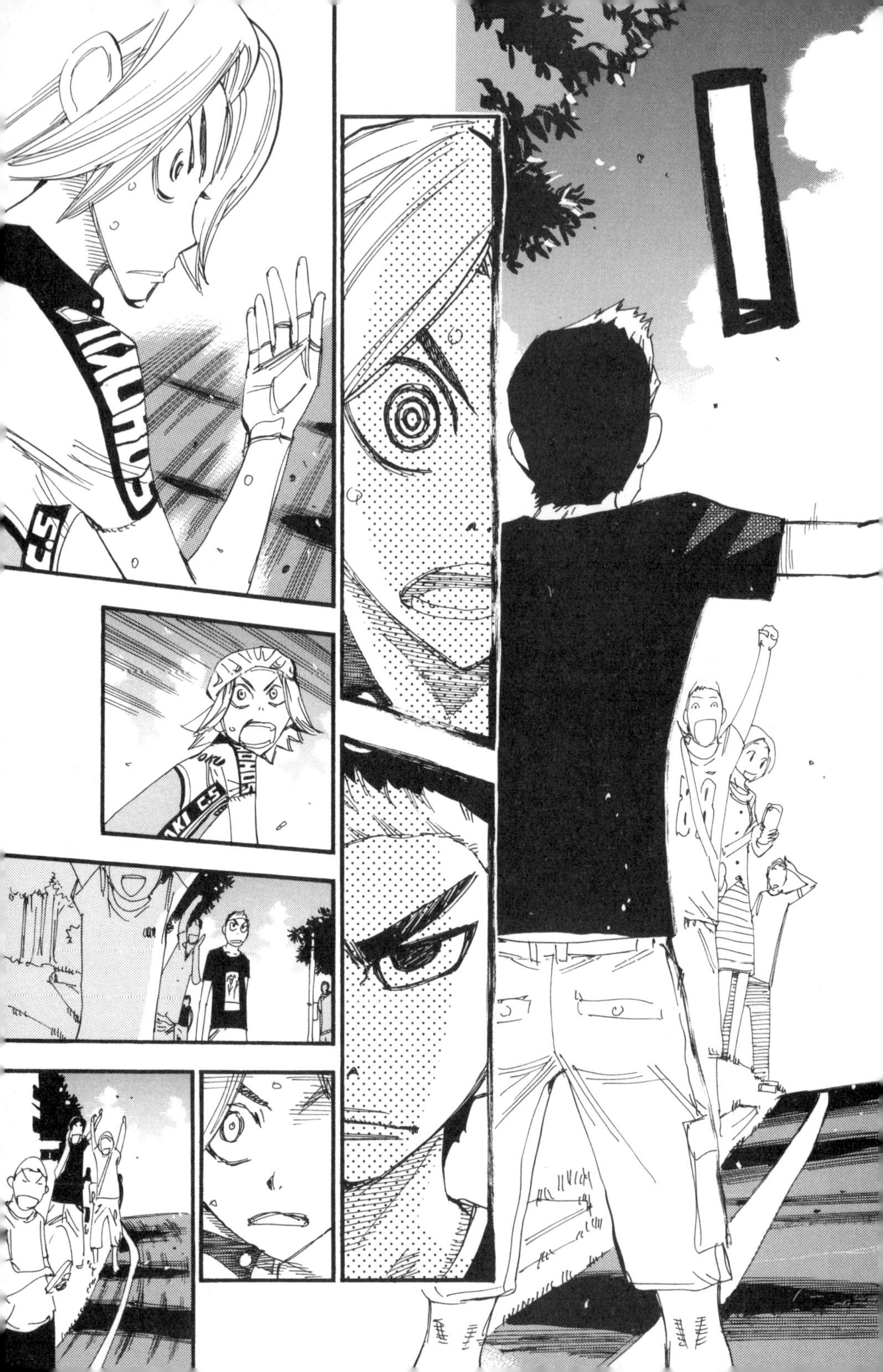

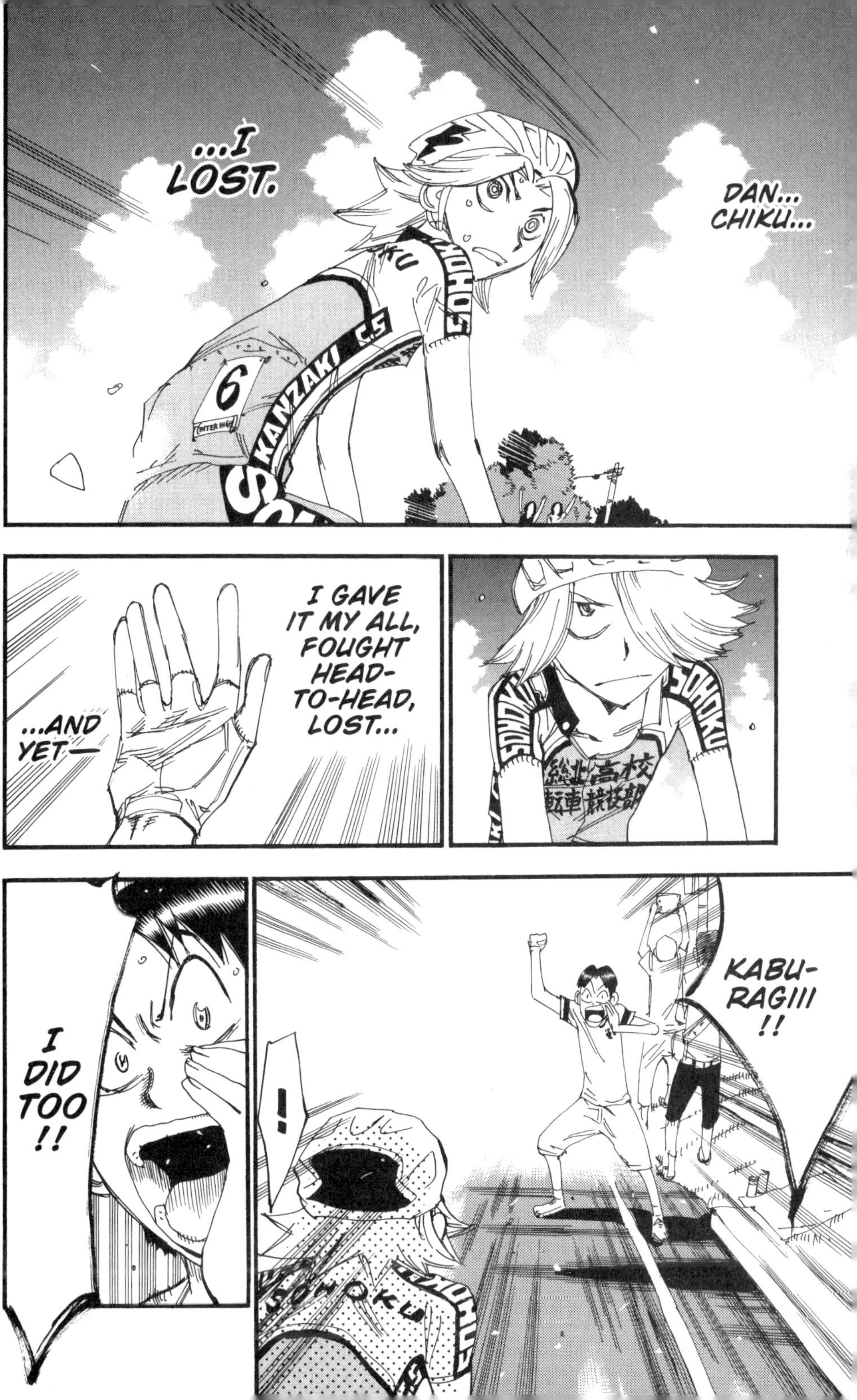
DAN... CHIKU...
...I LOST.
I GAVE IT MY ALL, FOUGHT HEAD-TO-HEAD, LOST...
...AND YET—
KABU-RAGIII !!
!
I DID TOO !!

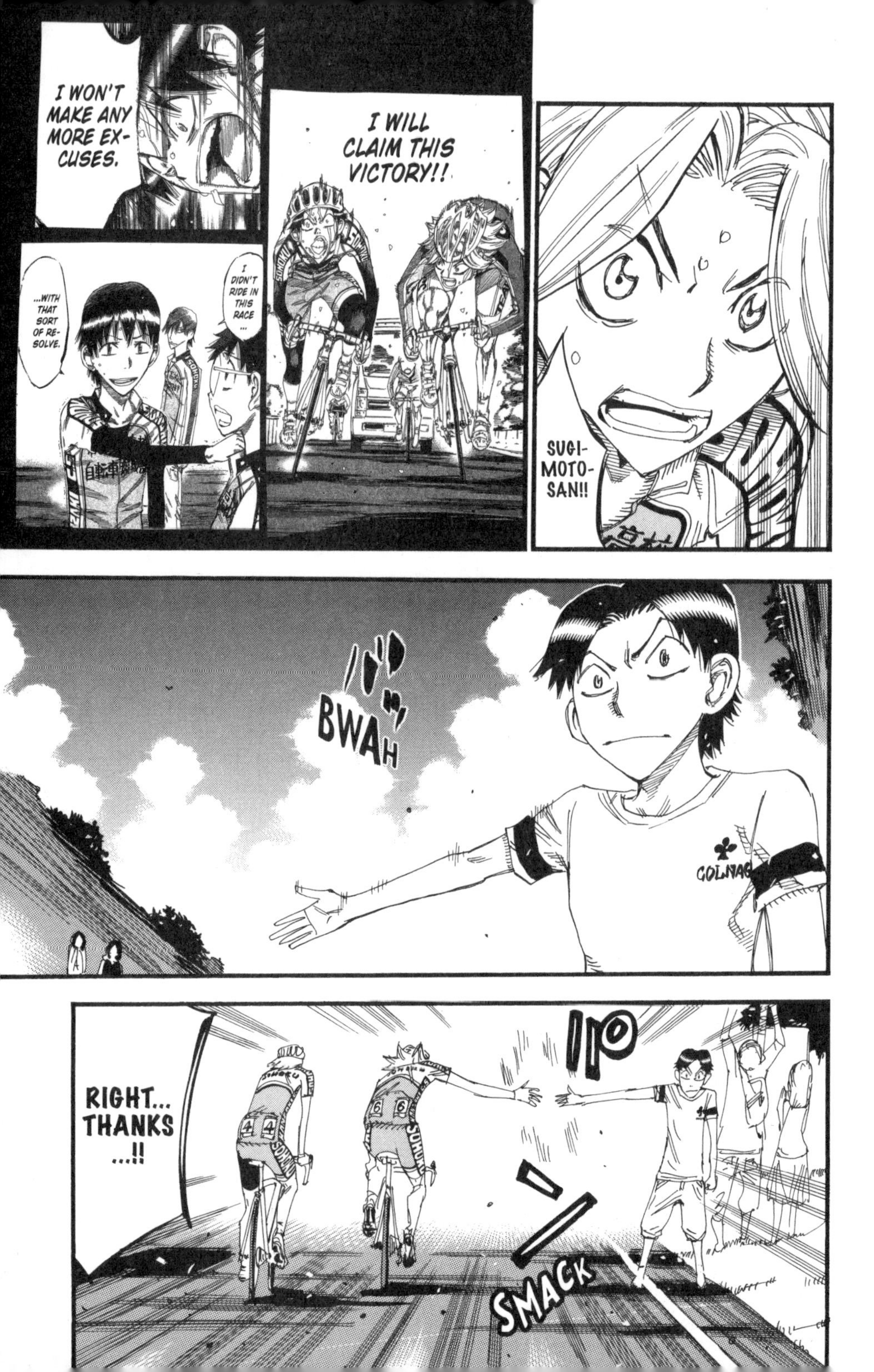
SUGI-MOTO-SAN!!
I WILL CLAIM THIS VICTORY!!
I WON'T MAKE ANY MORE EX-CUSES.
I DIDN'T RIDE IN THIS RACE ...
...WITH THAT SORT OF RE-SOLVE.
BWAH
SMACK
RIGHT... THANKS ...!!

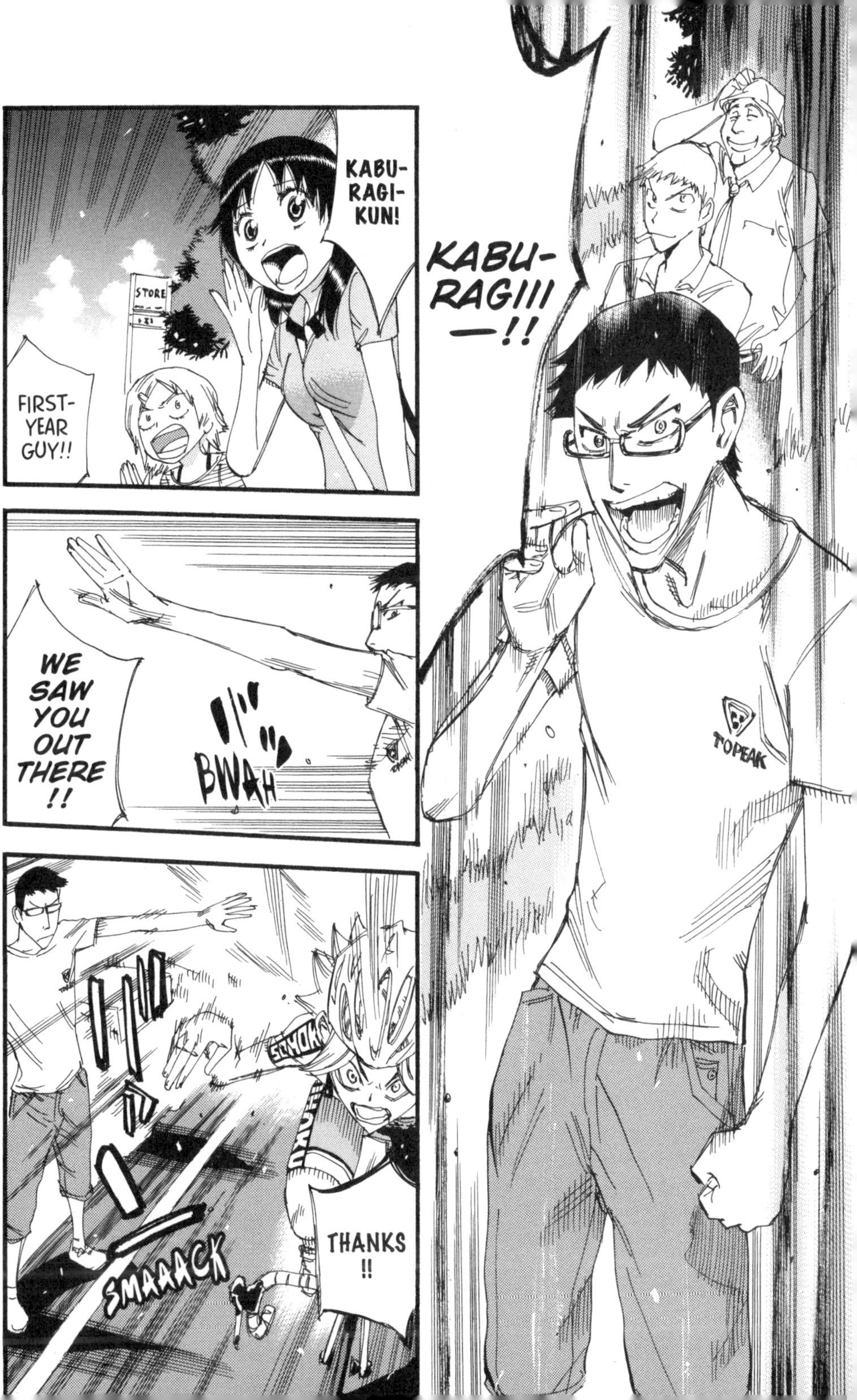
KABU-RAGI!!!—!!
TOPEAK
KABU-RAGI-KUN!
STORE
FIRST-YEAR GUY!!
WE SAW YOU OUT THERE!!
BWAH
THANKS!!
SMAAACK

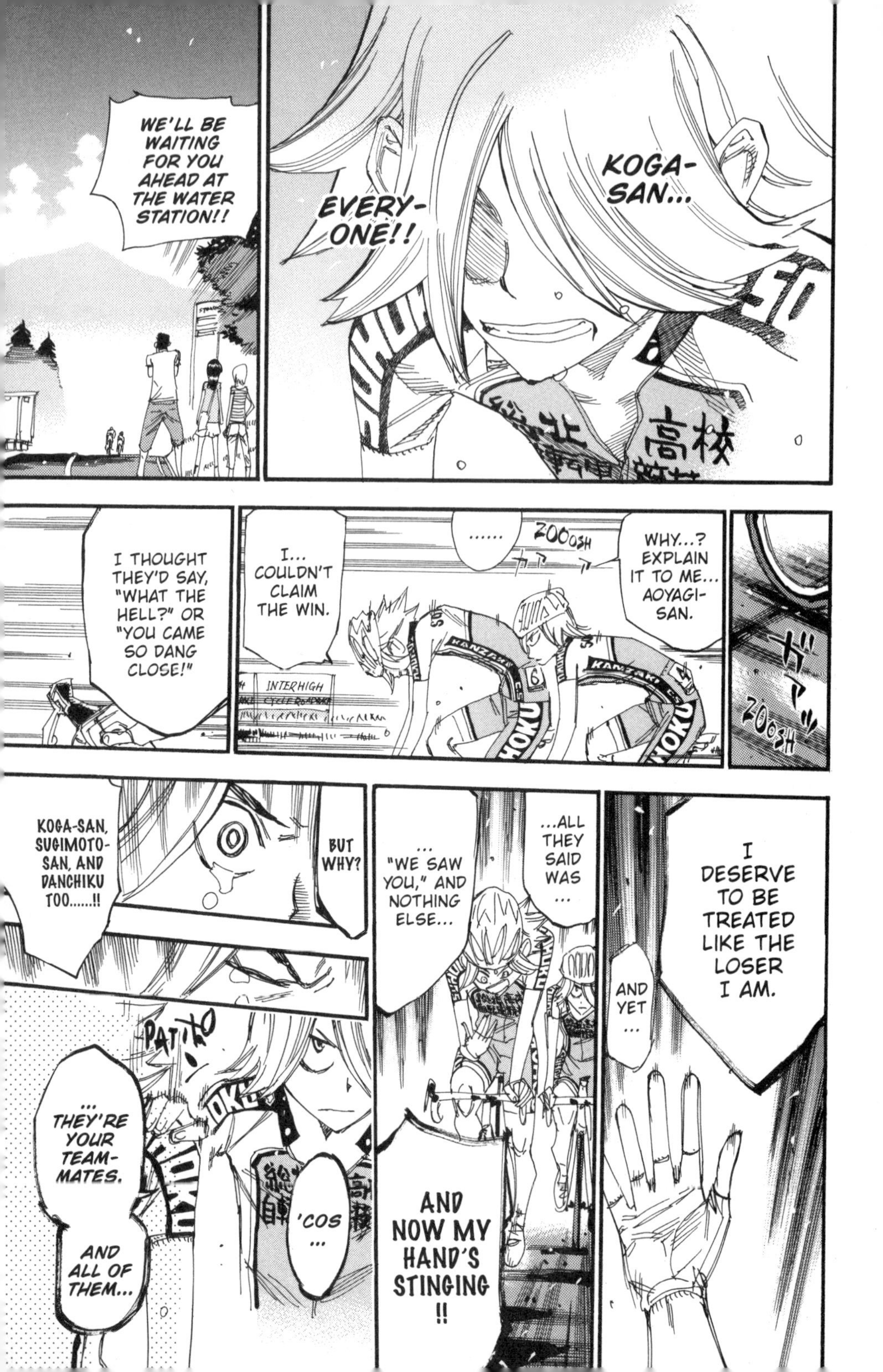
KOGA-SAN...
EVERY-ONE!!
WE'LL BE WAITING FOR YOU AHEAD AT THE WATER STATION!!
ZOOSH
WHY...? EXPLAIN IT TO ME... AOYAGI-SAN.
ZOOosh
......
I... COULDN'T CLAIM THE WIN.
INTERHIGH
I THOUGHT THEY'D SAY, "WHAT THE HELL?" OR "YOU CAME SO DANG CLOSE!"
I DESERVE TO BE TREATED LIKE THE LOSER I AM.
AND YET ...
...ALL THEY SAID WAS ...
... "WE SAW YOU," AND NOTHING ELSE...
AND NOW MY HAND'S STINGING !!
BUT WHY?
KOGA-SAN, SUGIMOTO-SAN, AND DANCHIKU TOO......!!
PATIKO
... THEY'RE YOUR TEAM-MATES.
'COS ...
AND ALL OF THEM...

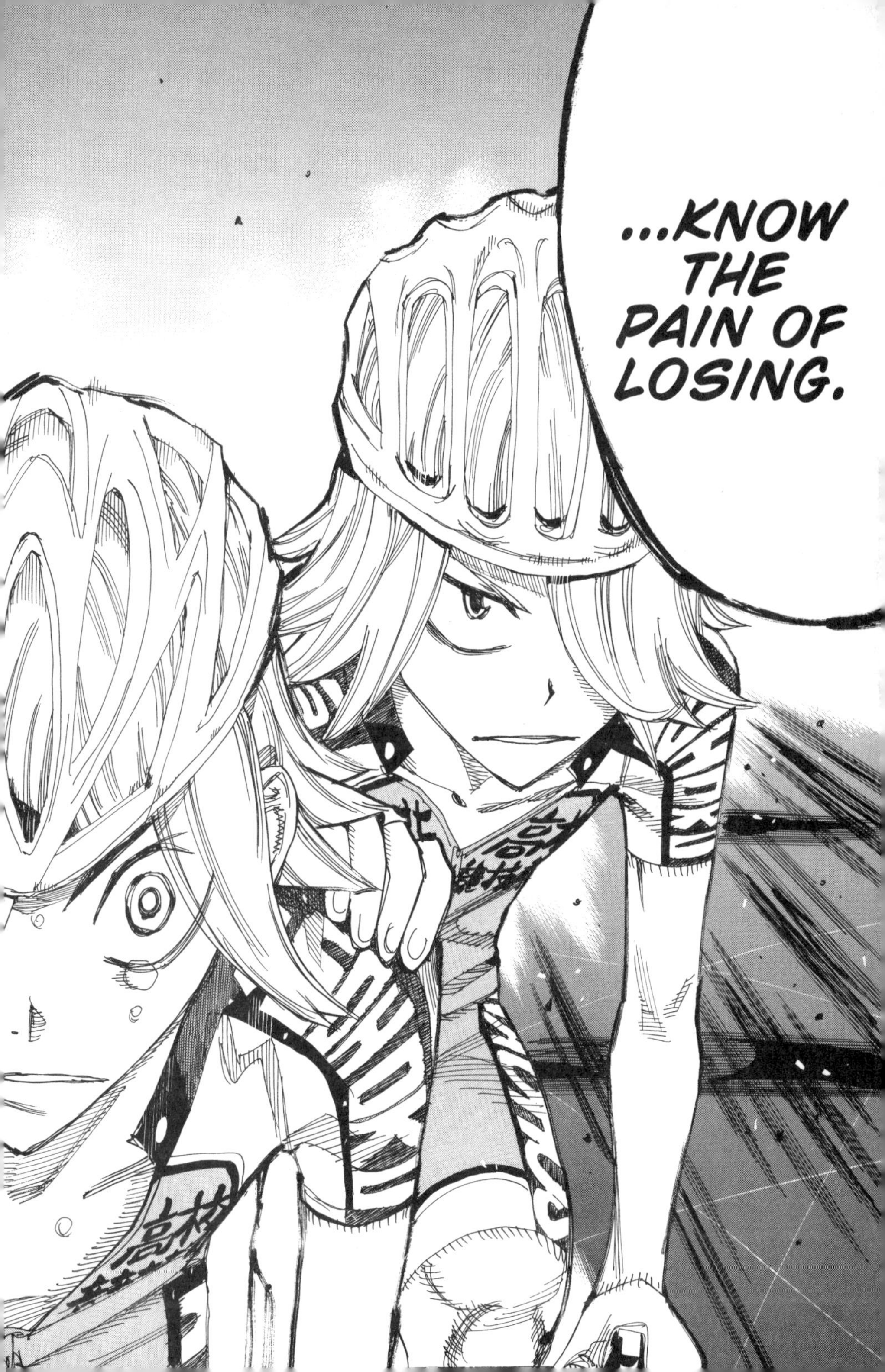
...KNOW THE PAIN OF LOSING.

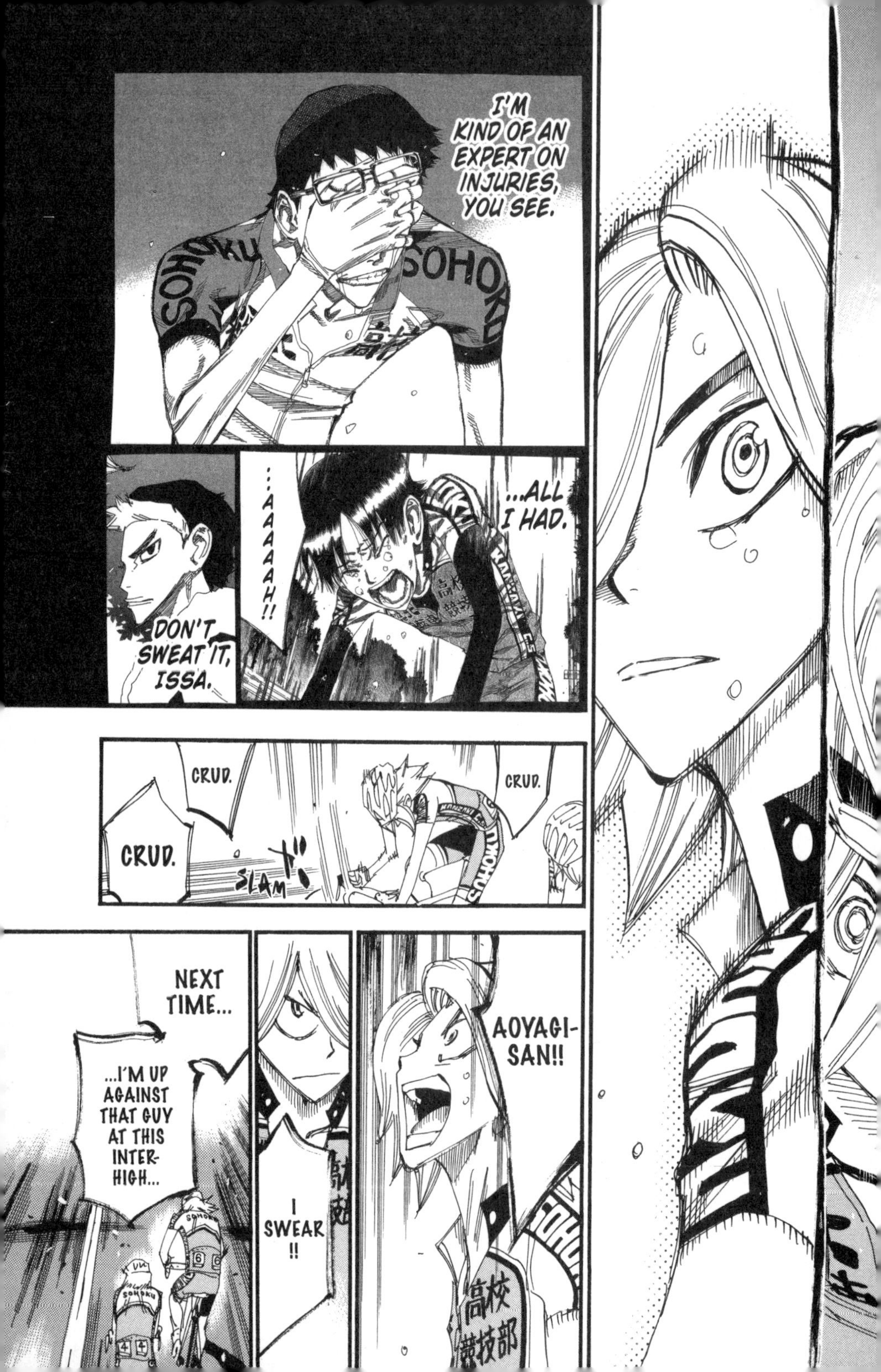
I'M KIND OF AN EXPERT ON INJURIES, YOU SEE.
...ALL I HAD.
...AAAAAAAH!!
DON'T SWEAT IT, ISSA.
CRUD.
CRUD.
CRUD.
SLAM
AOYAGI-SAN!!
I SWEAR!!
NEXT TIME...
...I'M UP AGAINST THAT GUY AT THIS INTER-HIGH...

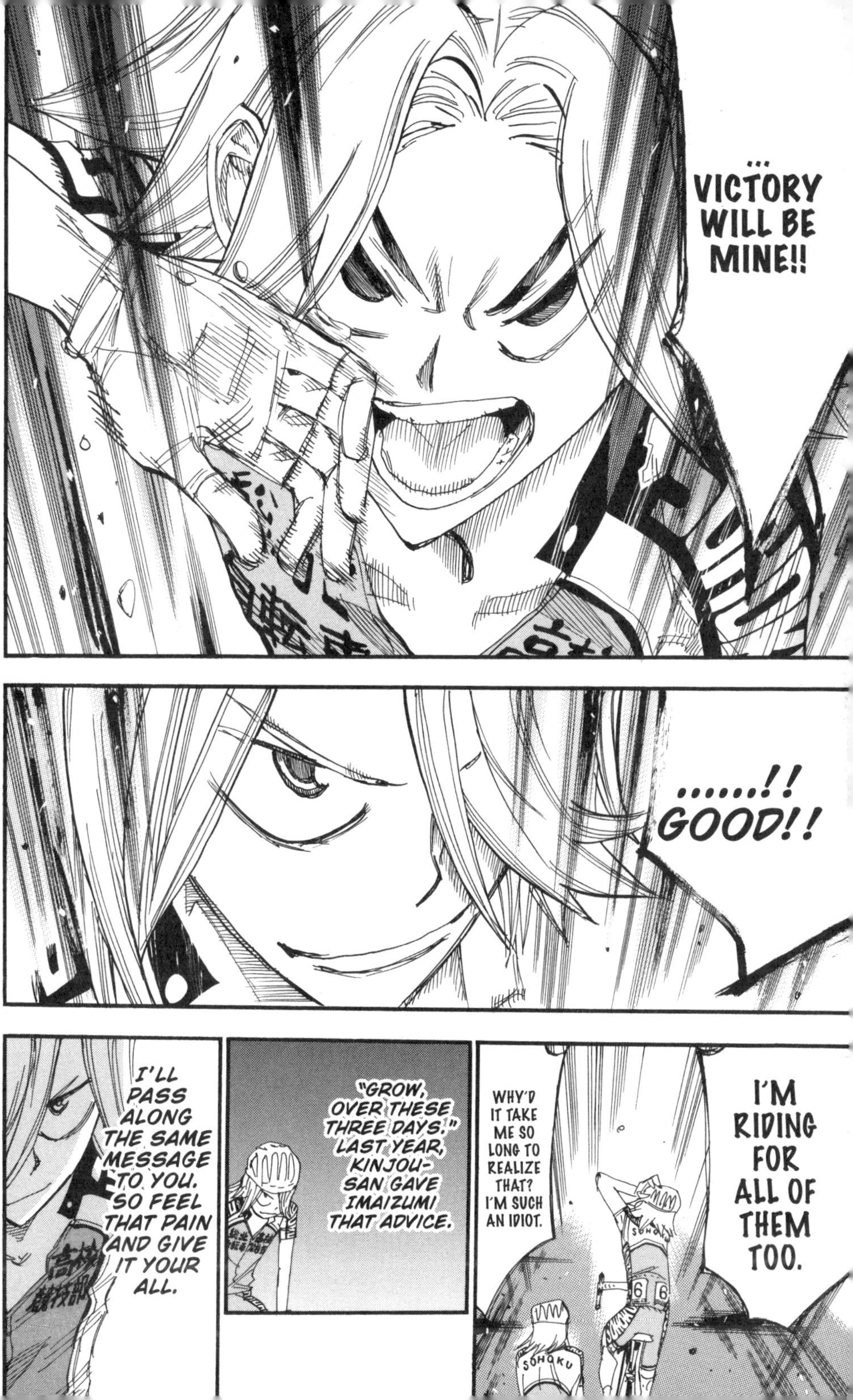
...VICTORY WILL BE MINE!!
......!! GOOD!!
I'M RIDING FOR ALL OF THEM TOO.
WHY'D IT TAKE ME SO LONG TO REALIZE THAT? I'M SUCH AN IDIOT.
"GROW, OVER THESE THREE DAYS." LAST YEAR, KINJOU-SAN GAVE IMAIZUMI THAT ADVICE.
I'LL PASS ALONG THE SAME MESSAGE TO YOU. SO FEEL THAT PAIN AND GIVE IT YOUR ALL.

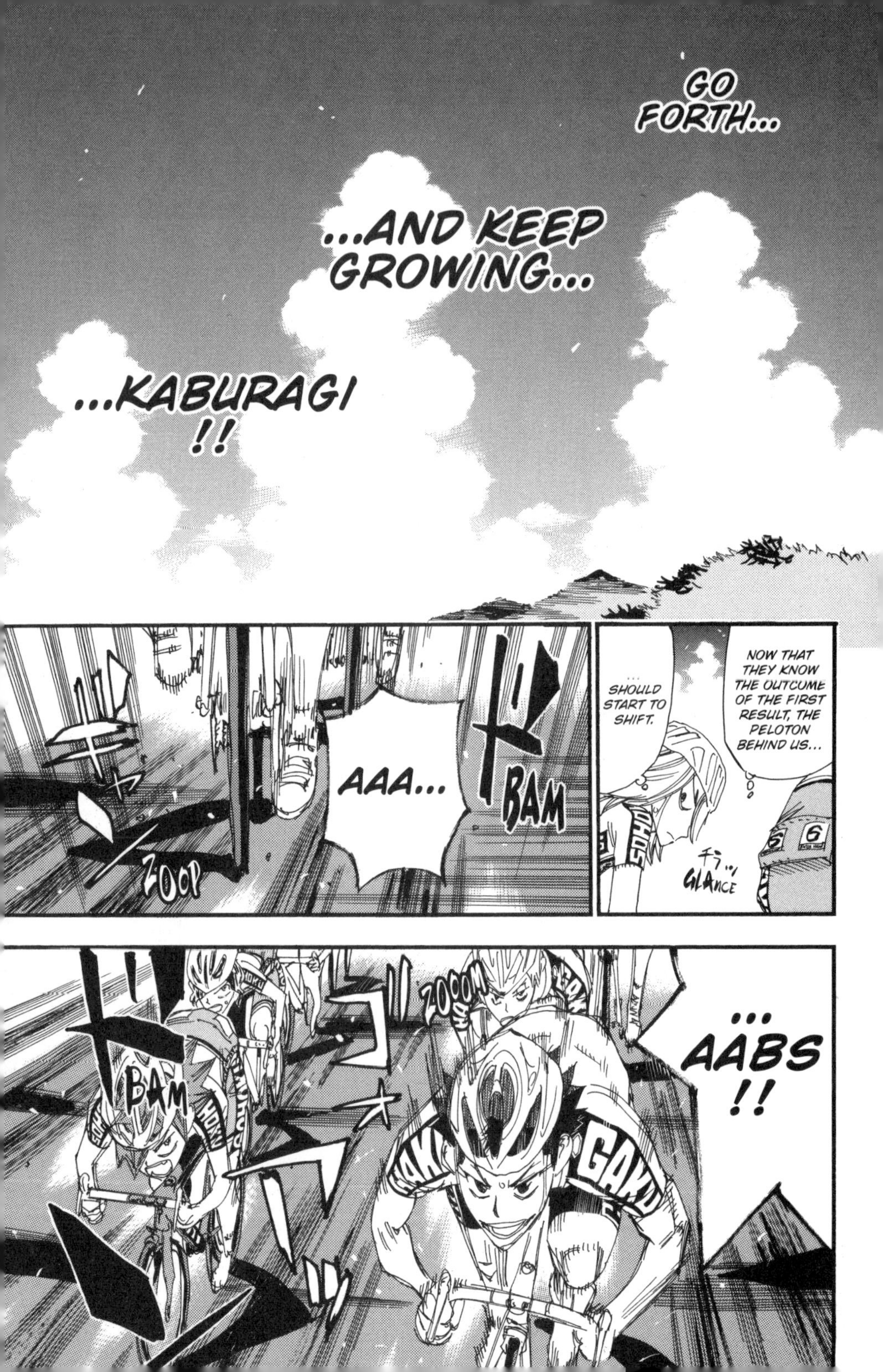
GO FORTH...
...AND KEEP GROWING...
...KABURAGI !!
NOW THAT THEY KNOW THE OUTCOME OF THE FIRST RESULT, THE PELOTON BEHIND US...
...SHOULD START TO SHIFT.
チラッ
GLANCE
BAM
AAA...
ZOOP
...AABS !!
ZOOOM
BAM

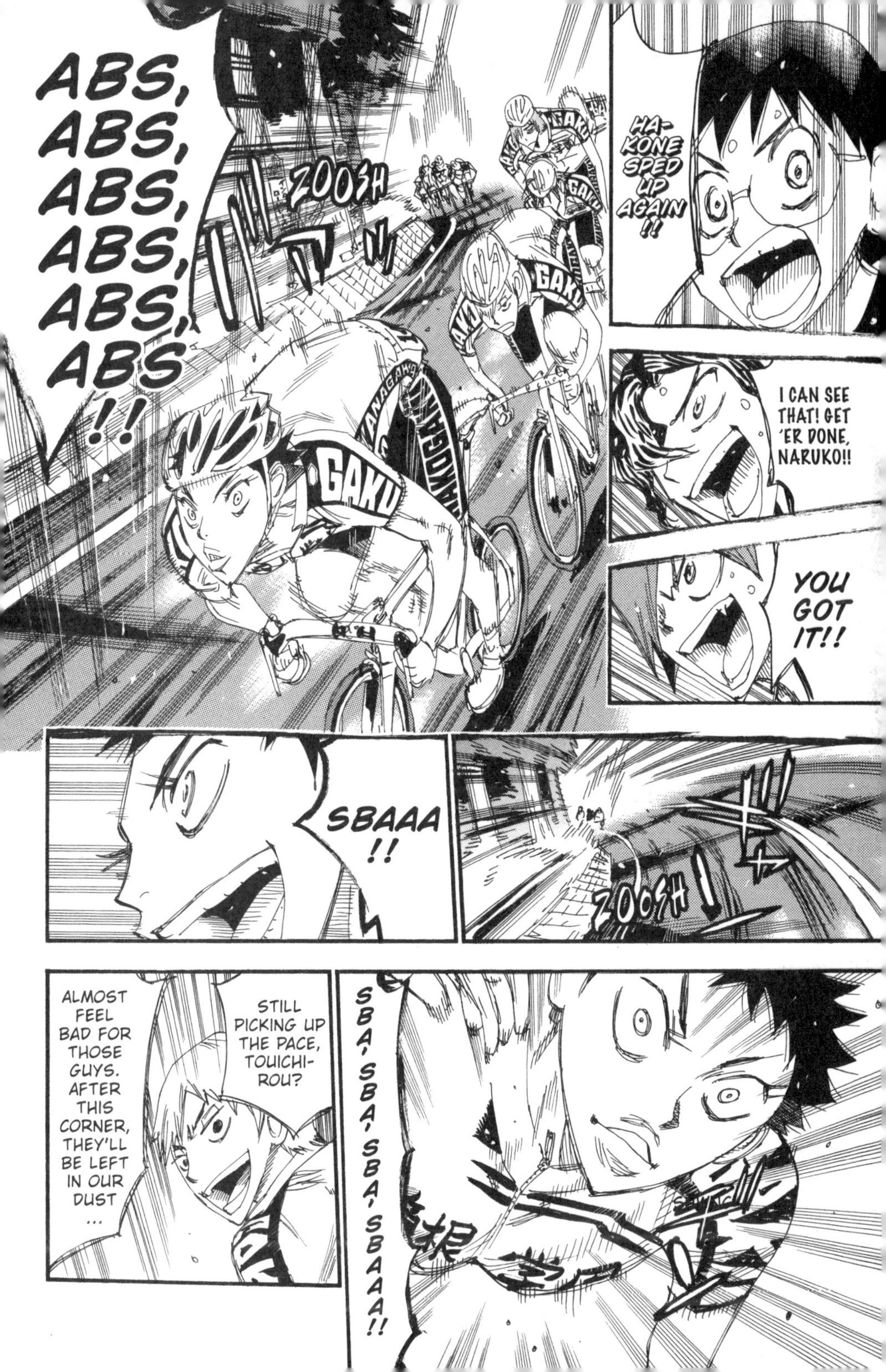
HA-KONE SPED UP AGAIN!!
I CAN SEE THAT! GET 'ER DONE, NARUKO!!
YOU GOT IT!!
ZOOSH
ABS, ABS, ABS, ABS, ABS, ABS!!
ZOOSH
SBAAA!!
SBA, SBA, SBA, SBAAA!!
STILL PICKING UP THE PACE, TOUICHI-ROU?
ALMOST FEEL BAD FOR THOSE GUYS. AFTER THIS CORNER, THEY'LL BE LEFT IN OUR DUST...

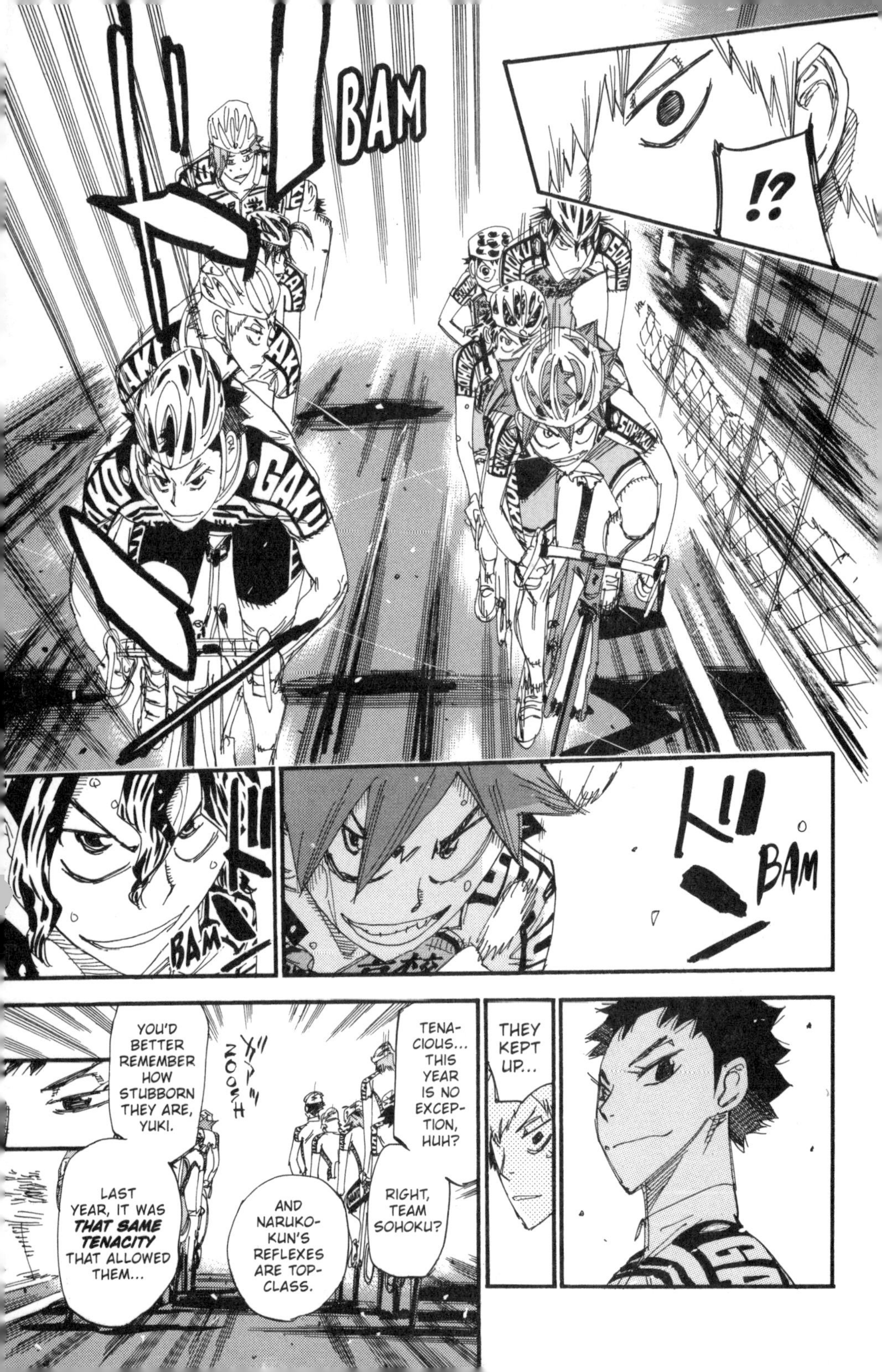
!?
BAM
BAM
BAM
THEY KEPT UP...
TENACIOUS... THIS YEAR IS NO EXCEPTION, HUH?
RIGHT, TEAM SOHOKU?
ZOOOSH
YOU'D BETTER REMEMBER HOW STUBBORN THEY ARE, YUKI.
AND NARUKO-KUN'S REFLEXES ARE TOP-CLASS.
LAST YEAR, IT WAS ***THAT SAME TENACITY*** THAT ALLOWED THEM...

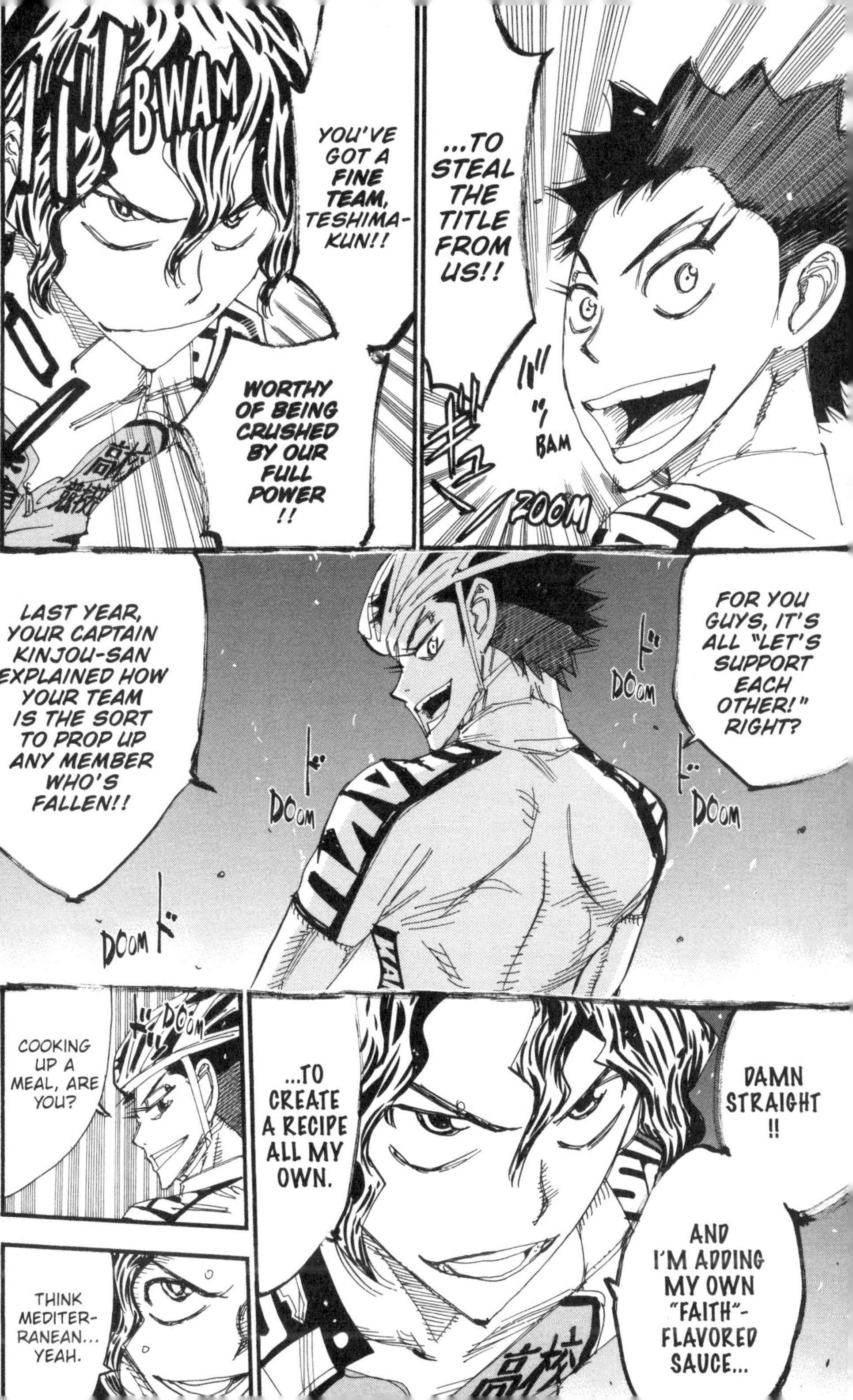
...TO STEAL THE TITLE FROM US!!
BAM
ZOOM
BWAM
YOU'VE GOT A FINE TEAM, TESHIMA-KUN!!
WORTHY OF BEING CRUSHED BY OUR FULL POWER!!
FOR YOU GUYS, IT'S ALL "LET'S SUPPORT EACH OTHER!" RIGHT?
DOOM
DOOM
LAST YEAR, YOUR CAPTAIN KINJOU-SAN EXPLAINED HOW YOUR TEAM IS THE SORT TO PROP UP ANY MEMBER WHO'S FALLEN!!
DOOM
DOOM
DAMN STRAIGHT!!
AND I'M ADDING MY OWN "FAITH"-FLAVORED SAUCE...
...TO CREATE A RECIPE ALL MY OWN.
DOOM
COOKING UP A MEAL, ARE YOU?
THINK MEDITERRANEAN... YEAH.

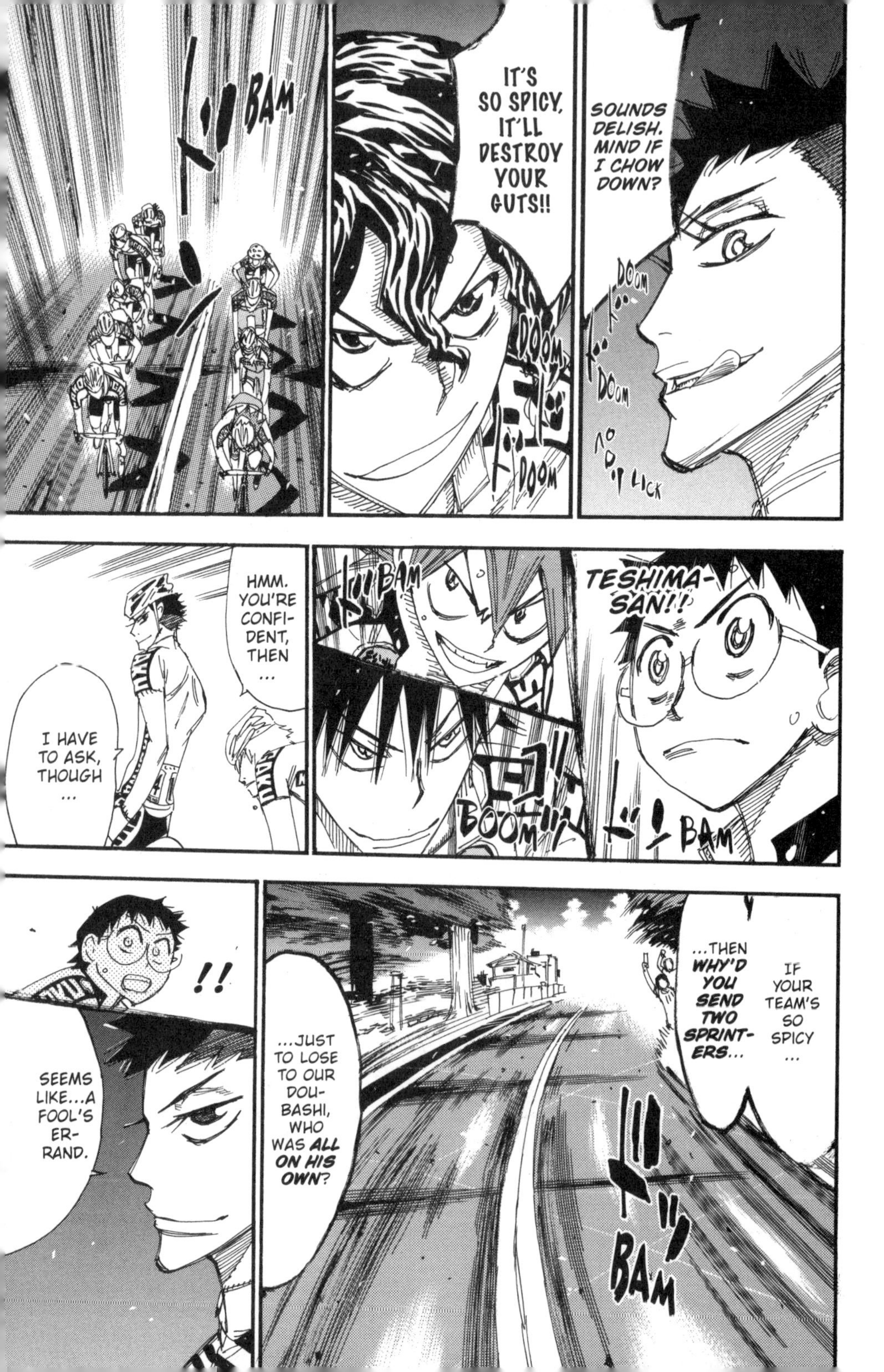
SOUNDS DELISH. MIND IF I CHOW DOWN?
DOOM
DOOM
LICK
IT'S SO SPICY, IT'LL DESTROY YOUR GUTS!!
DOOM
DOOM
BAM
TESHIMA-SAN!!
BAM
BAM
BOOM
HMM. YOU'RE CONFIDENT, THEN...
I HAVE TO ASK, THOUGH...
IF YOUR TEAM'S SO SPICY...
...THEN WHY'D YOU SEND TWO SPRINTERS...
BAM
...JUST TO LOSE TO OUR DOUBASHI, WHO WAS ALL ON HIS OWN?
!!
SEEMS LIKE...A FOOL'S ERRAND.

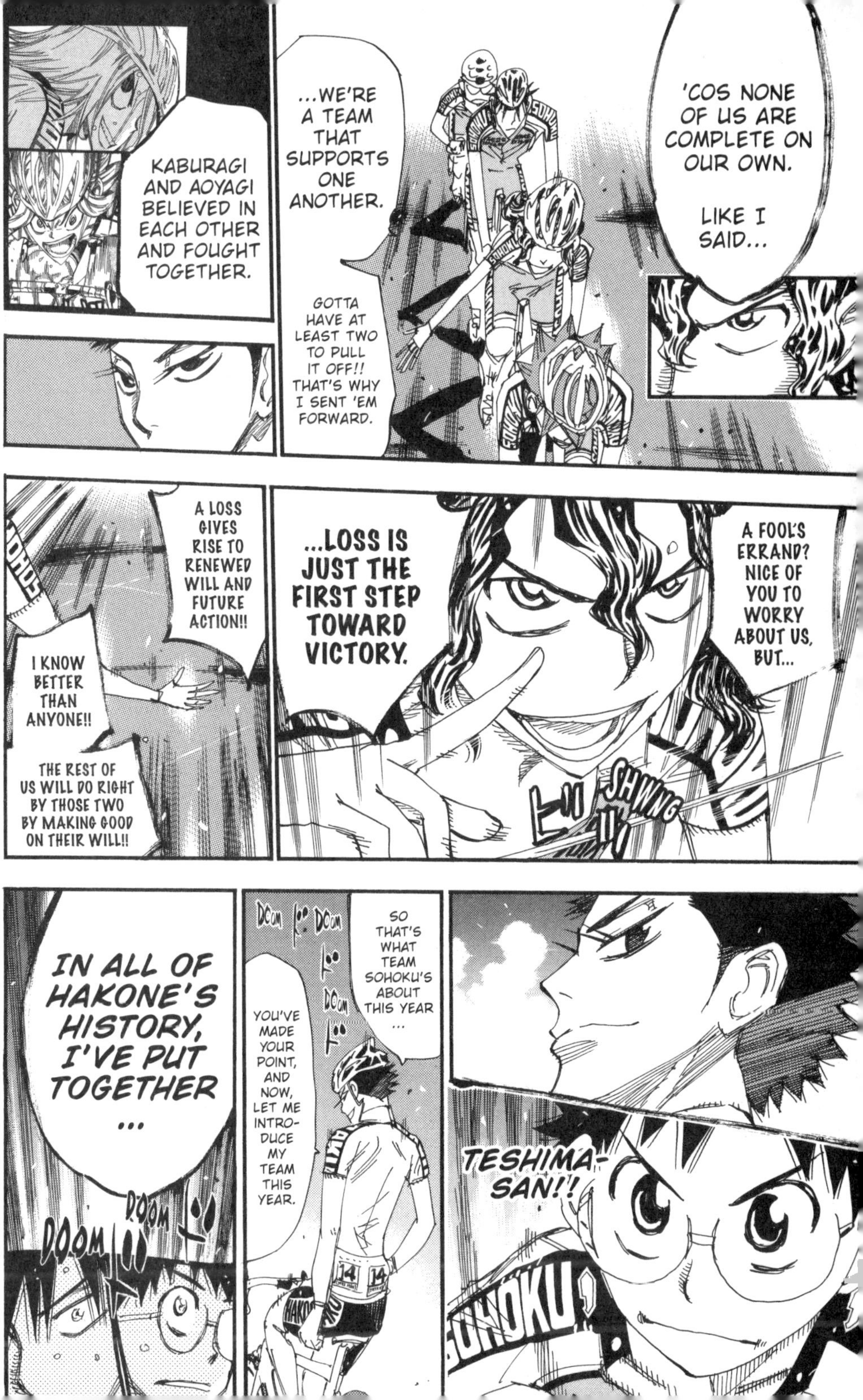
'COS NONE OF US ARE COMPLETE ON OUR OWN.
LIKE I SAID...
...WE'RE A TEAM THAT SUPPORTS ONE ANOTHER.
GOTTA HAVE AT LEAST TWO TO PULL IT OFF!! THAT'S WHY I SENT 'EM FORWARD.
KABURAGI AND AOYAGI BELIEVED IN EACH OTHER AND FOUGHT TOGETHER.
A FOOL'S ERRAND? NICE OF YOU TO WORRY ABOUT US, BUT...
...LOSS IS JUST THE FIRST STEP TOWARD VICTORY.
SHWING
A LOSS GIVES RISE TO RENEWED WILL AND FUTURE ACTION!!
I KNOW BETTER THAN ANYONE!!
THE REST OF US WILL DO RIGHT BY THOSE TWO BY MAKING GOOD ON THEIR WILL!!
TESHIMA-SAN!!
DOOM DOOM DOOM
SO THAT'S WHAT TEAM SOHOKU'S ABOUT THIS YEAR...
YOU'VE MADE YOUR POINT, AND NOW, LET ME INTRODUCE MY TEAM THIS YEAR.
IN ALL OF HAKONE'S HISTORY, I'VE PUT TOGETHER...
DOOM DOOM

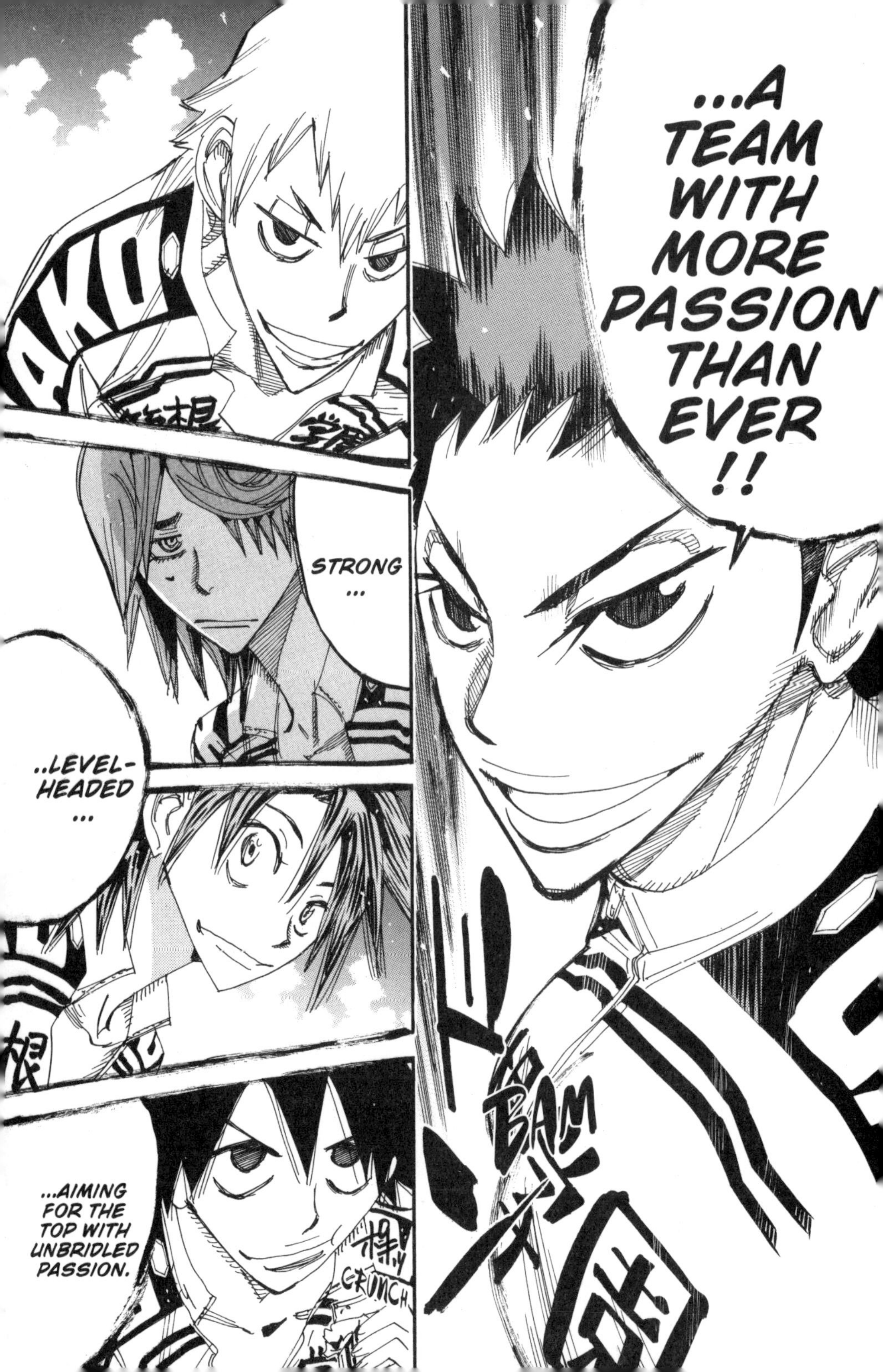
...A TEAM WITH MORE PASSION THAN EVER!!
BAM
STRONG...
..LEVEL-HEADED...
...AIMING FOR THE TOP WITH UNBRIDLED PASSION.
CRUNCH

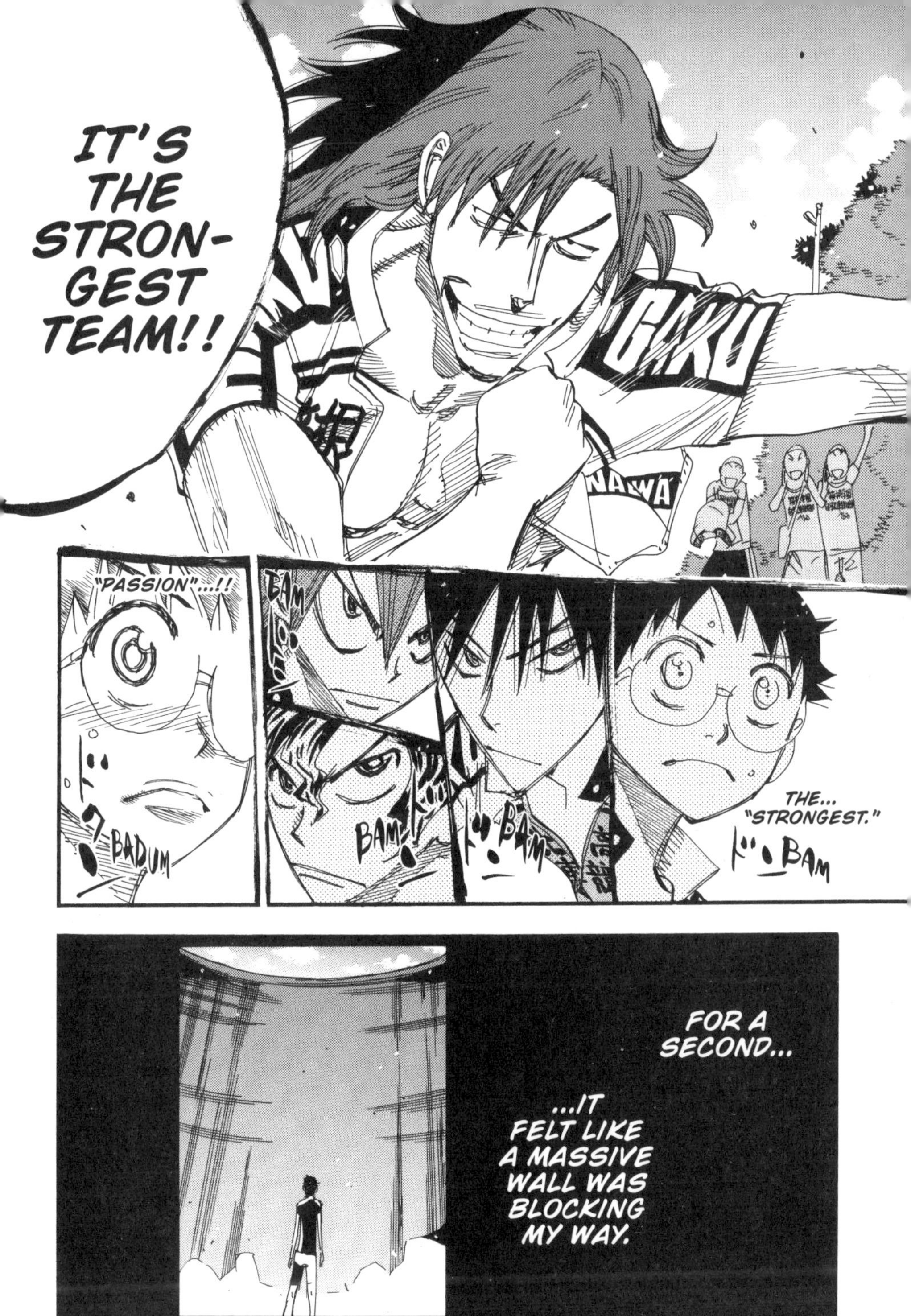
IT'S THE STRONGEST TEAM!!
GAKU
NAWA
BAM
THE... "STRONGEST."
BAM
BAM
BAM
"PASSION"...!!
BADUM
FOR A SECOND...
...IT FELT LIKE A MASSIVE WALL WAS BLOCKING MY WAY.

RIDE.315 THE FALL OF SAKAMICHI

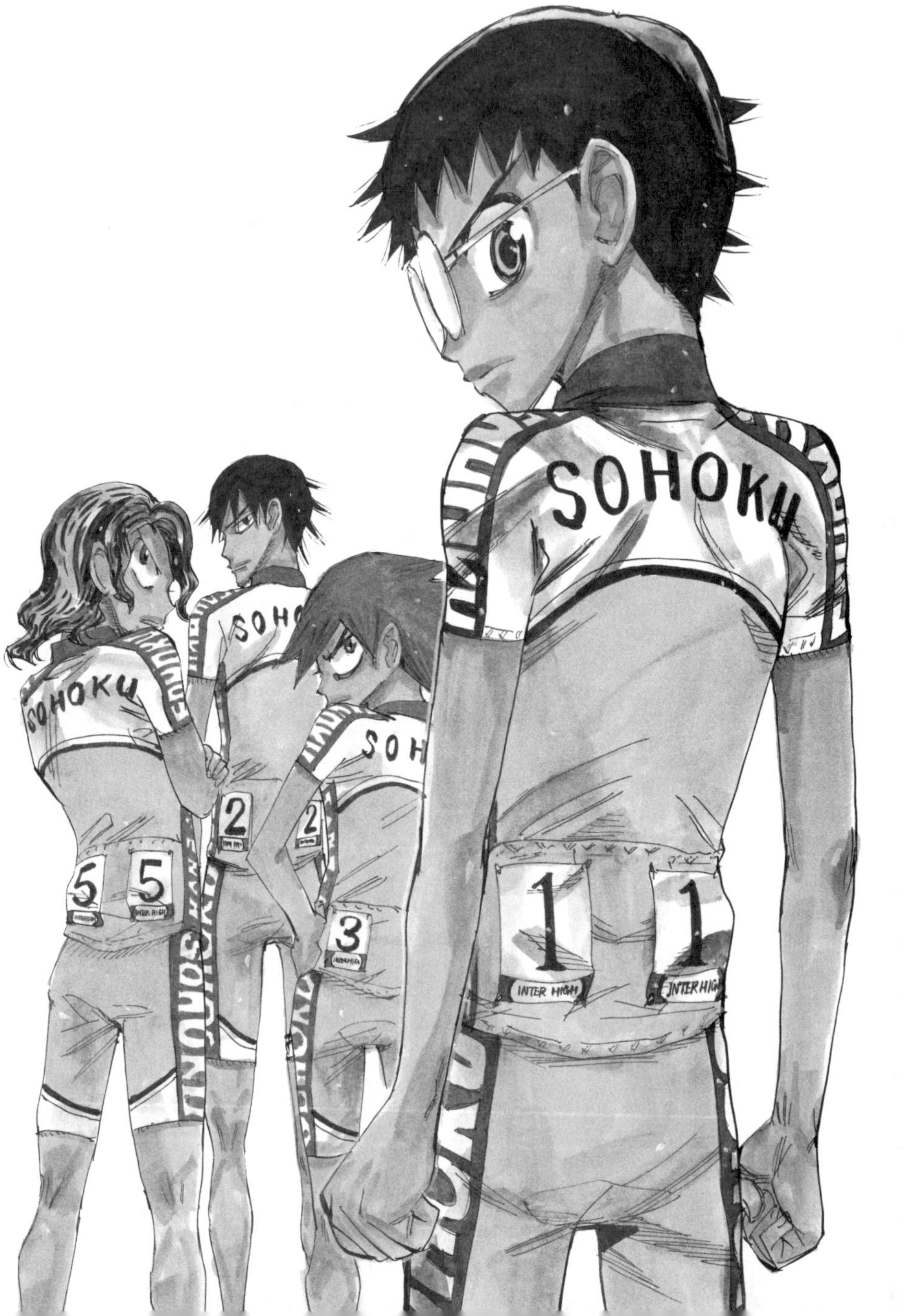
SOHOKU
SOHOKU
SOHO
SOH
5 5
INTER HIGH
2
2
3
1 1
INTER HIGH
INTER HIGH

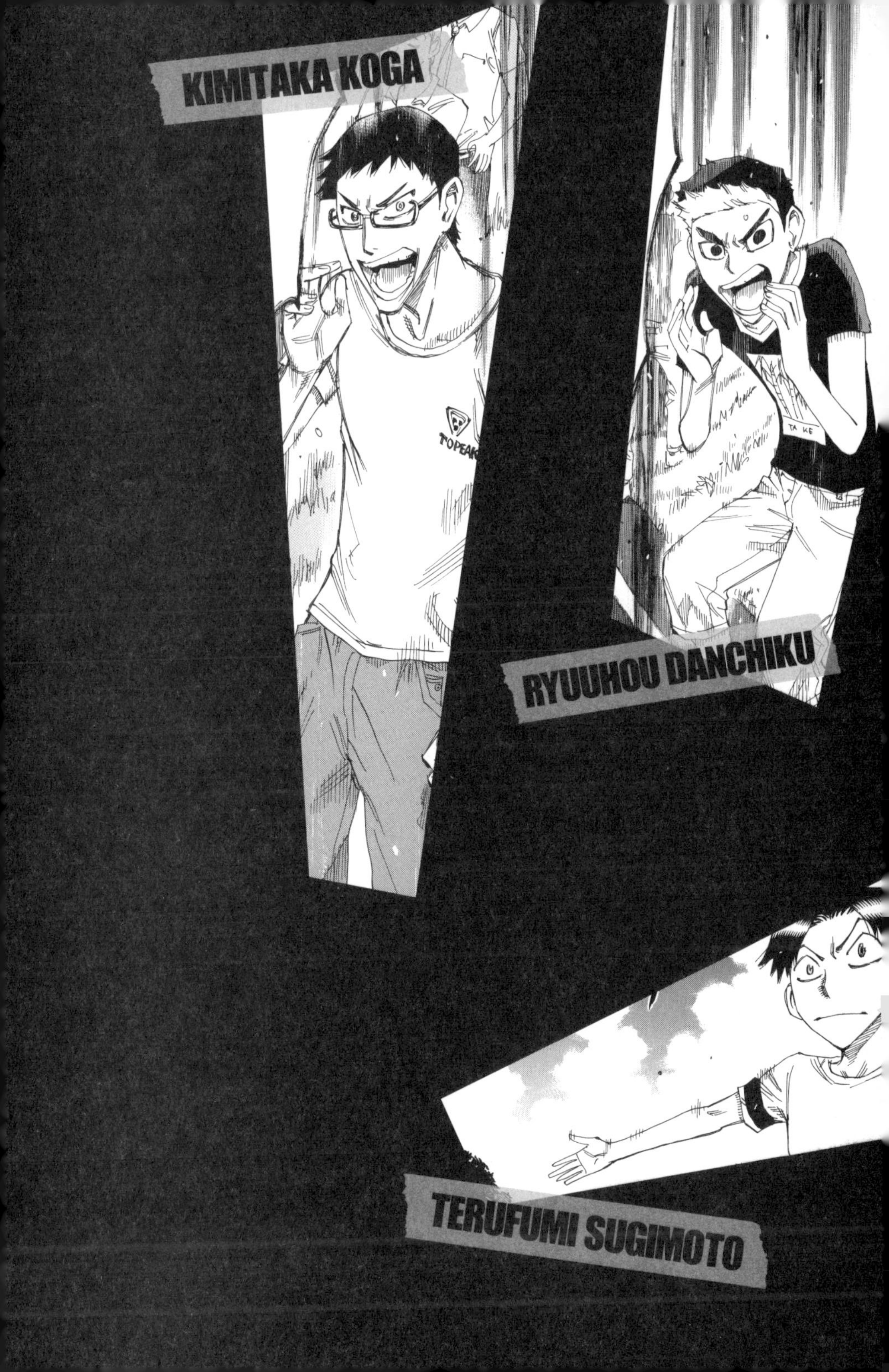
RYUUHOU DANCHIKU
KIMITAKA KOGA
TERUFUMI SUGIMOTO

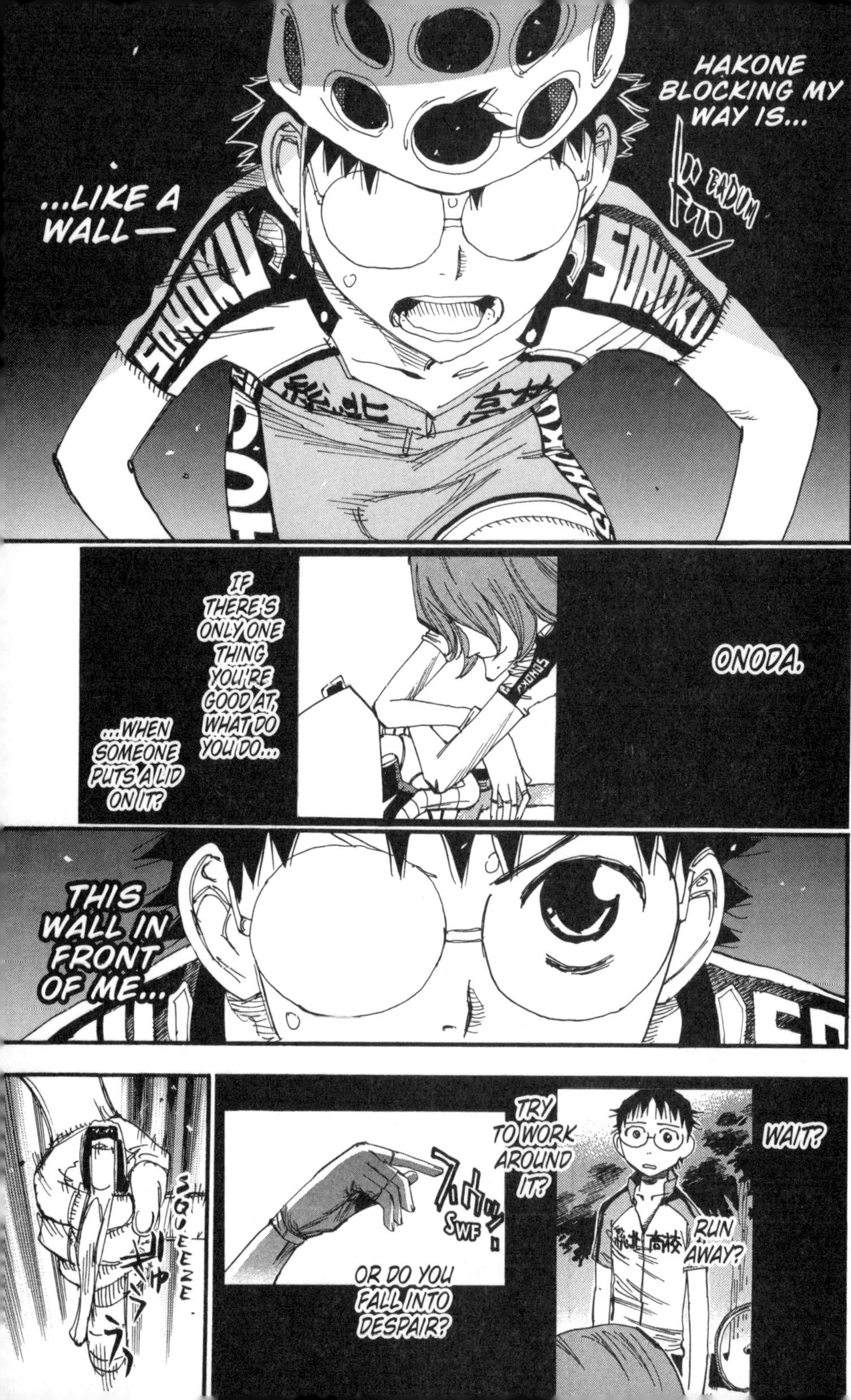
HAKONE BLOCKING MY WAY IS...
BADUM
...LIKE A WALL—
ONODA.
IF THERE'S ONLY ONE THING YOU'RE GOOD AT, WHAT DO YOU DO...
...WHEN SOMEONE PUTS A LID ON IT?
THIS WALL IN FRONT OF ME...
WAIT?
RUN AWAY?
TRY TO WORK AROUND IT?
SWF
OR DO YOU FALL INTO DESPAIR?
SQUEEZE

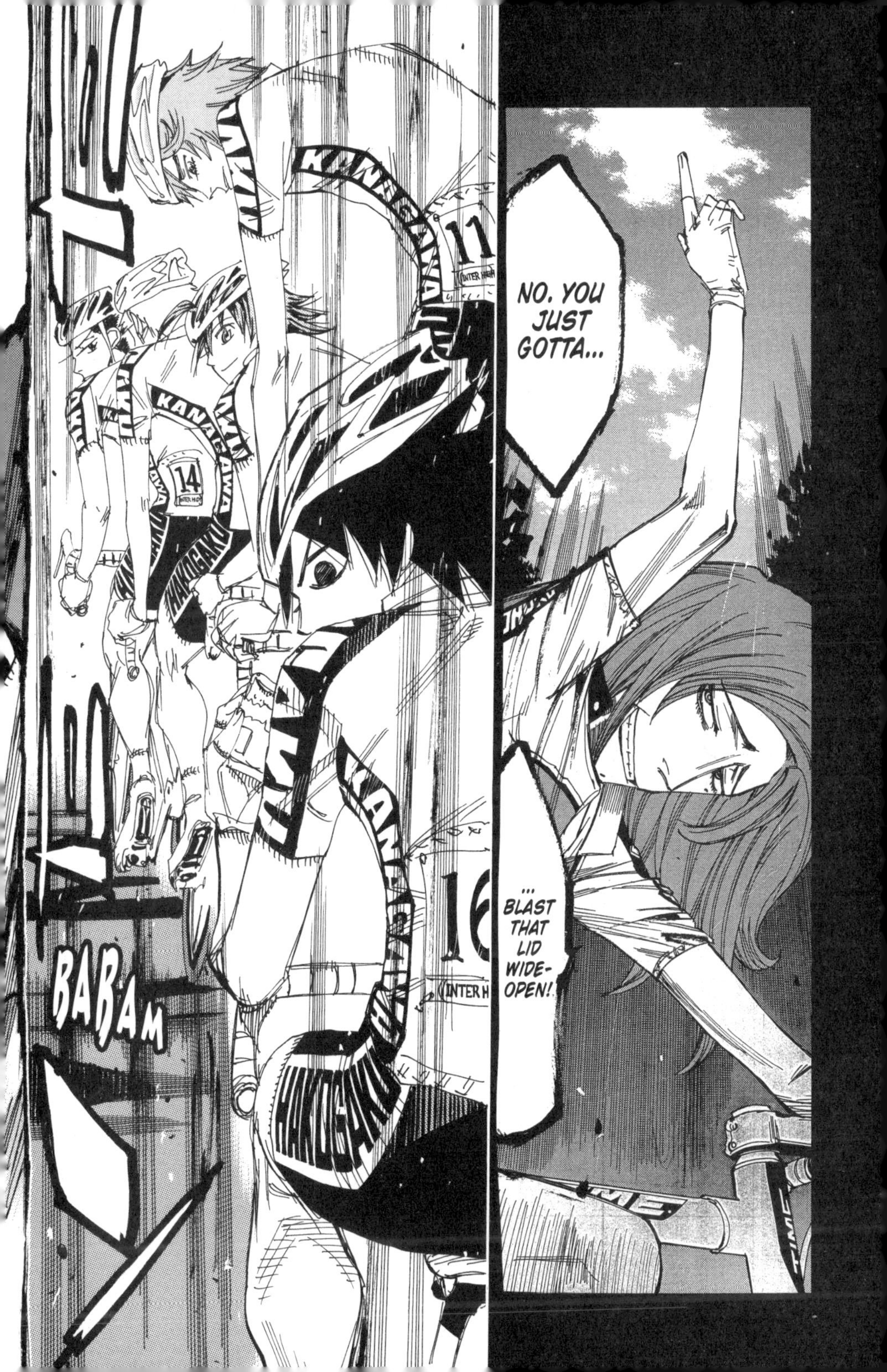
NO. YOU JUST GOTTA...
...BLAST THAT LID WIDE-OPEN!
BABAM

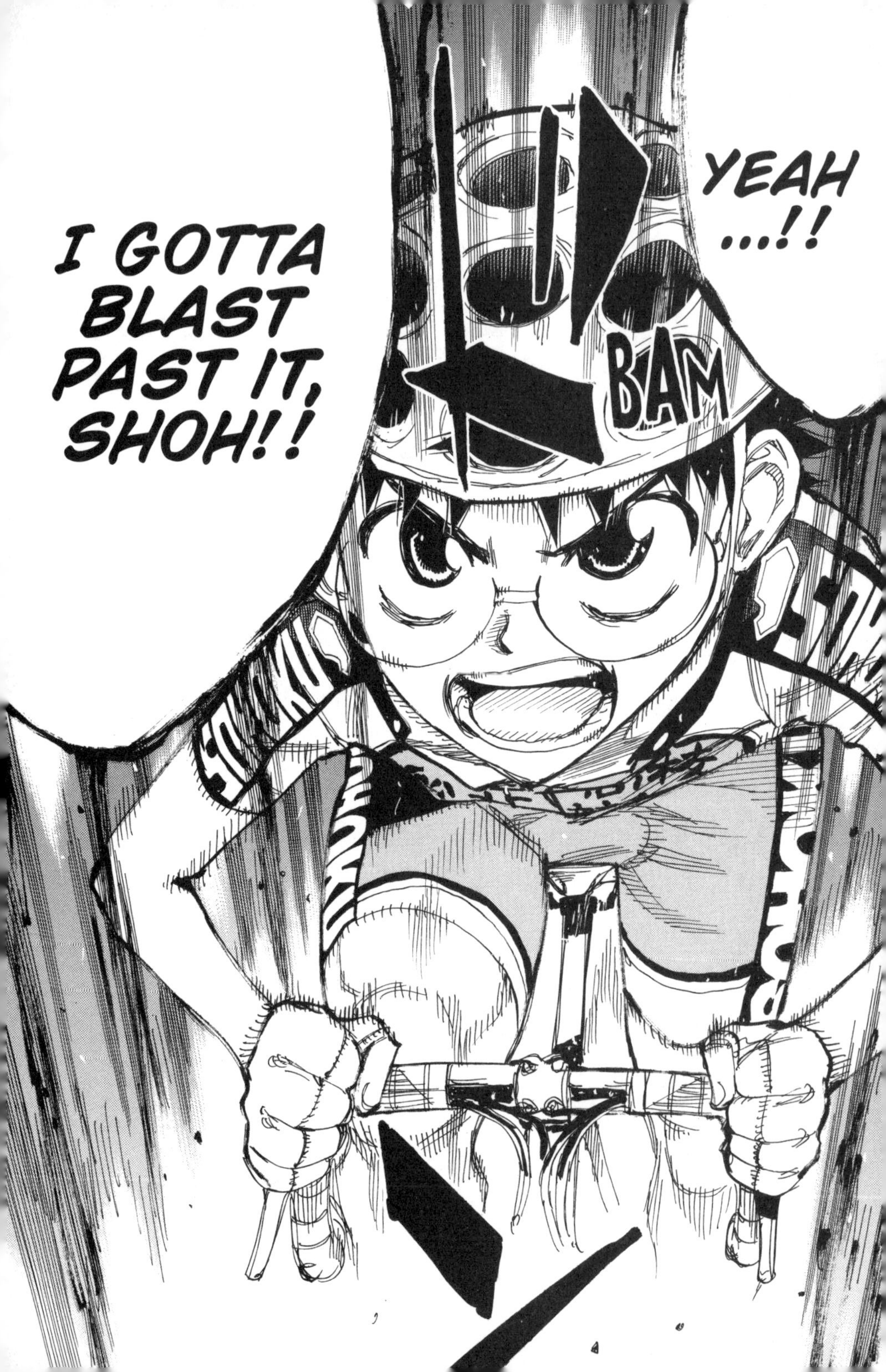
YEAH ...!!
I GOTTA BLAST PAST IT, SHOH!!
BAM

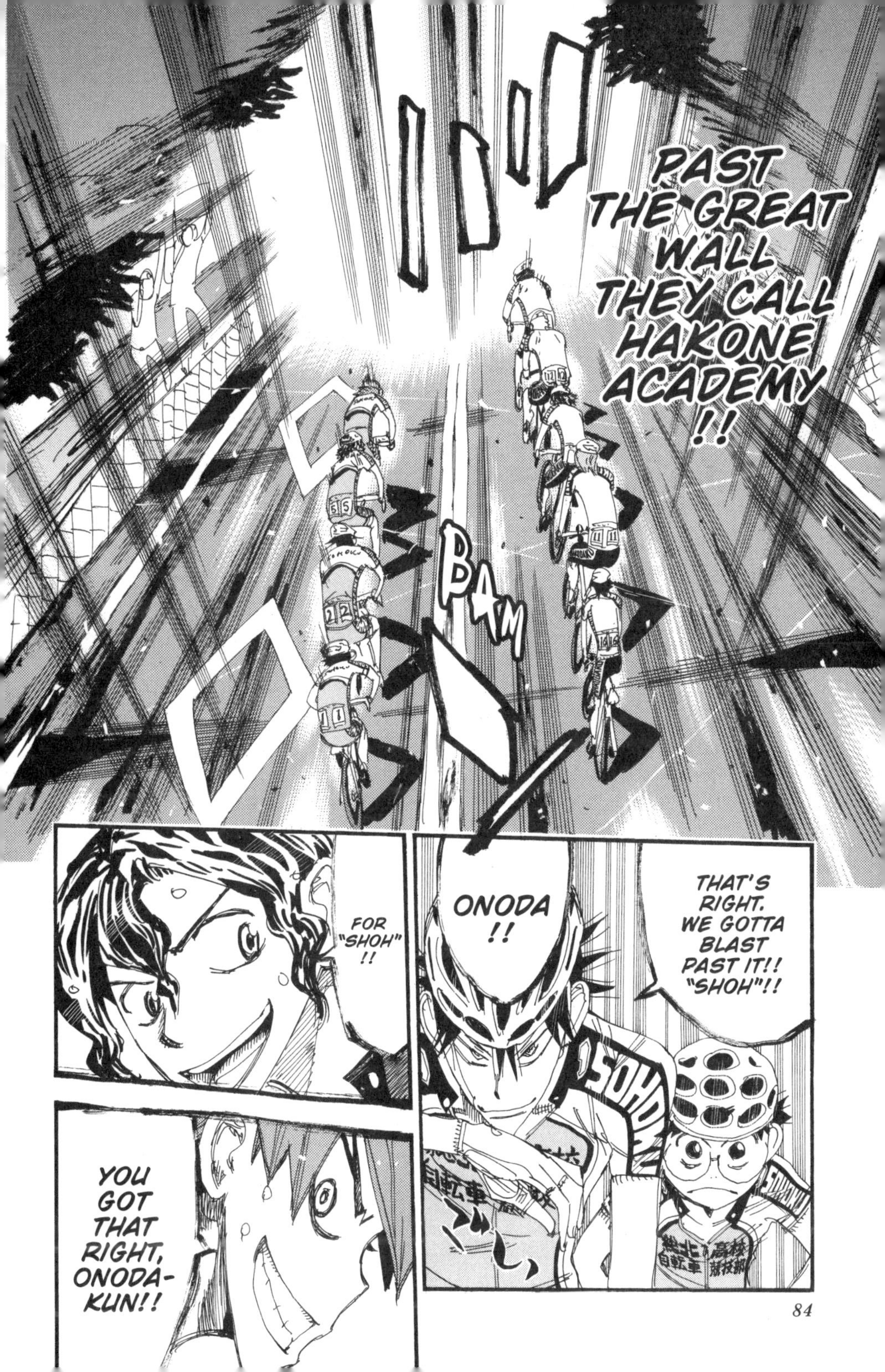
PAST THE GREAT WALL THEY CALL HAKONE ACADEMY!!
BAM
THAT'S RIGHT. WE GOTTA BLAST PAST IT!! "SHOH"!!
ONODA!!
FOR "SHOH"!!
YOU GOT THAT RIGHT, ONODA-KUN!!

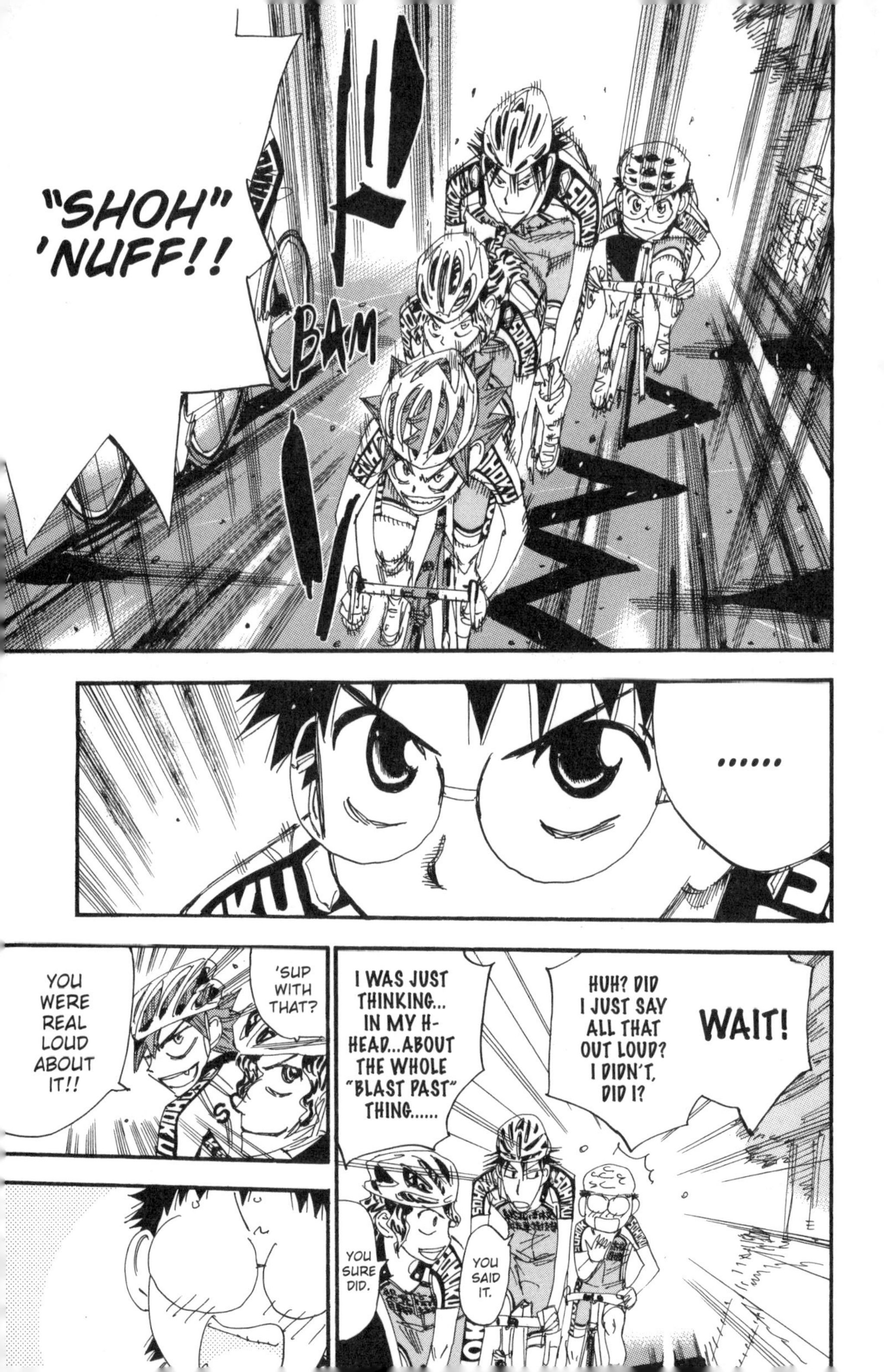
"SHOH" 'NUFF!!
BAM
......
WAIT!
HUH? DID I JUST SAY ALL THAT OUT LOUD? I DIDN'T, DID I?
I WAS JUST THINKING... IN MY H-HEAD...ABOUT THE WHOLE "BLAST PAST" THING......
YOU SAID IT.
YOU SURE DID.
'SUP WITH THAT?
YOU WERE REAL LOUD ABOUT IT!!

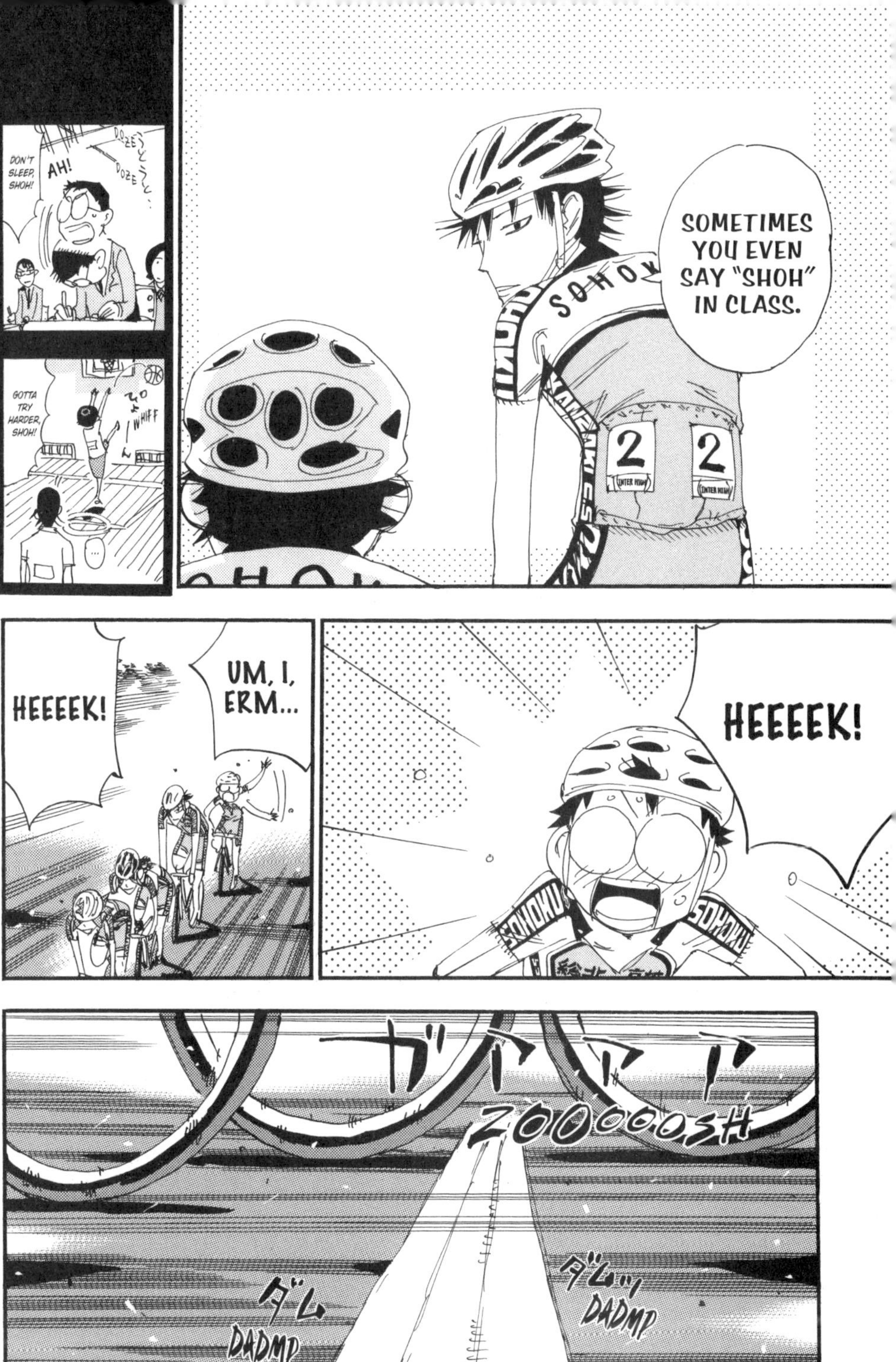
SOMETIMES YOU EVEN SAY "SHOH" IN CLASS.
DON'T SLEEP, SHOH!
AH!
DOZE
DOZE
GOTTA TRY HARDER, SHOH!
WHIFF
...
HEEEEK!
UM, I, ERM...
HEEEEK!
ZOOOOOOSH
DADMP
DADMP

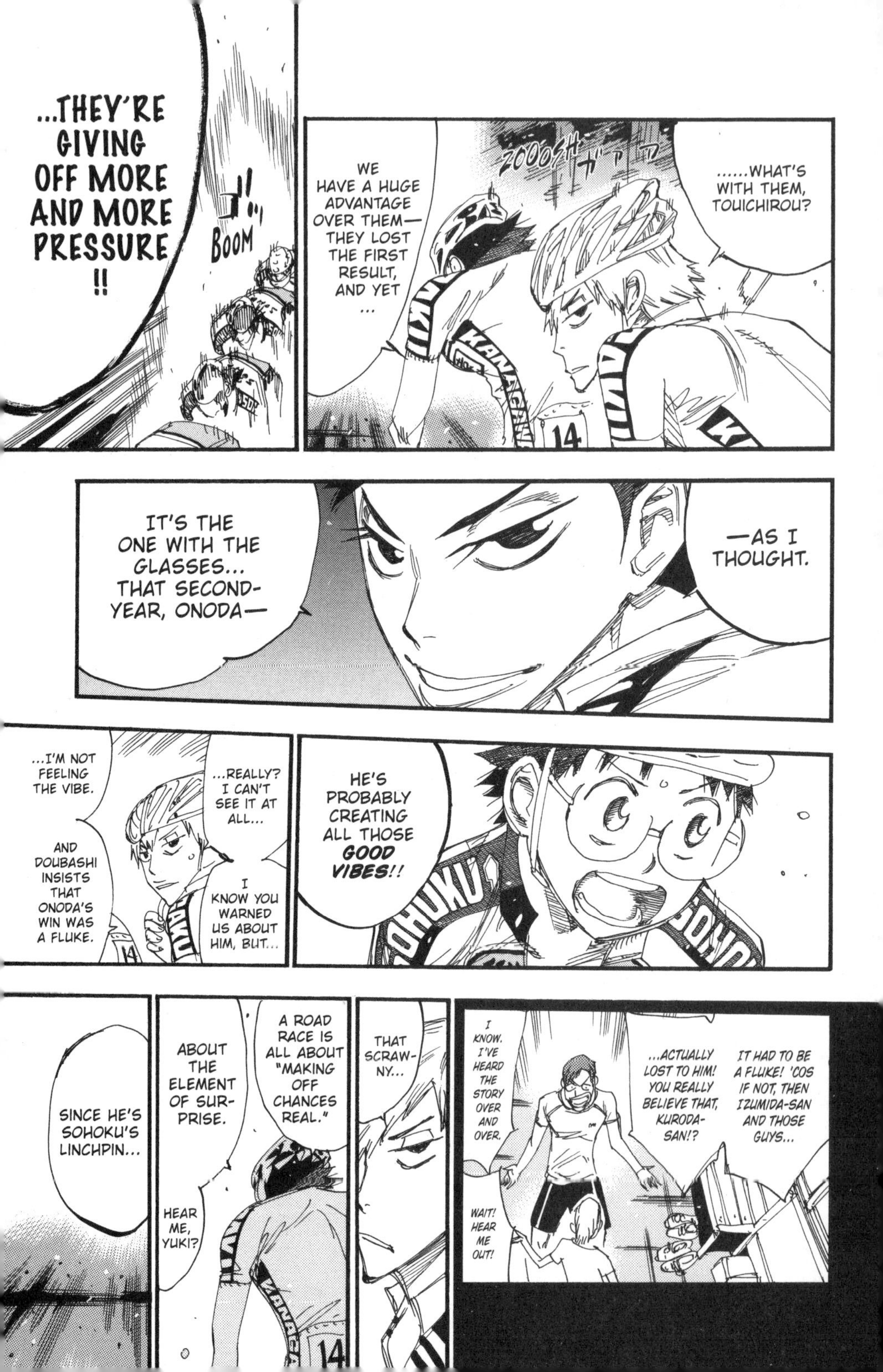
......WHAT'S WITH THEM, TOUICHIROU?
ZOOOSH
WE HAVE A HUGE ADVANTAGE OVER THEM—THEY LOST THE FIRST RESULT, AND YET...
...THEY'RE GIVING OFF MORE AND MORE PRESSURE!!
BOOM
—AS I THOUGHT.
IT'S THE ONE WITH THE GLASSES... THAT SECOND-YEAR, ONODA—
HE'S PROBABLY CREATING ALL THOSE GOOD VIBES!!
...REALLY? I CAN'T SEE IT AT ALL...
I KNOW YOU WARNED US ABOUT HIM, BUT...
...I'M NOT FEELING THE VIBE.
AND DOUBASHI INSISTS THAT ONODA'S WIN WAS A FLUKE.
IT HAD TO BE A FLUKE! 'COS IF NOT, THEN IZUMIDA-SAN AND THOSE GUYS...
...ACTUALLY LOST TO HIM! YOU REALLY BELIEVE THAT, KURODA-SAN!?
I KNOW. I'VE HEARD THE STORY OVER AND OVER.
WAIT! HEAR ME OUT!
THAT SCRAWNY...
A ROAD RACE IS ALL ABOUT "MAKING OFF CHANCES REAL."
ABOUT THE ELEMENT OF SURPRISE.
HEAR ME, YUKI?
SINCE HE'S SOHOKU'S LINCHPIN...

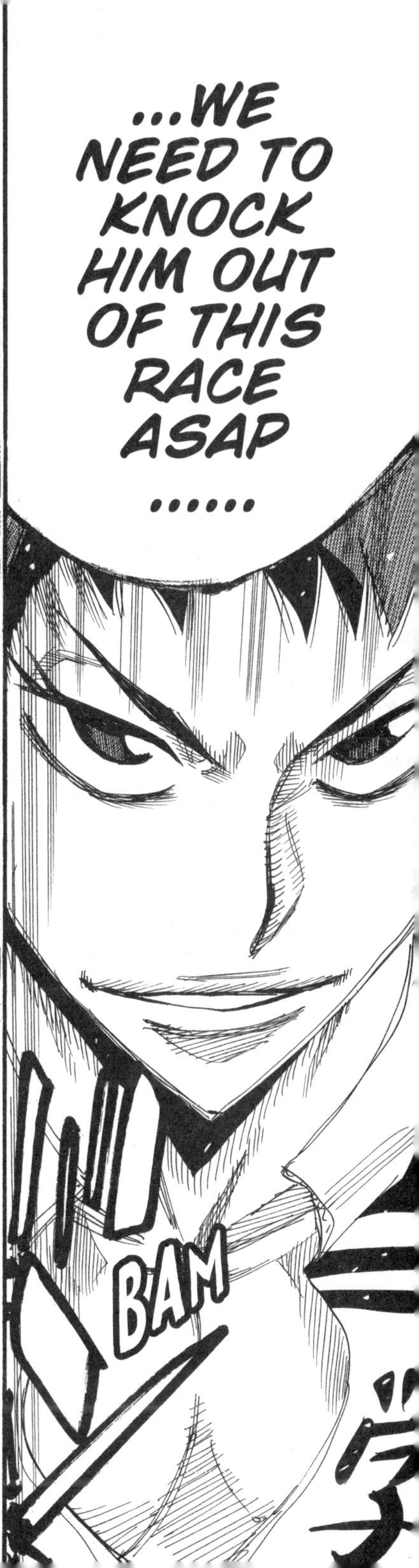
...WE NEED TO KNOCK HIM OUT OF THIS RACE ASAP ......
BAM
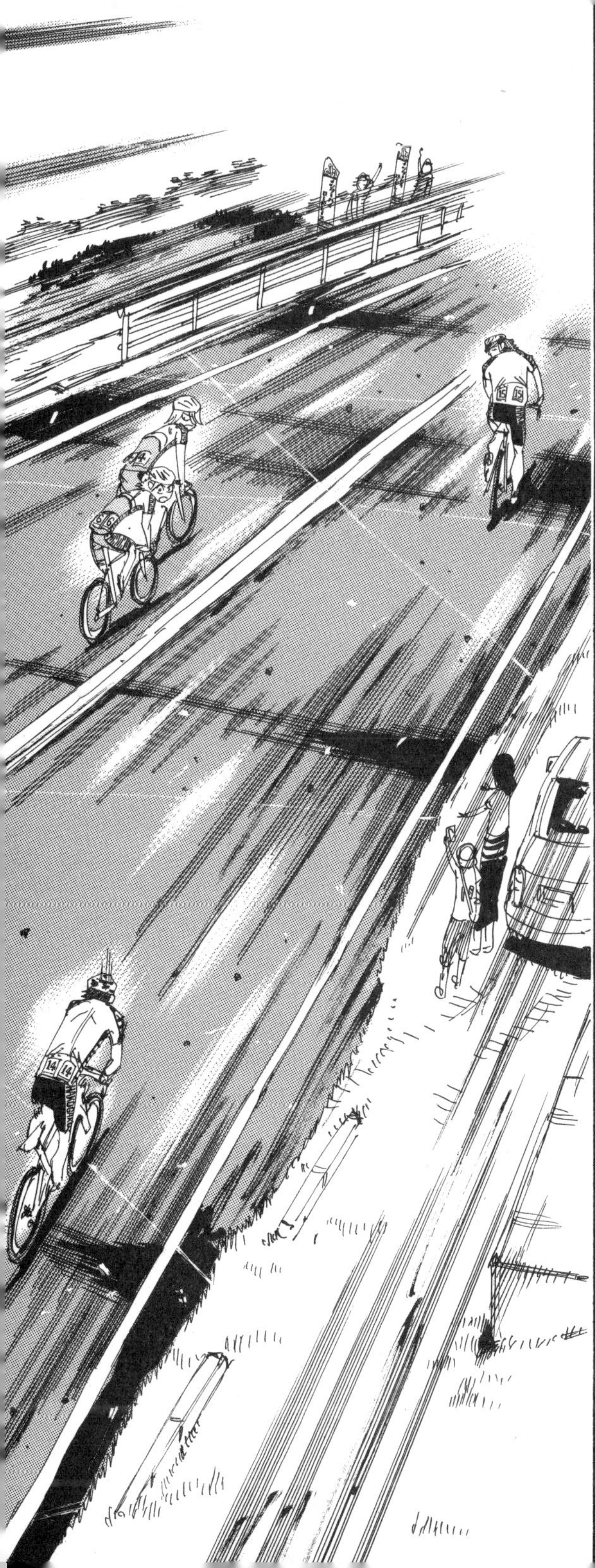

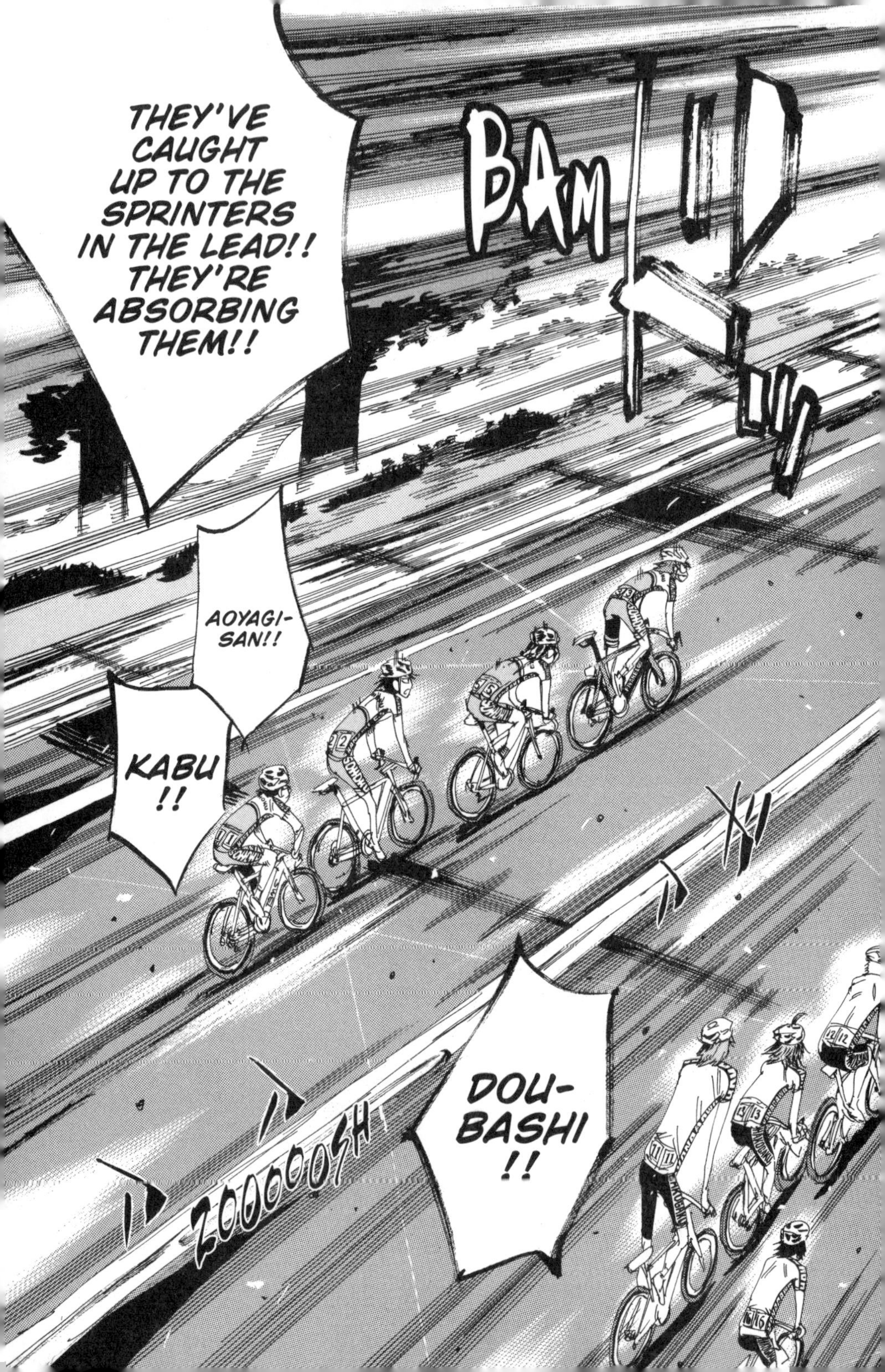
BAM
THEY'VE CAUGHT UP TO THE SPRINTERS IN THE LEAD!! THEY'RE ABSORBING THEM!!
AOYAGI-SAN!!
KABU!!
DOU-BASHI!!
ZOOOOOSH

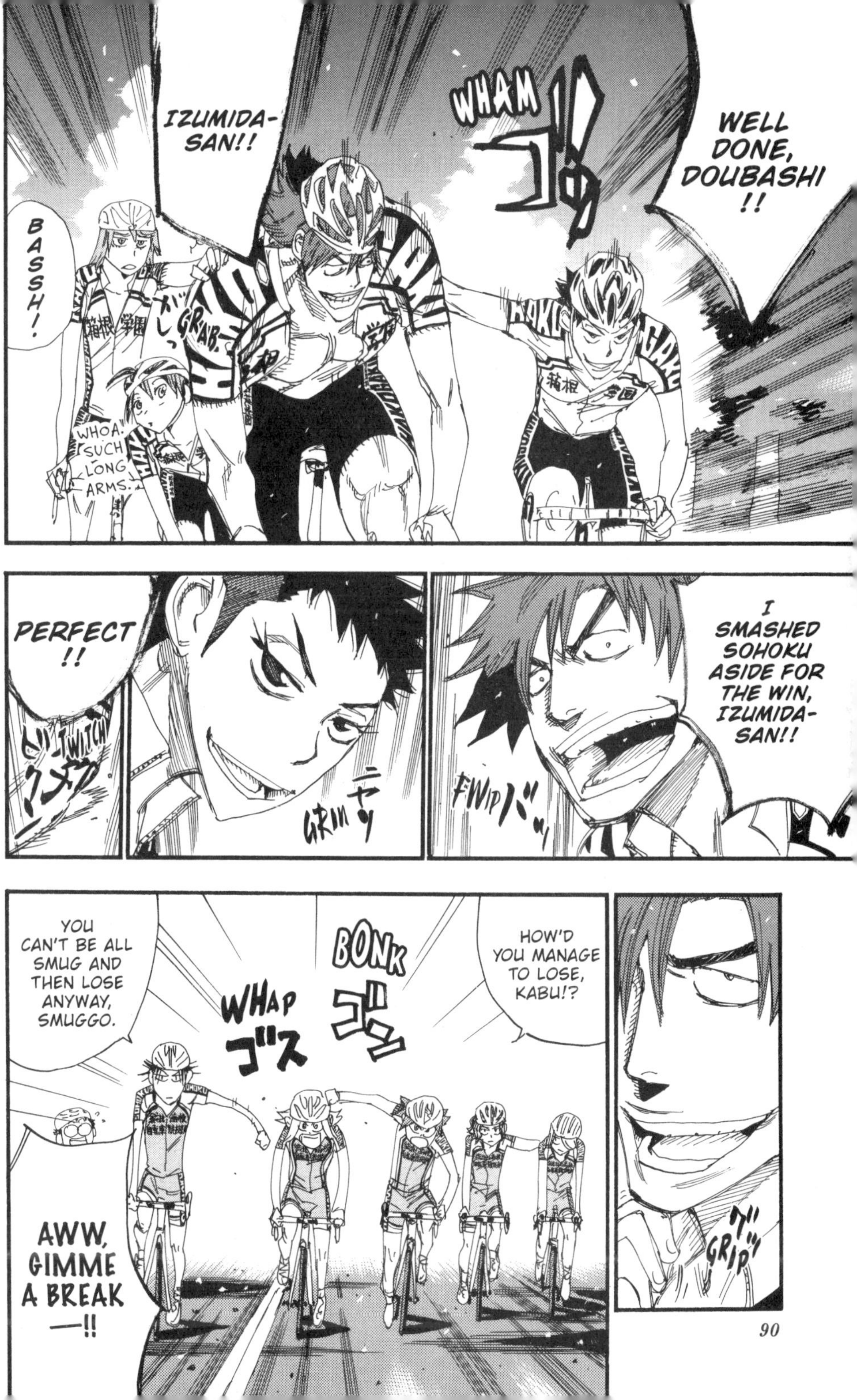
WELL DONE, DOUBASHI!!
WHAM
IZUMIDA-SAN!!
BASSH!
GRAB
WHOA. SUCH LONG ARMS.
I SMASHED SOHOKU ASIDE FOR THE WIN, IZUMIDA-SAN!!
FWIP
GRIN
PERFECT!!
TWITCH
GRIP
HOW'D YOU MANAGE TO LOSE, KABU!?
BONK
WHAP
YOU CAN'T BE ALL SMUG AND THEN LOSE ANYWAY, SMUGGO.
AWW, GIMME A BREAK—!!

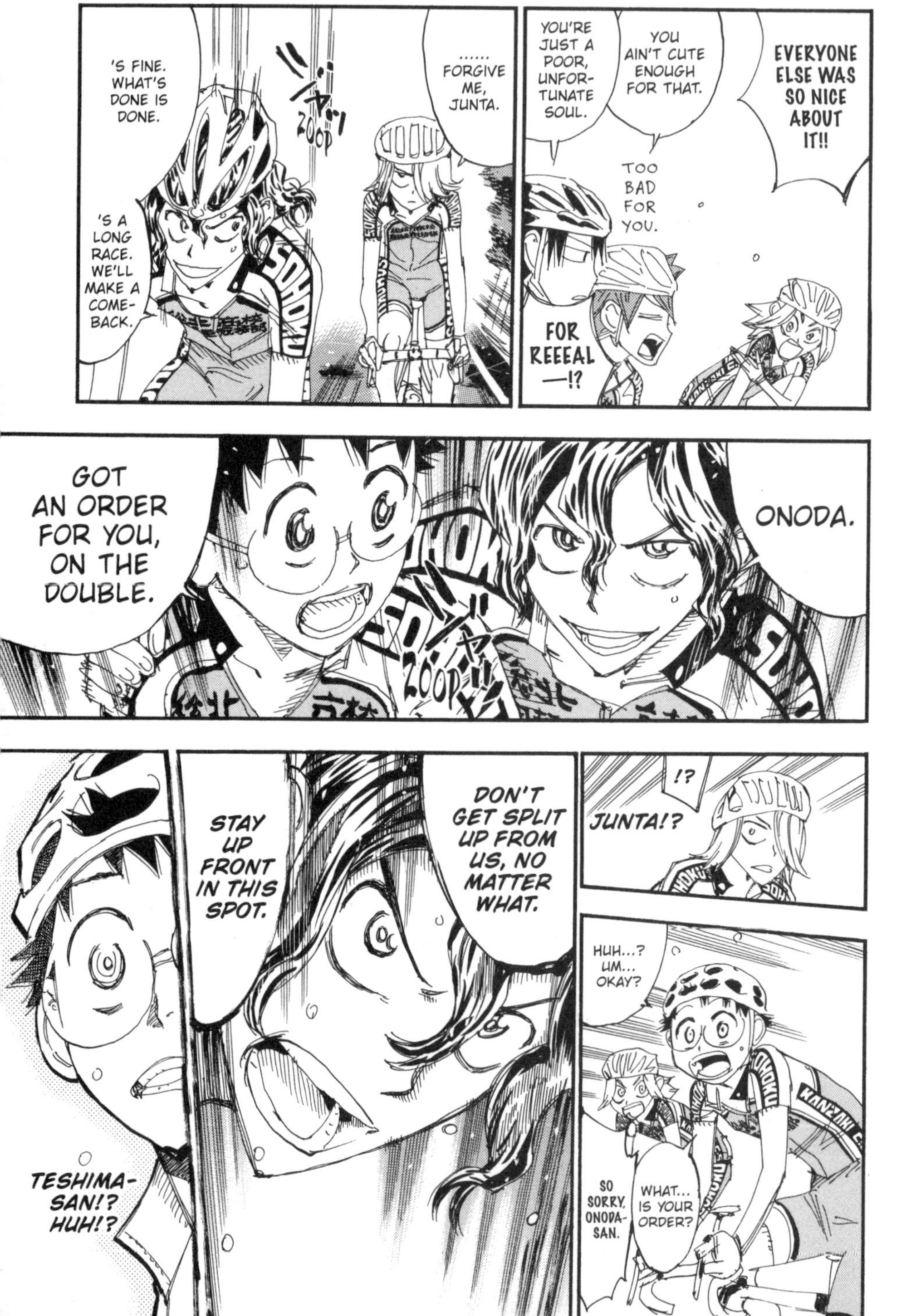
EVERYONE ELSE WAS SO NICE ABOUT IT!!
YOU AIN'T CUTE ENOUGH FOR THAT.
YOU'RE JUST A POOR, UNFORTUNATE SOUL.
TOO BAD FOR YOU.
FOR REEEAL—!?
......FORGIVE ME, JUNTA.
ZOOP
'S FINE. WHAT'S DONE IS DONE.
'S A LONG RACE. WE'LL MAKE A COMEBACK.
ONODA.
ZOOP
GOT AN ORDER FOR YOU, ON THE DOUBLE.
!?
JUNTA!?
HUH...? UM... OKAY?
WHAT... IS YOUR ORDER?
SO SORRY, ONODA-SAN.
DON'T GET SPLIT UP FROM US, NO MATTER WHAT.
STAY UP FRONT IN THIS SPOT.
TESHIMA-SAN!? HUH!?

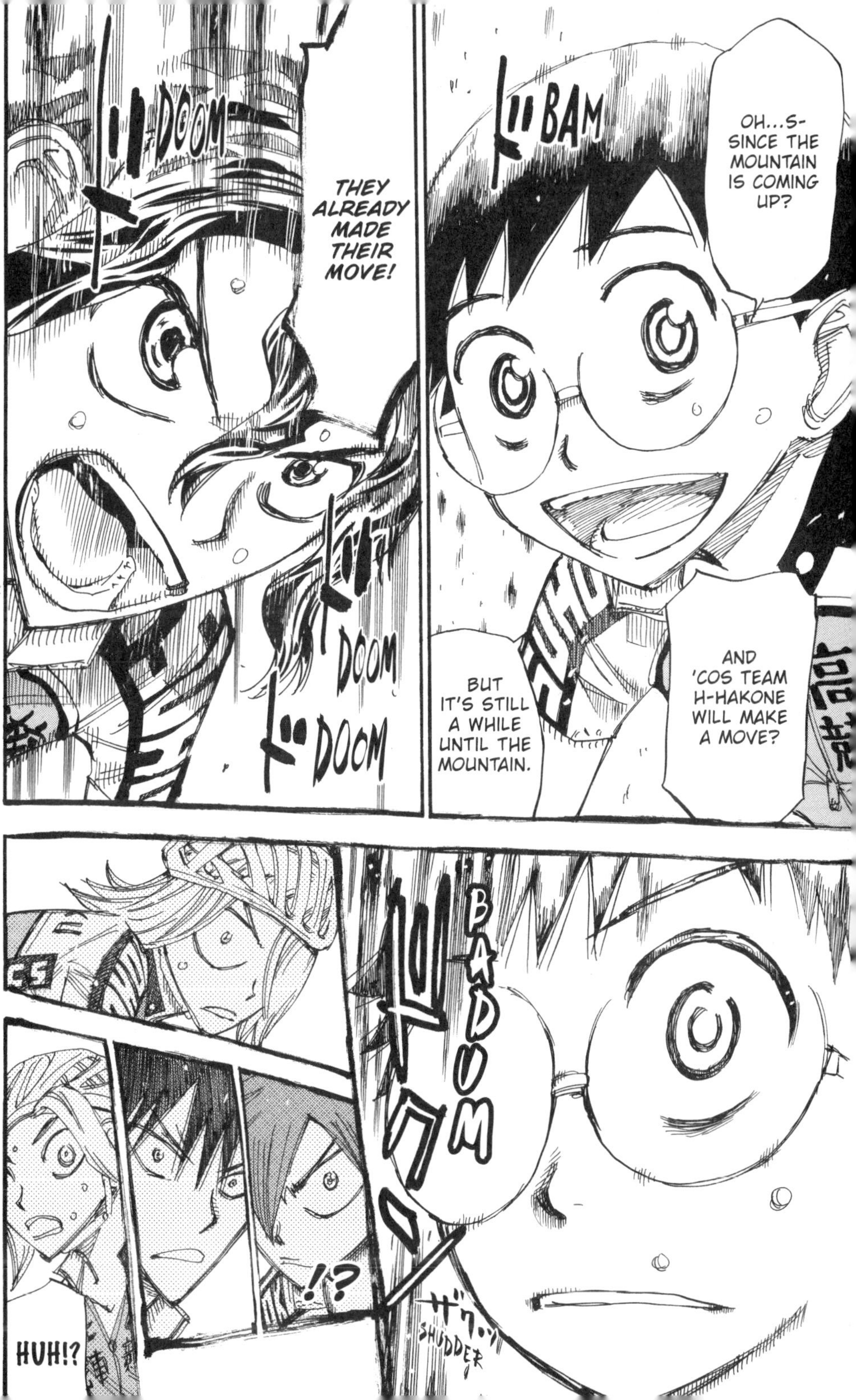
BAM
OH...S-SINCE THE MOUNTAIN IS COMING UP?
AND 'COS TEAM H-HAKONE WILL MAKE A MOVE?
BUT IT'S STILL A WHILE UNTIL THE MOUNTAIN.
DOOM
THEY ALREADY MADE THEIR MOVE!
DOOM
DOOM
BADUM
SHUDDER
!?
HUH!?

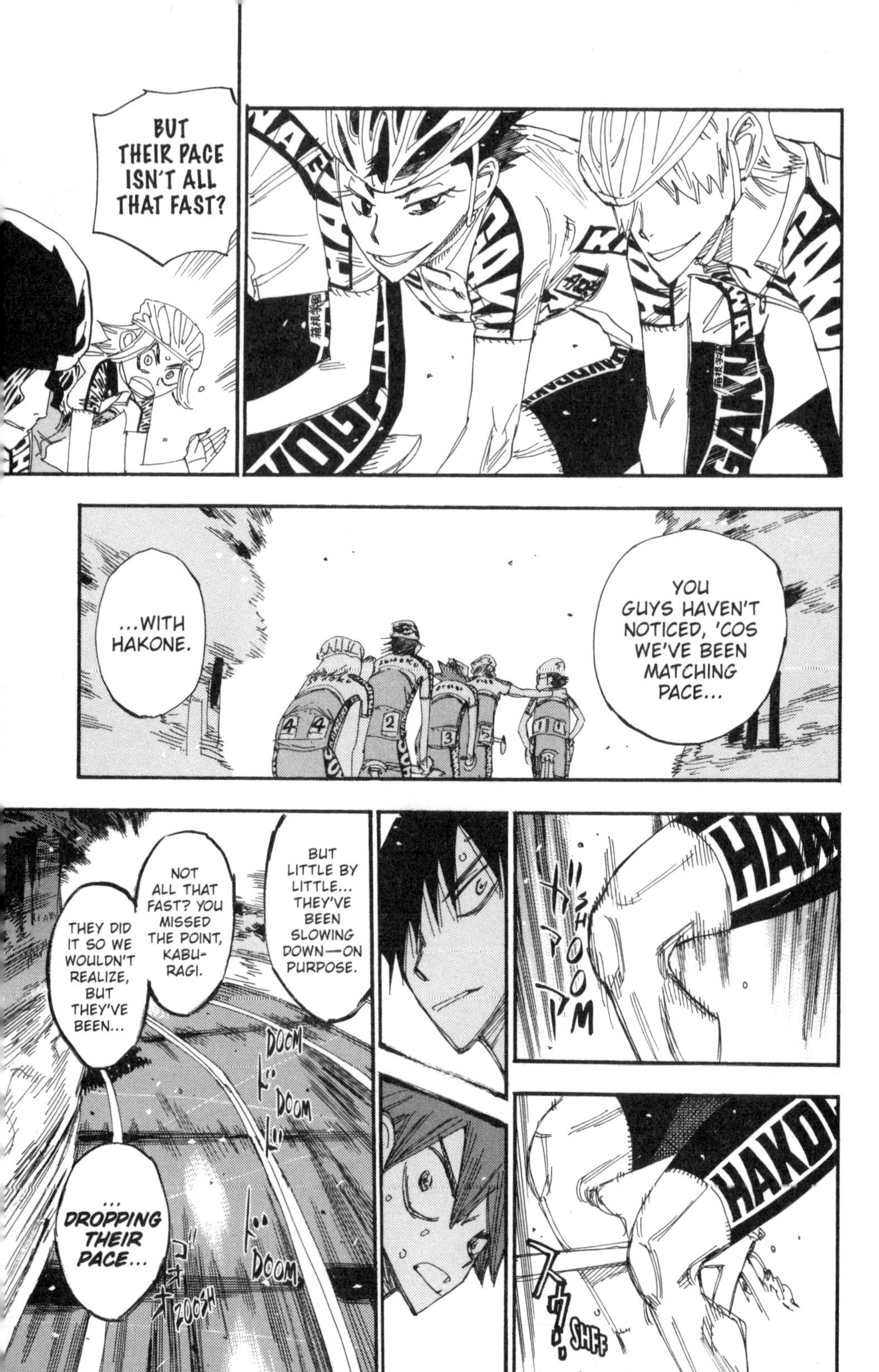

BUT THEIR PACE ISN'T ALL THAT FAST?
YOU GUYS HAVEN'T NOTICED, 'COS WE'VE BEEN MATCHING PACE…
…WITH HAKONE.
SHOOOM
SHFF
BUT LITTLE BY LITTLE… THEY'VE BEEN SLOWING DOWN—ON PURPOSE.
NOT ALL THAT FAST? YOU MISSED THE POINT, KABURAGI.
THEY DID IT SO WE WOULDN'T REALIZE, BUT THEY'VE BEEN…
DOOM
DOOM
DOOM
…DROPPING THEIR PACE…
ZOOSH

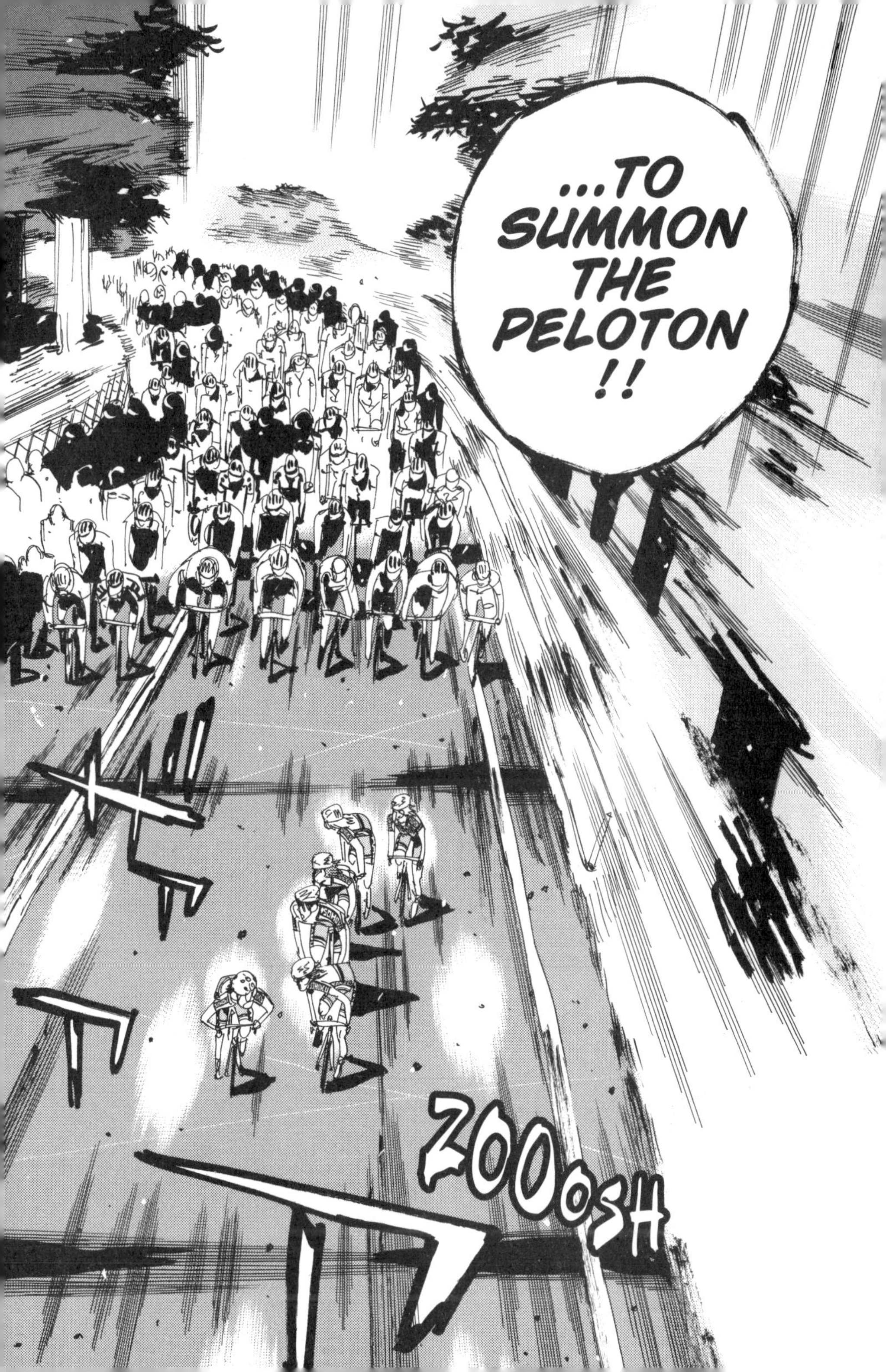
...TO SUMMON THE PELOTON!!
ZOOOSH

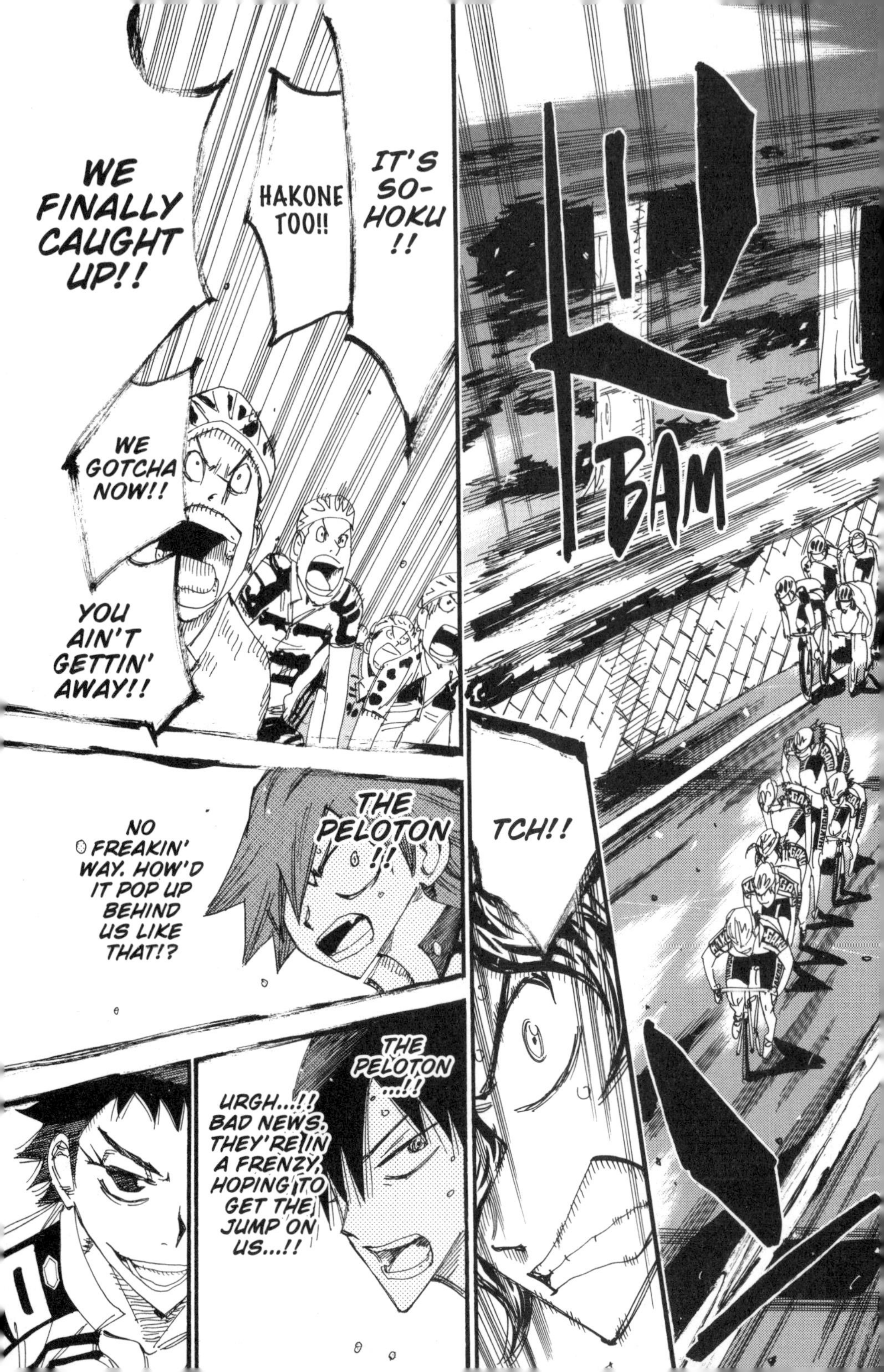
BAM
IT'S SO-HOKU!!
HAKONE TOO!!
WE FINALLY CAUGHT UP!!
WE GOTCHA NOW!!
YOU AIN'T GETTIN' AWAY!!
TCH!!
THE PELOTON!!
NO FREAKIN' WAY. HOW'D IT POP UP BEHIND US LIKE THAT!?
THE PELOTON...!!
URGH...!! BAD NEWS. THEY'RE IN A FRENZY, HOPING TO GET THE JUMP ON US...!!

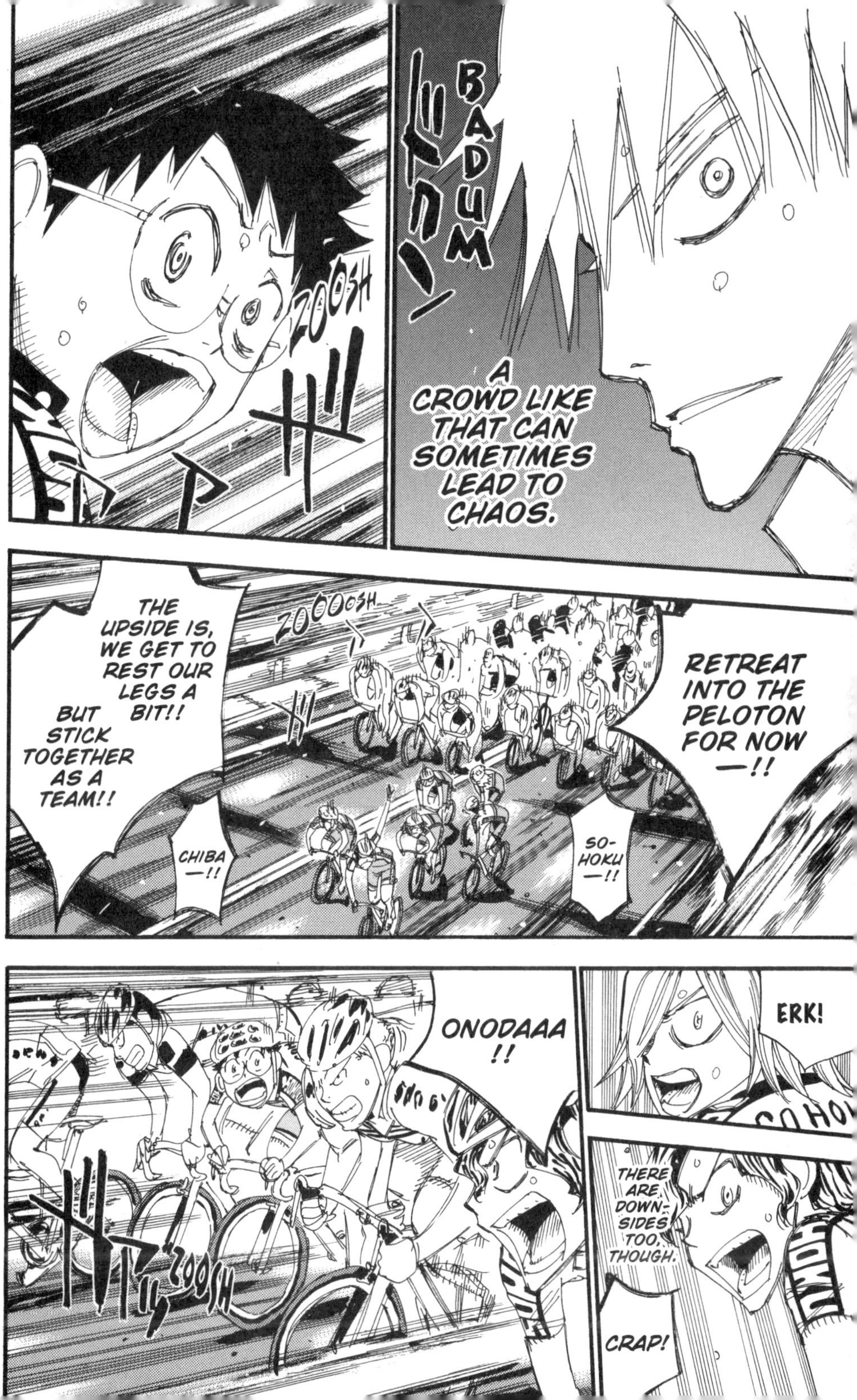
BADUM
A CROWD LIKE THAT CAN SOMETIMES LEAD TO CHAOS.
ZOOSH
RETREAT INTO THE PELOTON FOR NOW—!!
SO-HOKU—!!
ZOOOOSH
THE UPSIDE IS, WE GET TO REST OUR LEGS A BIT!!
BUT STICK TOGETHER AS A TEAM!!
CHIBA—!!
ERK!
THERE ARE DOWNSIDES TOO, THOUGH.
CRAP!
ONODAAA!!
ZOOSH

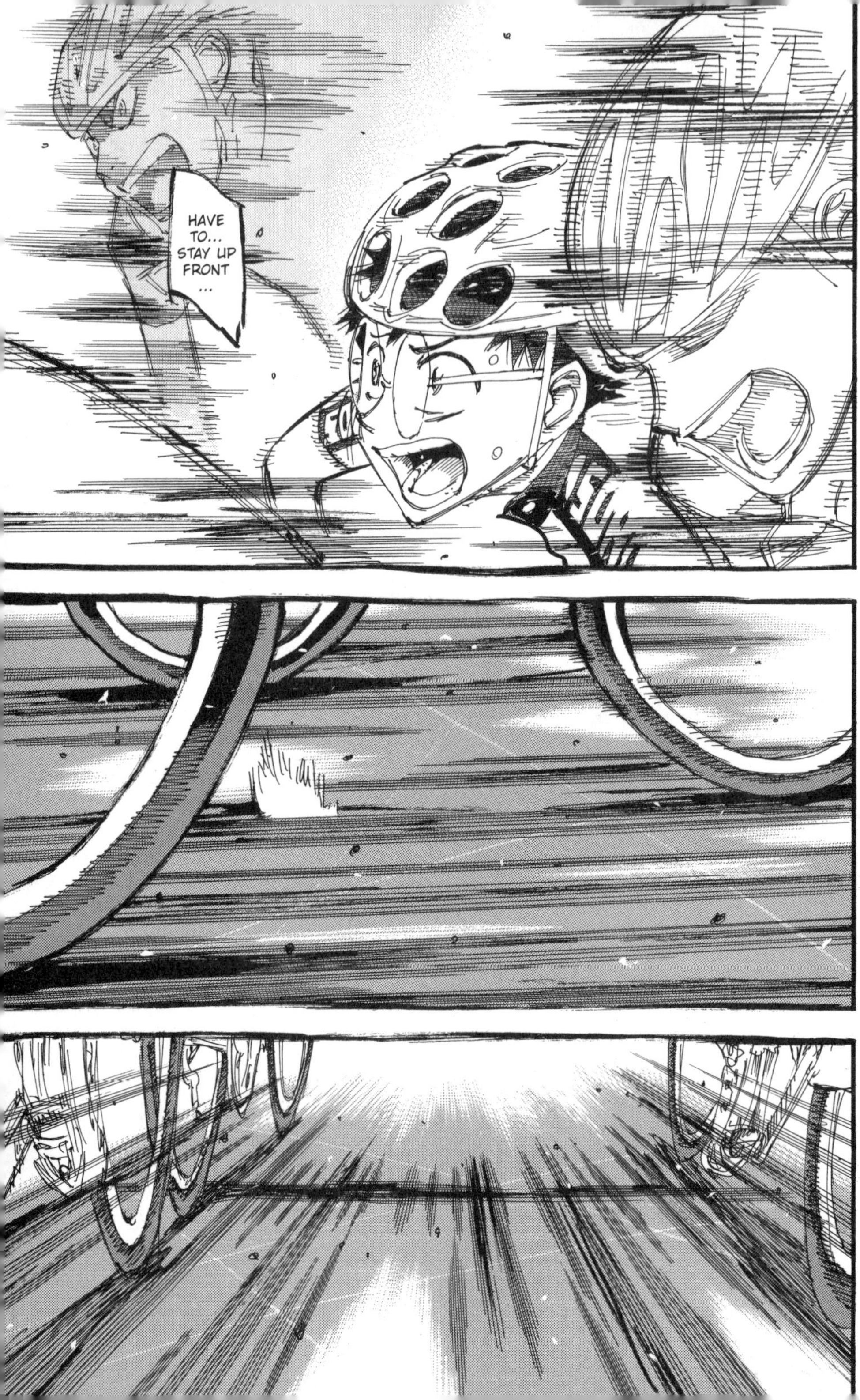
HAVE TO... STAY UP FRONT ...

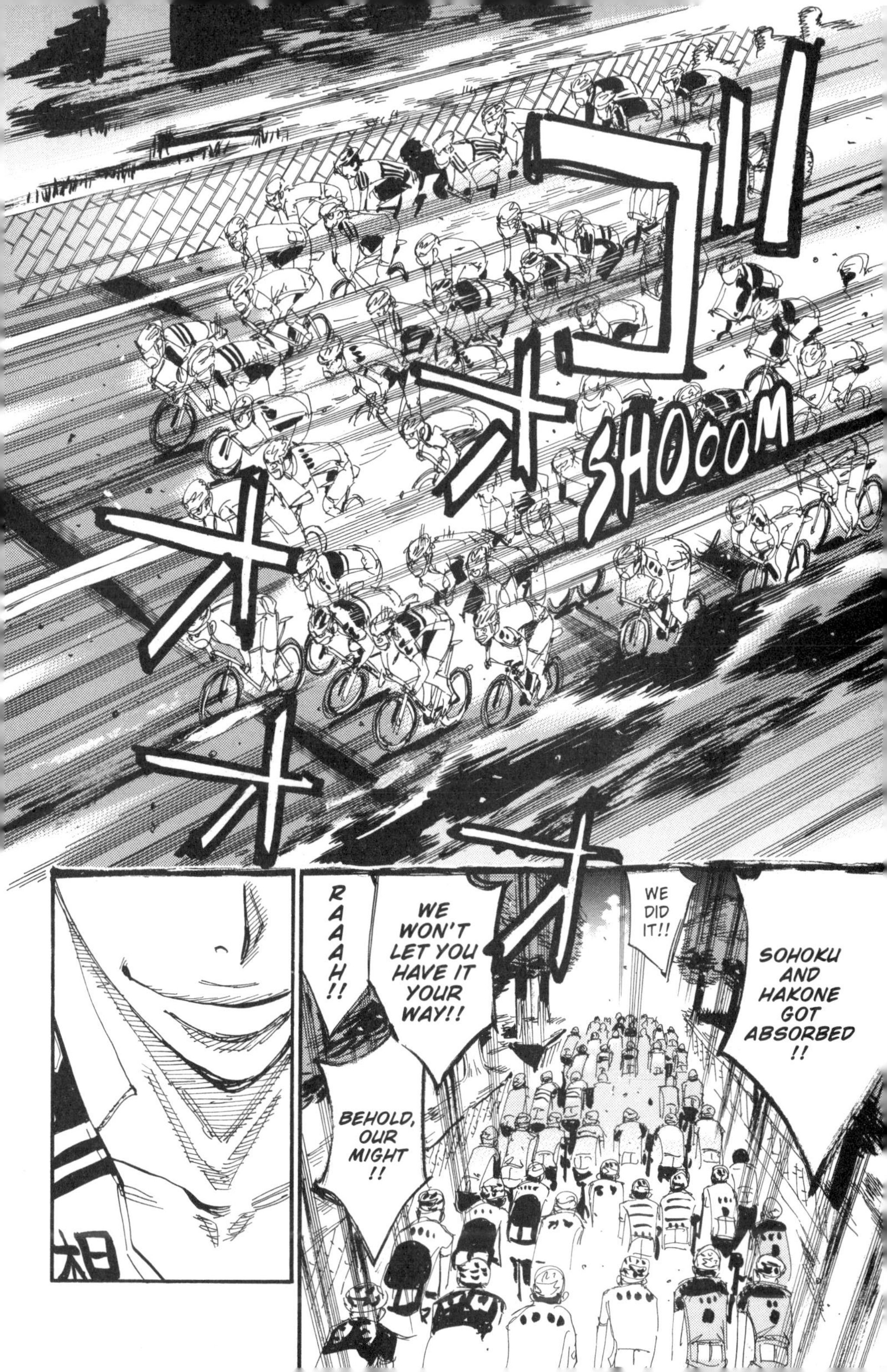
SHOOOM
SOHOKU AND HAKONE GOT ABSORBED!!
WE DID IT!!
WE WON'T LET YOU HAVE IT YOUR WAY!!
RAAAAH!!
BEHOLD, OUR MIGHT!!

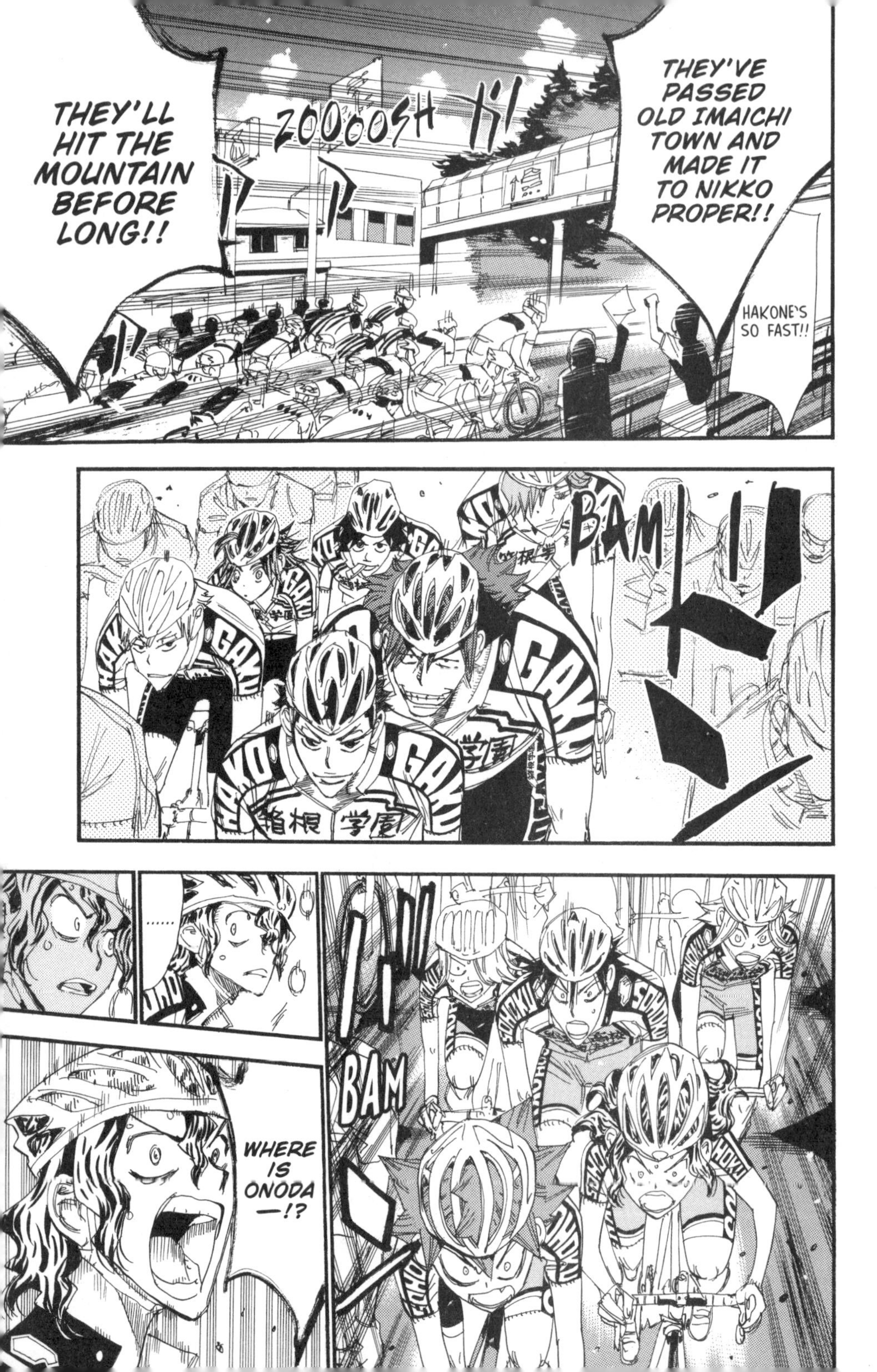
THEY'VE PASSED OLD IMAICHI TOWN AND MADE IT TO NIKKO PROPER!!
ZOOOOSH
HAKONE'S SO FAST!!
THEY'LL HIT THE MOUNTAIN BEFORE LONG!!
BAM
BAM
......
WHERE IS ONODA—!?

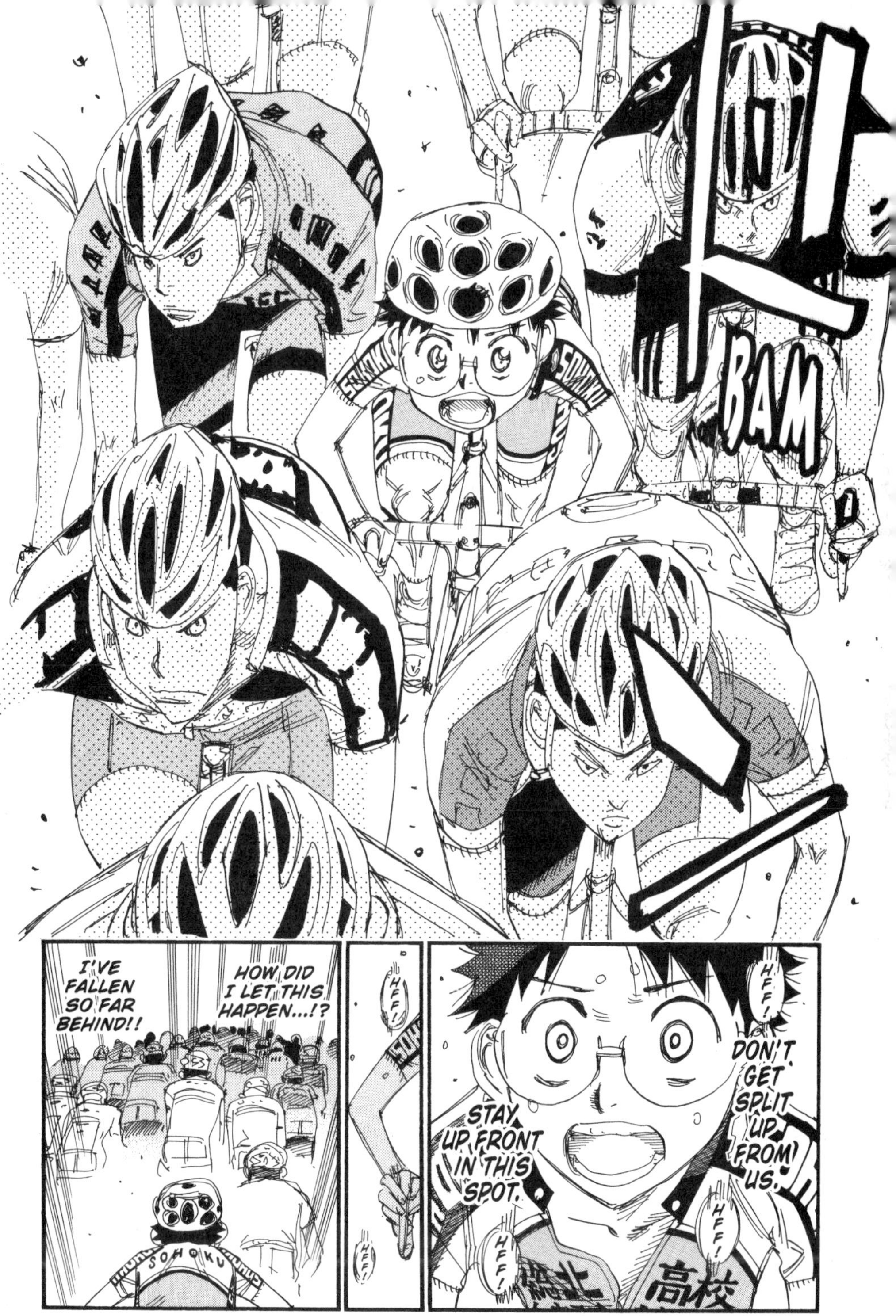
BAM
HFF!
DON'T GET SPLIT UP FROM US.
STAY UP FRONT IN THIS SPOT.
HFF!
HFF!
HFF!
HFF!
HOW DID I LET THIS HAPPEN...!?
I'VE FALLEN SO FAR BEHIND!!

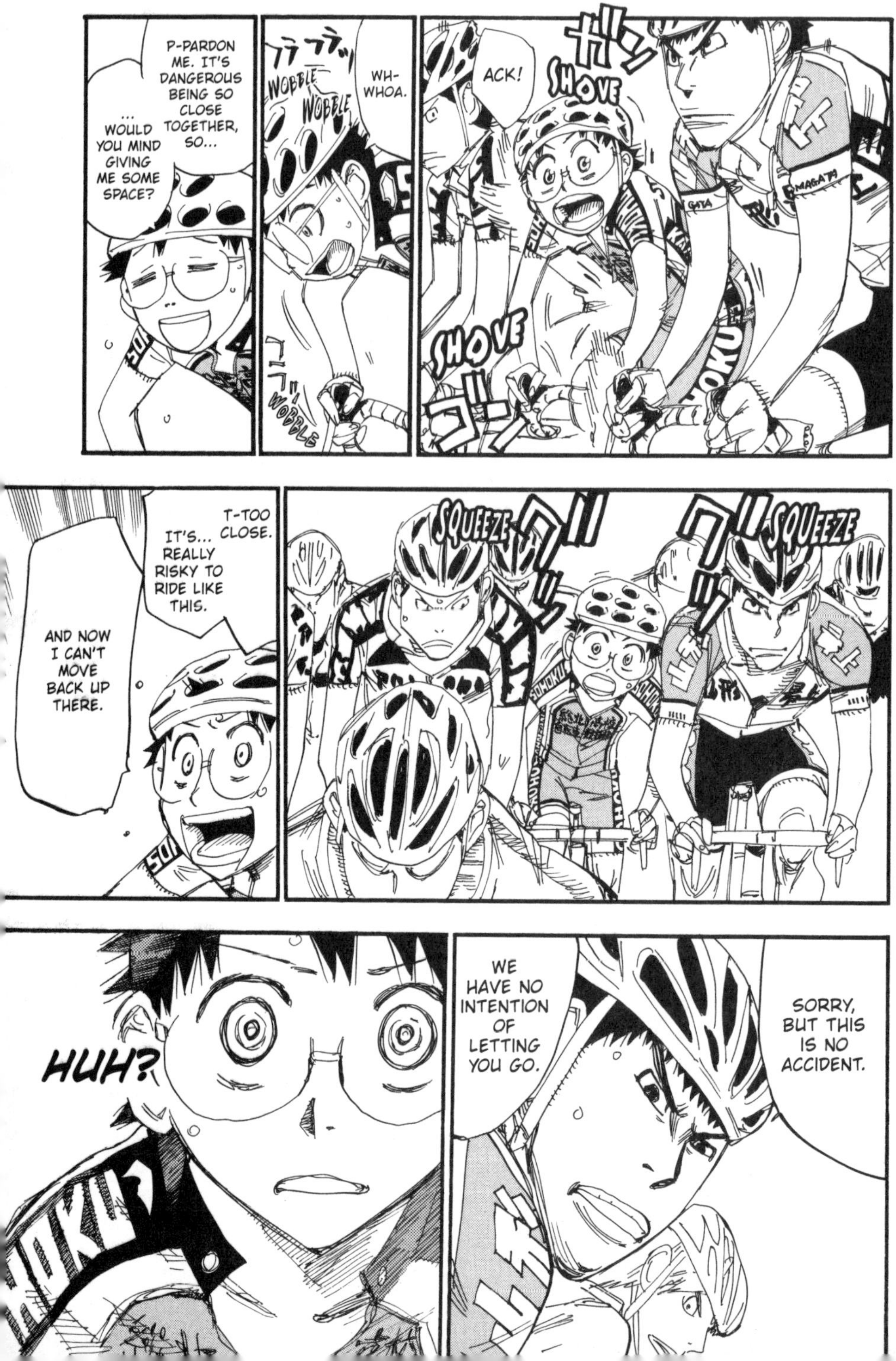
SHOVE
ACK!
SHOVE
WH-WHOA.
WOBBLE WOBBLE
WOBBLE
P-PARDON ME. IT'S DANGEROUS BEING SO CLOSE TOGETHER, SO...
... WOULD YOU MIND GIVING ME SOME SPACE?
SQUEEZE
SQUEEZE
T-TOO CLOSE.
IT'S... REALLY RISKY TO RIDE LIKE THIS.
AND NOW I CAN'T MOVE BACK UP THERE.
SORRY, BUT THIS IS NO ACCIDENT.
WE HAVE NO INTENTION OF LETTING YOU GO.
HUH?

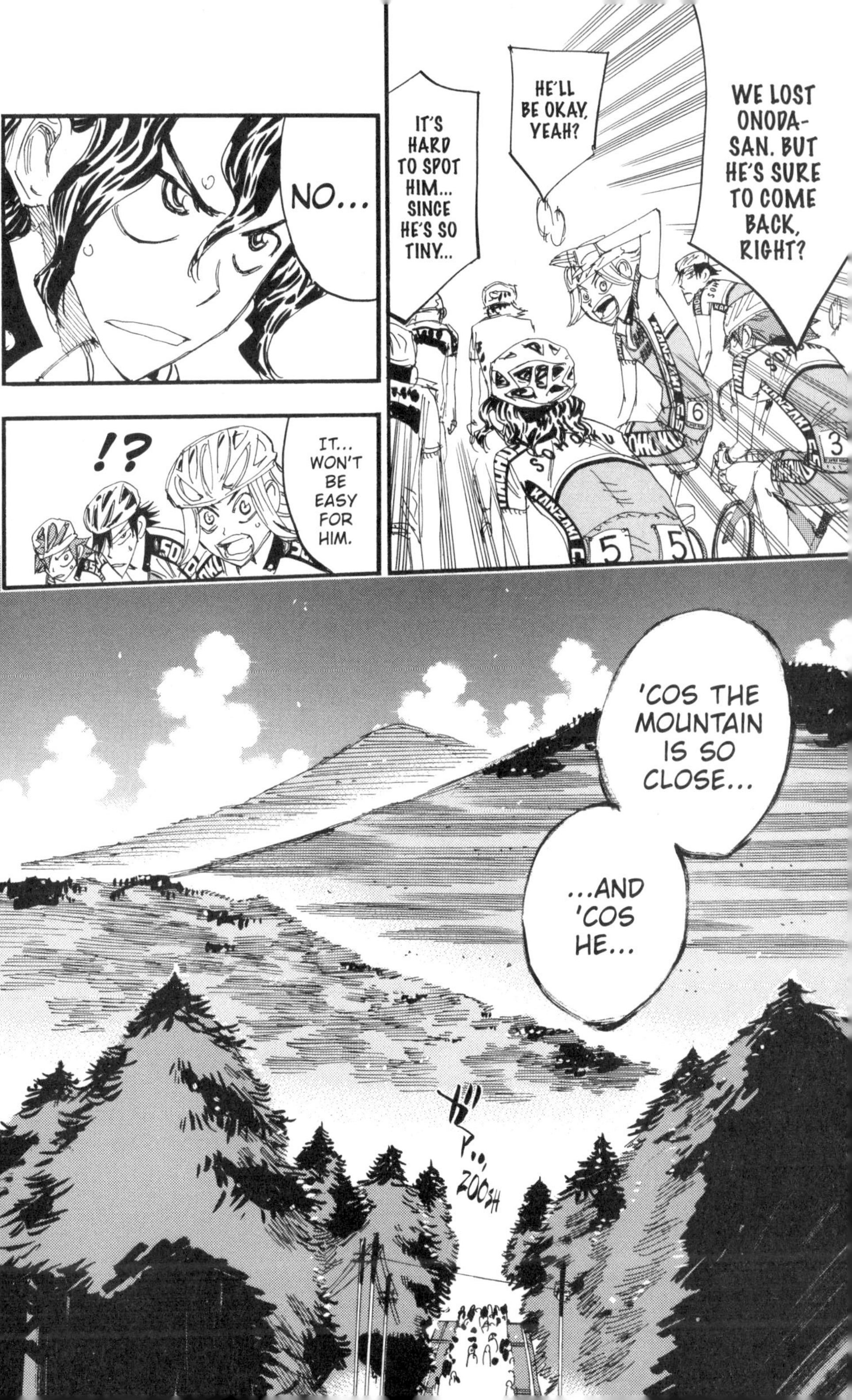
WE LOST ONODA-SAN. BUT HE'S SURE TO COME BACK, RIGHT?
HE'LL BE OKAY, YEAH?
IT'S HARD TO SPOT HIM... SINCE HE'S SO TINY...
NO...
!?
IT... WON'T BE EASY FOR HIM.
'COS THE MOUNTAIN IS SO CLOSE...
...AND 'COS HE...
ZOOSH

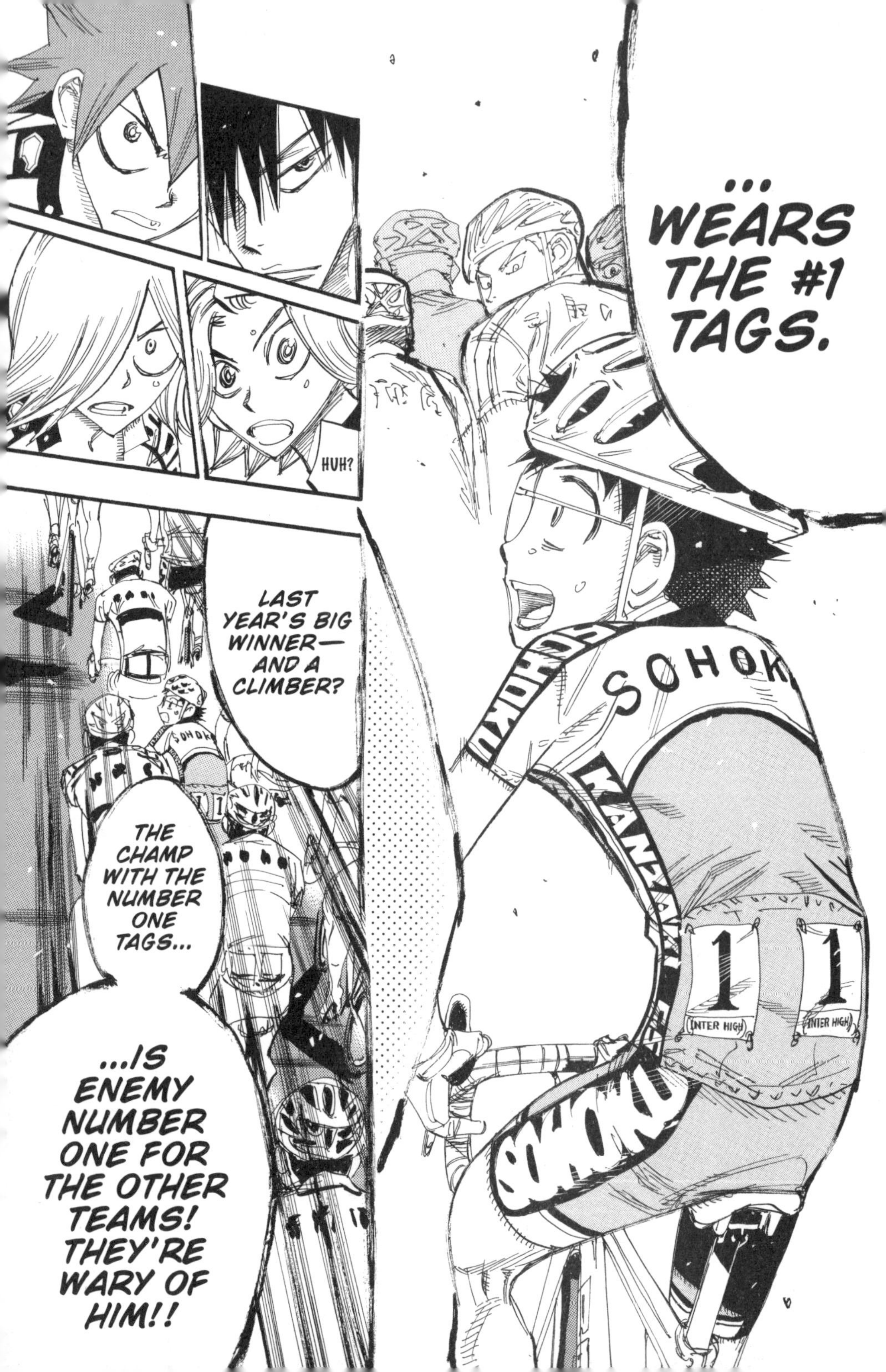
...WEARS THE #1 TAGS.
HUH?
LAST YEAR'S BIG WINNER—AND A CLIMBER?
THE CHAMP WITH THE NUMBER ONE TAGS...
...IS ENEMY NUMBER ONE FOR THE OTHER TEAMS! THEY'RE WARY OF HIM!!

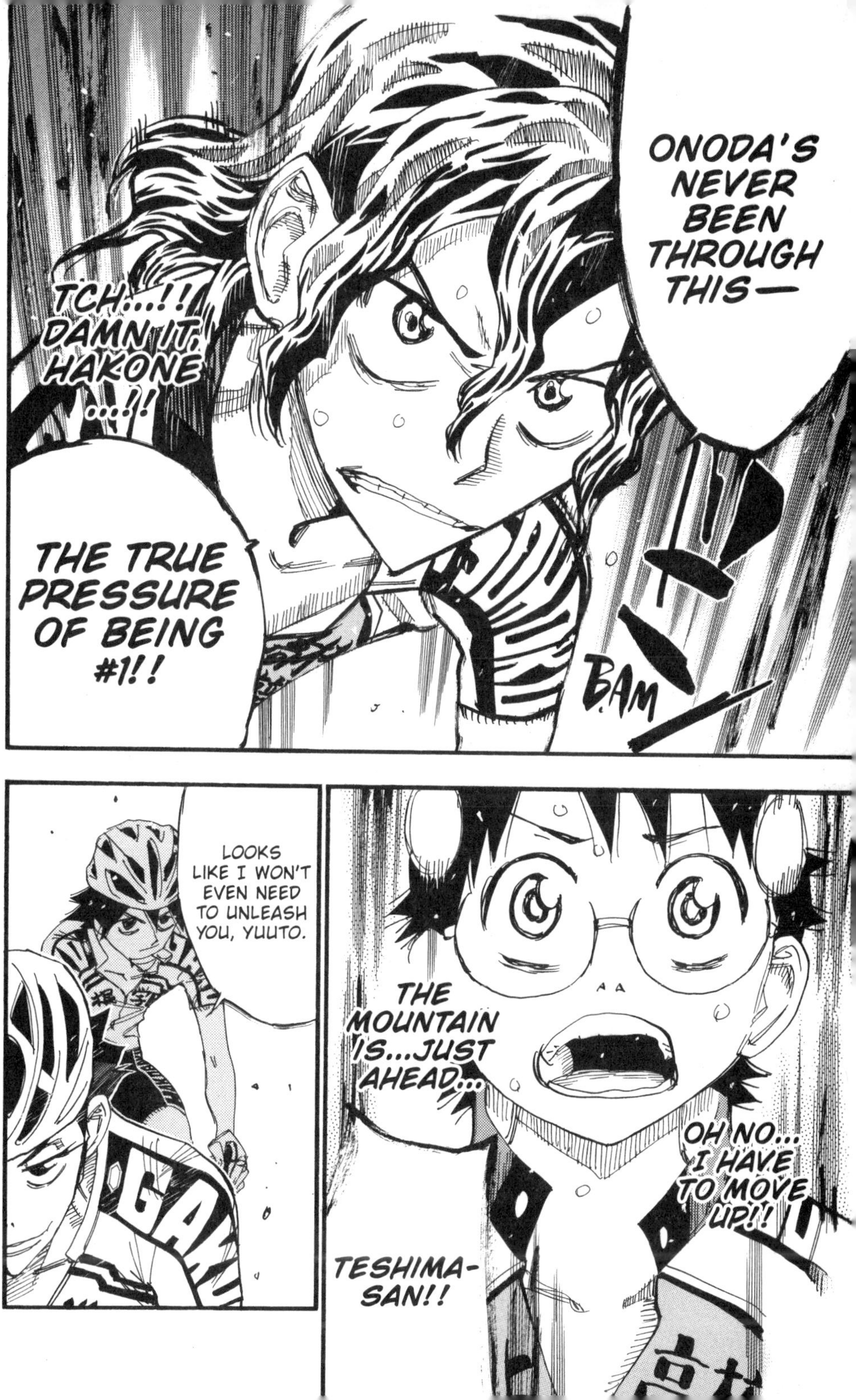
ONODA'S NEVER BEEN THROUGH THIS—
TCH...!! DAMN IT, HAKONE ...!!
THE TRUE PRESSURE OF BEING #1!!
BAM
THE MOUNTAIN IS...JUST AHEAD...
OH NO... I HAVE TO MOVE UP!!
TESHIMA-SAN!!
LOOKS LIKE I WON'T EVEN NEED TO UNLEASH YOU, YUUTO.

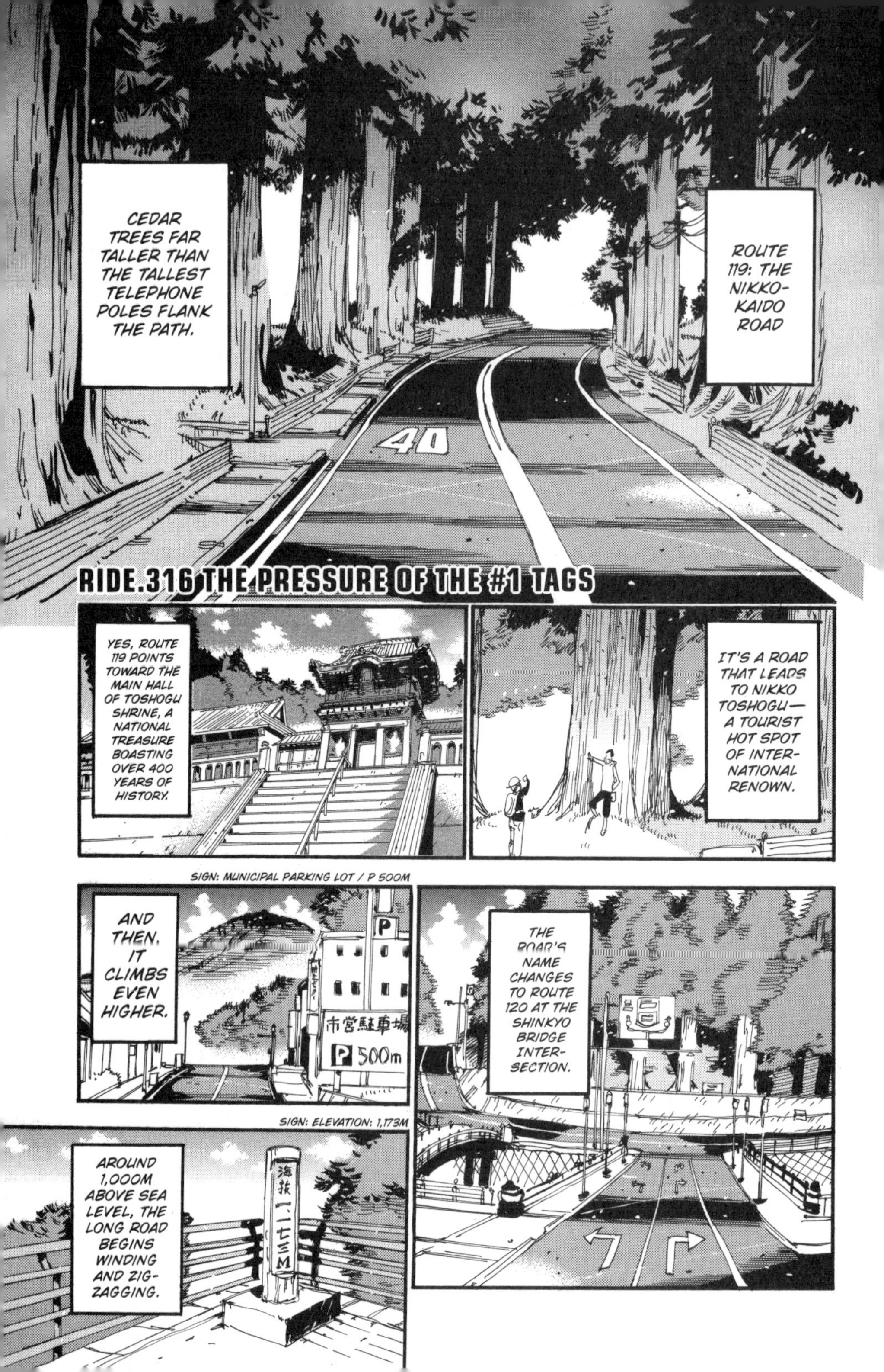
ROUTE 119: THE NIKKO-KAIDO ROAD
CEDAR TREES FAR TALLER THAN THE TALLEST TELEPHONE POLES FLANK THE PATH.
40
RIDE.316 THE PRESSURE OF THE #1 TAGS
IT'S A ROAD THAT LEADS TO NIKKO TOSHOGU—A TOURIST HOT SPOT OF INTER-NATIONAL RENOWN.
YES, ROUTE 119 POINTS TOWARD THE MAIN HALL OF TOSHOGU SHRINE, A NATIONAL TREASURE BOASTING OVER 400 YEARS OF HISTORY.
THE ROAD'S NAME CHANGES TO ROUTE 120 AT THE SHINKYO BRIDGE INTER-SECTION.
SIGN: MUNICIPAL PARKING LOT / P 500M
AND THEN, IT CLIMBS EVEN HIGHER.
市営駐車場
P 500m
SIGN: ELEVATION: 1,173M
AROUND 1,000M ABOVE SEA LEVEL, THE LONG ROAD BEGINS WINDING AND ZIG-ZAGGING.
海抜一一七三M

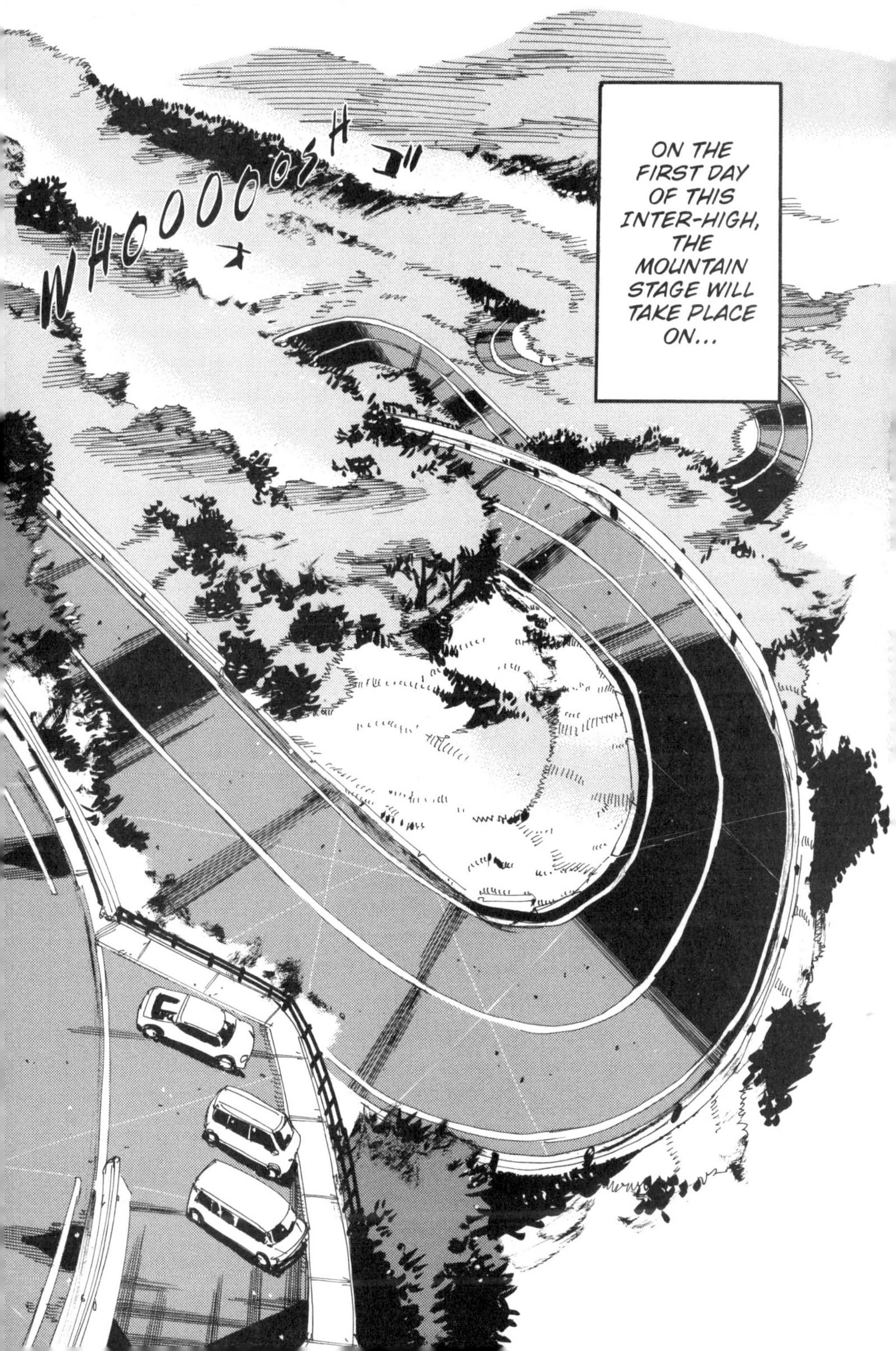
ON THE FIRST DAY OF THIS INTER-HIGH, THE MOUNTAIN STAGE WILL TAKE PLACE ON...
WHOOOOOSH

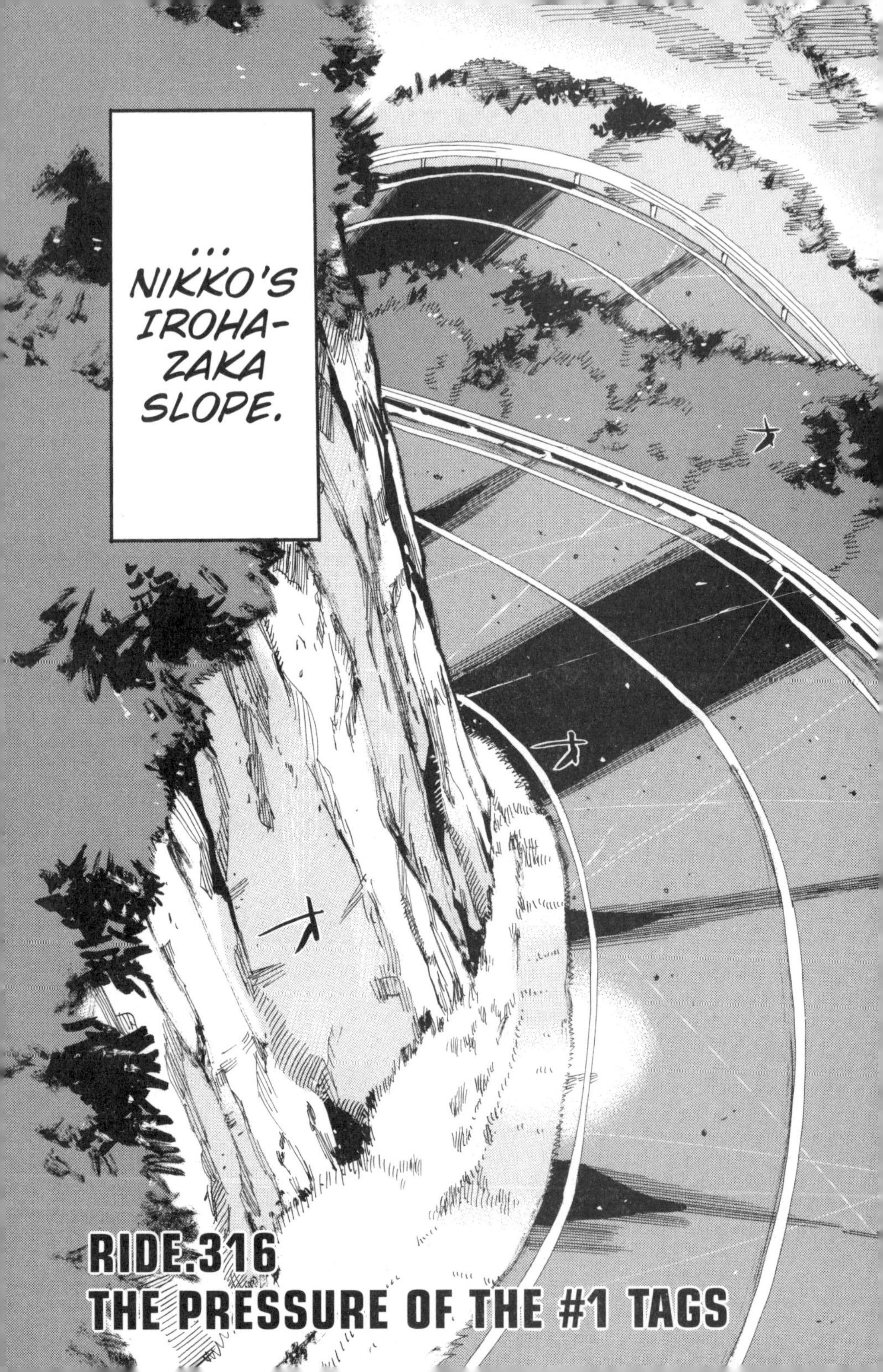
...NIKKO'S IROHA-ZAKA SLOPE.

RIDE.316 THE PRESSURE OF THE #1 TAGS

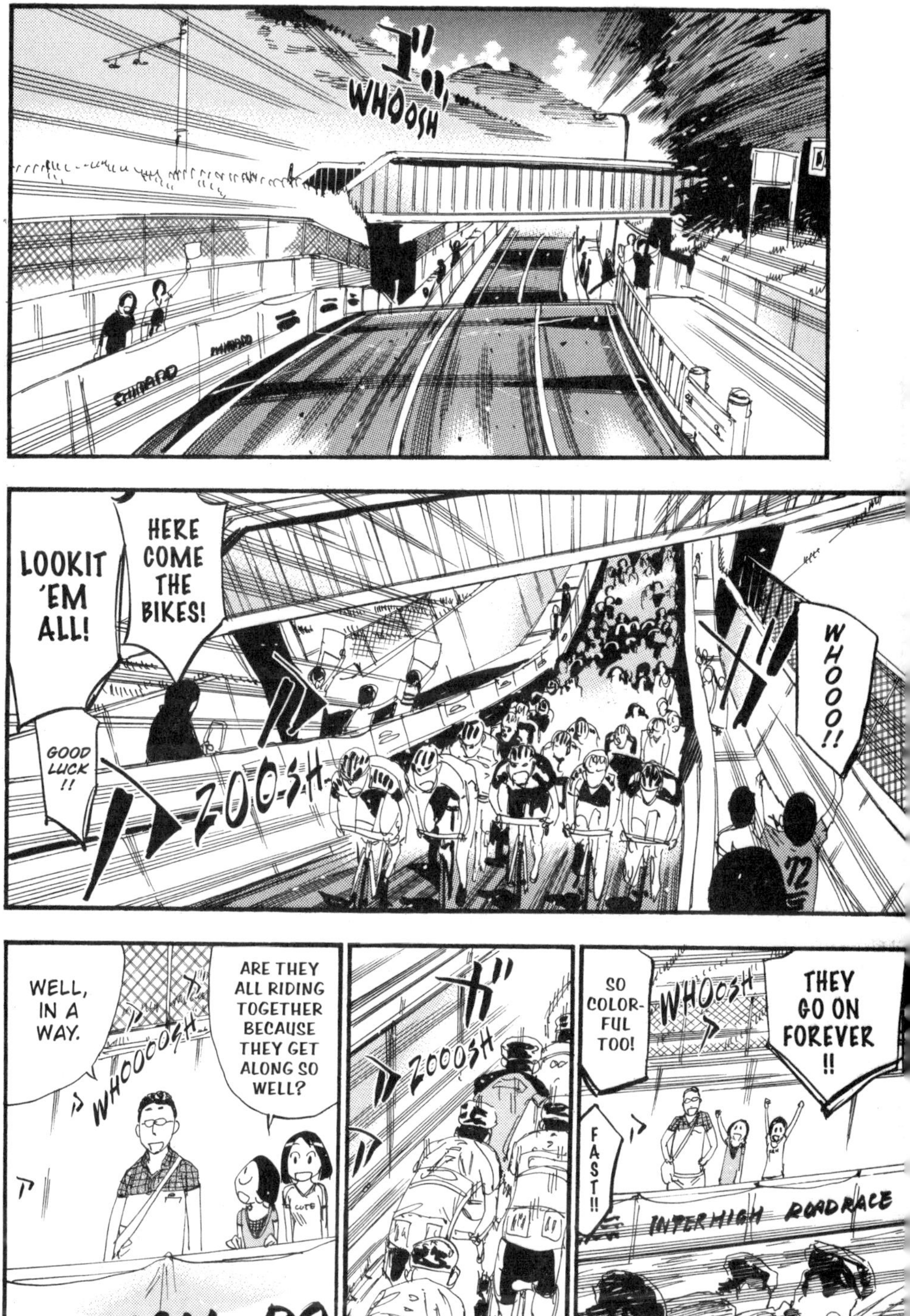
WHOOSH
WHOOOO!!
HERE COME THE BIKES!
LOOKIT 'EM ALL!
GOOD LUCK!!
ZOOSH
THEY GO ON FOREVER!!
WHOOSH
SO COLOR-FUL TOO!
FAST!!
INTERHIGH ROADRACE
ZOOOSH
ARE THEY ALL RIDING TOGETHER BECAUSE THEY GET ALONG SO WELL?
WELL, IN A WAY.
WHOOOOSH
WHOOOOSH
ER-HIGH RO

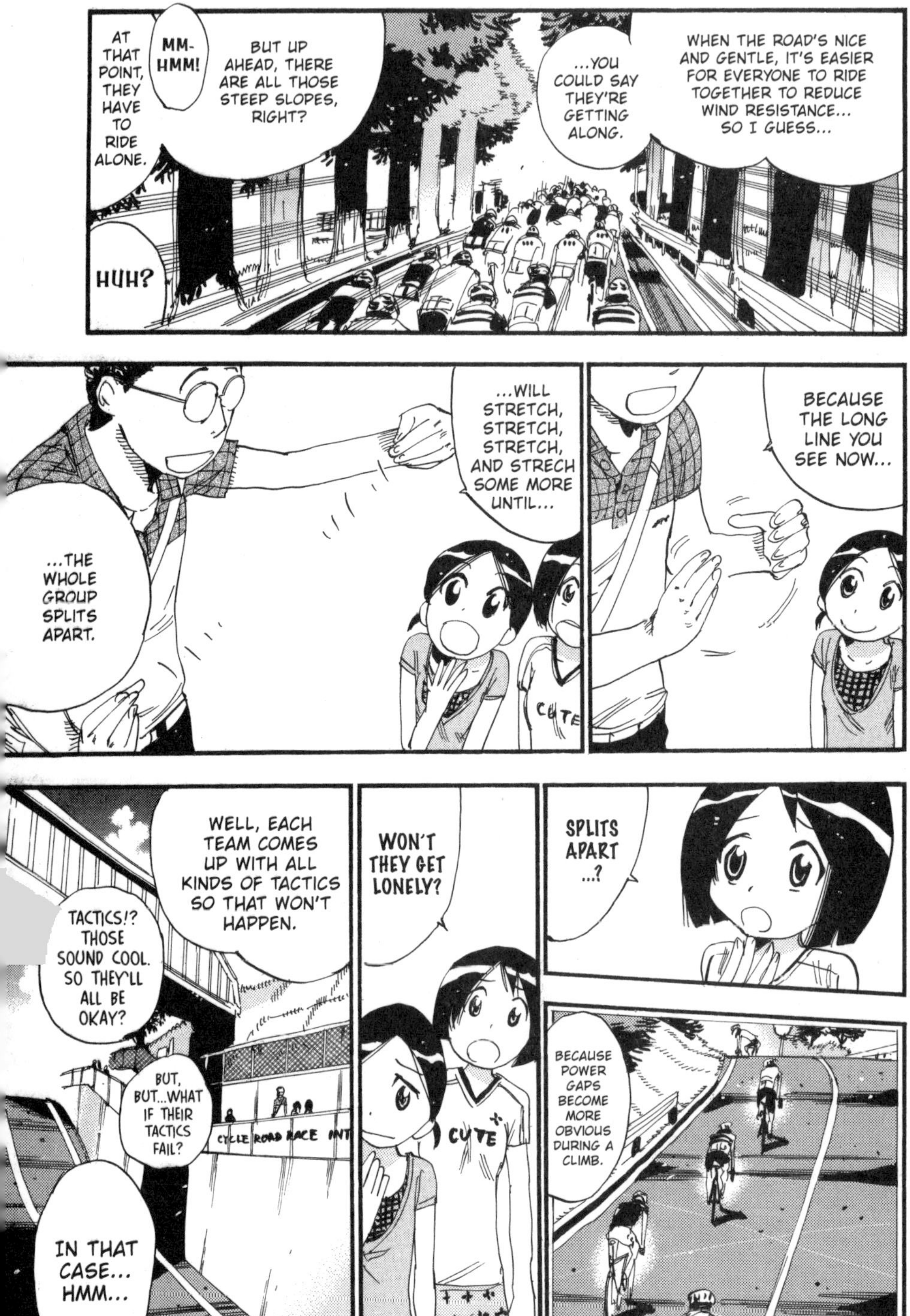
WHEN THE ROAD'S NICE AND GENTLE, IT'S EASIER FOR EVERYONE TO RIDE TOGETHER TO REDUCE WIND RESISTANCE... SO I GUESS...
...YOU COULD SAY THEY'RE GETTING ALONG.
BUT UP AHEAD, THERE ARE ALL THOSE STEEP SLOPES, RIGHT?
MM-HMM!
AT THAT POINT, THEY HAVE TO RIDE ALONE.
HUH?
BECAUSE THE LONG LINE YOU SEE NOW...
...WILL STRETCH, STRETCH, STRETCH, AND STRECH SOME MORE UNTIL...
...THE WHOLE GROUP SPLITS APART.
CUTE
SPLITS APART ...?
BECAUSE POWER GAPS BECOME MORE OBVIOUS DURING A CLIMB.
WON'T THEY GET LONELY?
CUTE
WELL, EACH TEAM COMES UP WITH ALL KINDS OF TACTICS SO THAT WON'T HAPPEN.
TACTICS!? THOSE SOUND COOL. SO THEY'LL ALL BE OKAY?
BUT, BUT...WHAT IF THEIR TACTICS FAIL?
CYCLE ROAD RACE INT
IN THAT CASE... HMM...

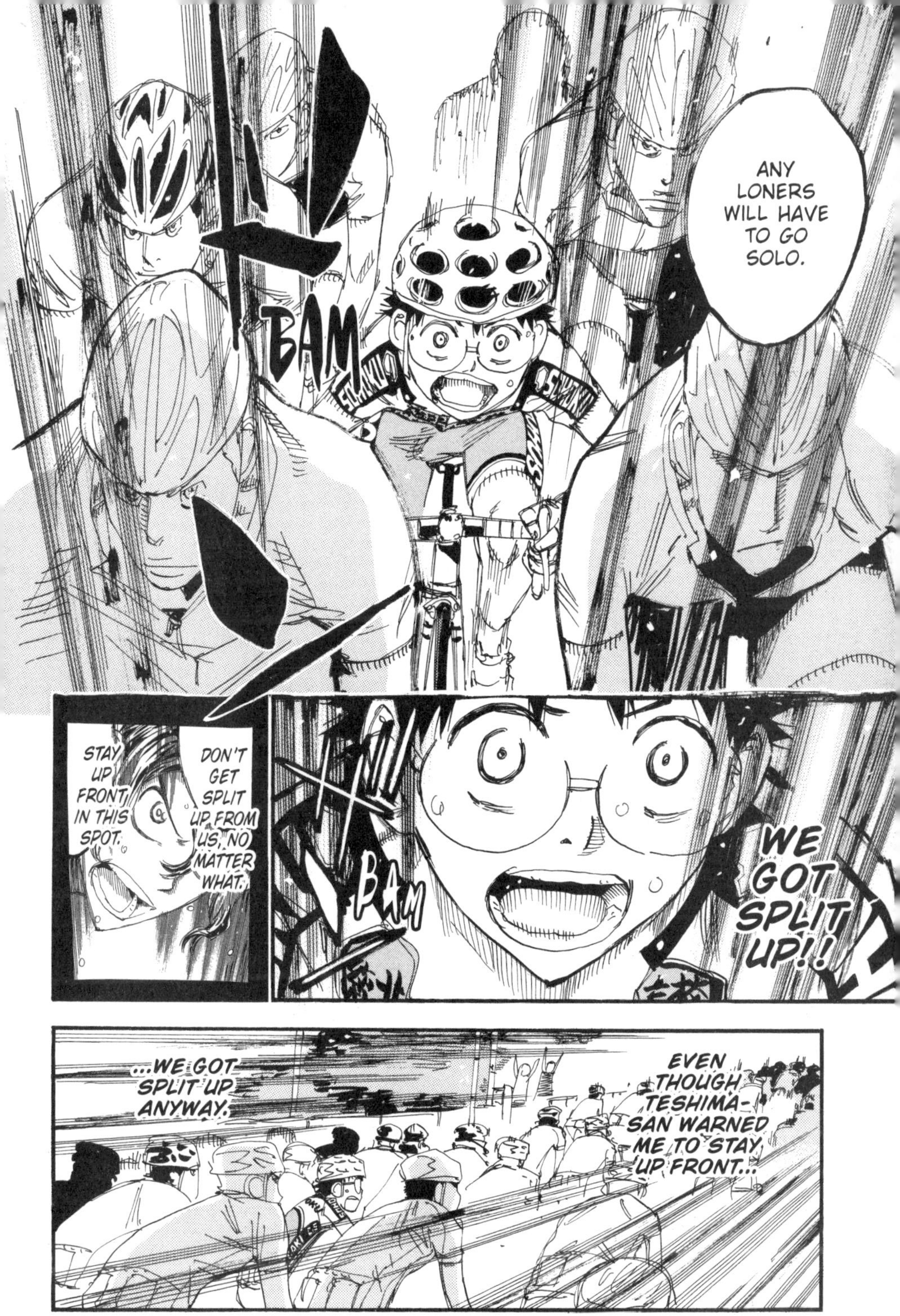
ANY LONERS WILL HAVE TO GO SOLO.
BAM
BAM
WE GOT SPLIT UP!!
DON'T GET SPLIT UP FROM US, NO MATTER WHAT.
STAY UP FRONT IN THIS SPOT.
EVEN THOUGH TESHIMA-SAN WARNED ME TO STAY UP FRONT...
...WE GOT SPLIT UP ANYWAY.

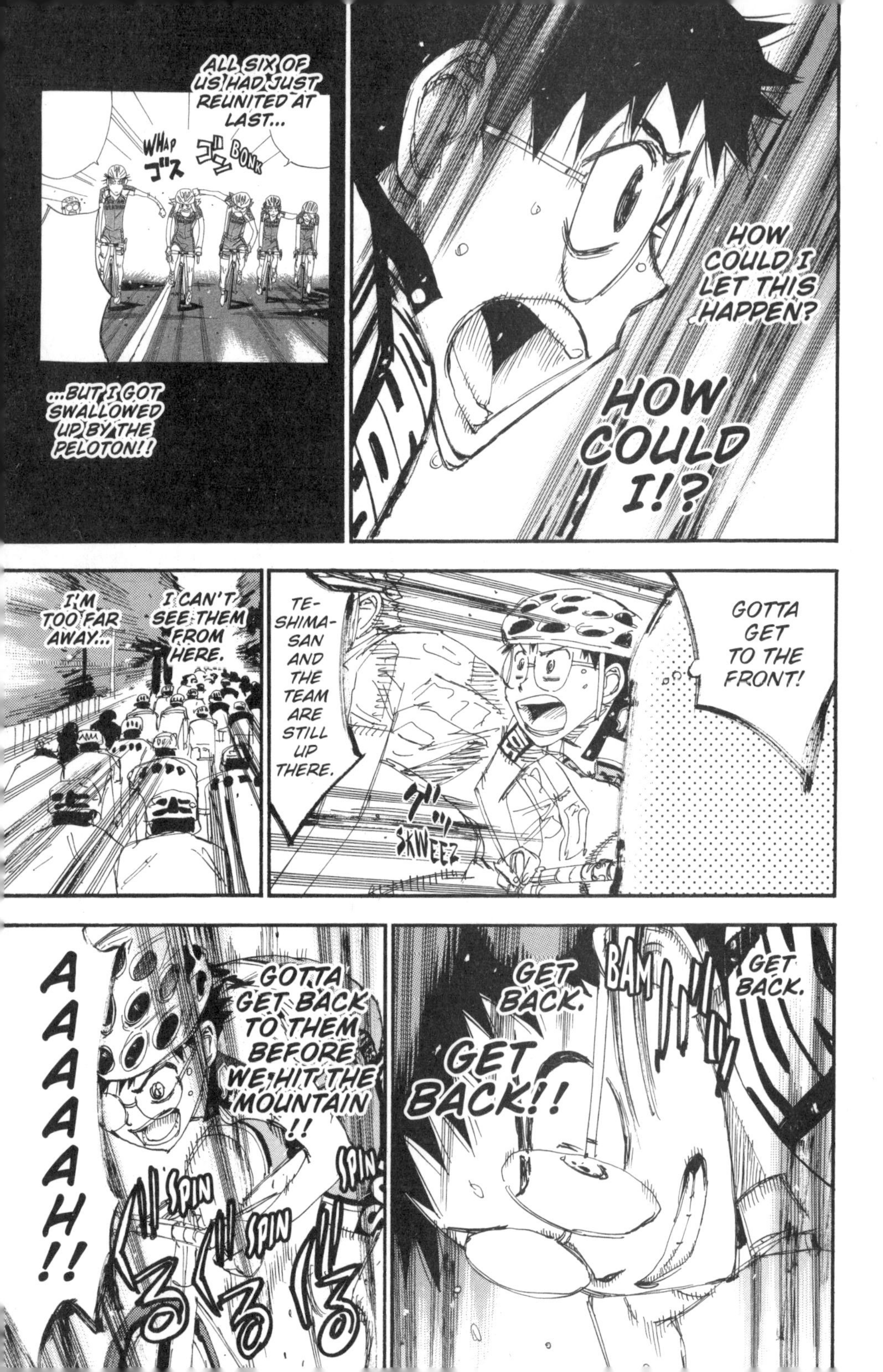
HOW COULD I LET THIS HAPPEN?
HOW COULD I!?
ALL SIX OF US HAD JUST REUNITED AT LAST...
WHAP ゴス
ゴン BONK
...BUT I GOT SWALLOWED UP BY THE PELOTON!!
GOTTA GET TO THE FRONT!
TE-SHIMA-SAN AND THE TEAM ARE STILL UP THERE.
グッ SKWEEZ
I CAN'T SEE THEM FROM HERE.
I'M TOO FAR AWAY...
GET BACK.
BAM
GET BACK.
GET BACK!!
GOTTA GET BACK TO THEM BEFORE WE HIT THE MOUNTAIN!!
AAAAAAAH!!
SPIN
SPIN
SPIN
SPIN

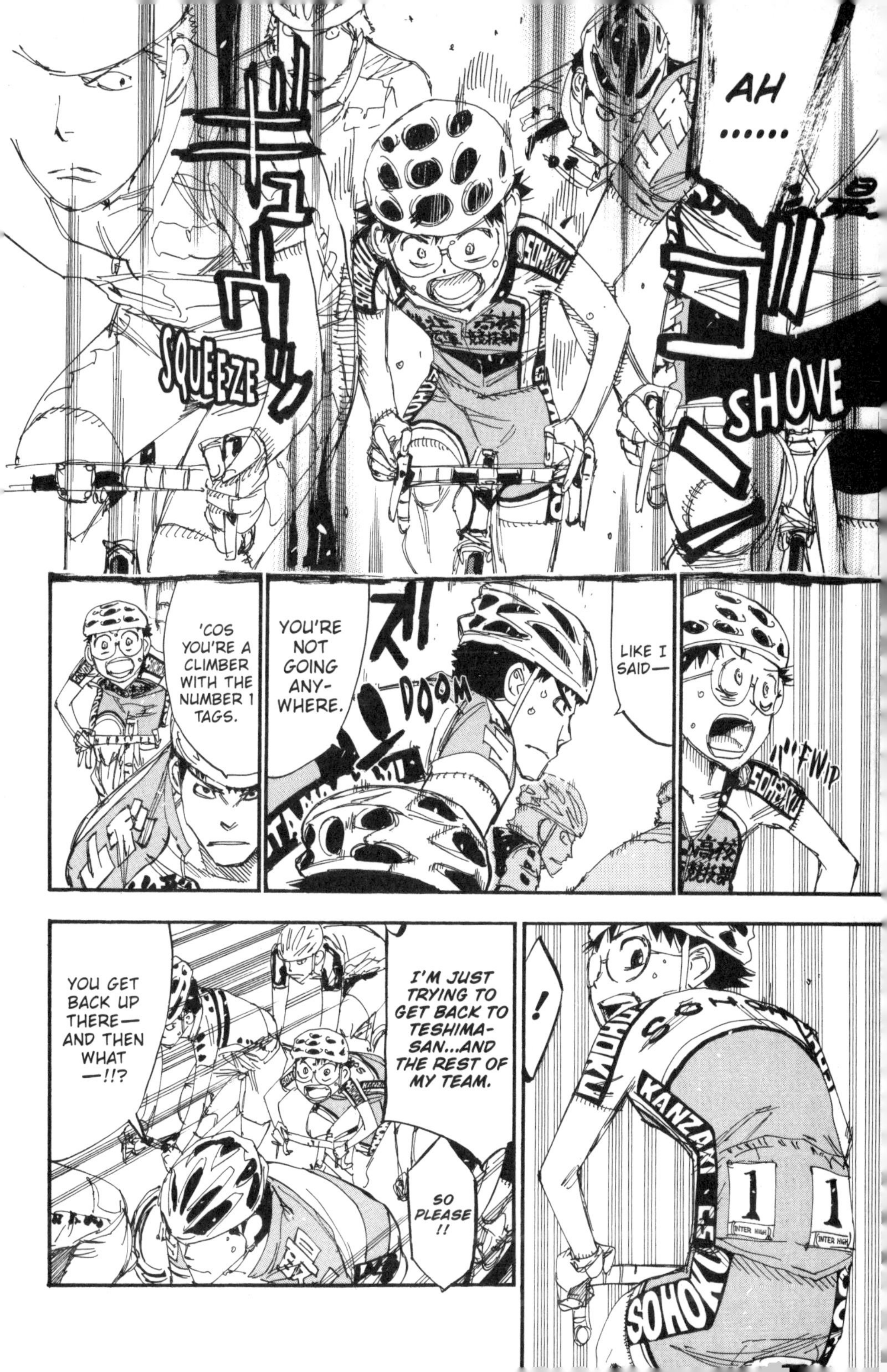
AH ......
SHOVE
SQUEEZE
LIKE I SAID—
FWIP
YOU'RE NOT GOING ANYWHERE.
DOOM
'COS YOU'RE A CLIMBER WITH THE NUMBER 1 TAGS.
!
I'M JUST TRYING TO GET BACK TO TESHIMA-SAN...AND THE REST OF MY TEAM.
YOU GET BACK UP THERE—AND THEN WHAT—!!?
SO PLEASE!!

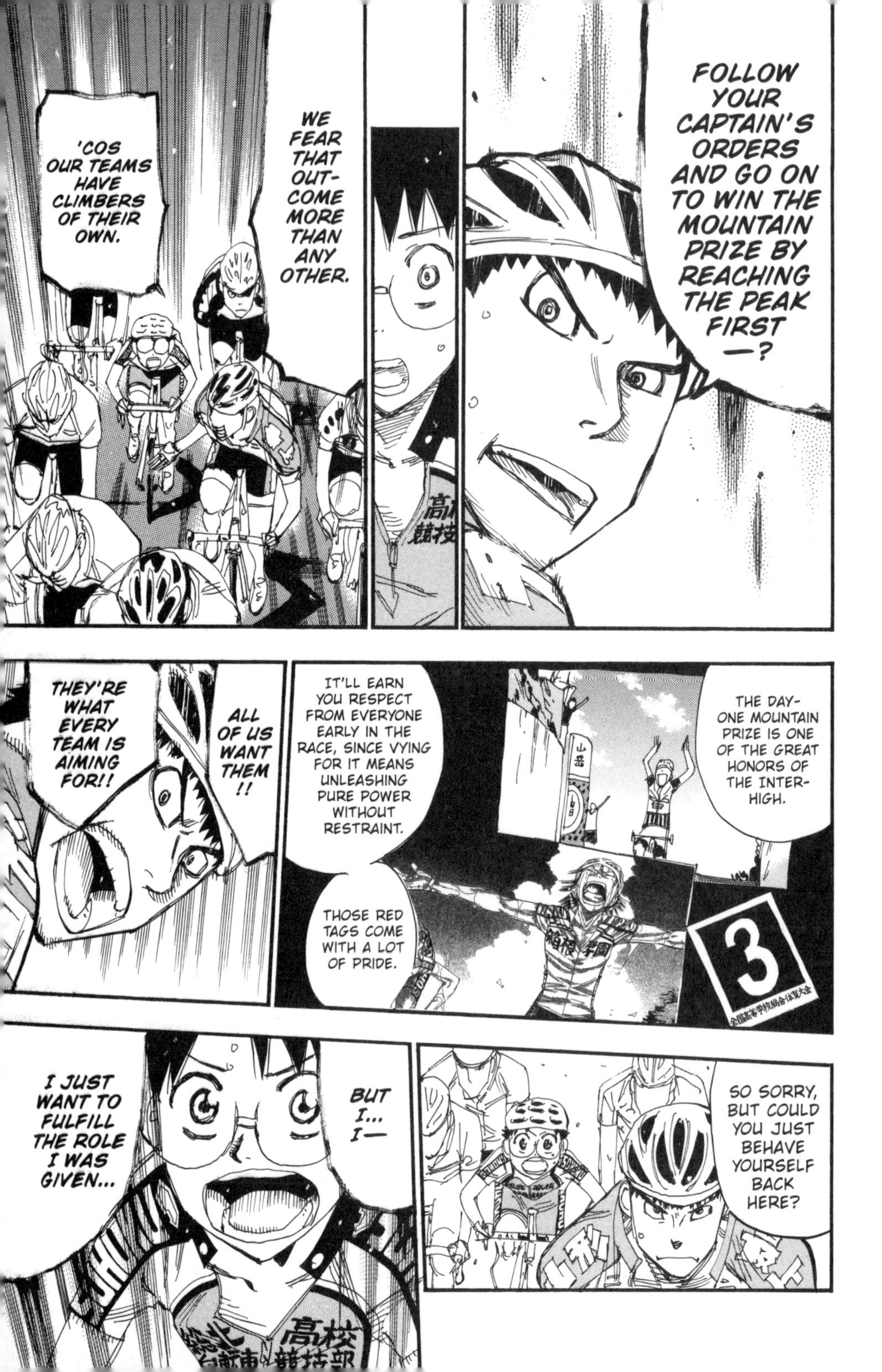
FOLLOW YOUR CAPTAIN'S ORDERS AND GO ON TO WIN THE MOUNTAIN PRIZE BY REACHING THE PEAK FIRST —?
WE FEAR THAT OUT-COME MORE THAN ANY OTHER.
'COS OUR TEAMS HAVE CLIMBERS OF THEIR OWN.
THE DAY-ONE MOUNTAIN PRIZE IS ONE OF THE GREAT HONORS OF THE INTER-HIGH.
IT'LL EARN YOU RESPECT FROM EVERYONE EARLY IN THE RACE, SINCE VYING FOR IT MEANS UNLEASHING PURE POWER WITHOUT RESTRAINT.
3
THOSE RED TAGS COME WITH A LOT OF PRIDE.
ALL OF US WANT THEM!!
THEY'RE WHAT EVERY TEAM IS AIMING FOR!!
SO SORRY, BUT COULD YOU JUST BEHAVE YOURSELF BACK HERE?
BUT I... I—
I JUST WANT TO FULFILL THE ROLE I WAS GIVEN...

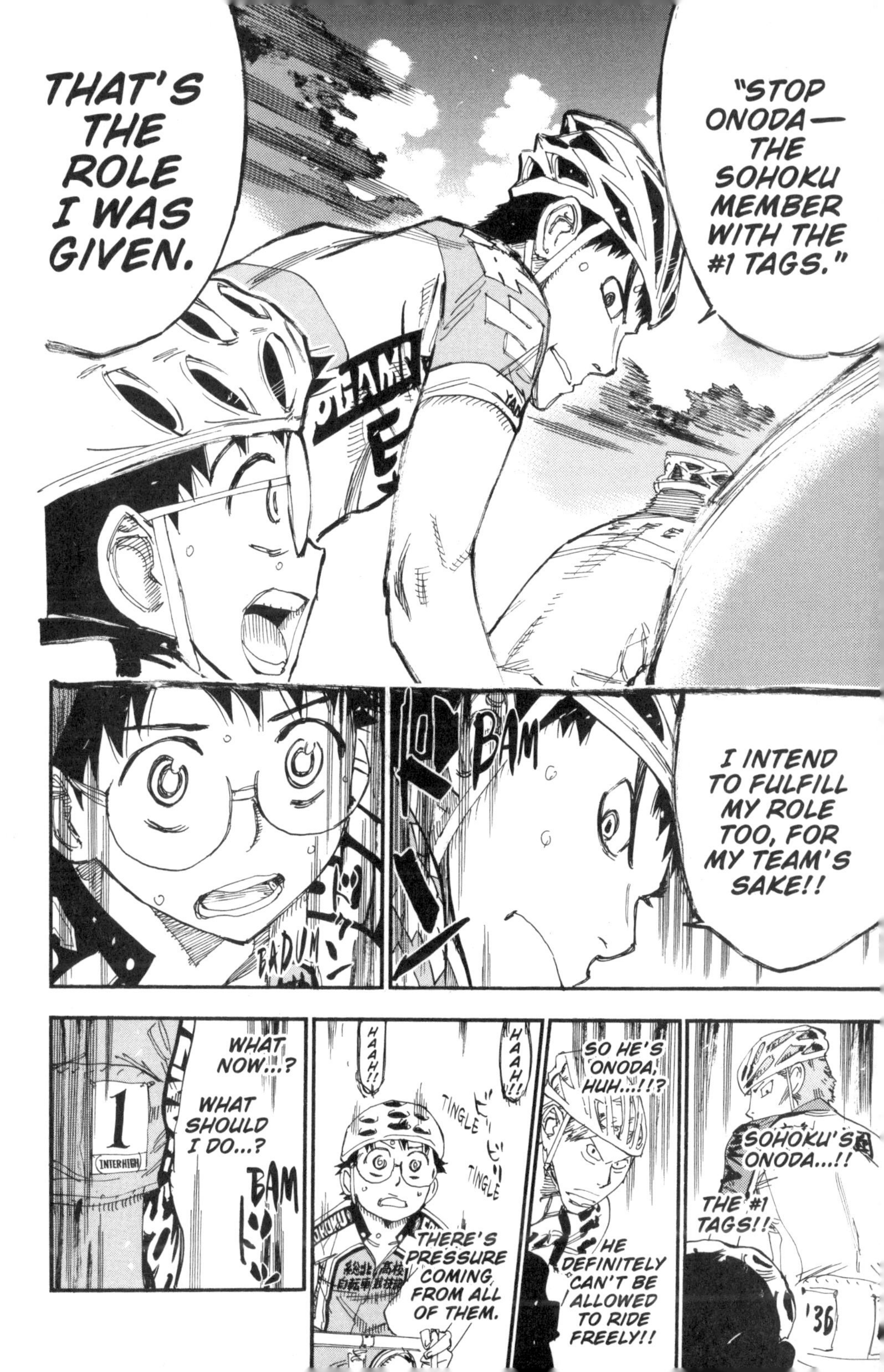
"STOP ONODA—THE SOHOKU MEMBER WITH THE #1 TAGS."
THAT'S THE ROLE I WAS GIVEN.
BAM
I INTEND TO FULFILL MY ROLE TOO, FOR MY TEAM'S SAKE!!
BADUM
SOHOKU'S ONODA...!!
THE #1 TAGS!!
36
SO HE'S ONODA, HUH...!!?
HE DEFINITELY CAN'T BE ALLOWED TO RIDE FREELY!!
HAAH!!
HAAH!!
TINGLE
TINGLE
THERE'S PRESSURE COMING FROM ALL OF THEM.
WHAT NOW...?
WHAT SHOULD I DO...?
BAM
1
INTERHIGH

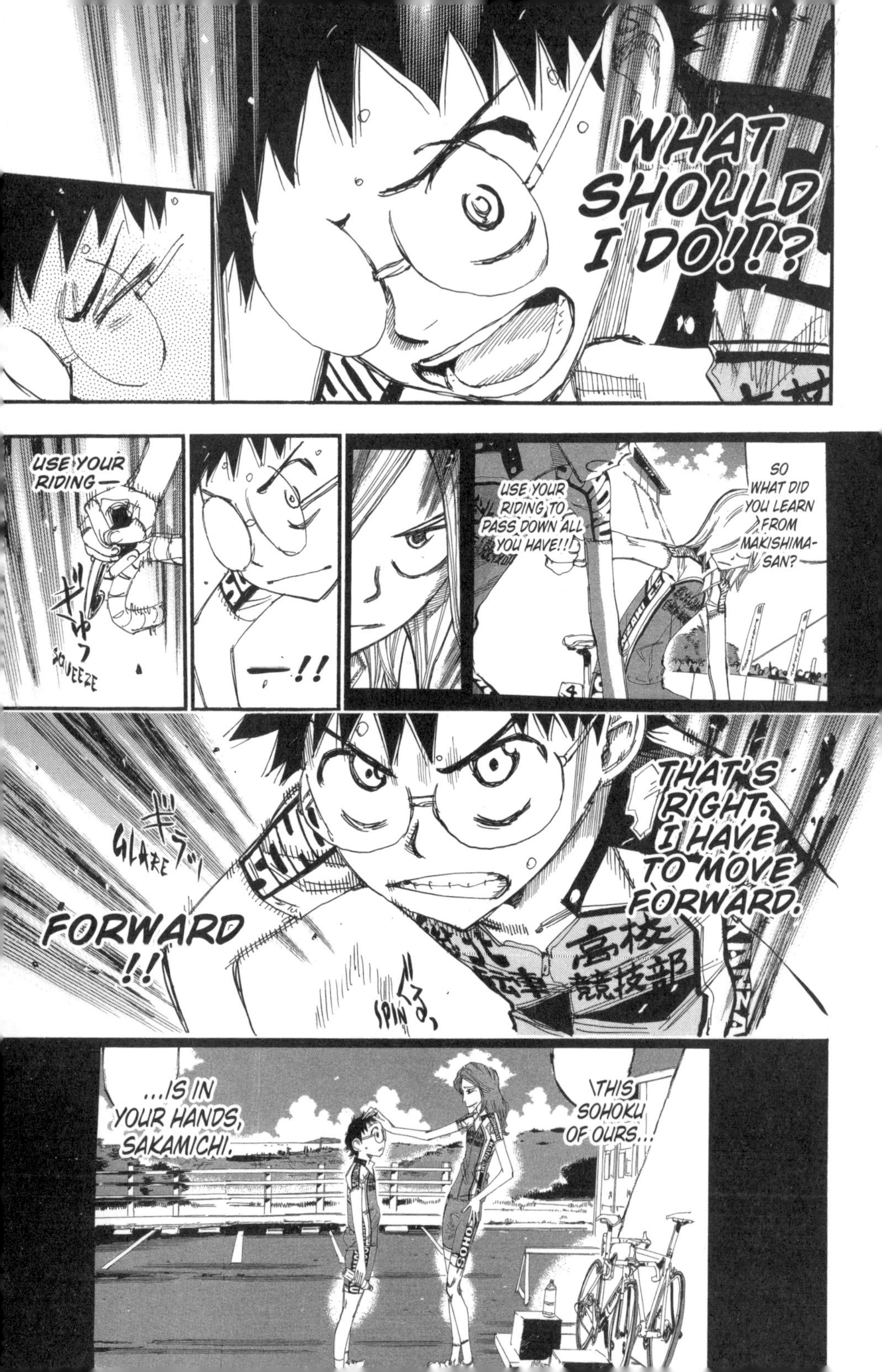
WHAT SHOULD I DO!!?
SO WHAT DID YOU LEARN FROM MAKISHIMA-SAN?
USE YOUR RIDING TO PASS DOWN ALL YOU HAVE!!!
—!!
USE YOUR RIDING—
SQUEEZE
THAT'S RIGHT. I HAVE TO MOVE FORWARD.
GLARE
FORWARD!!
SPIN
THIS SOHOKU OF OURS...
...IS IN YOUR HANDS, SAKAMICHI.

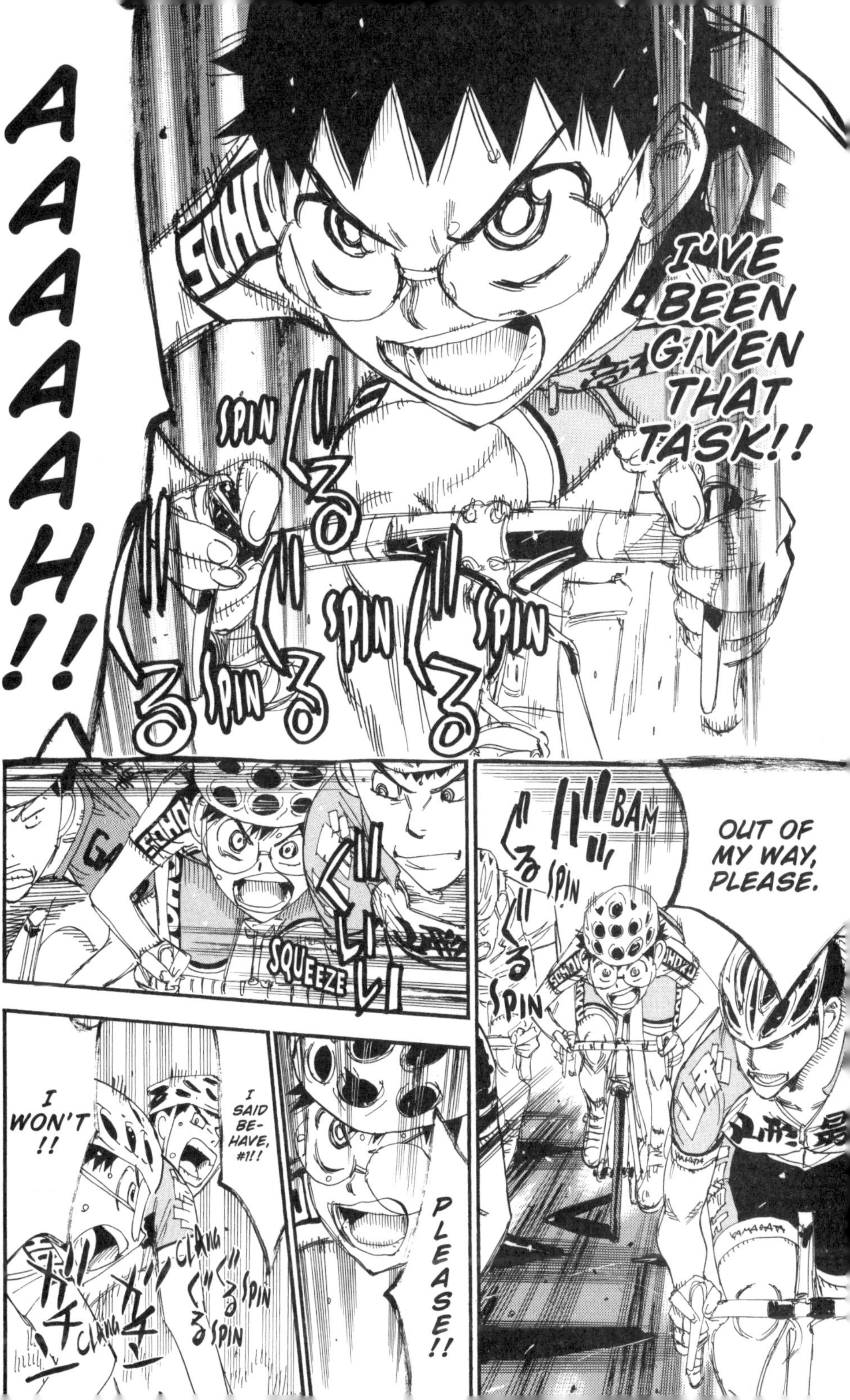

I'VE BEEN GIVEN THAT TASK!!
SPIN
SPIN
SPIN
SPIN
AAAAAH!!
BAM
SPIN
SPIN
OUT OF MY WAY, PLEASE.
SQUEEZE
PLEASE!!
I SAID BE-HAVE, #1!!
I WON'T!!
CLANG
CLANG
CLANG
SPIN
SPIN

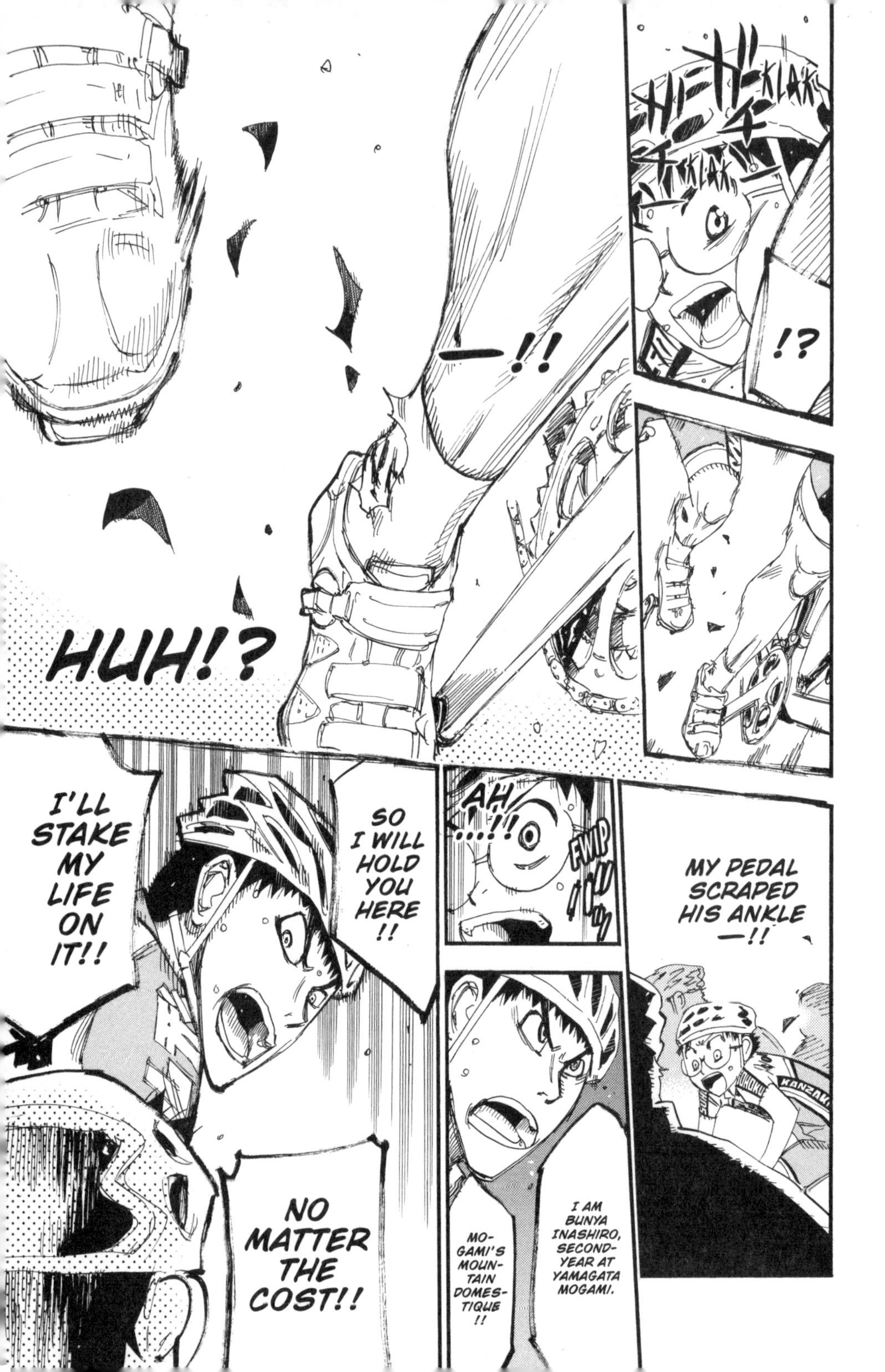
KLAK!
KLAK!!
!?
—!!
HUH!?
MY PEDAL SCRAPED HIS ANKLE—!!
AH...!!
FWIP
I AM BUNYA INASHIRO, SECOND-YEAR AT YAMAGATA MOGAMI.
MO-GAMI'S MOUN-TAIN DOMES-TIQUE!!
SO I WILL HOLD YOU HERE!!
I'LL STAKE MY LIFE ON IT!!
NO MATTER THE COST!!

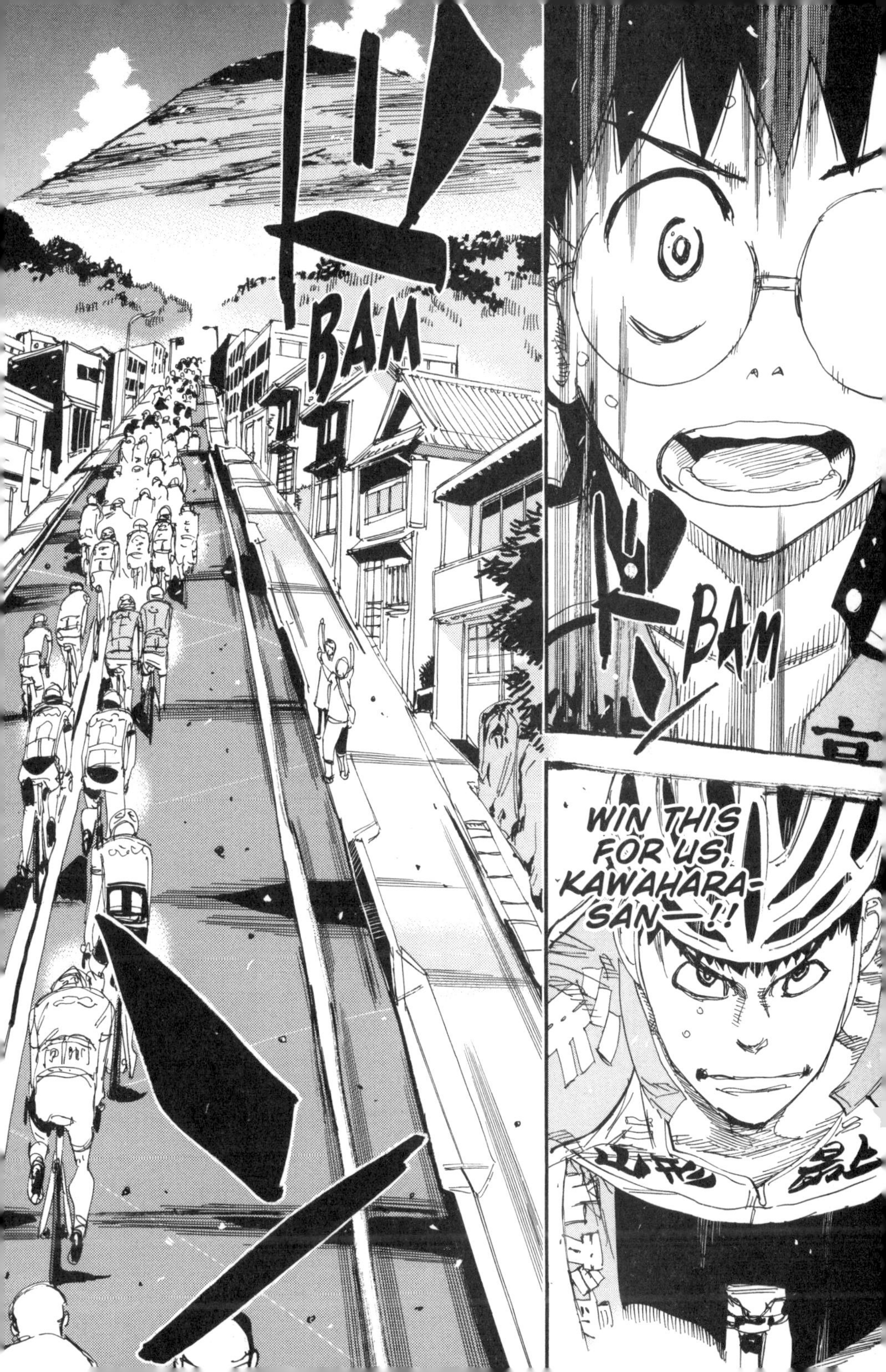
BAM
WIN THIS FOR US, KAWAHARA-SAN—!!
BAM

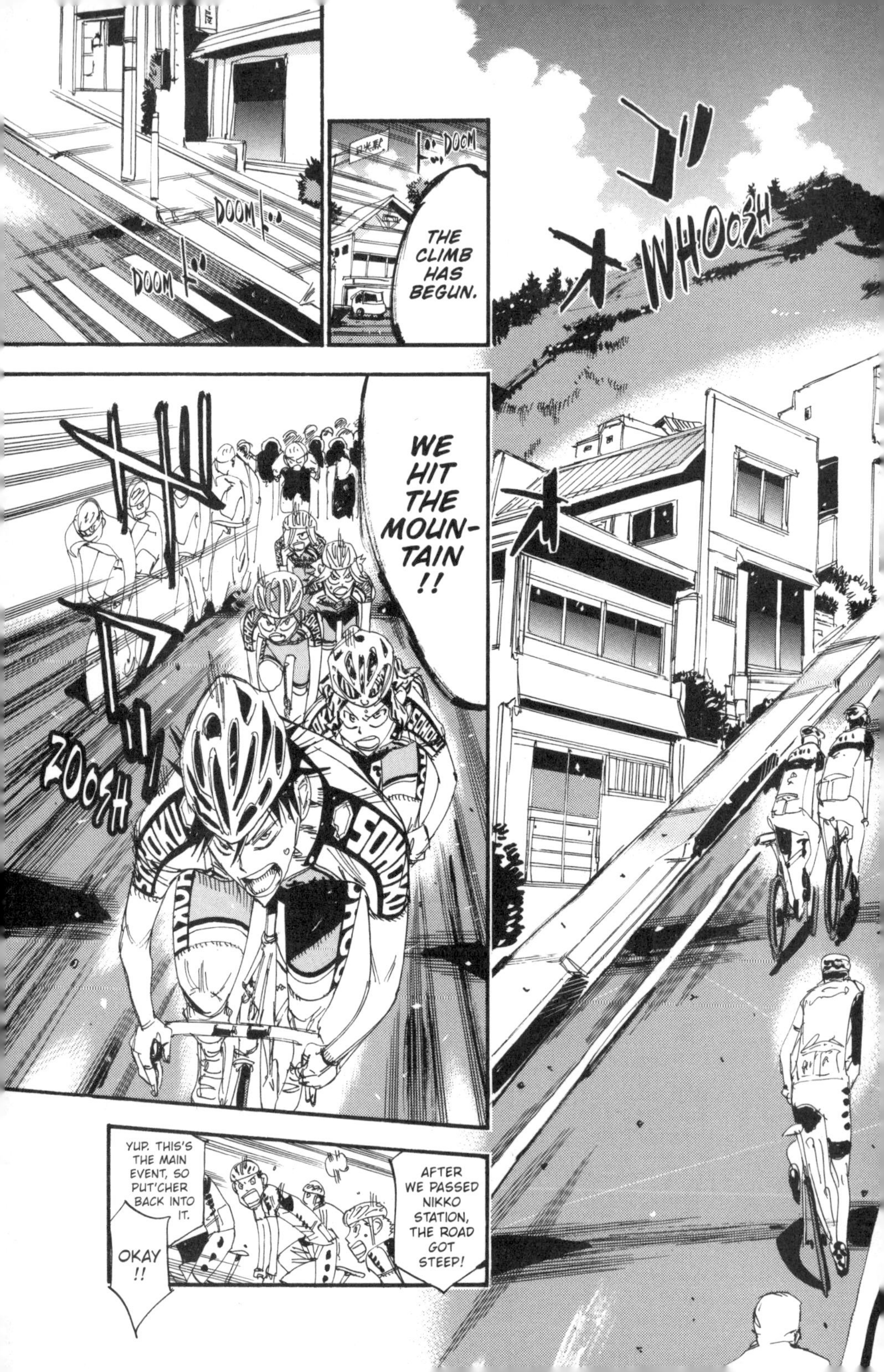
WHOOSH
DOOM
THE CLIMB HAS BEGUN.
DOOM
DOOM
WE HIT THE MOUNTAIN!!
ZOOSH
AFTER WE PASSED NIKKO STATION, THE ROAD GOT STEEP!
YUP. THIS'S THE MAIN EVENT, SO PUT'CHER BACK INTO IT.
OKAY!!

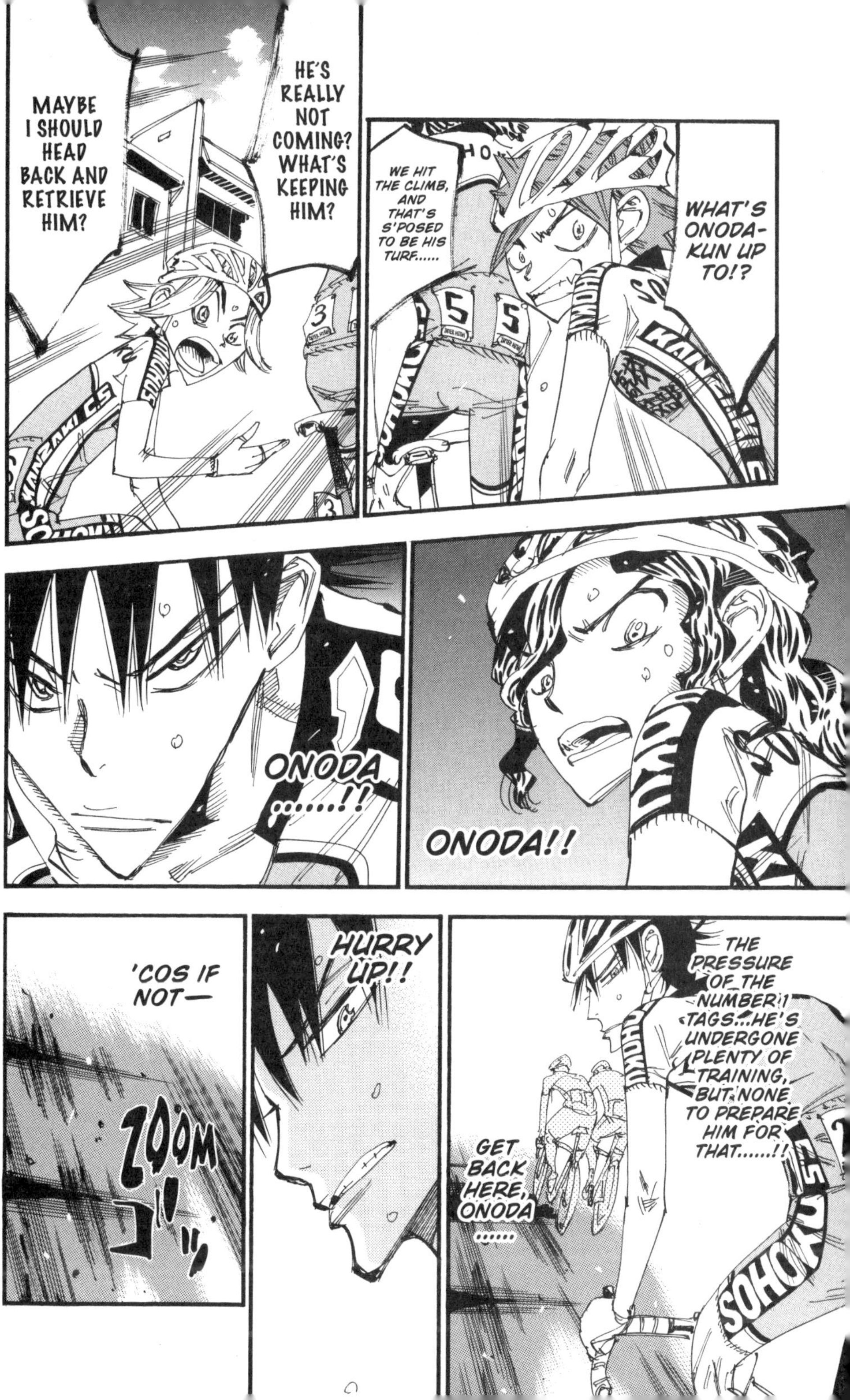
WHAT'S ONODA-KUN UP TO!?
WE HIT THE CLIMB, AND THAT'S S'POSED TO BE HIS TURF......
HE'S REALLY NOT COMING? WHAT'S KEEPING HIM?
MAYBE I SHOULD HEAD BACK AND RETRIEVE HIM?
ONODA!!
ONODA ......!!
THE PRESSURE OF THE NUMBER 1 TAGS...HE'S UNDERGONE PLENTY OF TRAINING, BUT NONE TO PREPARE HIM FOR THAT......!!
GET BACK HERE, ONODA ......
HURRY UP!!
'COS IF NOT—
ZOOM

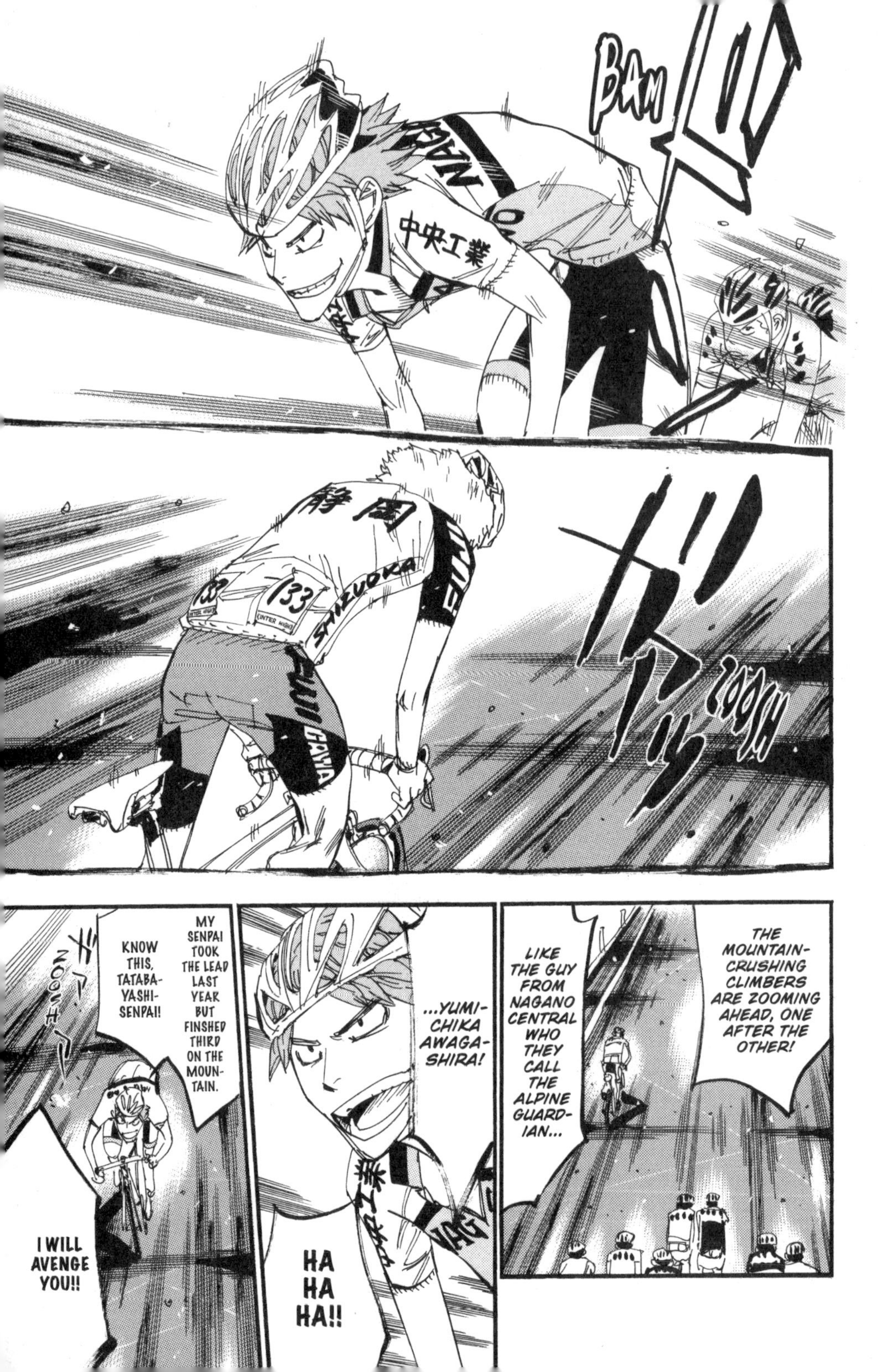
BAM
中央工業
静岡
SHIZUOKA
133
ZOOSH
THE MOUNTAIN-CRUSHING CLIMBERS ARE ZOOMING AHEAD, ONE AFTER THE OTHER!
LIKE THE GUY FROM NAGANO CENTRAL WHO THEY CALL THE ALPINE GUARDIAN...
...YUMICHIKA AWAGASHIRA!
HA HA HA!!
MY SENPAI TOOK THE LEAD LAST YEAR BUT FINSHED THIRD ON THE MOUNTAIN.
KNOW THIS, TATABAYASHI-SENPAI!
ZOOSH
I WILL AVENGE YOU!!

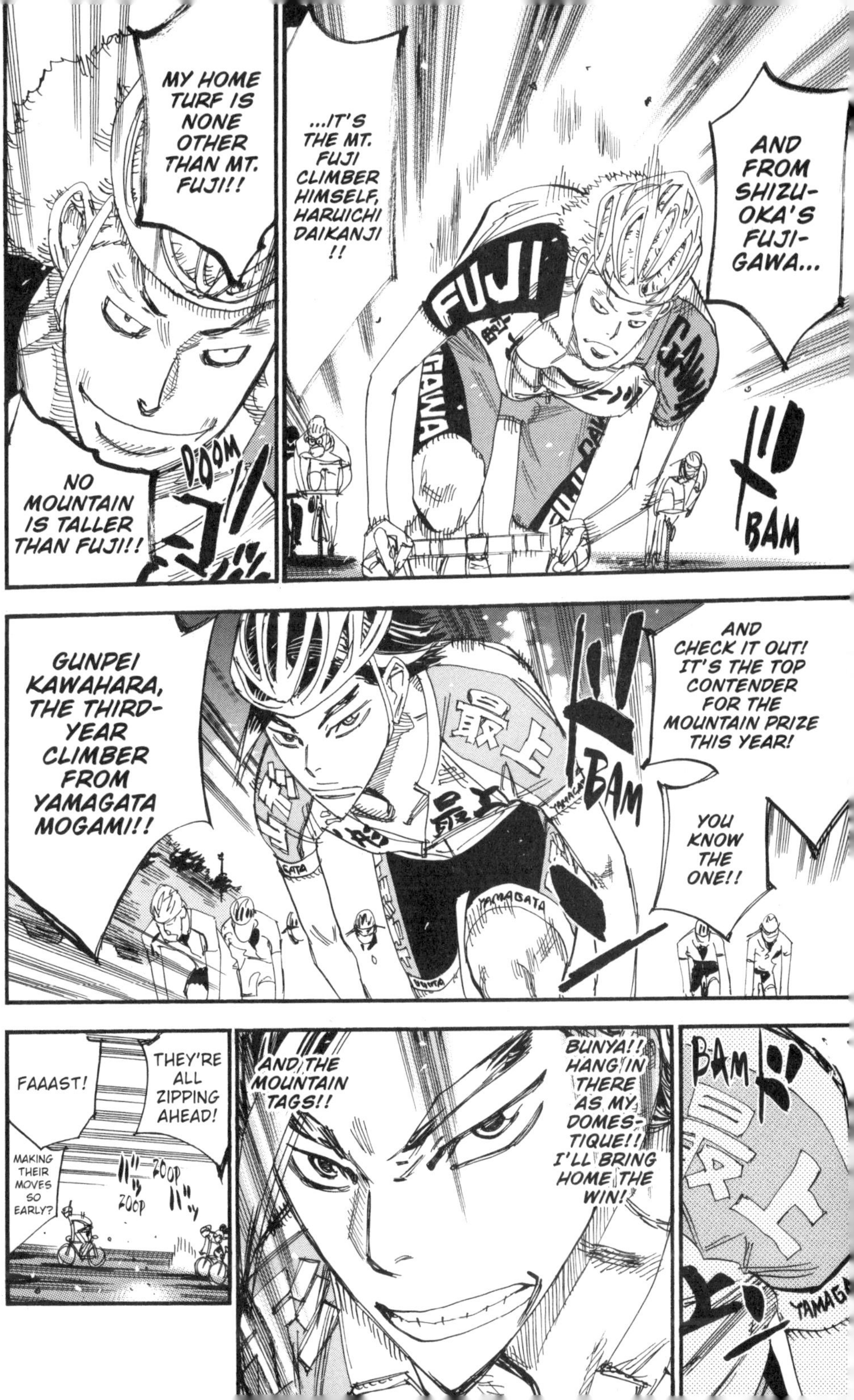
AND FROM SHIZUOKA'S FUJIGAWA...
...IT'S THE MT. FUJI CLIMBER HIMSELF, HARUICHI DAIKANJI!!
BAM
MY HOME TURF IS NONE OTHER THAN MT. FUJI!!
DOOM
NO MOUNTAIN IS TALLER THAN FUJI!!
AND CHECK IT OUT! IT'S THE TOP CONTENDER FOR THE MOUNTAIN PRIZE THIS YEAR!
YOU KNOW THE ONE!!
BAM
GUNPEI KAWAHARA, THE THIRD-YEAR CLIMBER FROM YAMAGATA MOGAMI!!
BAM
BUNYA!! HANG IN THERE AS MY DOMESTIQUE!! I'LL BRING HOME THE WIN!
AND THE MOUNTAIN TAGS!!
THEY'RE ALL ZIPPING AHEAD!
FAAAST!
ZOOP
ZOOP
MAKING THEIR MOVES SO EARLY?

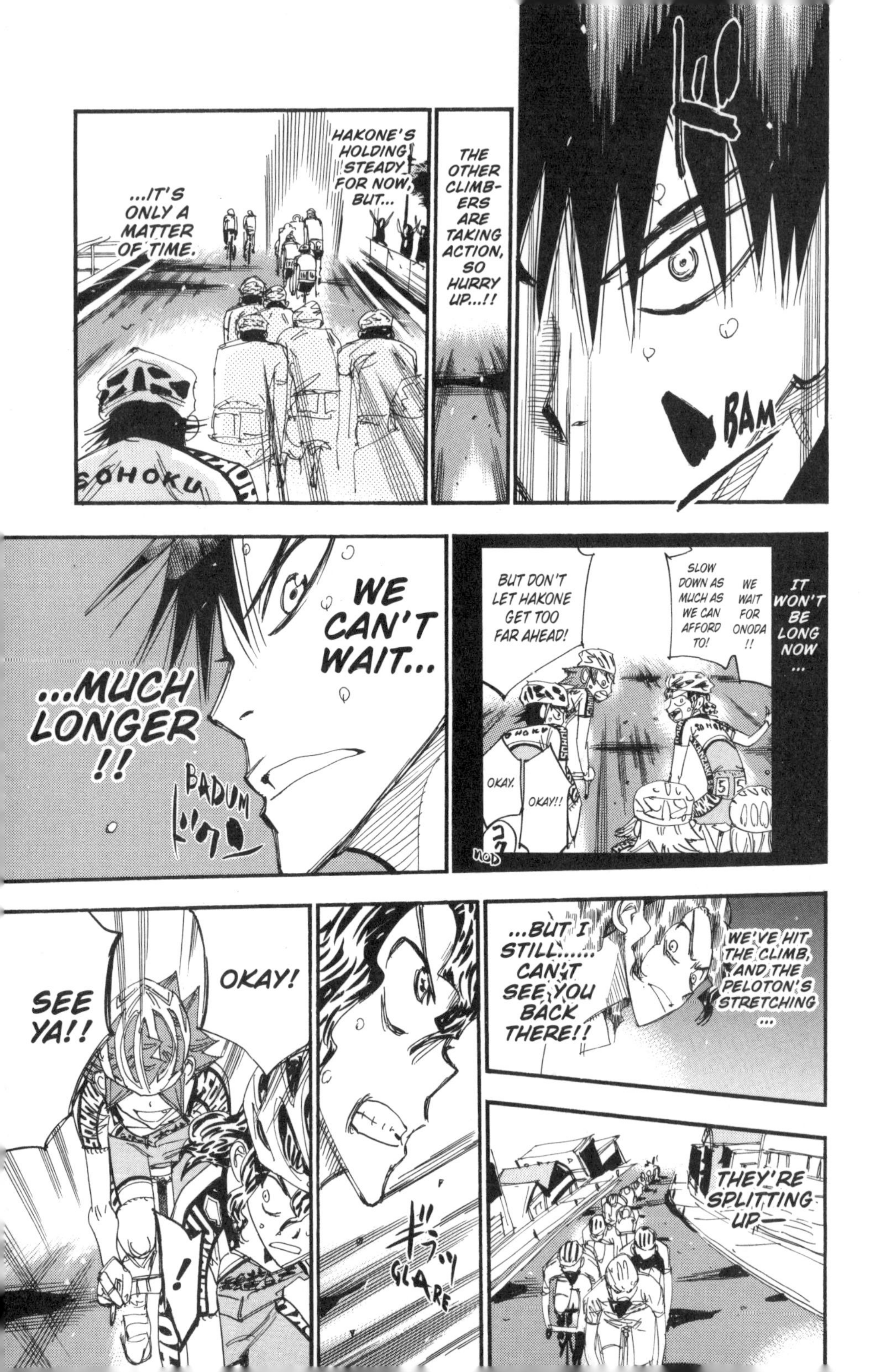
BAM
THE OTHER CLIMBERS ARE TAKING ACTION, SO HURRY UP...!!
HAKONE'S HOLDING STEADY FOR NOW, BUT...
...IT'S ONLY A MATTER OF TIME.
IT WON'T BE LONG NOW...
WE WAIT FOR ONODA!!
SLOW DOWN AS MUCH AS WE CAN AFFORD TO!
BUT DON'T LET HAKONE GET TOO FAR AHEAD!
OKAY.
OKAY!!
NOD
WE CAN'T WAIT...
...MUCH LONGER!!
BADUM
WE'VE HIT THE CLIMB, AND THE PELOTON'S STRETCHING...
...BUT I STILL...... CAN'T SEE YOU BACK THERE!!
THEY'RE SPLITTING UP—
GLARE
OKAY!
SEE YA!!
!

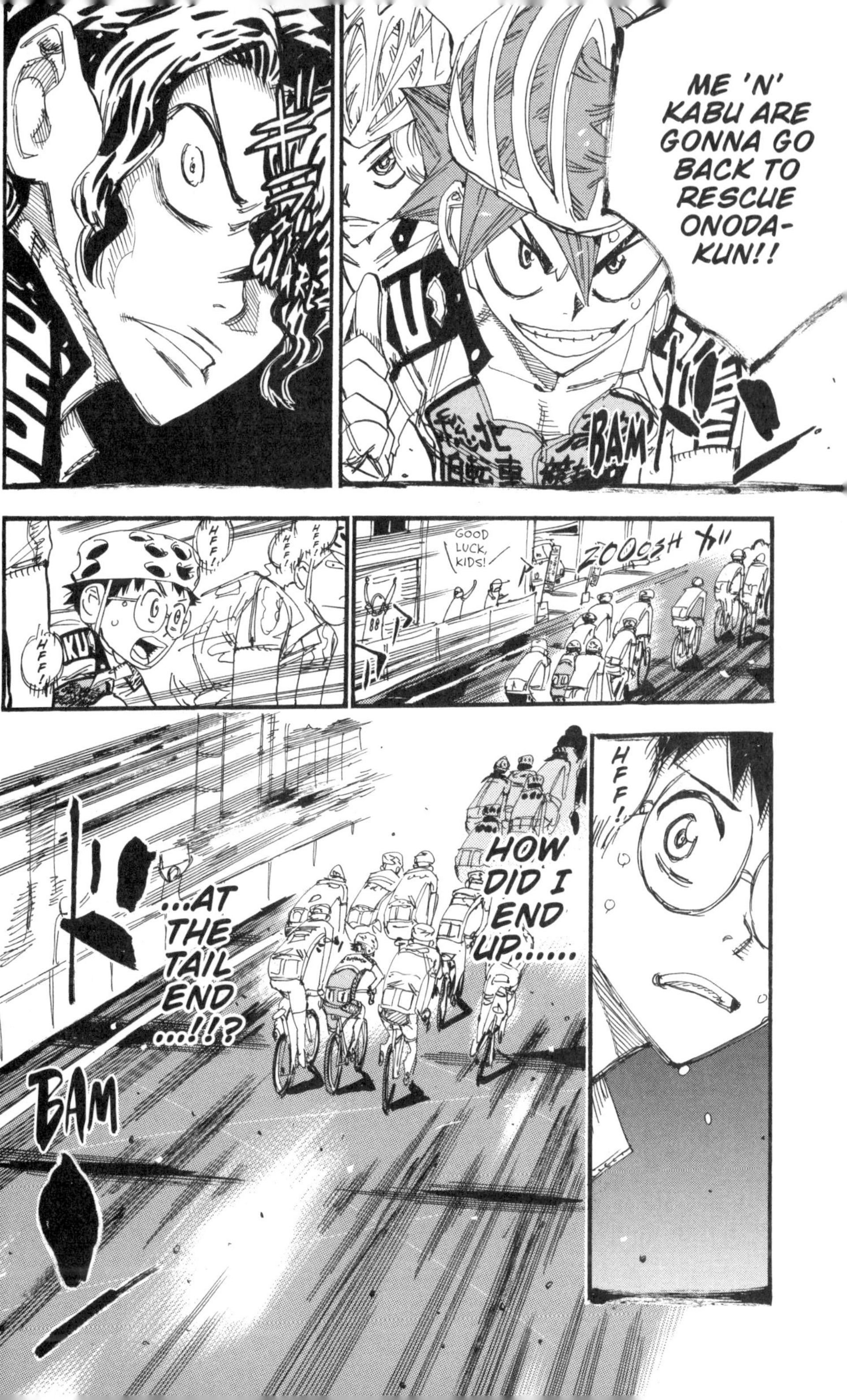
ME 'N' KABU ARE GONNA GO BACK TO RESCUE ONODA-KUN!!
BAM
GLARE
GOOD LUCK, KIDS!
ZOOOSH
HFF!
HFF!
HFF!
HFF!
HFF!
HOW DID I END UP......
...AT THE TAIL END ...!!?
BAM

RIDE.317 THE IMPENETRABLE BLOCKADE

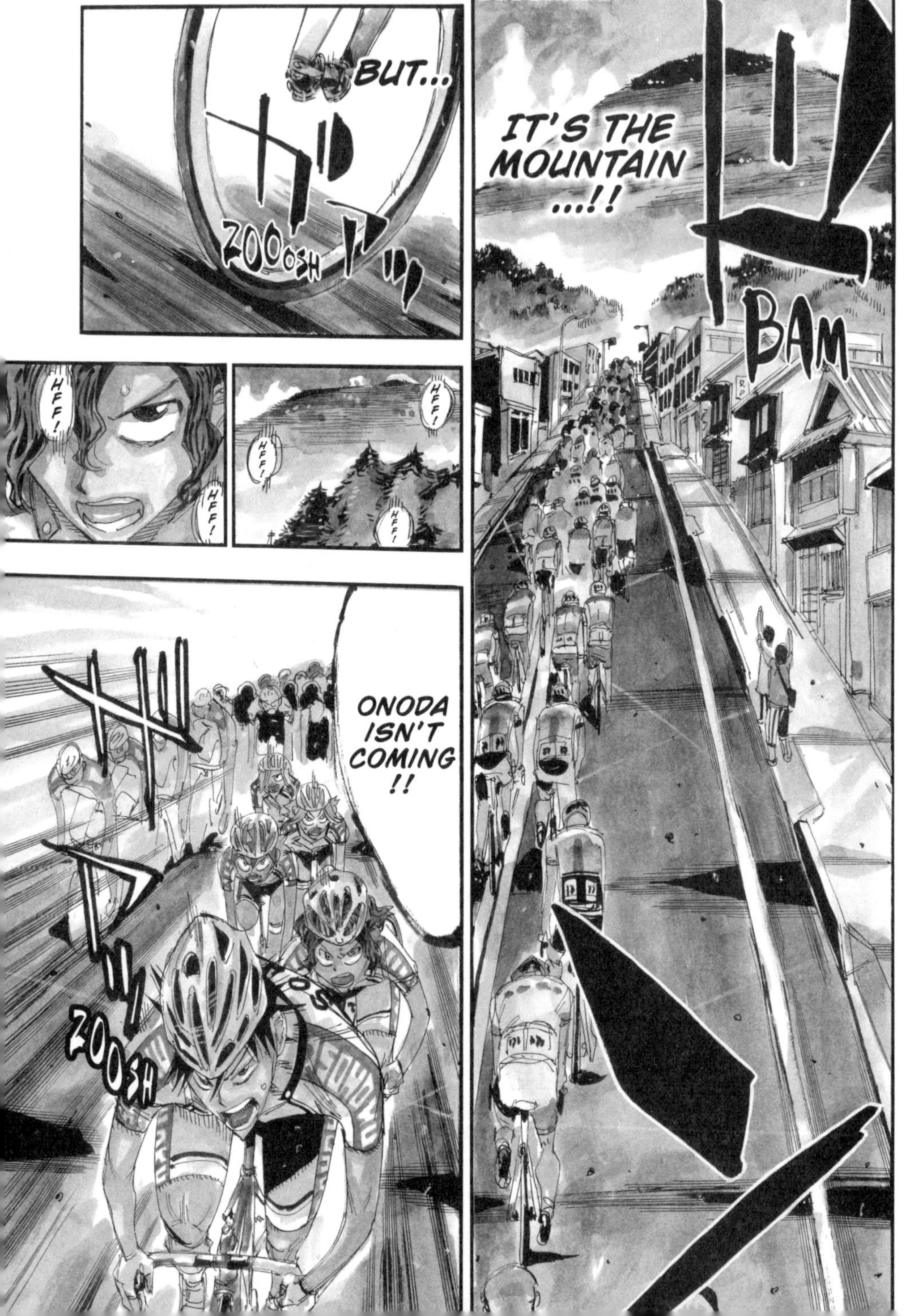
IT'S THE MOUNTAIN ...!!
BAM
BUT...
ZOOOSH
HFF!
HFF!
HFF!
HFF!
HFF!
ONODA ISN'T COMING !!
ZOOSH

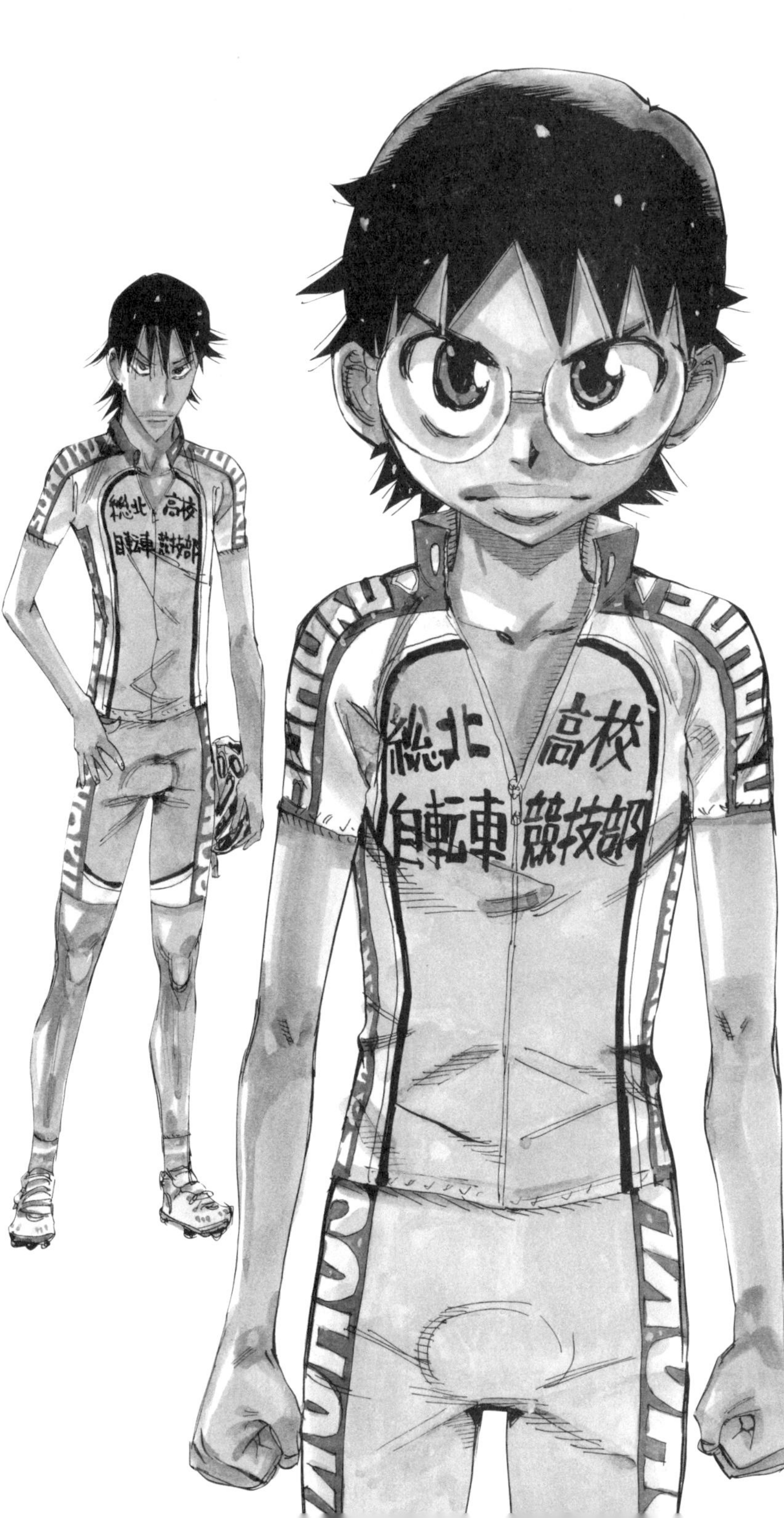
総北高校
自転車競技部

RIDE.317 THE IMPENETRABLE BLOCKADE

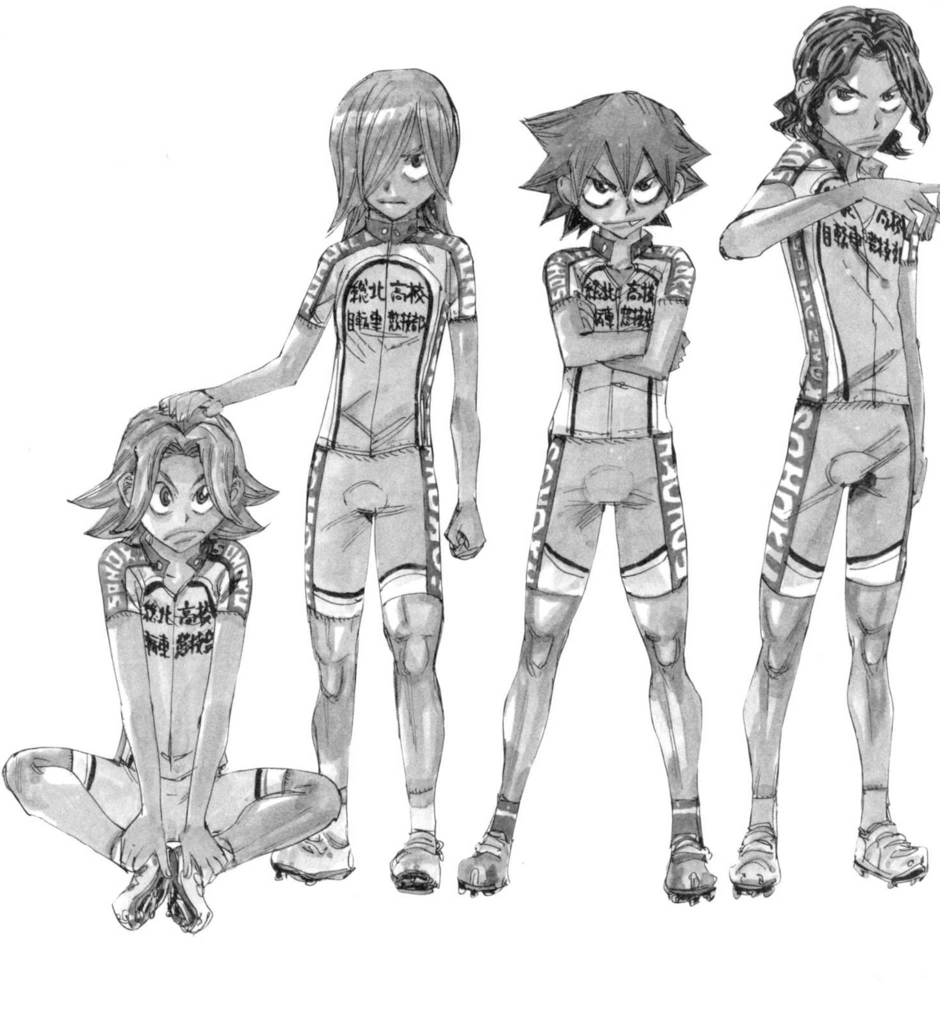

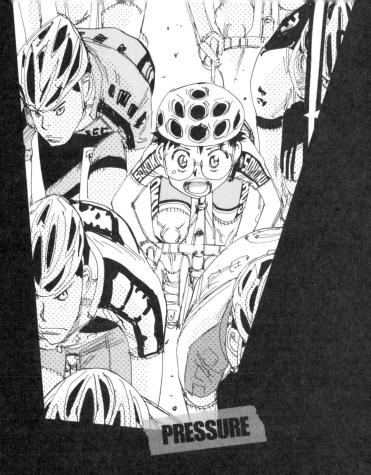

PRESSURE

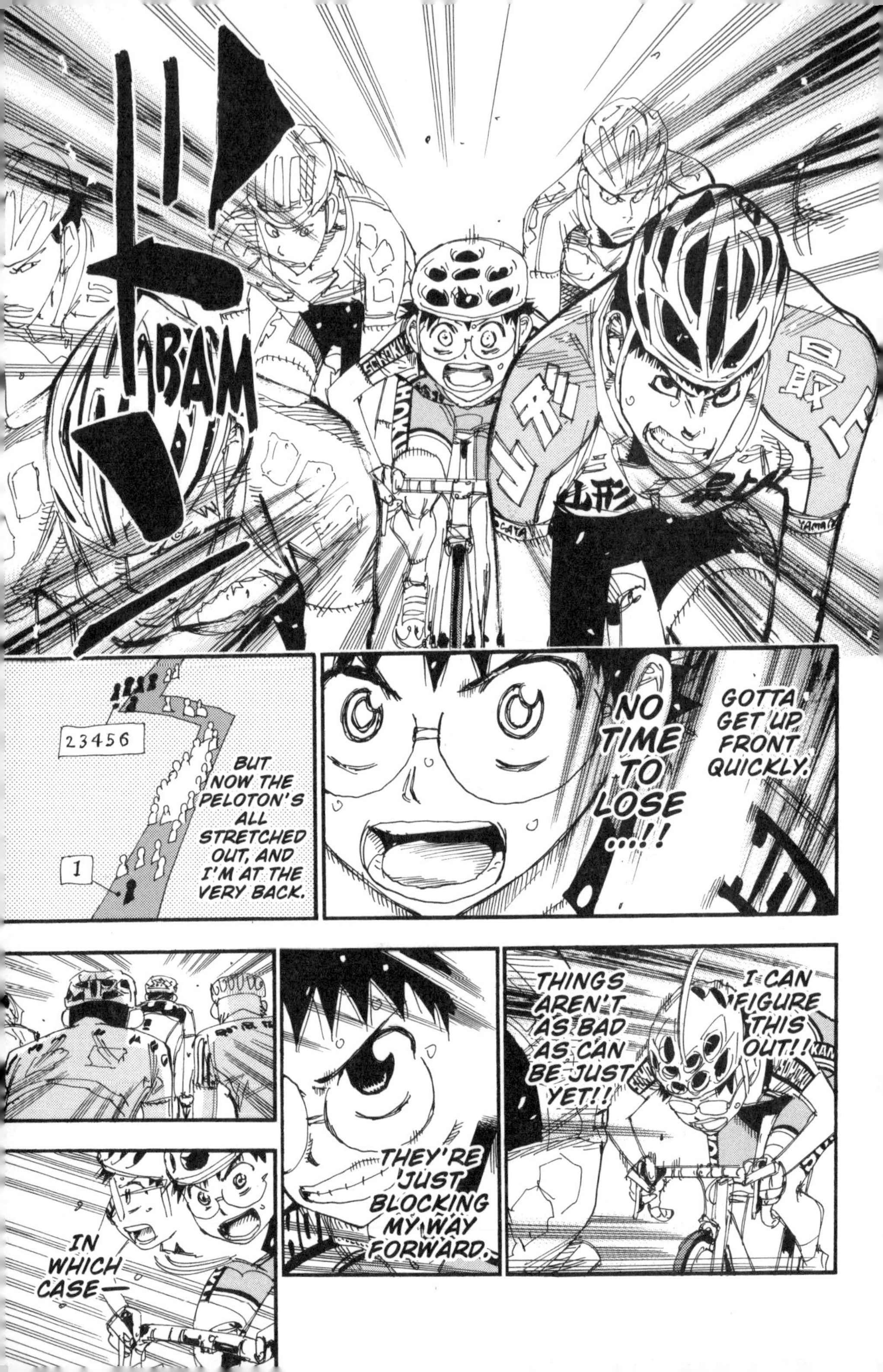
BAM
GOTTA GET UP FRONT QUICKLY.
NO TIME TO LOSE...!!
23456
1
BUT NOW THE PELOTON'S ALL STRETCHED OUT, AND I'M AT THE VERY BACK.
I CAN FIGURE THIS OUT!!
THINGS AREN'T AS BAD AS CAN BE JUST YET!!
THEY'RE JUST BLOCKING MY WAY FORWARD.
IN WHICH CASE—

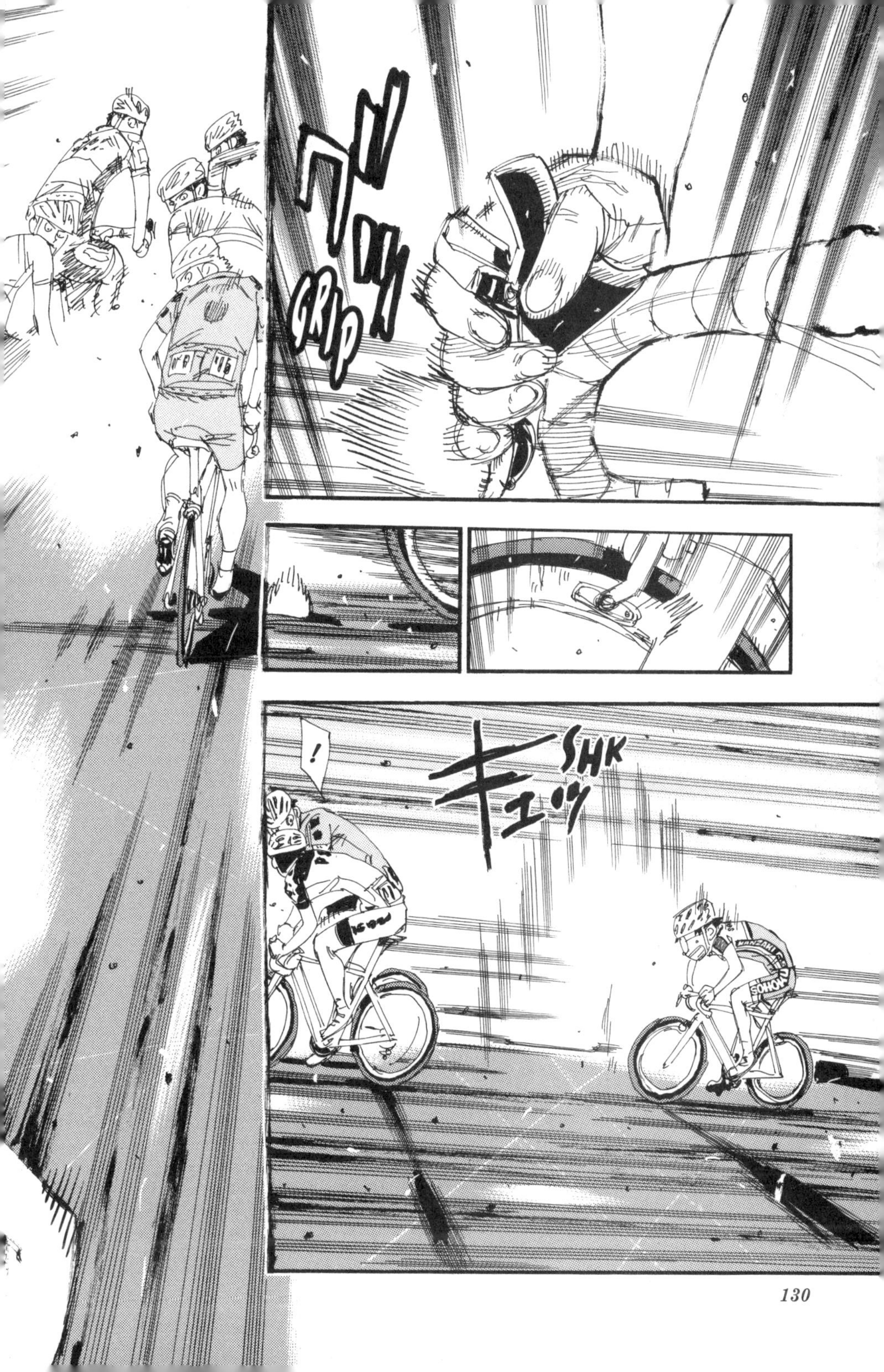
GRIP
!
SHK

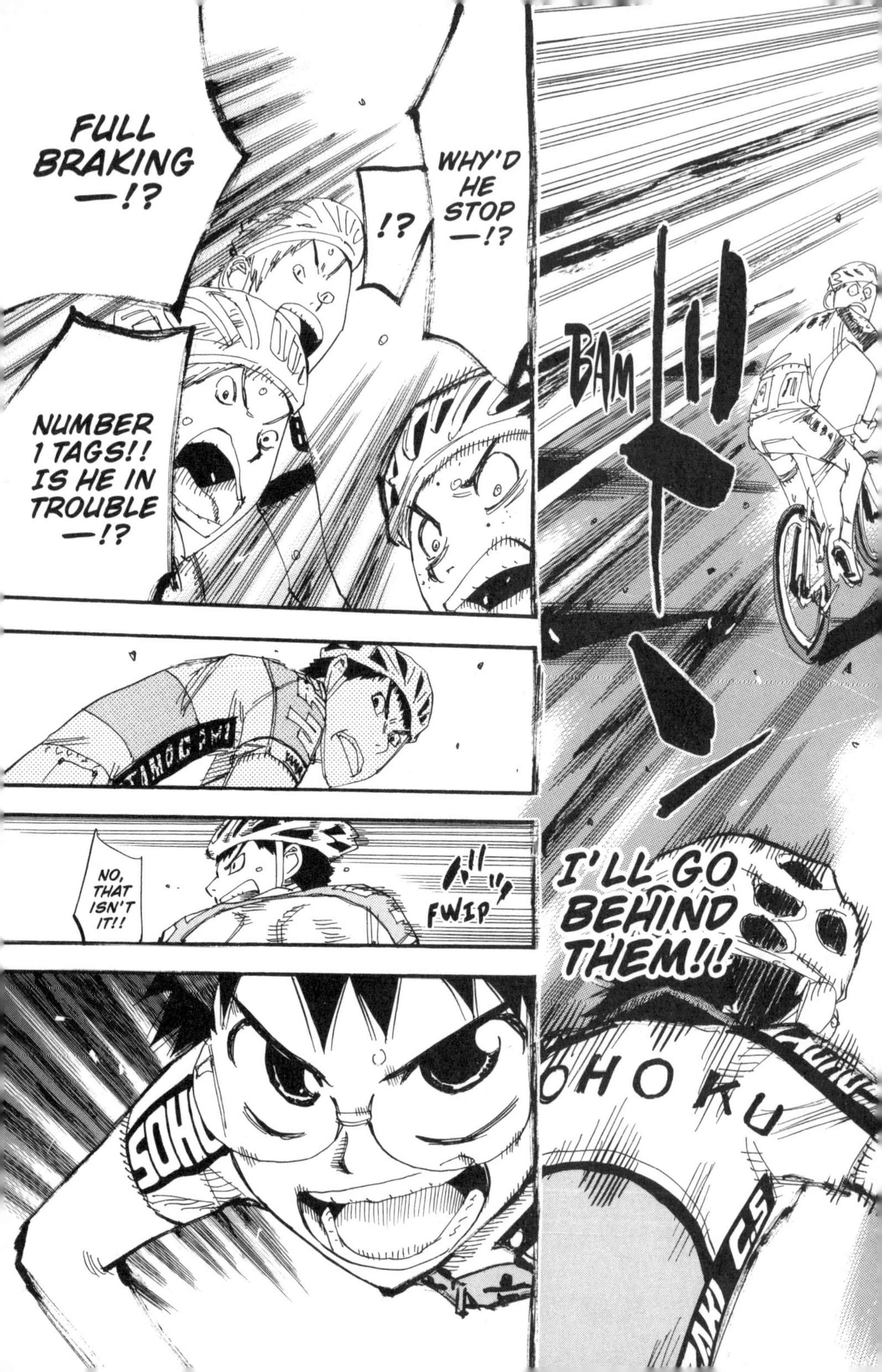
BAM
WHY'D HE STOP —!?
!?
FULL BRAKING —!?
NUMBER 1 TAGS!! IS HE IN TROUBLE —!?
FWIP
NO, THAT ISN'T IT!!
I'LL GO BEHIND THEM!!
SOHOKU

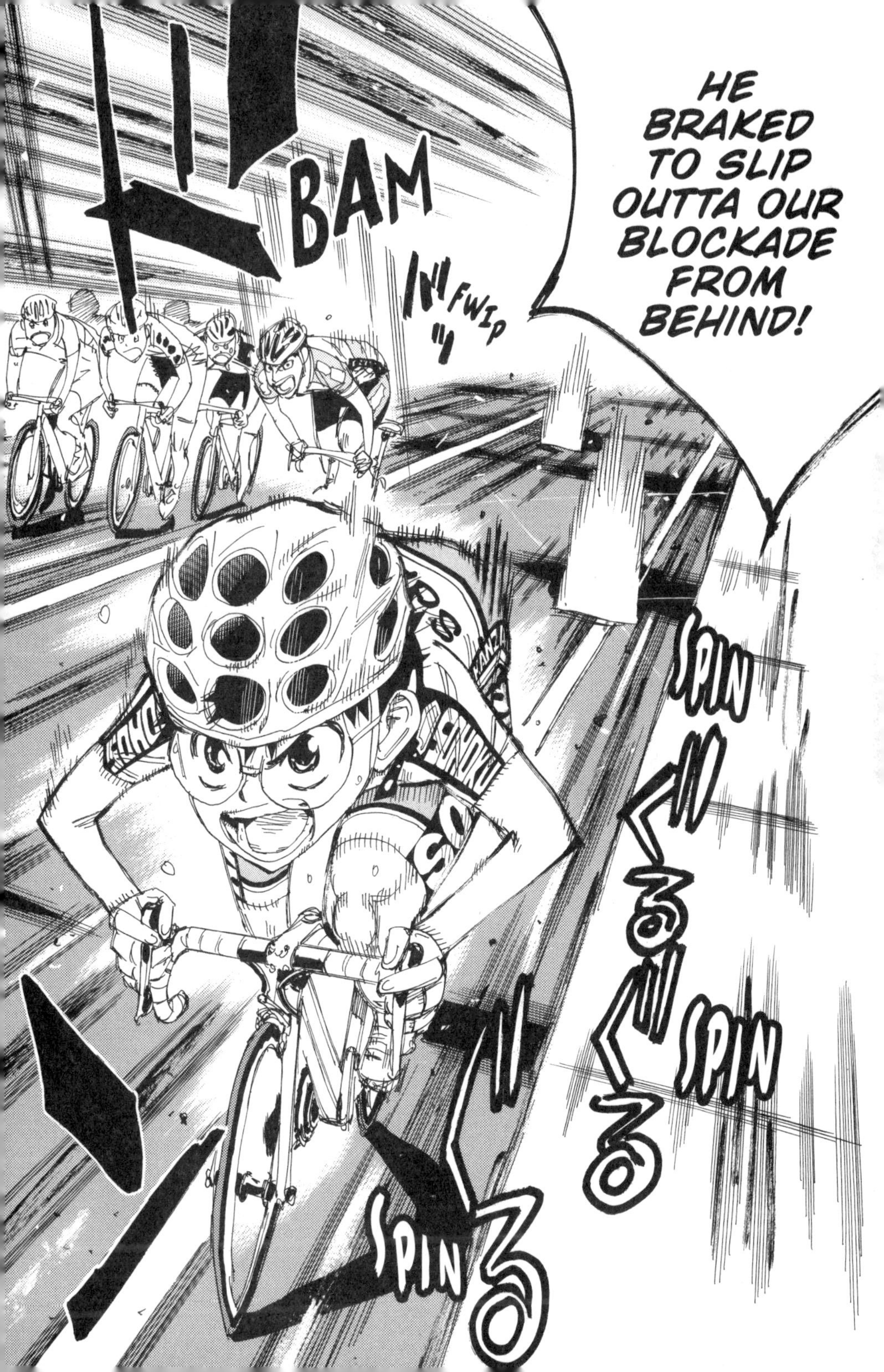
HE BRAKED TO SLIP OUTTA OUR BLOCKADE FROM BEHIND!
BAM
FWIP
SPIN
SPIN
SPIN

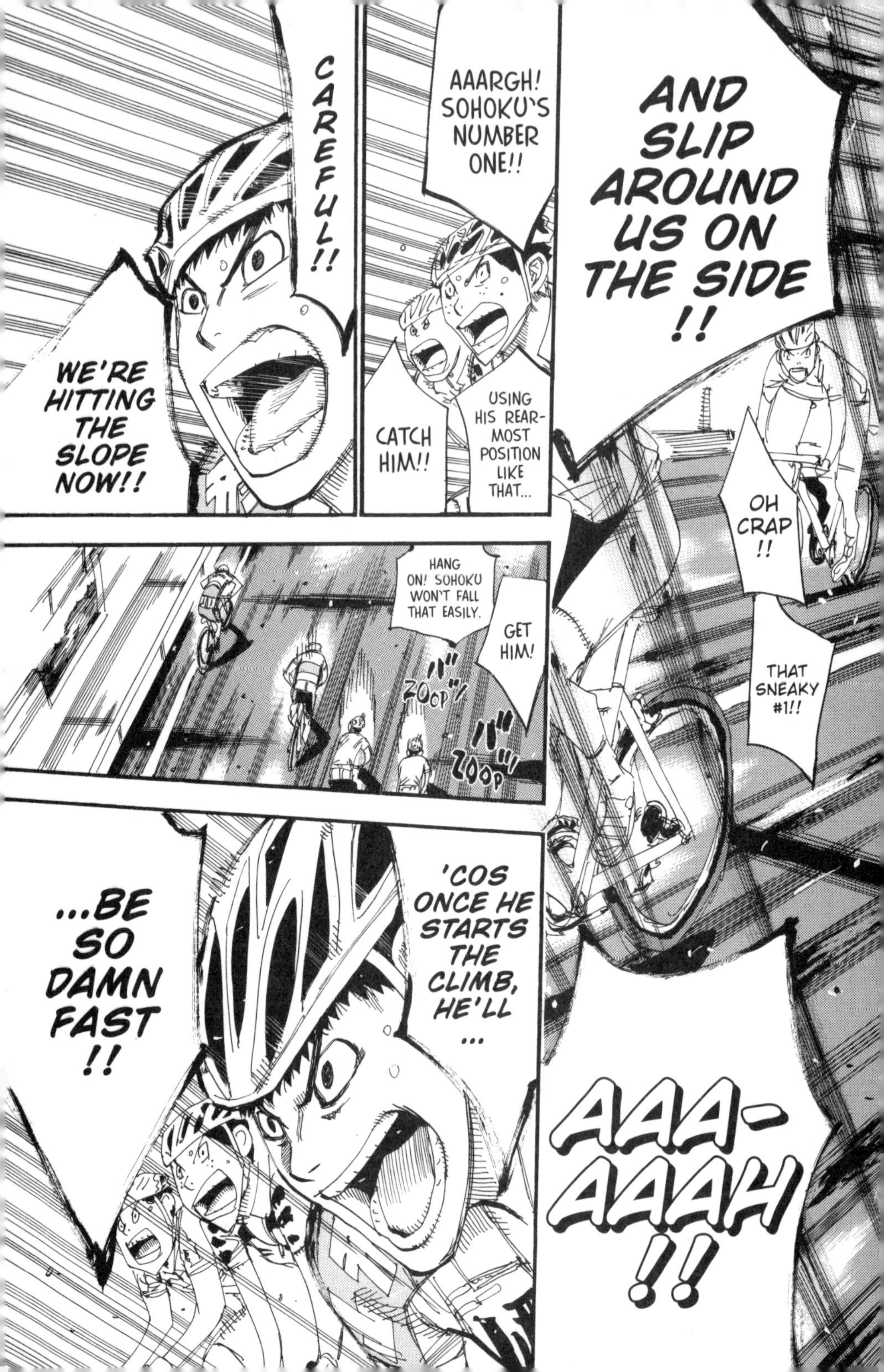
AND SLIP AROUND US ON THE SIDE!!
OH CRAP!!
THAT SNEAKY #1!!
AAAAAAH!!
AAARGH! SOHOKU'S NUMBER ONE!!
USING HIS REAR-MOST POSITION LIKE THAT...
CATCH HIM!!
CAREFUL!!
WE'RE HITTING THE SLOPE NOW!!
HANG ON! SOHOKU WON'T FALL THAT EASILY.
GET HIM!
ZOOP
ZOOP
'COS ONCE HE STARTS THE CLIMB, HE'LL...
...BE SO DAMN FAST!!

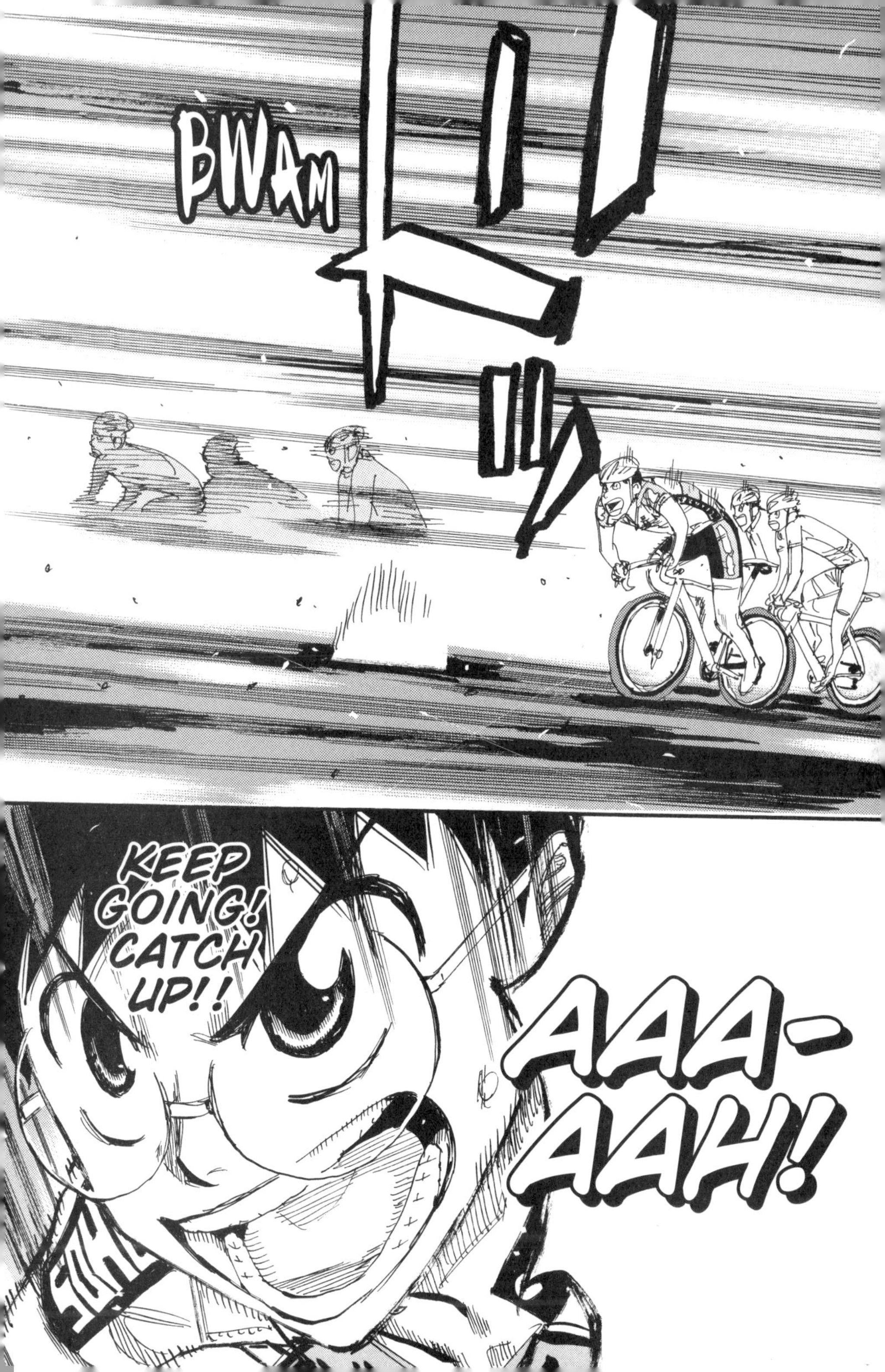
BWAM
AAA-AAAH!
KEEP GOING! CATCH UP!!

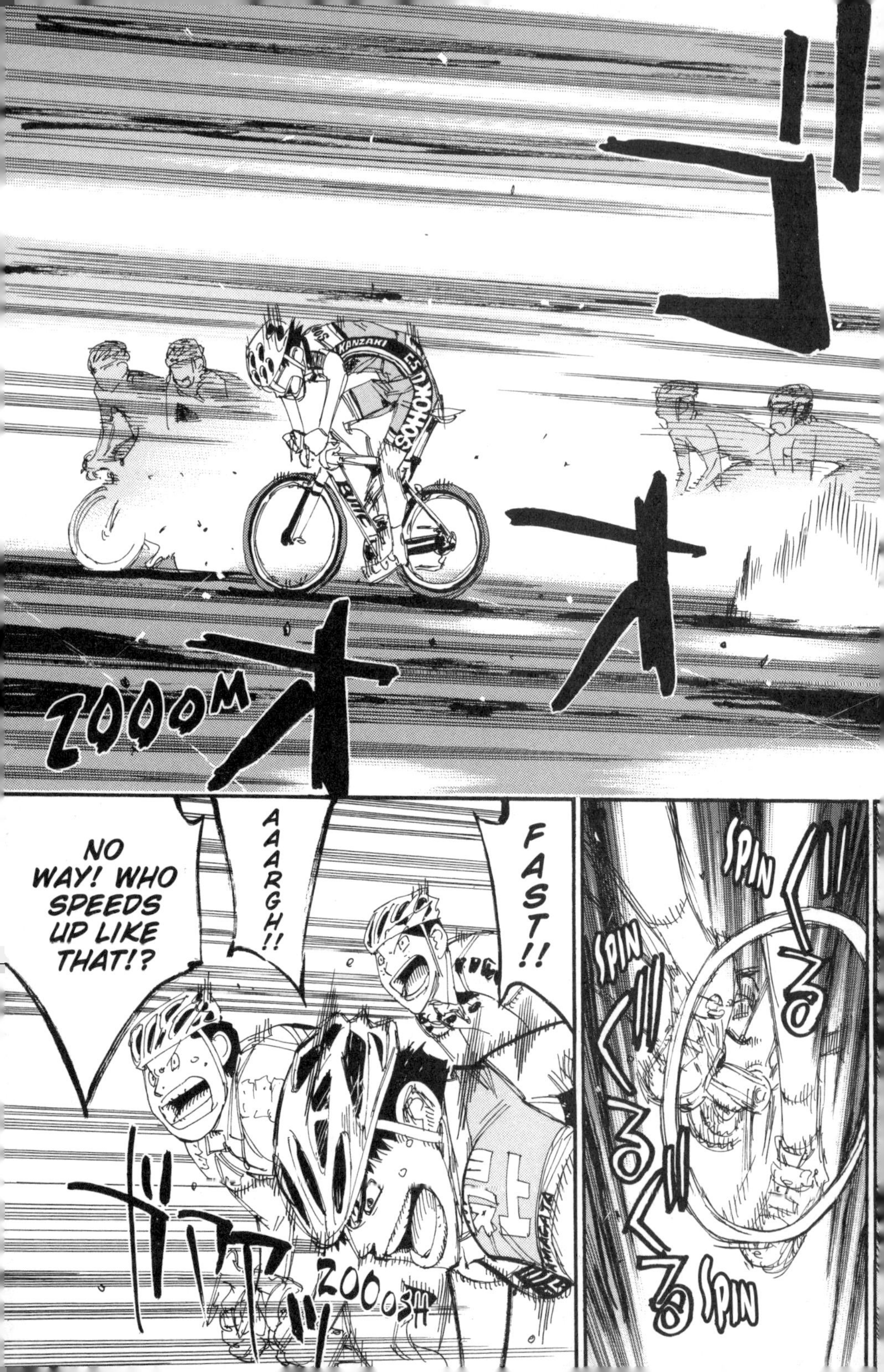

ZOOOM
SPIN
SPIN
SPIN
FAST!!
AAARGH!!
NO WAY! WHO SPEEDS UP LIKE THAT!?
ZOOOSH

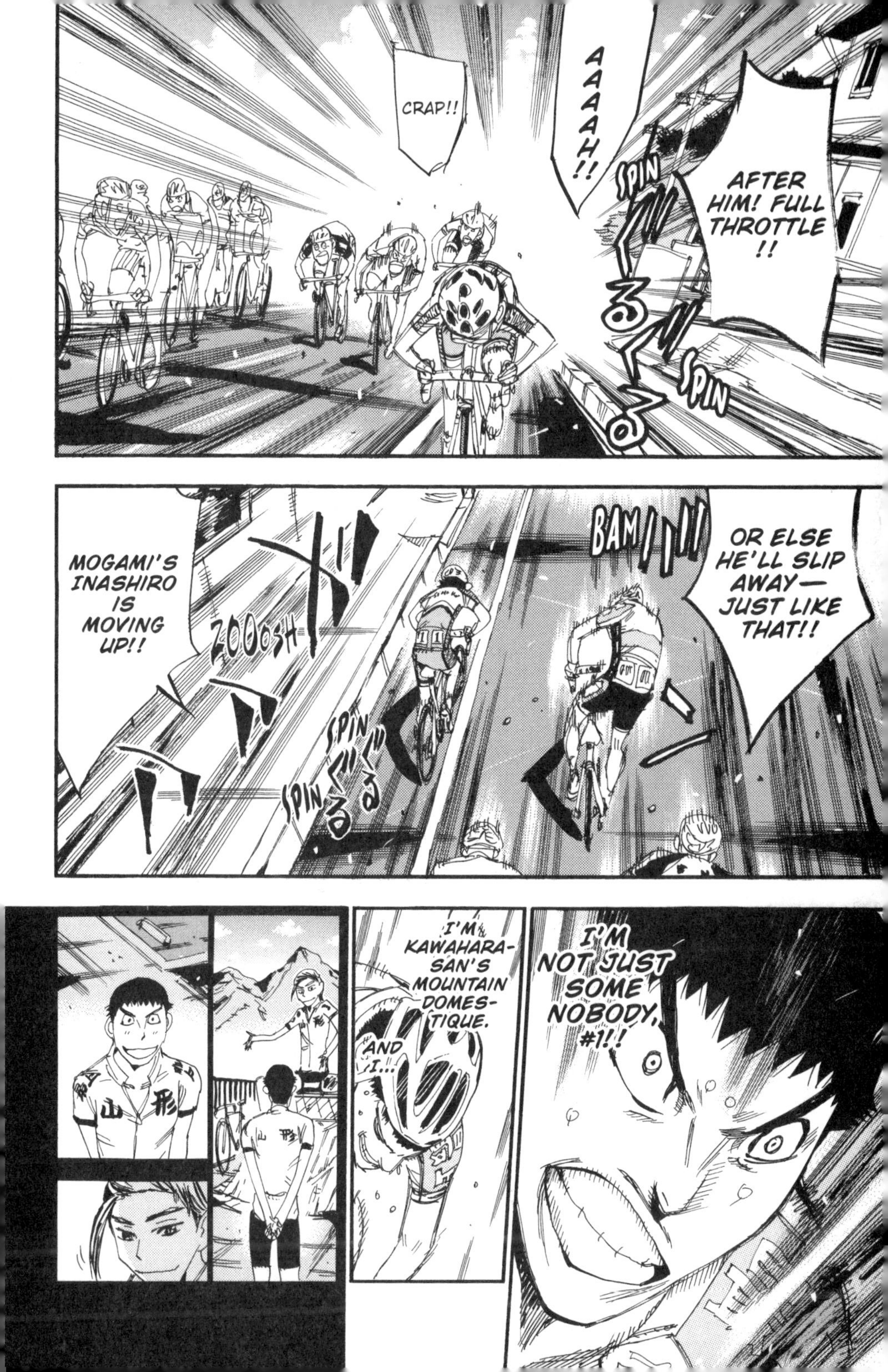
AFTER HIM! FULL THROTTLE!!
AAAAAH!!
SPIN
SPIN
CRAP!!
OR ELSE HE'LL SLIP AWAY— JUST LIKE THAT!!
BAM
MOGAMI'S INASHIRO IS MOVING UP!!
ZOOOSH
SPIN
SPIN
I'M NOT JUST SOME NOBODY, #1!!
I'M KAWAHARA-SAN'S MOUNTAIN DOMESTIQUE.
AND I...

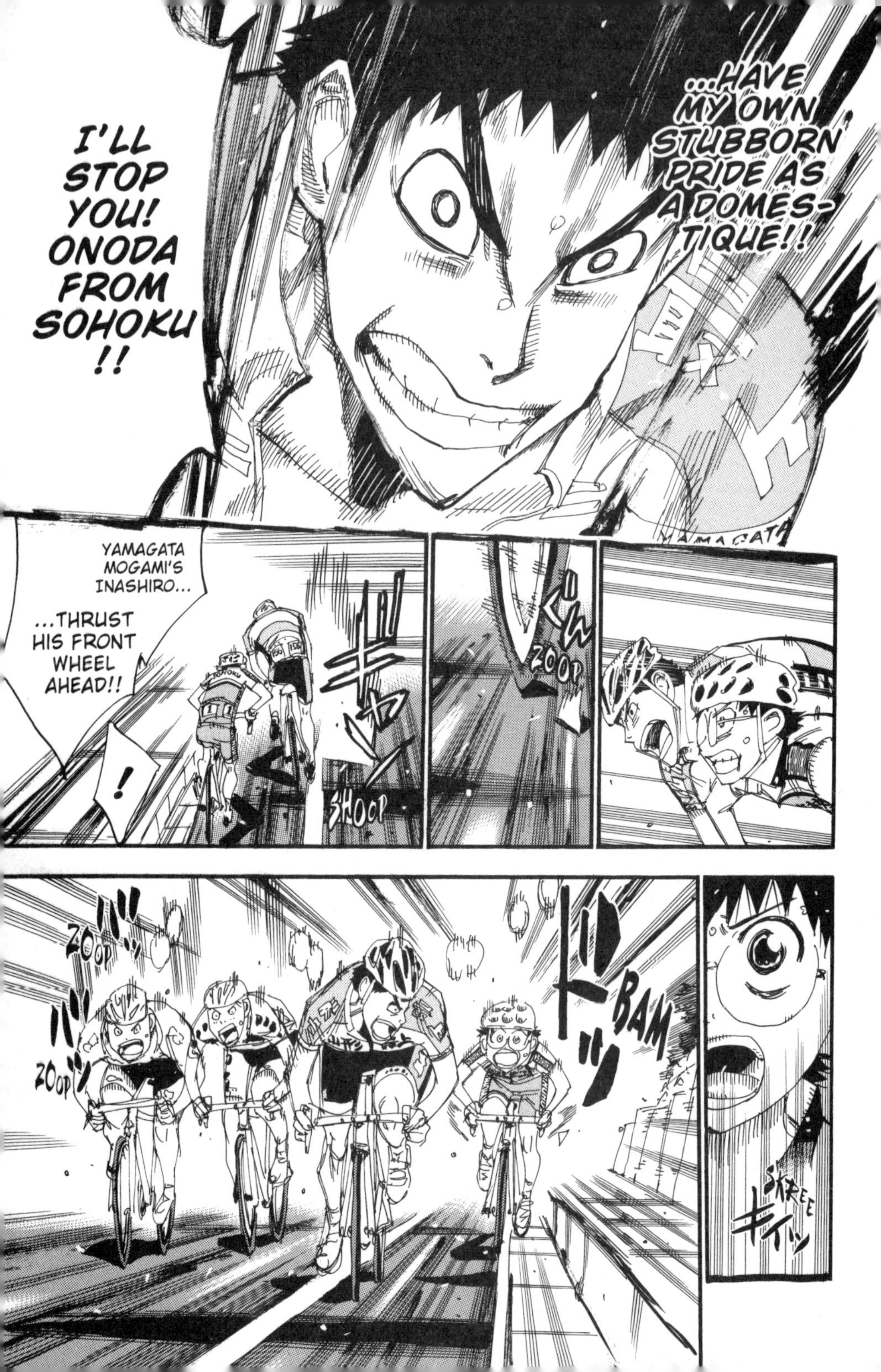
...HAVE MY OWN STUBBORN PRIDE AS A DOMES-TIQUE!!
I'LL STOP YOU! ONODA FROM SOHOKU!!
ZOOP
YAMAGATA MOGAMI'S INASHIRO...
...THRUST HIS FRONT WHEEL AHEAD!!
!
SHOOP
SKREE
BAM
ZOOP
ZOOP

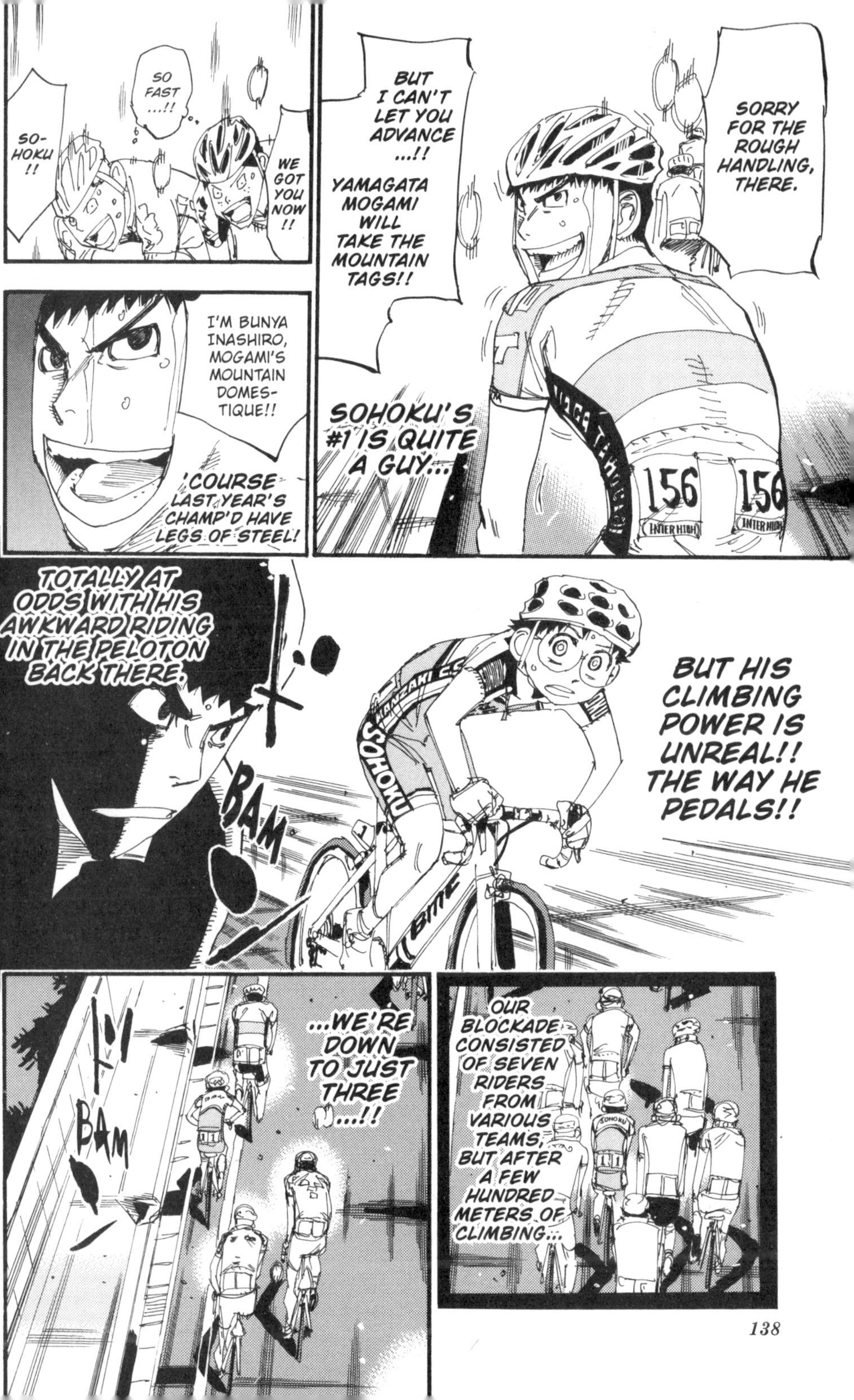
SORRY FOR THE ROUGH HANDLING, THERE.
BUT I CAN'T LET YOU ADVANCE ...!!
YAMAGATA MOGAMI WILL TAKE THE MOUNTAIN TAGS!!
SOHOKU'S #1 IS QUITE A GUY...
156
INTER HIGH
156
INTER HIGH
SO FAST ...!!
WE GOT YOU NOW !!
SO-HOKU !!
I'M BUNYA INASHIRO, MOGAMI'S MOUNTAIN DOMES-TIQUE!!
'COURSE LAST YEAR'S CHAMP'D HAVE LEGS OF STEEL!
BUT HIS CLIMBING POWER IS UNREAL!! THE WAY HE PEDALS!!
TOTALLY AT ODDS WITH HIS AWKWARD RIDING IN THE PELOTON BACK THERE.
BAM
SOHOKU
OUR BLOCKADE CONSISTED OF SEVEN RIDERS FROM VARIOUS TEAMS, BUT AFTER A FEW HUNDRED METERS OF CLIMBING...
...WE'RE DOWN TO JUST THREE ...!!
BAM

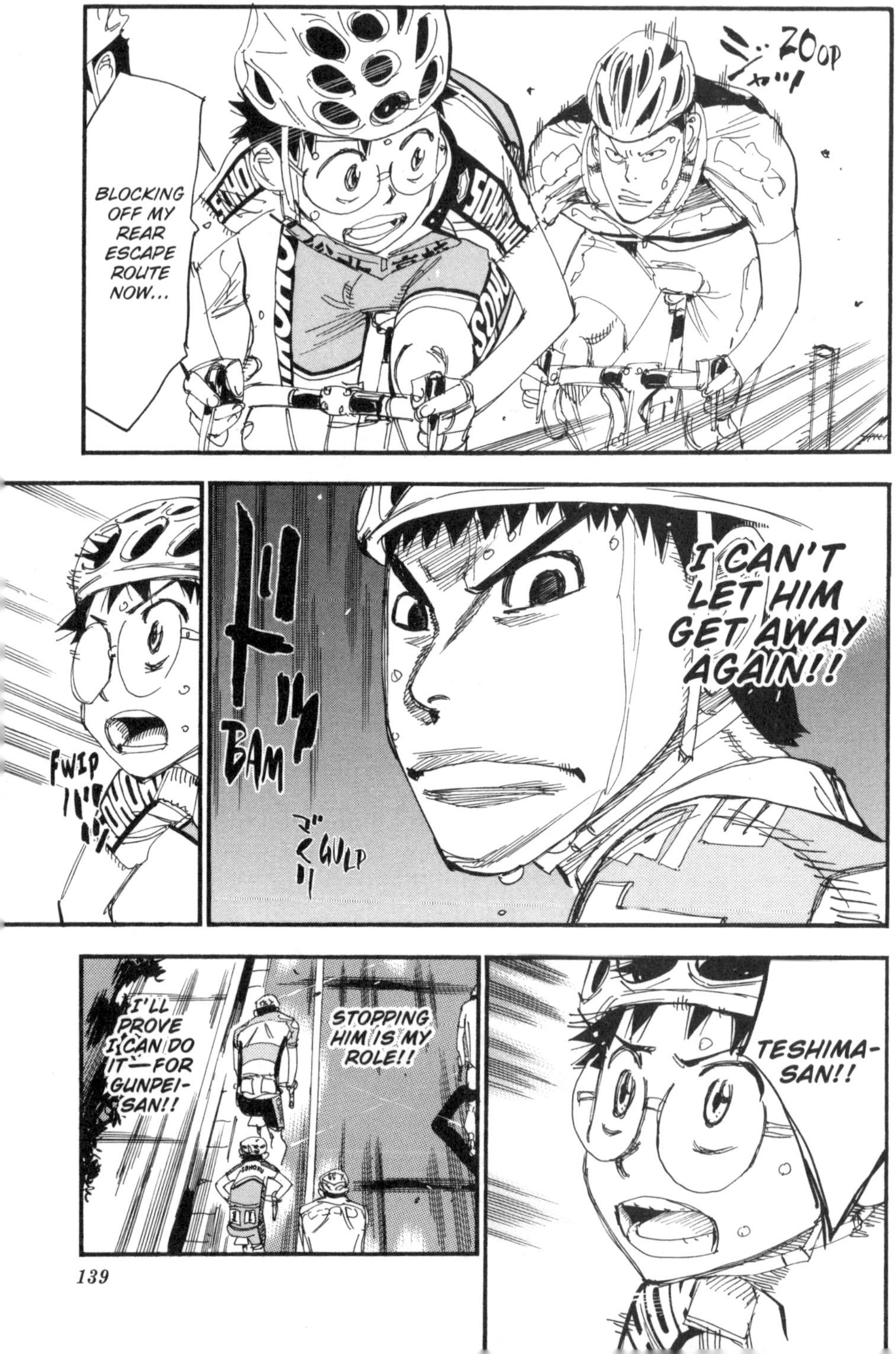
ZOOP
BLOCKING OFF MY REAR ESCAPE ROUTE NOW...
I CAN'T LET HIM GET AWAY AGAIN!!
BAM
GULP
FWIP
TESHIMA-SAN!!
STOPPING HIM IS MY ROLE!!
I'LL PROVE I CAN DO IT—FOR GUNPEI-SAN!!

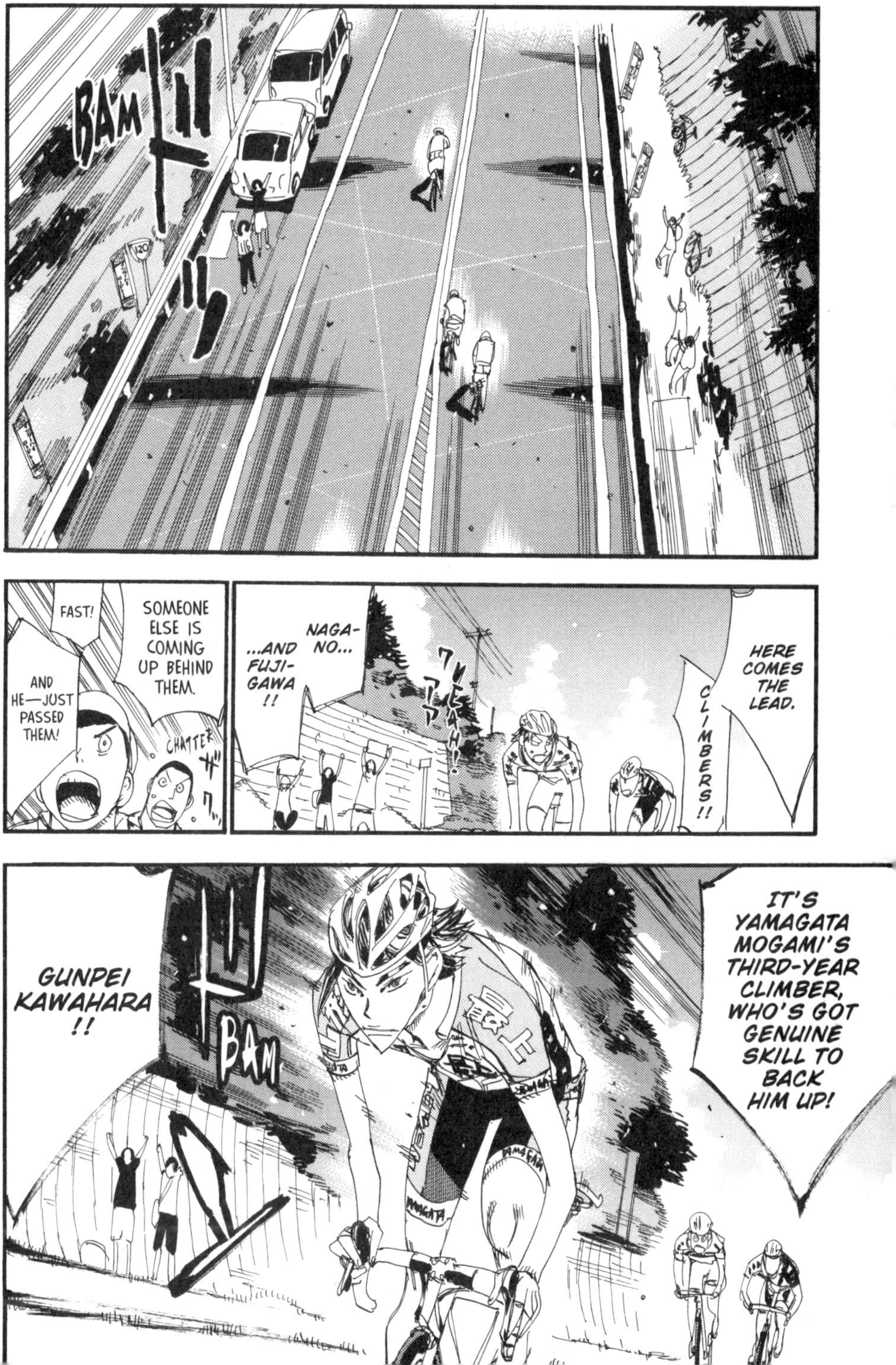
BAM
HERE COMES THE LEAD.
CLIMBERS!!
YEAH!
NAGANO...
...AND FUJIGAWA!!
SOMEONE ELSE IS COMING UP BEHIND THEM.
FAST!
AND HE—JUST PASSED THEM!
CHATTER
IT'S YAMAGATA MOGAMI'S THIRD-YEAR CLIMBER, WHO'S GOT GENUINE SKILL TO BACK HIM UP!
GUNPEI KAWAHARA!!
BAM

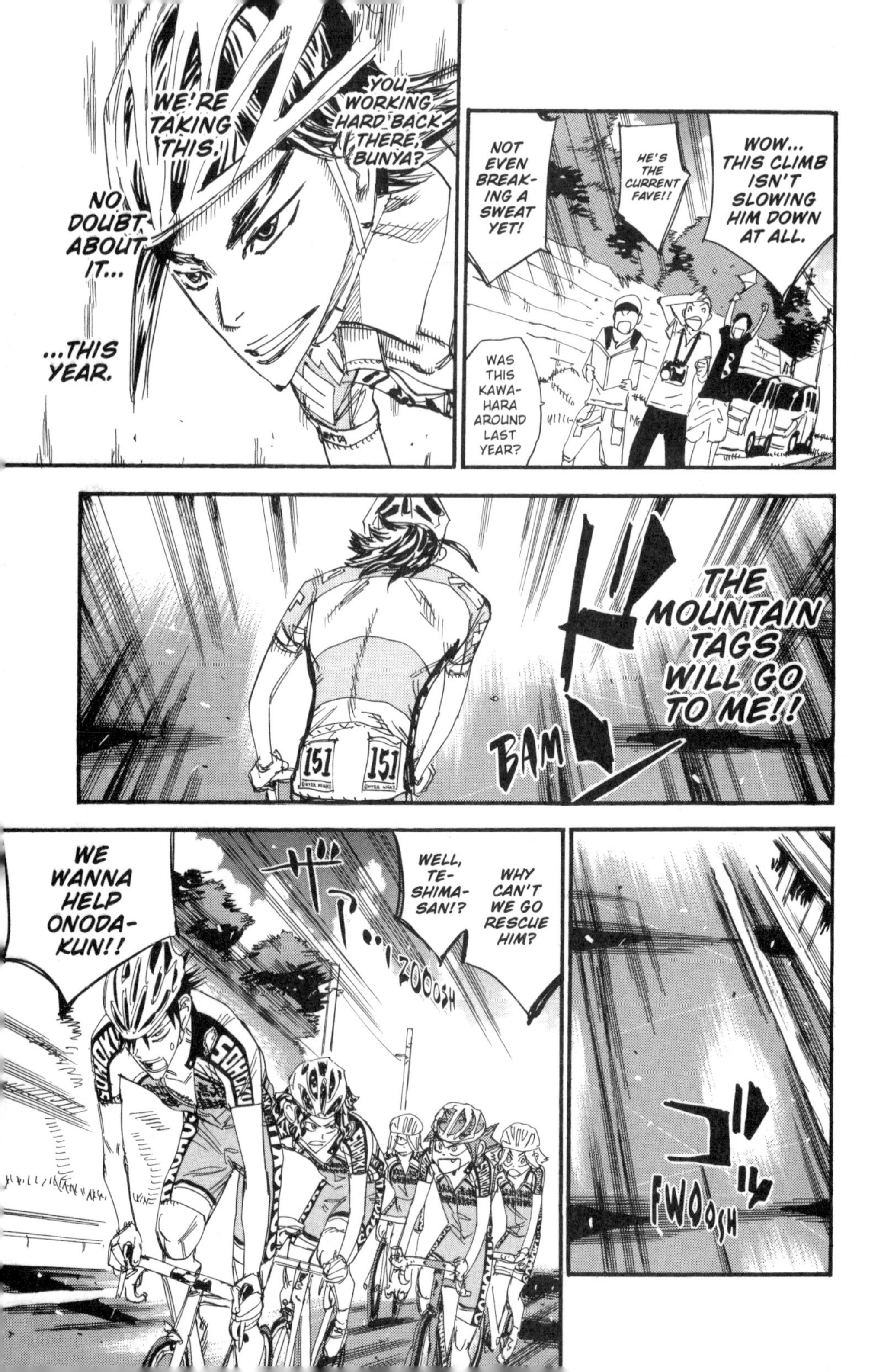
WOW... THIS CLIMB ISN'T SLOWING HIM DOWN AT ALL.
HE'S THE CURRENT FAVE!!
NOT EVEN BREAKING A SWEAT YET!
WAS THIS KAWAHARA AROUND LAST YEAR?
YOU WORKING HARD BACK THERE, BUNYA?
WE'RE TAKING THIS.
NO DOUBT ABOUT IT...
...THIS YEAR.
THE MOUNTAIN TAGS WILL GO TO ME!!
BAM
151
151
FWOOSH
WHY CAN'T WE GO RESCUE HIM?
WELL, TESHIMA-SAN!?
ZOOOSH
WE WANNA HELP ONODA-KUN!!

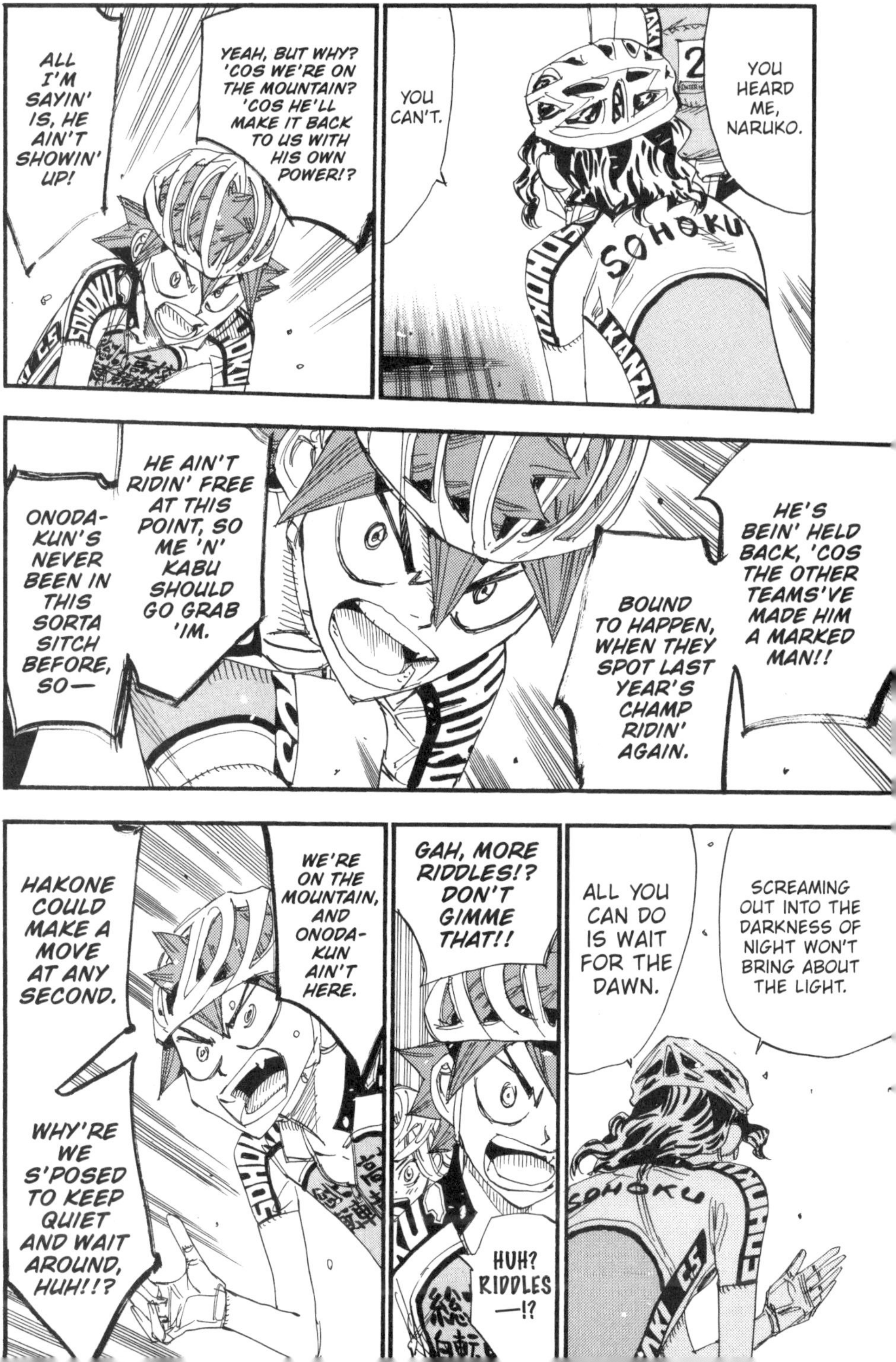
YOU HEARD ME, NARUKO.
YOU CAN'T.
YEAH, BUT WHY? 'COS WE'RE ON THE MOUNTAIN? 'COS HE'LL MAKE IT BACK TO US WITH HIS OWN POWER!?
ALL I'M SAYIN' IS, HE AIN'T SHOWIN' UP!
HE'S BEIN' HELD BACK, 'COS THE OTHER TEAMS'VE MADE HIM A MARKED MAN!!
BOUND TO HAPPEN, WHEN THEY SPOT LAST YEAR'S CHAMP RIDIN' AGAIN.
HE AIN'T RIDIN' FREE AT THIS POINT, SO ME 'N' KABU SHOULD GO GRAB 'IM.
ONODA-KUN'S NEVER BEEN IN THIS SORTA SITCH BEFORE, SO—
SCREAMING OUT INTO THE DARKNESS OF NIGHT WON'T BRING ABOUT THE LIGHT.
ALL YOU CAN DO IS WAIT FOR THE DAWN.
GAH, MORE RIDDLES!? DON'T GIMME THAT!!
HUH? MORE RIDDLES—!?
WE'RE ON THE MOUNTAIN, AND ONODA-KUN AIN'T HERE.
HAKONE COULD MAKE A MOVE AT ANY SECOND.
WHY'RE WE S'POSED TO KEEP QUIET AND WAIT AROUND, HUH!!?

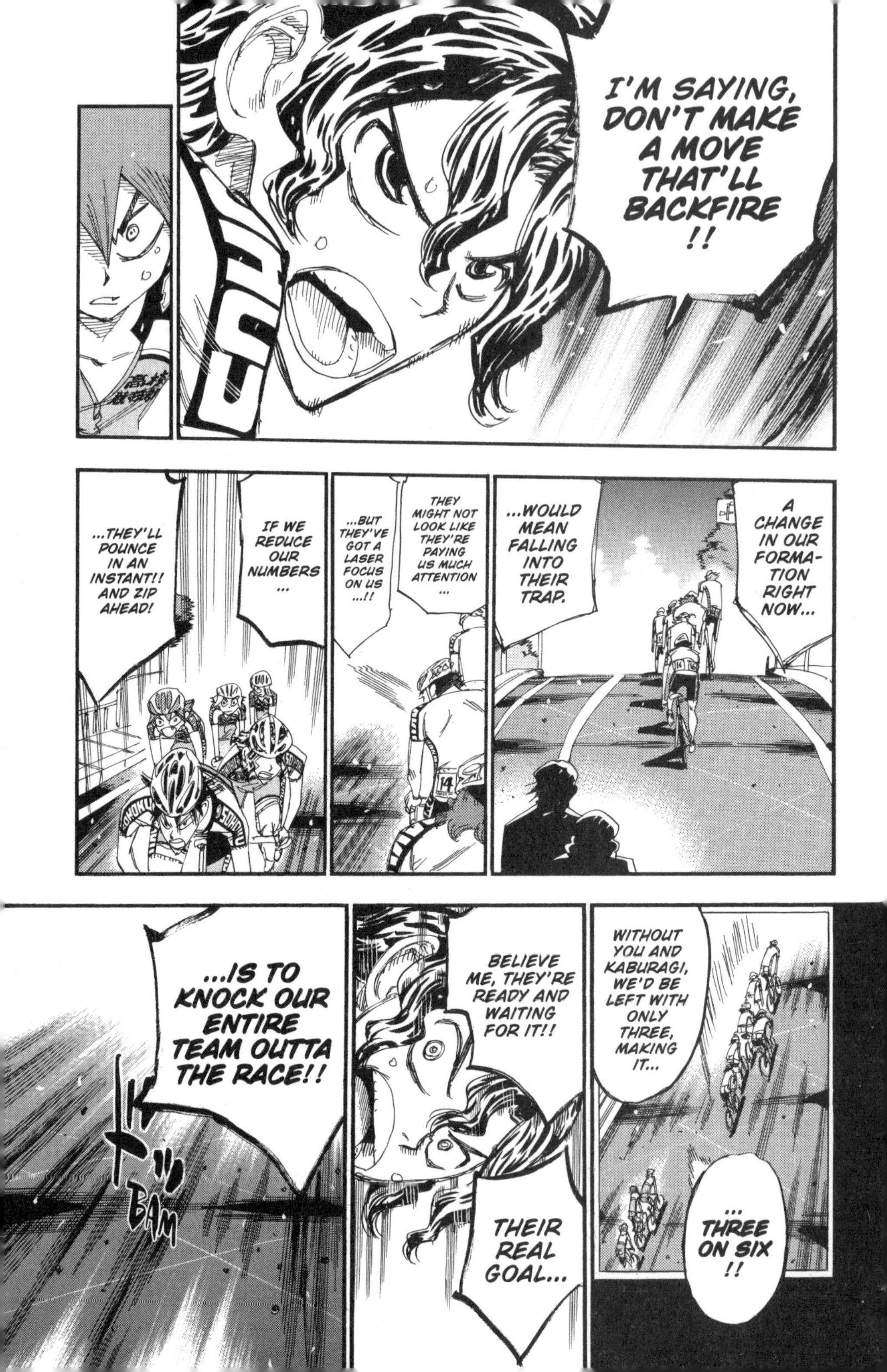
I'M SAYING, DON'T MAKE A MOVE THAT'LL BACKFIRE!!
A CHANGE IN OUR FORMATION RIGHT NOW...
...WOULD MEAN FALLING INTO THEIR TRAP.
THEY MIGHT NOT LOOK LIKE THEY'RE PAYING US MUCH ATTENTION...
...BUT THEY'VE GOT A LASER FOCUS ON US...!!
IF WE REDUCE OUR NUMBERS...
...THEY'LL POUNCE IN AN INSTANT!! AND ZIP AHEAD!
WITHOUT YOU AND KABURAGI, WE'D BE LEFT WITH ONLY THREE, MAKING IT...
...THREE ON SIX!!
BELIEVE ME, THEY'RE READY AND WAITING FOR IT!!
THEIR REAL GOAL...
...IS TO KNOCK OUR ENTIRE TEAM OUTTA THE RACE!!
BAM

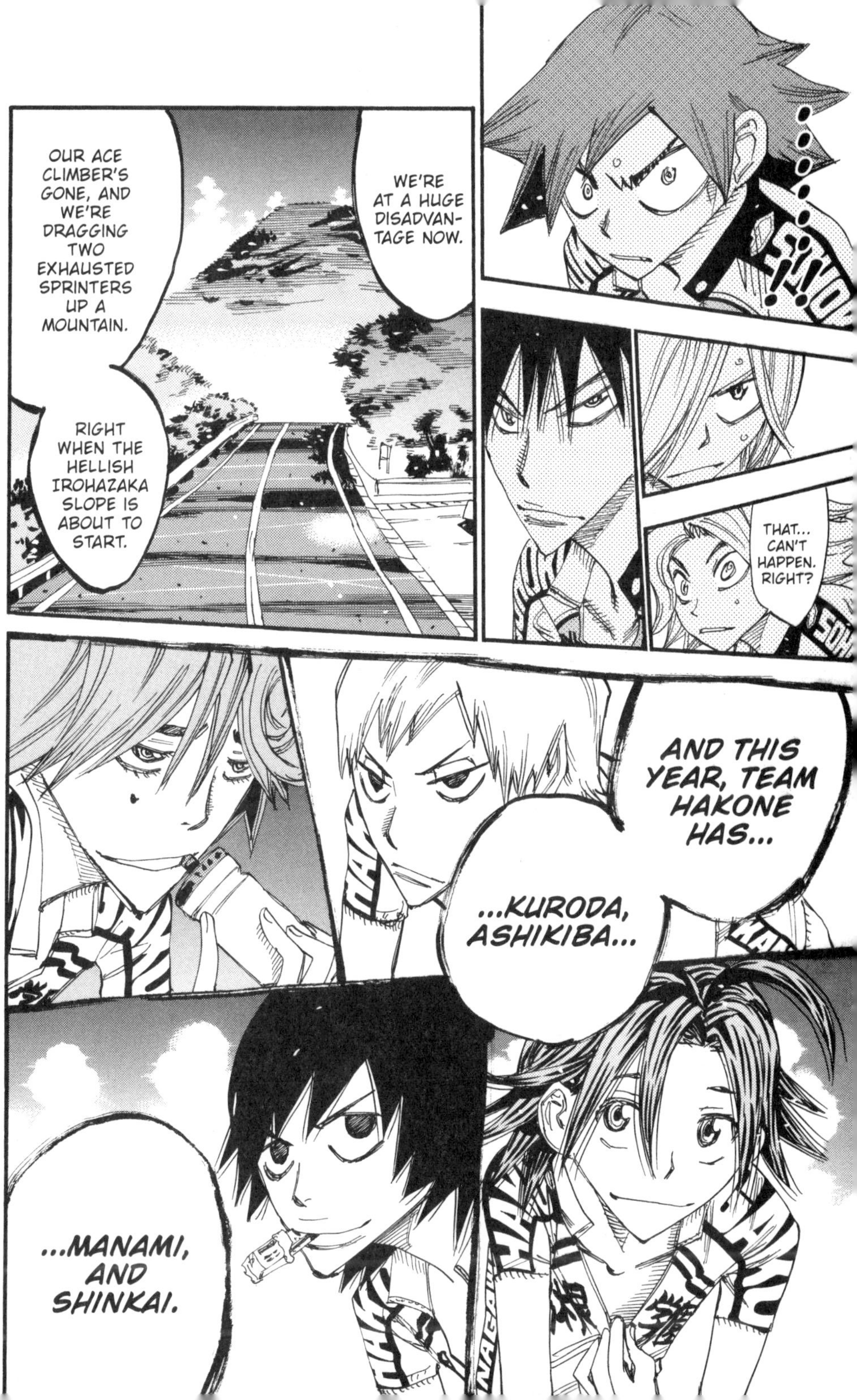
......!!
THAT... CAN'T HAPPEN. RIGHT?
WE'RE AT A HUGE DISADVANTAGE NOW.
OUR ACE CLIMBER'S GONE, AND WE'RE DRAGGING TWO EXHAUSTED SPRINTERS UP A MOUNTAIN.
RIGHT WHEN THE HELLISH IROHAZAKA SLOPE IS ABOUT TO START.
AND THIS YEAR, TEAM HAKONE HAS...
...KURODA, ASHIKIBA...
...MANAMI, AND SHINKAI.

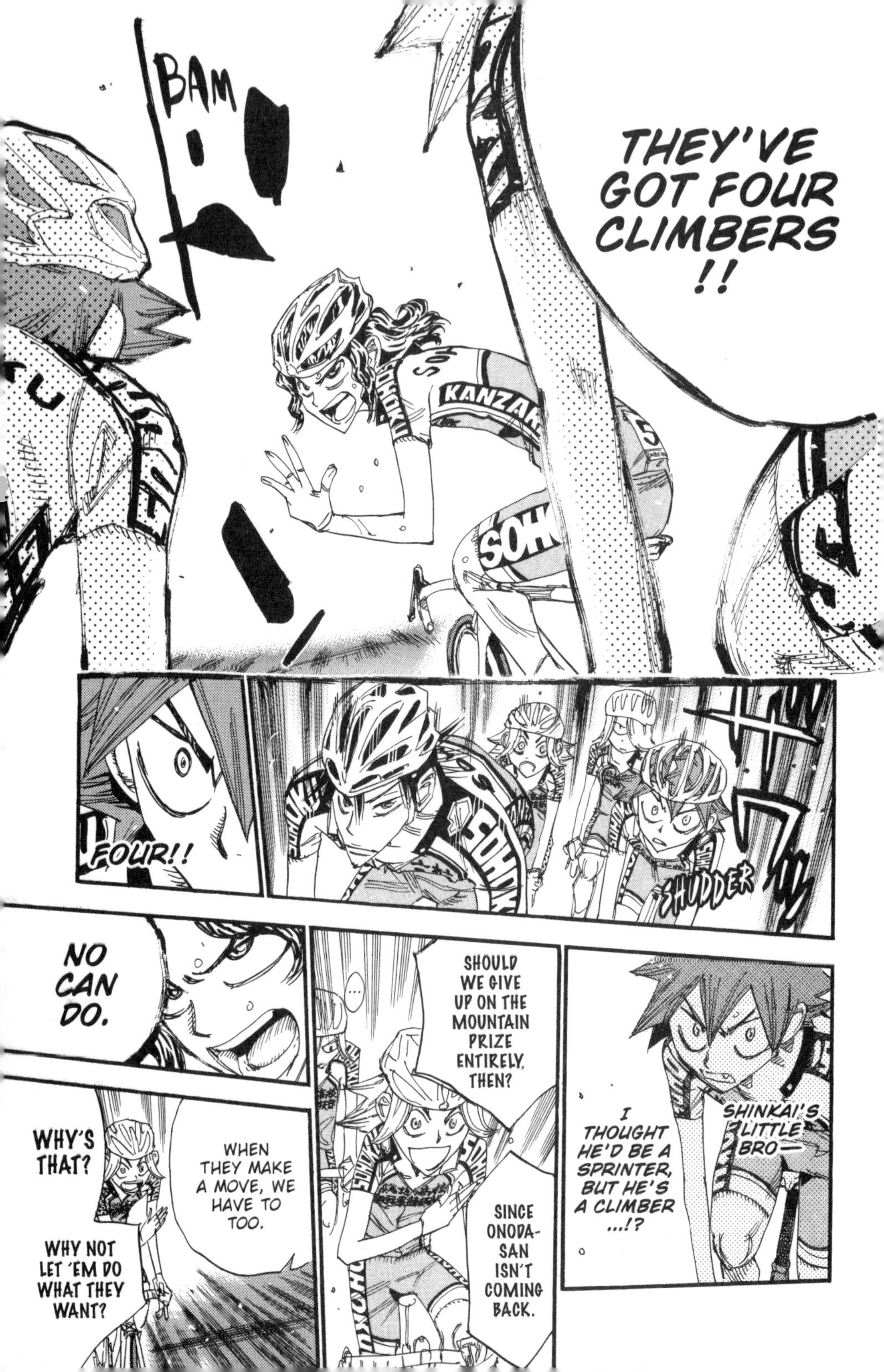
THEY'VE GOT FOUR CLIMBERS !!
BAM
SHUDDER
FOUR!!
SHINKAI'S LITTLE BRO—
I THOUGHT HE'D BE A SPRINTER, BUT HE'S A CLIMBER ...!?
...
SHOULD WE GIVE UP ON THE MOUNTAIN PRIZE ENTIRELY, THEN?
SINCE ONODA-SAN ISN'T COMING BACK.
NO CAN DO.
WHEN THEY MAKE A MOVE, WE HAVE TO TOO.
WHY'S THAT?
WHY NOT LET 'EM DO WHAT THEY WANT?

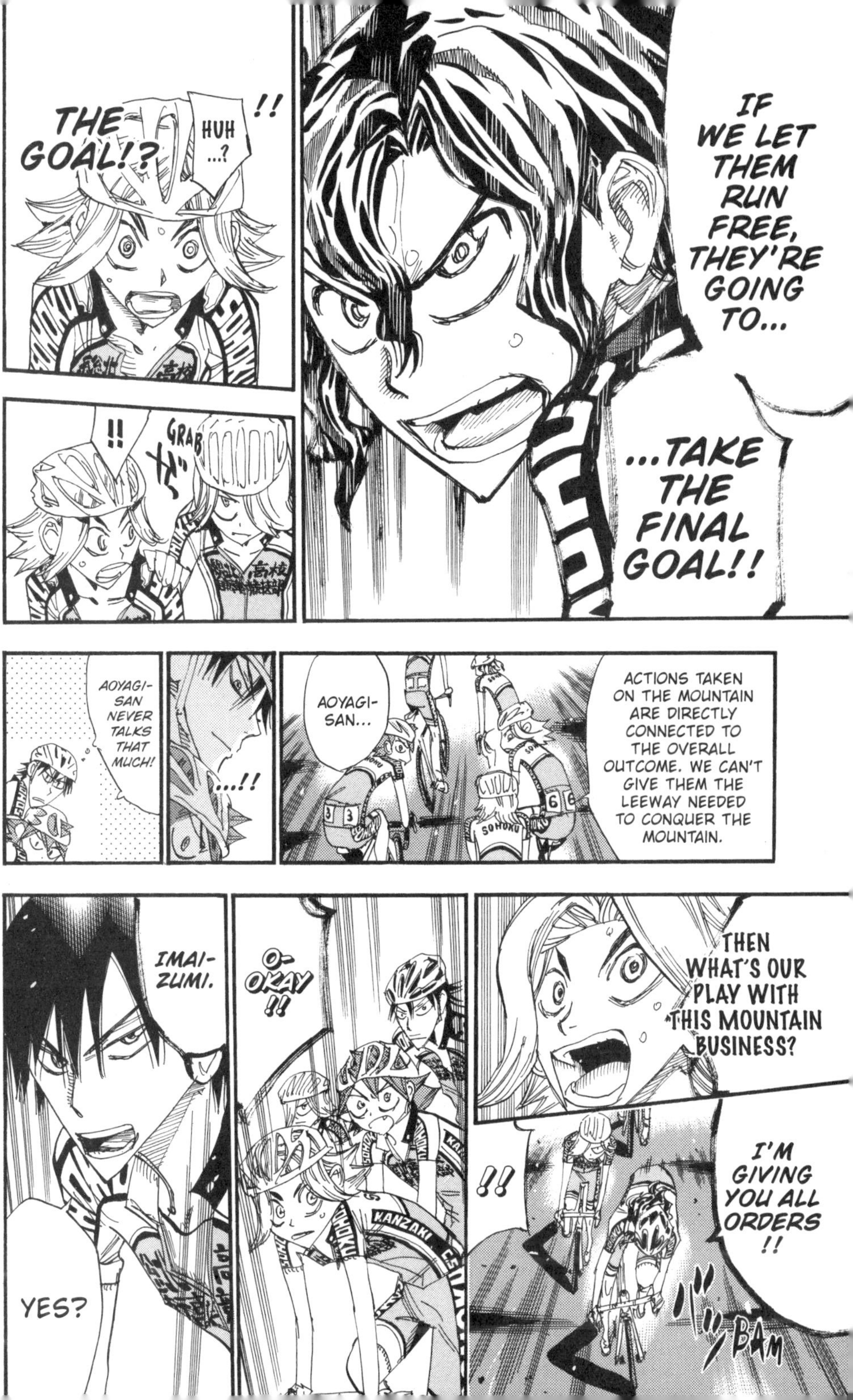
IF WE LET THEM RUN FREE, THEY'RE GOING TO...
...TAKE THE FINAL GOAL!!
!!
HUH ...?
THE GOAL!?
GRAB
!!
ACTIONS TAKEN ON THE MOUNTAIN ARE DIRECTLY CONNECTED TO THE OVERALL OUTCOME. WE CAN'T GIVE THEM THE LEEWAY NEEDED TO CONQUER THE MOUNTAIN.
AOYAGI-SAN...
...!!
AOYAGI-SAN NEVER TALKS THAT MUCH!
THEN WHAT'S OUR PLAY WITH THIS MOUNTAIN BUSINESS?
I'M GIVING YOU ALL ORDERS!!
!!
BAM
O-OKAY!!
IMAI-ZUMI.
YES?

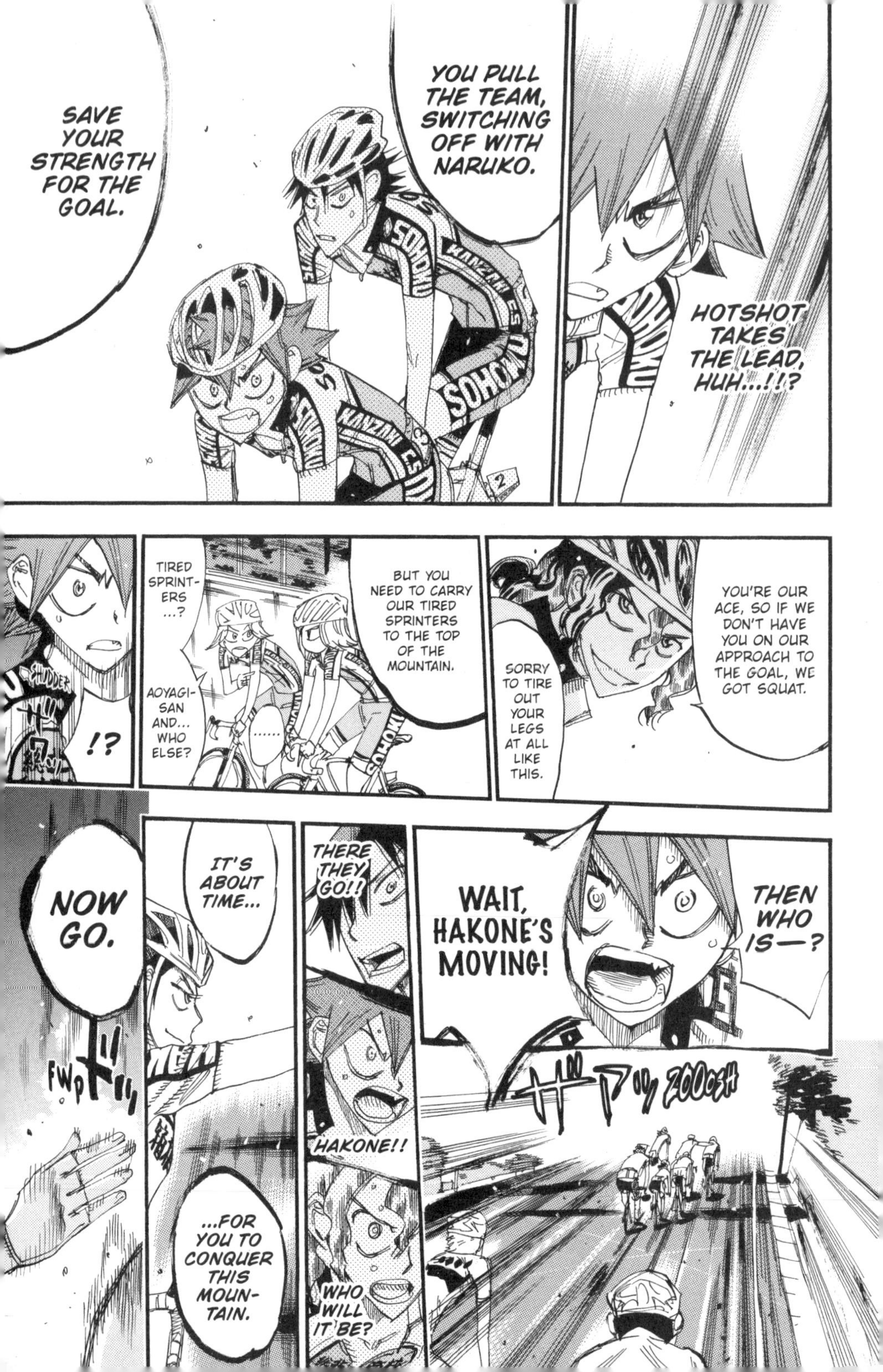
HOTSHOT TAKES THE LEAD, HUH...!!?
YOU PULL THE TEAM, SWITCHING OFF WITH NARUKO.
SAVE YOUR STRENGTH FOR THE GOAL.
YOU'RE OUR ACE, SO IF WE DON'T HAVE YOU ON OUR APPROACH TO THE GOAL, WE GOT SQUAT.
SORRY TO TIRE OUT YOUR LEGS AT ALL LIKE THIS.
BUT YOU NEED TO CARRY OUR TIRED SPRINTERS TO THE TOP OF THE MOUNTAIN.
TIRED SPRINTERS...?
......
AOYAGI-SAN AND... WHO ELSE?
SHUDDER
!?
THEN WHO IS—?
WAIT, HAKONE'S MOVING!
ZOOSH
THERE THEY GO!!
HAKONE!!
WHO WILL IT BE?
IT'S ABOUT TIME...
...FOR YOU TO CONQUER THIS MOUNTAIN.
NOW GO.
FWP

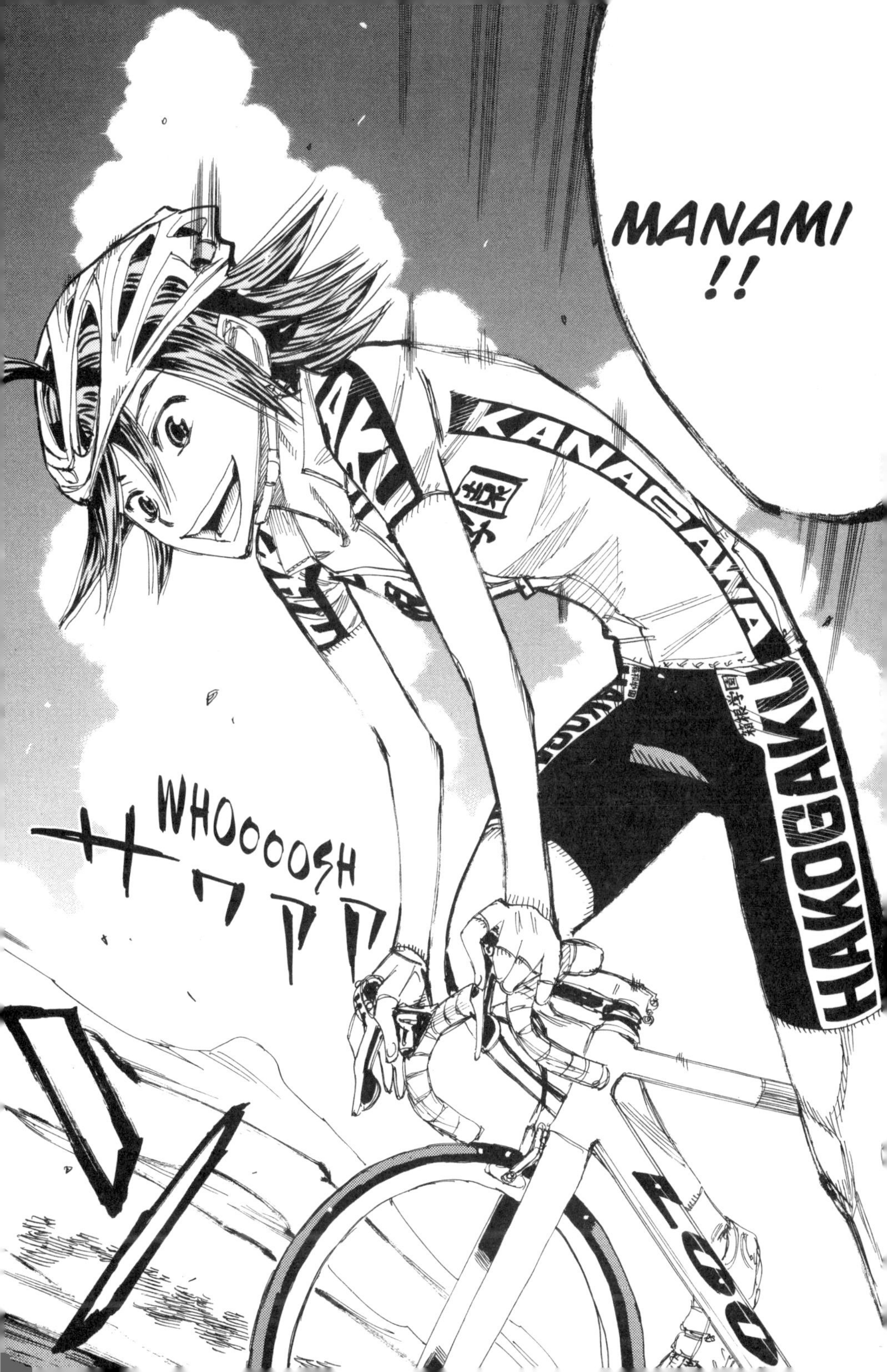
MANAMI!!
WHOOOOOSH

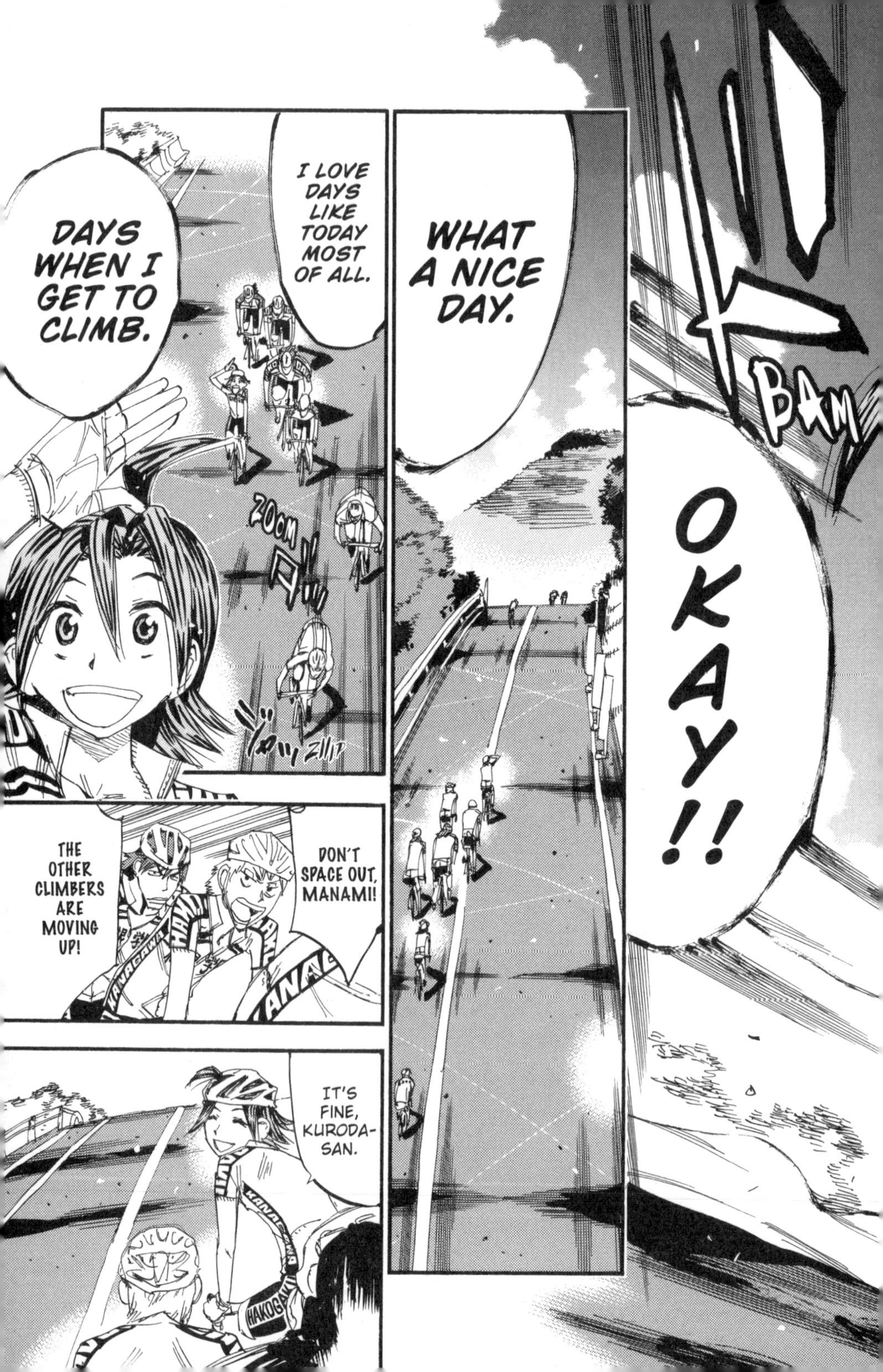
BAM
OKAY!!
WHAT A NICE DAY.
I LOVE DAYS LIKE TODAY MOST OF ALL.
DAYS WHEN I GET TO CLIMB.
ZOOM
ZIIP
DON'T SPACE OUT, MANAMI!
THE OTHER CLIMBERS ARE MOVING UP!
IT'S FINE, KURODA-SAN.

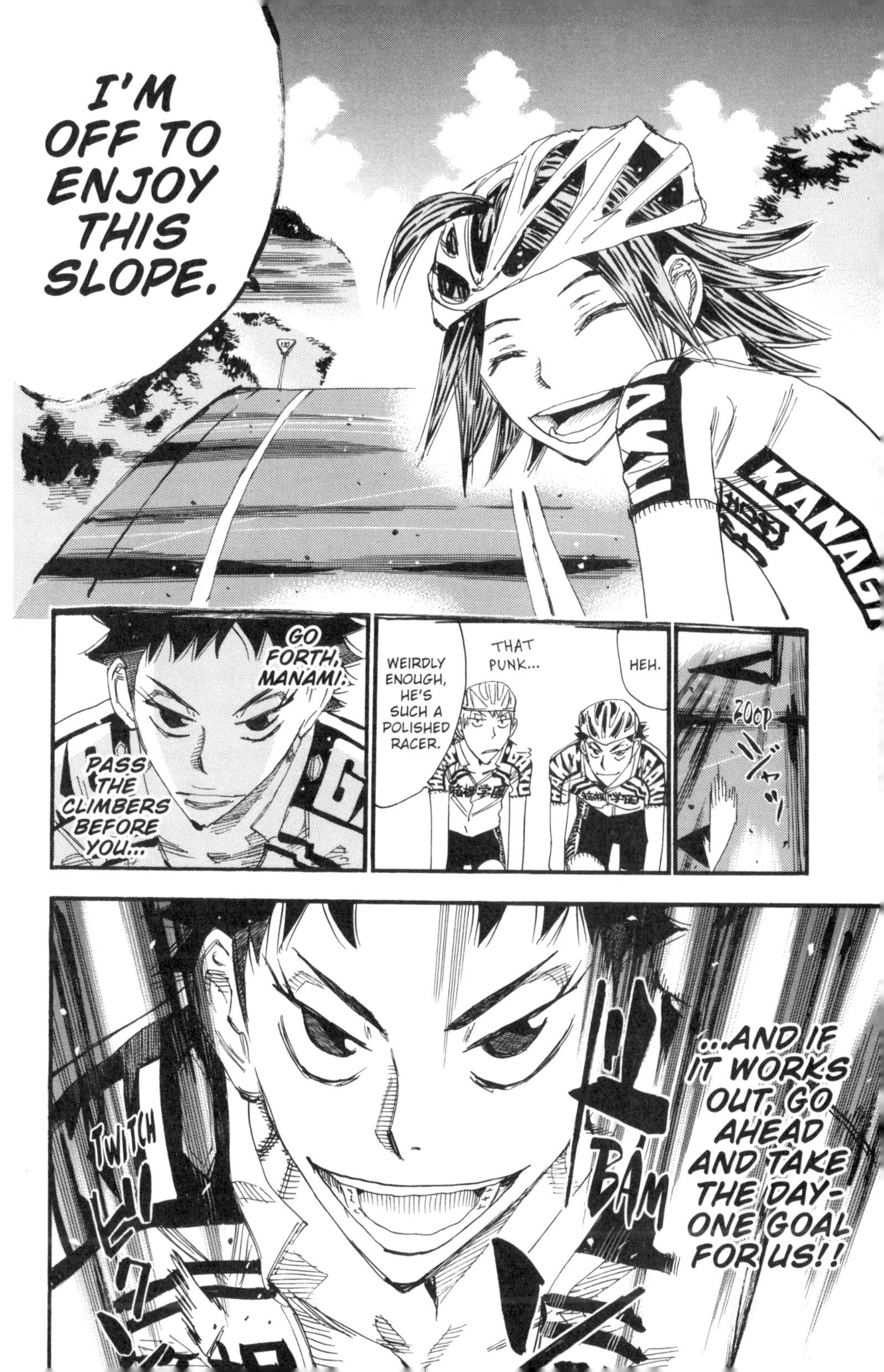
I'M OFF TO ENJOY THIS SLOPE.
ZOOP
HEH.
THAT PUNK...
WEIRDLY ENOUGH, HE'S SUCH A POLISHED RACER.
GO FORTH, MANAMI.
PASS THE CLIMBERS BEFORE YOU...
...AND IF IT WORKS OUT, GO AHEAD AND TAKE THE DAY-ONE GOAL FOR US!!
BAM
TWITCH

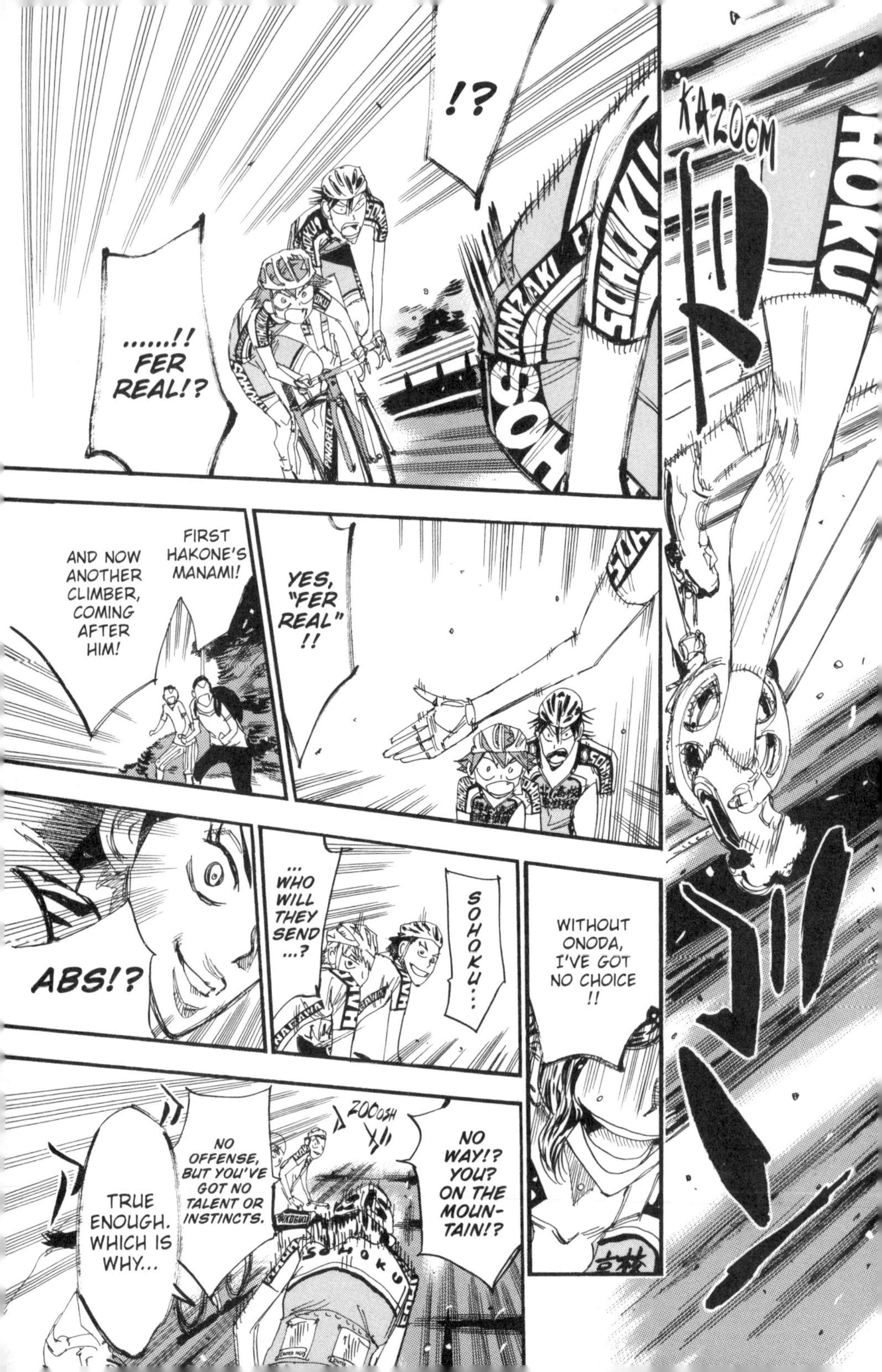
KAZOOM
!?
......!! FER REAL!?
YES, "FER REAL"!!
FIRST HAKONE'S MANAMI!
AND NOW ANOTHER CLIMBER, COMING AFTER HIM!
WITHOUT ONODA, I'VE GOT NO CHOICE!!
SOHOKU...
...WHO WILL THEY SEND...?
ABS!?
NO WAY!? YOU? ON THE MOUNTAIN!?
ZOOOSH
NO OFFENSE, BUT YOU'VE GOT NO TALENT OR INSTINCTS.
TRUE ENOUGH. WHICH IS WHY...

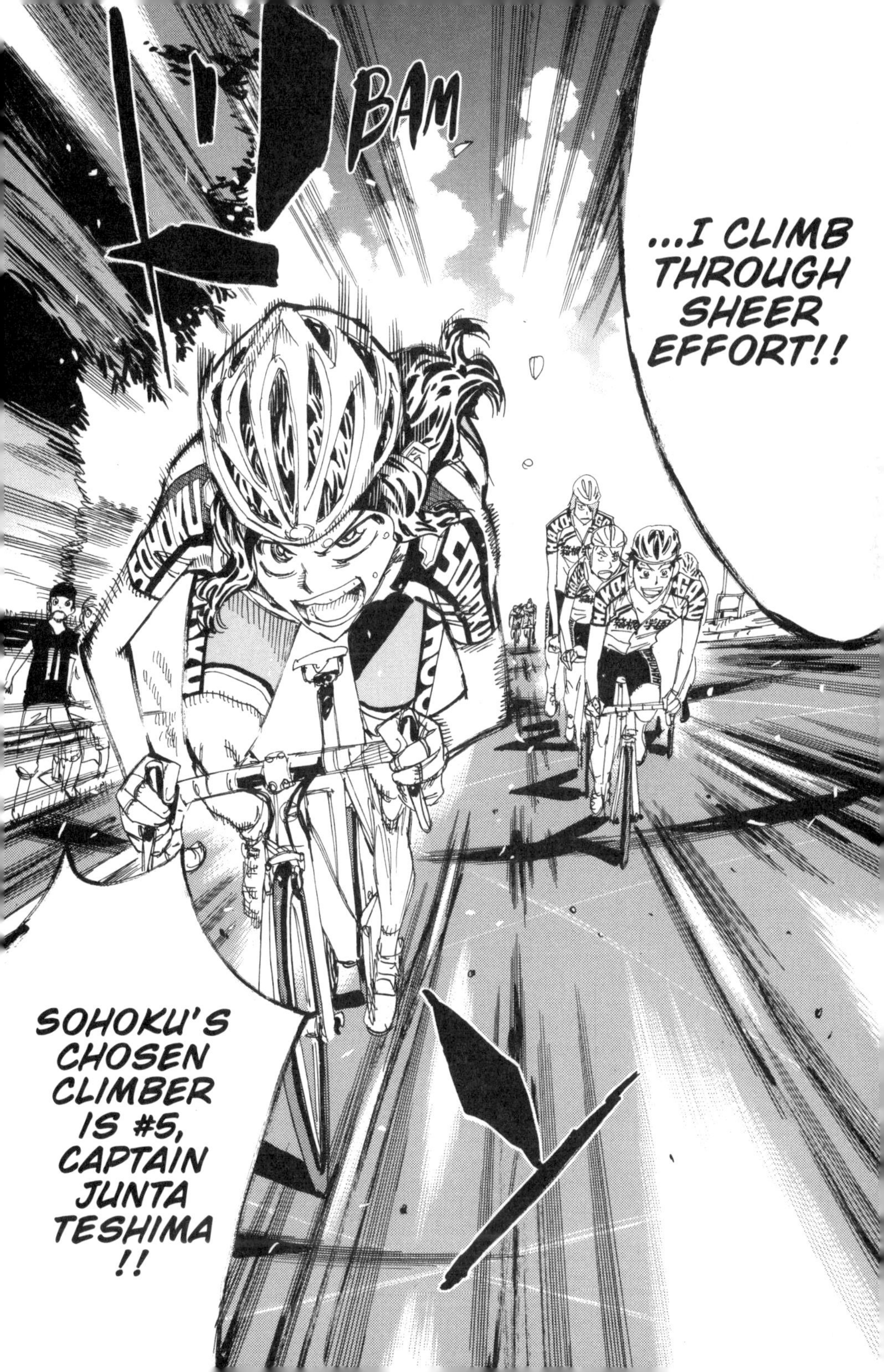
...I CLIMB THROUGH SHEER EFFORT!!
BAM
SOHOKU'S CHOSEN CLIMBER IS #5, CAPTAIN JUNTA TESHIMA !!

RIDE.318 JUNTA TESHIMA!

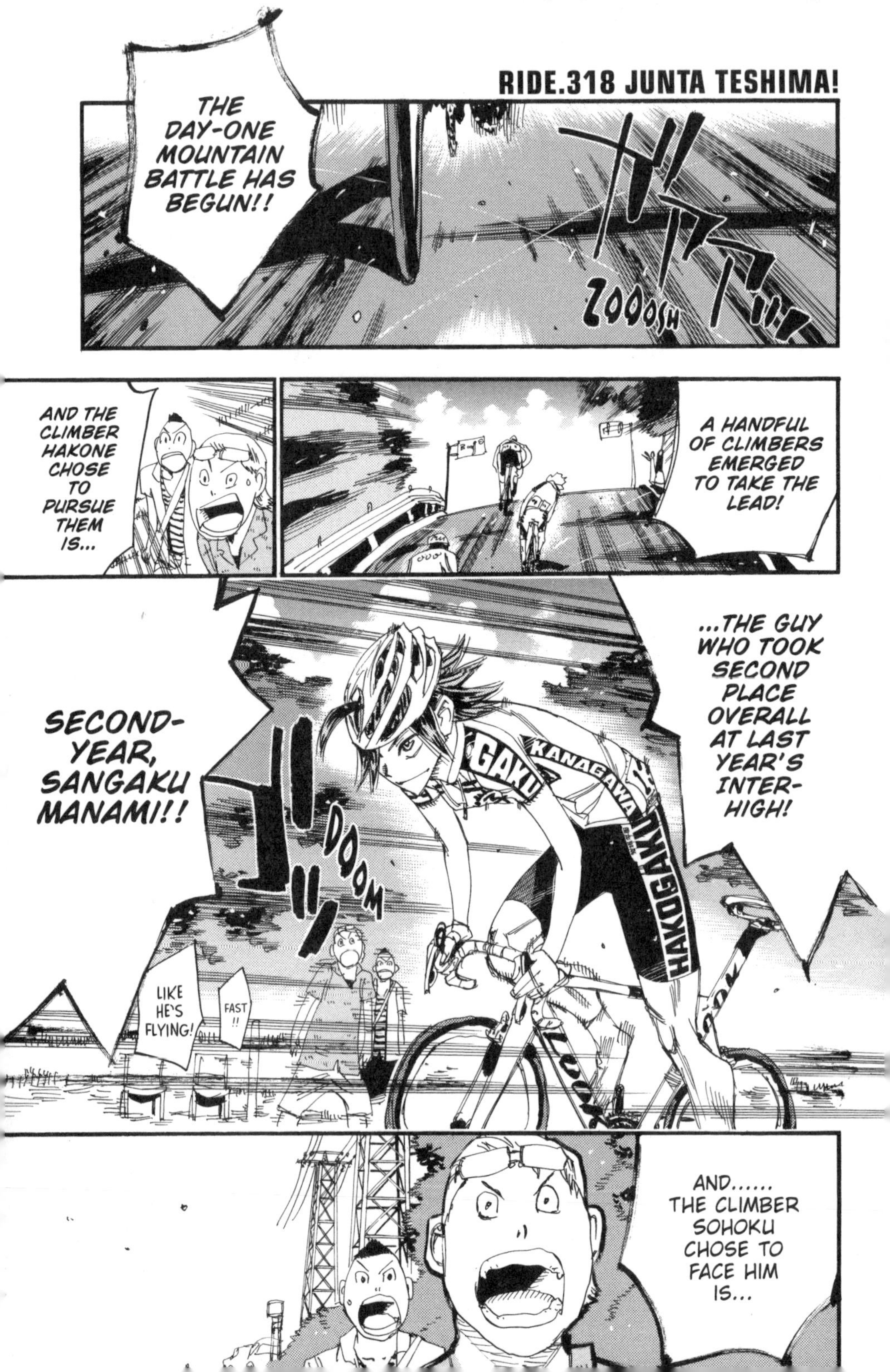
THE DAY-ONE MOUNTAIN BATTLE HAS BEGUN!!
ZOOOSH
A HANDFUL OF CLIMBERS EMERGED TO TAKE THE LEAD!
AND THE CLIMBER HAKONE CHOSE TO PURSUE THEM IS...
...THE GUY WHO TOOK SECOND PLACE OVERALL AT LAST YEAR'S INTER-HIGH!
SECOND-YEAR, SANGAKU MANAMI!!
DOOOM
FAST!!
LIKE HE'S FLYING!
AND...... THE CLIMBER SOHOKU CHOSE TO FACE HIM IS...

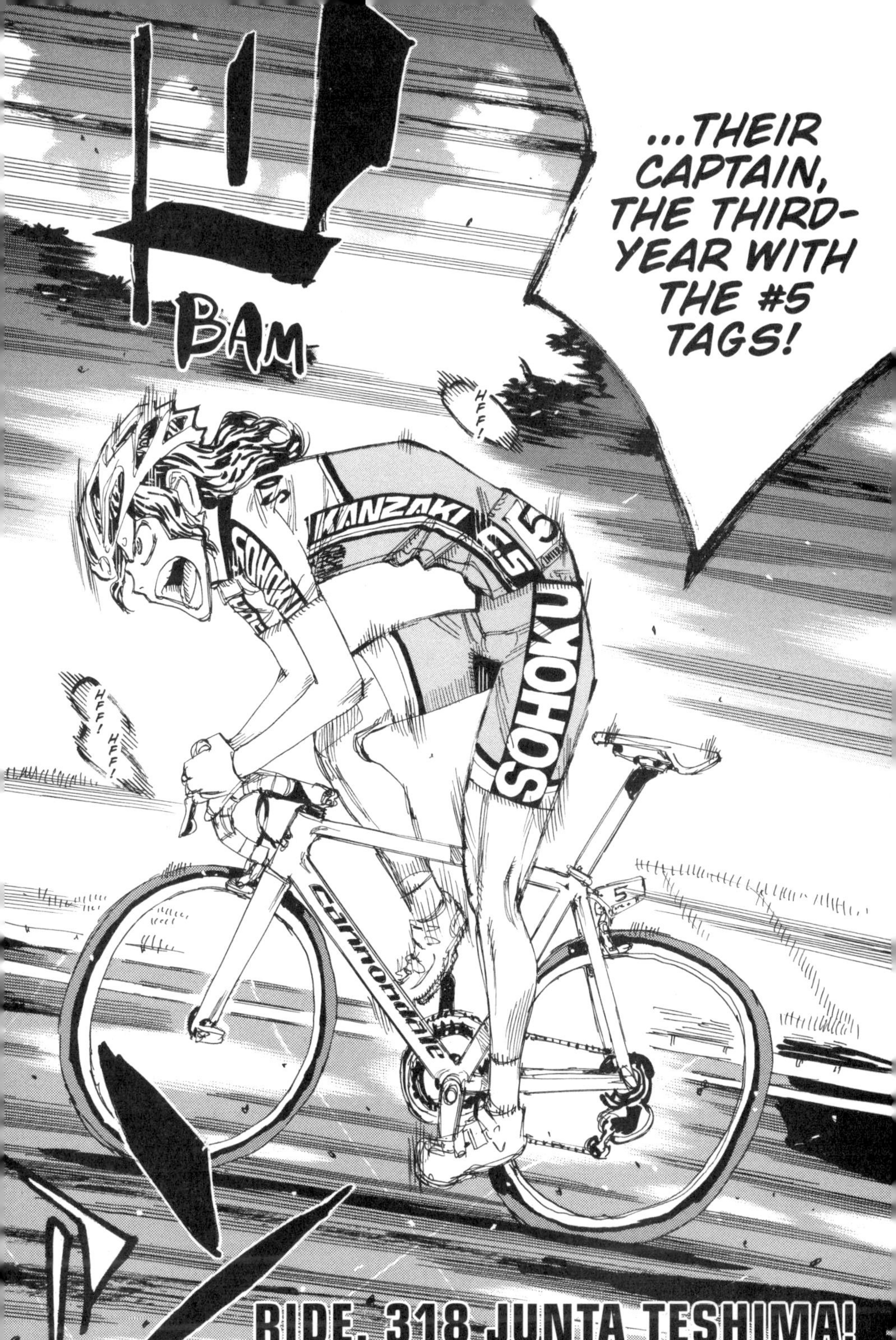
...THEIR CAPTAIN, THE THIRD-YEAR WITH THE #5 TAGS!
BAM
HFF!
HFF! HFF!
KANZAKI
SOHOKU
SOHOKU
5
cannondale

RIDE. 318 JUNTA TESHIMA!

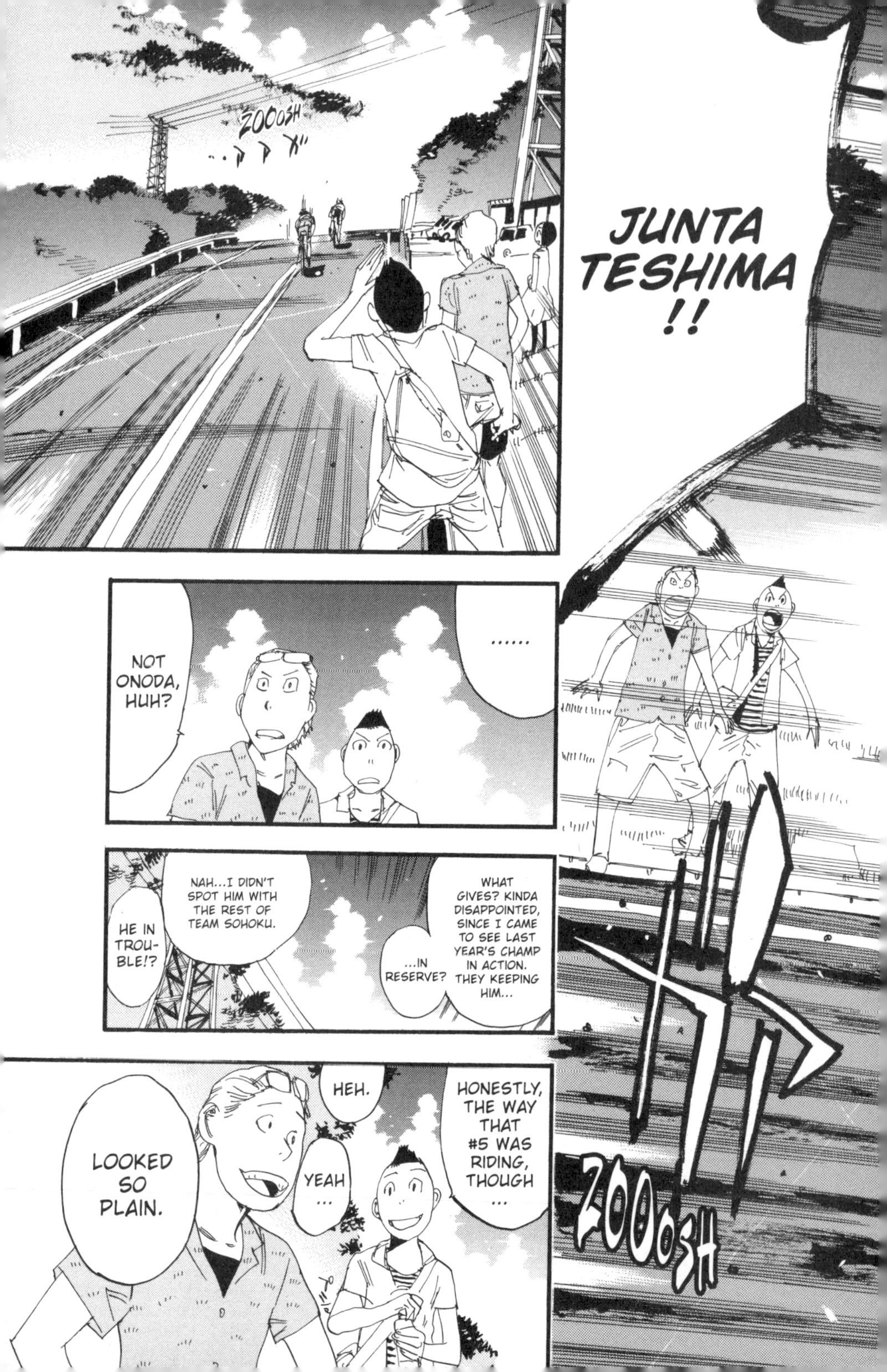
JUNTA TESHIMA!!
ZOOOSH
ZOOOSH
......
NOT ONODA, HUH?
WHAT GIVES? KINDA DISAPPOINTED, SINCE I CAME TO SEE LAST YEAR'S CHAMP IN ACTION. THEY KEEPING HIM...
...IN RESERVE?
NAH...I DIDN'T SPOT HIM WITH THE REST OF TEAM SOHOKU.
HE IN TROU-BLE!?
HONESTLY, THE WAY THAT #5 WAS RIDING, THOUGH ...
HEH.
YEAH ...
LOOKED SO PLAIN.

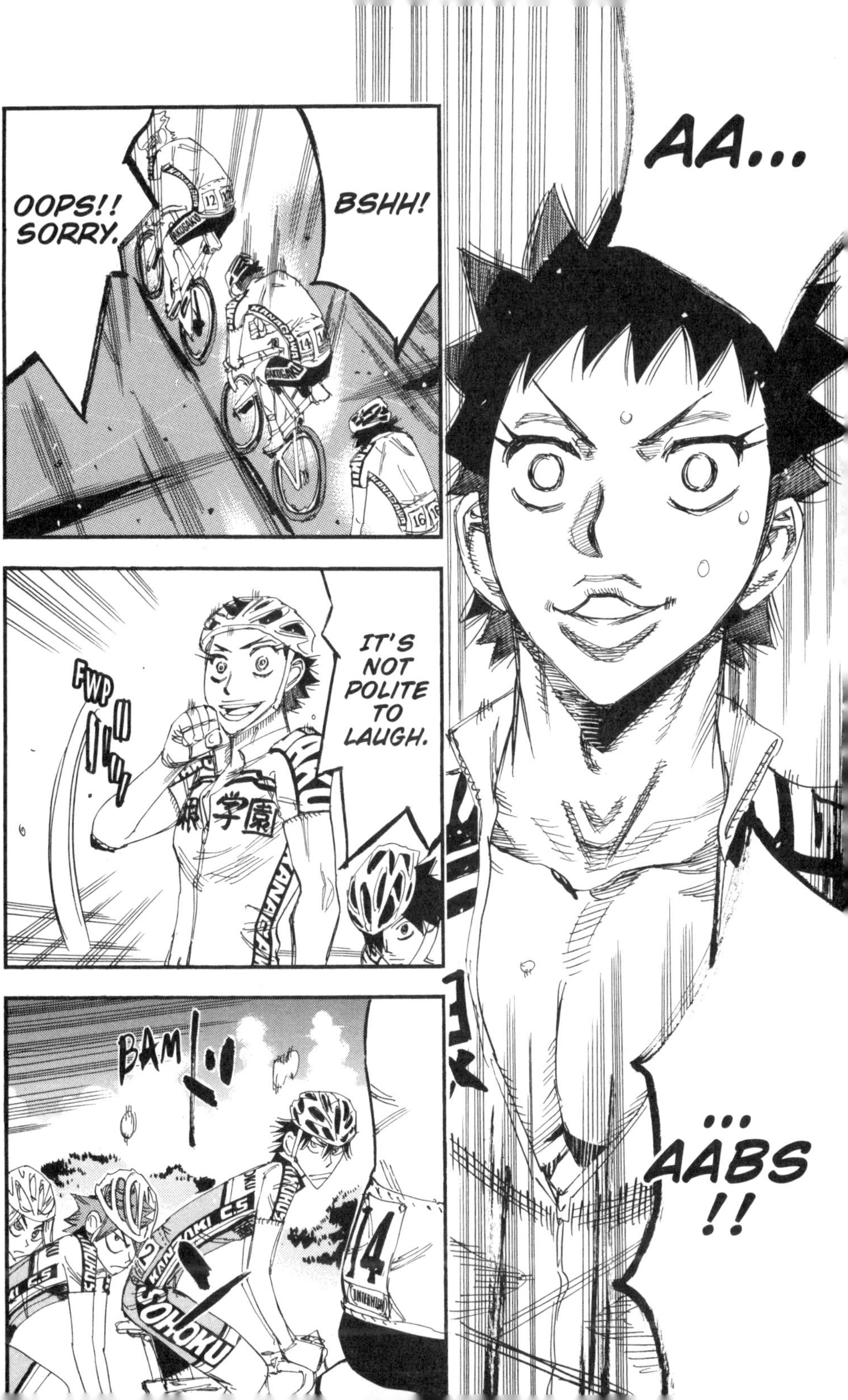
AA...
...AABS!!
BSHH!
OOPS!! SORRY.
IT'S NOT POLITE TO LAUGH.
FWP
BAM

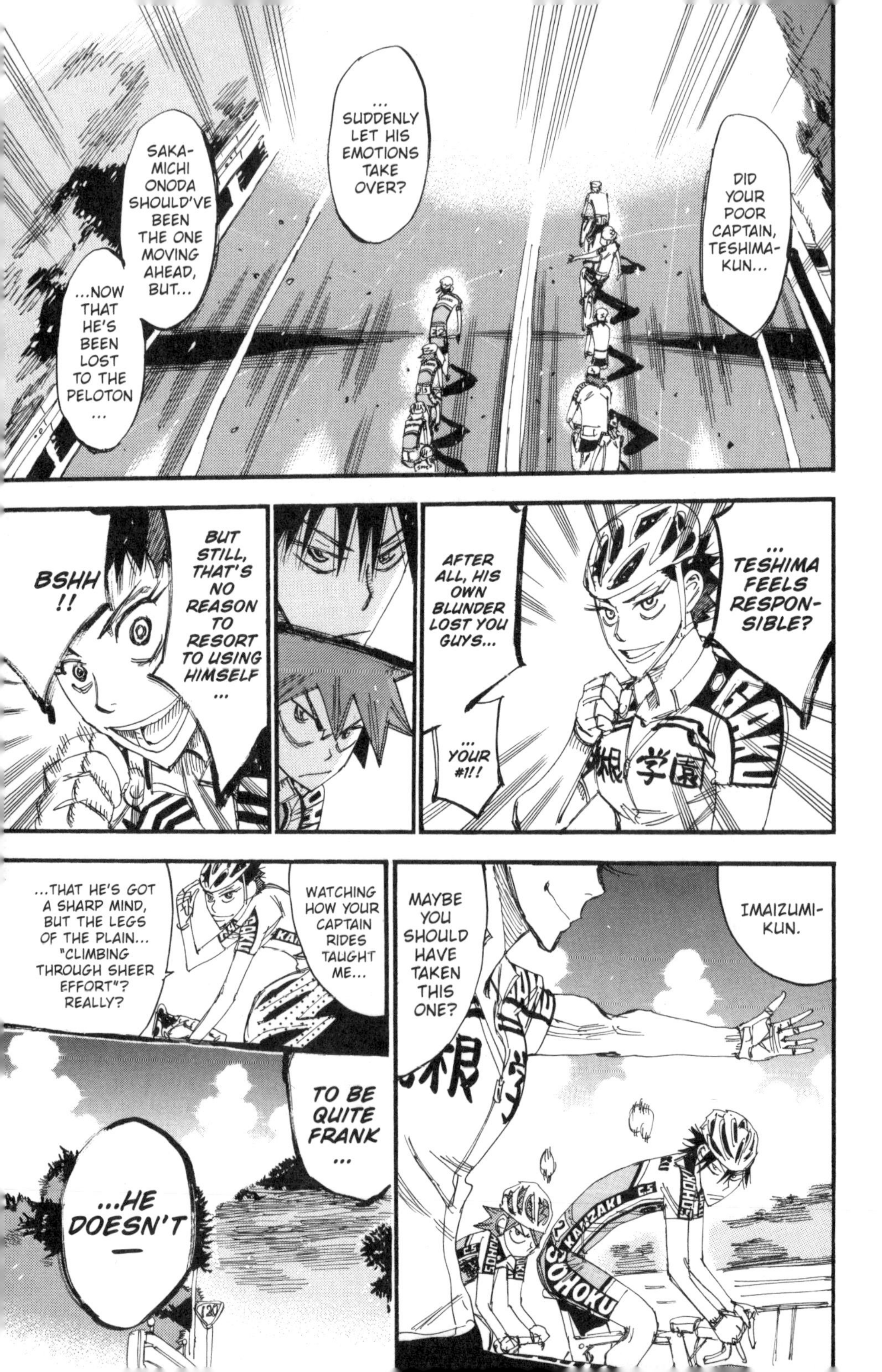
DID YOUR POOR CAPTAIN, TESHIMA-KUN...
...SUDDENLY LET HIS EMOTIONS TAKE OVER?
SAKA-MICHI ONODA SHOULD'VE BEEN THE ONE MOVING AHEAD, BUT...
...NOW THAT HE'S BEEN LOST TO THE PELOTON...
...TESHIMA FEELS RESPON-SIBLE?
AFTER ALL, HIS OWN BLUNDER LOST YOU GUYS...
...YOUR #1!!
BUT STILL, THAT'S NO REASON TO RESORT TO USING HIMSELF...
BSHH!!
IMAIZUMI-KUN.
MAYBE YOU SHOULD HAVE TAKEN THIS ONE?
WATCHING HOW YOUR CAPTAIN RIDES TAUGHT ME...
...THAT HE'S GOT A SHARP MIND, BUT THE LEGS OF THE PLAIN... "CLIMBING THROUGH SHEER EFFORT"? REALLY?
TO BE QUITE FRANK...
...HE DOESN'T—

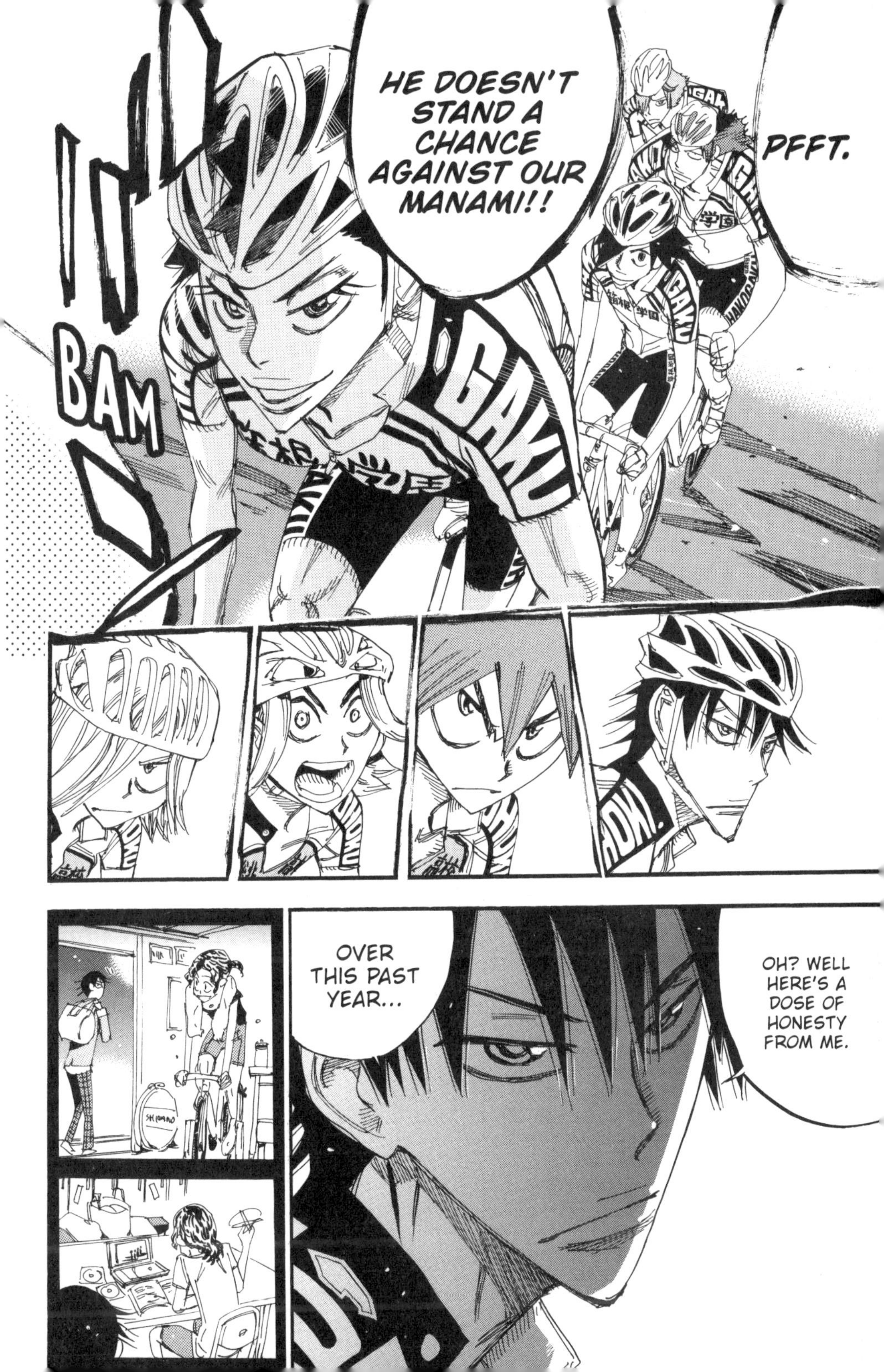
HE DOESN'T STAND A CHANCE AGAINST OUR MANAMI!!
PFFT.
BAM
OH? WELL HERE'S A DOSE OF HONESTY FROM ME.
OVER THIS PAST YEAR...

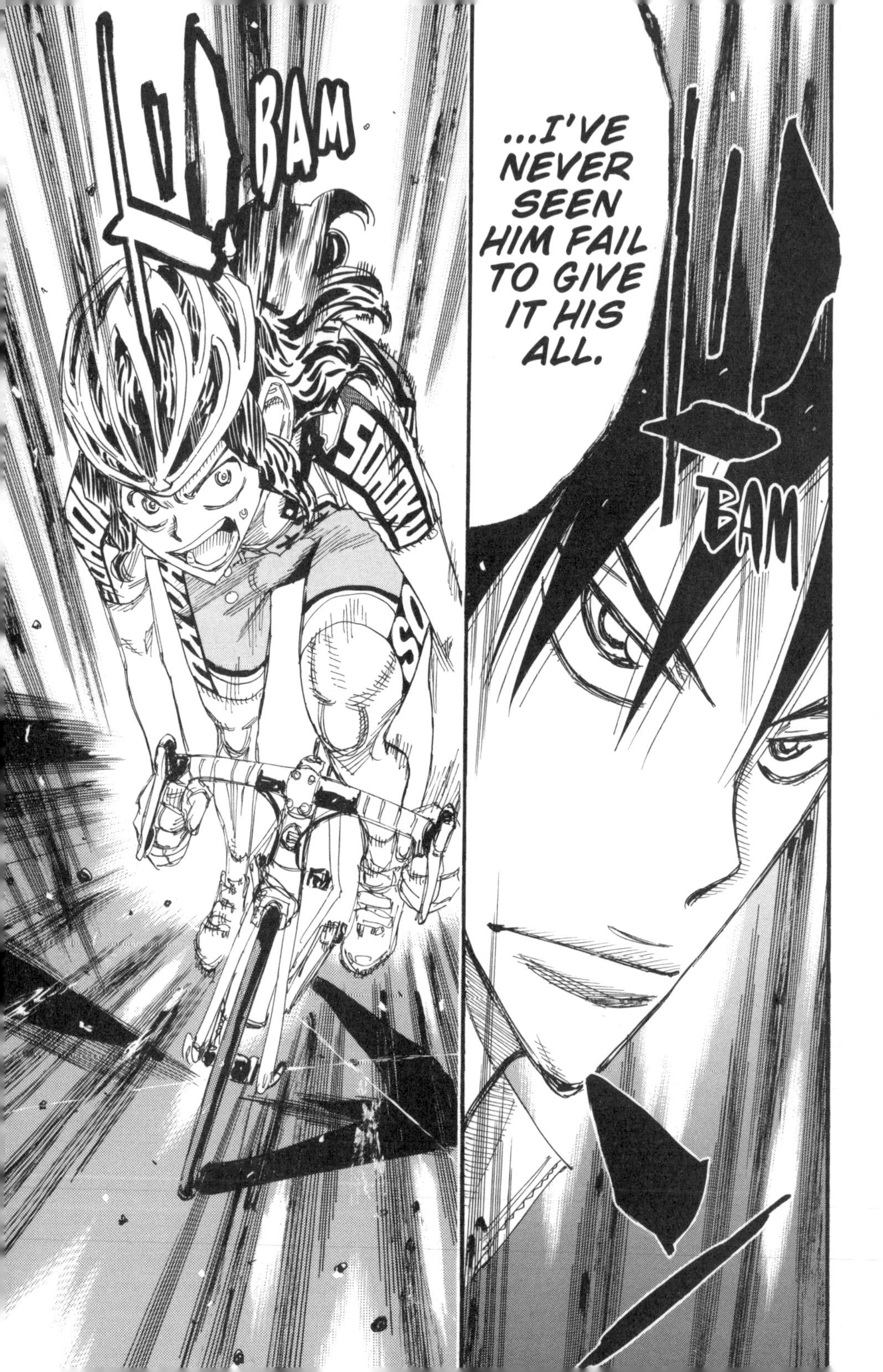
...I'VE NEVER SEEN HIM FAIL TO GIVE IT HIS ALL.
BAM
BAM

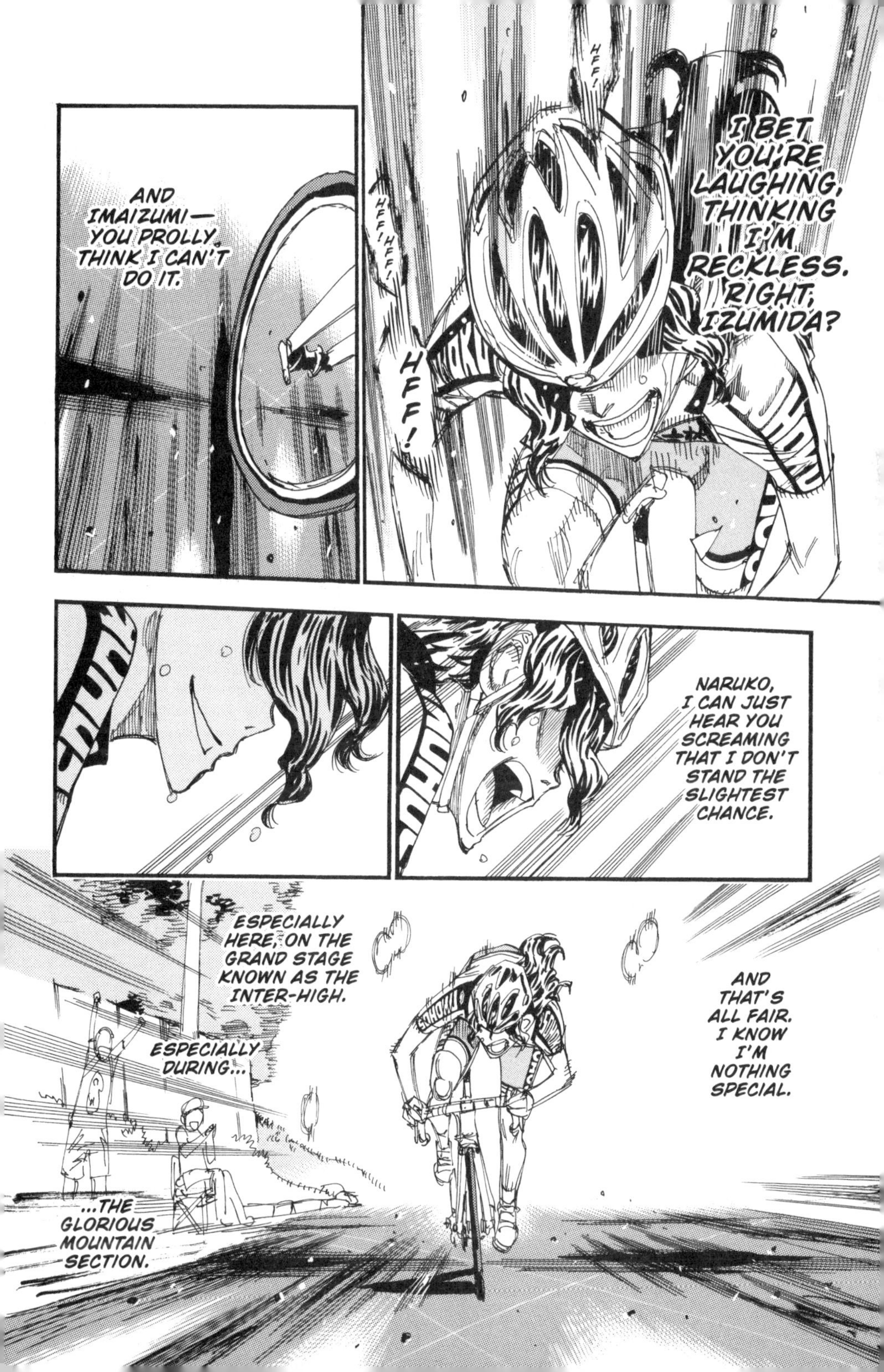
HFF!
I BET YOU'RE LAUGHING, THINKING I'M RECKLESS. RIGHT, IZUMIDA?
HFF! HFF!
HFF!
AND IMAIZUMI— YOU PROLLY THINK I CAN'T DO IT.
NARUKO, I CAN JUST HEAR YOU SCREAMING THAT I DON'T STAND THE SLIGHTEST CHANCE.
AND THAT'S ALL FAIR. I KNOW I'M NOTHING SPECIAL.
ESPECIALLY HERE, ON THE GRAND STAGE KNOWN AS THE INTER-HIGH.
ESPECIALLY DURING...
...THE GLORIOUS MOUNTAIN SECTION.

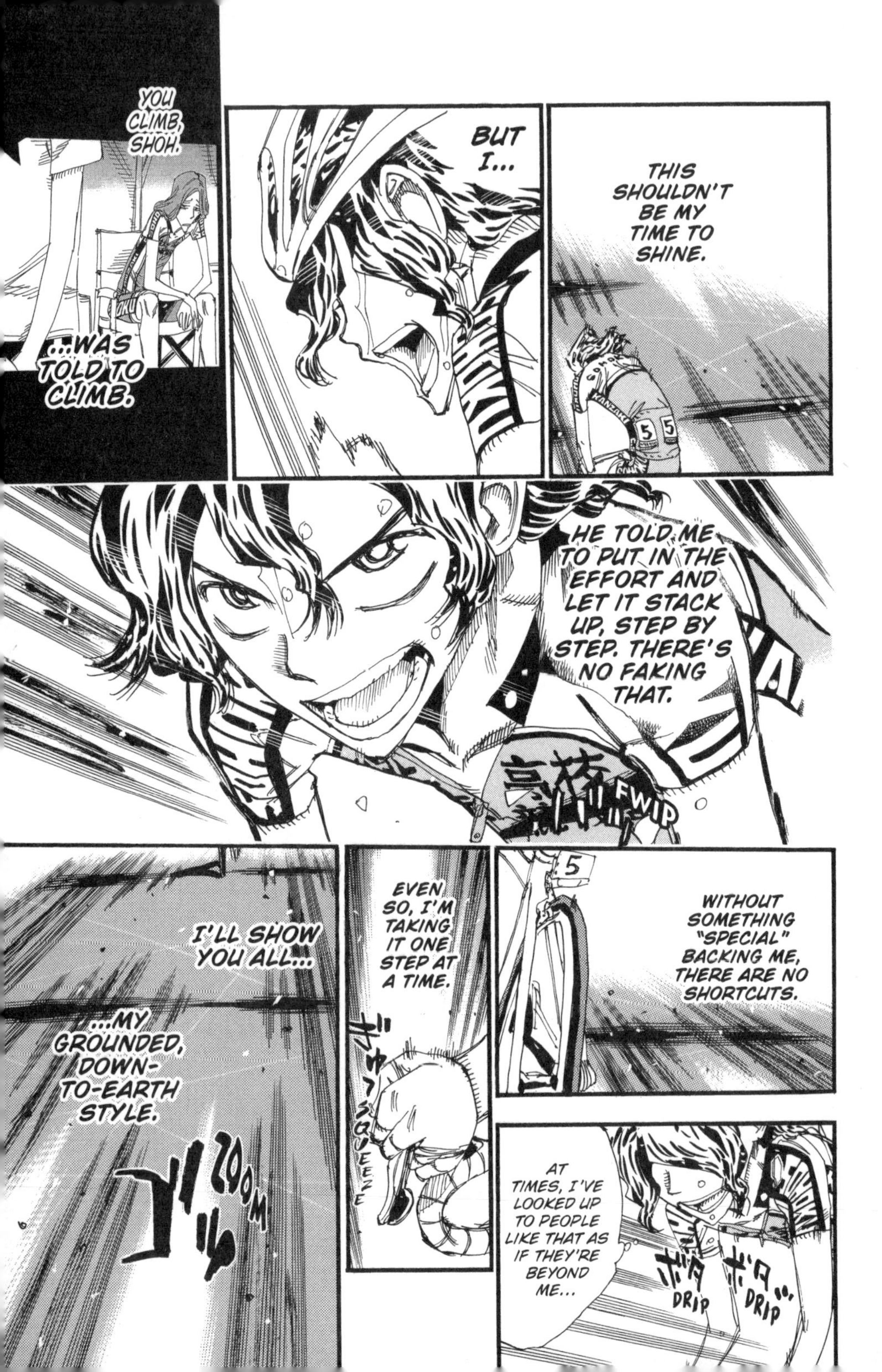
THIS SHOULDN'T BE MY TIME TO SHINE.
BUT I...
YOU CLIMB, SHOH.
...WAS TOLD TO CLIMB.
HE TOLD ME TO PUT IN THE EFFORT AND LET IT STACK UP, STEP BY STEP. THERE'S NO FAKING THAT.
FWIP
WITHOUT SOMETHING "SPECIAL" BACKING ME, THERE ARE NO SHORTCUTS.
AT TIMES, I'VE LOOKED UP TO PEOPLE LIKE THAT AS IF THEY'RE BEYOND ME...
DRIP
DRIP
EVEN SO, I'M TAKING IT ONE STEP AT A TIME.
SQUEEZE
I'LL SHOW YOU ALL...
...MY GROUNDED, DOWN-TO-EARTH STYLE.
ZOOM

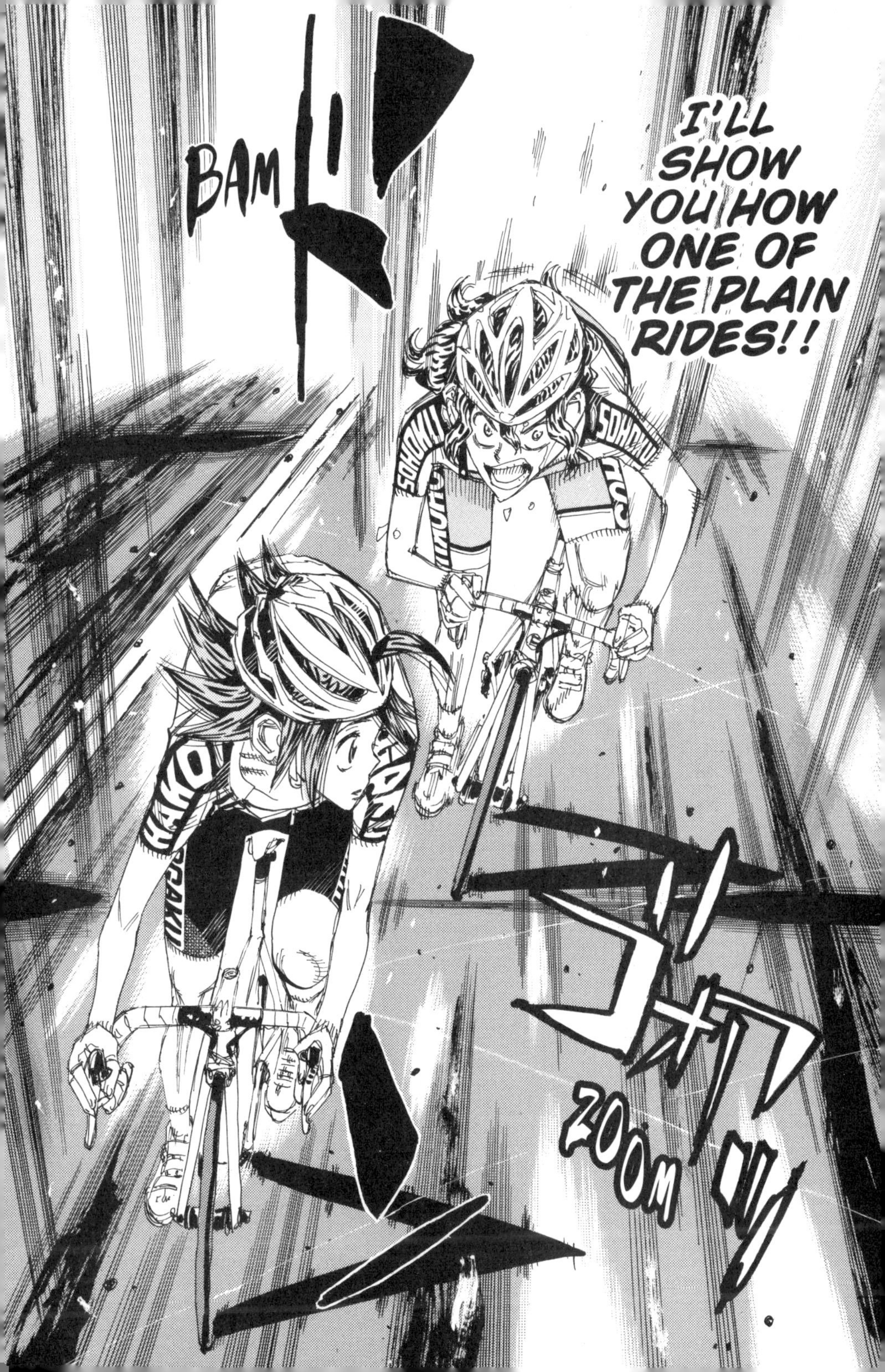
I'LL SHOW YOU HOW ONE OF THE PLAIN RIDES!!
BAM
ZOOM

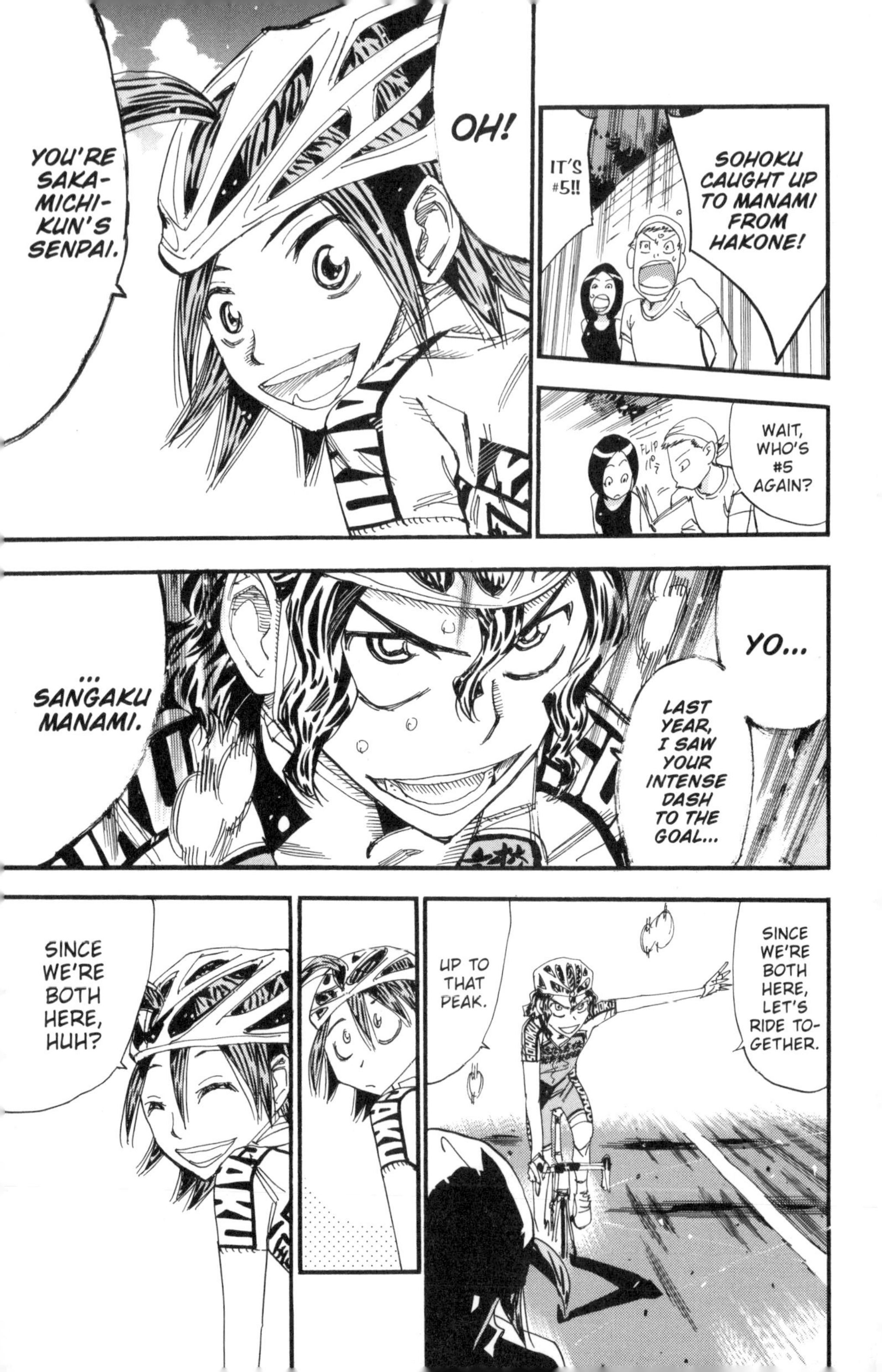
SOHOKU CAUGHT UP TO MANAMI FROM HAKONE!
IT'S #5!!
WAIT, WHO'S #5 AGAIN?
FLIP
OH!
YOU'RE SAKA-MICHI-KUN'S SENPAI.
YO...
LAST YEAR, I SAW YOUR INTENSE DASH TO THE GOAL...
...SANGAKU MANAMI.
SINCE WE'RE BOTH HERE, LET'S RIDE TO-GETHER.
UP TO THAT PEAK.
SINCE WE'RE BOTH HERE, HUH?

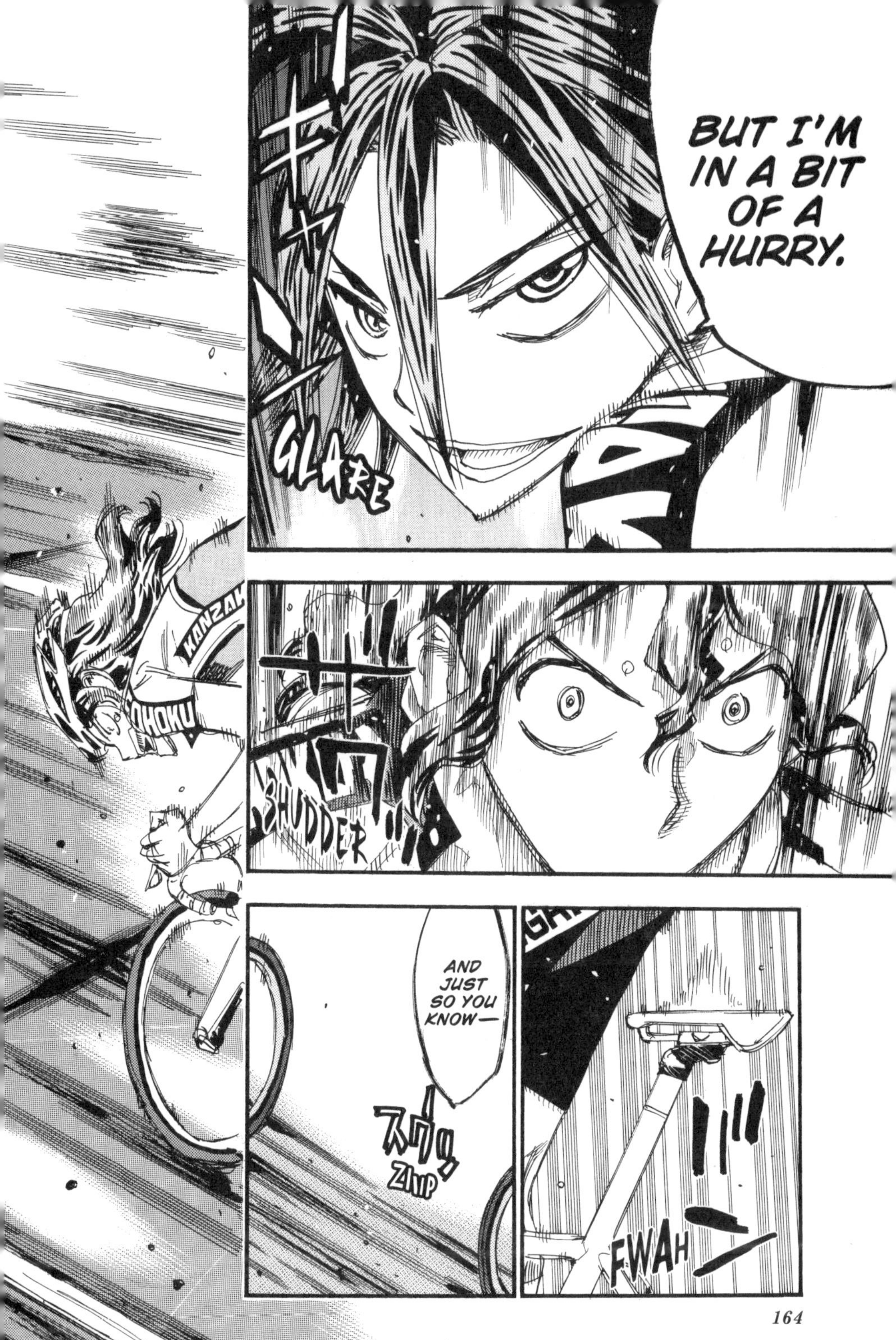
BUT I'M IN A BIT OF A HURRY.
GLARE
SHUDDER
FWAH
AND JUST SO YOU KNOW—
ZIP

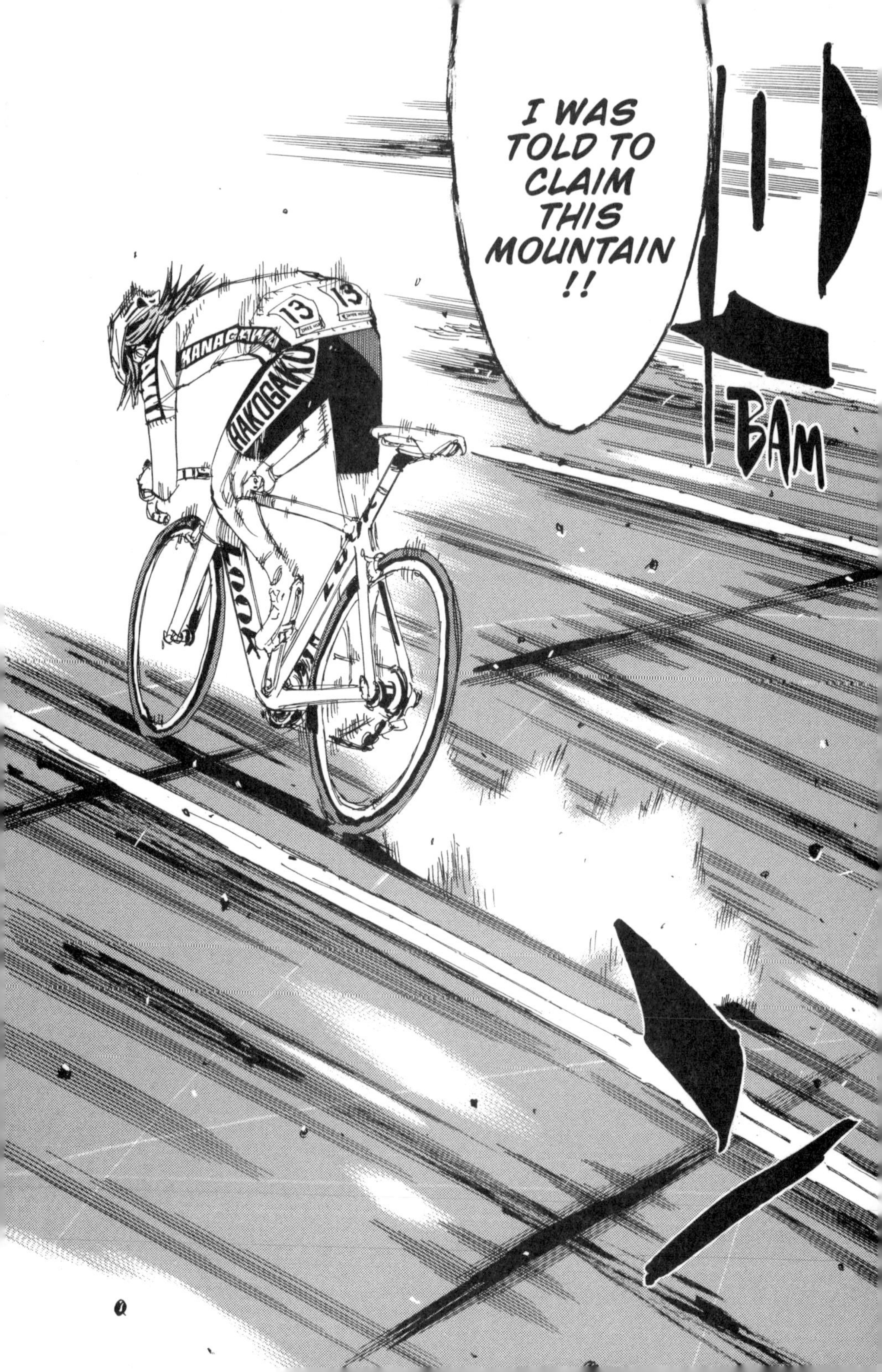
I WAS TOLD TO CLAIM THIS MOUNTAIN!!
BAM

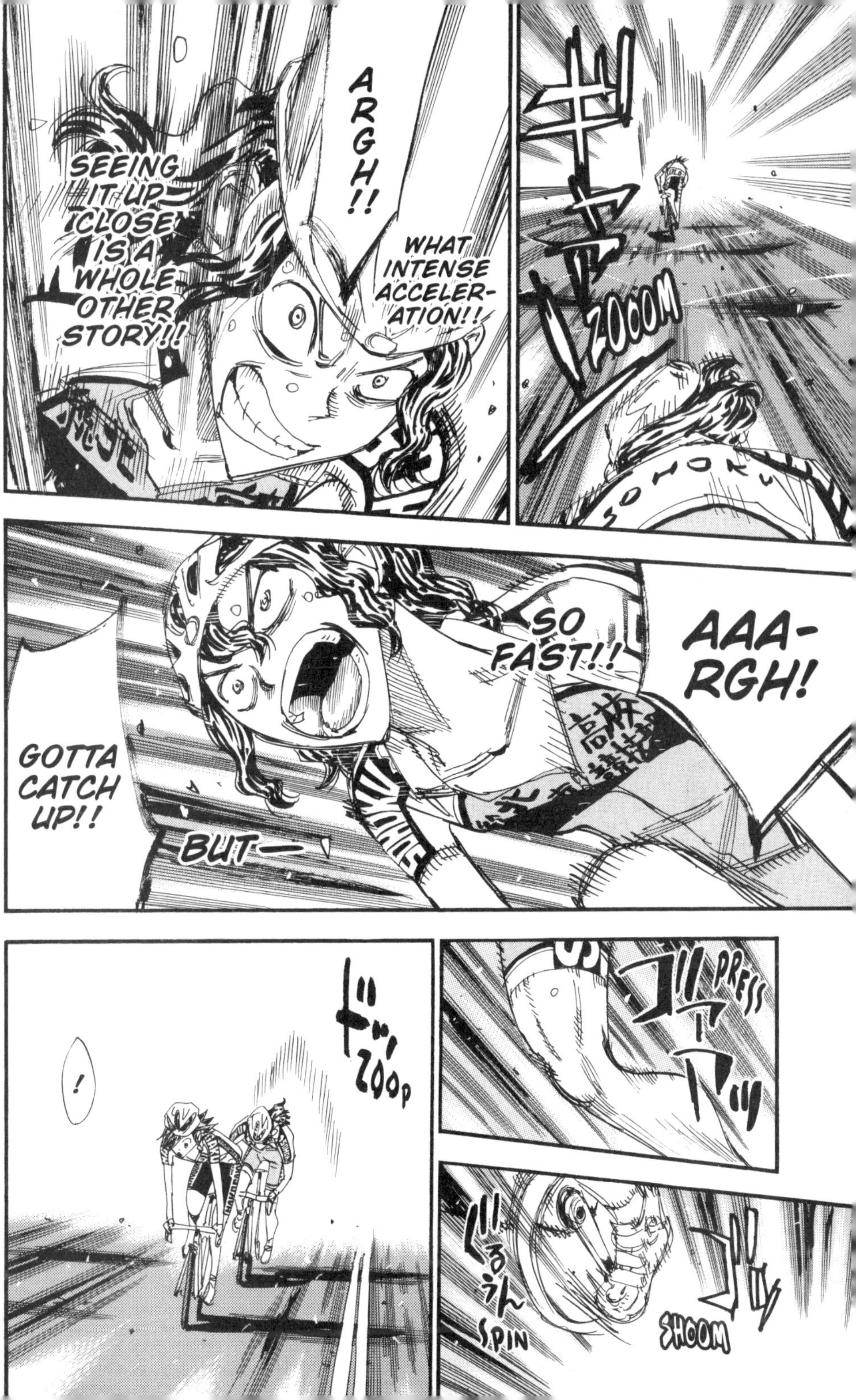
ZOOOM
ARGH!!
WHAT INTENSE ACCELER-ATION!!
SEEING IT UP CLOSE IS A WHOLE OTHER STORY!!
AAA-RGH!
SO FAST!!
GOTTA CATCH UP!!
BUT—
PRESS
SHOOM
SPIN
ZOOP
!

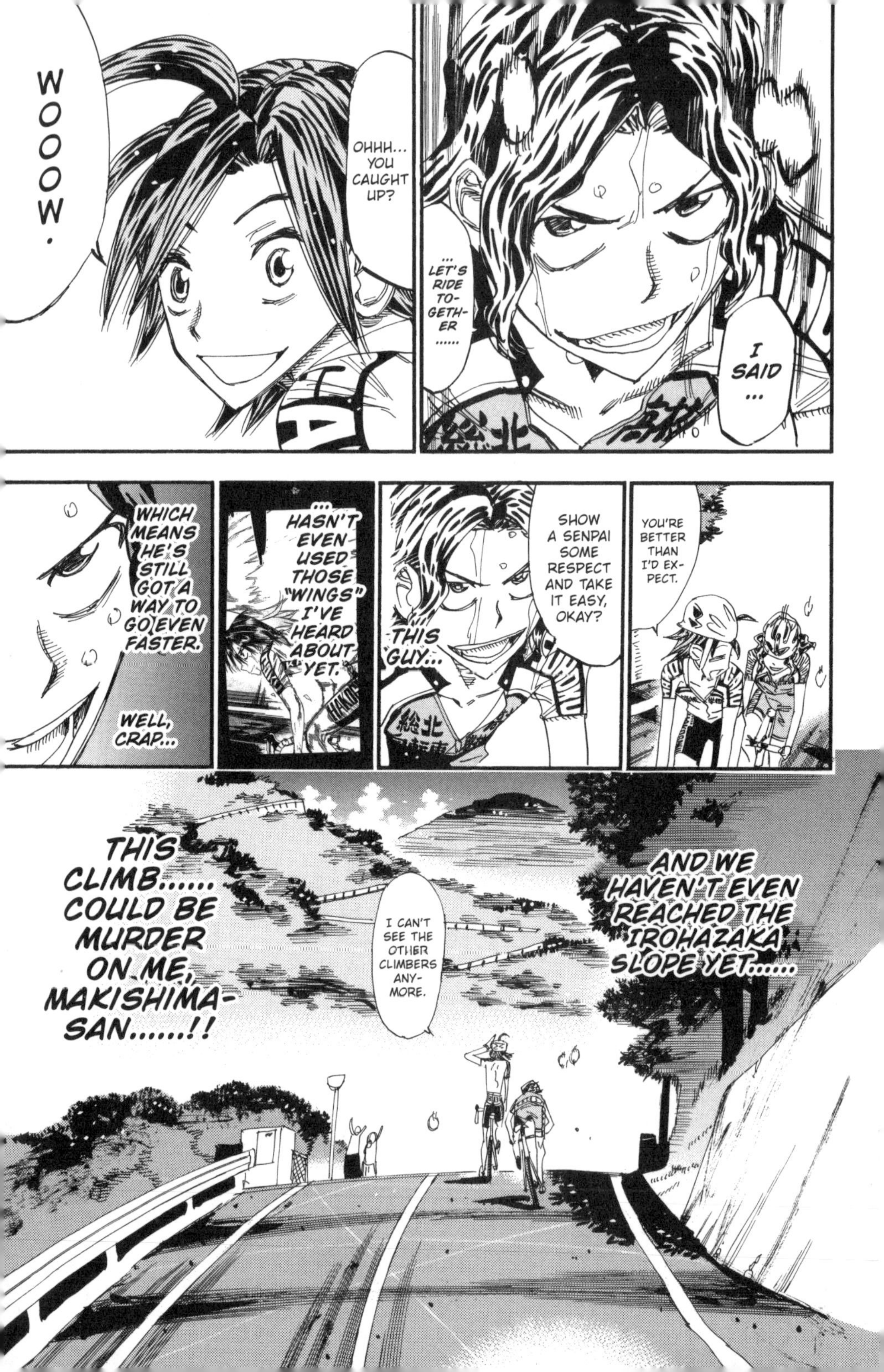
I SAID ...
... LET'S RIDE TO-GETH-ER ......
OHHH... YOU CAUGHT UP?
WOOOOW.
YOU'RE BETTER THAN I'D EX-PECT.
SHOW A SENPAI SOME RESPECT AND TAKE IT EASY, OKAY?
THIS GUY...
... HASN'T EVEN USED THOSE "WINGS" I'VE HEARD ABOUT YET.
WHICH MEANS HE'S STILL GOT A WAY TO GO EVEN FASTER.
WELL, CRAP...
AND WE HAVEN'T EVEN REACHED THE IROHAZAKA SLOPE YET......
I CAN'T SEE THE OTHER CLIMBERS ANY-MORE.
THIS CLIMB...... COULD BE MURDER ON ME, MAKISHIMA-SAN......!!

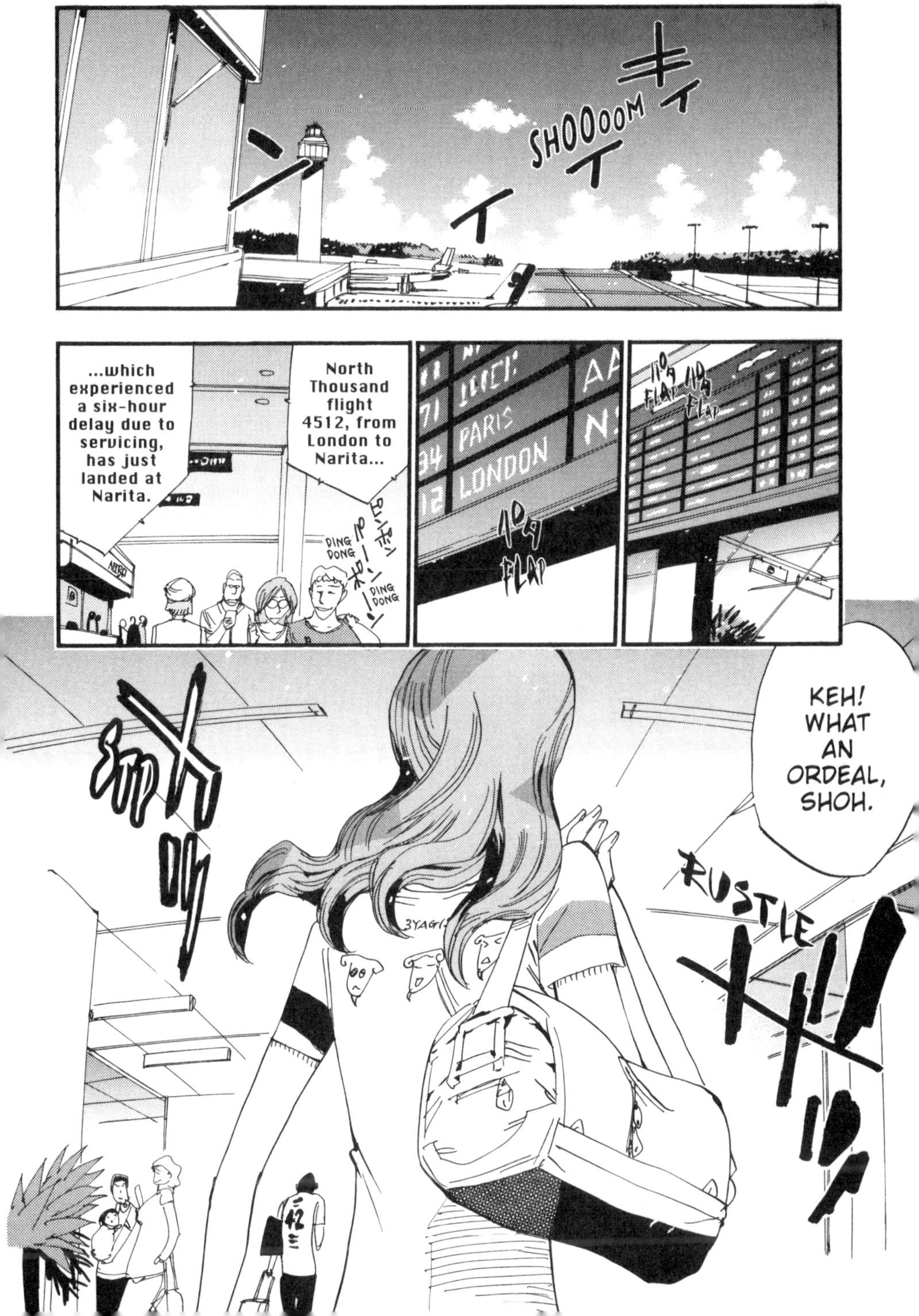
SHOOoom
FLAP FLAP
PARIS
LONDON
FLAP
North Thousand flight 4512, from London to Narita...
...which experienced a six-hour delay due to servicing, has just landed at Narita.
DING DONG
DING DONG
KEH! WHAT AN ORDEAL, SHOH.
RUSTLE

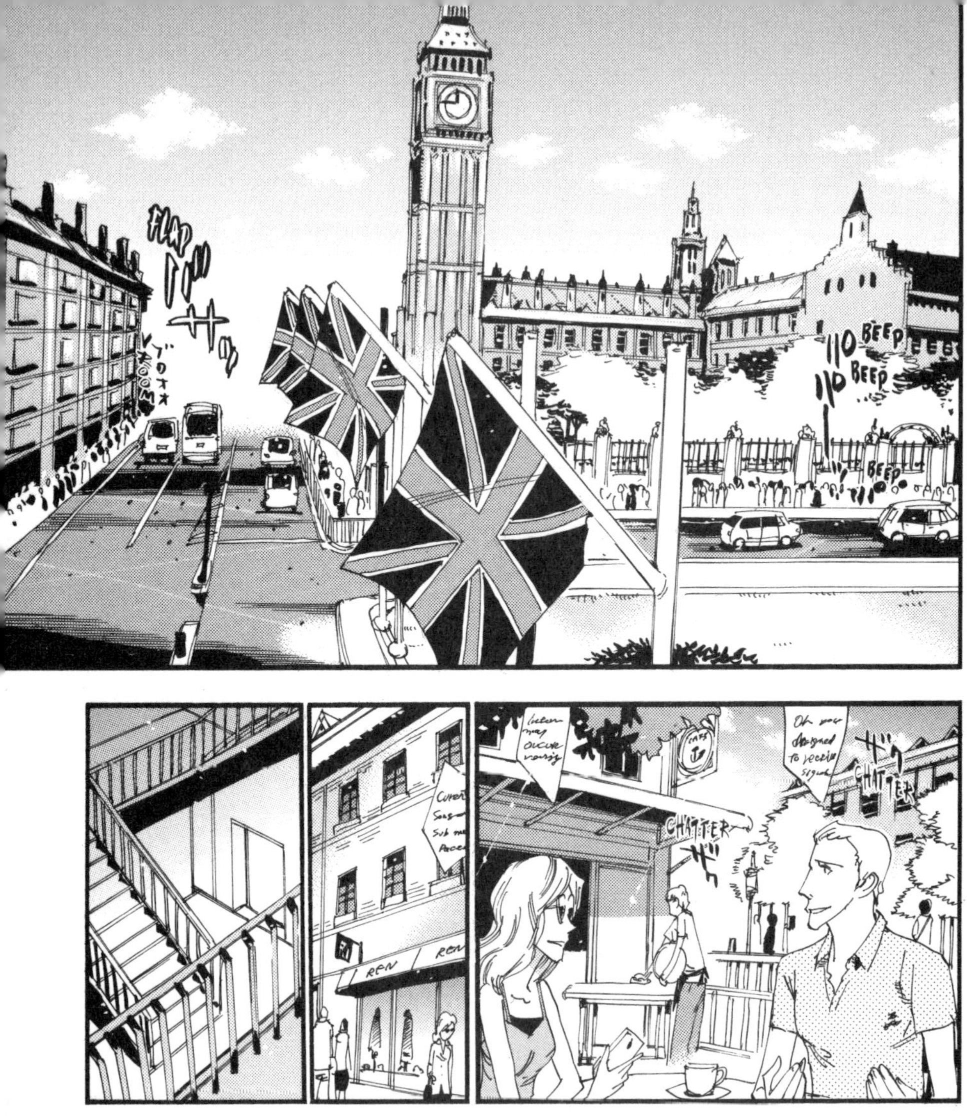
BEEP
BEEP
BEEP
FLAP
ROOM
CHATTER
CHATTER
REN
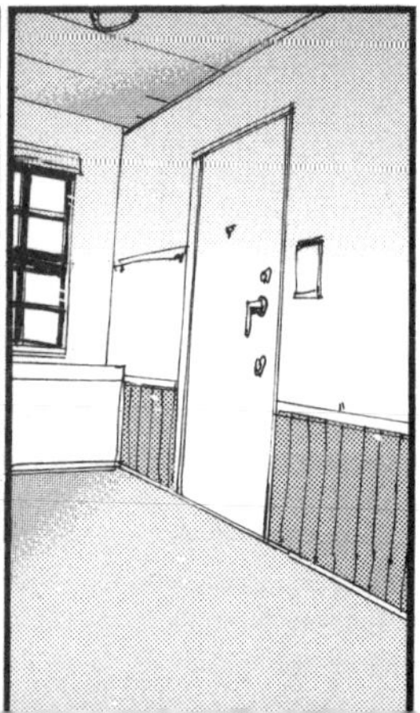
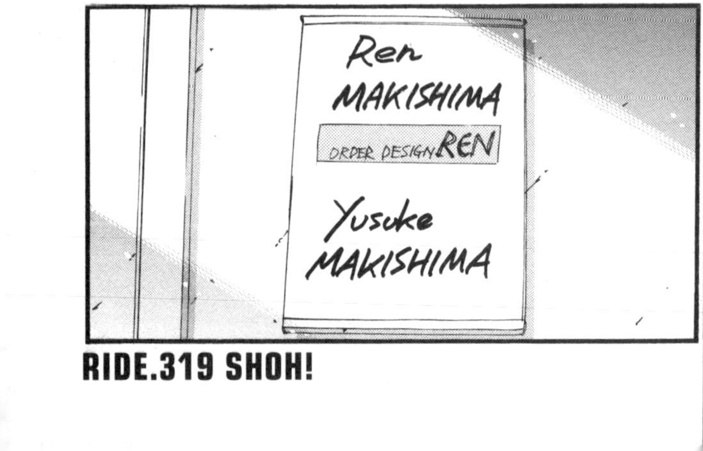
Ren
MAKISHIMA
ORDER DESIGN REN
Yusuke
MAKISHIMA

RIDE.319 SHOH!

RIDE.319 SHOH!

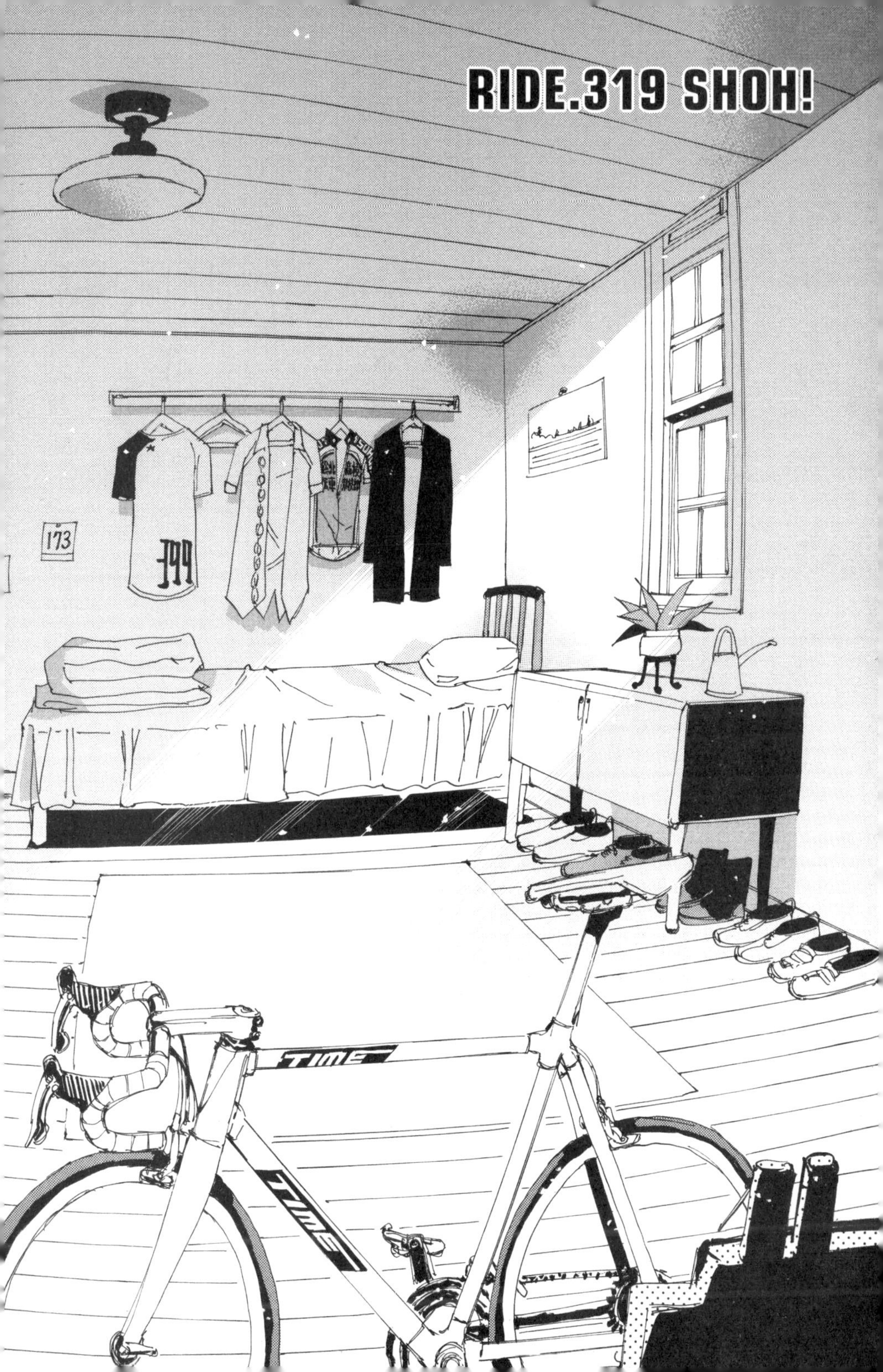
173
TIME
TIME

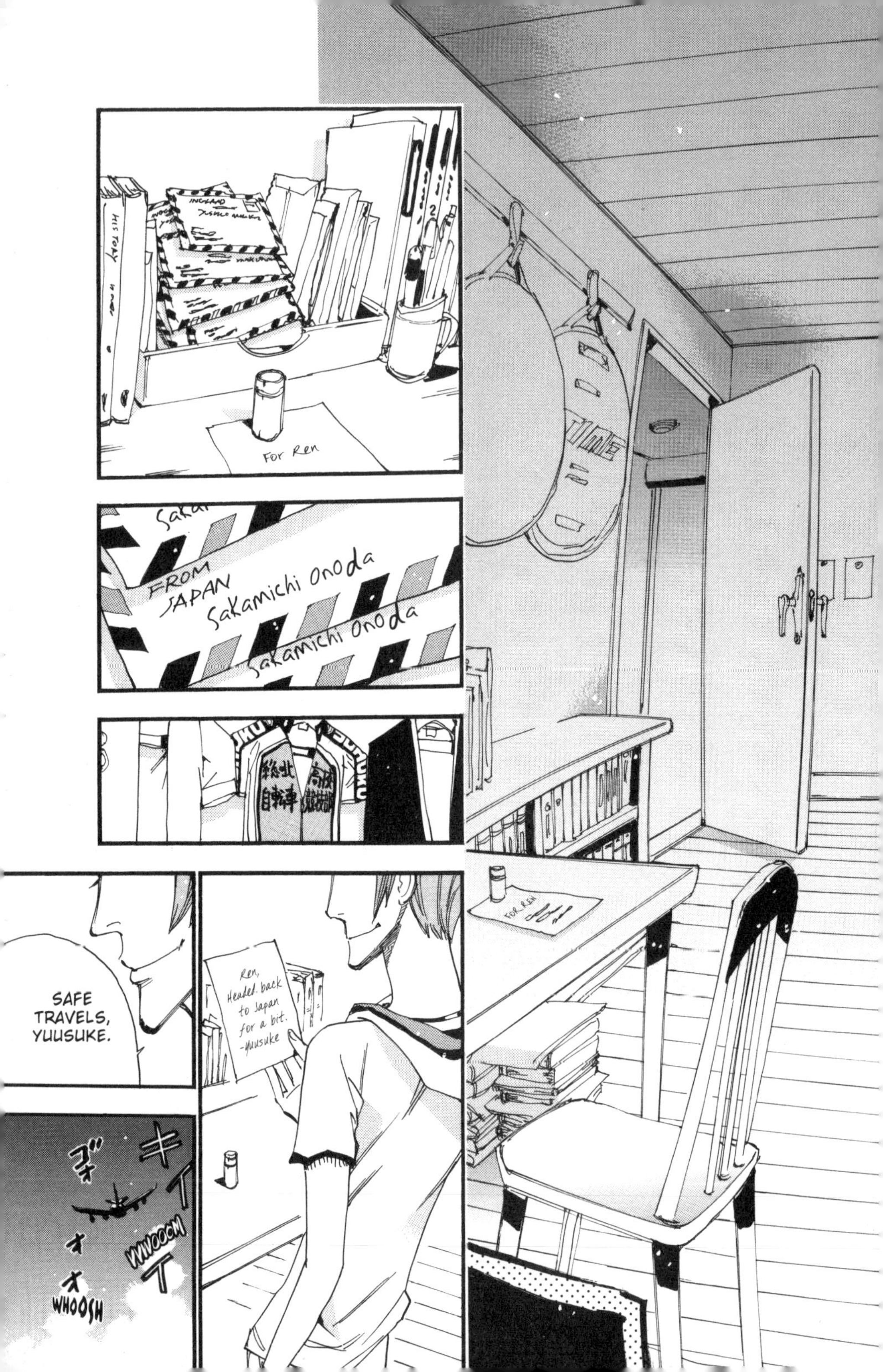
FOR REN
HISTORY
For Ren
FROM JAPAN
Sakamichi Onoda
Sakamichi Onoda
総北高校自転車競技部
Ren, Headed back to Japan for a bit. -Yuusuke
SAFE TRAVELS, YUUSUKE.
キイイ
VWOOOM
ゴオオ
WHOOSH

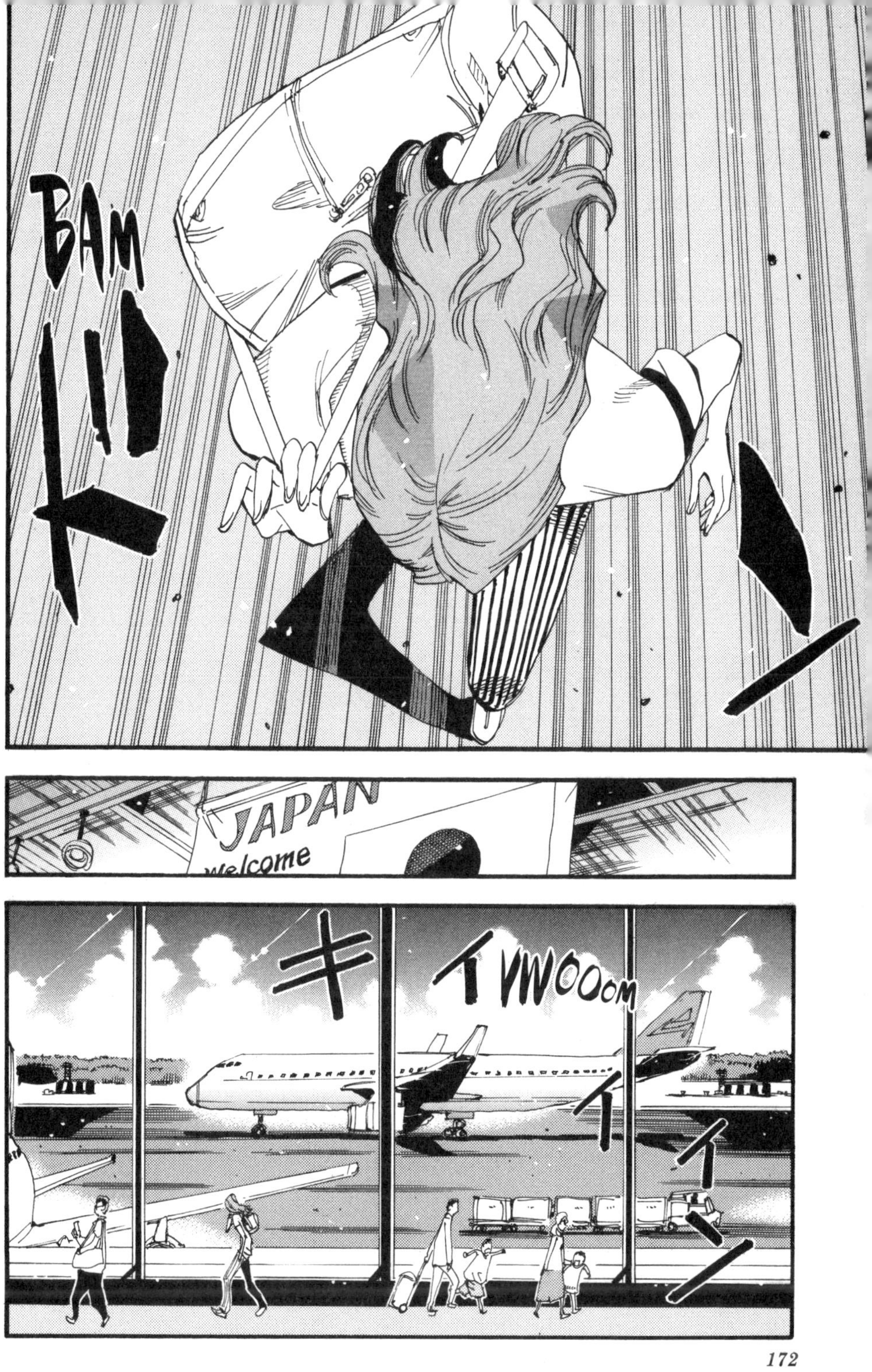
BAM
JAPAN
Welcome
VWOOOM

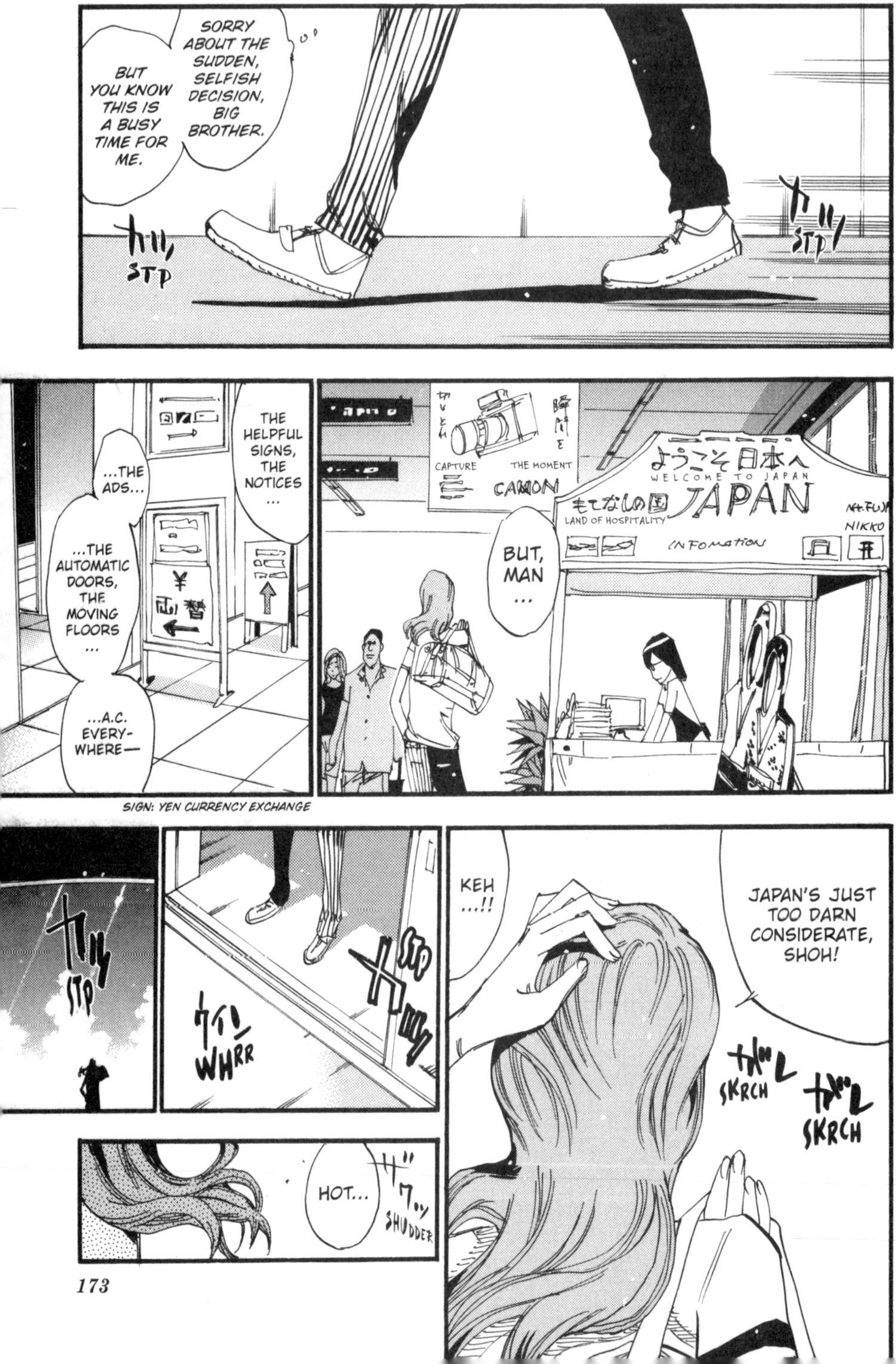
SORRY ABOUT THE SUDDEN, SELFISH DECISION, BIG BROTHER.
BUT YOU KNOW THIS IS A BUSY TIME FOR ME.
STP
STP
CAPTURE THE MOMENT
CAMON
ようこそ日本へ
WELCOME TO JAPAN
もてなしの国
LAND OF HOSPITALITY
JAPAN
Mt.FUJI
NIKKO
INFOMATION
BUT, MAN...
THE HELPFUL SIGNS, THE NOTICES...
...THE ADS...
...THE AUTOMATIC DOORS, THE MOVING FLOORS...
...A.C. EVERYWHERE—
SIGN: YEN CURRENCY EXCHANGE
JAPAN'S JUST TOO DARN CONSIDERATE, SHOH!
KEH...!!
SKRCH
SKRCH
STP
WHRR
STP
HOT...
SHUDDER

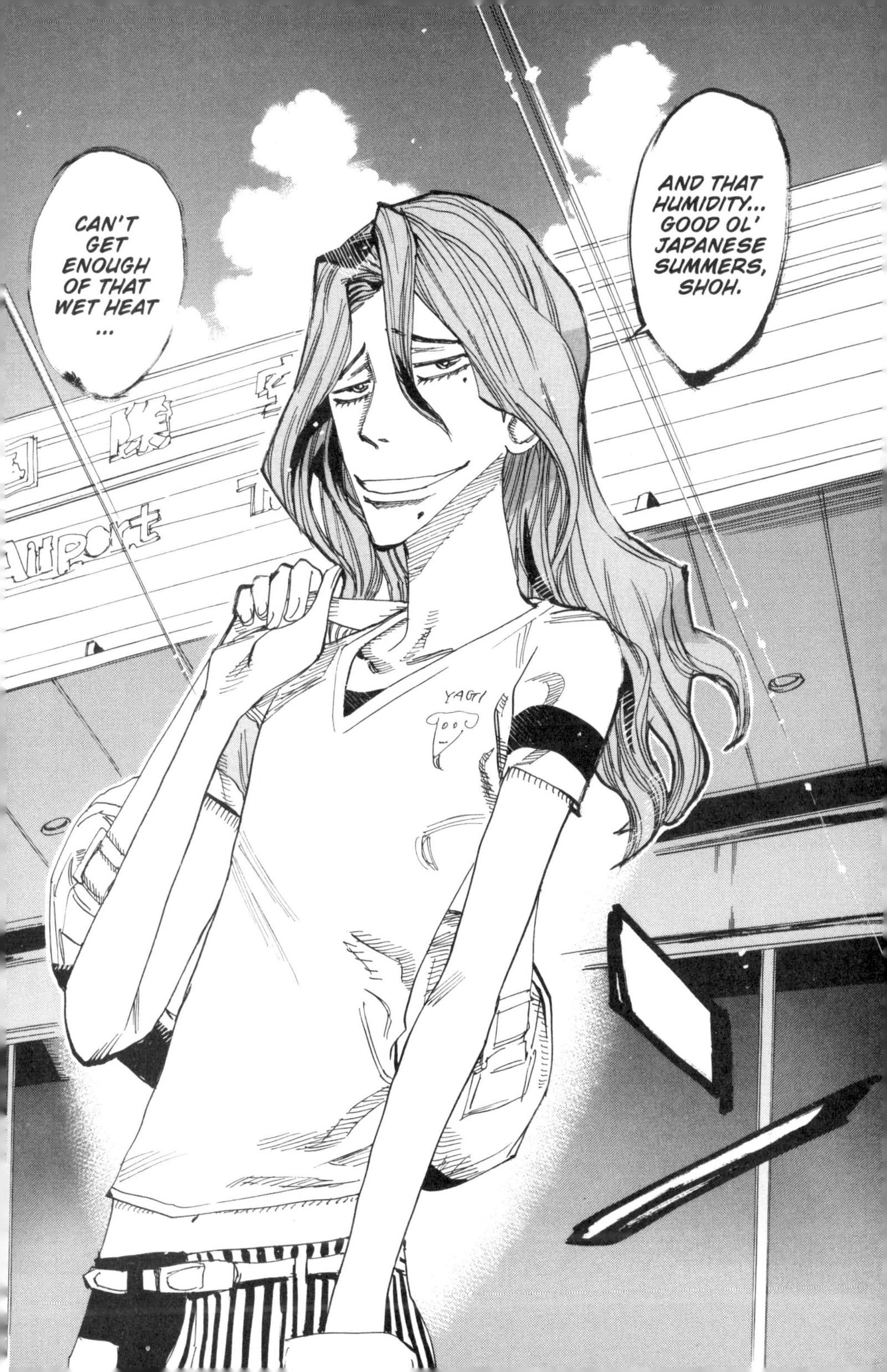
AND THAT HUMIDITY... GOOD OL' JAPANESE SUMMERS, SHOH.
CAN'T GET ENOUGH OF THAT WET HEAT ...
YAGI

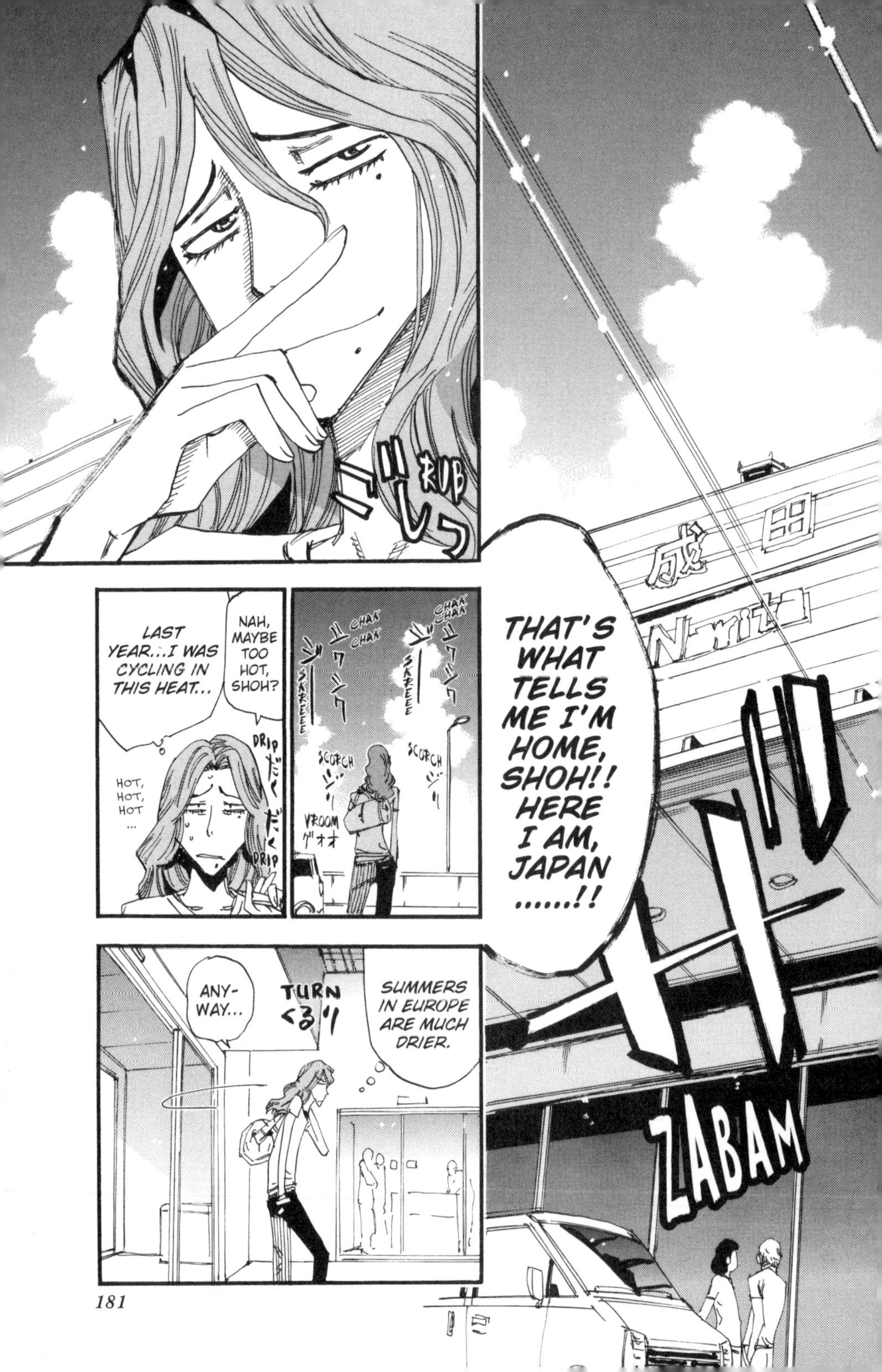
THAT'S WHAT TELLS ME I'M HOME, SHOH!! HERE I AM, JAPAN......!!
ZABAM
RUB
ゴシッ
CHAK CHAK
CHAK
SKREEE
SCORCH
SCORCH
VROOM
NAH, MAYBE TOO HOT, SHOH?
LAST YEAR...I WAS CYCLING IN THIS HEAT...
DRIP
DRIP
HOT, HOT, HOT ...
SUMMERS IN EUROPE ARE MUCH DRIER.
TURN
くるり
ANY-WAY...

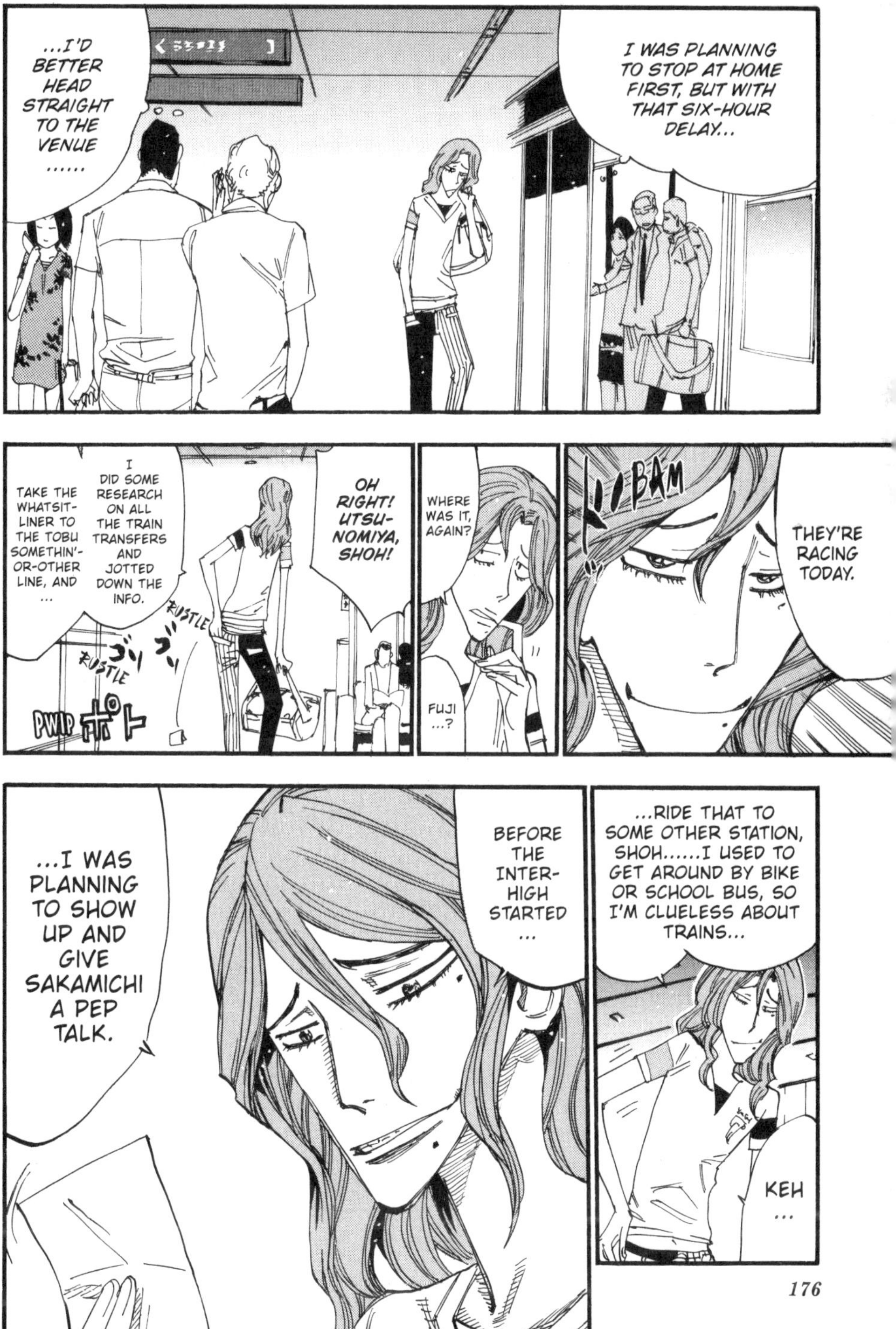
I WAS PLANNING TO STOP AT HOME FIRST, BUT WITH THAT SIX-HOUR DELAY...
...I'D BETTER HEAD STRAIGHT TO THE VENUE ......
BAM
THEY'RE RACING TODAY.
WHERE WAS IT, AGAIN?
FUJI ...?
OH RIGHT! UTSU-NOMIYA, SHOH!
I DID SOME RESEARCH ON ALL THE TRAIN TRANSFERS AND JOTTED DOWN THE INFO.
TAKE THE WHATSIT-LINER TO THE TOBU SOMETHIN'-OR-OTHER LINE, AND ...
RUSTLE
RUSTLE
PWIP
...RIDE THAT TO SOME OTHER STATION, SHOH......I USED TO GET AROUND BY BIKE OR SCHOOL BUS, SO I'M CLUELESS ABOUT TRAINS...
KEH ...
BEFORE THE INTER-HIGH STARTED ...
...I WAS PLANNING TO SHOW UP AND GIVE SAKAMICHI A PEP TALK.

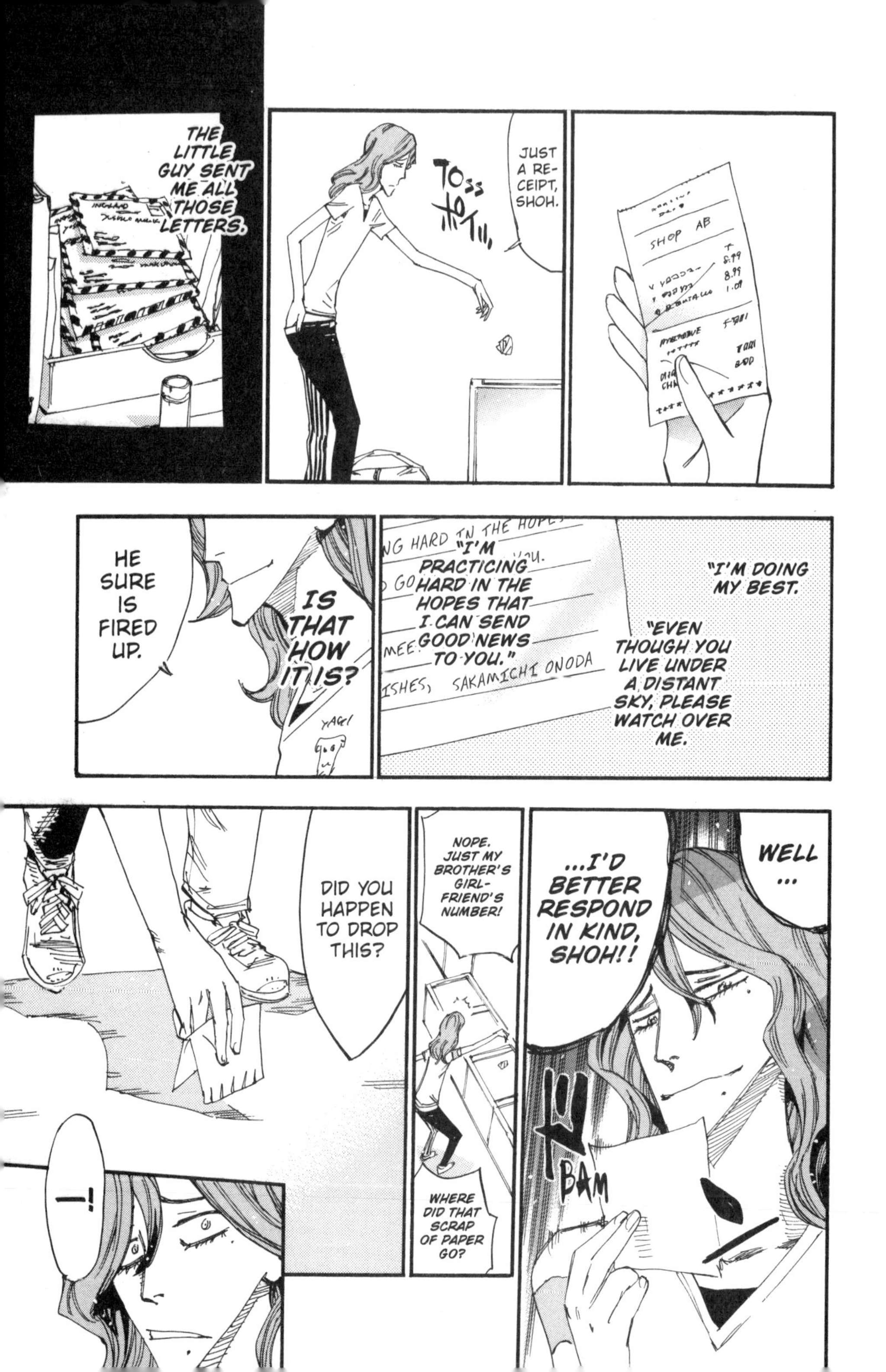
SHOP AB
JUST A RE-CEIPT, SHOH.
TOSS
THE LITTLE GUY SENT ME ALL THOSE LETTERS.
"I'M DOING MY BEST.
"EVEN THOUGH YOU LIVE UNDER A DISTANT SKY, PLEASE WATCH OVER ME.
"I'M PRACTICING HARD IN THE HOPES THAT I CAN SEND GOOD NEWS TO YOU."
SAKAMICHI ONODA
IS THAT HOW IT IS?
HE SURE IS FIRED UP.
WELL ...
...I'D BETTER RESPOND IN KIND, SHOH!!
BAM
NOPE. JUST MY BROTHER'S GIRL-FRIEND'S NUMBER!
WHERE DID THAT SCRAP OF PAPER GO?
DID YOU HAPPEN TO DROP THIS?
—!

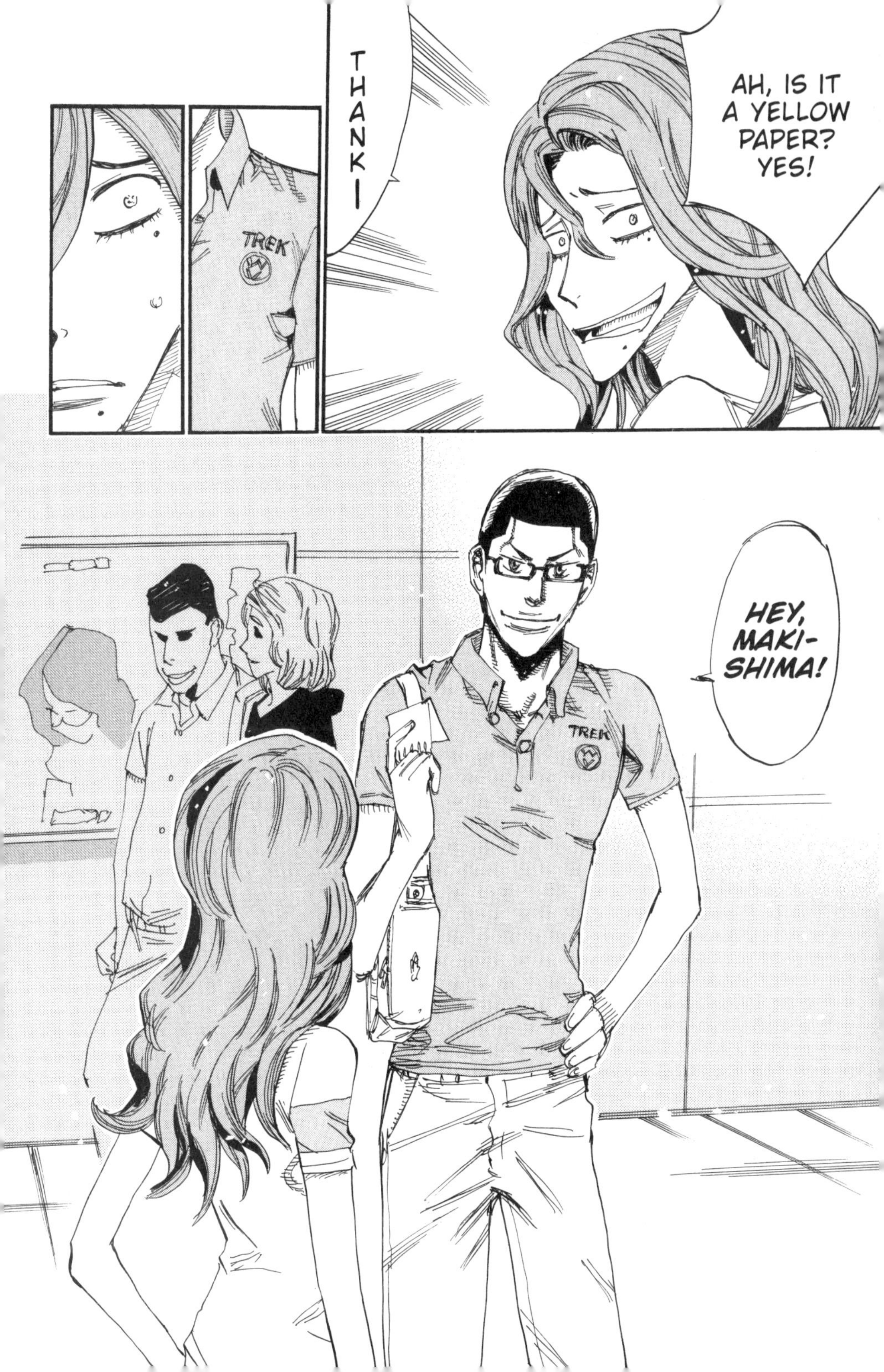
AH, IS IT A YELLOW PAPER? YES!
THANK—
TREK
TREK
HEY, MAKI-SHIMA!

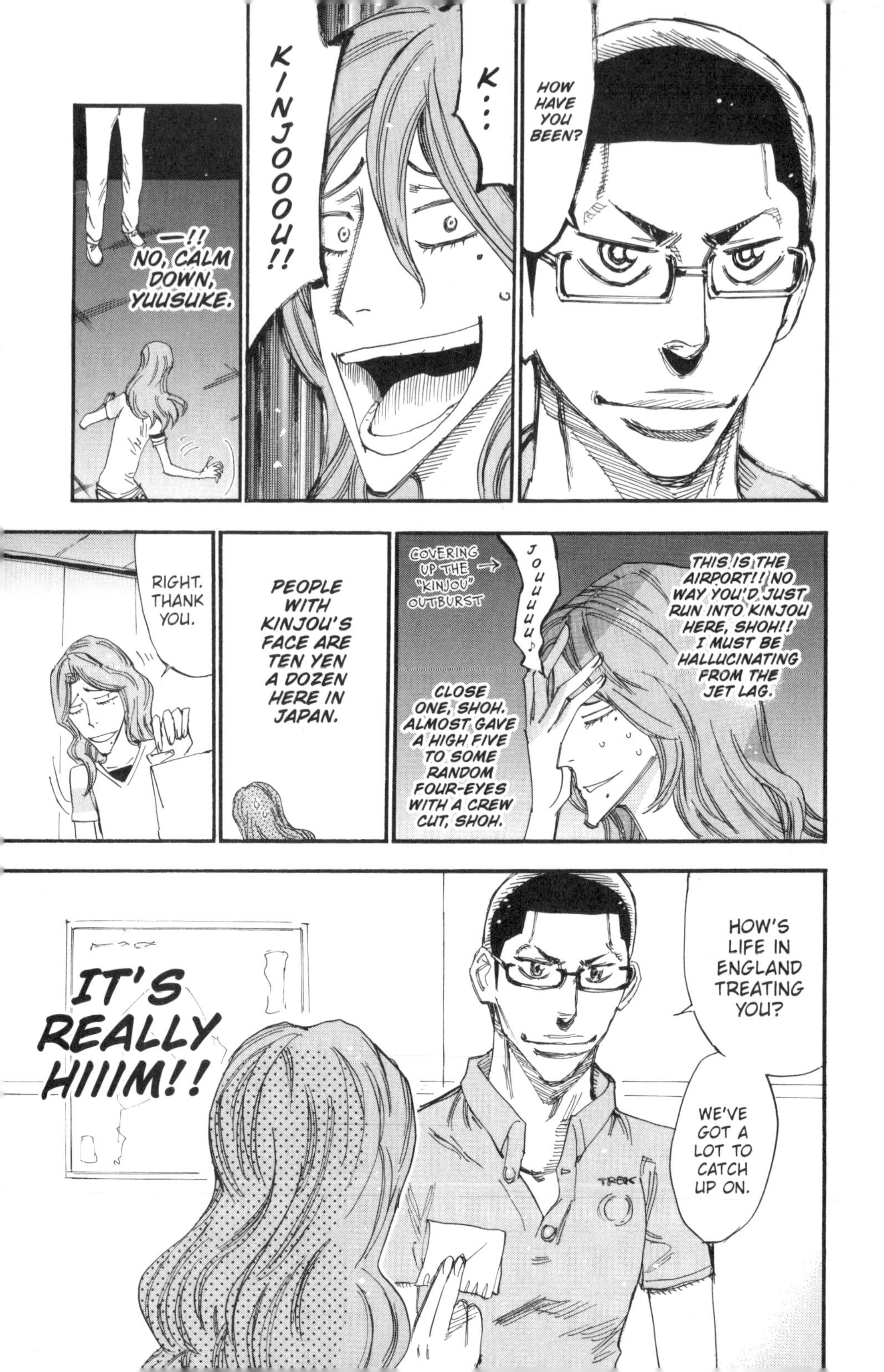
HOW HAVE YOU BEEN?
K...
KINJOOOOU!!
—!! NO, CALM DOWN, YUUSUKE.
THIS IS THE AIRPORT!! NO WAY YOU'D JUST RUN INTO KINJOU HERE, SHOH!! I MUST BE HALLUCINATING FROM THE JET LAG.
Jouuuuu♪
COVERING UP THE "KINJOU" OUTBURST →
CLOSE ONE, SHOH. ALMOST GAVE A HIGH FIVE TO SOME RANDOM FOUR-EYES WITH A CREW CUT, SHOH.
PEOPLE WITH KINJOU'S FACE ARE TEN YEN A DOZEN HERE IN JAPAN.
RIGHT. THANK YOU.
HOW'S LIFE IN ENGLAND TREATING YOU?
WE'VE GOT A LOT TO CATCH UP ON.
IT'S REALLY HIIIM!!

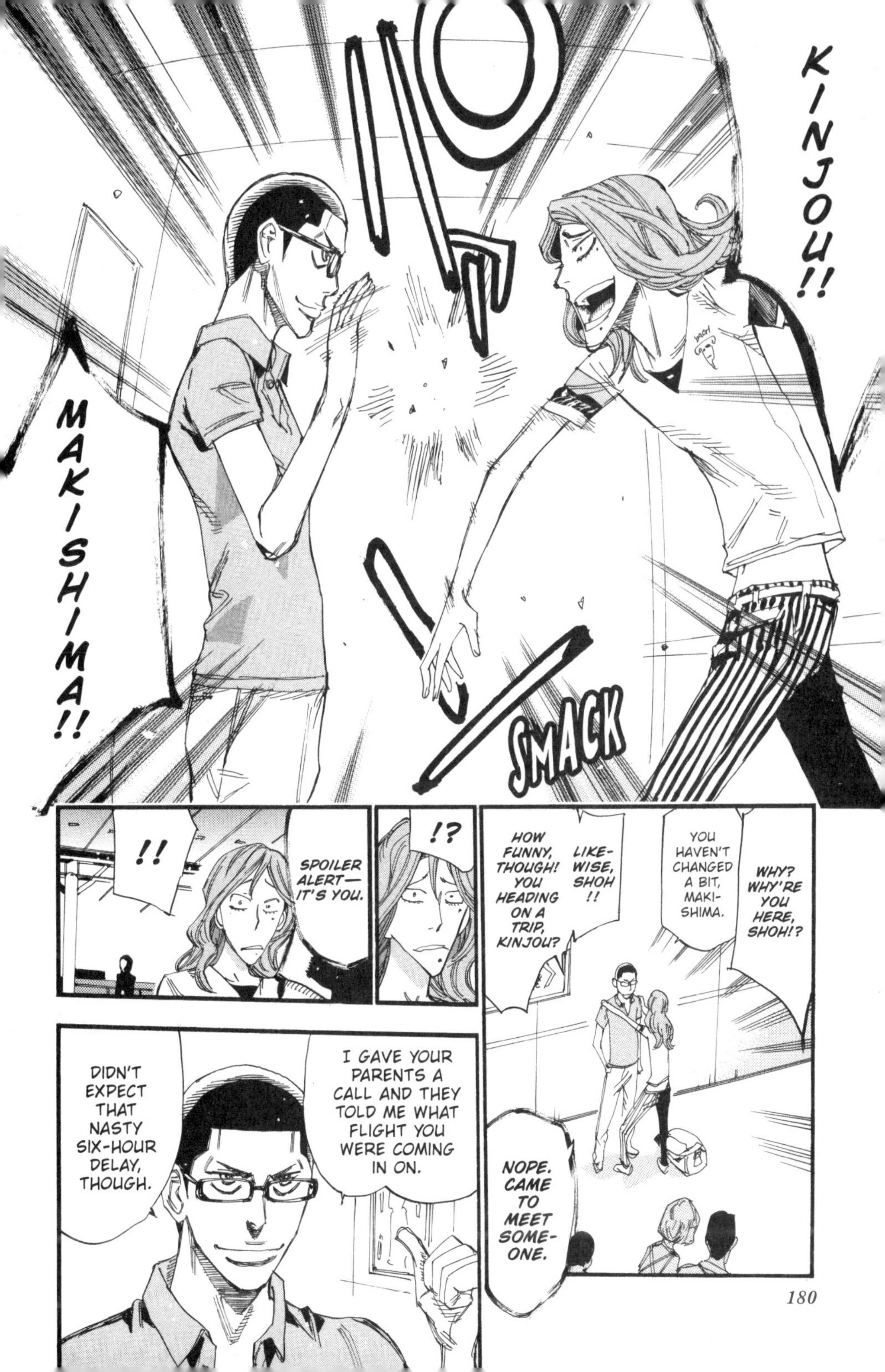
KINJOU!!
MAKISHIMA!!
SMACK
WHY? WHY'RE YOU HERE, SHOH!?
YOU HAVEN'T CHANGED A BIT, MAKI-SHIMA.
LIKE-WISE, SHOH!!
HOW FUNNY, THOUGH! YOU HEADING ON A TRIP, KINJOU?
NOPE. CAME TO MEET SOME-ONE.
!?
SPOILER ALERT—IT'S YOU.
!!
I GAVE YOUR PARENTS A CALL AND THEY TOLD ME WHAT FLIGHT YOU WERE COMING IN ON.
DIDN'T EXPECT THAT NASTY SIX-HOUR DELAY, THOUGH.

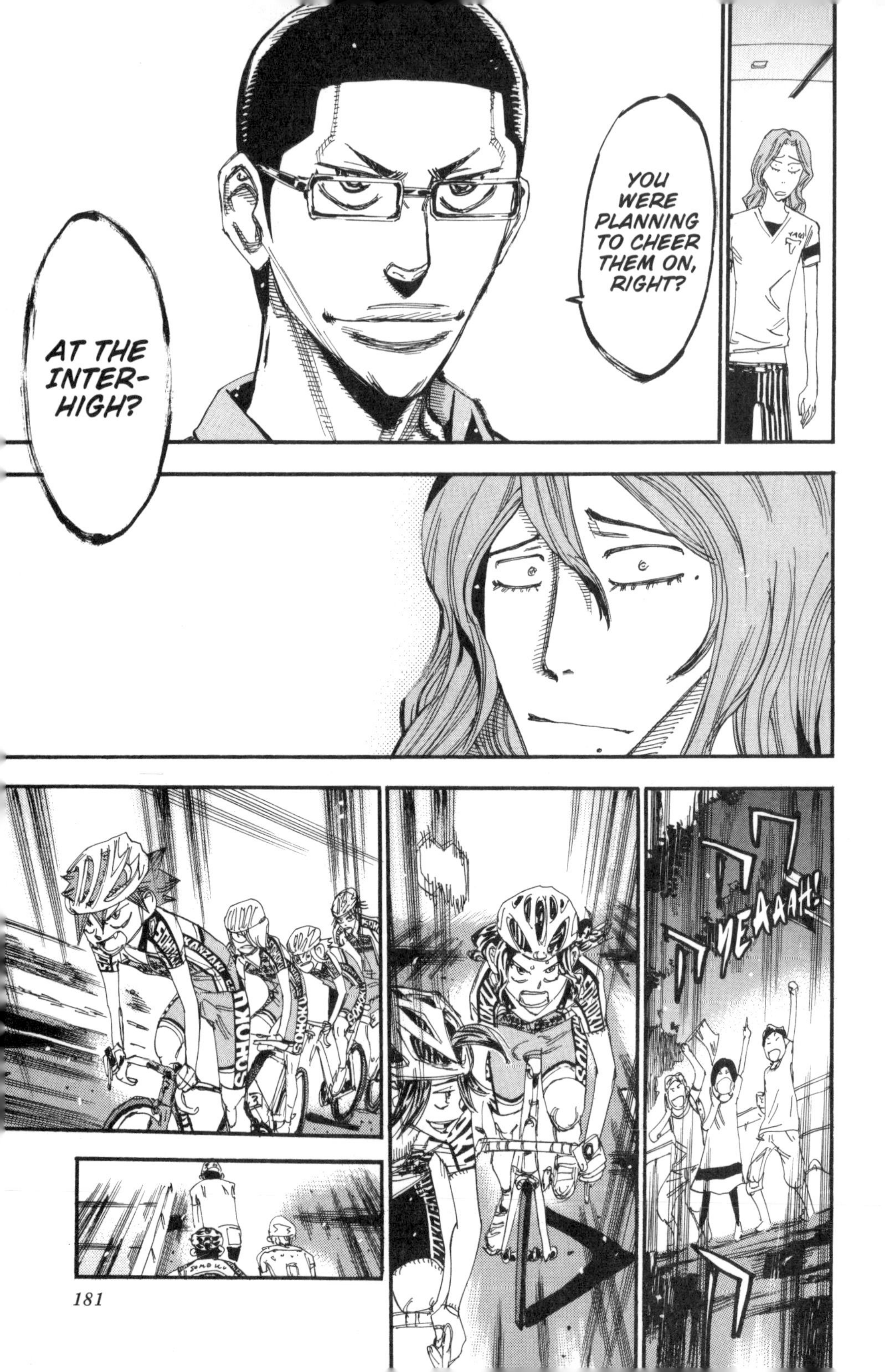
YOU WERE PLANNING TO CHEER THEM ON, RIGHT?
AT THE INTER-HIGH?
YEAAAH!

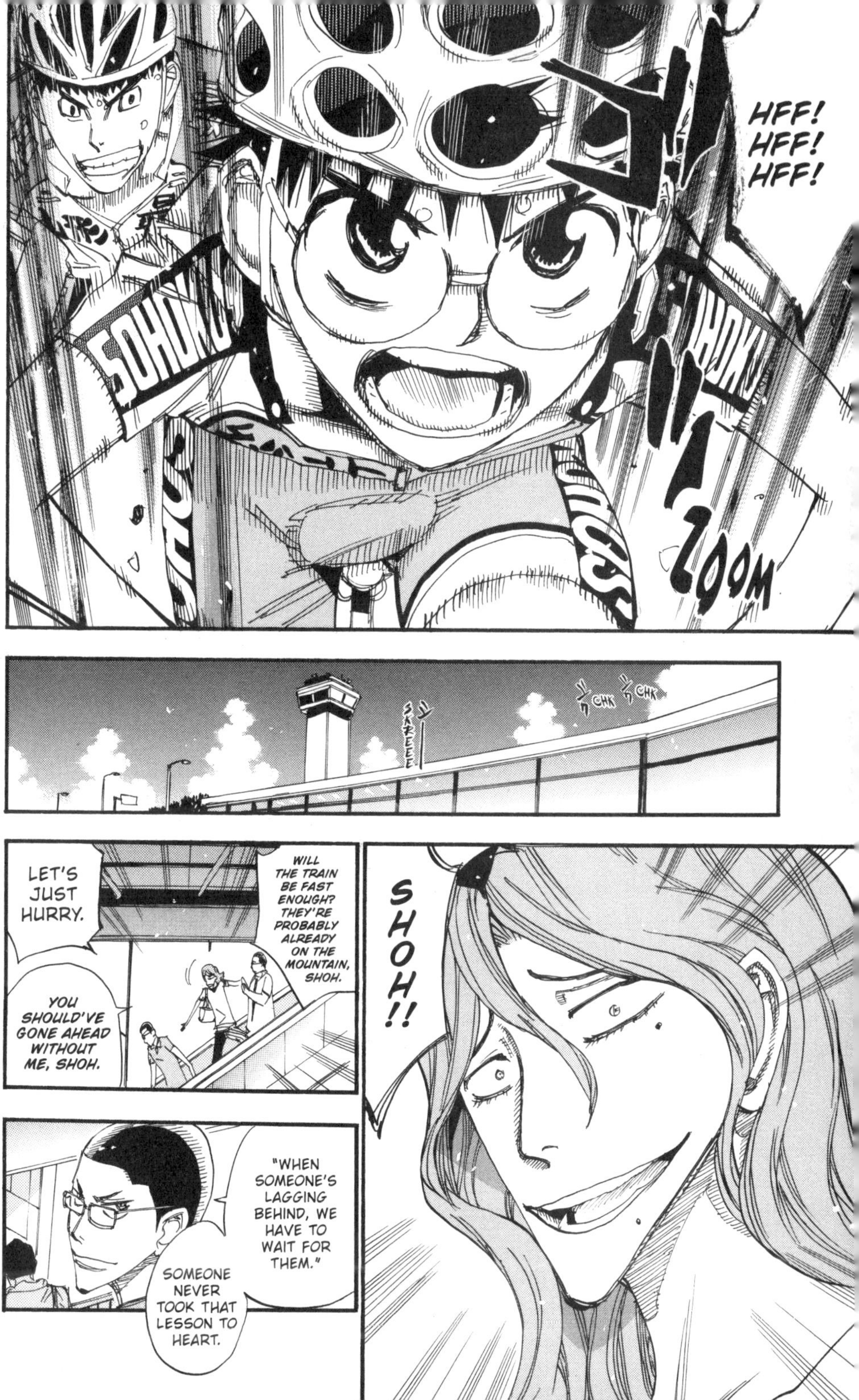
HFF! HFF! HFF!
ZOOM
SKREEE
CHK CHK
SHOH!!
WILL THE TRAIN BE FAST ENOUGH? THEY'RE PROBABLY ALREADY ON THE MOUNTAIN, SHOH.
LET'S JUST HURRY.
YOU SHOULD'VE GONE AHEAD WITHOUT ME, SHOH.
"WHEN SOMEONE'S LAGGING BEHIND, WE HAVE TO WAIT FOR THEM."
SOMEONE NEVER TOOK THAT LESSON TO HEART.

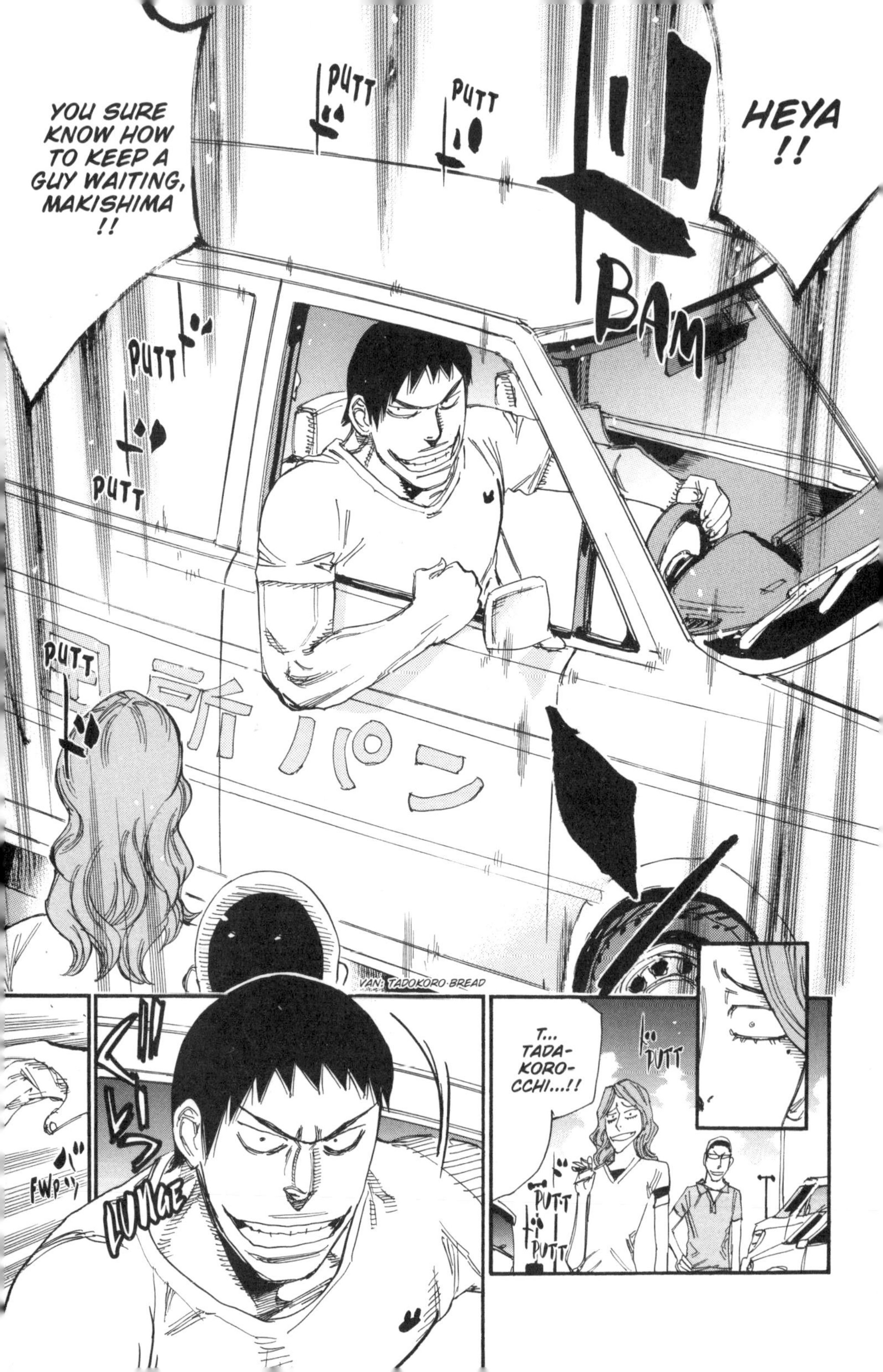
HEYA !!
BAM
PUTT
PUTT
YOU SURE KNOW HOW TO KEEP A GUY WAITING, MAKISHIMA !!
PUTT
PUTT
PUTT
VAN: TADOKORO BREAD
PUTT
T... TADA-KORO-CCHI...!!
PUTT
PUTT
LUNGE
FWP

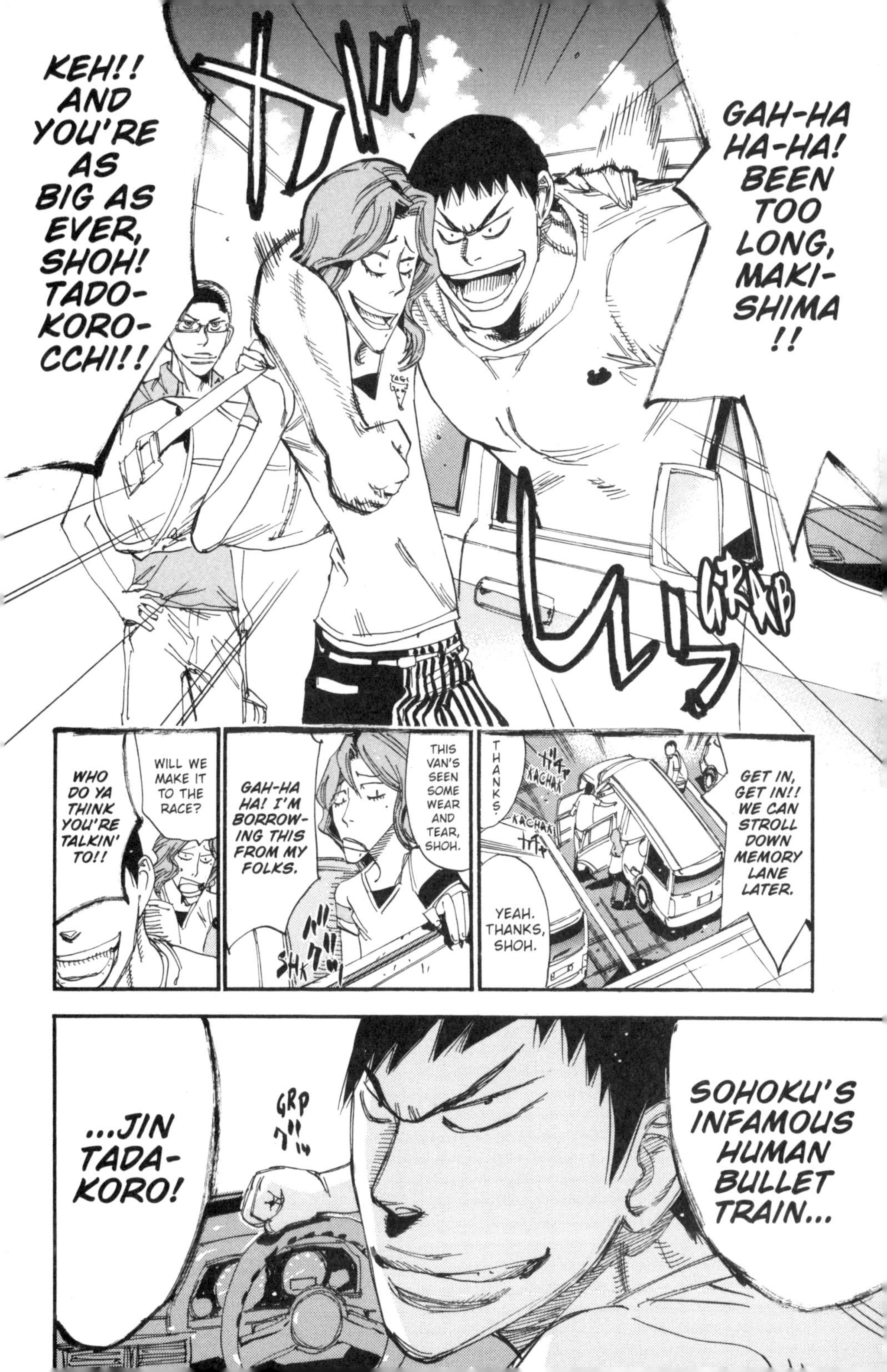
GAH-HA HA-HA! BEEN TOO LONG, MAKI-SHIMA!!
GRAB
KEH!! AND YOU'RE AS BIG AS EVER, SHOH! TADO-KOROCCHI!!
GET IN, GET IN!! WE CAN STROLL DOWN MEMORY LANE LATER.
KACHAK
KACHAK
THANKS.
YEAH. THANKS, SHOH.
THIS VAN'S SEEN SOME WEAR AND TEAR, SHOH.
GAH-HA HA! I'M BORROWING THIS FROM MY FOLKS.
SHK
WILL WE MAKE IT TO THE RACE?
WHO DO YA THINK YOU'RE TALKIN' TO!!
SOHOKU'S INFAMOUS HUMAN BULLET TRAIN...
GRP
...JIN TADA-KORO!

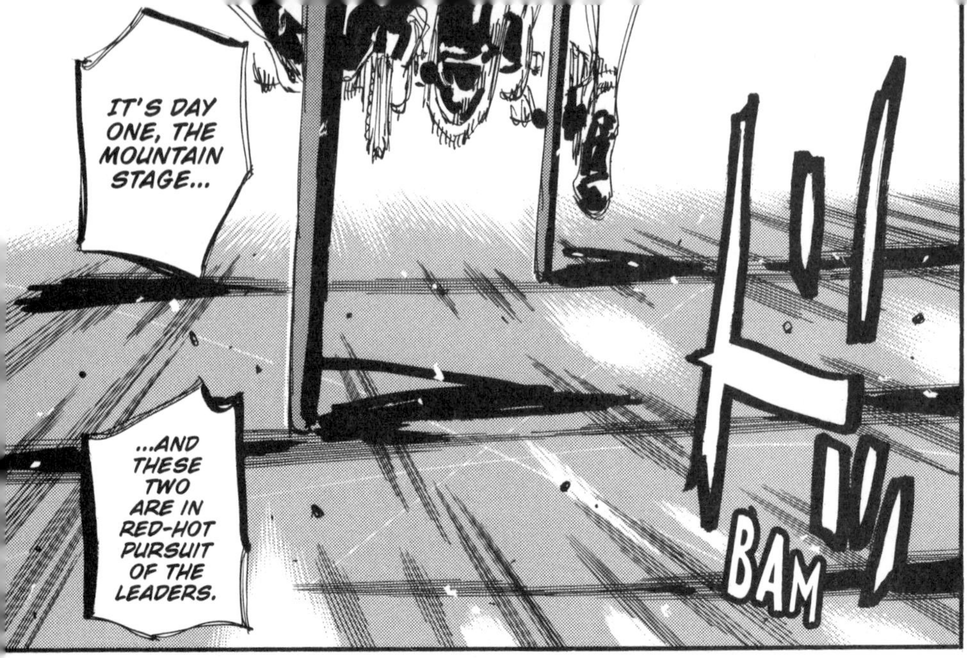
IT'S DAY ONE, THE MOUNTAIN STAGE...
...AND THESE TWO ARE IN RED-HOT PURSUIT OF THE LEADERS.
BAM

FLAGS: INTER-HIGH ROAD RACE, NIKKO-KAIDO

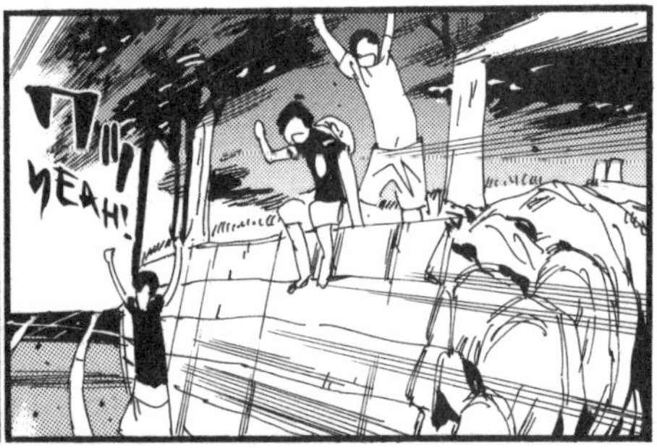
YEAH!

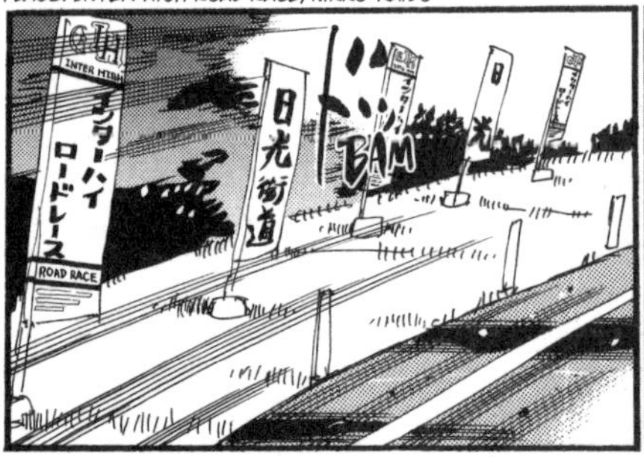
INTER HIGH
ROAD RACE
BAM

SIGN: IROHAZAKA JUST AHEAD

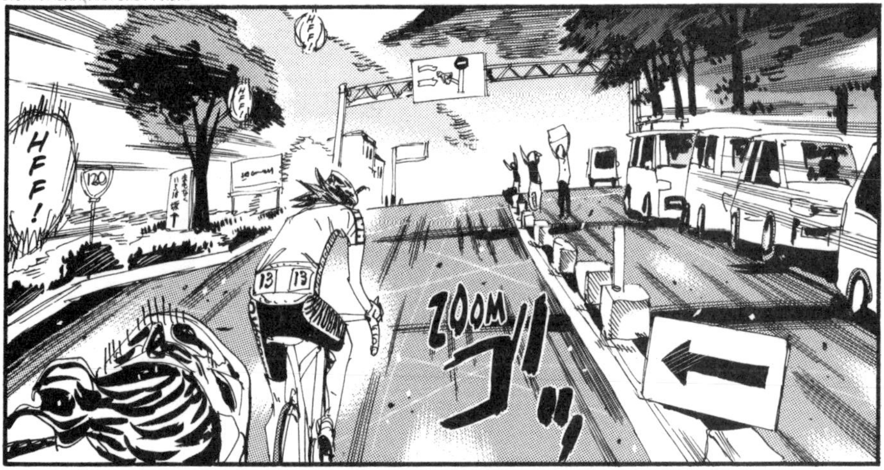
HFF!
HFF!
HFF!
13
ZOOM

RIDE.320 TESHIMA'S CHALLENGE!!

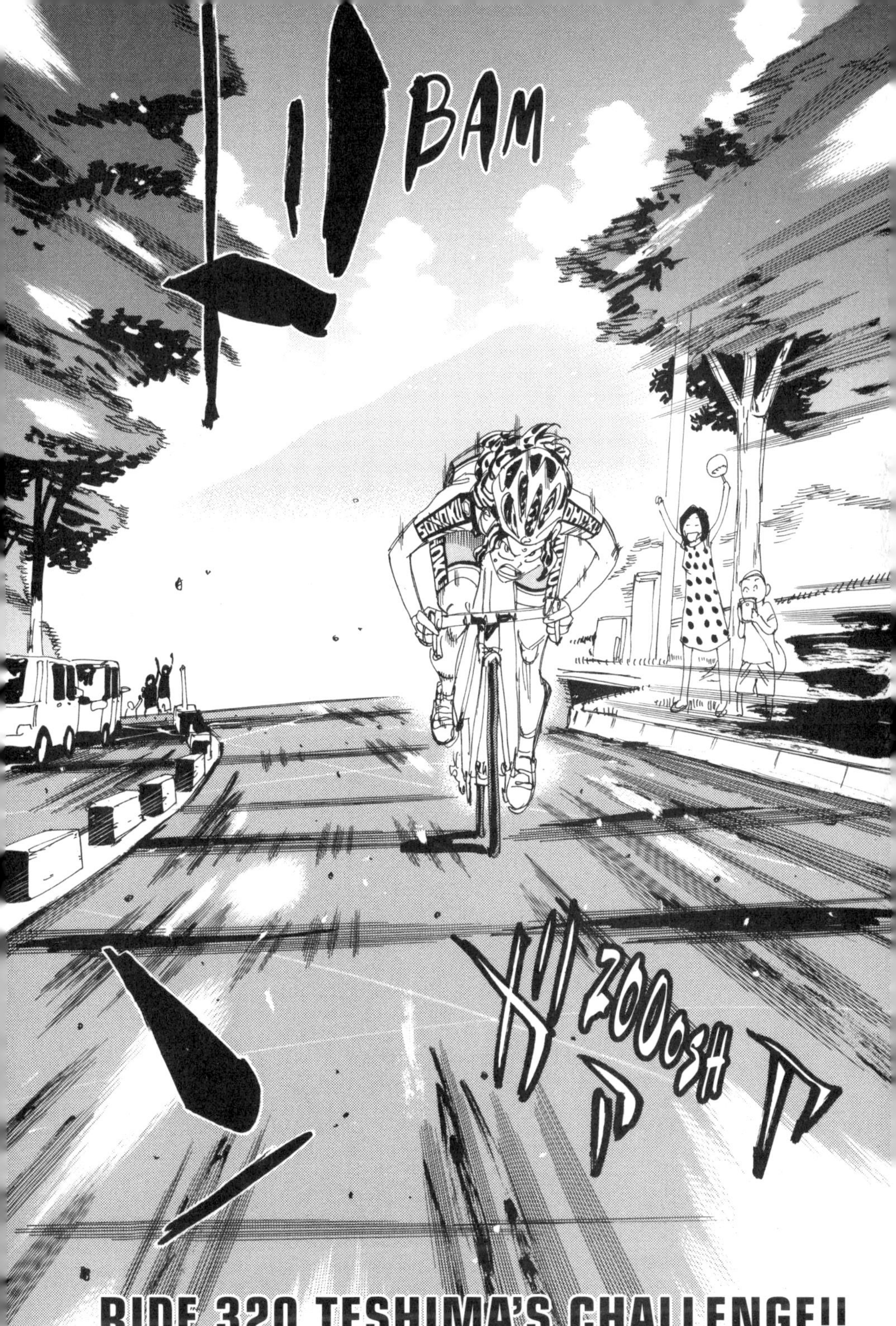
BAM
ZOOOSH

RIDE.320 TESHIMA'S CHALLENGE!!

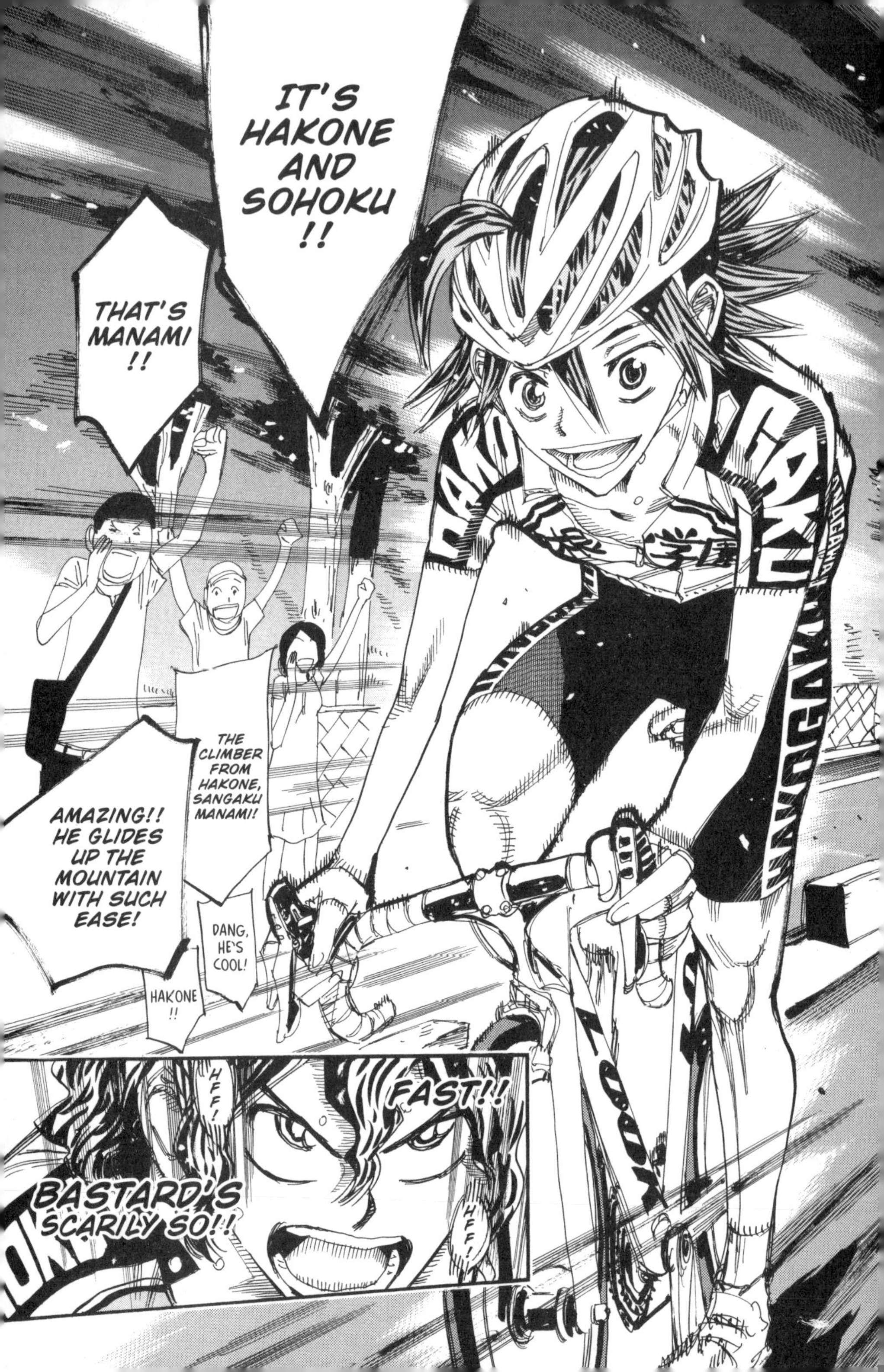
IT'S HAKONE AND SOHOKU!!
THAT'S MANAMI!!
THE CLIMBER FROM HAKONE, SANGAKU MANAMI!
AMAZING!! HE GLIDES UP THE MOUNTAIN WITH SUCH EASE!
DANG, HE'S COOL!
HAKONE!!
HFF!
FAST!!
BASTARD'S SCARILY SO!!
HFF!

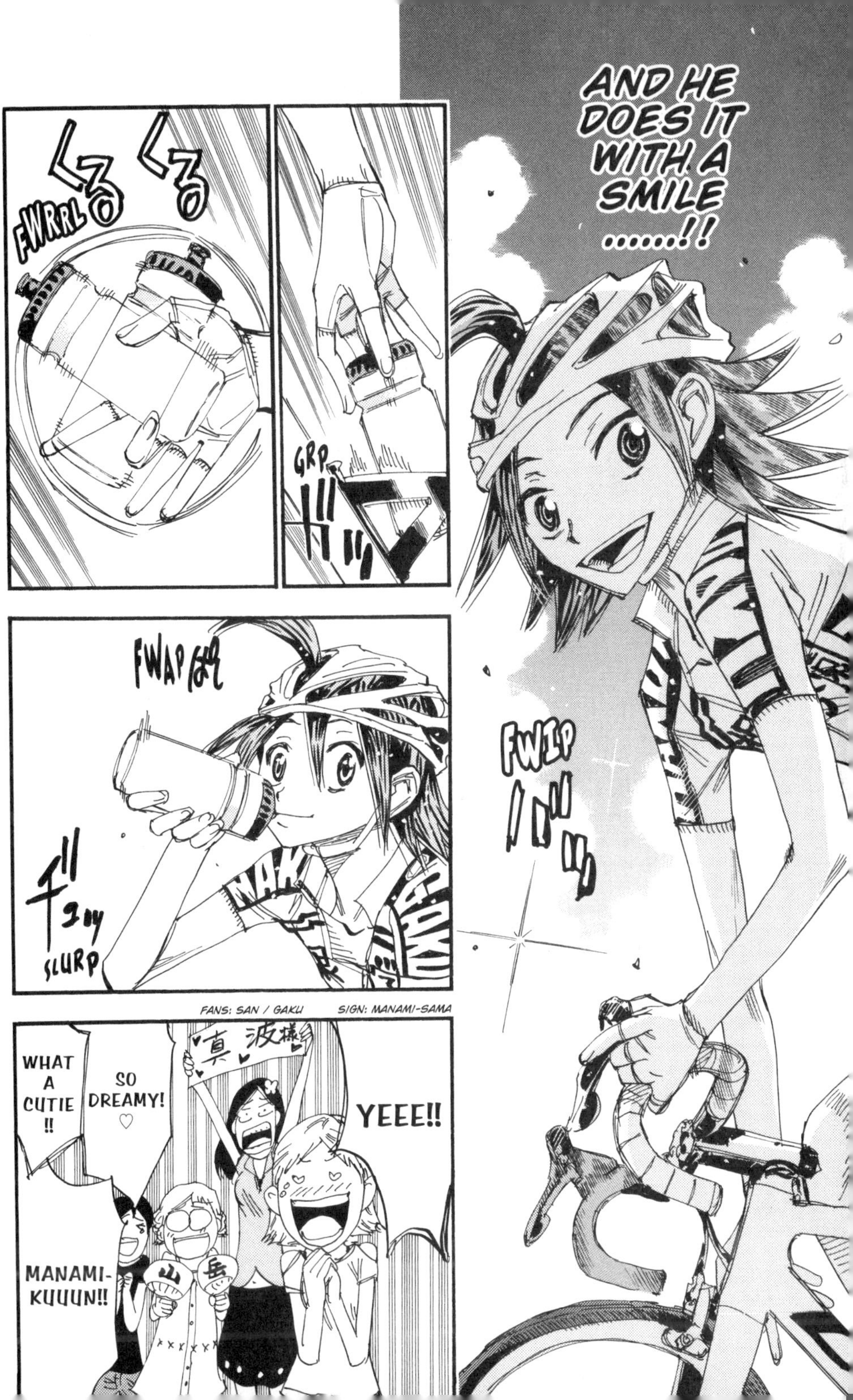
AND HE DOES IT WITH A SMILE ......!!
FWIP
GRP
くるくる
FWRRL
FWAP
SLURP
FANS: SAN / GAKU
SIGN: MANAMI-SAMA
真波様
YEEE!!
SO DREAMY! ♡
WHAT A CUTIE !!
MANAMI-KUUUN!!

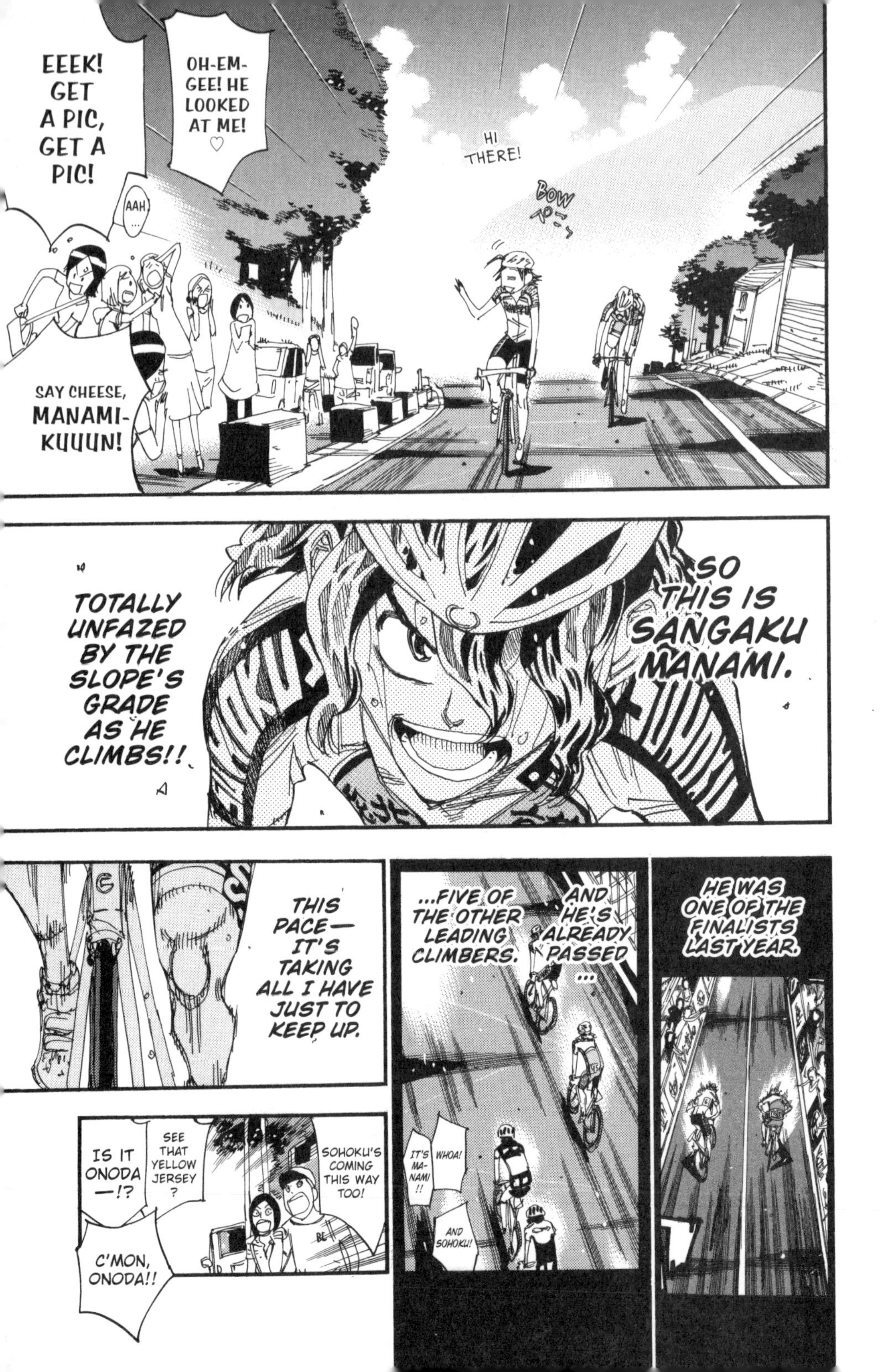
HI THERE!
BOW
OH-EM-GEE! HE LOOKED AT ME! ♡
EEEK! GET A PIC, GET A PIC!
AAH ...
SAY CHEESE, MANAMI-KUUUN!
SO THIS IS SANGAKU MANAMI.
TOTALLY UNFAZED BY THE SLOPE'S GRADE AS HE CLIMBS!!
HE WAS ONE OF THE FINALISTS LAST YEAR.
AND HE'S ALREADY PASSED ...
...FIVE OF THE OTHER LEADING CLIMBERS.
WHOA!
IT'S MANAMI!!
AND SOHOKU!
THIS PACE— IT'S TAKING ALL I HAVE JUST TO KEEP UP.
SOHOKU'S COMING THIS WAY TOO!
SEE THAT YELLOW JERSEY?
IS IT ONODA—!?
C'MON, ONODA!!

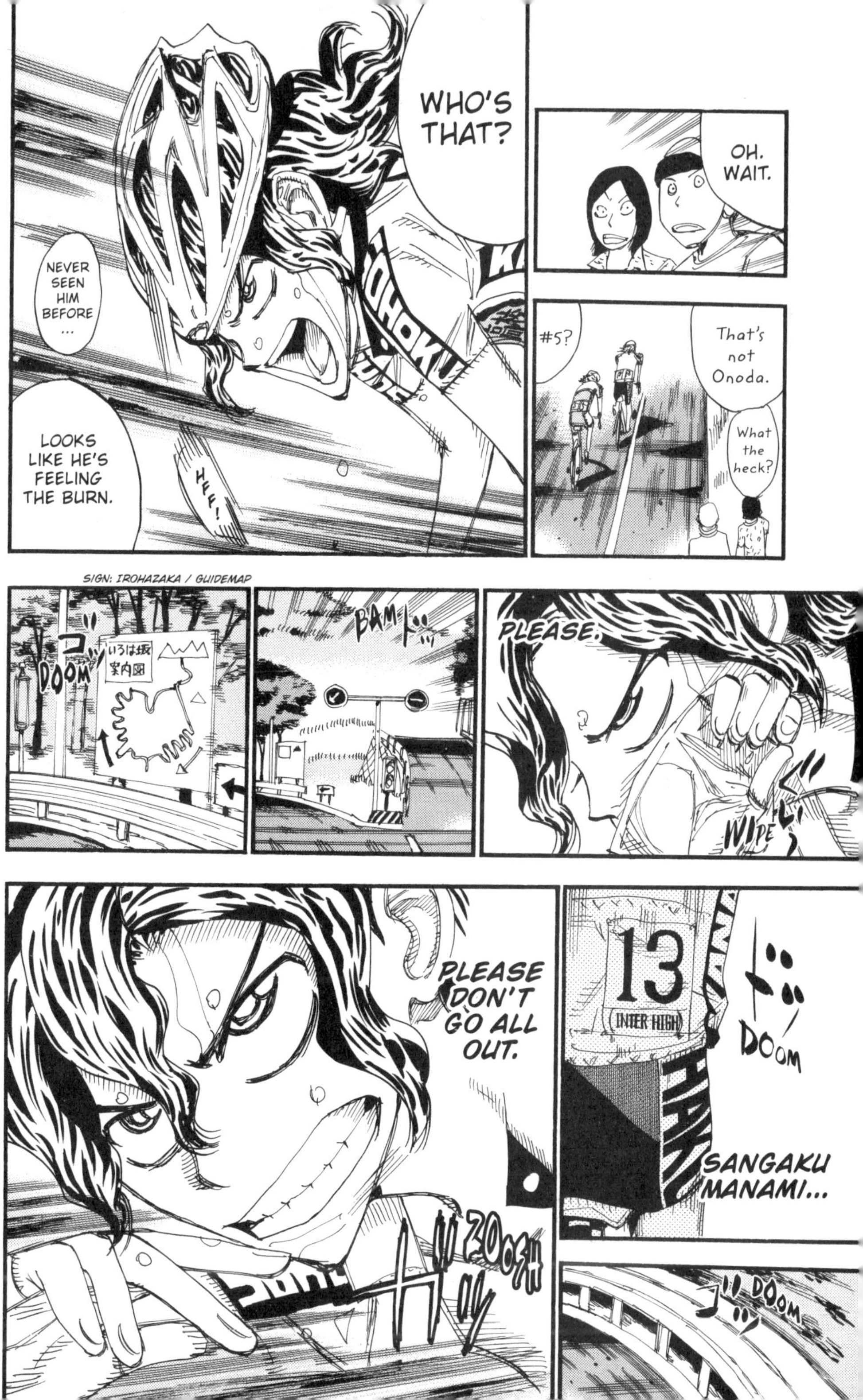
OH. WAIT.
That's not Onoda.
#5?
What the heck?
WHO'S THAT?
NEVER SEEN HIM BEFORE ...
LOOKS LIKE HE'S FEELING THE BURN.
HFF!
SIGN: IROHAZAKA / GUIDEMAP
PLEASE.
WIPE
BAM
DOOM
いろは坂
案内図
13
INTER HIGH
DOOM
SANGAKU MANAMI...
DOOM
PLEASE DON'T GO ALL OUT.
ZOOFH

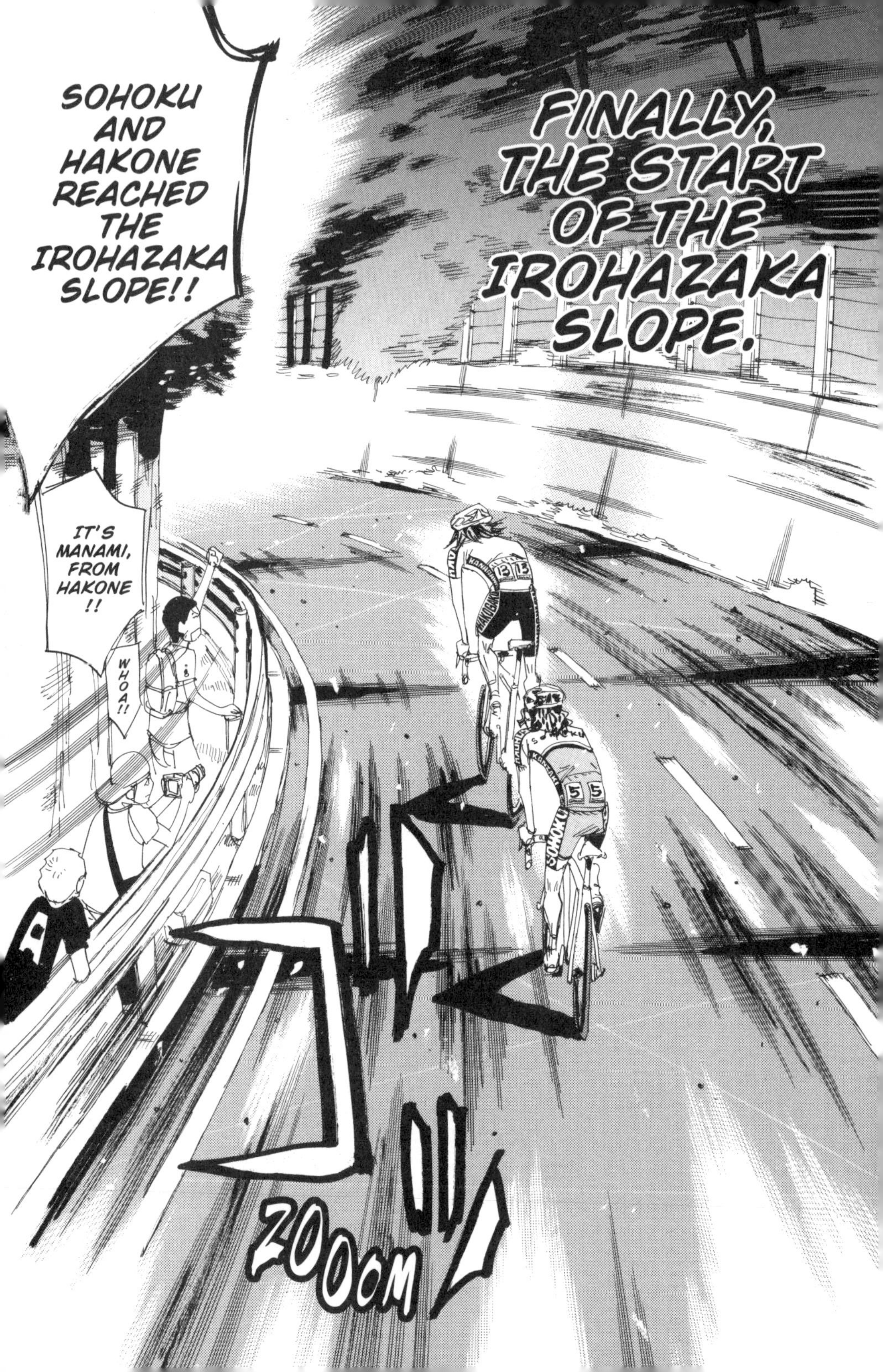
FINALLY, THE START OF THE IROHAZAKA SLOPE.
SOHOKU AND HAKONE REACHED THE IROHAZAKA SLOPE!!
IT'S MANAMI, FROM HAKONE!!
WHOA!!
ZOOOM

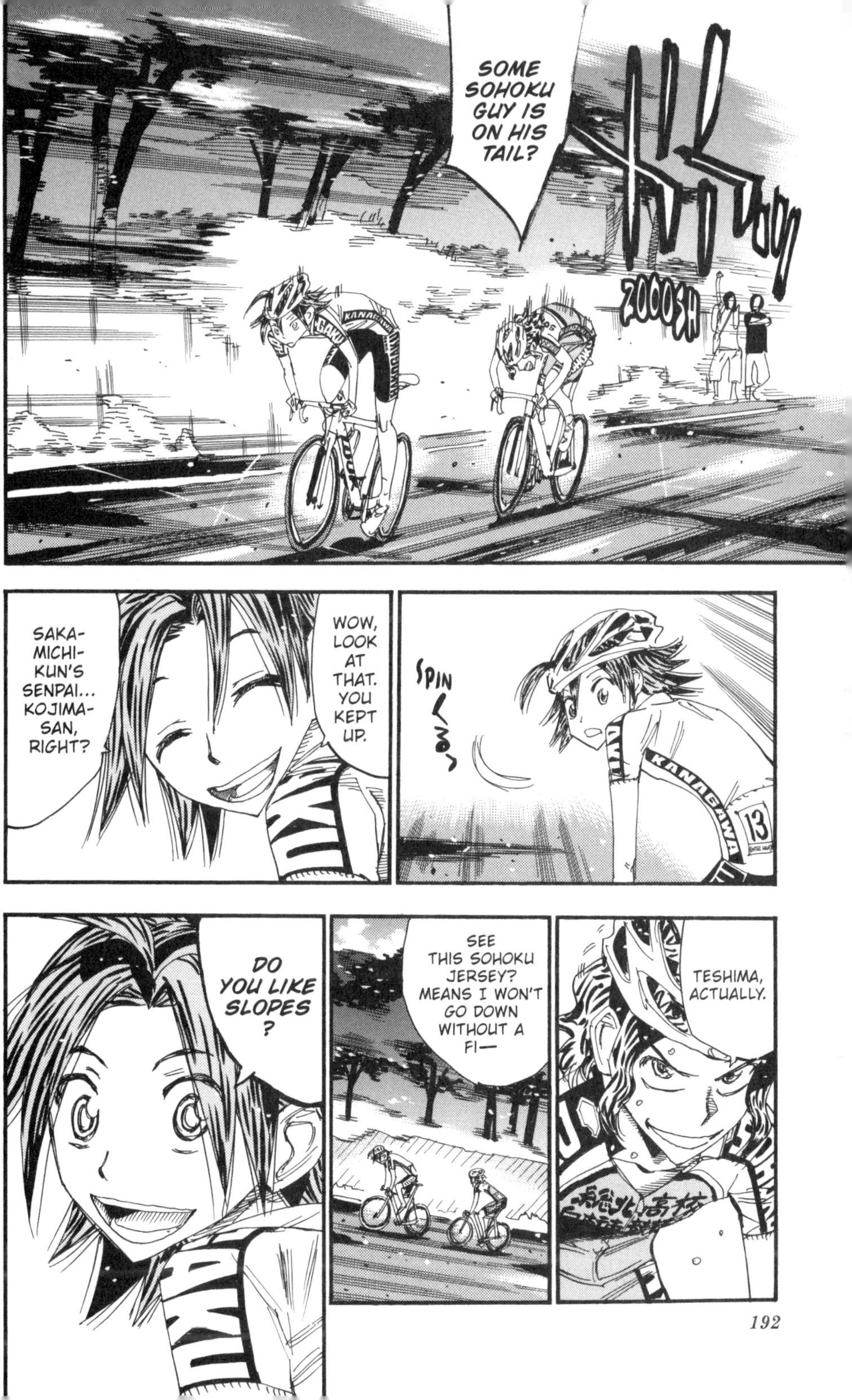
SOME SOHOKU GUY IS ON HIS TAIL?
ZOOOSH
SPIN
WOW, LOOK AT THAT. YOU KEPT UP.
SAKA-MICHI-KUN'S SENPAI... KOJIMA-SAN, RIGHT?
TESHIMA, ACTUALLY.
SEE THIS SOHOKU JERSEY? MEANS I WON'T GO DOWN WITHOUT A FI—
DO YOU LIKE SLOPES?

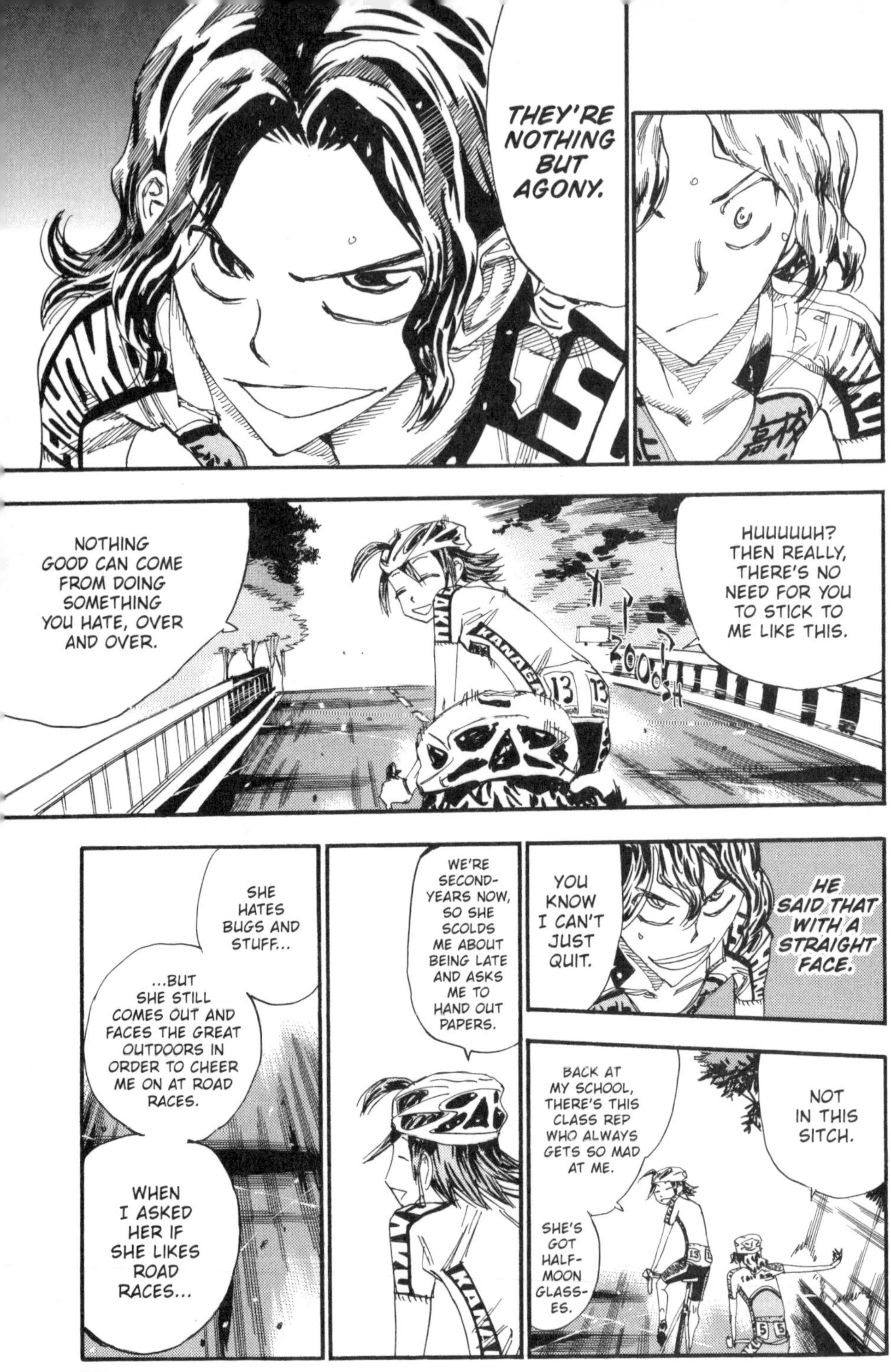
THEY'RE NOTHING BUT AGONY.
HUUUUUH? THEN REALLY, THERE'S NO NEED FOR YOU TO STICK TO ME LIKE THIS.
NOTHING GOOD CAN COME FROM DOING SOMETHING YOU HATE, OVER AND OVER.
HE SAID THAT WITH A STRAIGHT FACE.
YOU KNOW I CAN'T JUST QUIT.
NOT IN THIS SITCH.
BACK AT MY SCHOOL, THERE'S THIS CLASS REP WHO ALWAYS GETS SO MAD AT ME.
SHE'S GOT HALF-MOON GLASS-ES.
WE'RE SECOND-YEARS NOW, SO SHE SCOLDS ME ABOUT BEING LATE AND ASKS ME TO HAND OUT PAPERS.
SHE HATES BUGS AND STUFF...
...BUT SHE STILL COMES OUT AND FACES THE GREAT OUTDOORS IN ORDER TO CHEER ME ON AT ROAD RACES.
WHEN I ASKED HER IF SHE LIKES ROAD RACES...

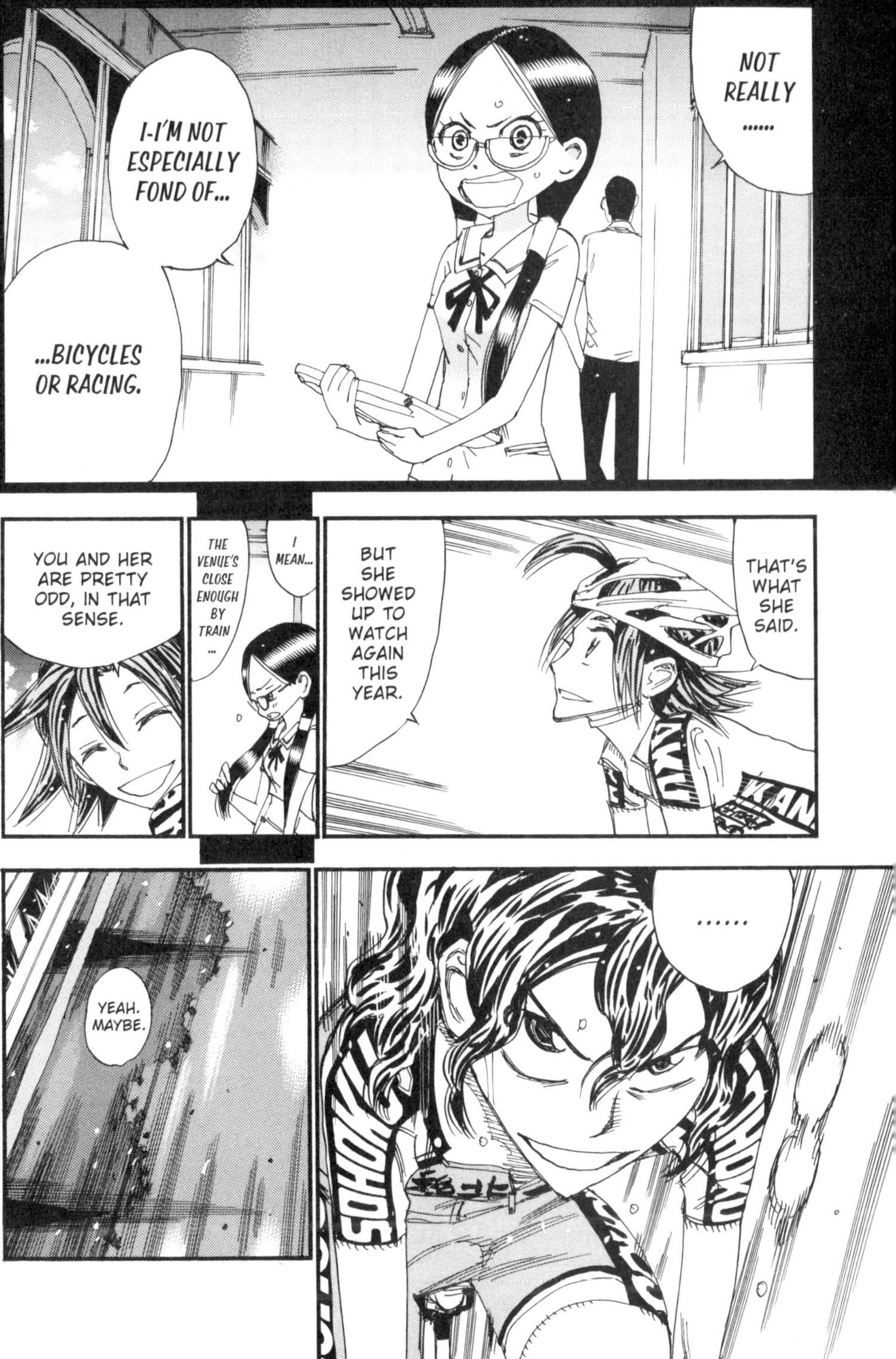
NOT REALLY ......
I-I'M NOT ESPECIALLY FOND OF...
...BICYCLES OR RACING.
THAT'S WHAT SHE SAID.
BUT SHE SHOWED UP TO WATCH AGAIN THIS YEAR.
I MEAN...
THE VENUE'S CLOSE ENOUGH BY TRAIN ...
YOU AND HER ARE PRETTY ODD, IN THAT SENSE.
......
YEAH. MAYBE.

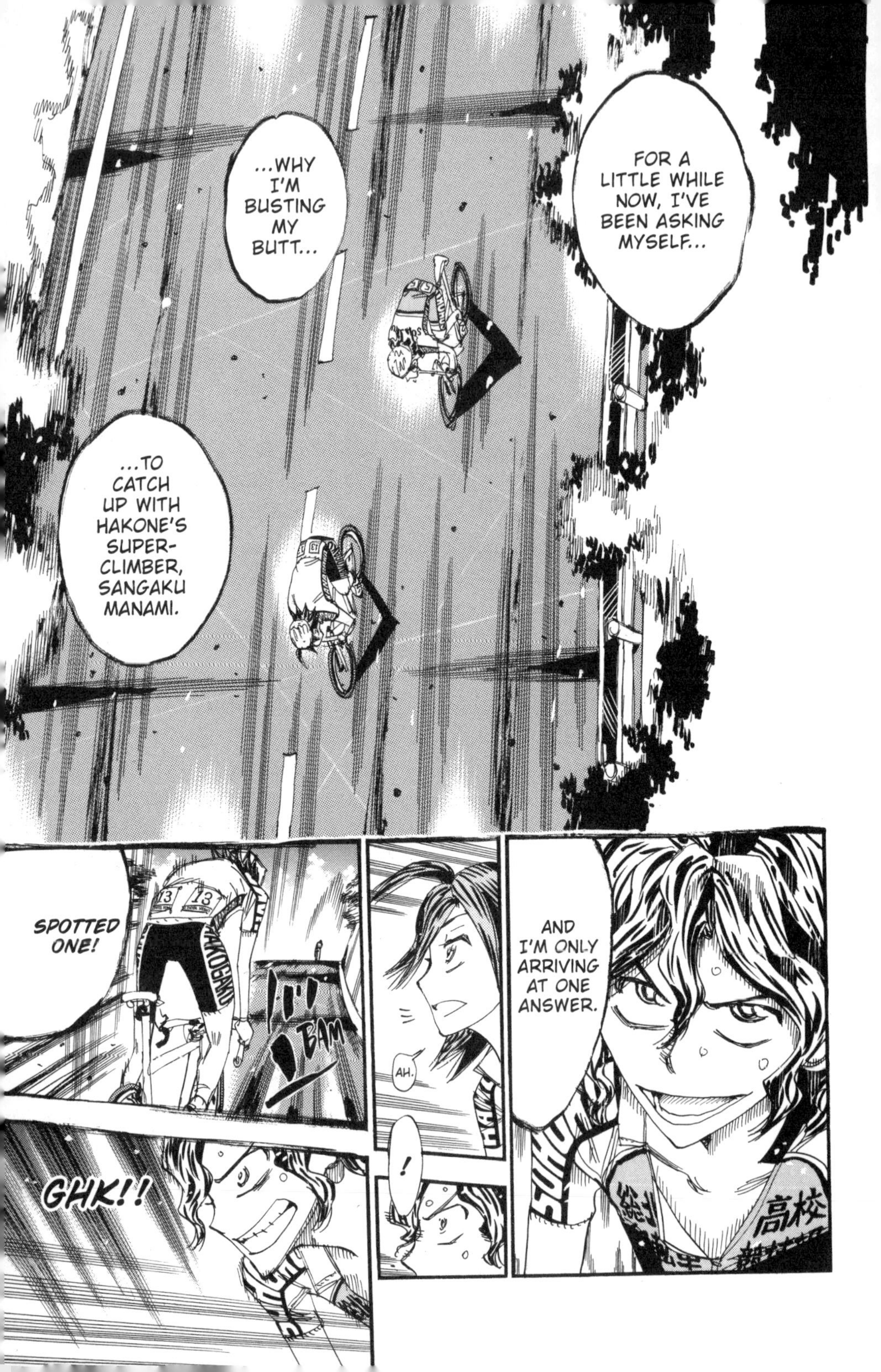
FOR A LITTLE WHILE NOW, I'VE BEEN ASKING MYSELF...
...WHY I'M BUSTING MY BUTT...
...TO CATCH UP WITH HAKONE'S SUPER-CLIMBER, SANGAKU MANAMI.
AND I'M ONLY ARRIVING AT ONE ANSWER.
AH.
SPOTTED ONE!
BAM
!
GHK!!

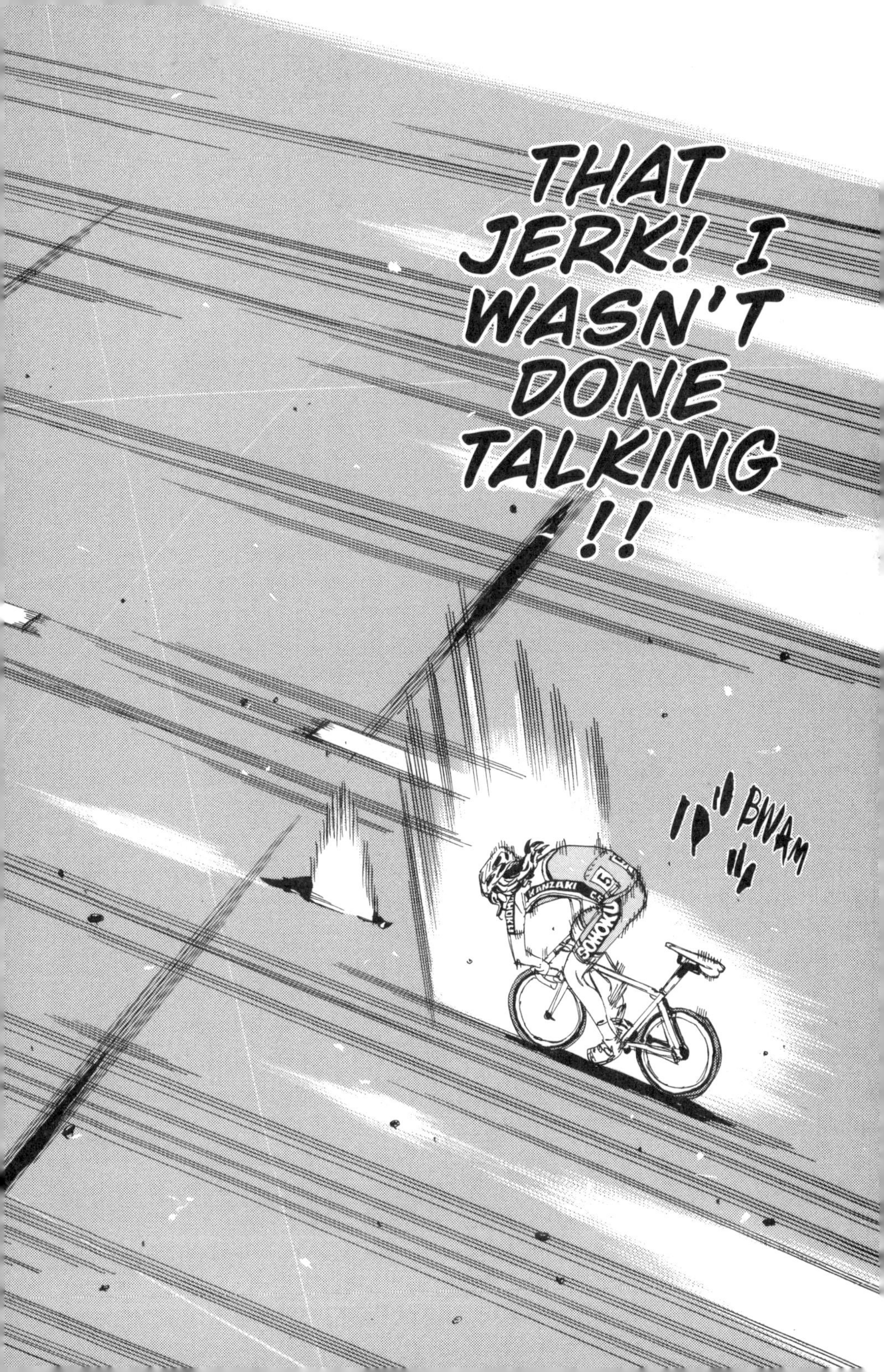
THAT JERK! I WASN'T DONE TALKING!!
BWAM

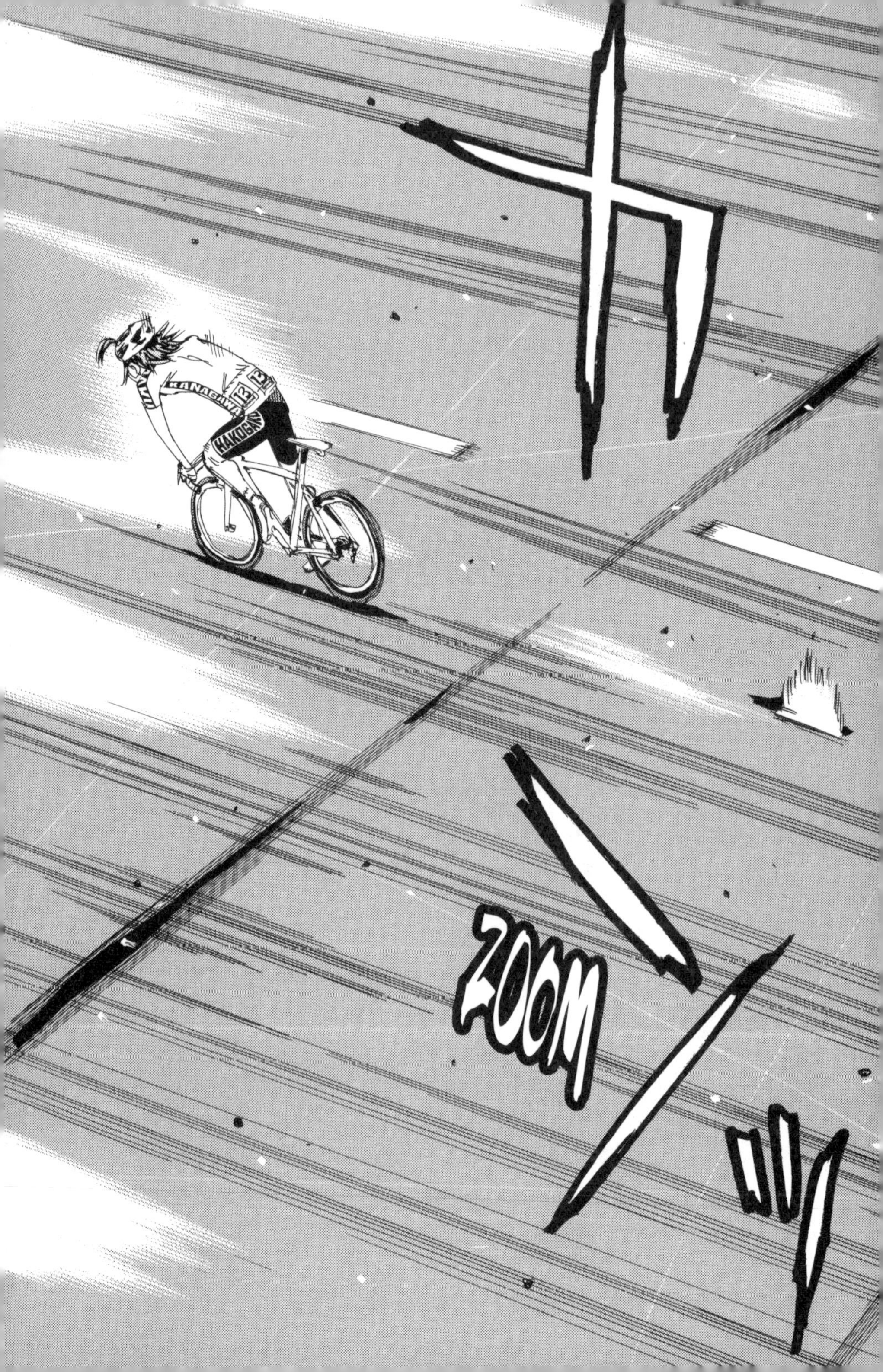
KANAGAWA
ZOOM

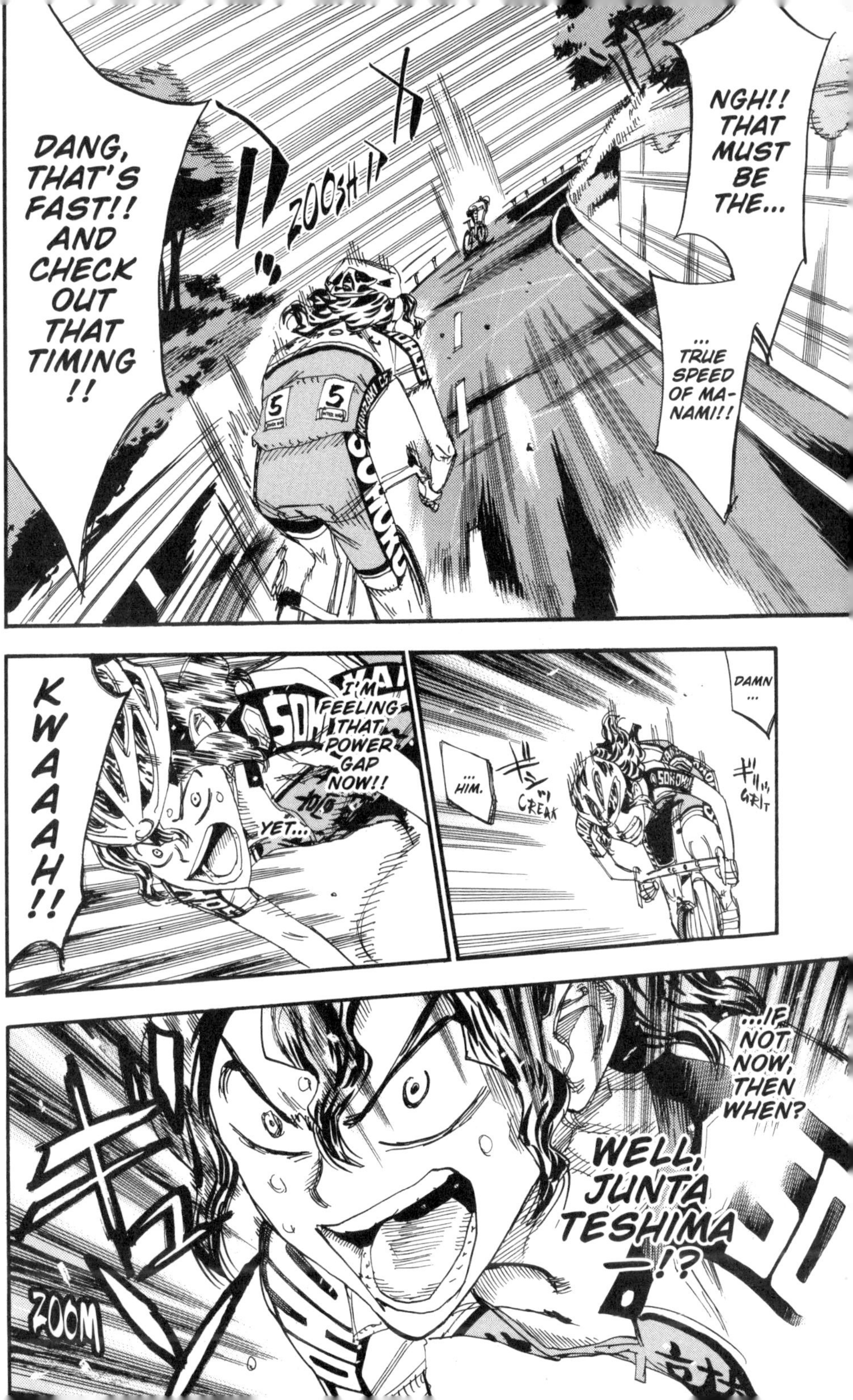
NGH!! THAT MUST BE THE...
...TRUE SPEED OF MA-NAMI!!
ZOOSH
DANG, THAT'S FAST!! AND CHECK OUT THAT TIMING!!
DAMN...
...HIM.
CREAK
GRIT
I'M FEELING THAT POWER GAP NOW!!
YET...
KWAAAAAH!!
...IF NOT NOW, THEN WHEN?
WELL, JUNTA TESHIMA—!?
ZOOM

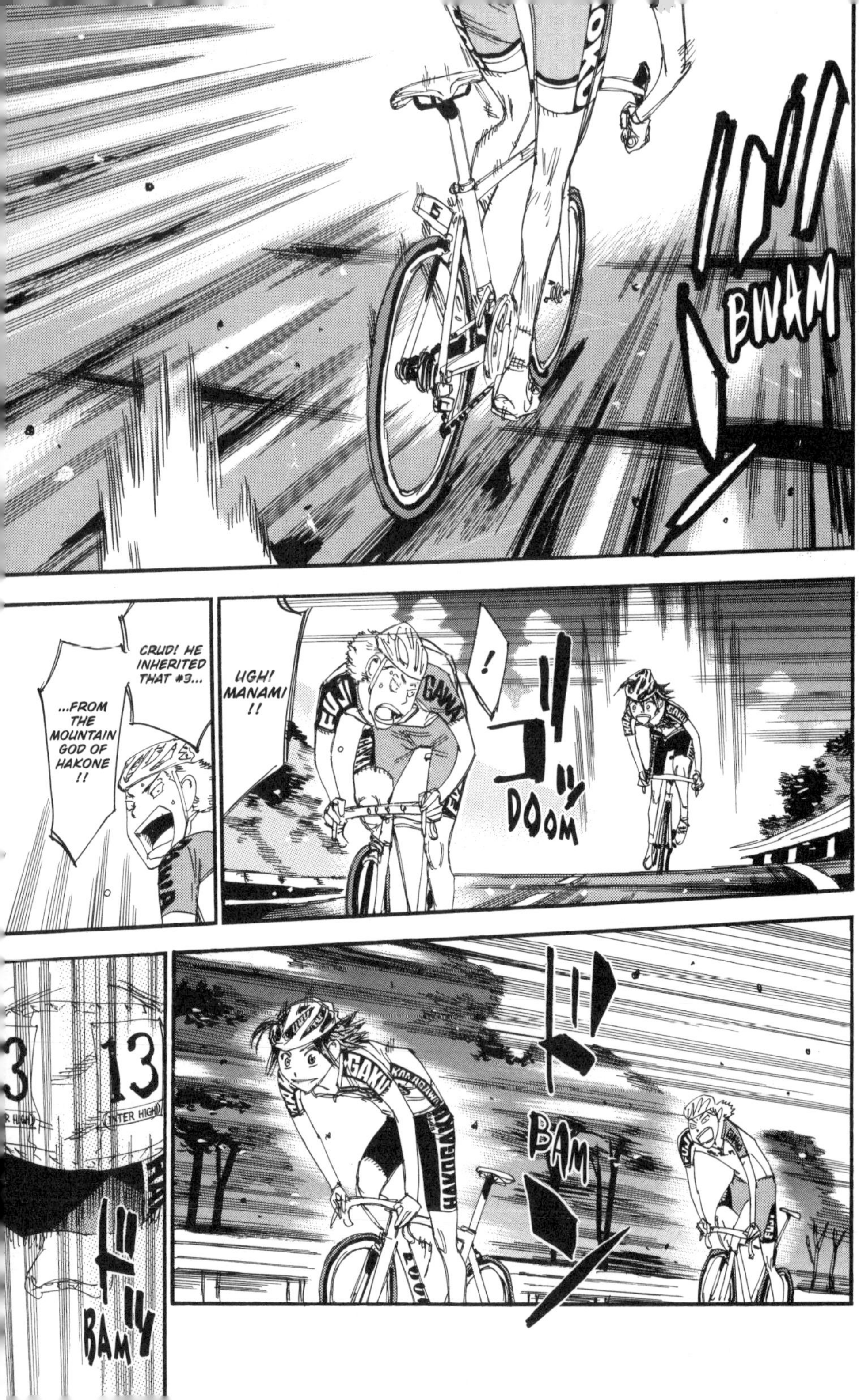
BWAM
!
DOOM
UGH! MANAMI!!
CRUD! HE INHERITED THAT #3...
...FROM THE MOUNTAIN GOD OF HAKONE!!
BAM
13
INTER HIGH
BAM

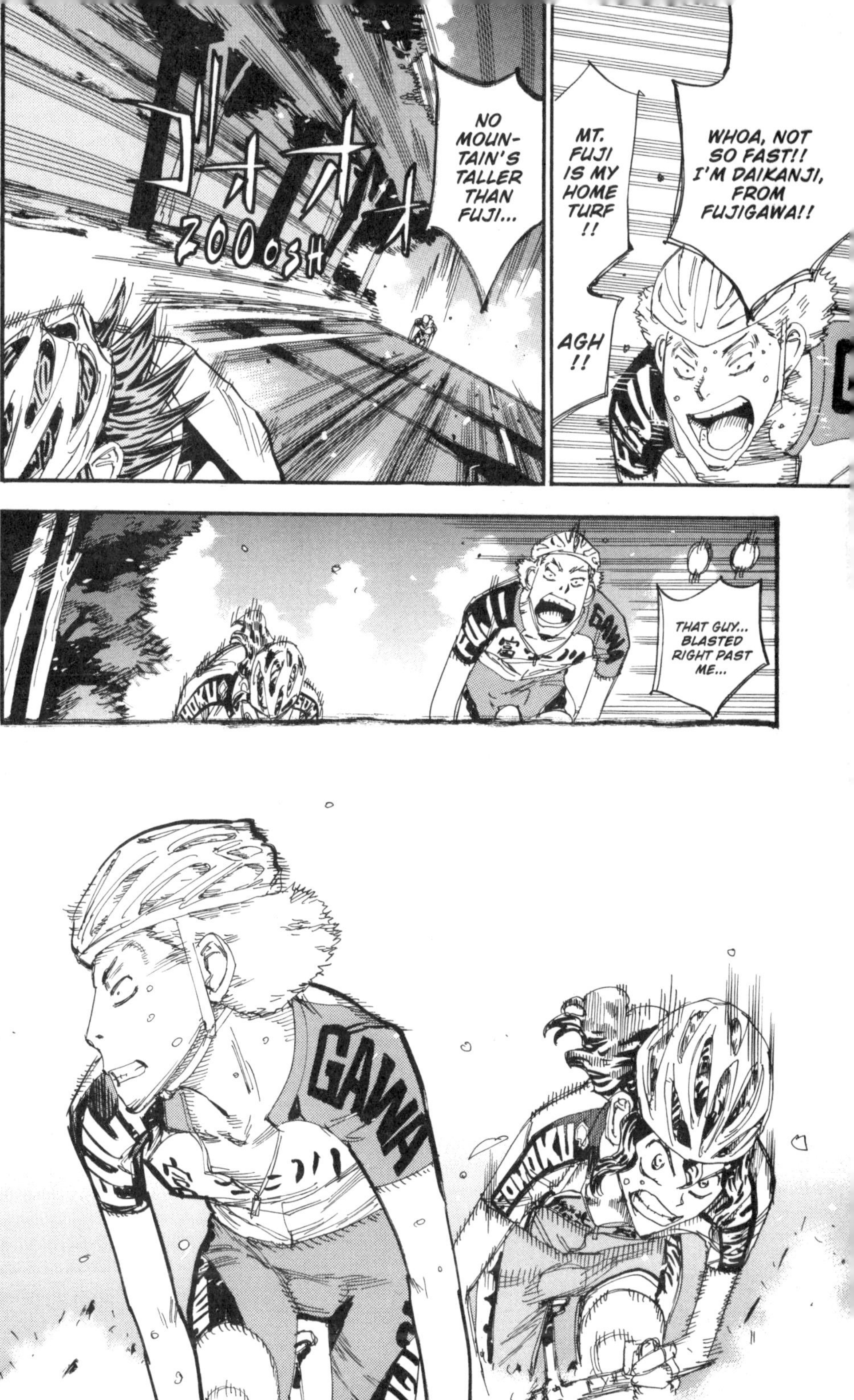
WHOA, NOT SO FAST!! I'M DAIKANJI, FROM FUJIGAWA!!
MT. FUJI IS MY HOME TURF!!
AGH!!
NO MOUN-TAIN'S TALLER THAN FUJI...
ZOOOSH
THAT GUY... BLASTED RIGHT PAST ME...

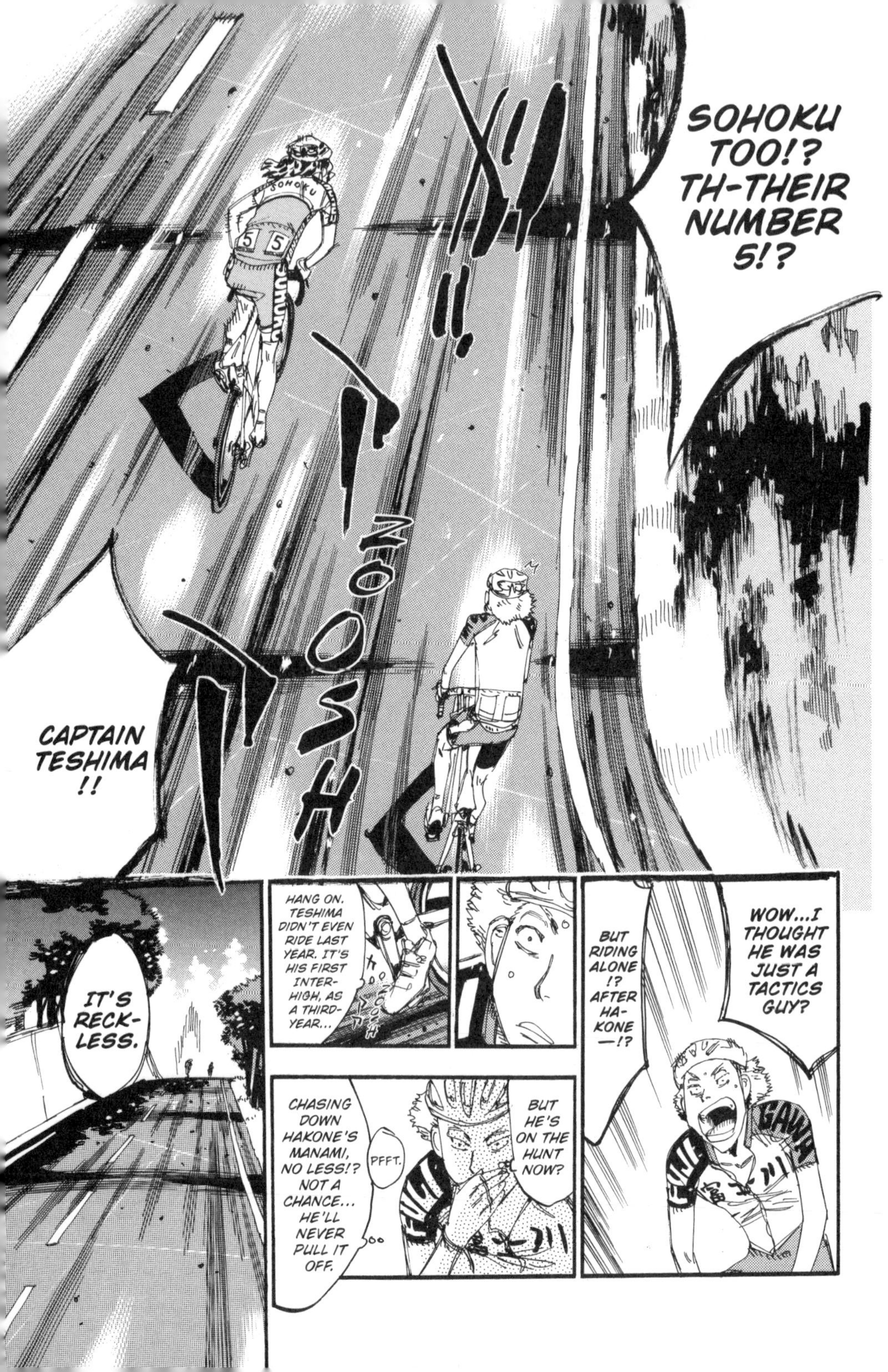
SOHOKU TOO!? TH-THEIR NUMBER 5!?
ZOOOSH
CAPTAIN TESHIMA!!
WOW...I THOUGHT HE WAS JUST A TACTICS GUY?
BUT RIDING ALONE!? AFTER HAKONE—!?
HANG ON. TESHIMA DIDN'T EVEN RIDE LAST YEAR. IT'S HIS FIRST INTER-HIGH, AS A THIRD-YEAR...
BUT HE'S ON THE HUNT NOW?
PFFT.
CHASING DOWN HAKONE'S MANAMI, NO LESS!? NOT A CHANCE... HE'LL NEVER PULL IT OFF.
IT'S RECK-LESS.

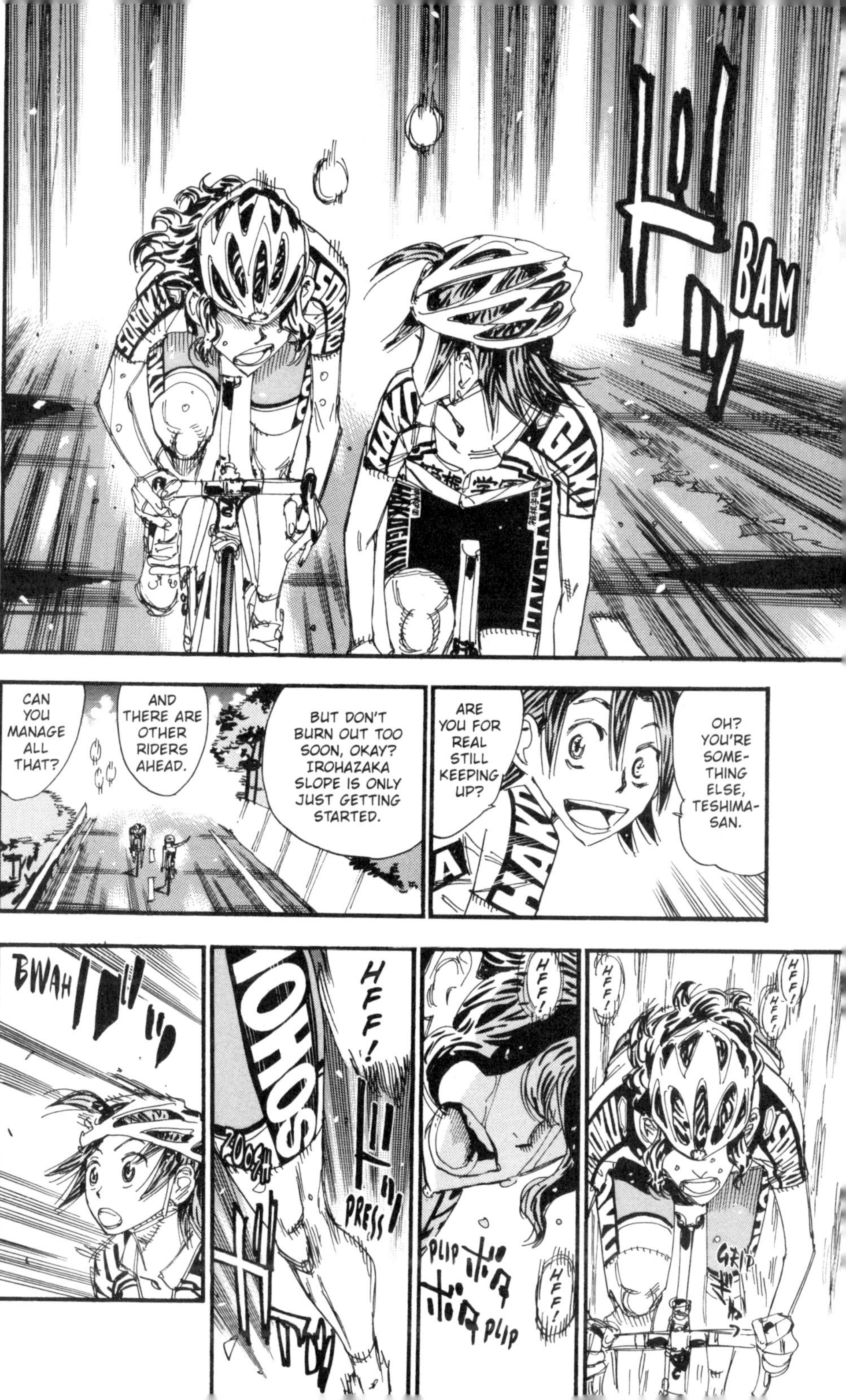
BAM
OH? YOU'RE SOMETHING ELSE, TESHIMA-SAN.
ARE YOU FOR REAL STILL KEEPING UP?
BUT DON'T BURN OUT TOO SOON, OKAY? IROHAZAKA SLOPE IS ONLY JUST GETTING STARTED.
AND THERE ARE OTHER RIDERS AHEAD.
CAN YOU MANAGE ALL THAT?
HFF!
HFF!
HFF!
GRIP
HFF!
HFF!
PLIP
PLIP
HFF!
PRESS
BWAH

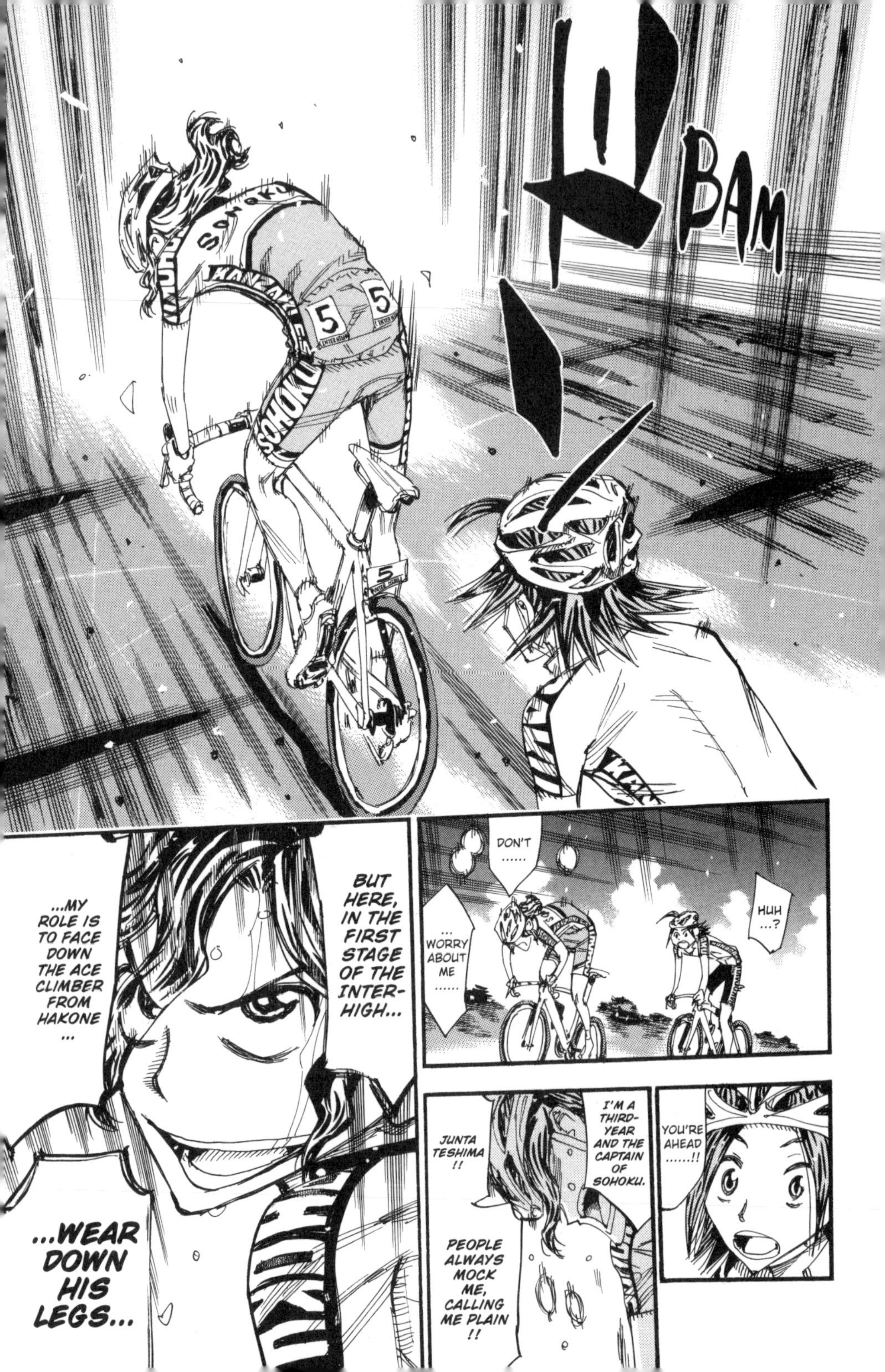
BAM
DON'T ......
... WORRY ABOUT ME ......
HUH ...?
YOU'RE AHEAD ......!!
I'M A THIRD-YEAR AND THE CAPTAIN OF SOHOKU.
JUNTA TESHIMA !!
PEOPLE ALWAYS MOCK ME, CALLING ME PLAIN !!
BUT HERE, IN THE FIRST STAGE OF THE INTER-HIGH...
...MY ROLE IS TO FACE DOWN THE ACE CLIMBER FROM HAKONE ...
...WEAR DOWN HIS LEGS...

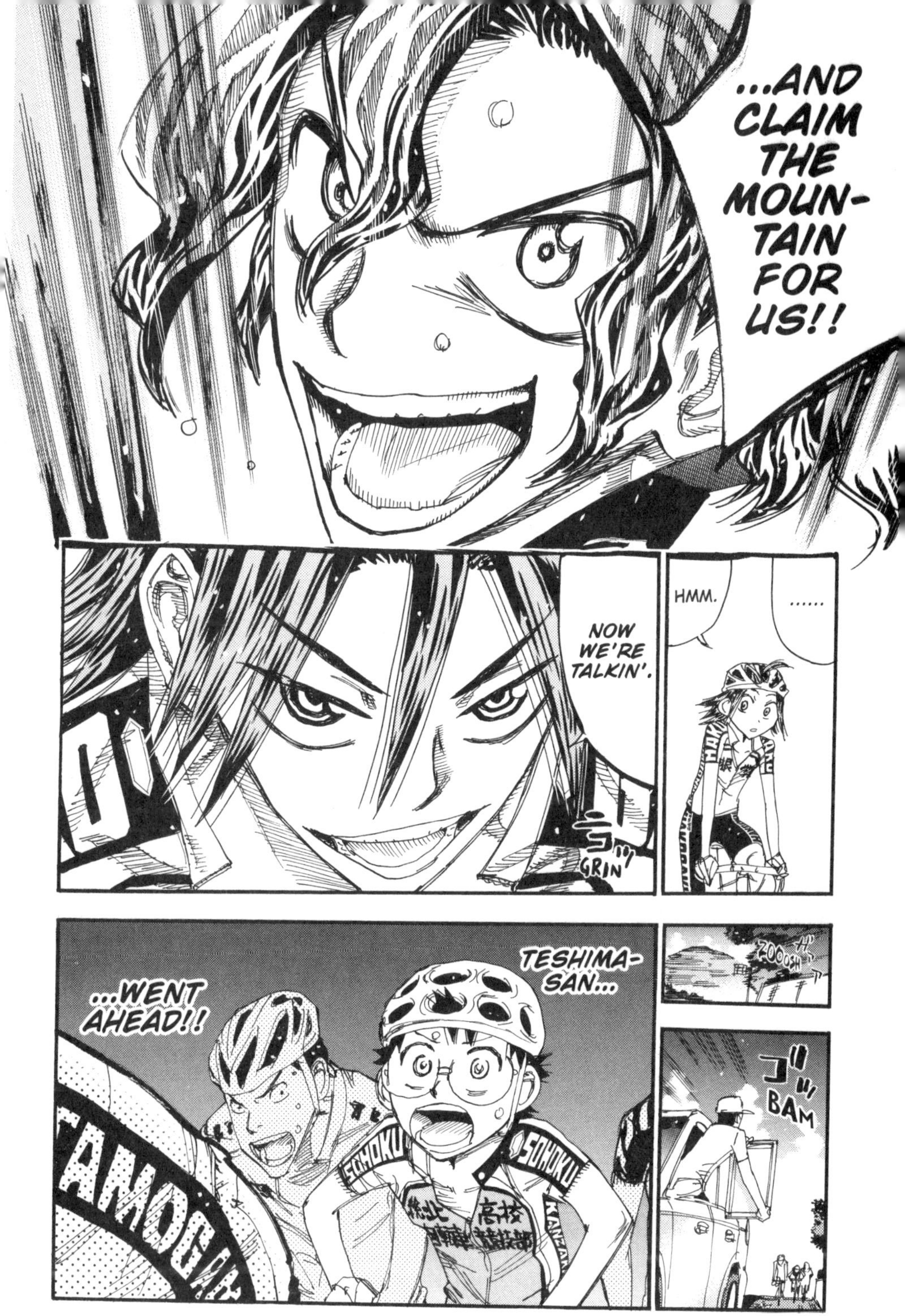
...AND CLAIM THE MOUNTAIN FOR US!!
......
HMM.
NOW WE'RE TALKIN'.
GRIN
ZOOOSH
BAM
TESHIMA-SAN...
...WENT AHEAD!!

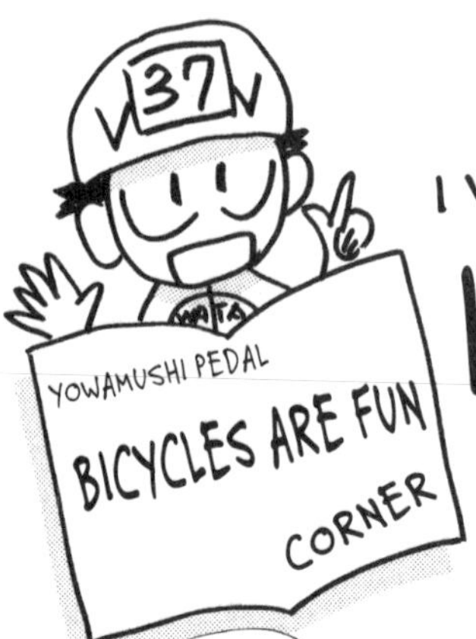
37
WATA
YOWAMUSHI PEDAL
BICYCLES ARE FUN
CORNER

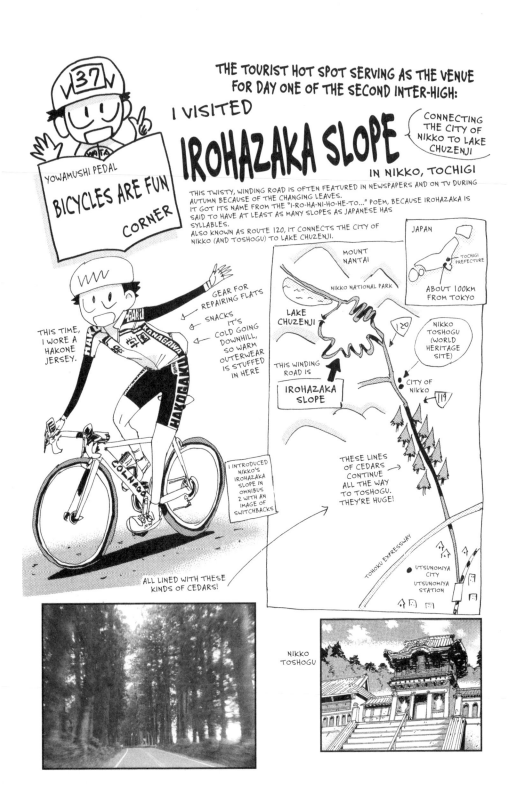

THE TOURIST HOT SPOT SERVING AS THE VENUE FOR DAY ONE OF THE SECOND INTER-HIGH:

I VISITED

IROHAZAKA SLOPE

(CONNECTING THE CITY OF NIKKO TO LAKE CHUZENJI)

IN NIKKO, TOCHIGI

THIS TWISTY, WINDING ROAD IS OFTEN FEATURED IN NEWSPAPERS AND ON TV DURING AUTUMN BECAUSE OF THE CHANGING LEAVES.
IT GOT ITS NAME FROM THE "I-RO-HA-NI-HO-HE-TO..." POEM, BECAUSE IROHAZAKA IS SAID TO HAVE AT LEAST AS MANY SLOPES AS JAPANESE HAS SYLLABLES.
ALSO KNOWN AS ROUTE 120, IT CONNECTS THE CITY OF NIKKO (AND TOSHOGU) TO LAKE CHUZENJI.

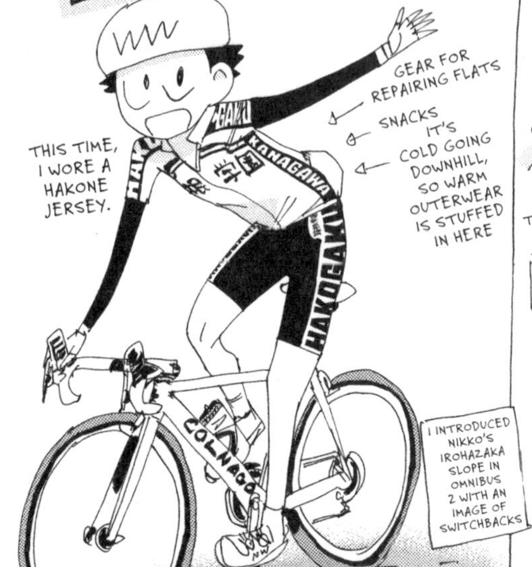
THIS TIME, I WORE A HAKONE JERSEY.
GEAR FOR REPAIRING FLATS
SNACKS
IT'S COLD GOING DOWNHILL, SO WARM OUTERWEAR IS STUFFED IN HERE
HAKOGAKU
KANAGAWA
COLNAGO
I INTRODUCED NIKKO'S IROHAZAKA SLOPE IN OMNIBUS 2 WITH AN IMAGE OF SWITCHBACKS

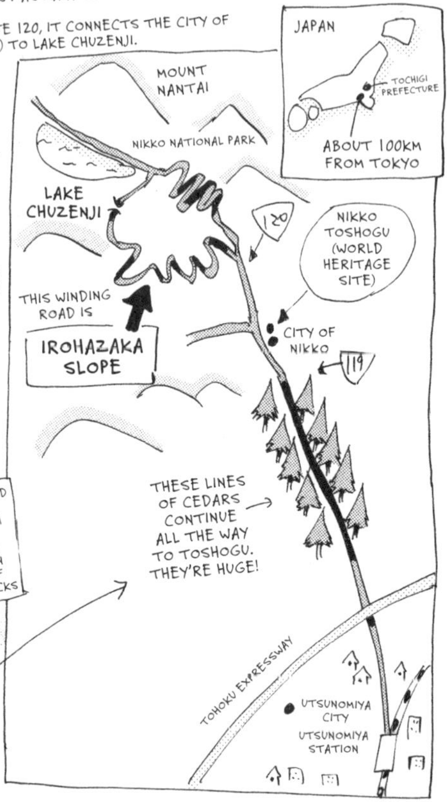
JAPAN
TOCHIGI PREFECTURE
ABOUT 100KM FROM TOKYO
MOUNT NANTAI
NIKKO NATIONAL PARK
LAKE CHUZENJI
120
NIKKO TOSHOGU (WORLD HERITAGE SITE)
THIS WINDING ROAD IS
IROHAZAKA SLOPE
CITY OF NIKKO
119
THESE LINES OF CEDARS CONTINUE ALL THE WAY TO TOSHOGU. THEY'RE HUGE!
TOHOKU EXPRESSWAY
UTSUNOMIYA CITY
UTSUNOMIYA STATION

ALL LINED WITH THESE KINDS OF CEDARS!

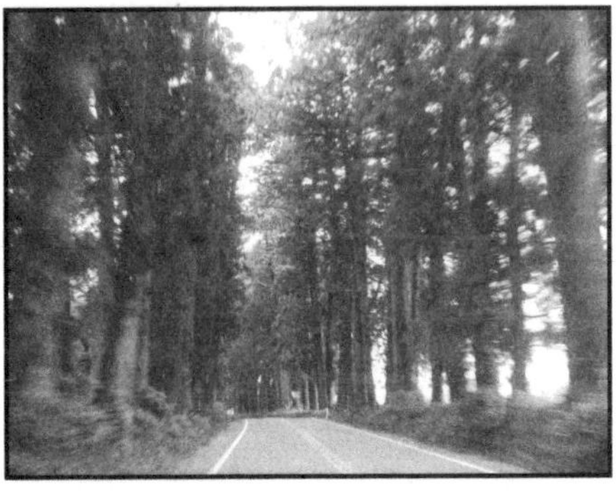

NIKKO TOSHOGU

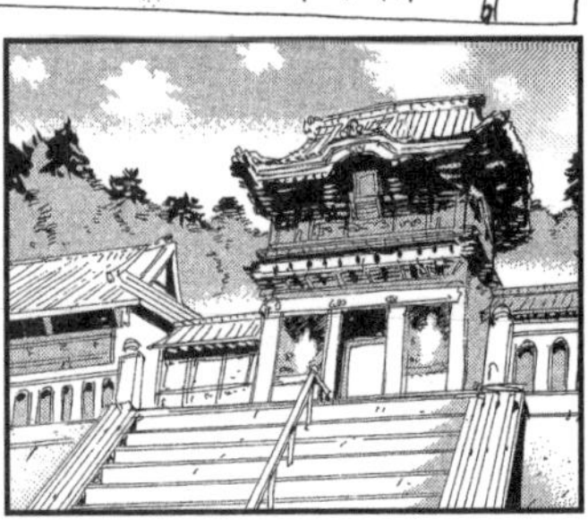

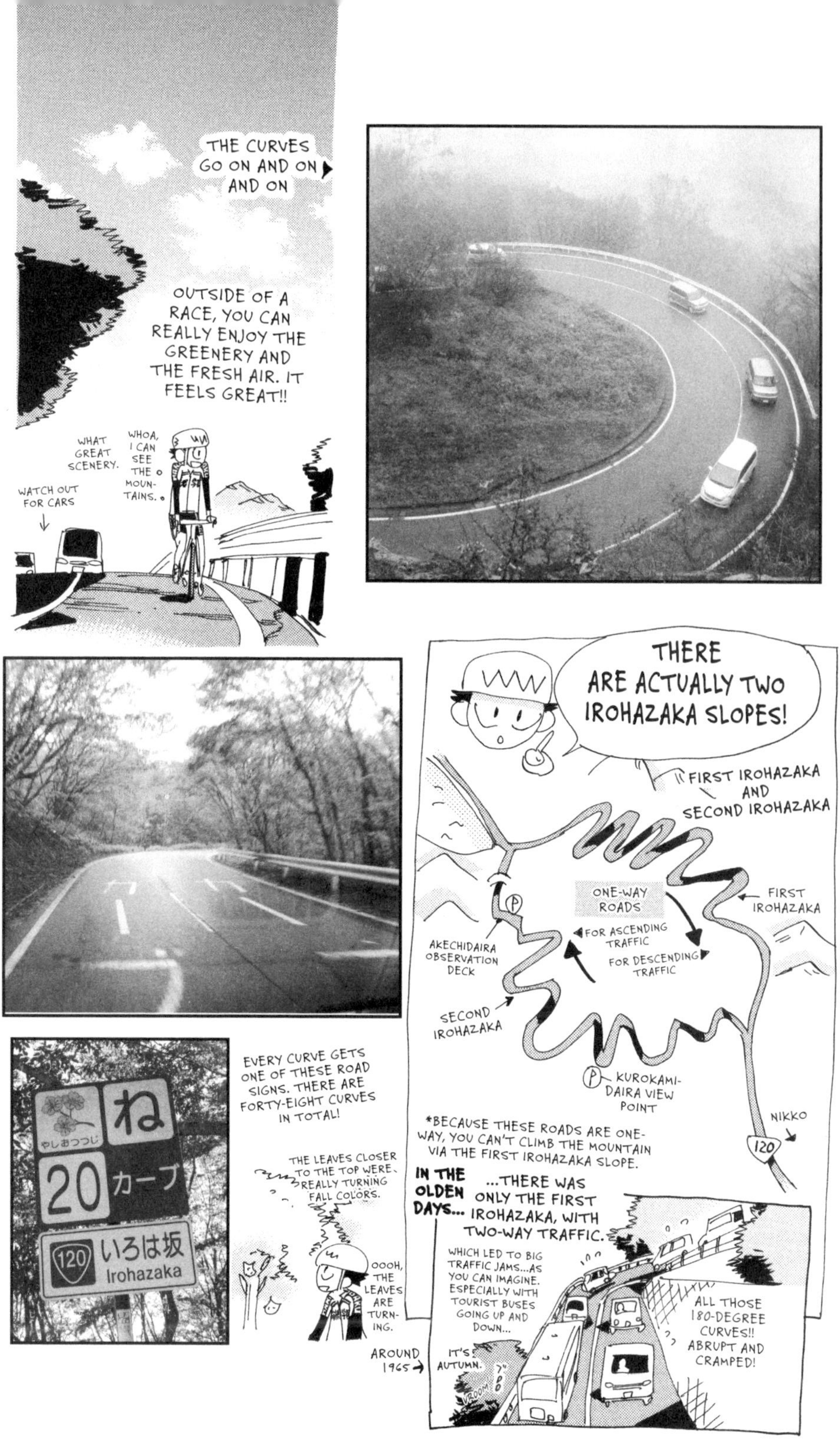
THE CURVES GO ON AND ON AND ON
OUTSIDE OF A RACE, YOU CAN REALLY ENJOY THE GREENERY AND THE FRESH AIR. IT FEELS GREAT!!
WHOA, I CAN SEE THE MOUNTAINS.
WHAT GREAT SCENERY.
WATCH OUT FOR CARS
THERE ARE ACTUALLY TWO IROHAZAKA SLOPES!
FIRST IROHAZAKA AND SECOND IROHAZAKA
ONE-WAY ROADS
FOR ASCENDING TRAFFIC
FOR DESCENDING TRAFFIC
FIRST IROHAZAKA
AKECHIDAIRA OBSERVATION DECK
SECOND IROHAZAKA
KUROKAMI-DAIRA VIEW POINT
NIKKO
120
*BECAUSE THESE ROADS ARE ONE-WAY, YOU CAN'T CLIMB THE MOUNTAIN VIA THE FIRST IROHAZAKA SLOPE.
IN THE OLDEN DAYS...
...THERE WAS ONLY THE FIRST IROHAZAKA, WITH TWO-WAY TRAFFIC.
WHICH LED TO BIG TRAFFIC JAMS...AS YOU CAN IMAGINE. ESPECIALLY WITH TOURIST BUSES GOING UP AND DOWN...
ALL THOSE 180-DEGREE CURVES!! ABRUPT AND CRAMPED!
IT'S AUTUMN.
AROUND 1965
ね
20 カーブ
やしおつつじ
120 いろは坂
Irohazaka
EVERY CURVE GETS ONE OF THESE ROAD SIGNS. THERE ARE FORTY-EIGHT CURVES IN TOTAL!
THE LEAVES CLOSER TO THE TOP WERE REALLY TURNING FALL COLORS.
OOOH, THE LEAVES ARE TURNING.

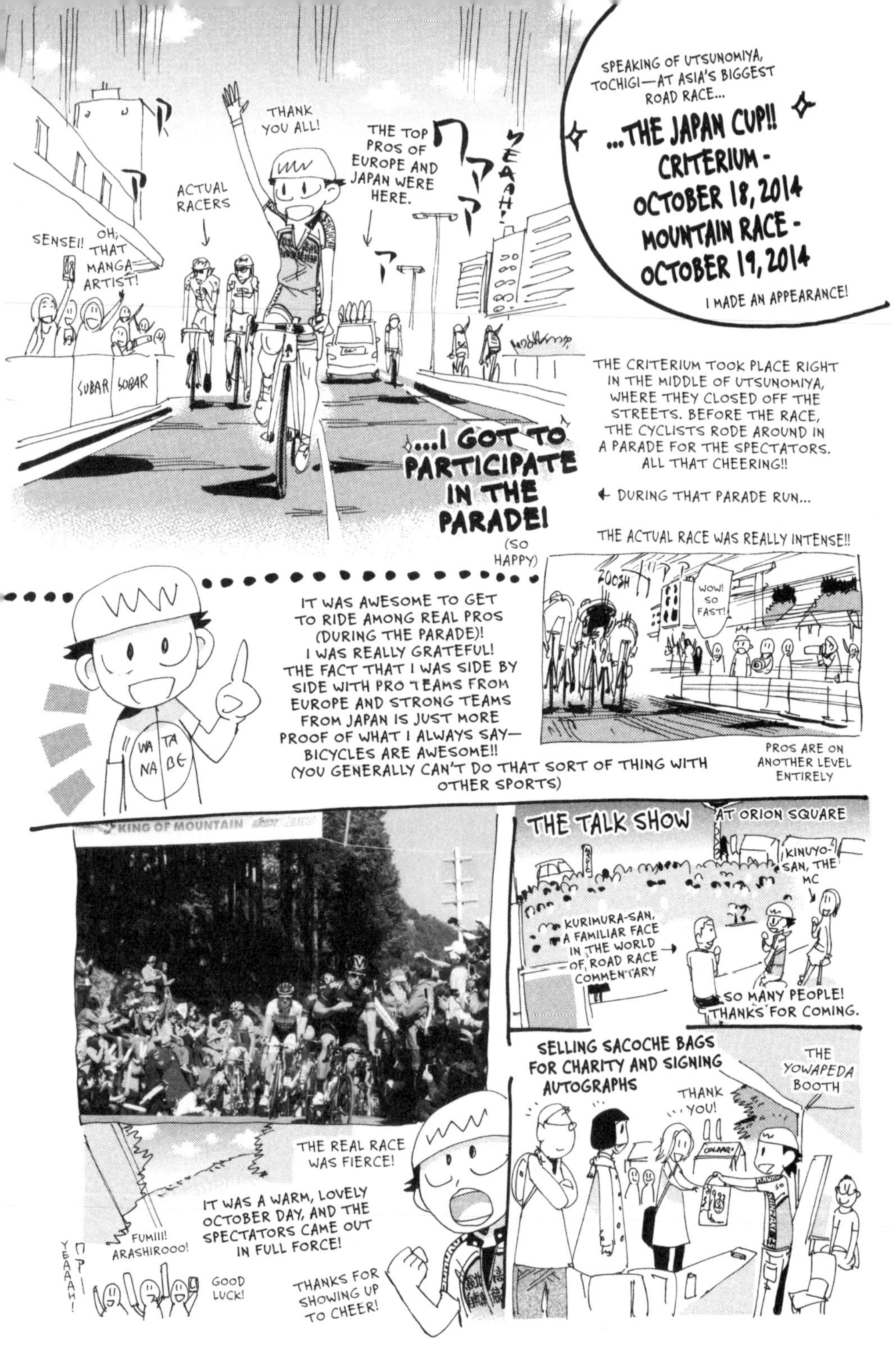

SPEAKING OF UTSUNOMIYA, TOCHIGI—AT ASIA'S BIGGEST ROAD RACE...
...THE JAPAN CUP!!
CRITERIUM - OCTOBER 18, 2014
MOUNTAIN RACE - OCTOBER 19, 2014
I MADE AN APPEARANCE!
YEAAAH!
THE TOP PROS OF EUROPE AND JAPAN WERE HERE.
THANK YOU ALL!
ACTUAL RACERS
OH, THAT MANGA ARTIST!
SENSEI!!
SUBAR SUBAR
THE CRITERIUM TOOK PLACE RIGHT IN THE MIDDLE OF UTSUNOMIYA, WHERE THEY CLOSED OFF THE STREETS. BEFORE THE RACE, THE CYCLISTS RODE AROUND IN A PARADE FOR THE SPECTATORS. ALL THAT CHEERING!!
← DURING THAT PARADE RUN...
...I GOT TO PARTICIPATE IN THE PARADE!
(SO HAPPY)
THE ACTUAL RACE WAS REALLY INTENSE!!
WOW! SO FAST!
ZOOSH
PROS ARE ON ANOTHER LEVEL ENTIRELY
IT WAS AWESOME TO GET TO RIDE AMONG REAL PROS (DURING THE PARADE)! I WAS REALLY GRATEFUL! THE FACT THAT I WAS SIDE BY SIDE WITH PRO TEAMS FROM EUROPE AND STRONG TEAMS FROM JAPAN IS JUST MORE PROOF OF WHAT I ALWAYS SAY—BICYCLES ARE AWESOME!! (YOU GENERALLY CAN'T DO THAT SORT OF THING WITH OTHER SPORTS)
WA TA NA BE
THE TALK SHOW
AT ORION SQUARE
KINUYO-SAN, THE MC
KURIMURA-SAN, A FAMILIAR FACE IN THE WORLD OF ROAD RACE COMMENTARY →
SO MANY PEOPLE! THANKS FOR COMING.
SELLING SACOCHE BAGS FOR CHARITY AND SIGNING AUTOGRAPHS
THE YOWAPEDA BOOTH
THANK YOU!
KING OF MOUNTAIN
THE REAL RACE WAS FIERCE!
IT WAS A WARM, LOVELY OCTOBER DAY, AND THE SPECTATORS CAME OUT IN FULL FORCE!
FUMIII! ARASHIROOO!
YEAAAH!
GOOD LUCK!
THANKS FOR SHOWING UP TO CHEER!

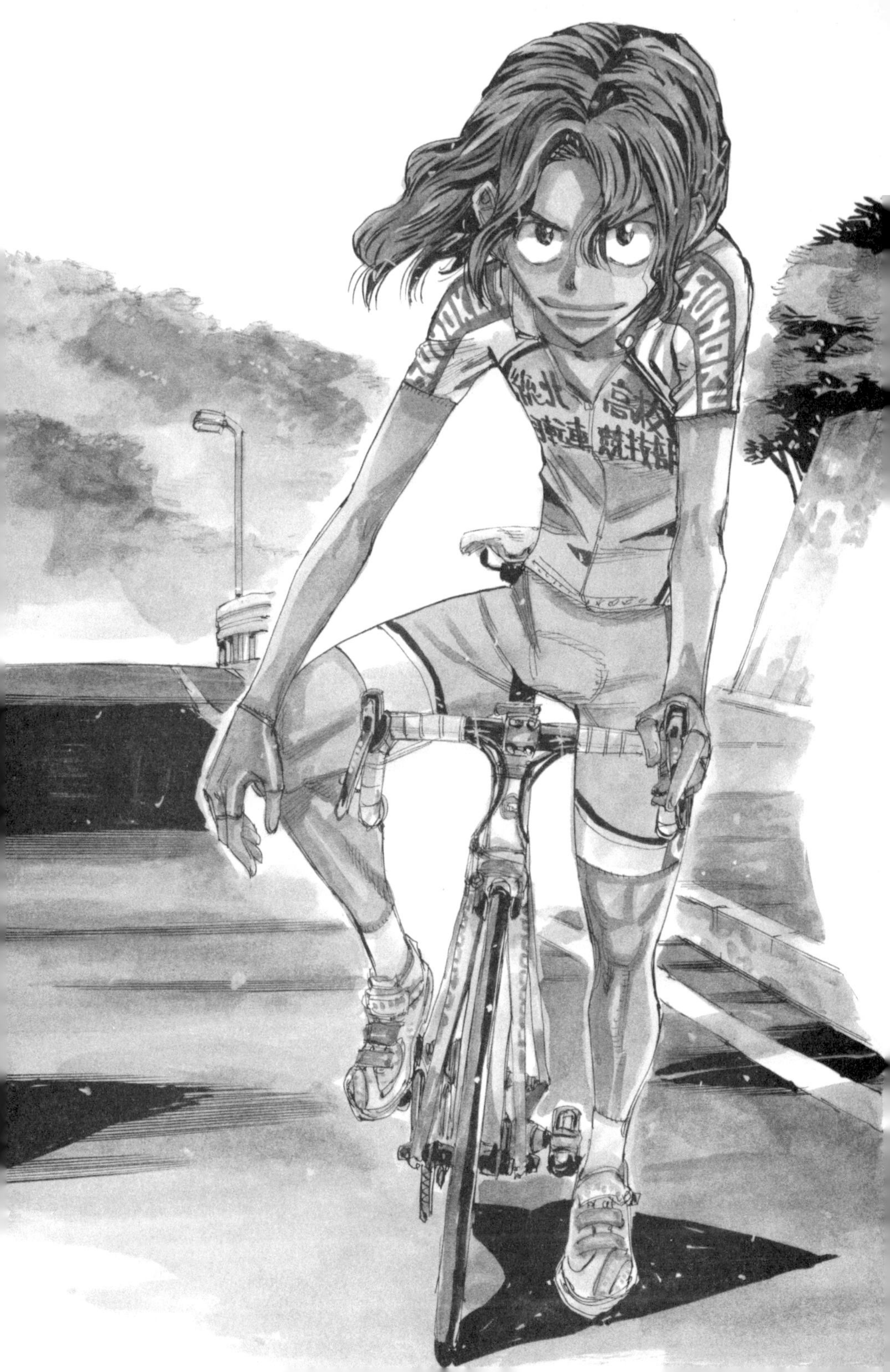

RIDE.321 MESSAGE

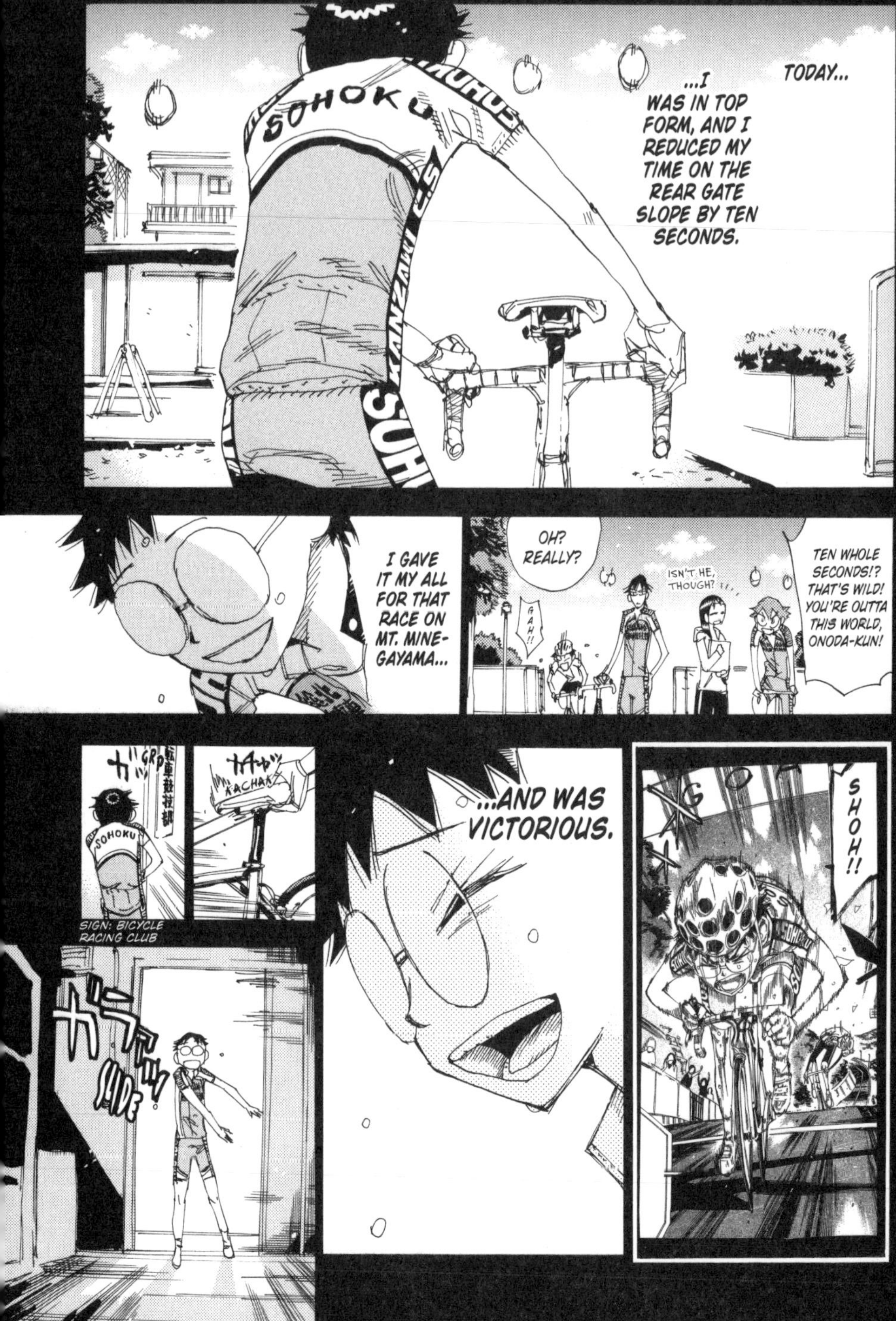

TODAY...
...I WAS IN TOP FORM, AND I REDUCED MY TIME ON THE REAR GATE SLOPE BY TEN SECONDS.
TEN WHOLE SECONDS!? THAT'S WILD! YOU'RE OUTTA THIS WORLD, ONODA-KUN!
ISN'T HE, THOUGH?
OH? REALLY?
GAH!!
I GAVE IT MY ALL FOR THAT RACE ON MT. MINE-GAYAMA...
GOAL
SHOH!!
...AND WAS VICTORIOUS.
KACHAK
GRP
SIGN: BICYCLE RACING CLUB
SLIDE

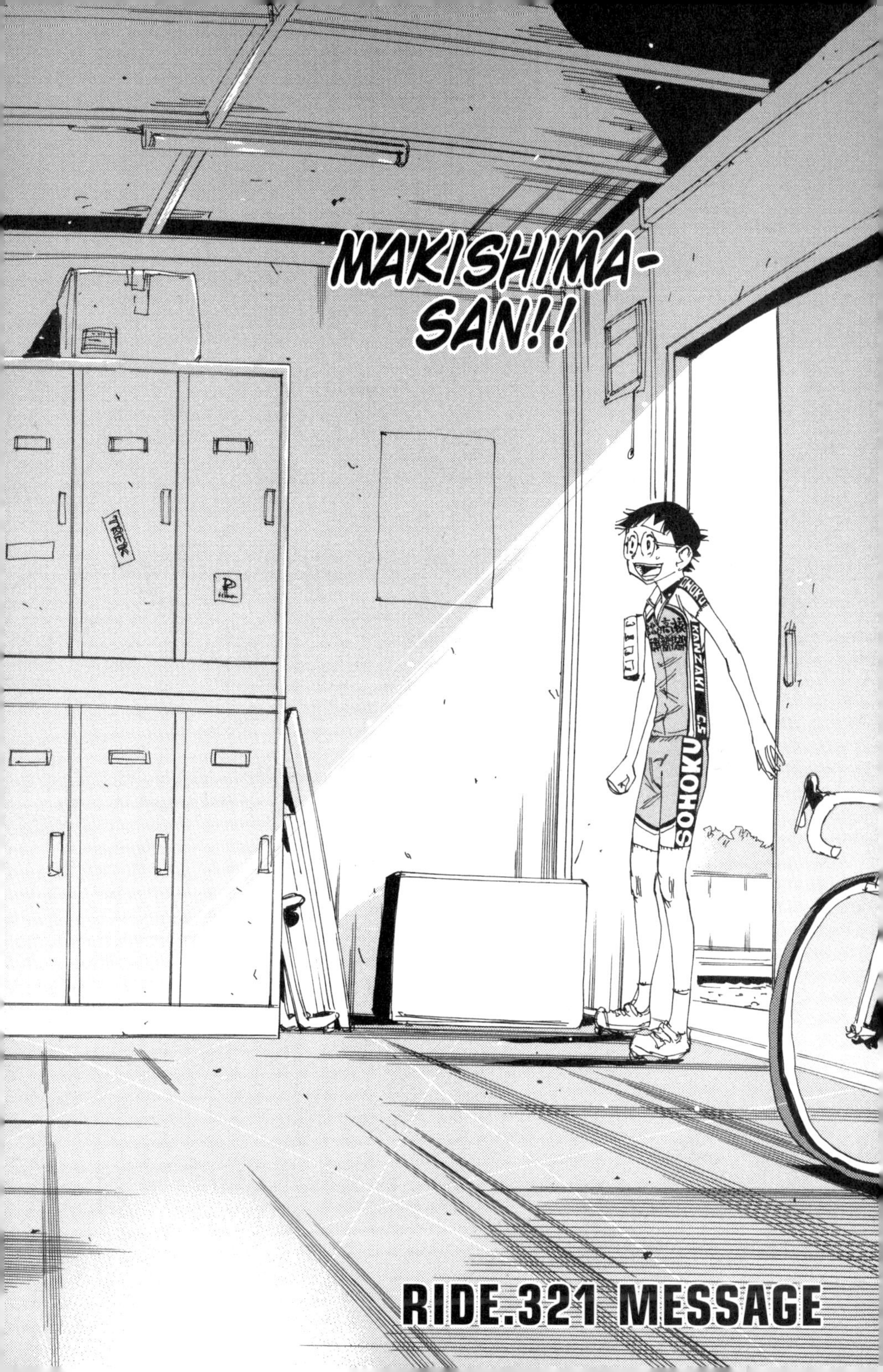
MAKISHIMA-SAN!!
TREK
RIDE.321 MESSAGE

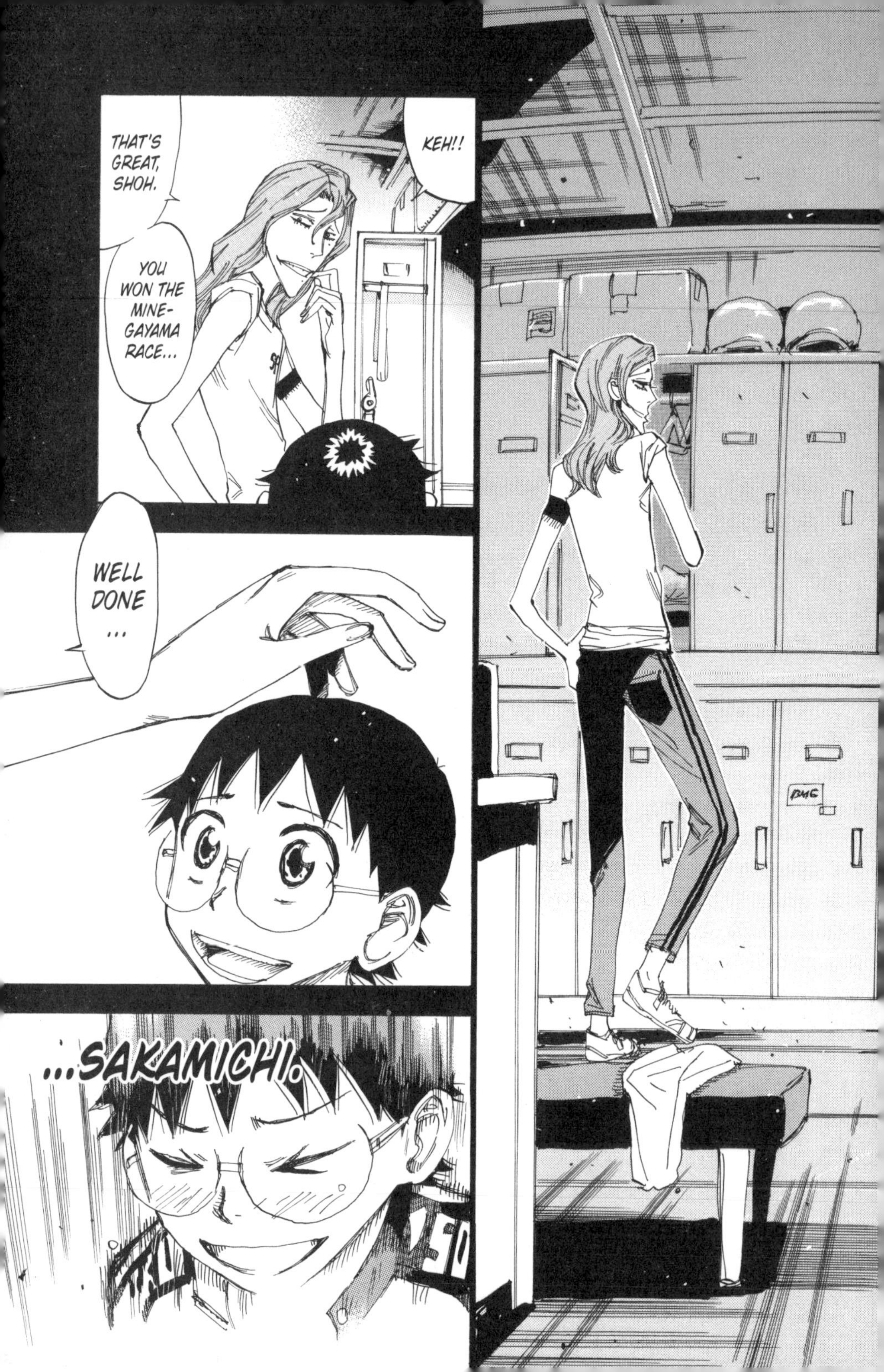
KEH!!
THAT'S GREAT, SHOH.
YOU WON THE MINE-GAYAMA RACE...
WELL DONE ...
...SAKAMICHI.

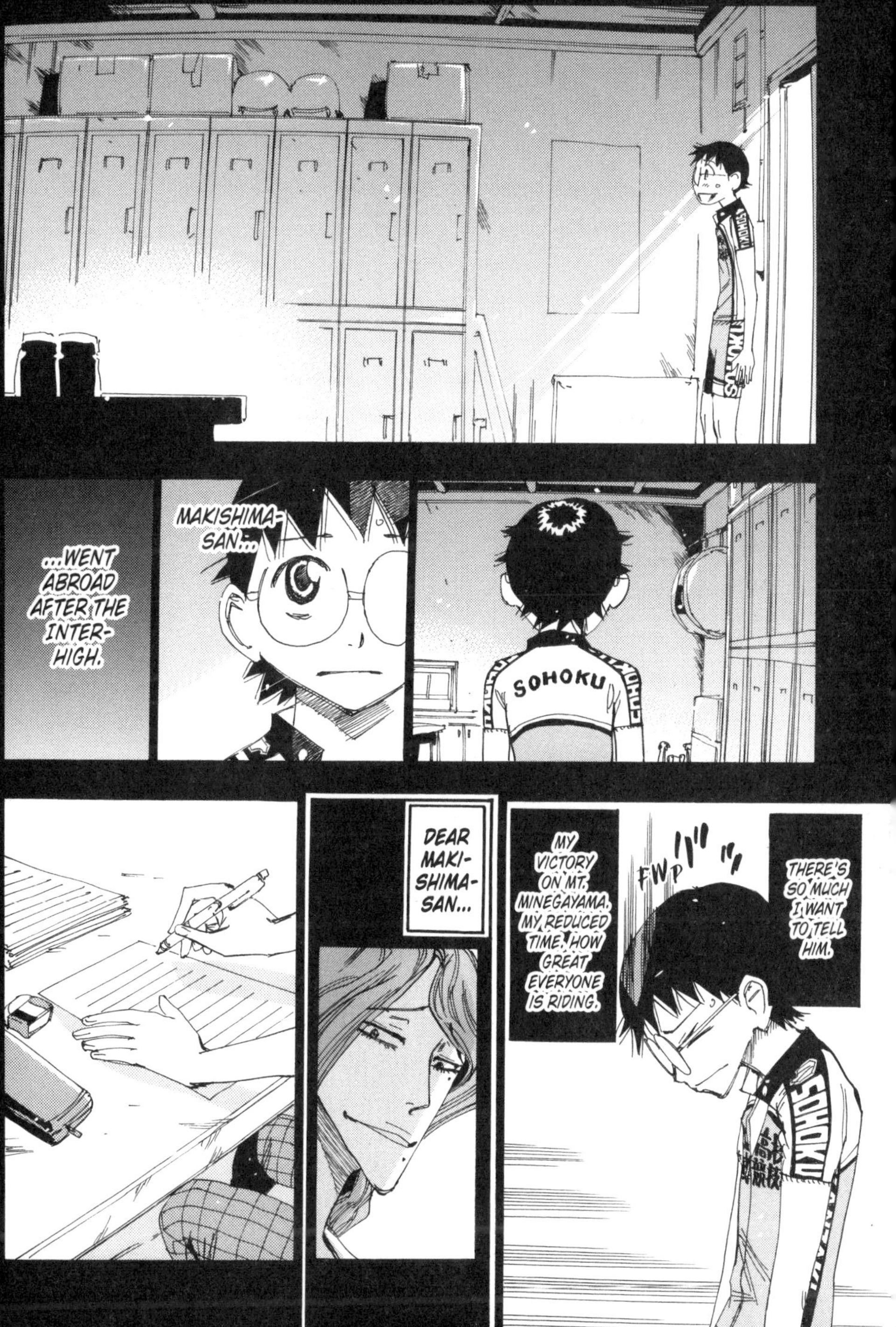
SOHOKU
MAKISHIMA-SAN...
...WENT ABROAD AFTER THE INTER-HIGH.
THERE'S SO MUCH I WANT TO TELL HIM.
FWP
MY VICTORY ON MT. MINEGAYAMA, MY REDUCED TIME, HOW GREAT EVERYONE IS RIDING.
DEAR MAKI-SHIMA-SAN...

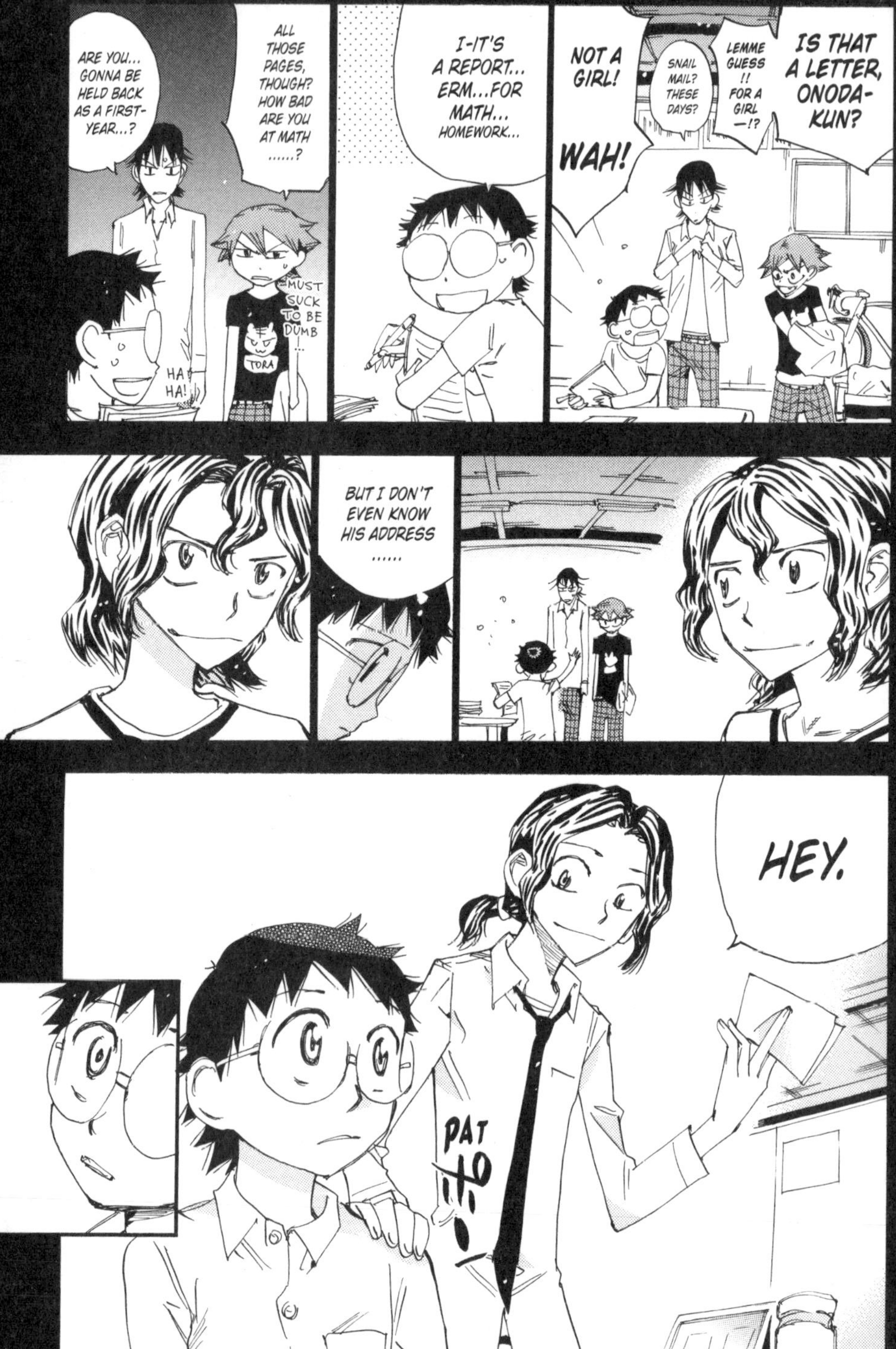
IS THAT A LETTER, ONODA-KUN?
LEMME GUESS!! FOR A GIRL—!?
SNAIL MAIL? THESE DAYS?
NOT A GIRL!
WAH!
I-IT'S A REPORT... ERM...FOR MATH... HOMEWORK...
ALL THOSE PAGES, THOUGH? HOW BAD ARE YOU AT MATH ......?
ARE YOU... GONNA BE HELD BACK AS A FIRST-YEAR...?
MUST SUCK TO BE DUMB...
TORA
HA HA!
BUT I DON'T EVEN KNOW HIS ADDRESS ......
HEY.
PAT

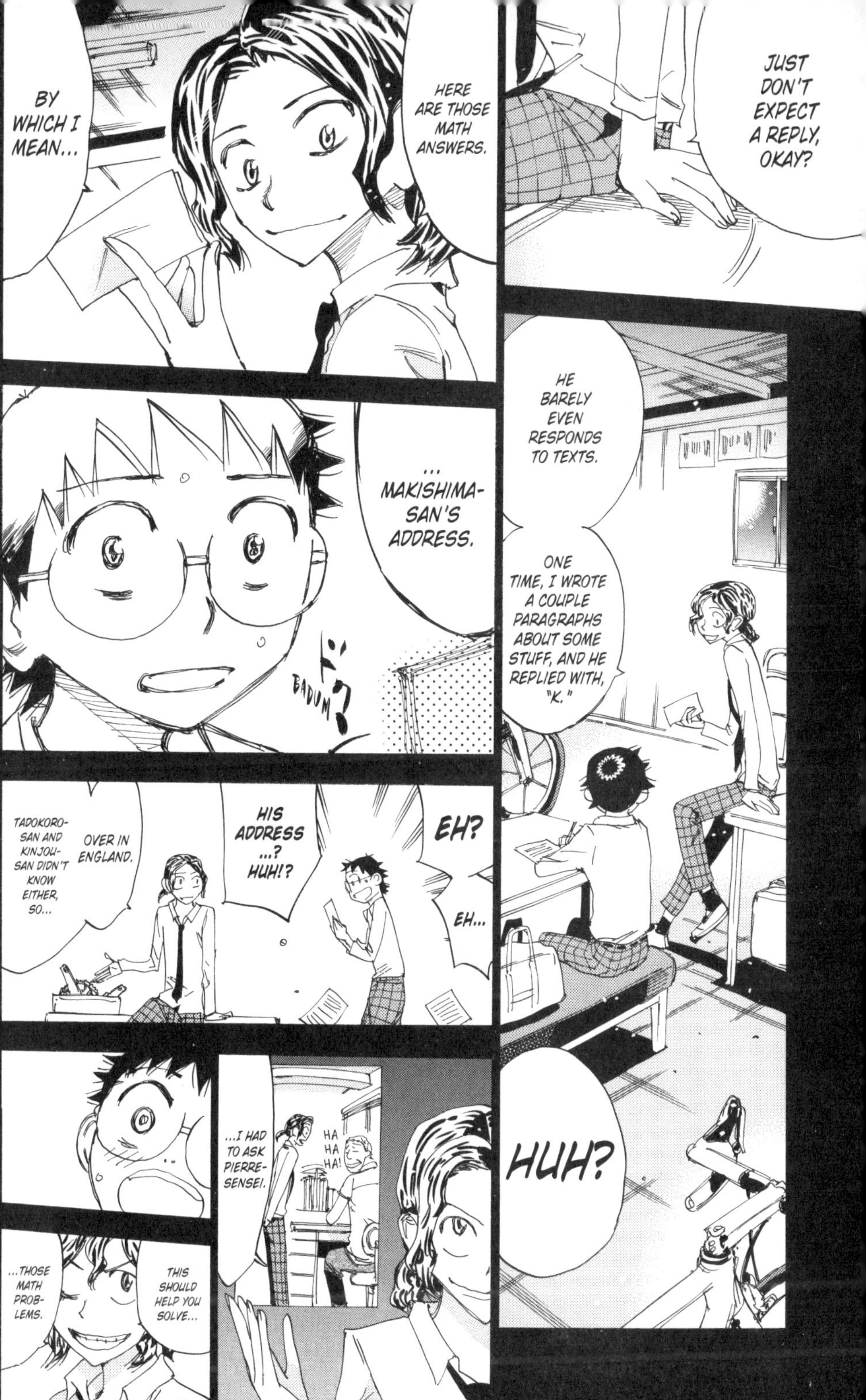

JUST DON'T EXPECT A REPLY, OKAY?
HERE ARE THOSE MATH ANSWERS.
BY WHICH I MEAN...
HE BARELY EVEN RESPONDS TO TEXTS.
ONE TIME, I WROTE A COUPLE PARAGRAPHS ABOUT SOME STUFF, AND HE REPLIED WITH, "K."
...MAKISHIMA-SAN'S ADDRESS.
BADUM
EH?
EH...
HIS ADDRESS ...? HUH!?
OVER IN ENGLAND.
TADOKORO-SAN AND KINJOU-SAN DIDN'T KNOW EITHER, SO...
HUH?
HA HA HA!
...I HAD TO ASK PIERRE-SENSEI.
THIS SHOULD HELP YOU SOLVE...
...THOSE MATH PROBLEMS.

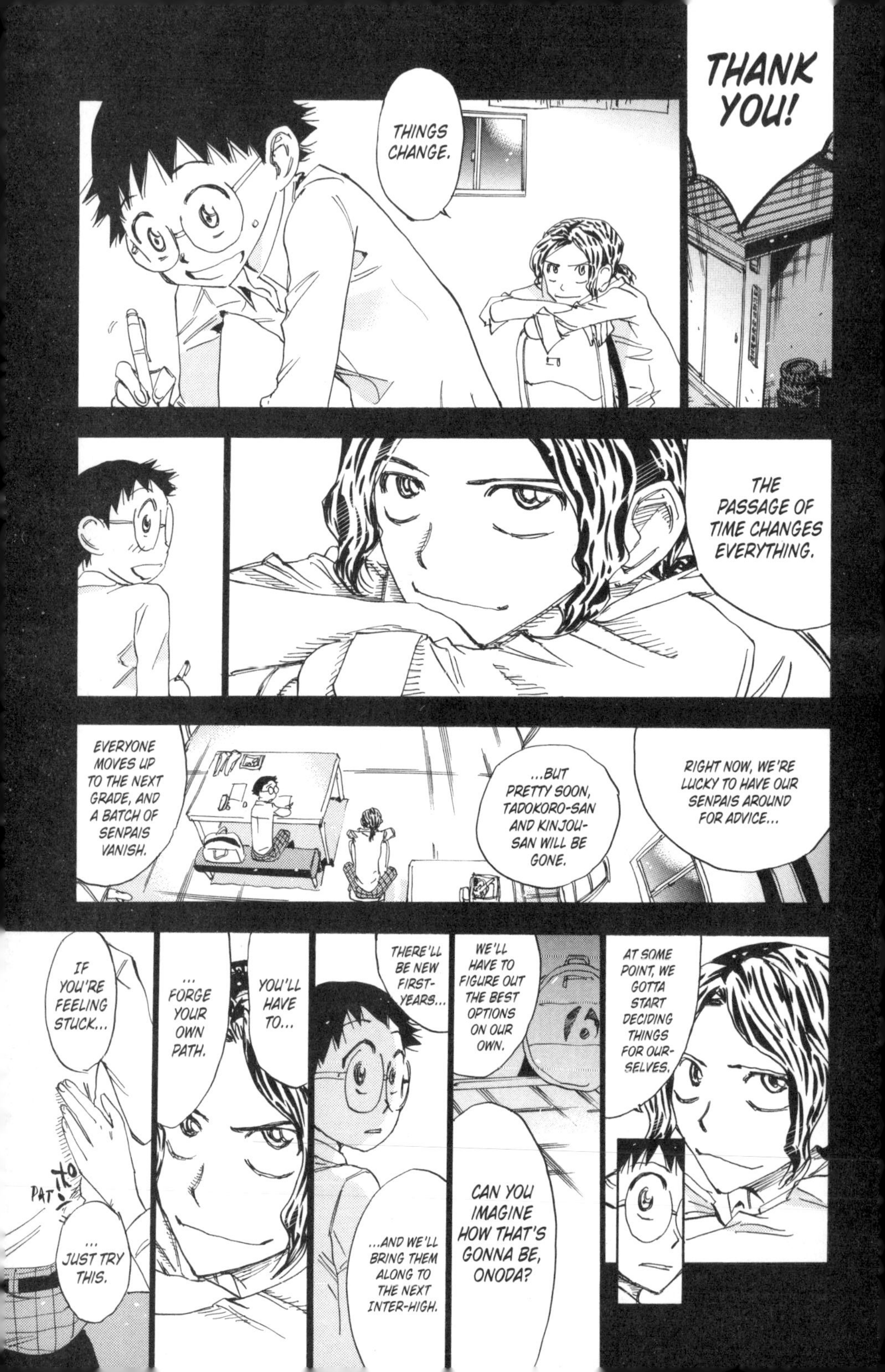
THANK YOU!
THINGS CHANGE.
THE PASSAGE OF TIME CHANGES EVERYTHING.
RIGHT NOW, WE'RE LUCKY TO HAVE OUR SENPAIS AROUND FOR ADVICE...
...BUT PRETTY SOON, TADOKORO-SAN AND KINJOU-SAN WILL BE GONE.
EVERYONE MOVES UP TO THE NEXT GRADE, AND A BATCH OF SENPAIS VANISH.
AT SOME POINT, WE GOTTA START DECIDING THINGS FOR OUR-SELVES.
WE'LL HAVE TO FIGURE OUT THE BEST OPTIONS ON OUR OWN.
CAN YOU IMAGINE HOW THAT'S GONNA BE, ONODA?
THERE'LL BE NEW FIRST-YEARS...
...AND WE'LL BRING THEM ALONG TO THE NEXT INTER-HIGH.
YOU'LL HAVE TO...
...FORGE YOUR OWN PATH.
IF YOU'RE FEELING STUCK...
...JUST TRY THIS.
PAT

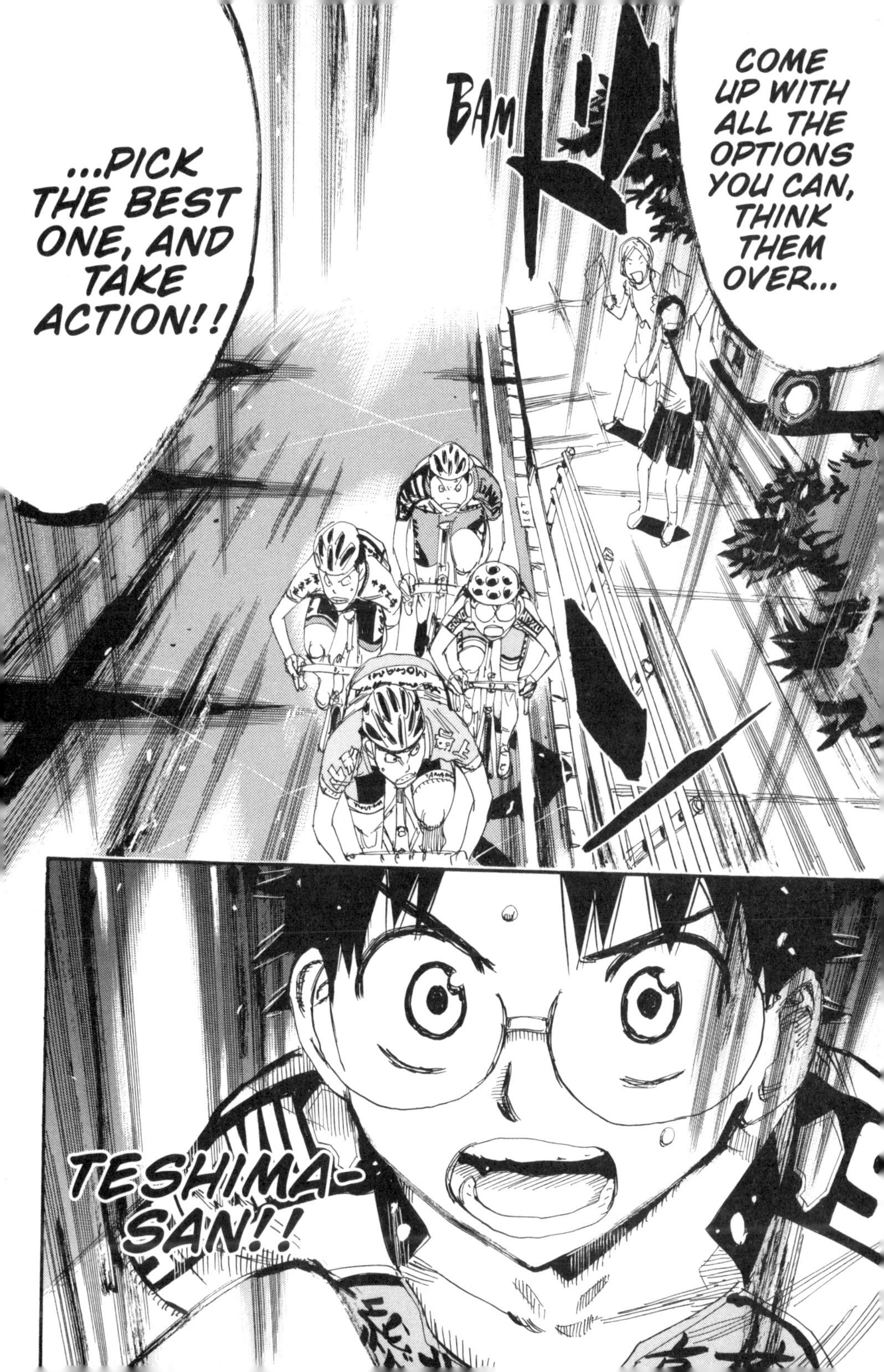
COME UP WITH ALL THE OPTIONS YOU CAN, THINK THEM OVER...
BAM
...PICK THE BEST ONE, AND TAKE ACTION!!
TESHIMA-SAN!!

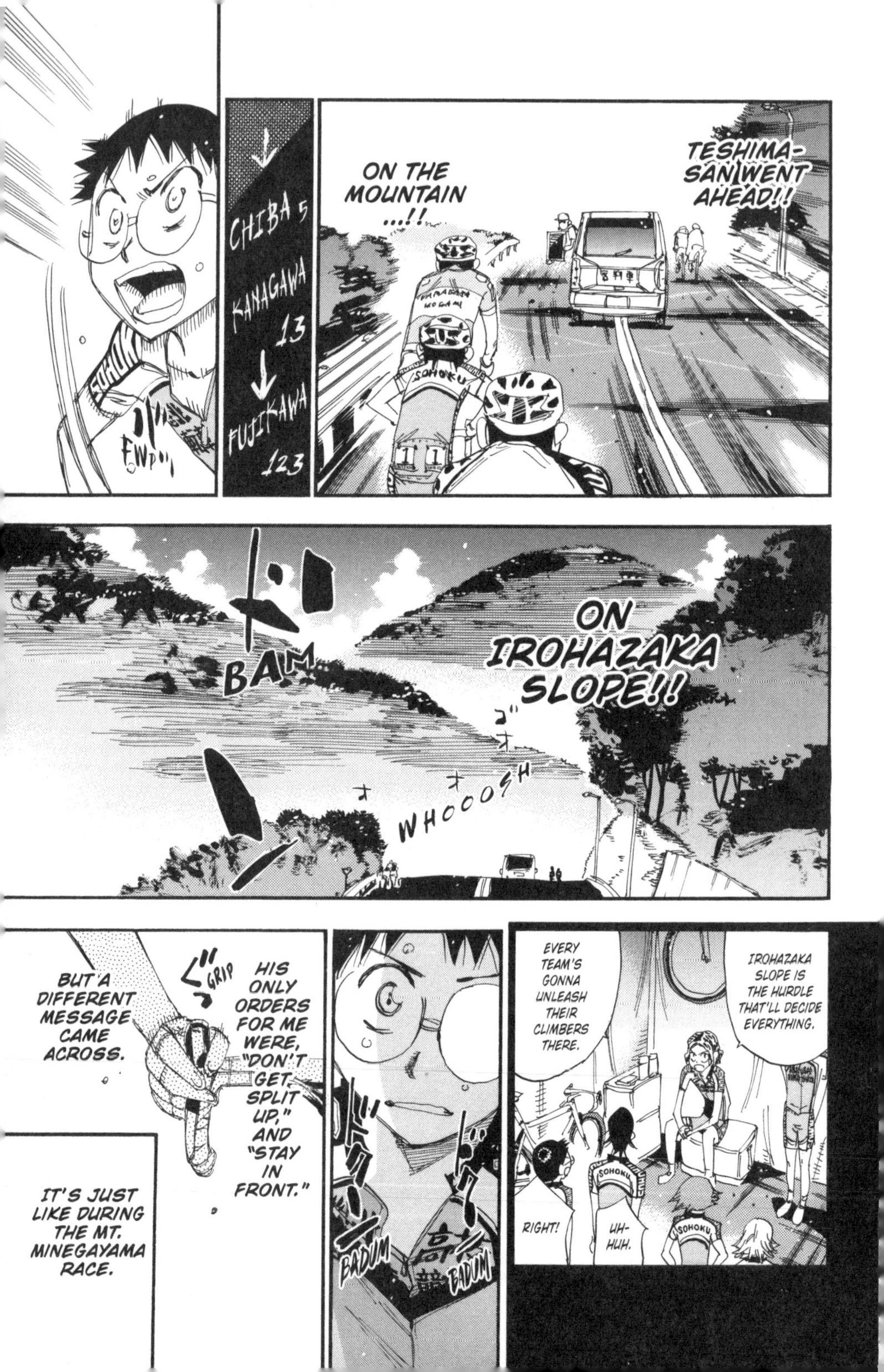

TESHIMA-SAN WENT AHEAD!!
ON THE MOUNTAIN ...!!
CHIBA 5
KANAGAWA 13
FUJIKAWA 123
FWP
ON IROHAZAKA SLOPE!!
BAM
WHOOOSH
IROHAZAKA SLOPE IS THE HURDLE THAT'LL DECIDE EVERYTHING.
EVERY TEAM'S GONNA UNLEASH THEIR CLIMBERS THERE.
UH-HUH.
RIGHT!
BADUM
BADUM
HIS ONLY ORDERS FOR ME WERE, "DON'T GET SPLIT UP," AND "STAY IN FRONT."
GRIP
BUT A DIFFERENT MESSAGE CAME ACROSS.
IT'S JUST LIKE DURING THE MT. MINEGAYAMA RACE.

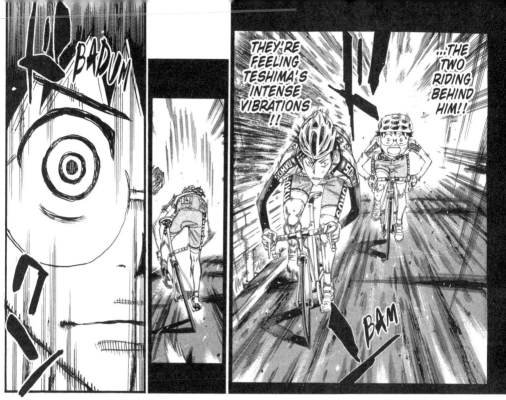

THEY'RE FEELING TESHIMA'S INTENSE VIBRATIONS!!

...THE TWO RIDING BEHIND HIM!!

BADUM

BAM

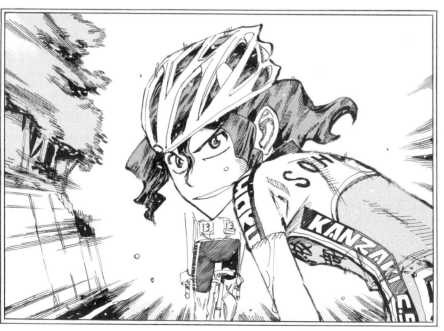

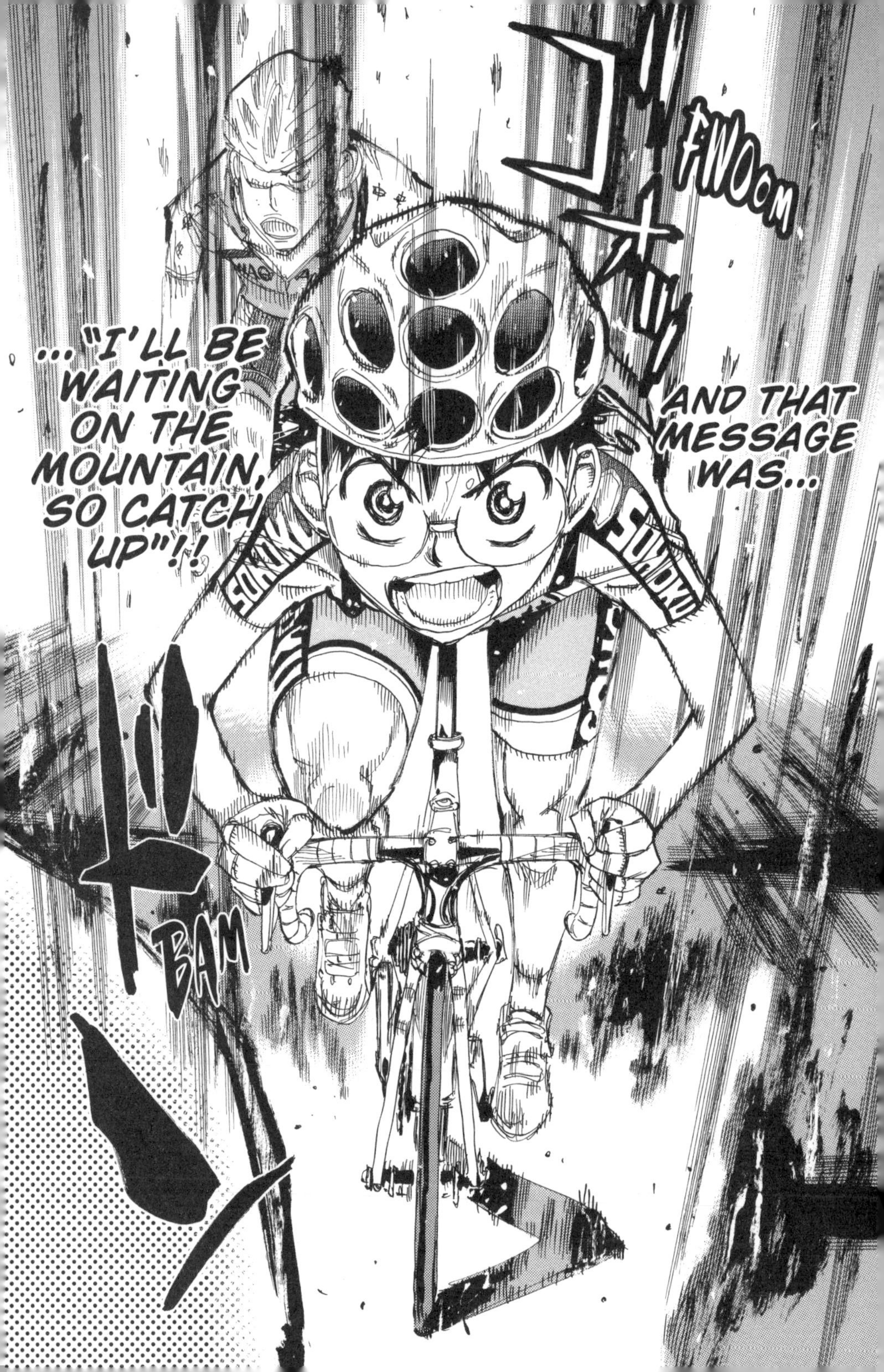
FWOOM
AND THAT MESSAGE WAS...
..."I'LL BE WAITING ON THE MOUNTAIN, SO CATCH UP"!!
BAM

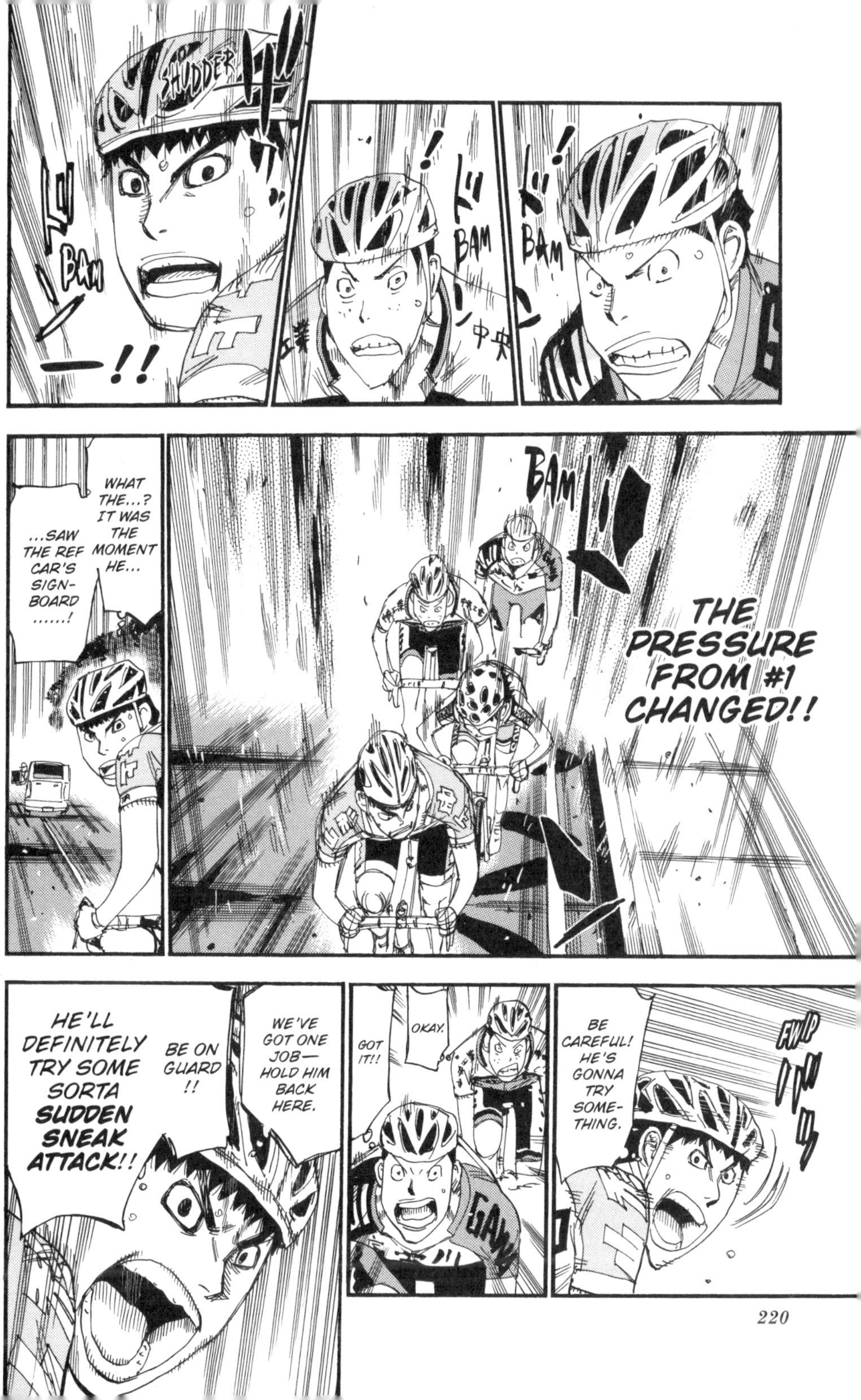
BAM
BAM
SHUDDER
BAM
BAM
THE PRESSURE FROM #1 CHANGED!!
WHAT THE...? IT WAS THE MOMENT HE...
...SAW THE REF CAR'S SIGN-BOARD......!
FWIP
BE CAREFUL! HE'S GONNA TRY SOME-THING.
OKAY.
GOT IT!!
WE'VE GOT ONE JOB—HOLD HIM BACK HERE.
BE ON GUARD!!
HE'LL DEFINITELY TRY SOME SORTA **SUDDEN SNEAK ATTACK!!**

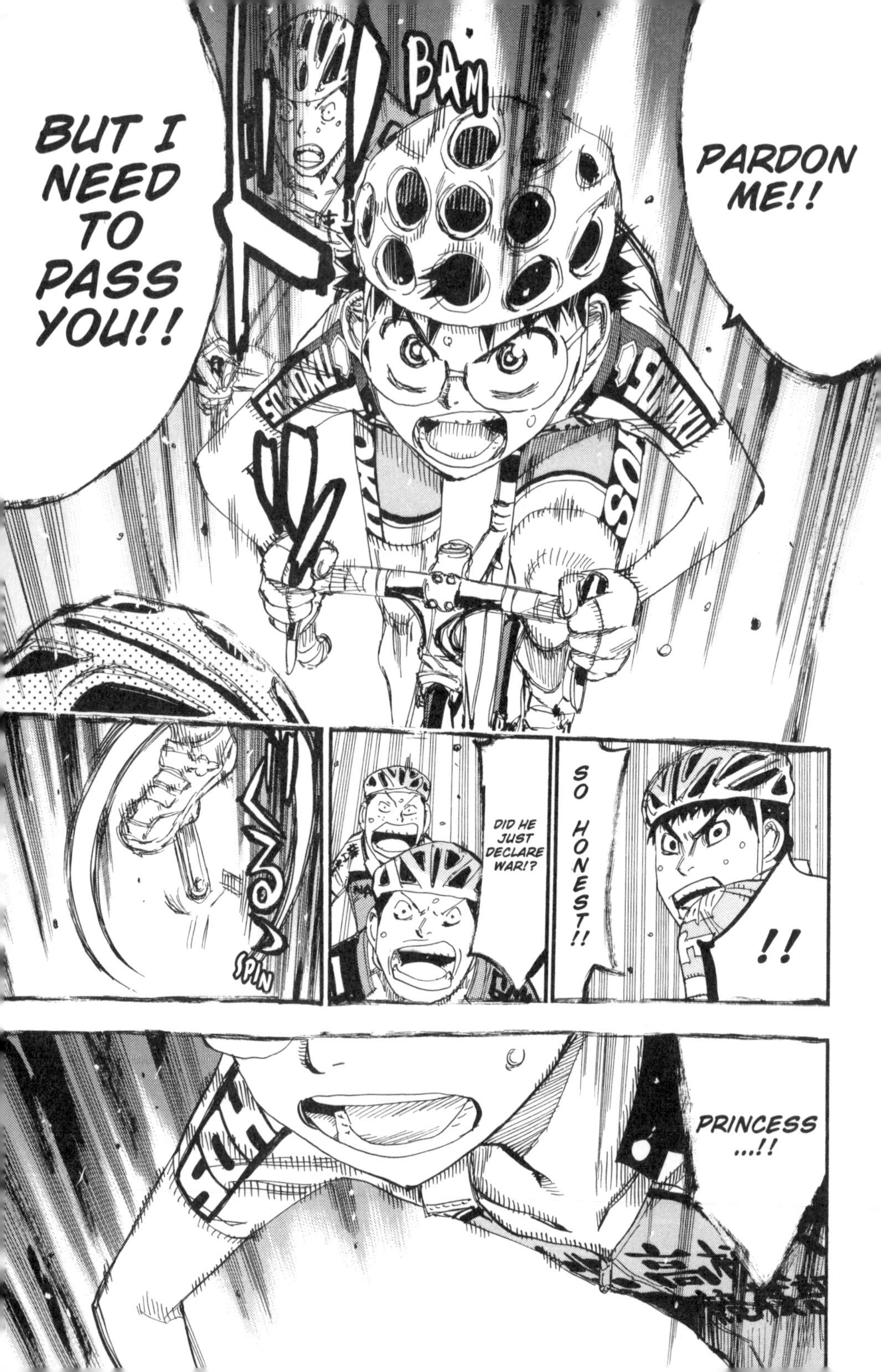
PARDON ME!!
BAM
BUT I NEED TO PASS YOU!!
SO HONEST!!
!!
DID HE JUST DECLARE WAR!?
SPIN
PRINCESS ...!!

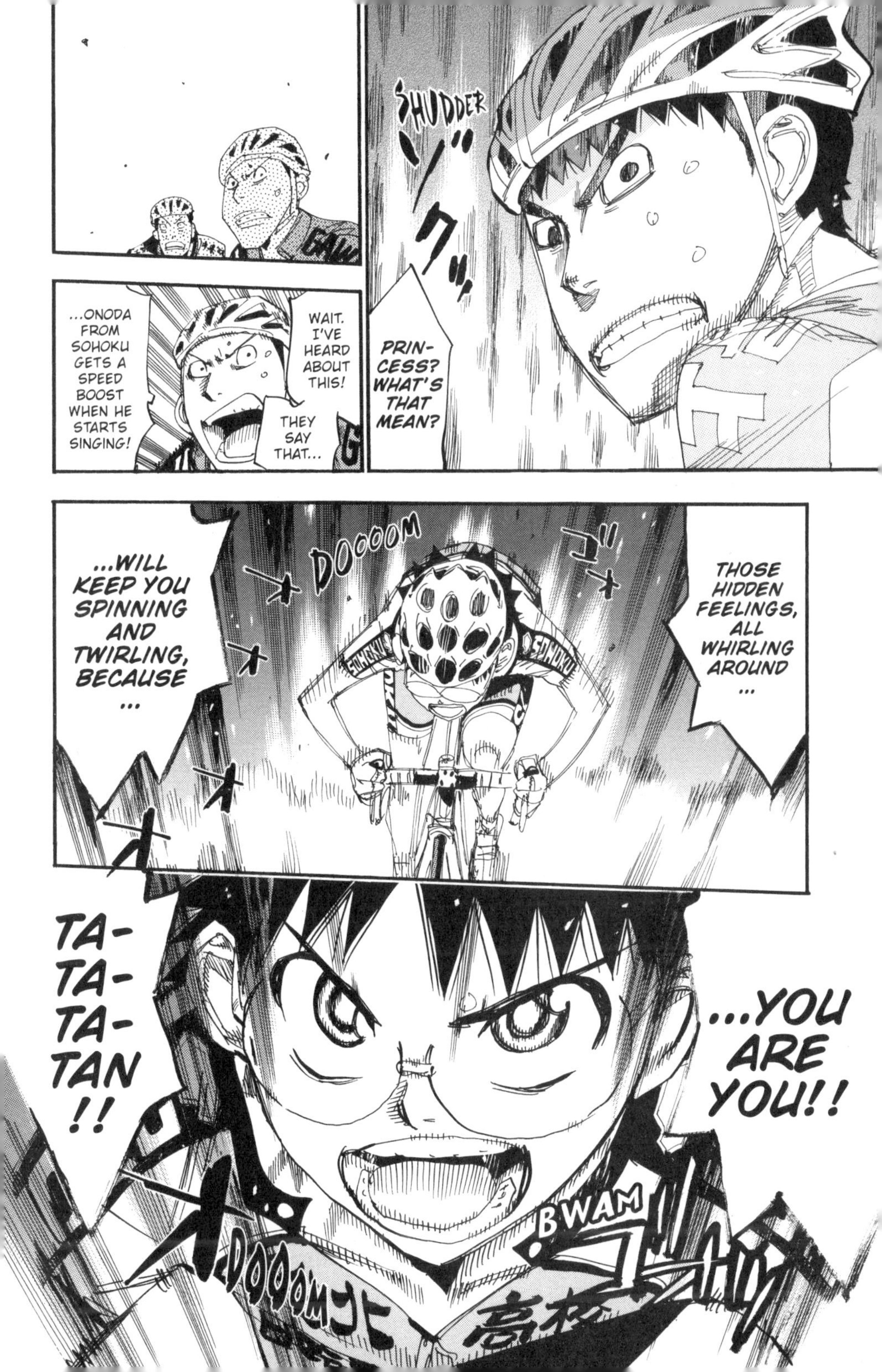
SHUDDER
PRIN-CESS? WHAT'S THAT MEAN?
WAIT. I'VE HEARD ABOUT THIS!
THEY SAY THAT...
...ONODA FROM SOHOKU GETS A SPEED BOOST WHEN HE STARTS SINGING!
THOSE HIDDEN FEELINGS, ALL WHIRLING AROUND...
DOOOOM
...WILL KEEP YOU SPINNING AND TWIRLING, BECAUSE...
...YOU ARE YOU!!
TA-TA-TA-TAN!!
BWAM
DOOOOM

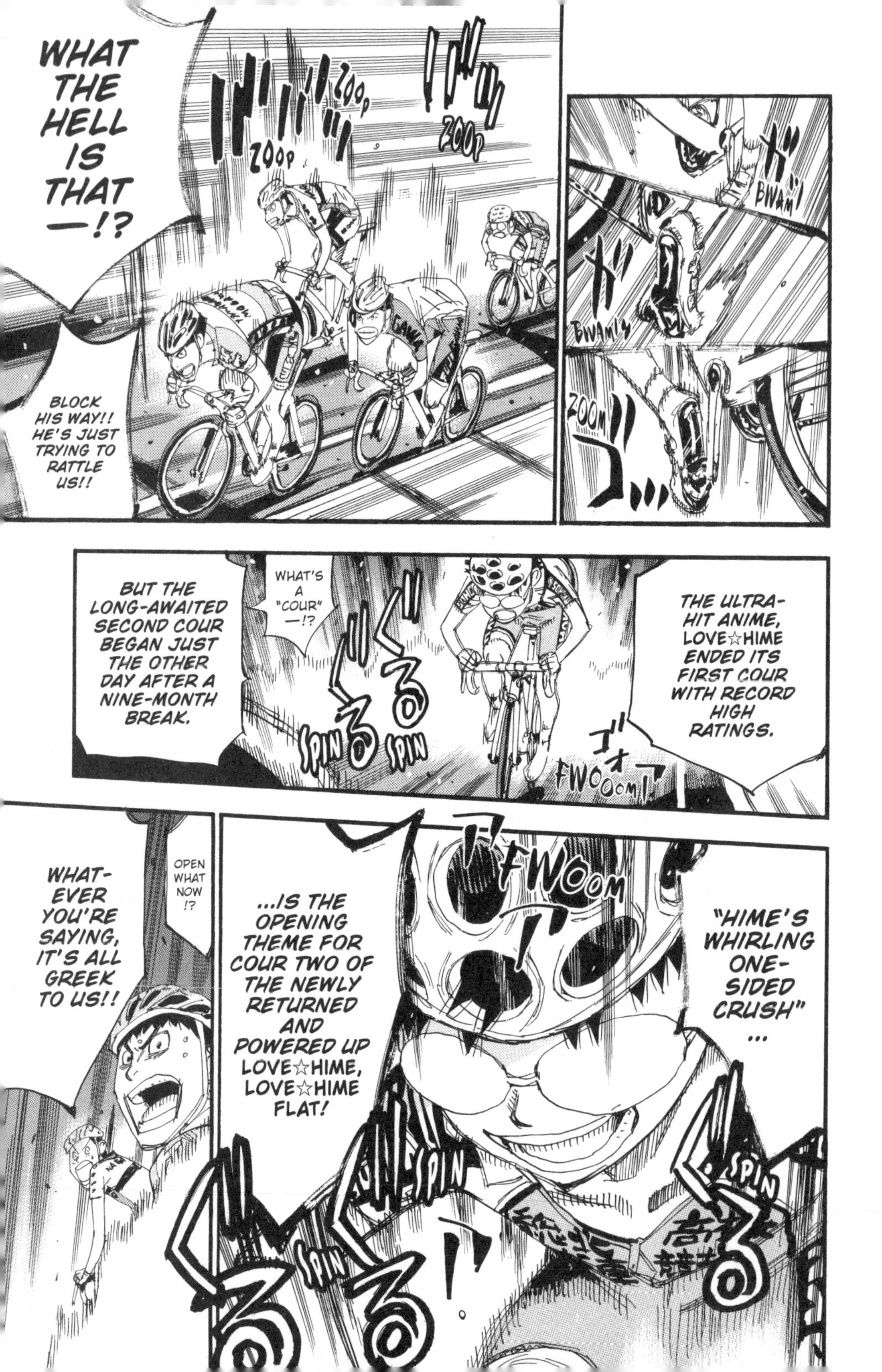
BWAM!
BWAM!
ZOOM!
ZOOP
ZOOP
ZOOP
WHAT THE HELL IS THAT—!?
BLOCK HIS WAY!! HE'S JUST TRYING TO RATTLE US!!
THE ULTRA-HIT ANIME, LOVE☆HIME ENDED ITS FIRST COUR WITH RECORD HIGH RATINGS.
FWOOOM!
WHAT'S A "COUR"—!?
SPIN
SPIN
BUT THE LONG-AWAITED SECOND COUR BEGAN JUST THE OTHER DAY AFTER A NINE-MONTH BREAK.
"HIME'S WHIRLING ONE-SIDED CRUSH"...
FWOOM!
...IS THE OPENING THEME FOR COUR TWO OF THE NEWLY RETURNED AND POWERED UP LOVE☆HIME, LOVE☆HIME FLAT!
SPIN
SPIN
SPIN
OPEN WHAT NOW!?
WHATEVER YOU'RE SAYING, IT'S ALL GREEK TO US!!

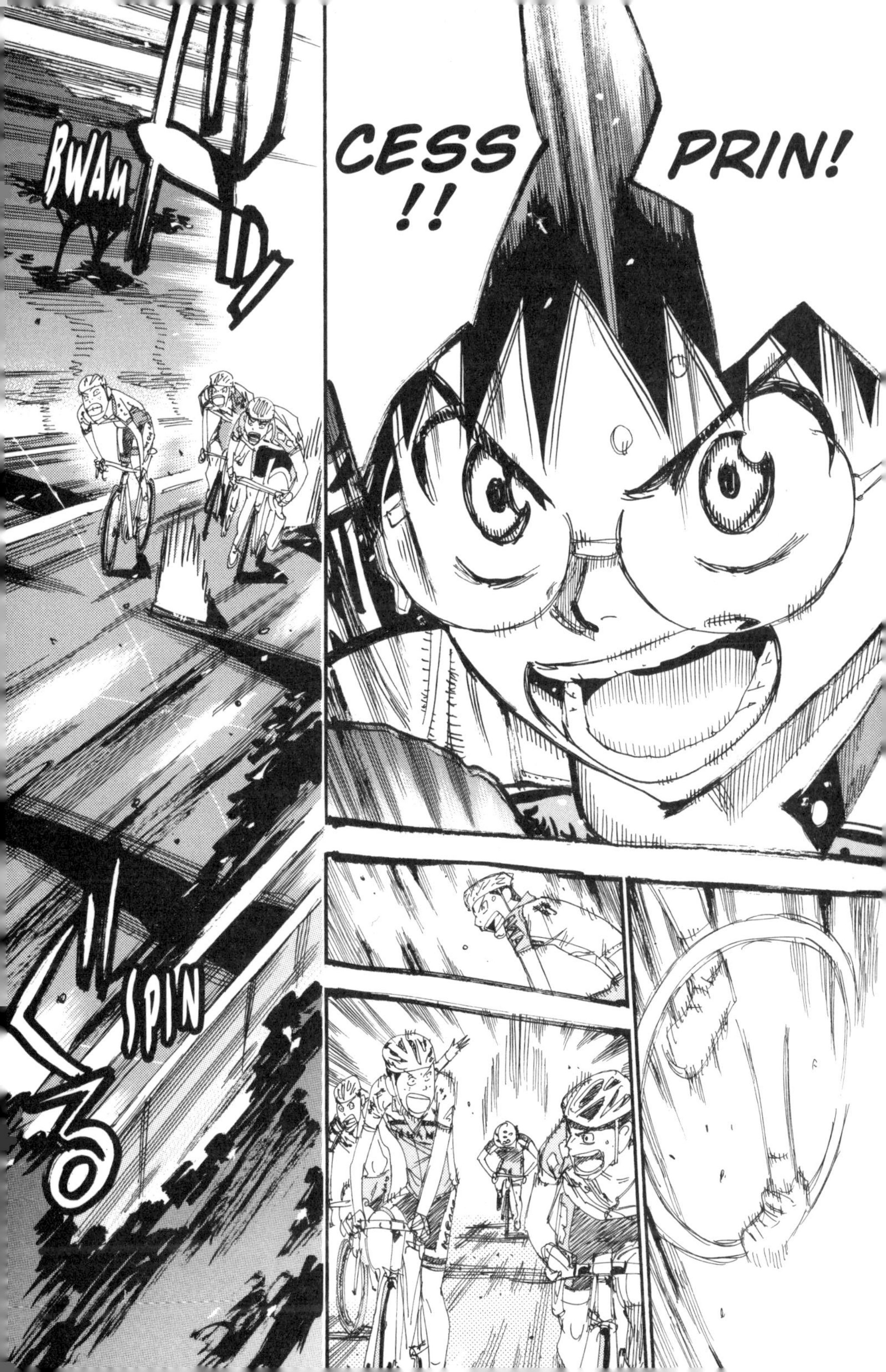
PRIN!
CESS
!!
BWAM
SPIN

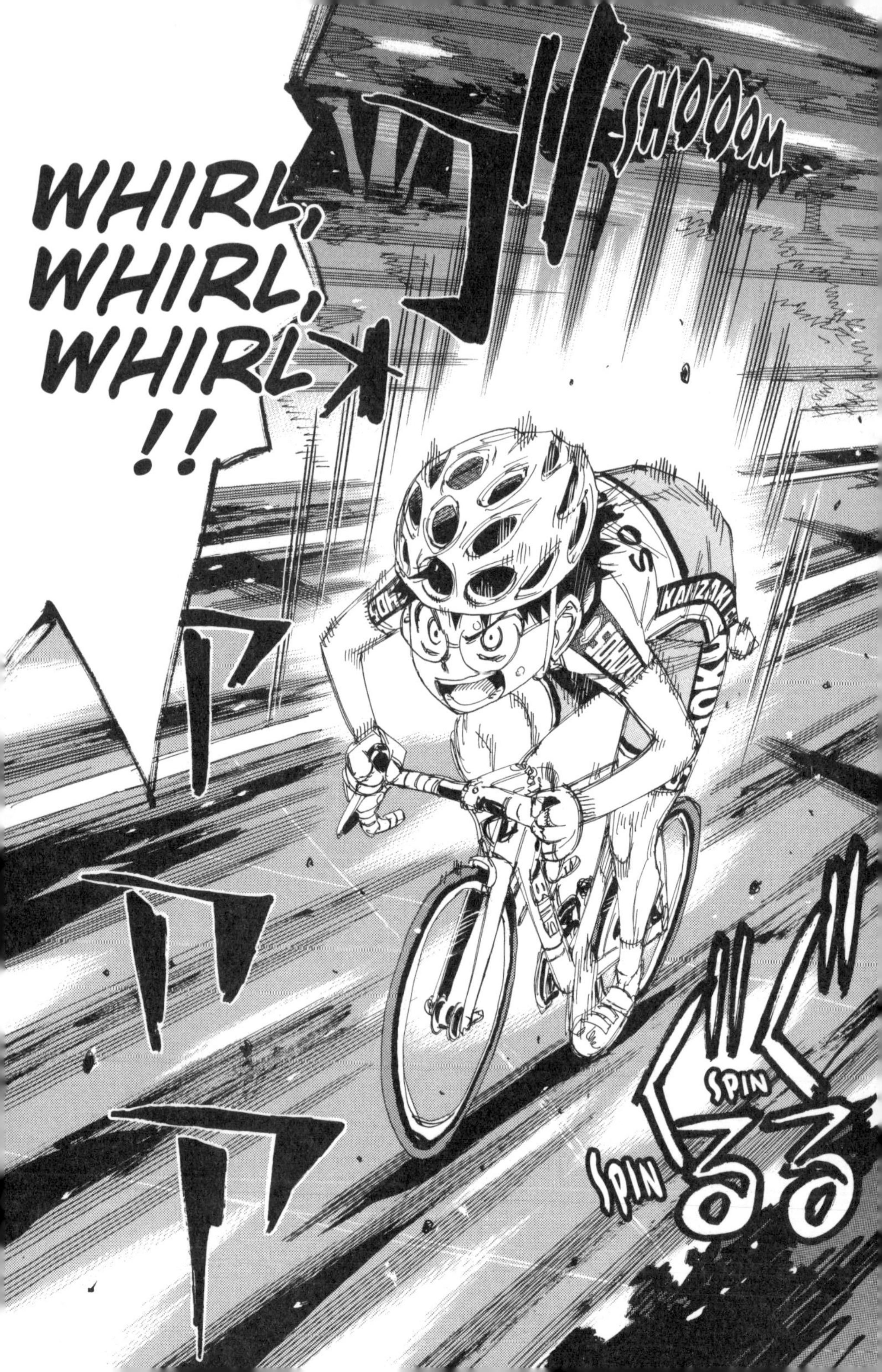
SHOOOM
WHIRL, WHIRL, WHIRL!!
SPIN
SPIN

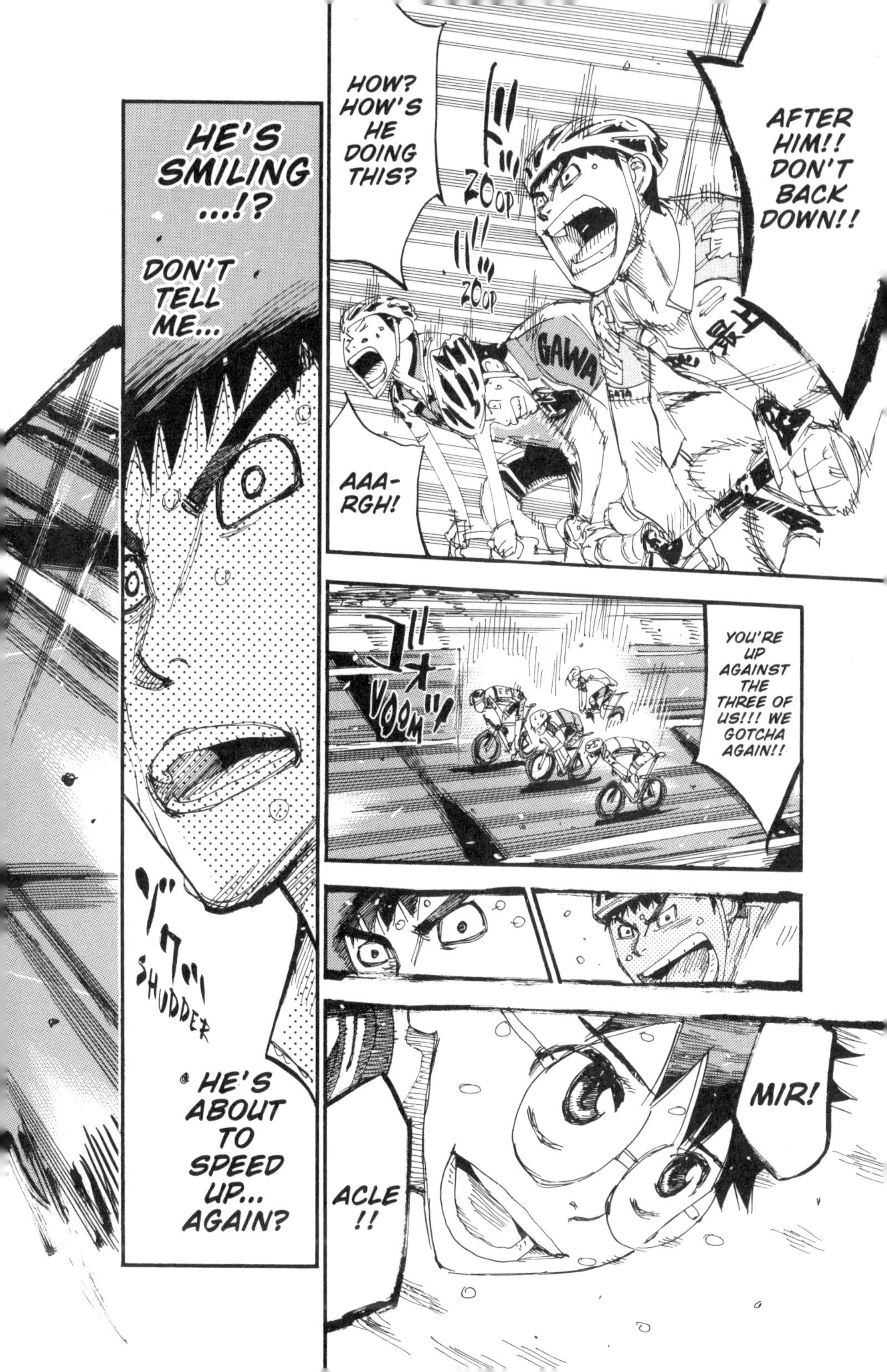
AFTER HIM!! DON'T BACK DOWN!!
HOW? HOW'S HE DOING THIS?
ZOOP
ZOOP
AAA-RGH!
VROOM
YOU'RE UP AGAINST THE THREE OF US!!! WE GOTCHA AGAIN!!
MIR!
ACLE!!
HE'S SMILING...!?
DON'T TELL ME...
SHUDDER
HE'S ABOUT TO SPEED UP... AGAIN?

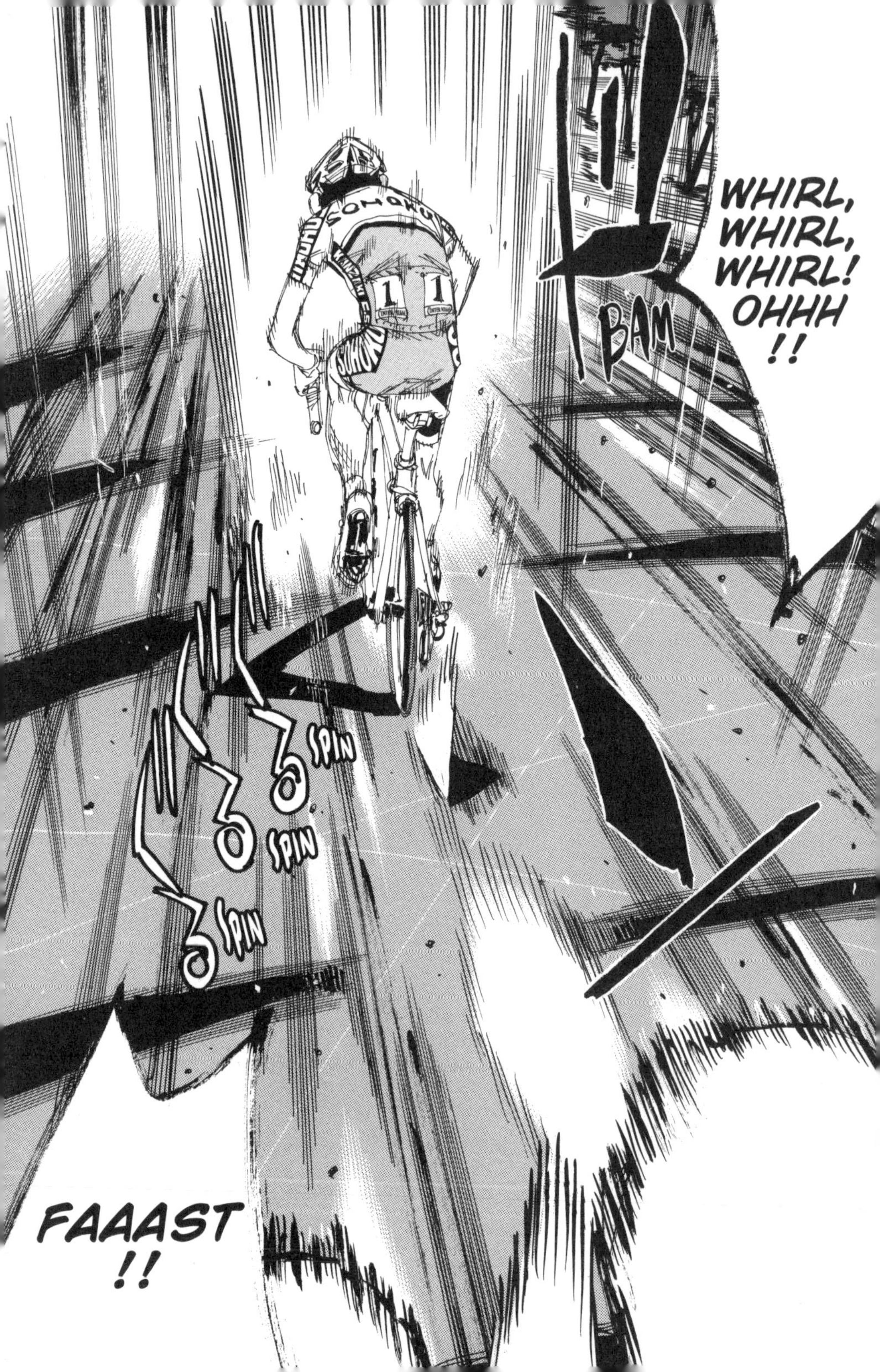
WHIRL, WHIRL, WHIRL! OHHH !!
BAM
SPIN
SPIN
SPIN
FAAAST !!

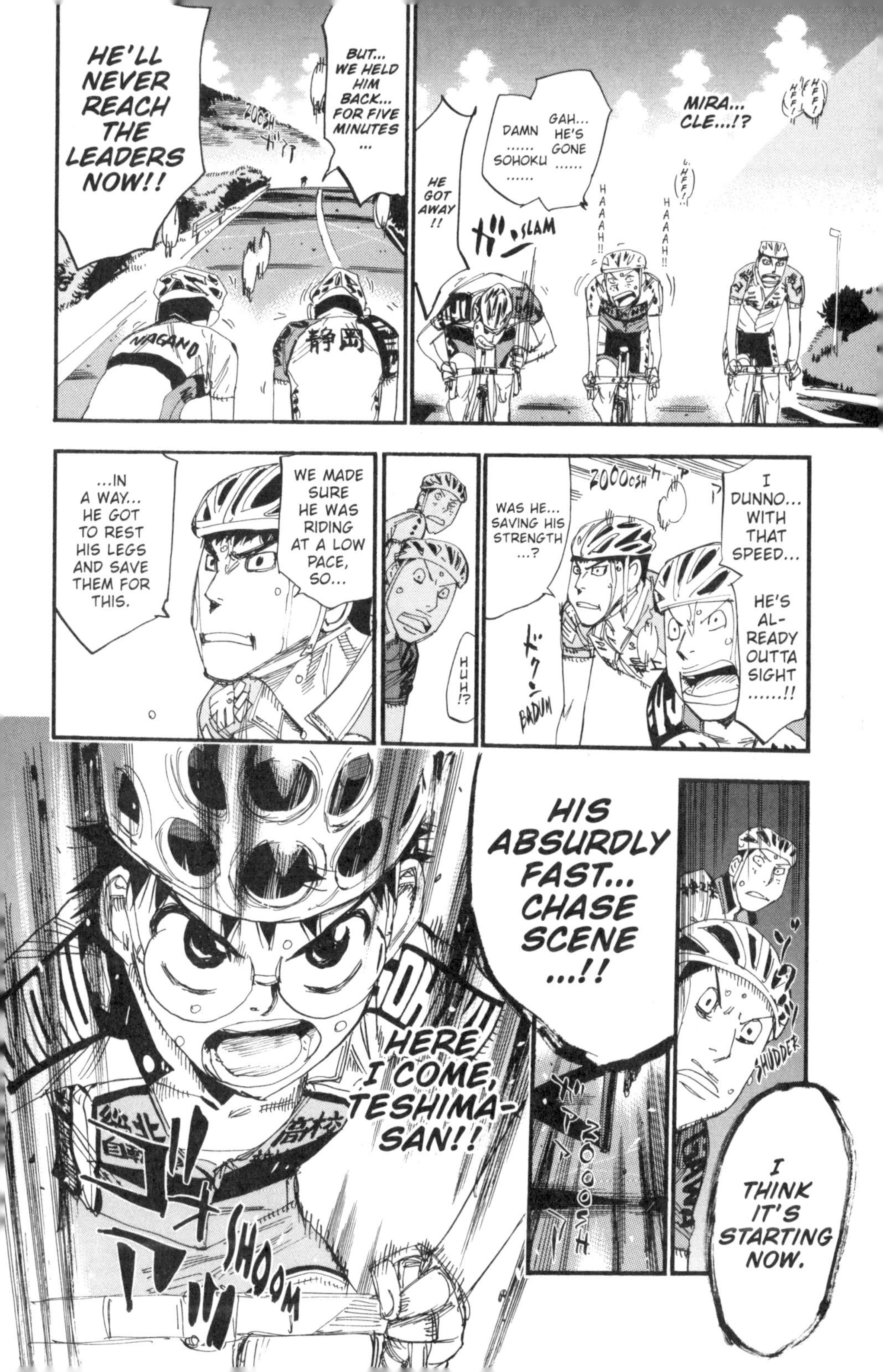
HFF! HFF!
MIRA... CLE...!?
HFF!
HAAAAH!!
HAAAAH!!
GAH... HE'S GONE ......
DAMN ...... SOHOKU ......
HE GOT AWAY!!
SLAM
BUT... WE HELD HIM BACK... FOR FIVE MINUTES ...
HE'LL NEVER REACH THE LEADERS NOW!!
ZOOSH
I DUNNO... WITH THAT SPEED...
ZOOOOSH
WAS HE... SAVING HIS STRENGTH ...?
HE'S AL-READY OUTTA SIGHT ......!!
BADUM
HUH!?
WE MADE SURE HE WAS RIDING AT A LOW PACE, SO...
...IN A WAY... HE GOT TO REST HIS LEGS AND SAVE THEM FOR THIS.
HIS ABSURDLY FAST... CHASE SCENE ...!!
SHUDDER
I THINK IT'S STARTING NOW.
WOOOOSH
HERE I COME, TESHIMA-SAN!!
SHOOM

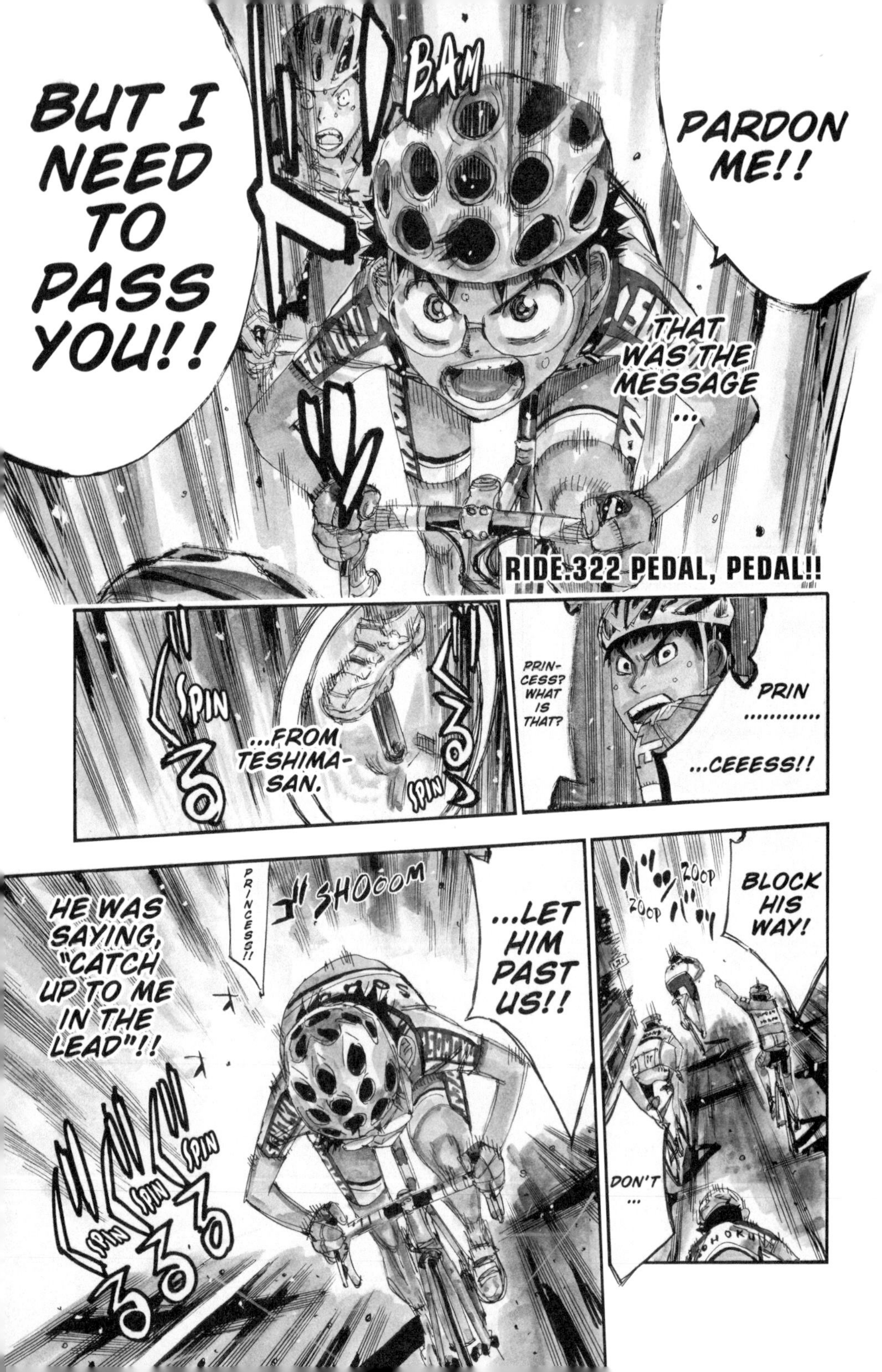
PARDON ME!!
BAM
BUT I NEED TO PASS YOU!!
THAT WAS THE MESSAGE ...
RIDE.322 PEDAL, PEDAL!!
PRIN ....CEEESS!!
PRIN-CESS? WHAT IS THAT?
SPIN
...FROM TESHIMA-SAN.
SPIN
BLOCK HIS WAY!
ZOOP
ZOOP
DON'T ...
...LET HIM PAST US!!
SHOOOM
PRINCESS!!
HE WAS SAYING, "CATCH UP TO ME IN THE LEAD"!!
SPIN
SPIN
SPIN
SPIN

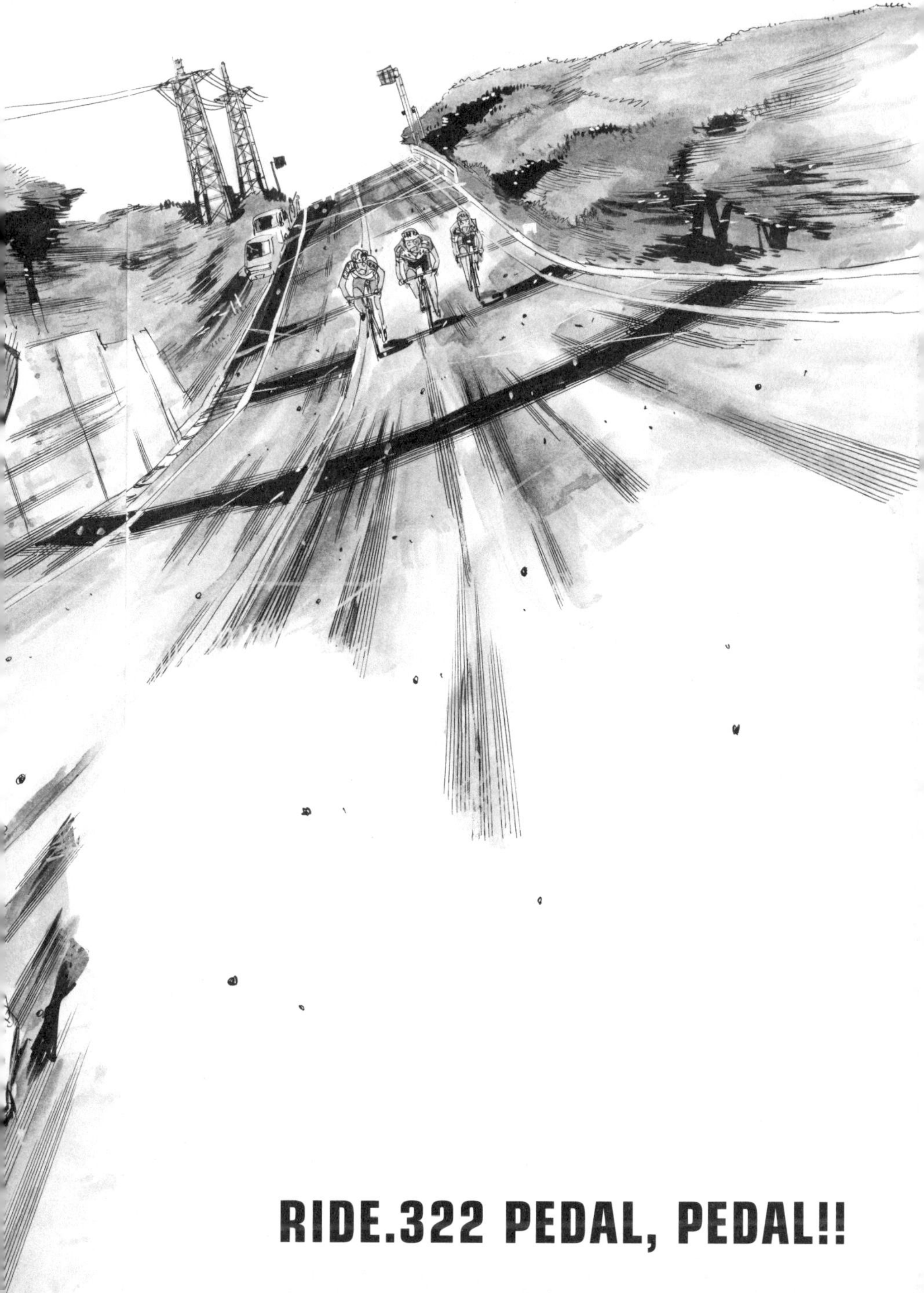

RIDE.322 PEDAL, PEDAL!!

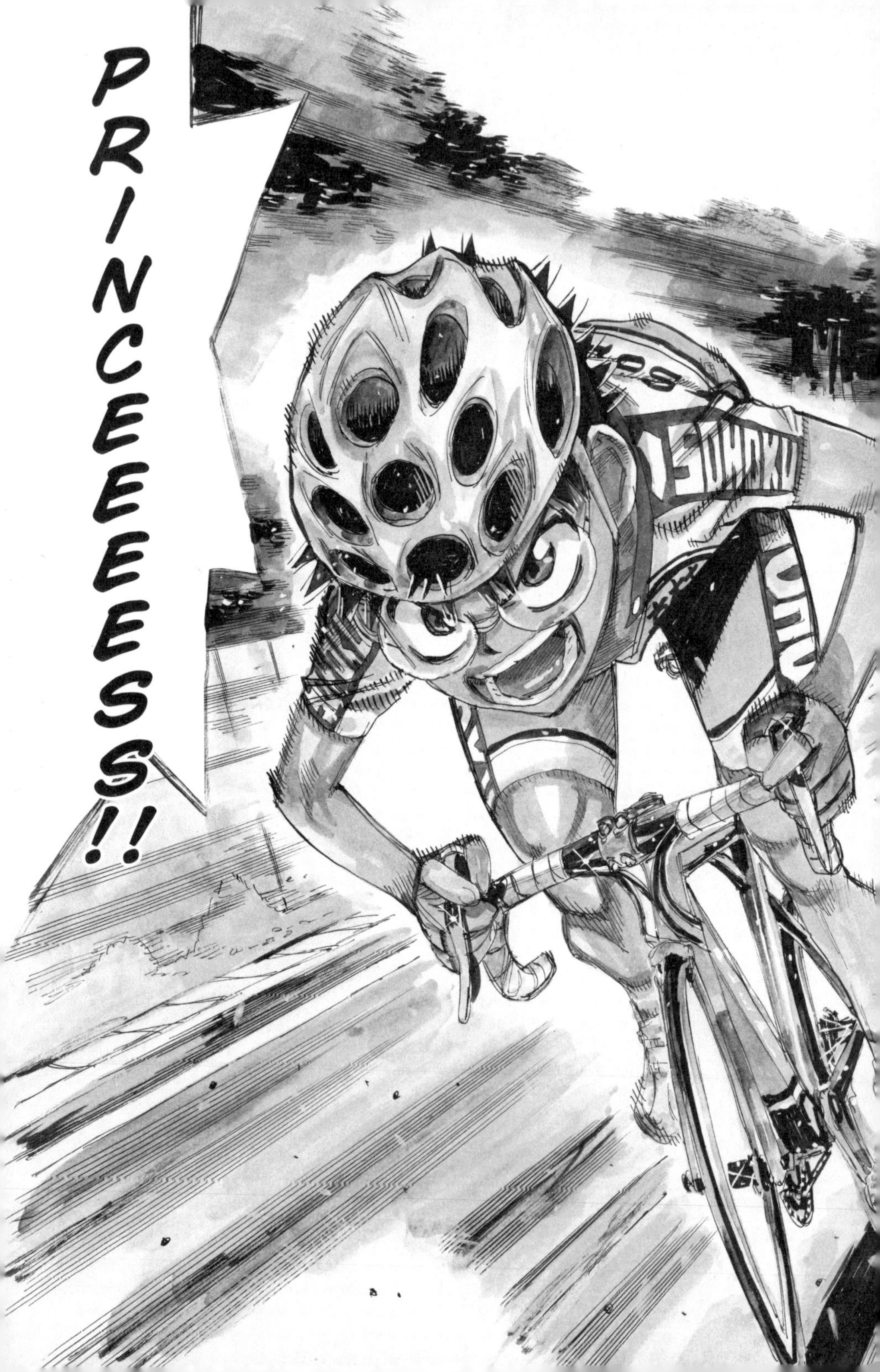
PRINCEEEESS!!

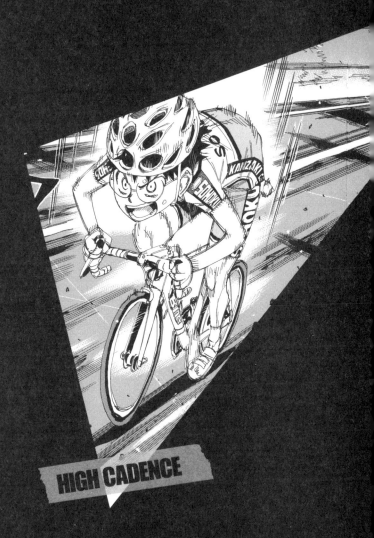

HIGH CADENCE

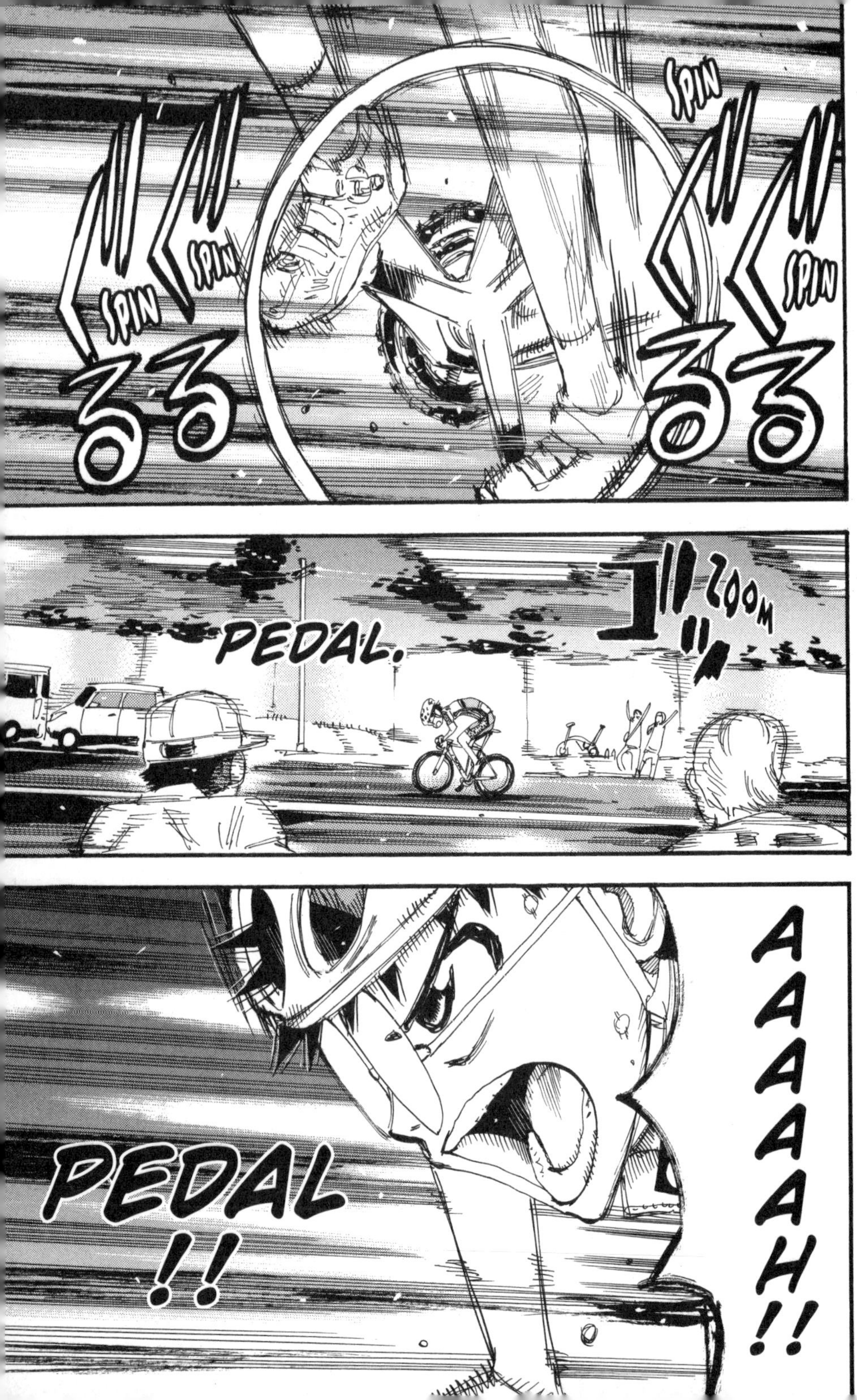
SPIN
SPIN
るる
SPIN
SPIN
るる
ZOOM
PEDAL.
AAAAAAH!!
PEDAL!!

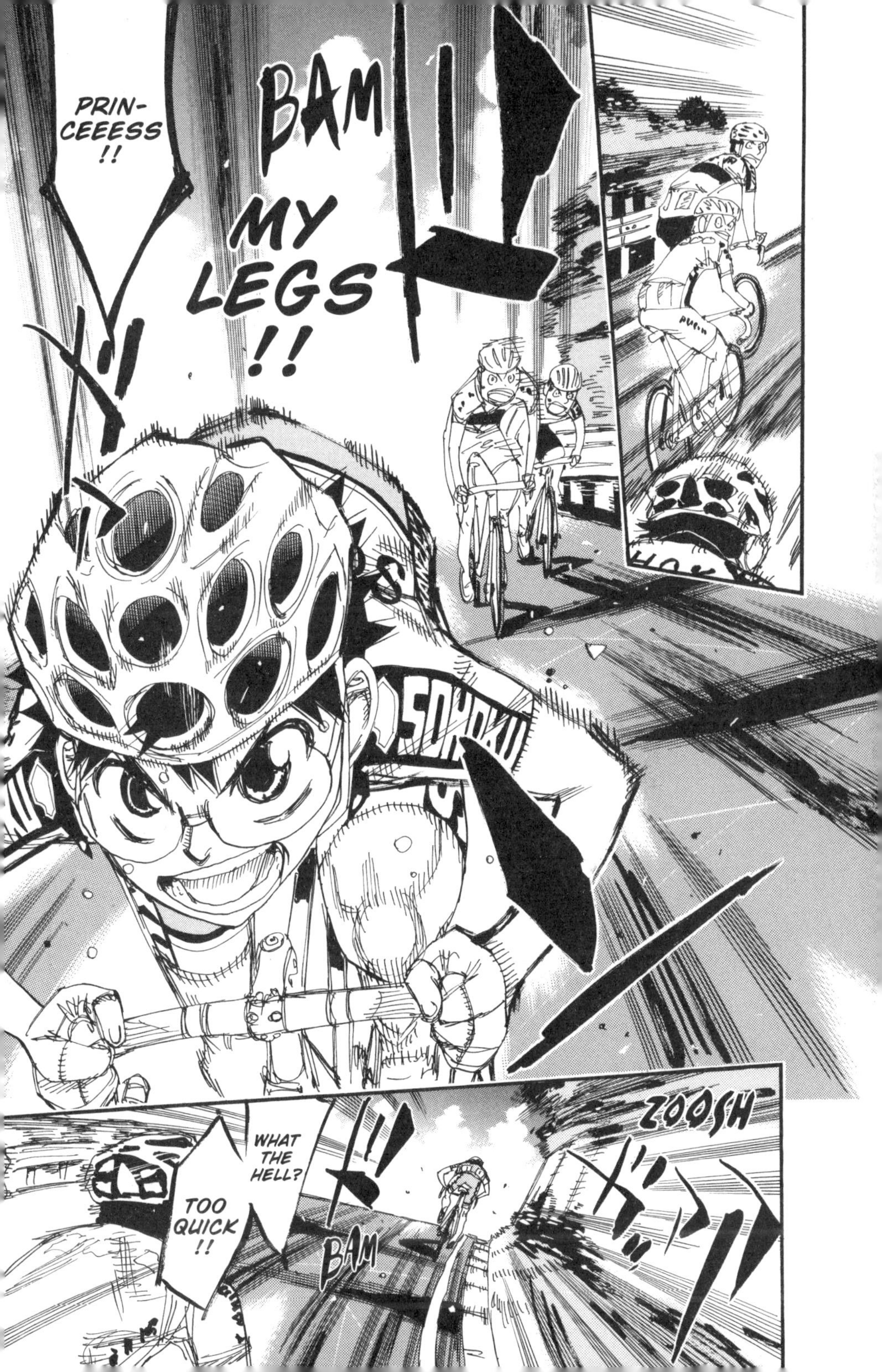
BAM
MY LEGS !!
PRIN-CEEESS !!
ZOOSH
WHAT THE HELL?
TOO QUICK !!
BAM

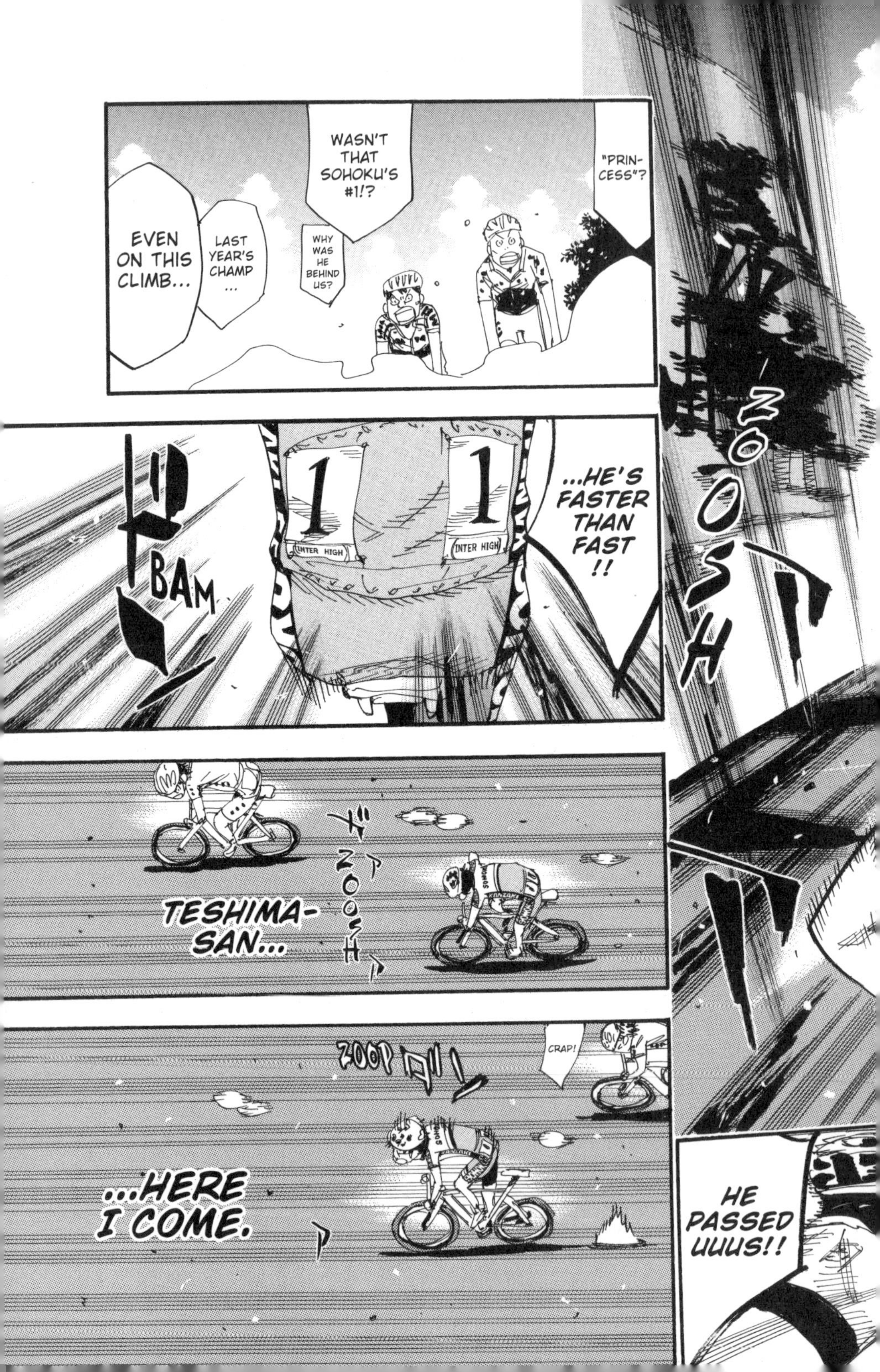
ZOOOSH
HE PASSED UUUS!!
"PRIN-CESS"?
WASN'T THAT SOHOKU'S #1!?
WHY WAS HE BEHIND US?
LAST YEAR'S CHAMP...
EVEN ON THIS CLIMB...
...HE'S FASTER THAN FAST!!
1
INTER HIGH
1
INTER HIGH
BAM
ZOOOSH
TESHIMA-SAN...
CRAP!
ZOOP
...HERE I COME.

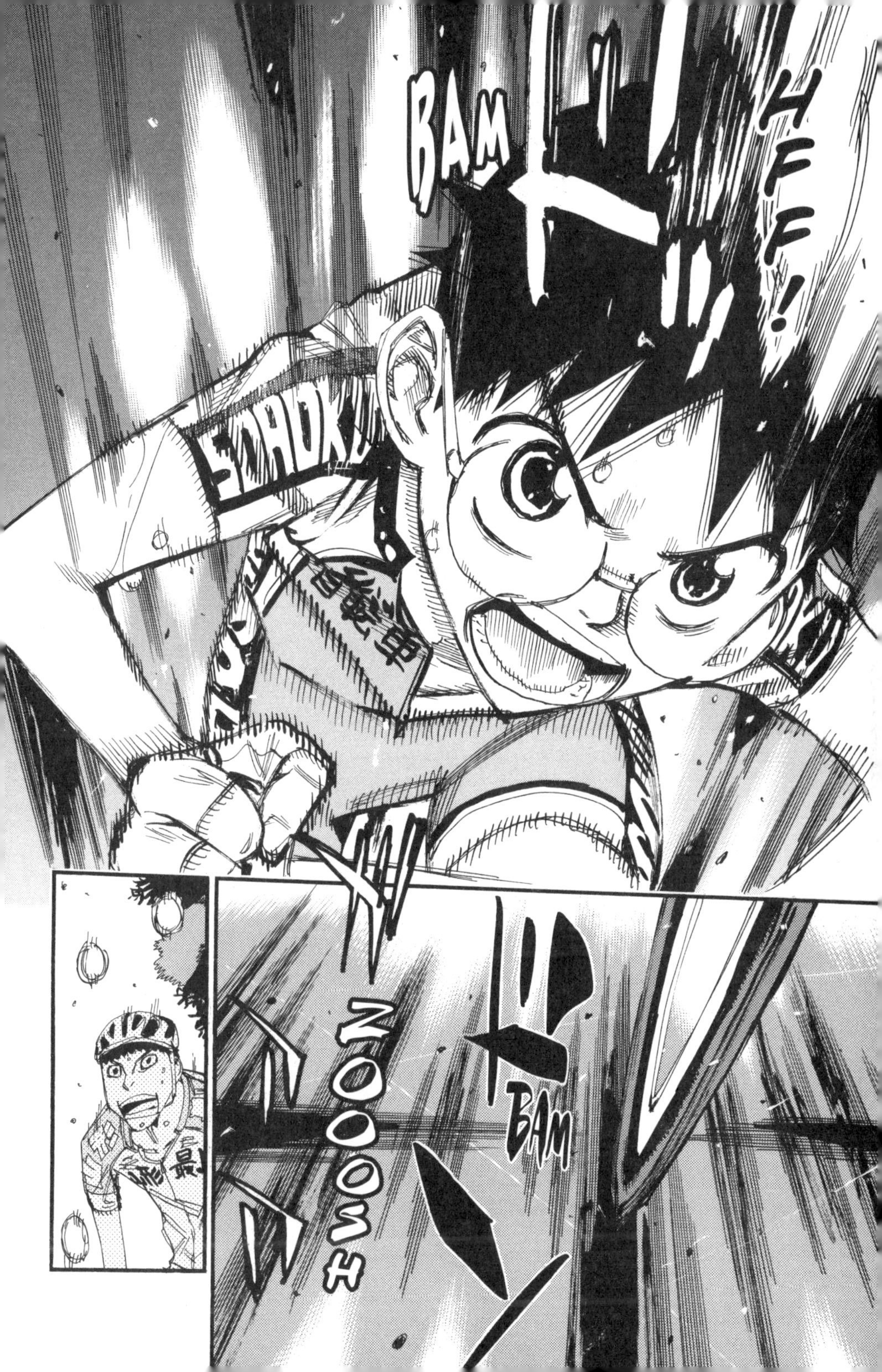
BAM
HUFF!
BAM
WHOOOOSH

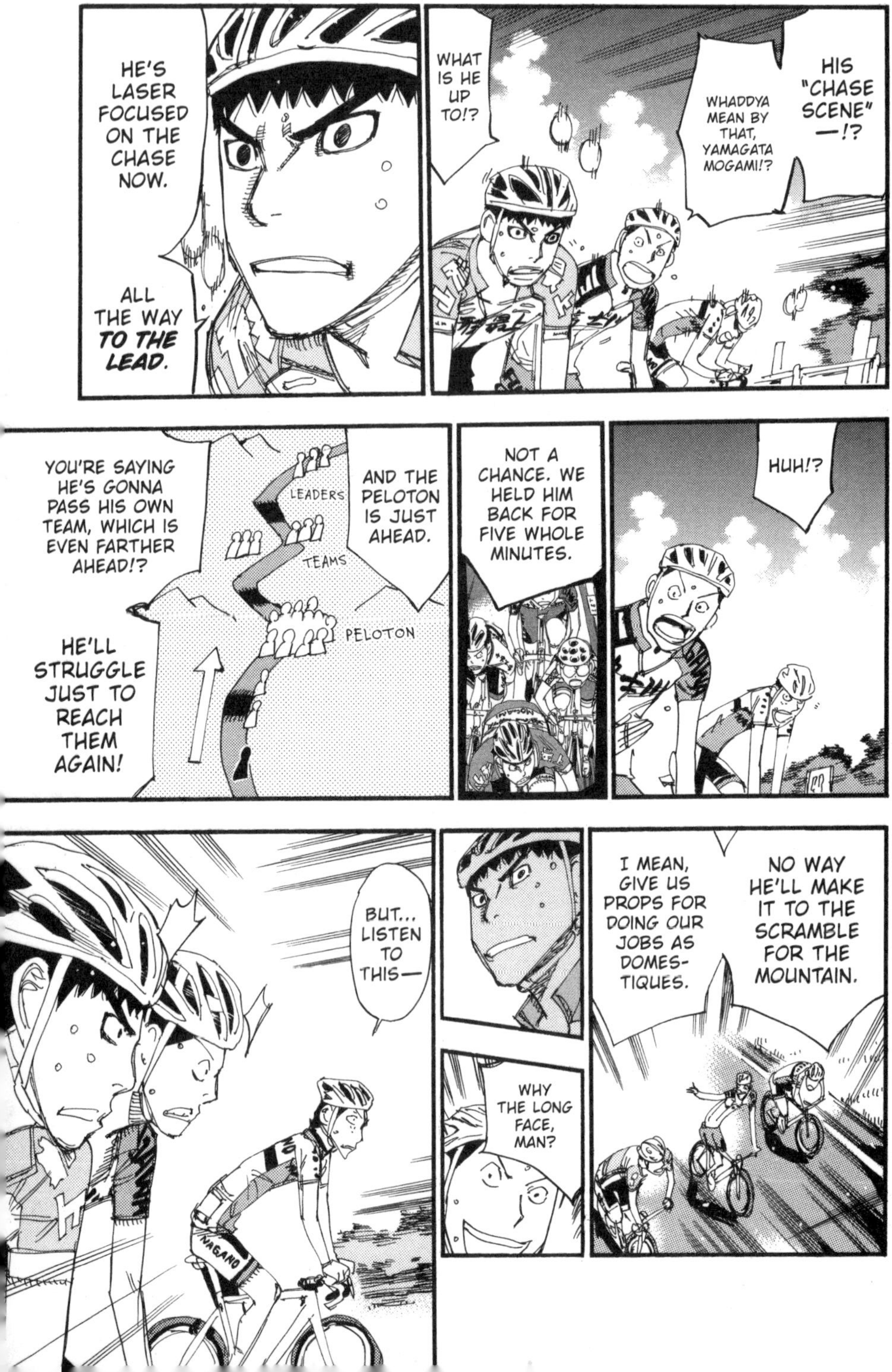
HIS "CHASE SCENE" —!?
WHADDYA MEAN BY THAT, YAMAGATA MOGAMI!?
WHAT IS HE UP TO!?
HE'S LASER FOCUSED ON THE CHASE NOW.
ALL THE WAY ***TO THE LEAD.***
HUH!?
NOT A CHANCE. WE HELD HIM BACK FOR FIVE WHOLE MINUTES.
AND THE PELOTON IS JUST AHEAD.
YOU'RE SAYING HE'S GONNA PASS HIS OWN TEAM, WHICH IS EVEN FARTHER AHEAD!?
LEADERS
TEAMS
PELOTON
HE'LL STRUGGLE JUST TO REACH THEM AGAIN!
NO WAY HE'LL MAKE IT TO THE SCRAMBLE FOR THE MOUNTAIN.
I MEAN, GIVE US PROPS FOR DOING OUR JOBS AS DOMESTIQUES.
WHY THE LONG FACE, MAN?
BUT... LISTEN TO THIS—
NAGANO

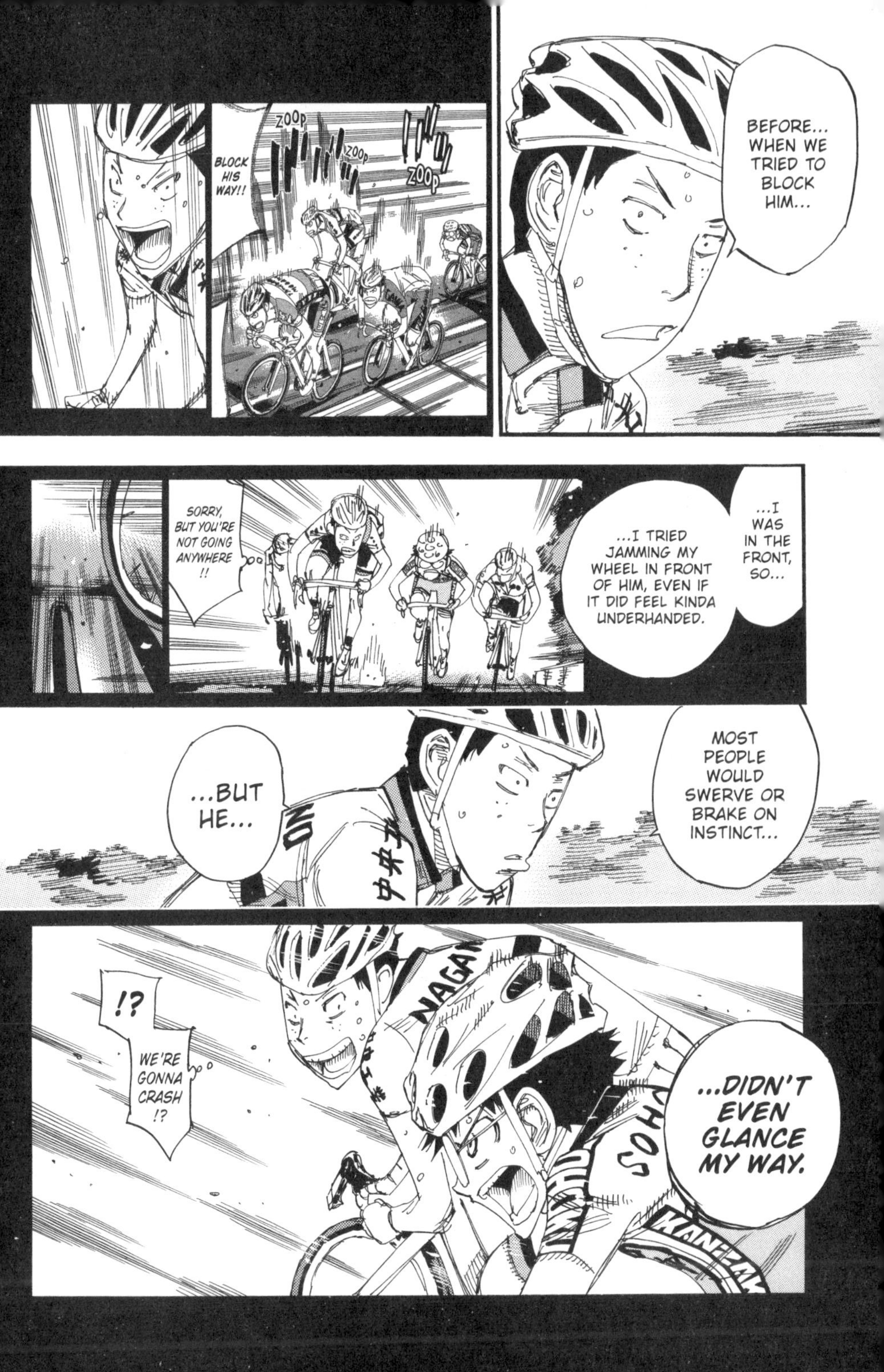
BEFORE... WHEN WE TRIED TO BLOCK HIM...
ZOOP
ZOOP
ZOOP
BLOCK HIS WAY!!
...I WAS IN THE FRONT, SO...
...I TRIED JAMMING MY WHEEL IN FRONT OF HIM, EVEN IF IT DID FEEL KINDA UNDERHANDED.
SORRY, BUT YOU'RE NOT GOING ANYWHERE!!
MOST PEOPLE WOULD SWERVE OR BRAKE ON INSTINCT...
...BUT HE...
...DIDN'T EVEN GLANCE MY WAY.
!?
WE'RE GONNA CRASH!?

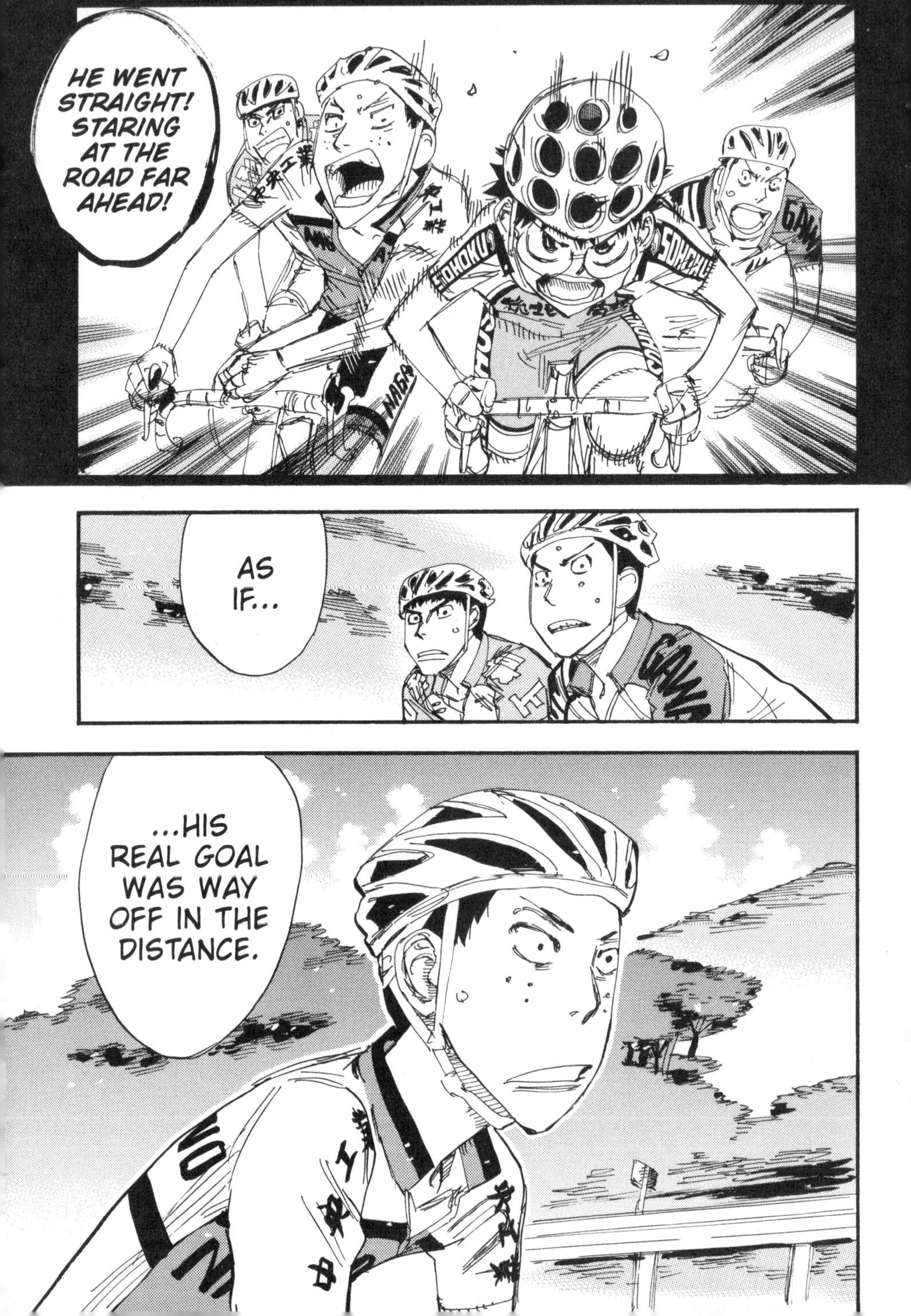
HE WENT STRAIGHT! STARING AT THE ROAD FAR AHEAD!
AS IF...
...HIS REAL GOAL WAS WAY OFF IN THE DISTANCE.

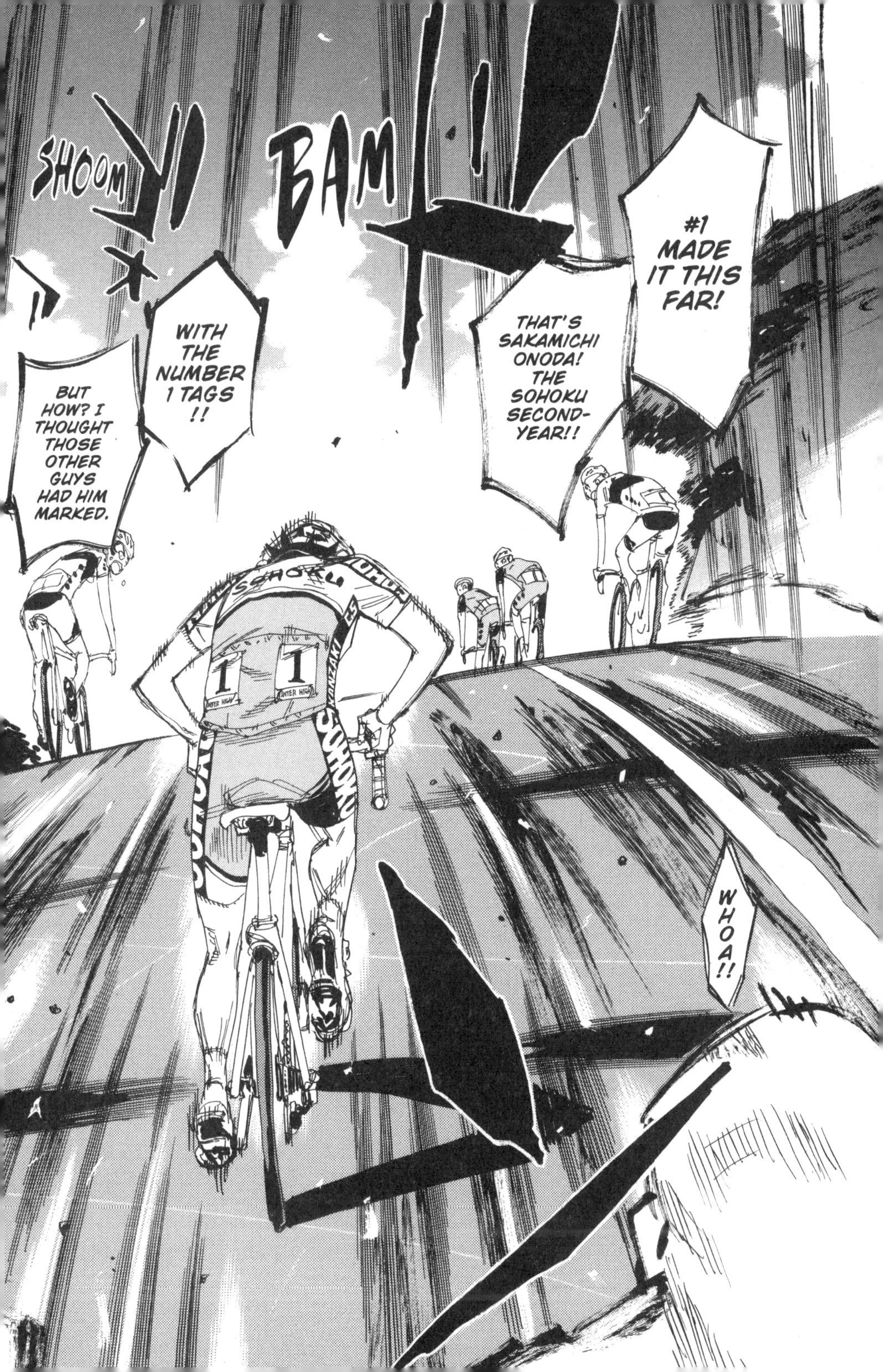
#1 MADE IT THIS FAR!
BAM
THAT'S SAKAMICHI ONODA! THE SOHOKU SECOND-YEAR!!
WITH THE NUMBER 1 TAGS!!
SHOOM
BUT HOW? I THOUGHT THOSE OTHER GUYS HAD HIM MARKED.
WHOA!!

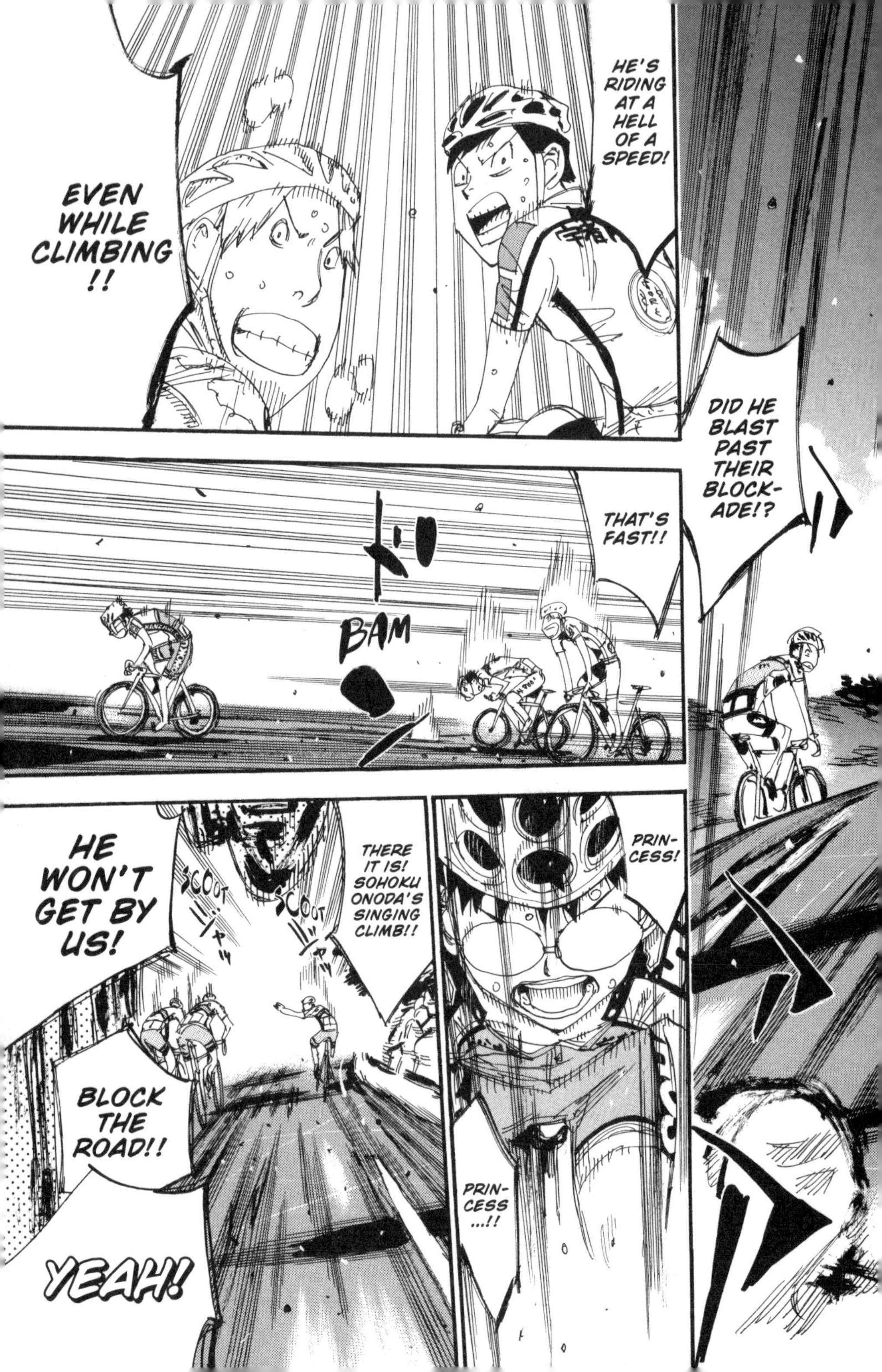
DID HE BLAST PAST THEIR BLOCK-ADE!?
HE'S RIDING AT A HELL OF A SPEED!
EVEN WHILE CLIMBING!!
THAT'S FAST!!
BAM
PRIN-CESS!
PRIN-CESS...!!
THERE IT IS! SOHOKU ONODA'S SINGING CLIMB!!
HE WON'T GET BY US!
SCOOT
SCOOT
BLOCK THE ROAD!!
YEAH!

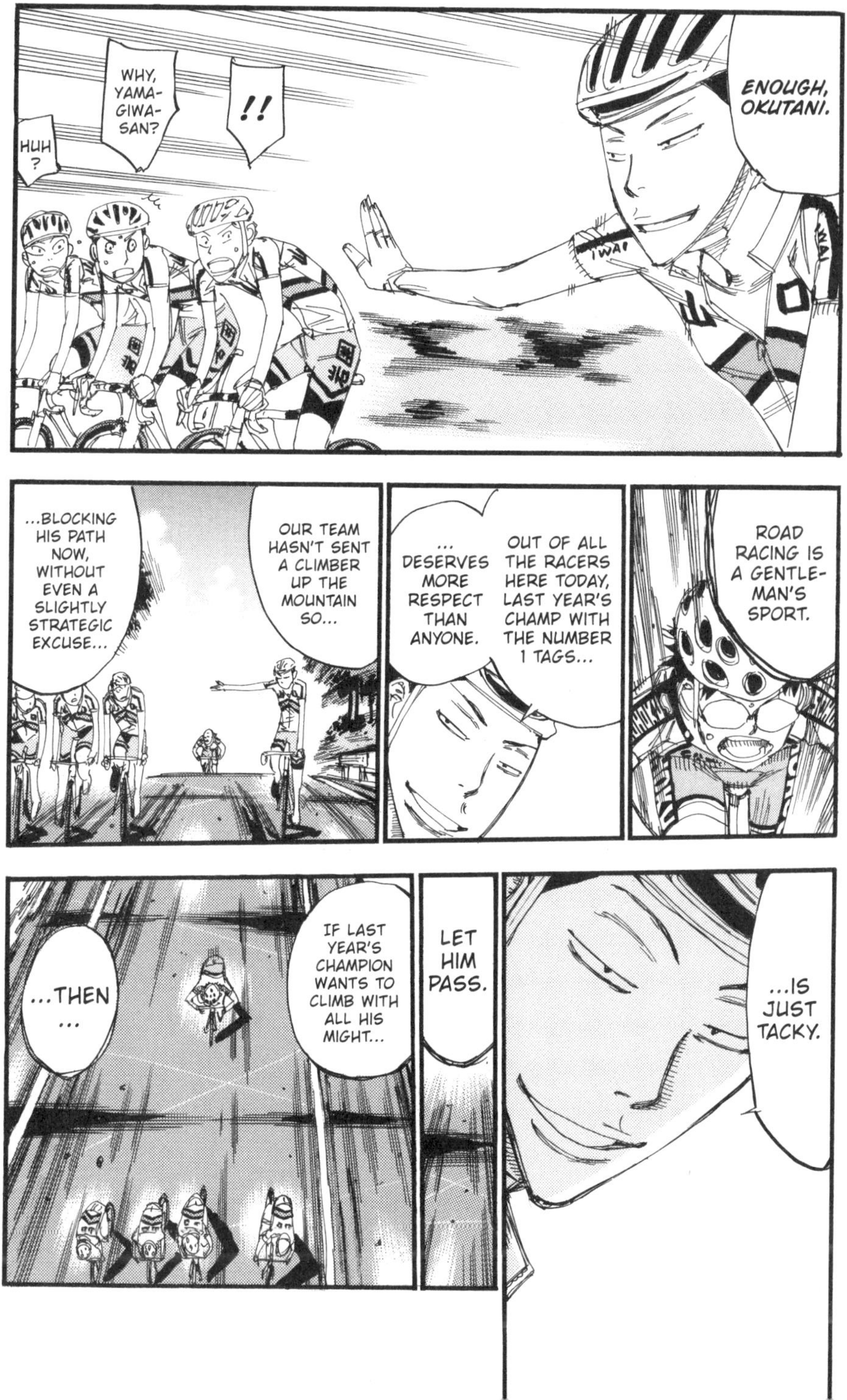
ENOUGH, OKUTANI.
!!
WHY, YAMAGIWA-SAN?
HUH?
ROAD RACING IS A GENTLEMAN'S SPORT.
OUT OF ALL THE RACERS HERE TODAY, LAST YEAR'S CHAMP WITH THE NUMBER 1 TAGS...
...DESERVES MORE RESPECT THAN ANYONE.
OUR TEAM HASN'T SENT A CLIMBER UP THE MOUNTAIN SO...
...BLOCKING HIS PATH NOW, WITHOUT EVEN A SLIGHTLY STRATEGIC EXCUSE...
...IS JUST TACKY.
LET HIM PASS.
IF LAST YEAR'S CHAMPION WANTS TO CLIMB WITH ALL HIS MIGHT...
...THEN...

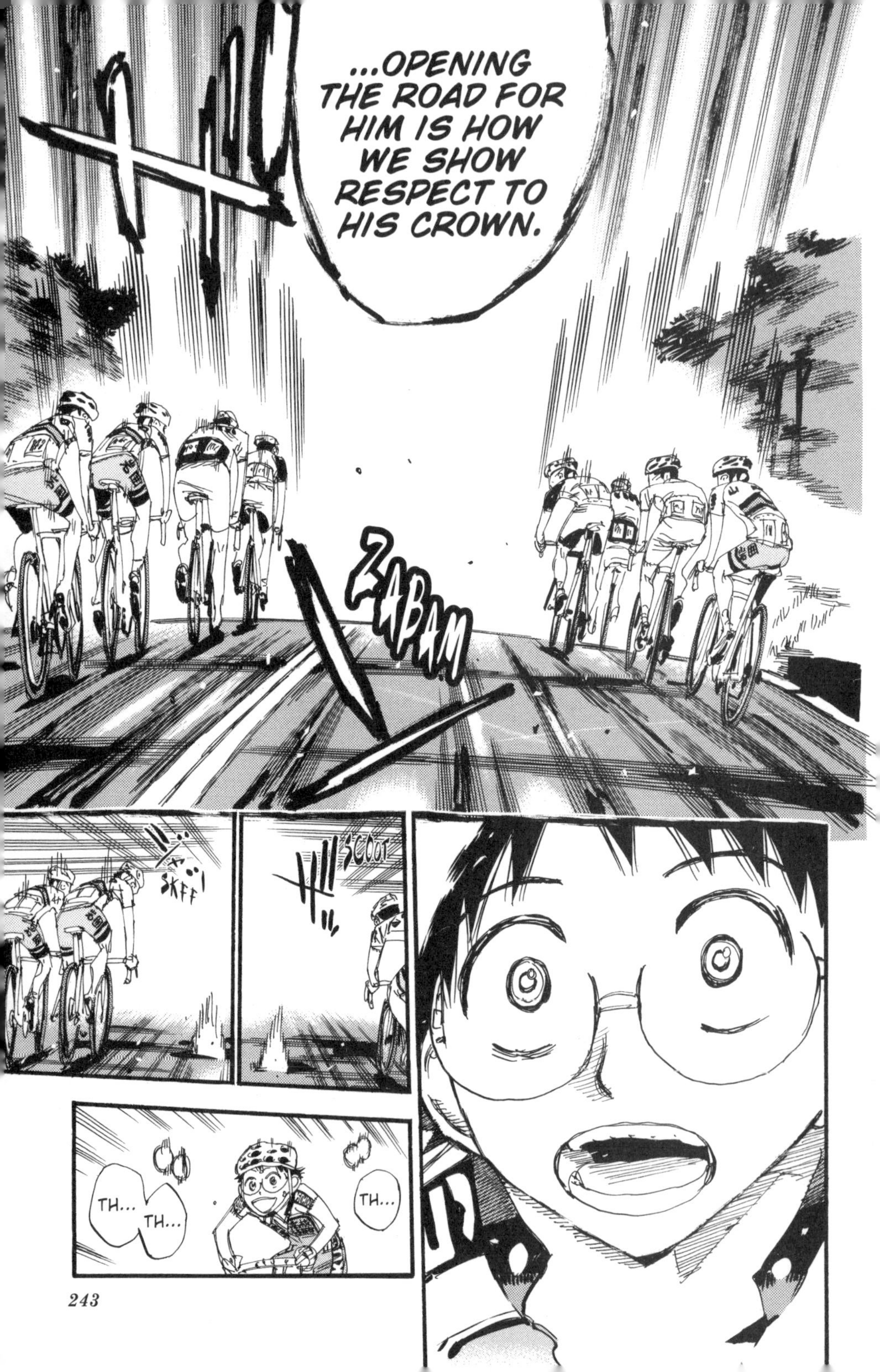
...OPENING THE ROAD FOR HIM IS HOW WE SHOW RESPECT TO HIS CROWN.
ZABAM
SCOOT
SKFF
TH...
TH...
TH...

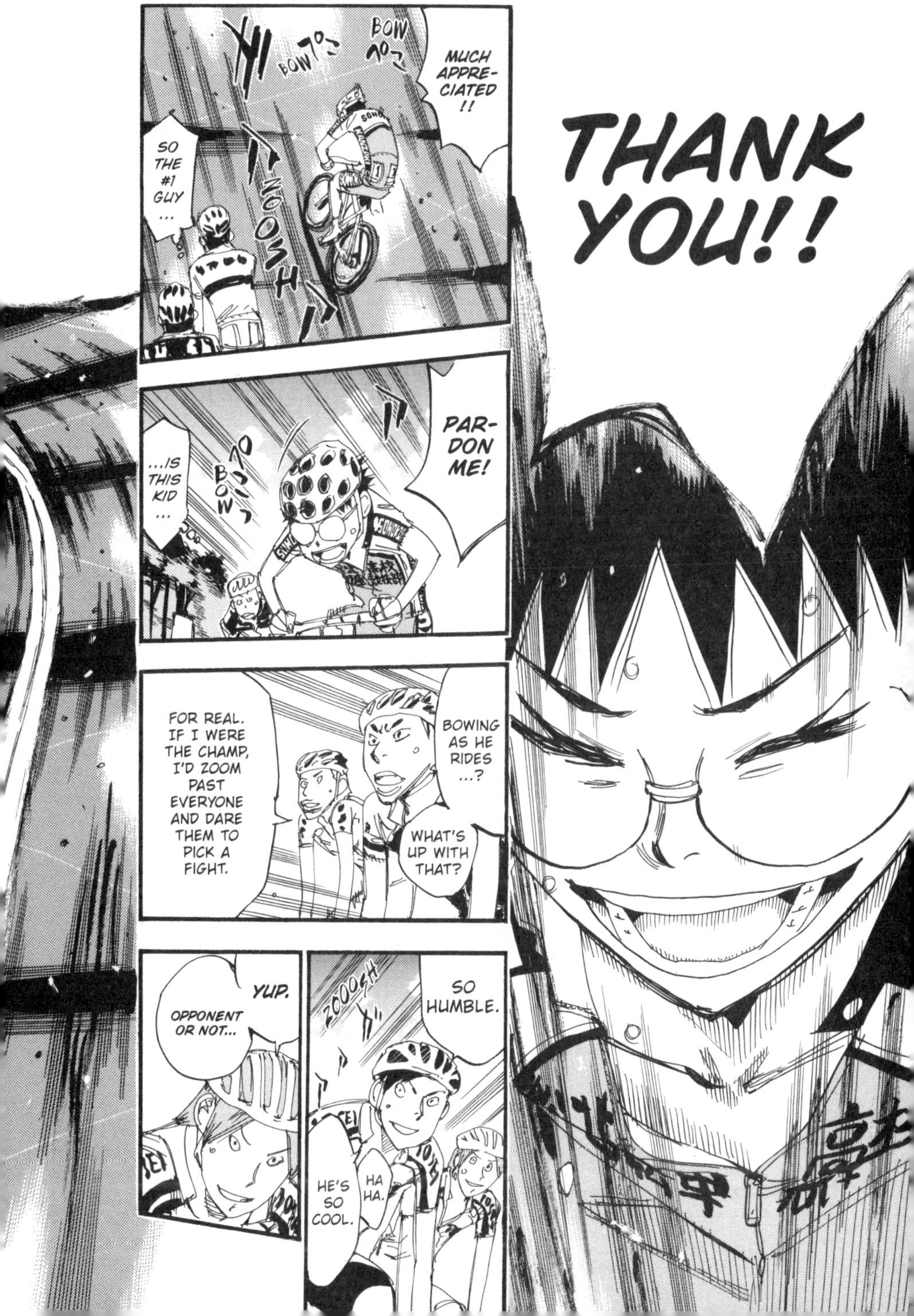
THANK YOU!!
MUCH APPRECIATED!!
BOW BOW
ZOOOSH
SO THE #1 GUY...
PARDON ME!
BOW BOW
...IS THIS KID...
BOWING AS HE RIDES...?
WHAT'S UP WITH THAT?
FOR REAL. IF I WERE THE CHAMP, I'D ZOOM PAST EVERYONE AND DARE THEM TO PICK A FIGHT.
SO HUMBLE.
ZOOOSH
HA HA.
HE'S SO COOL.
YUP.
OPPONENT OR NOT...

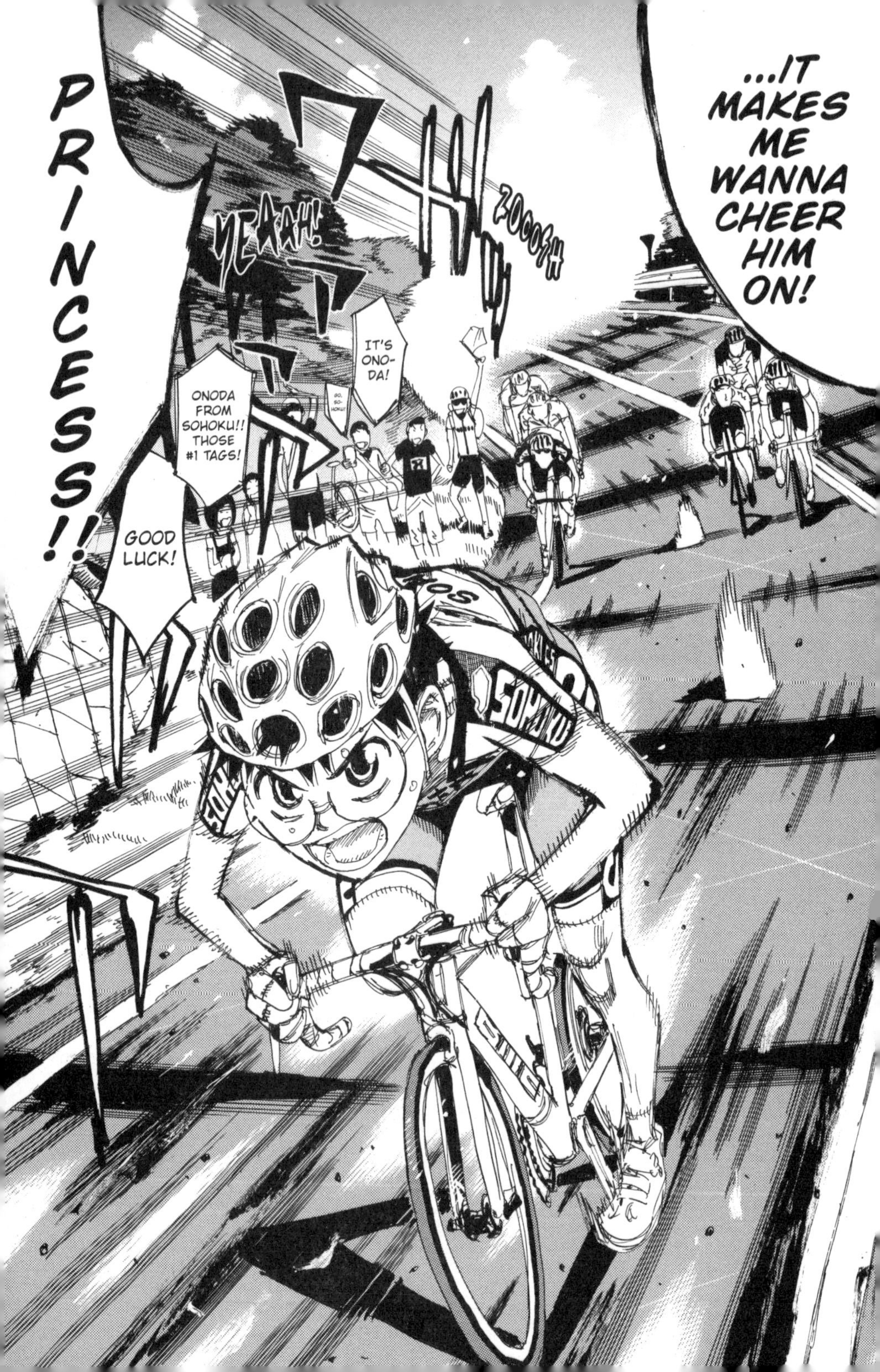
...IT MAKES ME WANNA CHEER HIM ON!
ZOOOOSH
IT'S ONO-DA!
GO, SO-HOKU!
ONODA FROM SOHOKU!! THOSE #1 TAGS!
YEAAH!
GOOD LUCK!
PRINCESS!!

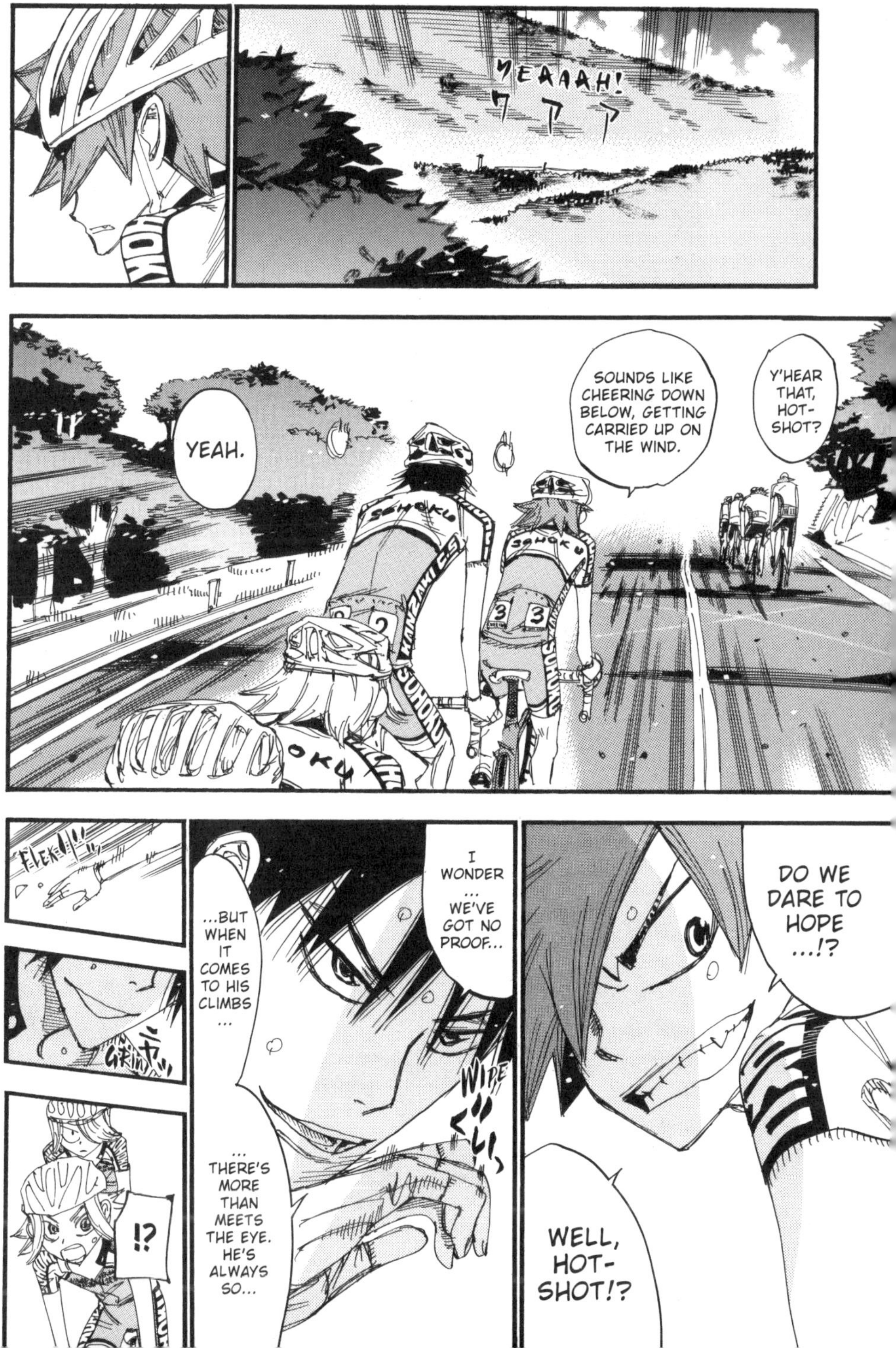
YEAAAH!
ワアア
Y'HEAR THAT, HOT-SHOT?
SOUNDS LIKE CHEERING DOWN BELOW, GETTING CARRIED UP ON THE WIND.
YEAH.
DO WE DARE TO HOPE ...!?
WELL, HOT-SHOT!?
I WONDER ... WE'VE GOT NO PROOF...
...BUT WHEN IT COMES TO HIS CLIMBS ...
WIPE
... THERE'S MORE THAN MEETS THE EYE. HE'S ALWAYS SO...
GRIN
!?

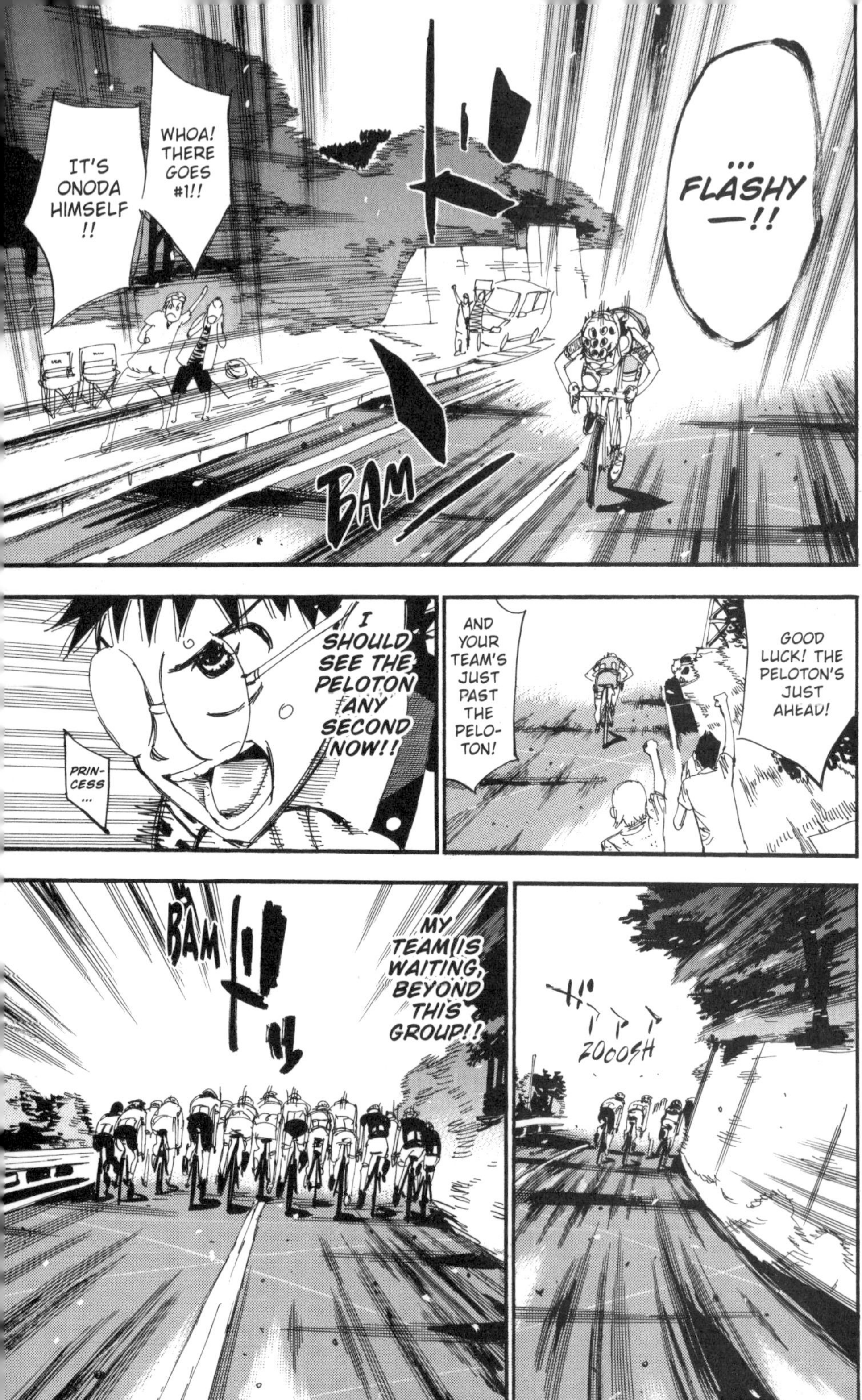
...FLÄSHY—!!
WHOA! THERE GOES #1!!
IT'S ONODA HIMSELF!!
BAM
GOOD LUCK! THE PELOTON'S JUST AHEAD!
AND YOUR TEAM'S JUST PAST THE PELOTON!
I SHOULD SEE THE PELOTON ANY SECOND NOW!!
PRINCESS...
ZOOOSH
MY TEAM IS WAITING, BEYOND THIS GROUP!!
BAM

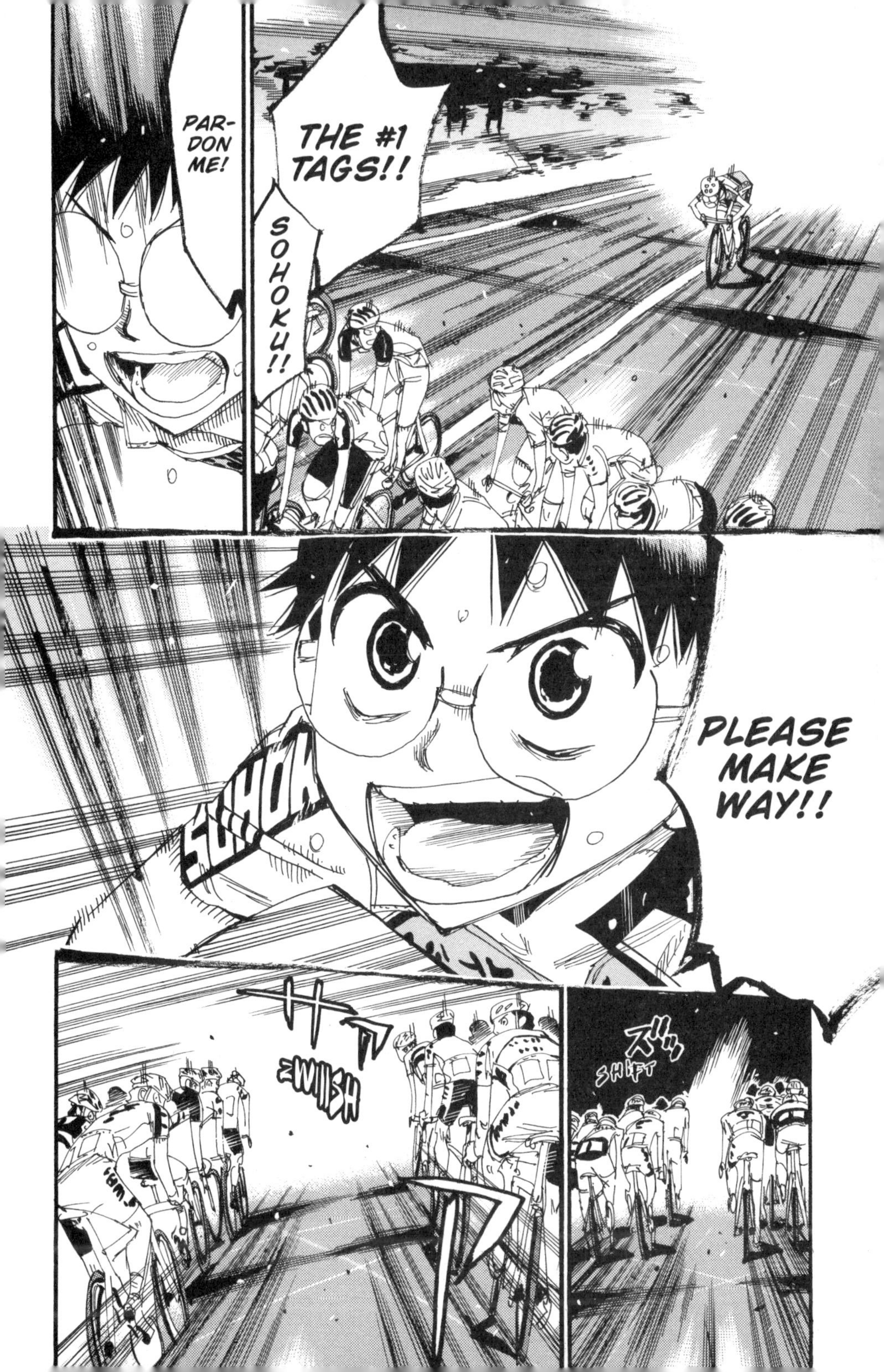
THE #1 TAGS!!
SOHOKU!!
PAR-DON ME!
PLEASE MAKE WAY!!
SHIFT
SWISH

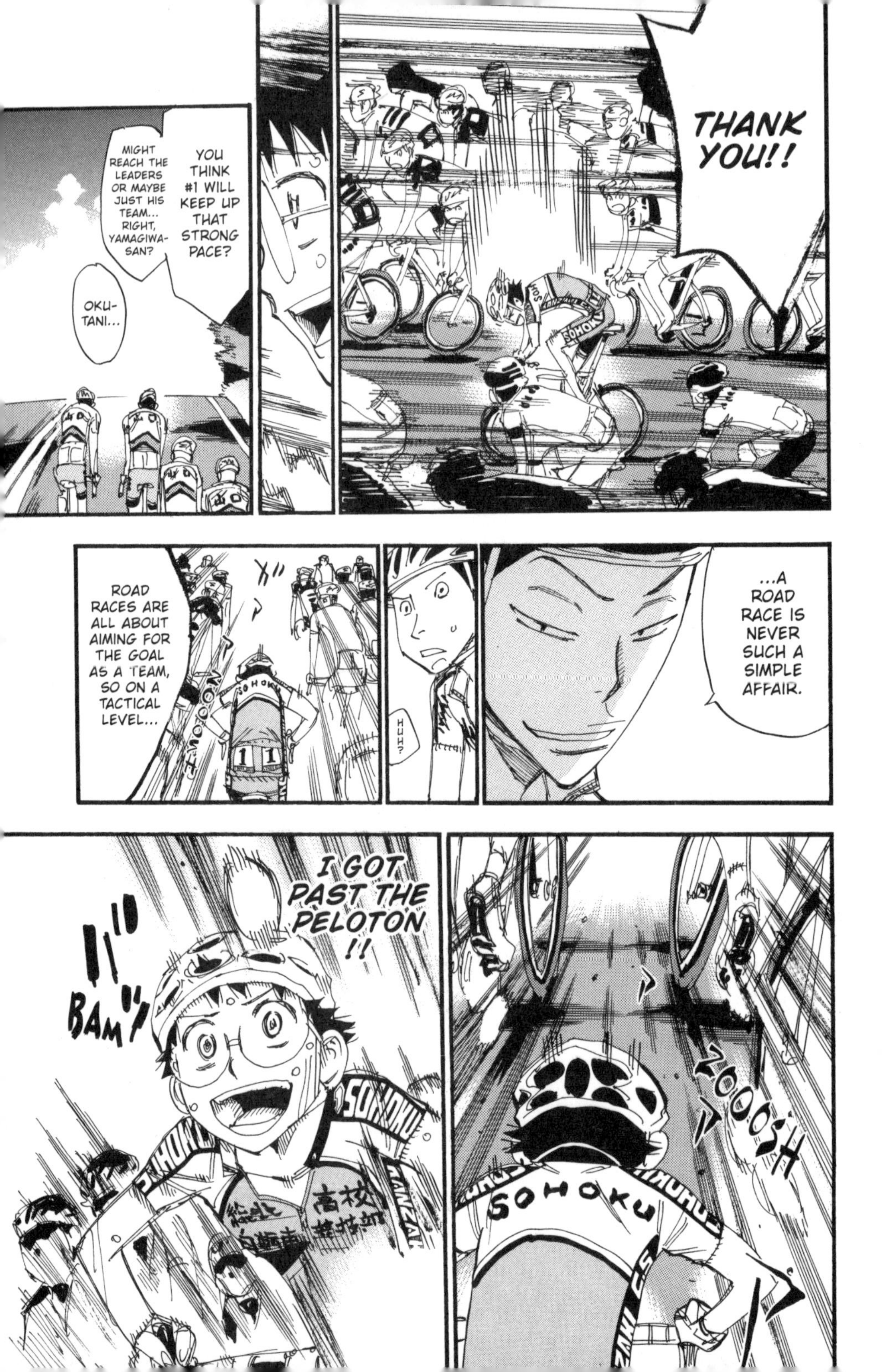

THANK YOU!!
YOU THINK #1 WILL KEEP UP THAT STRONG PACE?
MIGHT REACH THE LEADERS OR MAYBE JUST HIS TEAM... RIGHT, YAMAGIWA-SAN?
OKU-TANI...
...A ROAD RACE IS NEVER SUCH A SIMPLE AFFAIR.
HUH?
ROAD RACES ARE ALL ABOUT AIMING FOR THE GOAL AS A TEAM, SO ON A TACTICAL LEVEL...
ZOOOSH
I GOT PAST THE PELOTON!!
BAM

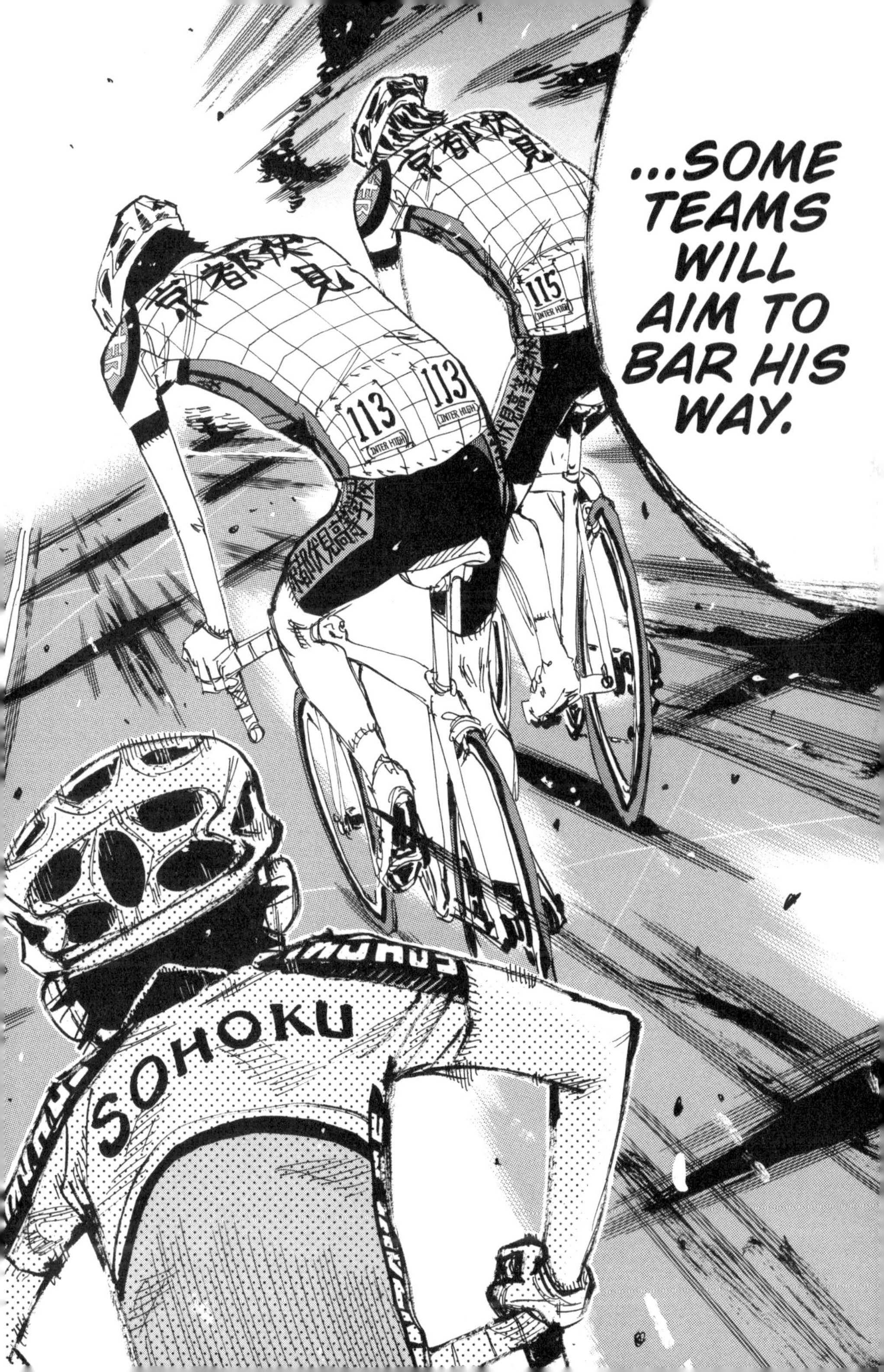
...SOME TEAMS WILL AIM TO BAR HIS WAY.
京都伏見
115
113
113
SOHOKU

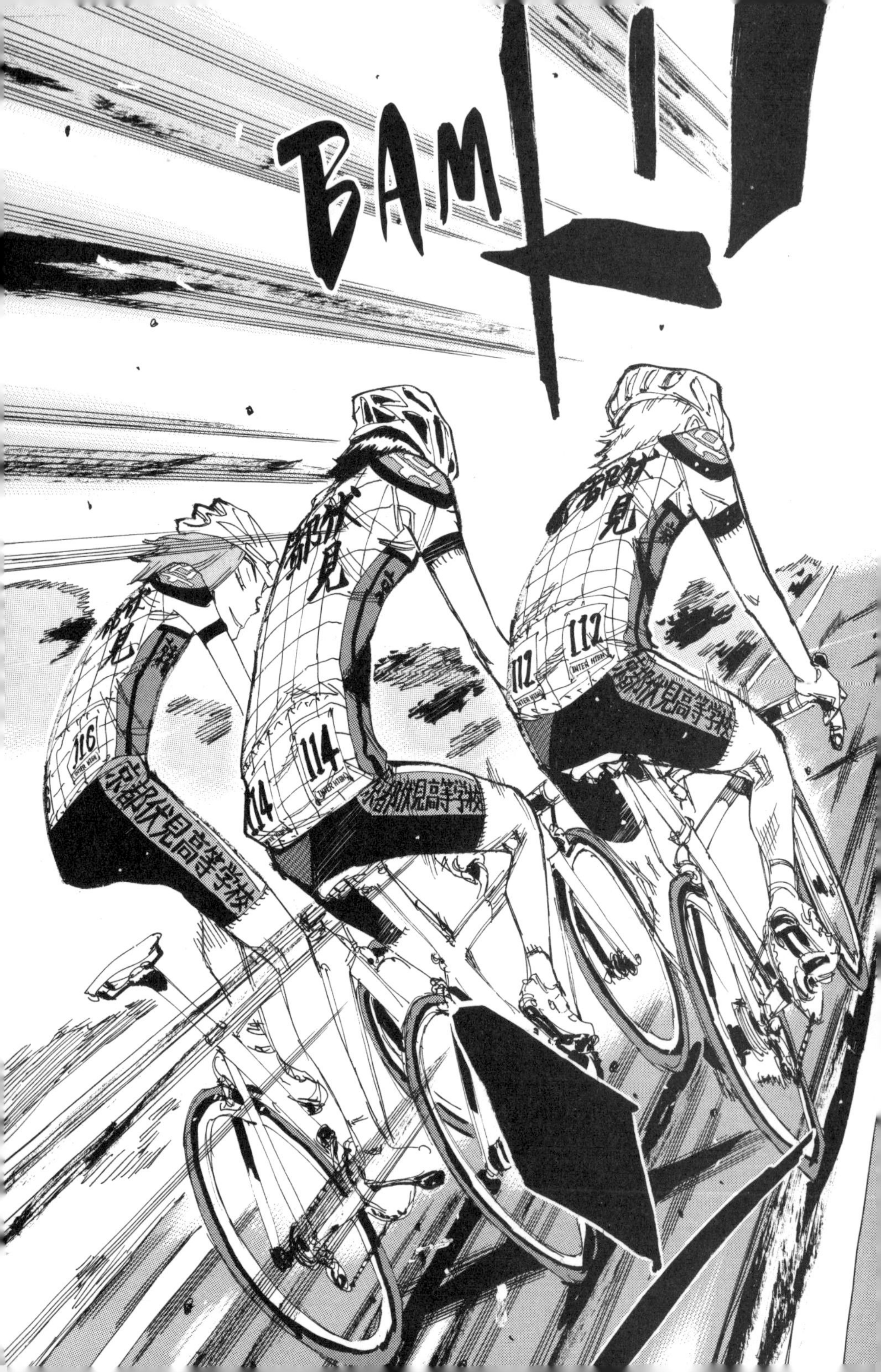
BAM!!
京都伏見高等学校

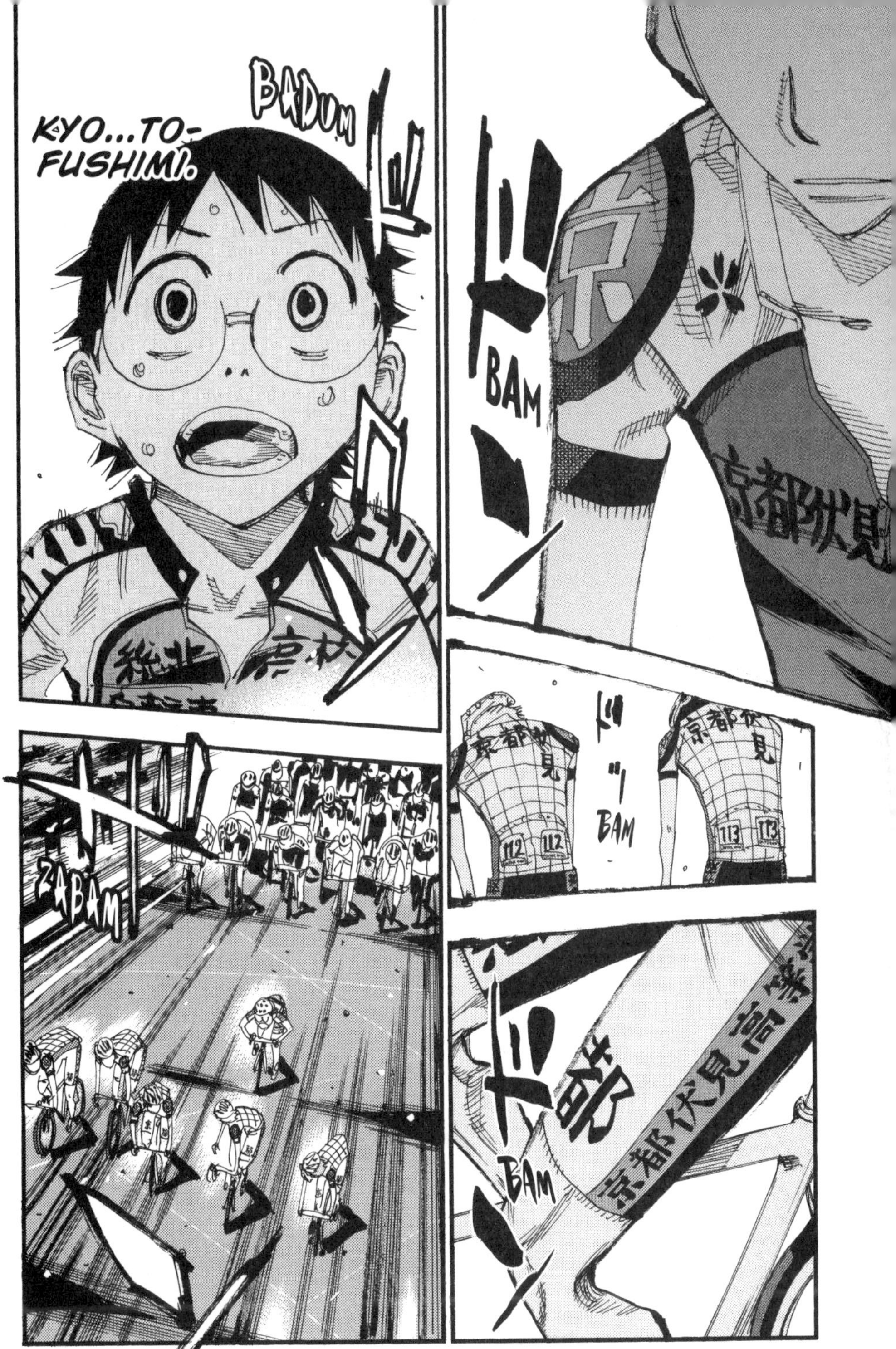
BAM
KYO...TO-FUSHIMI.
BADUM
BAM
BAM
ZABAM

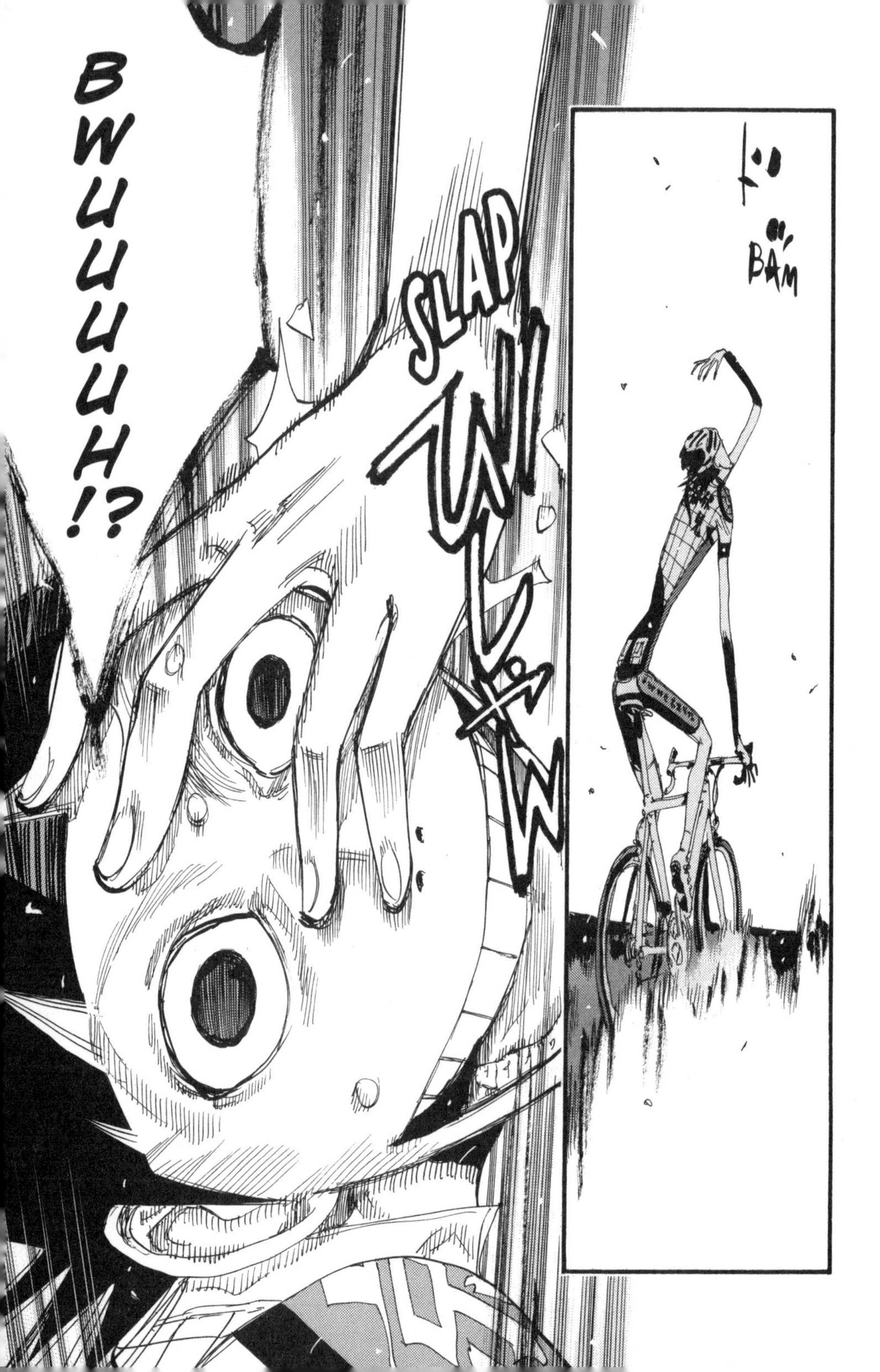
BAM
SLAP
BWUUUUH!?

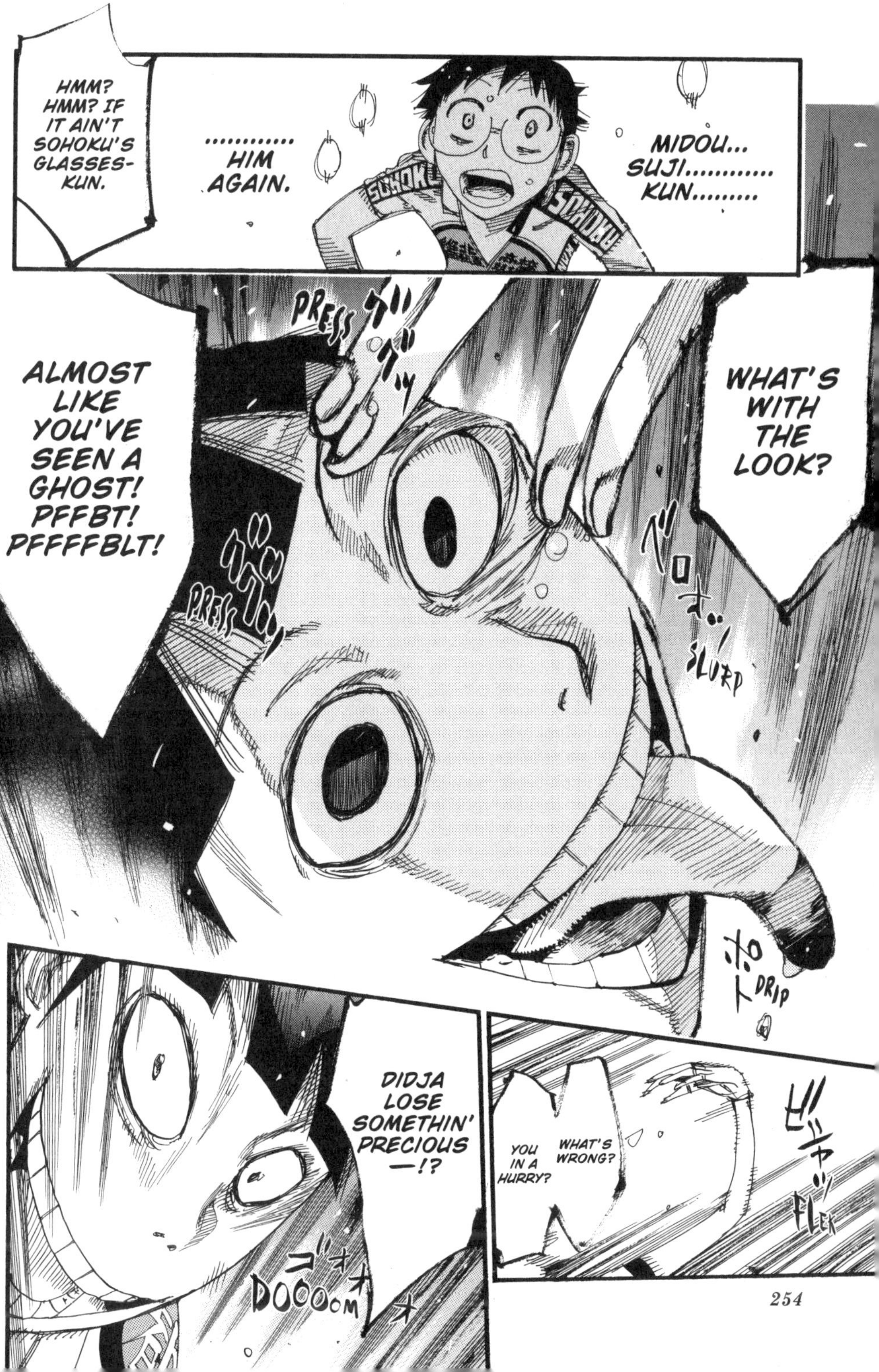

MIDOU... SUJI........... KUN.........
.... HIM AGAIN.
HMM? HMM? IF IT AIN'T SOHOKU'S GLASSES-KUN.
WHAT'S WITH THE LOOK?
PRESS
SLURP
ALMOST LIKE YOU'VE SEEN A GHOST! PFFBT! PFFFFBLT!
PRESS
DRIP
FLEK
WHAT'S WRONG?
YOU IN A HURRY?
DIDJA LOSE SOMETHIN' PRECIOUS—!?
DOOOOOM

RIDE.323 KYOTO-FUSHIMI

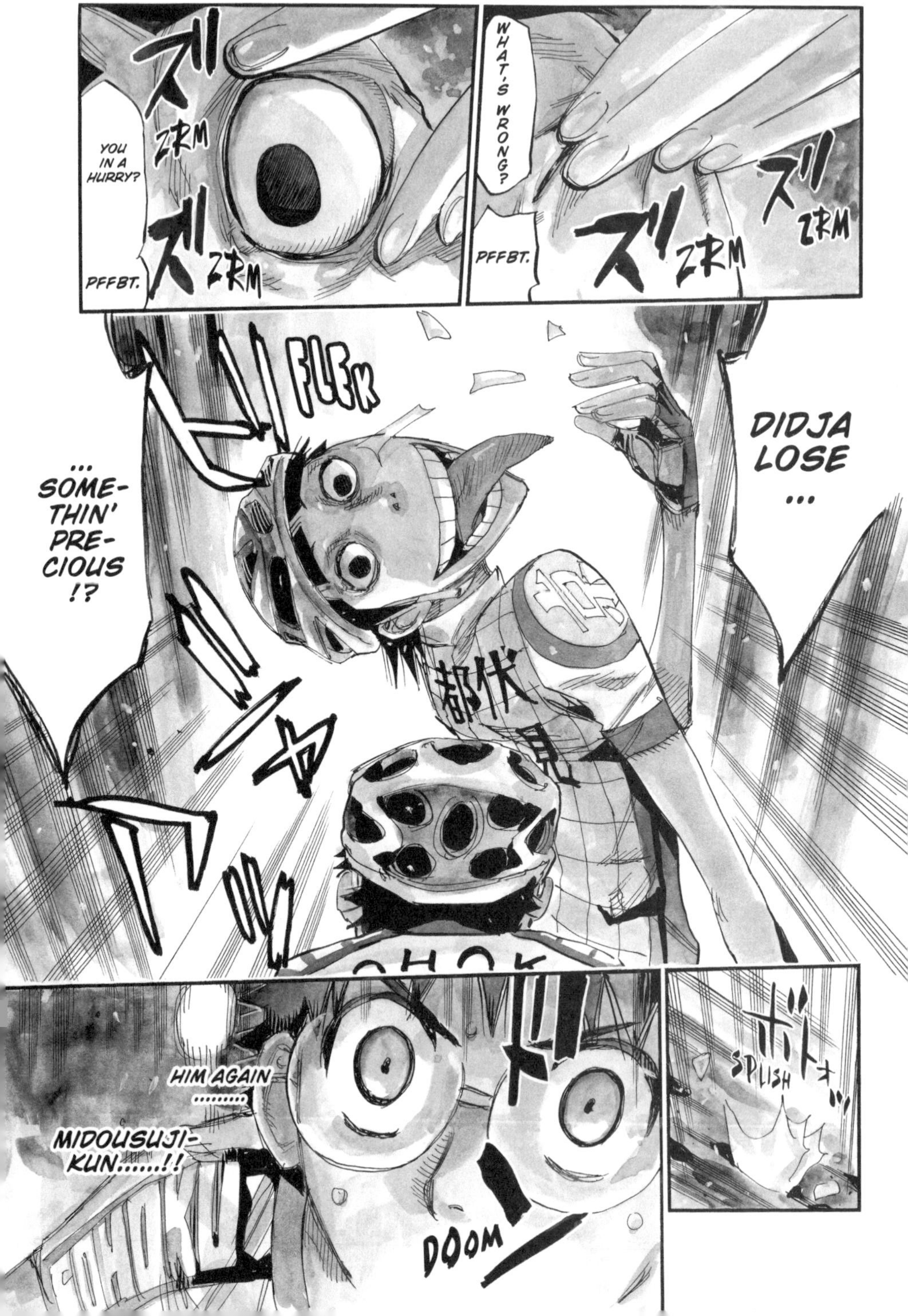
WHAT'S WRONG?
PFFBT.
ZRM
ZRM
YOU IN A HURRY?
ZRM
PFFBT.
ZRM
DIDJA LOSE ...
... SOME-THIN' PRE-CIOUS !?
FLEK
SPLISH
HIM AGAIN ....
MIDOUSUJI-KUN.......!!
DOOM

RIDE.323 KYOTO-FUSHIMI

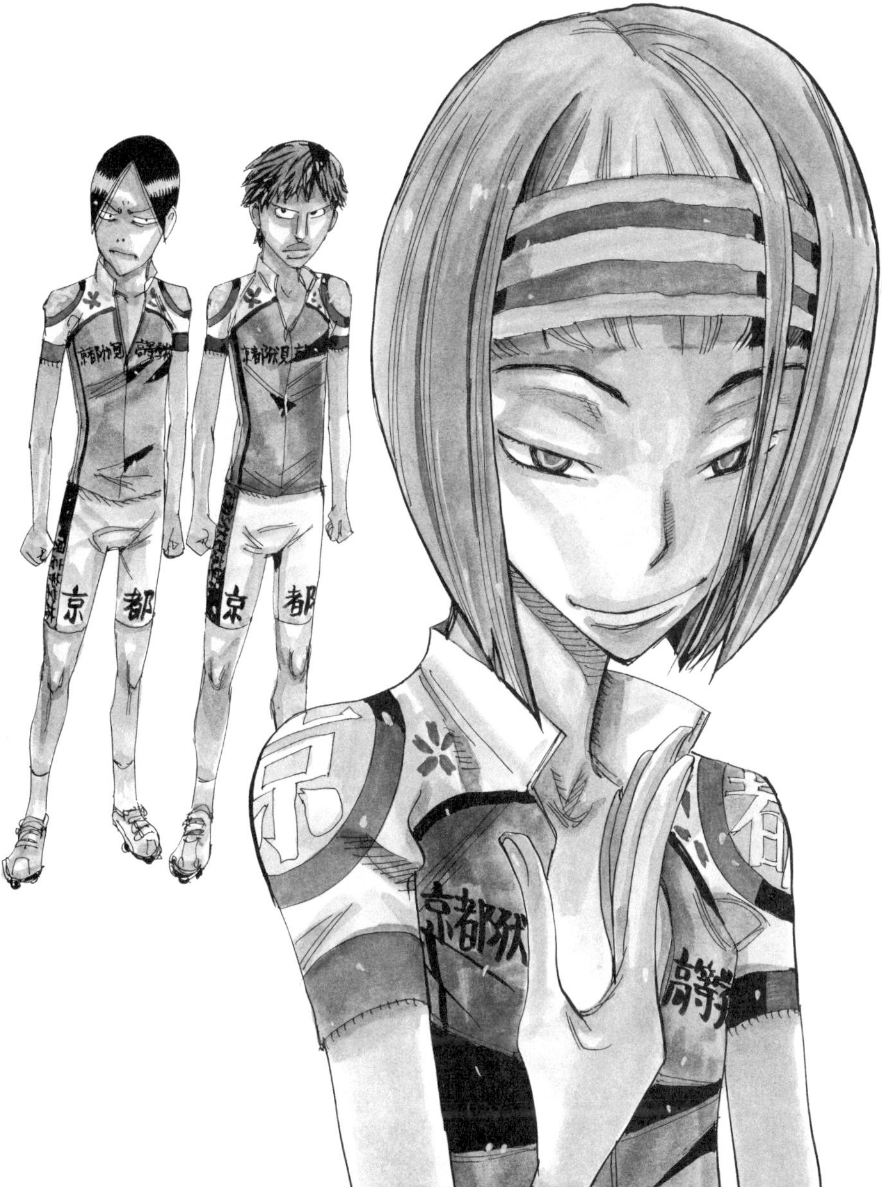

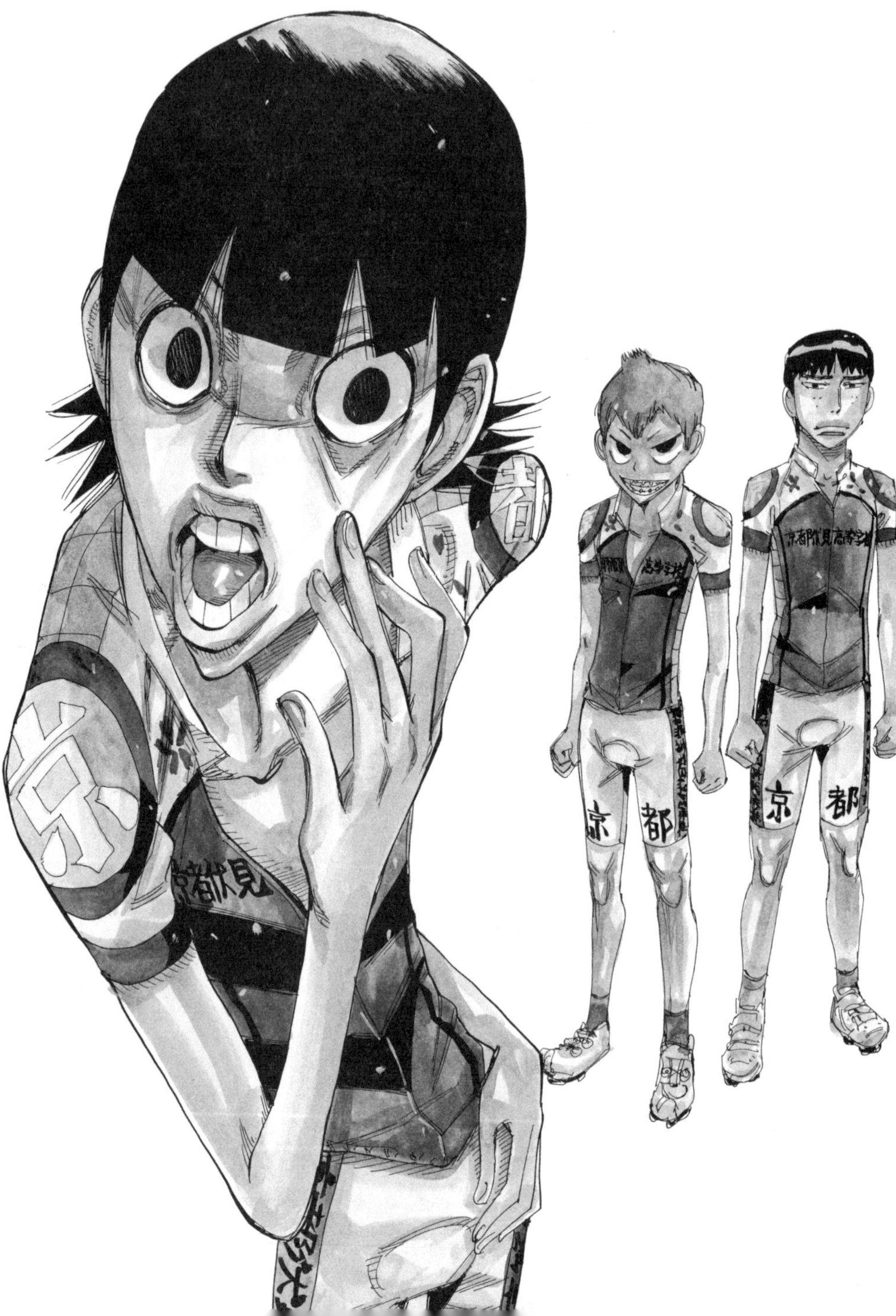
京都
京都

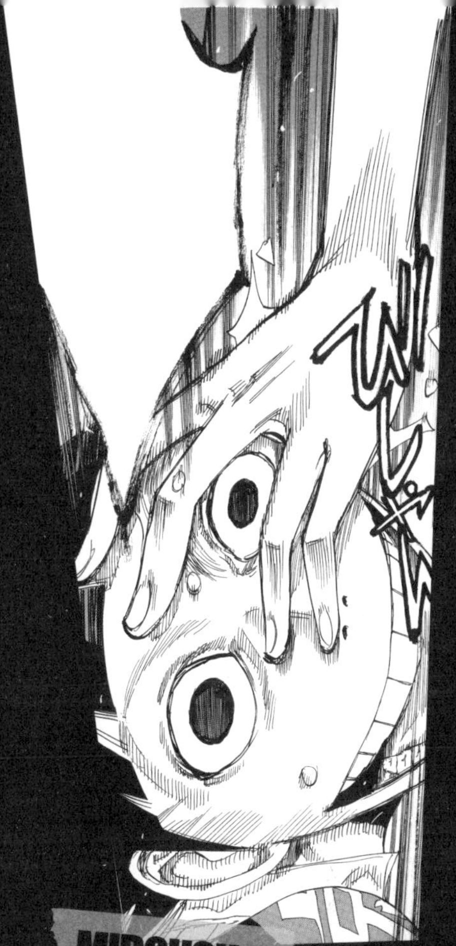
MIDOUSUJI

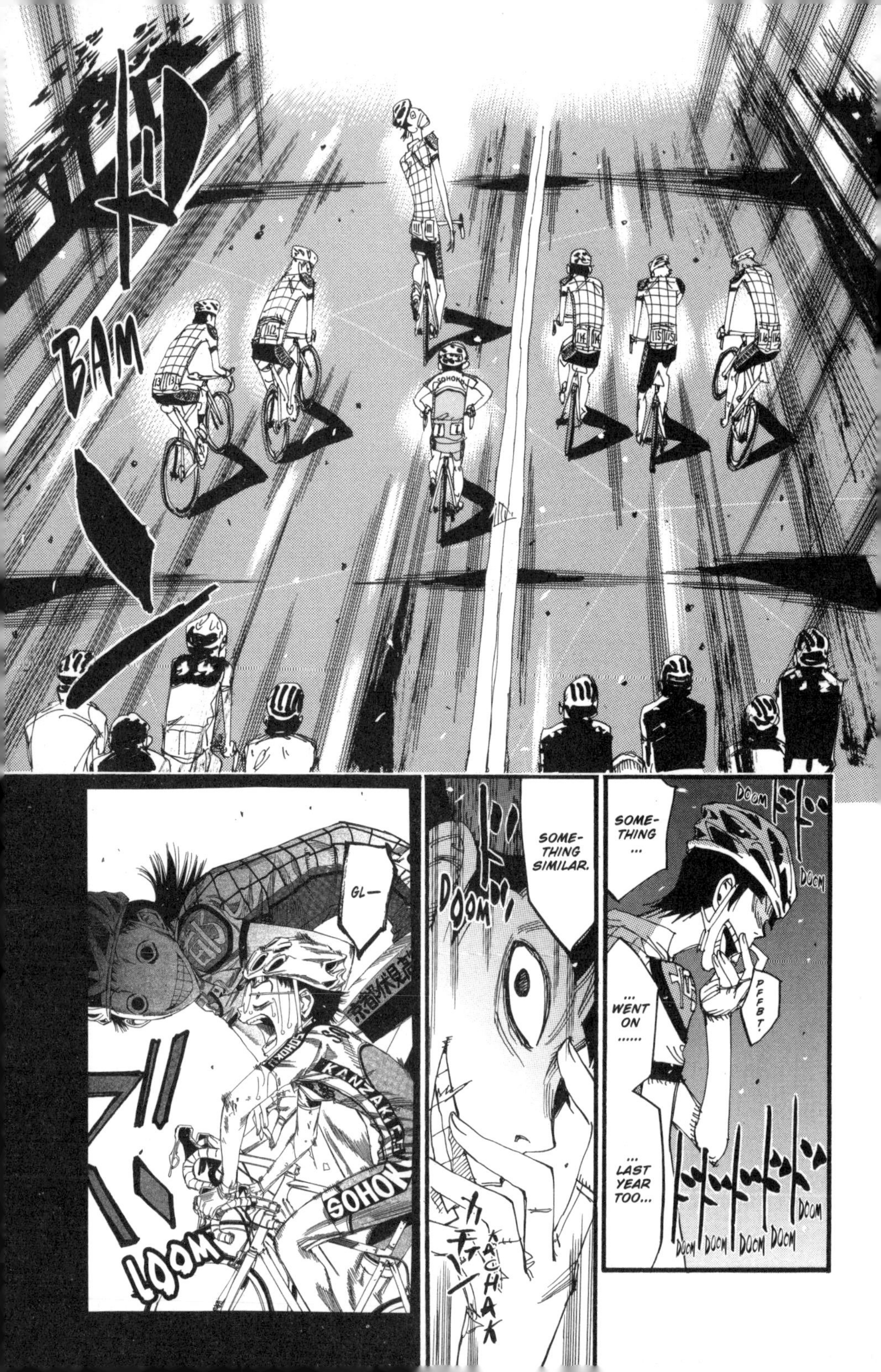
BAM
DOOM
DOOM
SOMETHING...
PFFBT.
...WENT ON ......
...LAST YEAR TOO...
DOOM
DOOM DOOM DOOM DOOM
SOMETHING SIMILAR.
DOOM
KACHAK
GL—

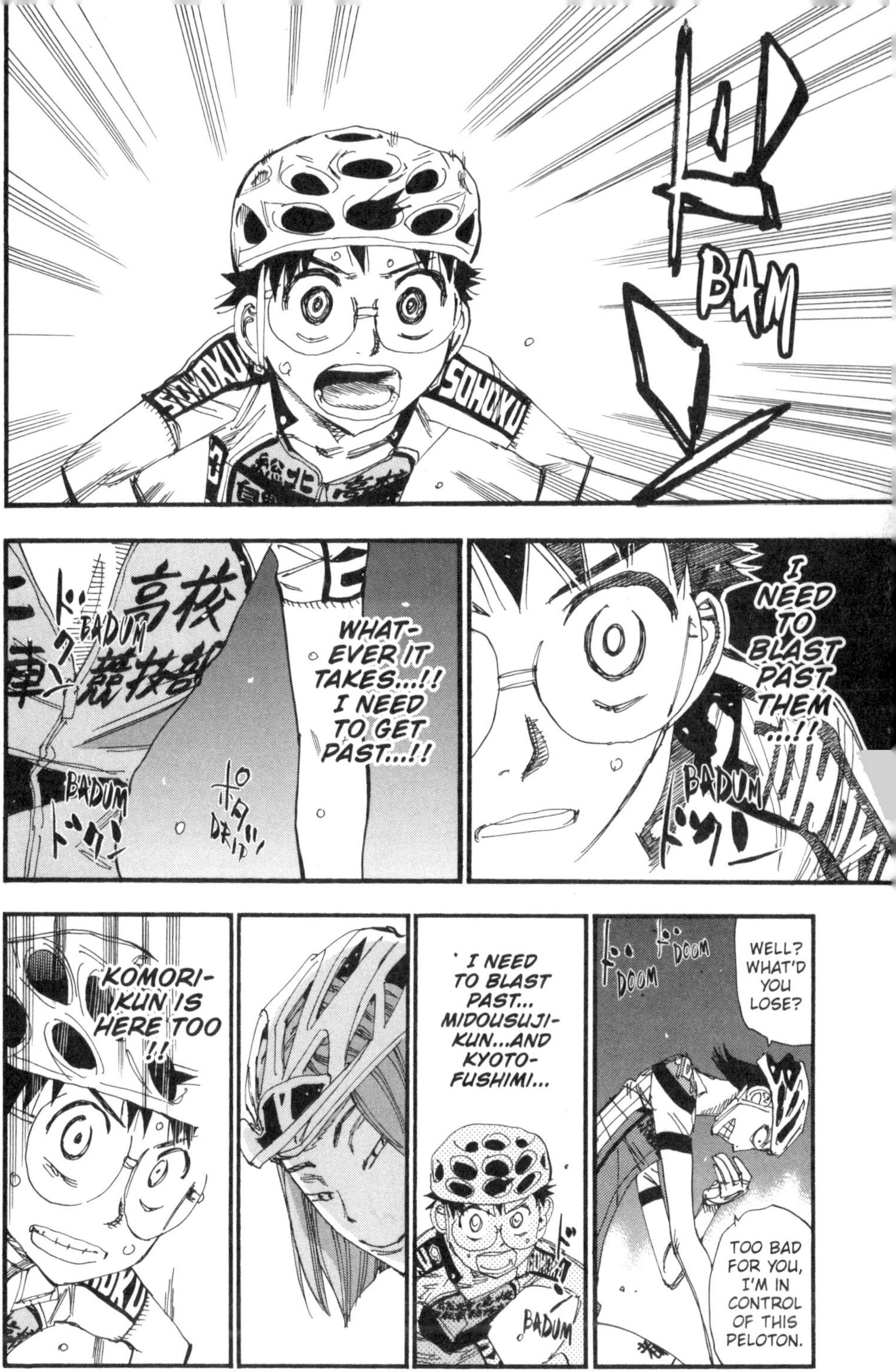
BAM
I NEED TO BLAST PAST THEM...!!
BADUM
WHAT-EVER IT TAKES...!! I NEED TO GET PAST...!!
BADUM
BADUM
DRIP
DOOM
DOOM
WELL? WHAT'D YOU LOSE?
TOO BAD FOR YOU, I'M IN CONTROL OF THIS PELOTON.
I NEED TO BLAST PAST... MIDOUSUJI-KUN...AND KYOTO-FUSHIMI...
BADUM
KOMORI-KUN IS HERE TOO!!

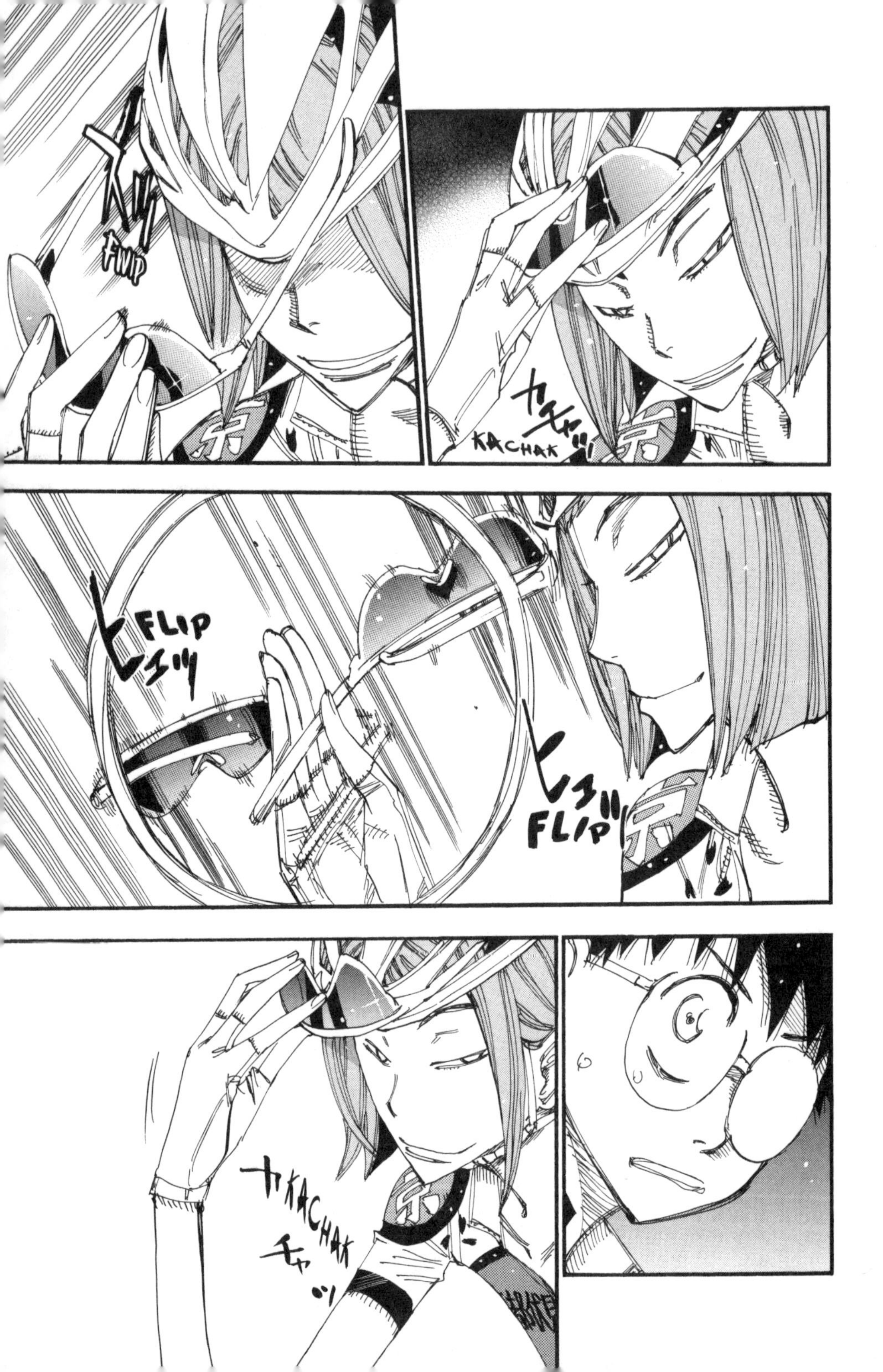
KACHAK
FLIP
FLIP
FLIP
KACHAK

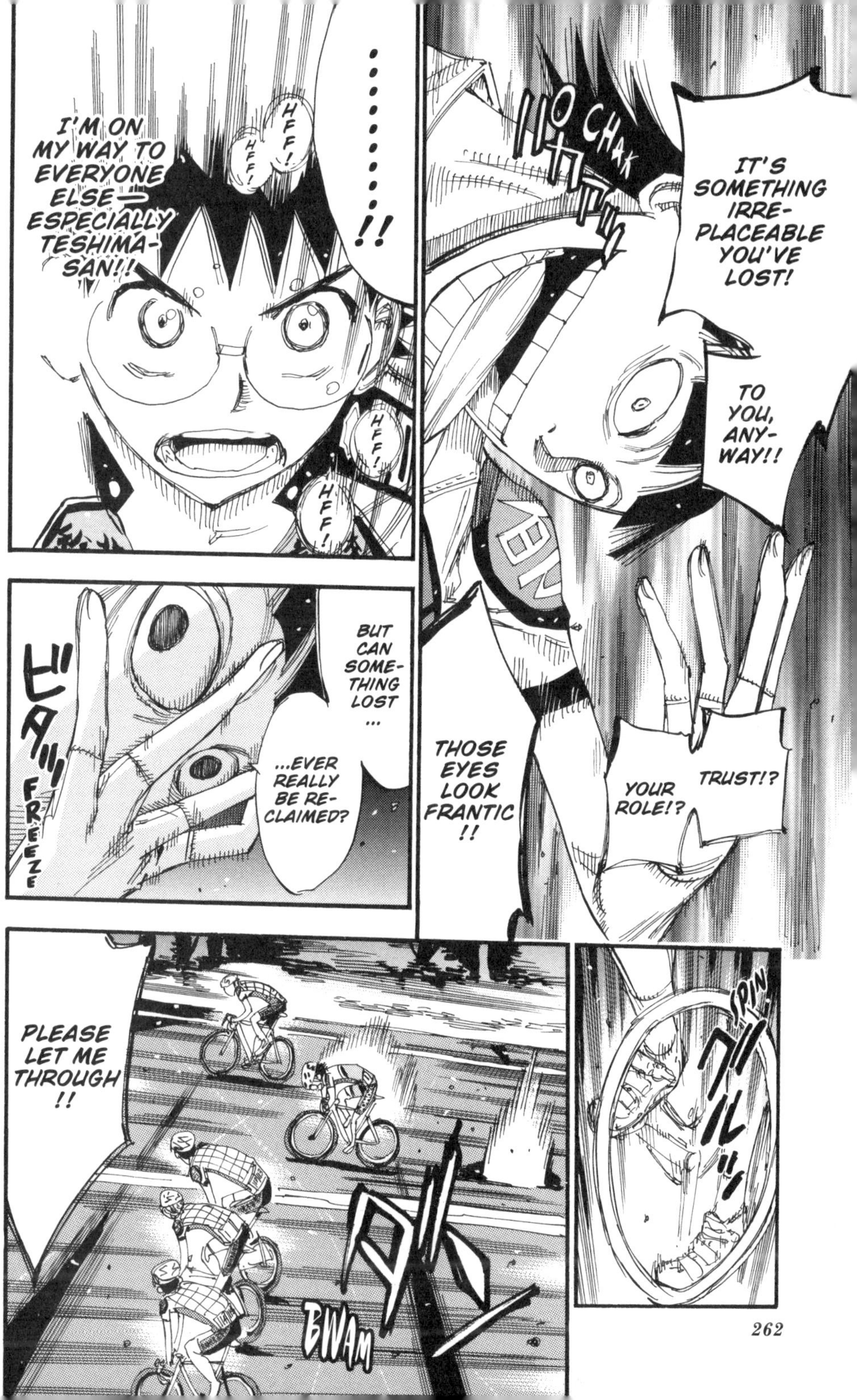
CHAK
IT'S SOMETHING IRRE-PLACEABLE YOU'VE LOST!
TO YOU, ANYWAY!!
TRUST!?
YOUR ROLE!?
THOSE EYES LOOK FRANTIC!!
.........!!
HFF! HFF!
I'M ON MY WAY TO EVERYONE ELSE—ESPECIALLY TESHIMA-SAN!!
HFF! HFF!
BUT CAN SOMETHING LOST...
...EVER REALLY BE RE-CLAIMED?
FREEZE
SPIN
PLEASE LET ME THROUGH!!
BWAM

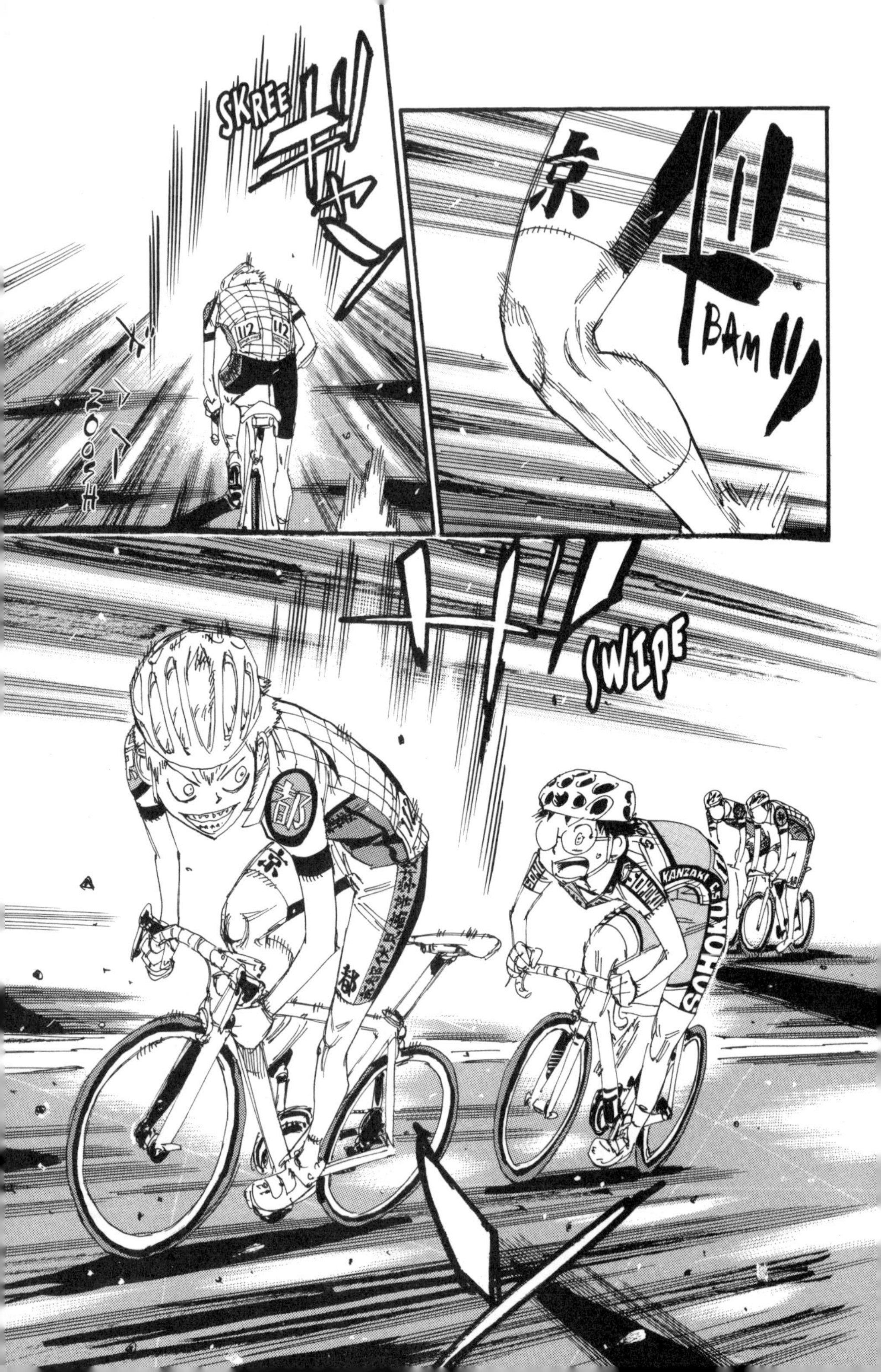
BAM
SKREE
WHOOSH
SWIPE

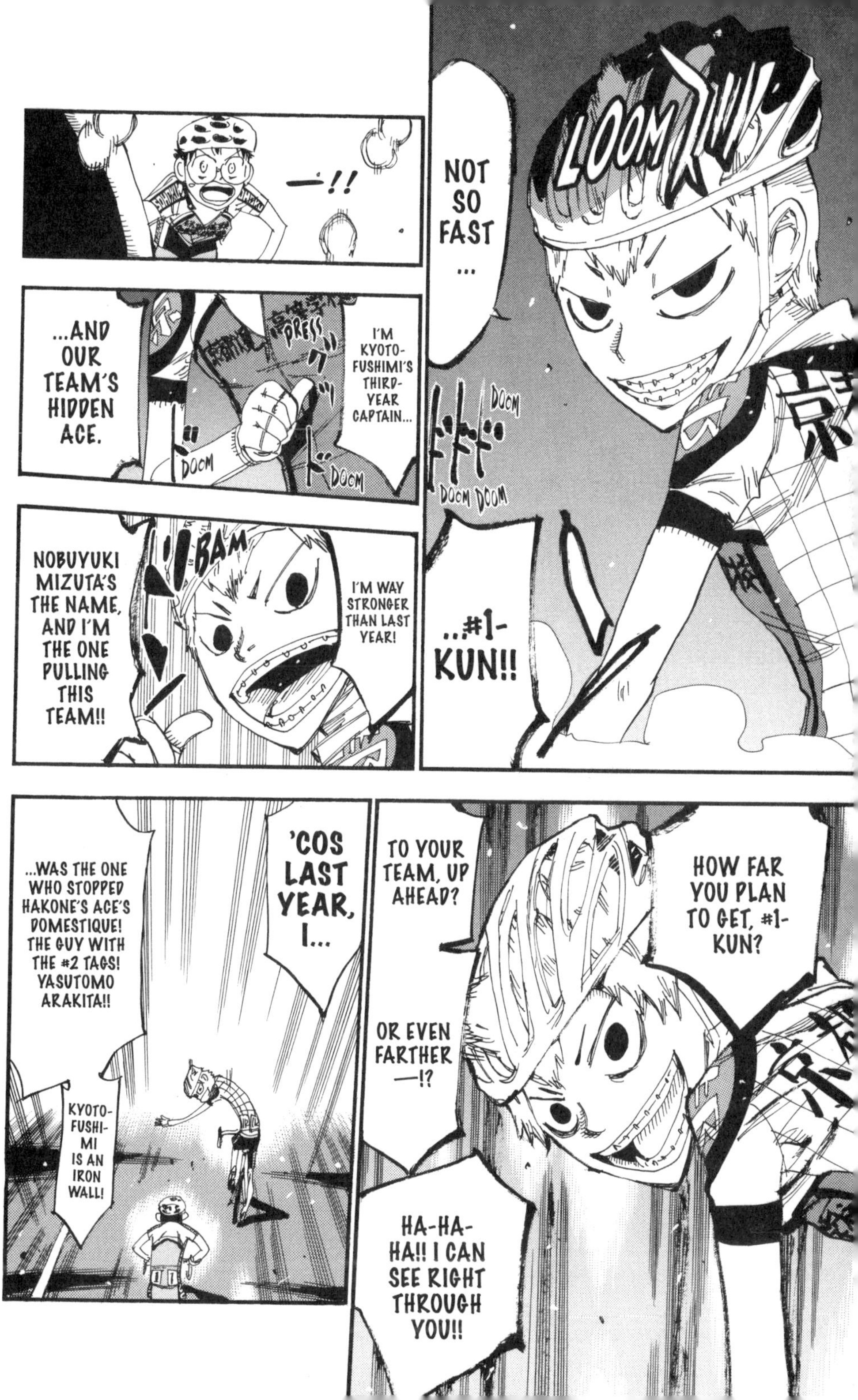

NOT SO FAST ...
LOOM
DOOM
DOOM DOOM
...#1-KUN!!
—!!
I'M KYOTO-FUSHIMI'S THIRD-YEAR CAPTAIN...
PRESS
...AND OUR TEAM'S HIDDEN ACE.
DOOM
DOOM
BAM
I'M WAY STRONGER THAN LAST YEAR!
NOBUYUKI MIZUTA'S THE NAME, AND I'M THE ONE PULLING THIS TEAM!!
HOW FAR YOU PLAN TO GET, #1-KUN?
TO YOUR TEAM, UP AHEAD?
OR EVEN FARTHER—!?
HA-HA-HA!! I CAN SEE RIGHT THROUGH YOU!!
'COS LAST YEAR, I...
...WAS THE ONE WHO STOPPED HAKONE'S ACE'S DOMESTIQUE! THE GUY WITH THE #2 TAGS! YASUTOMO ARAKITA!!
KYOTO-FUSHIMI IS AN IRON WALL!

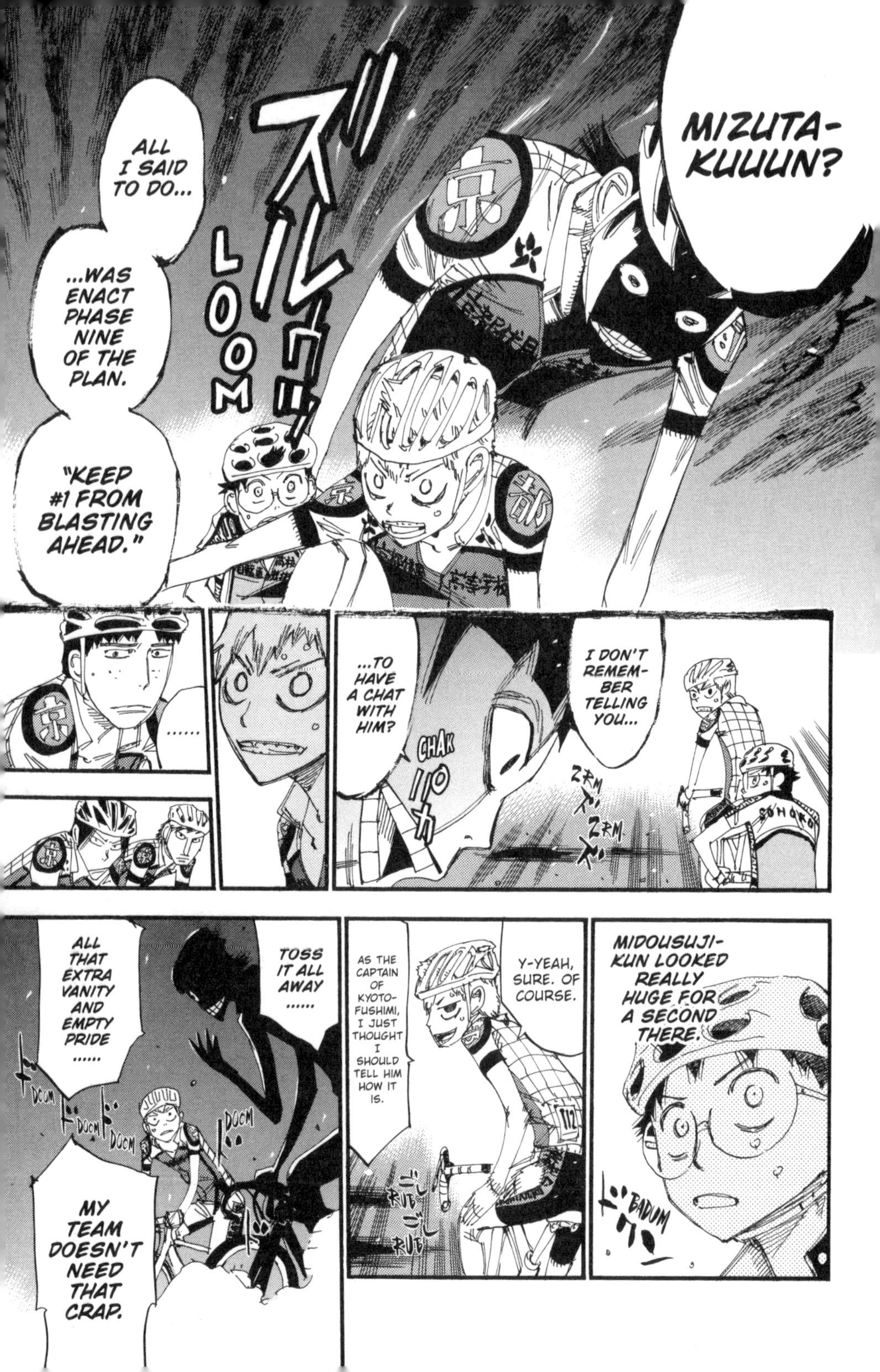
MIZUTA-KUUUN?
ALL I SAID TO DO...
...WAS ENACT PHASE NINE OF THE PLAN.
"KEEP #1 FROM BLASTING AHEAD."
LOOOM
I DON'T REMEMBER TELLING YOU...
...TO HAVE A CHAT WITH HIM?
CHAK
ZRM ZRM
......
MIDOUSUJI-KUN LOOKED REALLY HUGE FOR A SECOND THERE.
BADUM
Y-YEAH, SURE. OF COURSE.
AS THE CAPTAIN OF KYOTO-FUSHIMI, I JUST THOUGHT I SHOULD TELL HIM HOW IT IS.
RUB RUB
TOSS IT ALL AWAY ......
ALL THAT EXTRA VANITY AND EMPTY PRIDE ......
DOOM DOOM DOOM DOOM
MY TEAM DOESN'T NEED THAT CRAP.

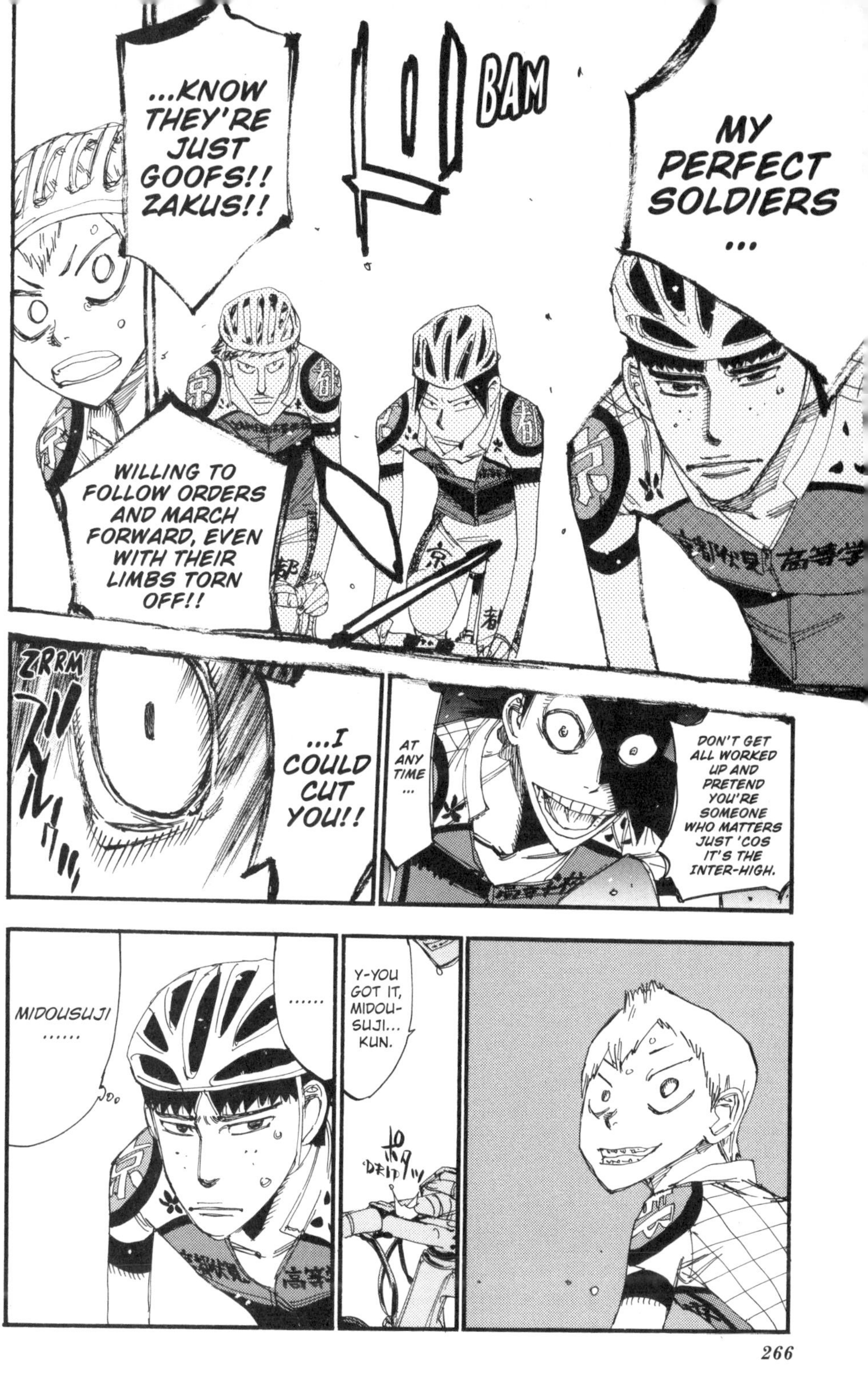
MY PERFECT SOLDIERS ...
BAM
...KNOW THEY'RE JUST GOOFS!! ZAKUS!!
WILLING TO FOLLOW ORDERS AND MARCH FORWARD, EVEN WITH THEIR LIMBS TORN OFF!!
DON'T GET ALL WORKED UP AND PRETEND YOU'RE SOMEONE WHO MATTERS JUST 'COS IT'S THE INTER-HIGH.
AT ANY TIME ...
...I COULD CUT YOU!!
ZRRM
Y-YOU GOT IT, MIDOU-SUJI... KUN.
DRIP
......
MIDOUSUJI ......

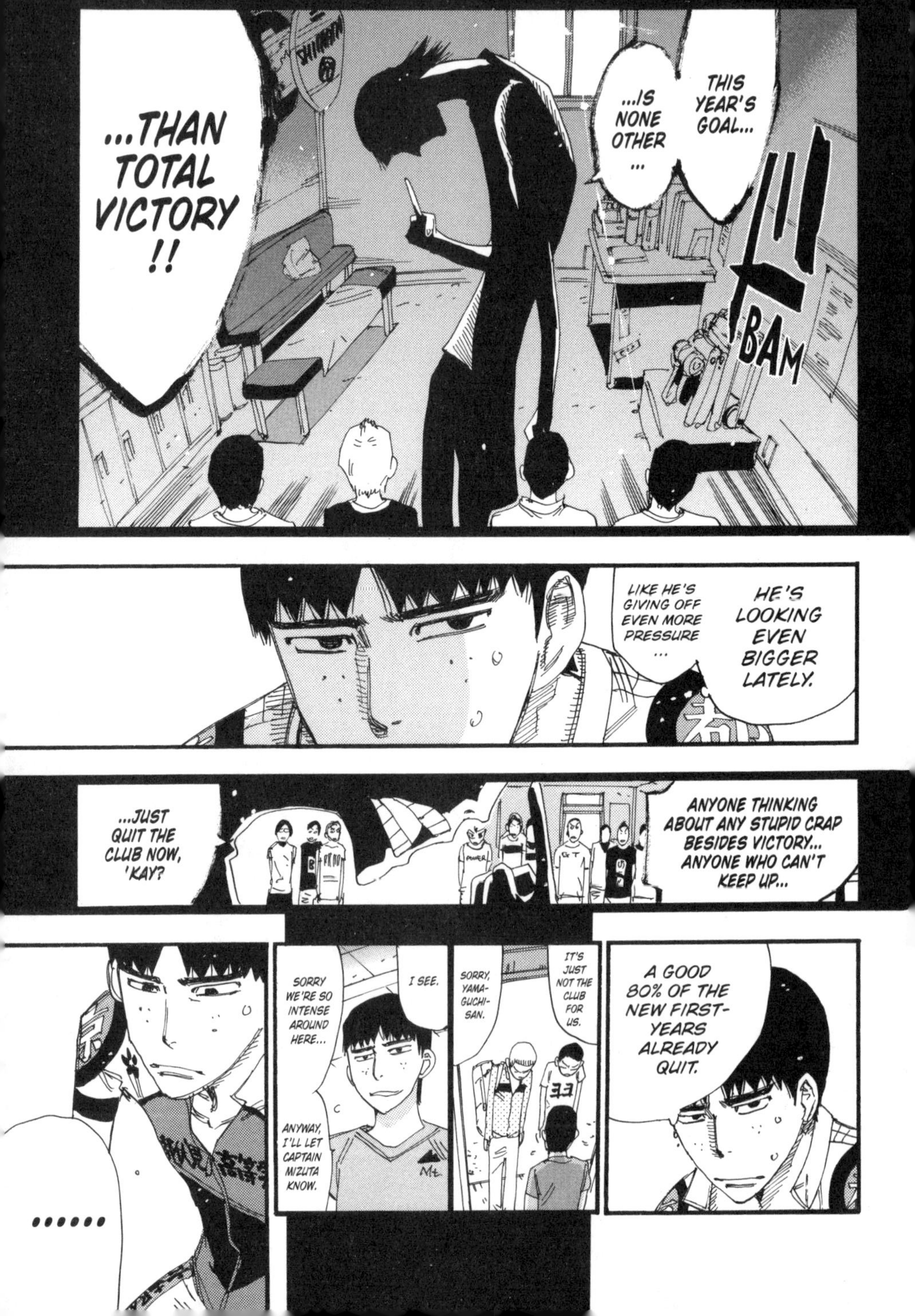
THIS YEAR'S GOAL...
...IS NONE OTHER ...
...THAN TOTAL VICTORY!!
BAM
HE'S LOOKING EVEN BIGGER LATELY.
LIKE HE'S GIVING OFF EVEN MORE PRESSURE ...
ANYONE THINKING ABOUT ANY STUPID CRAP BESIDES VICTORY... ANYONE WHO CAN'T KEEP UP...
...JUST QUIT THE CLUB NOW, 'KAY?
A GOOD 80% OF THE NEW FIRST-YEARS ALREADY QUIT.
IT'S JUST NOT THE CLUB FOR US.
SORRY, YAMAGUCHI-SAN.
I SEE.
SORRY WE'RE SO INTENSE AROUND HERE...
ANYWAY, I'LL LET CAPTAIN MIZUTA KNOW.
......

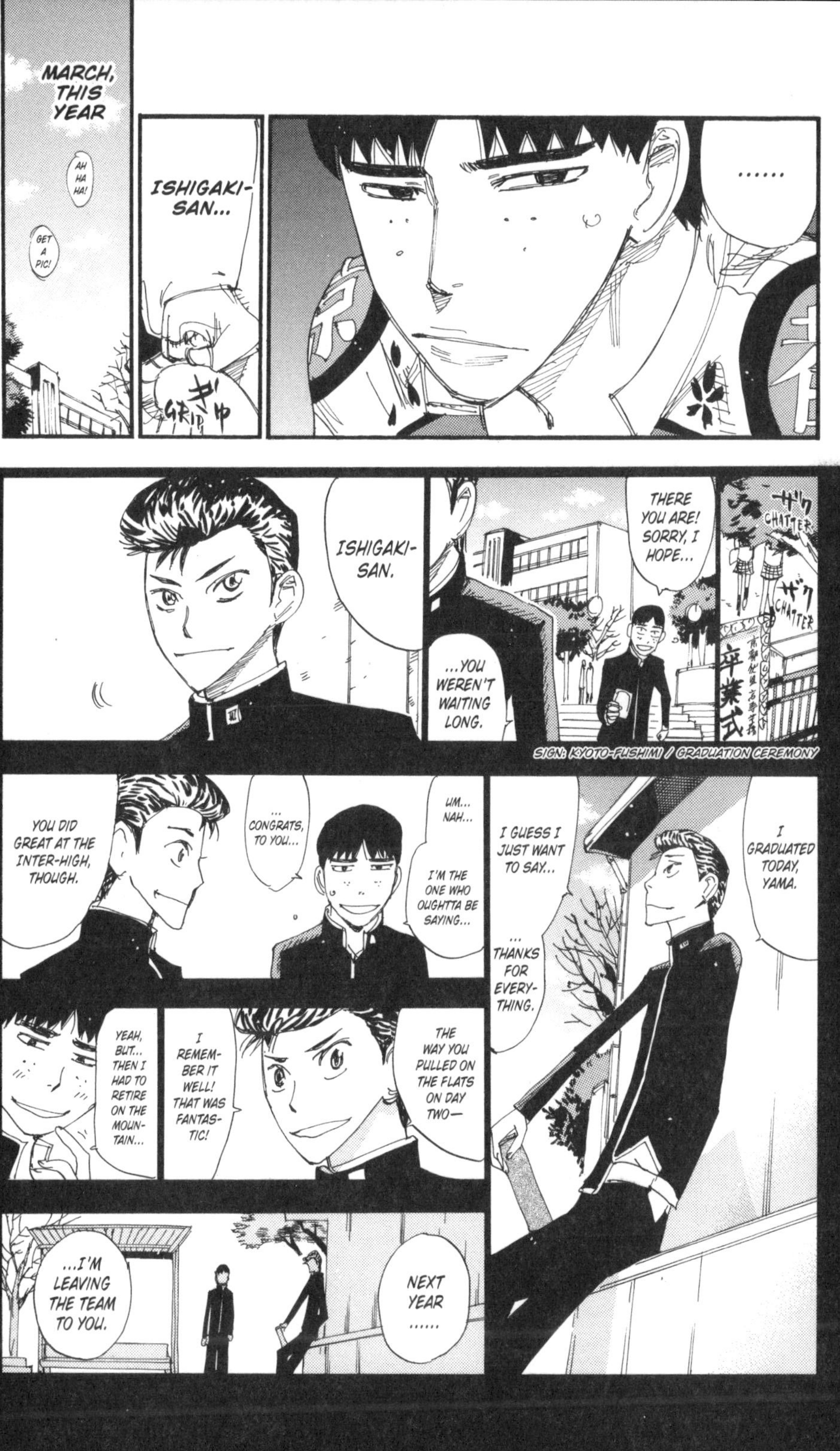
......
ISHIGAKI-SAN...
GRIP
MARCH, THIS YEAR
AH HA HA!
GET A PIC!
THERE YOU ARE! SORRY, I HOPE...
CHATTER
CHATTER
...YOU WEREN'T WAITING LONG.
SIGN: KYOTO-FUSHIMI / GRADUATION CEREMONY
ISHIGAKI-SAN.
I GRADUATED TODAY, YAMA.
I GUESS I JUST WANT TO SAY...
...THANKS FOR EVERYTHING.
UM... NAH...
I'M THE ONE WHO OUGHTTA BE SAYING...
...CONGRATS, TO YOU...
YOU DID GREAT AT THE INTER-HIGH, THOUGH.
THE WAY YOU PULLED ON THE FLATS ON DAY TWO—
I REMEMBER IT WELL! THAT WAS FANTASTIC!
YEAH, BUT... THEN I HAD TO RETIRE ON THE MOUNTAIN...
NEXT YEAR......
...I'M LEAVING THE TEAM TO YOU.

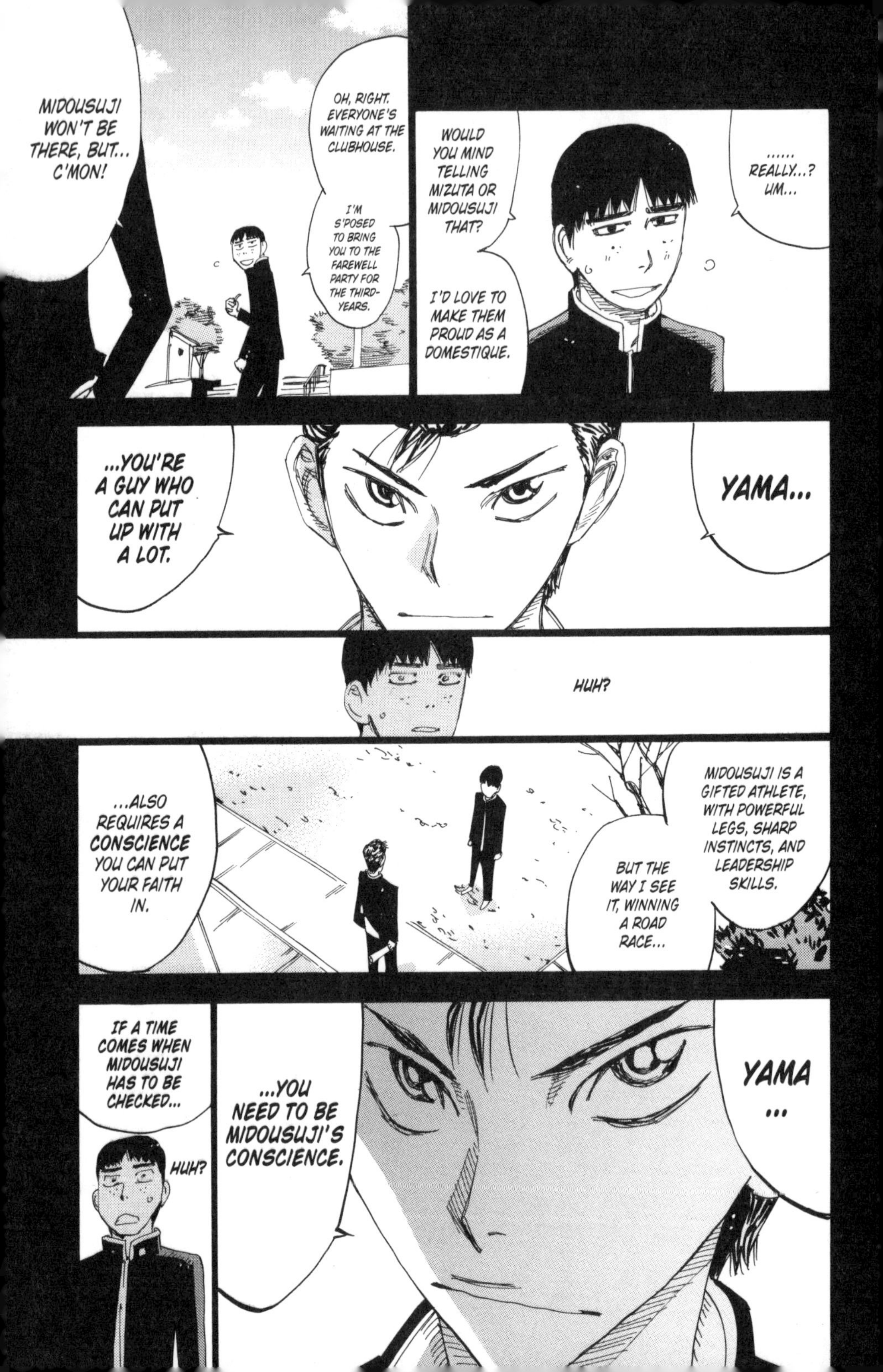

...... REALLY...? UM...
WOULD YOU MIND TELLING MIZUTA OR MIDOUSUJI THAT?
I'D LOVE TO MAKE THEM PROUD AS A DOMESTIQUE.
OH, RIGHT. EVERYONE'S WAITING AT THE CLUBHOUSE.
I'M S'POSED TO BRING YOU TO THE FAREWELL PARTY FOR THE THIRD-YEARS.
MIDOUSUJI WON'T BE THERE, BUT... C'MON!
YAMA...
...YOU'RE A GUY WHO CAN PUT UP WITH A LOT.
HUH?
MIDOUSUJI IS A GIFTED ATHLETE, WITH POWERFUL LEGS, SHARP INSTINCTS, AND LEADERSHIP SKILLS.
BUT THE WAY I SEE IT, WINNING A ROAD RACE...
...ALSO REQUIRES A CONSCIENCE YOU CAN PUT YOUR FAITH IN.
YAMA...
IF A TIME COMES WHEN MIDOUSUJI HAS TO BE CHECKED...
HUH?
...YOU NEED TO BE MIDOUSUJI'S CONSCIENCE.

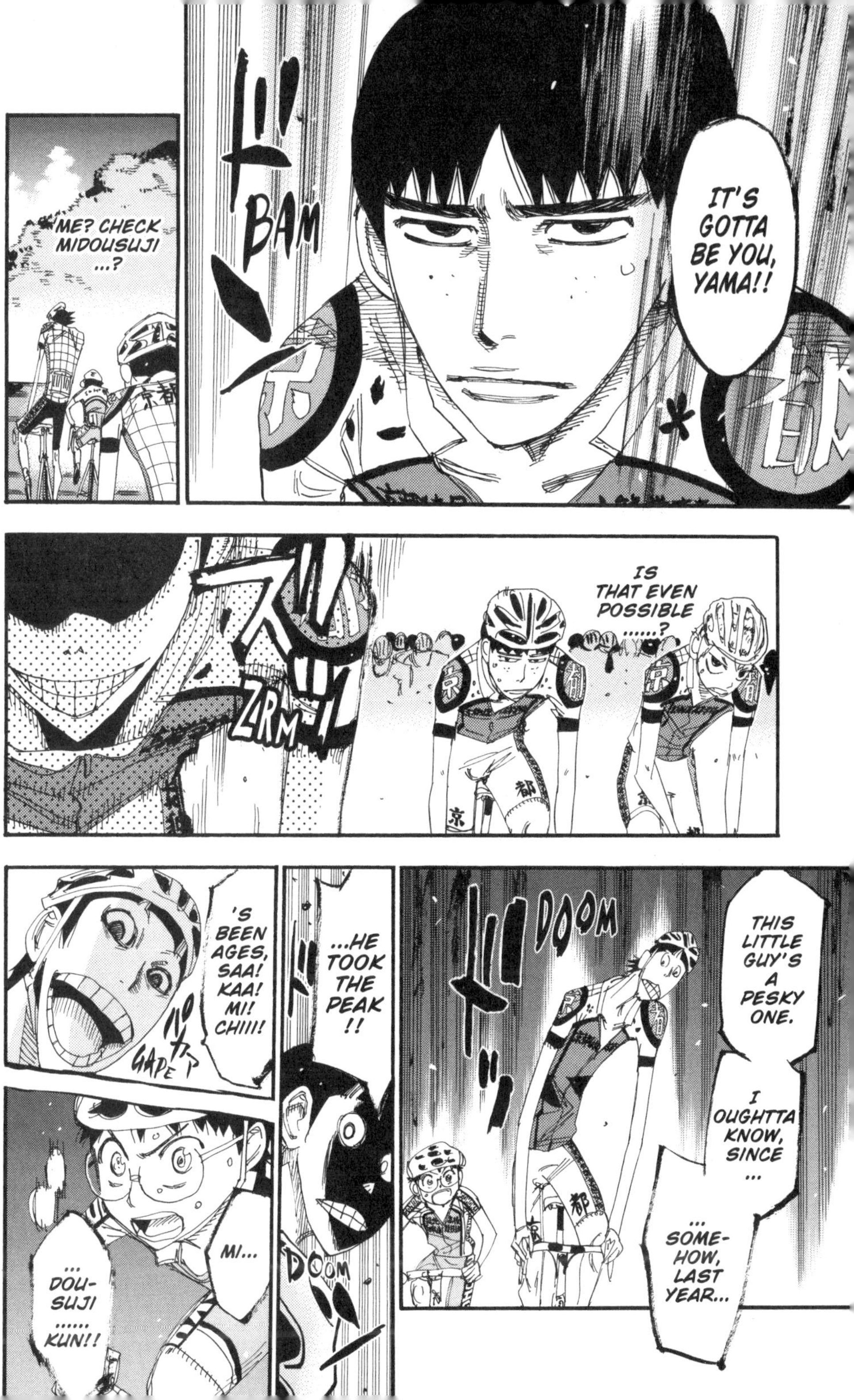
BAM
IT'S GOTTA BE YOU, YAMA!!
ME? CHECK MIDOUSUJI ...?
IS THAT EVEN POSSIBLE ......?
ZRM
DOOM
THIS LITTLE GUY'S A PESKY ONE.
I OUGHTTA KNOW, SINCE ...
... SOME-HOW, LAST YEAR...
...HE TOOK THE PEAK!!
MI...
DOOM
'S BEEN AGES, SAA! KAA! MI! CHIII!
GAPE
... DOU-SUJI ...... KUN!!

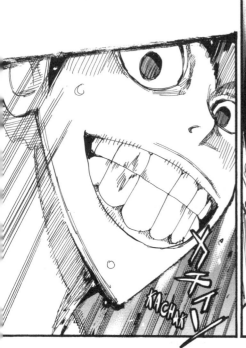
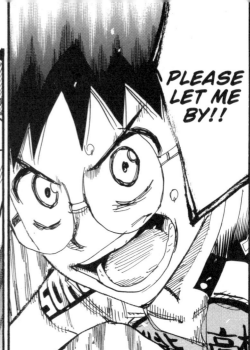

PLEASE LET ME BY!!

KACHAK

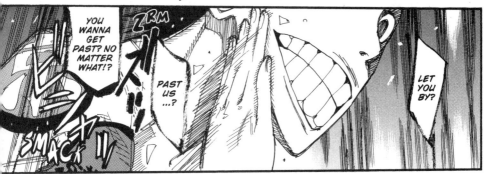

YOU WANNA GET PAST? NO MATTER WHAT!?

ZRM

PAST US ...?

SMACK

LET YOU BY?

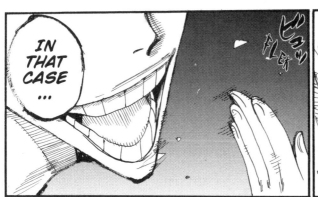

IN THAT CASE ...

FLEX

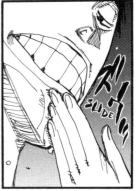

SLIDE

271

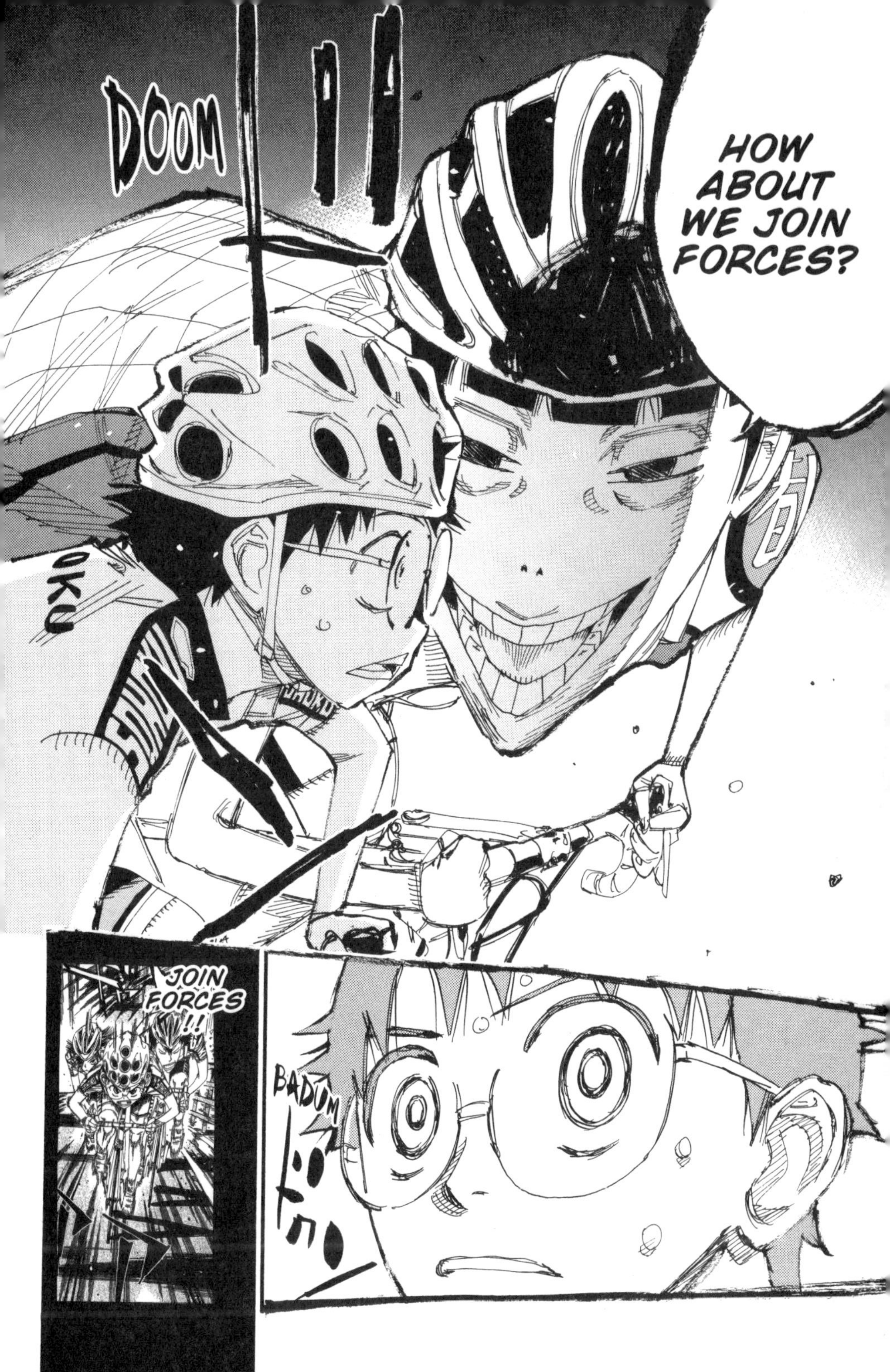
HOW ABOUT WE JOIN FORCES?
DOOM
BADUM
JOIN FORCES!!

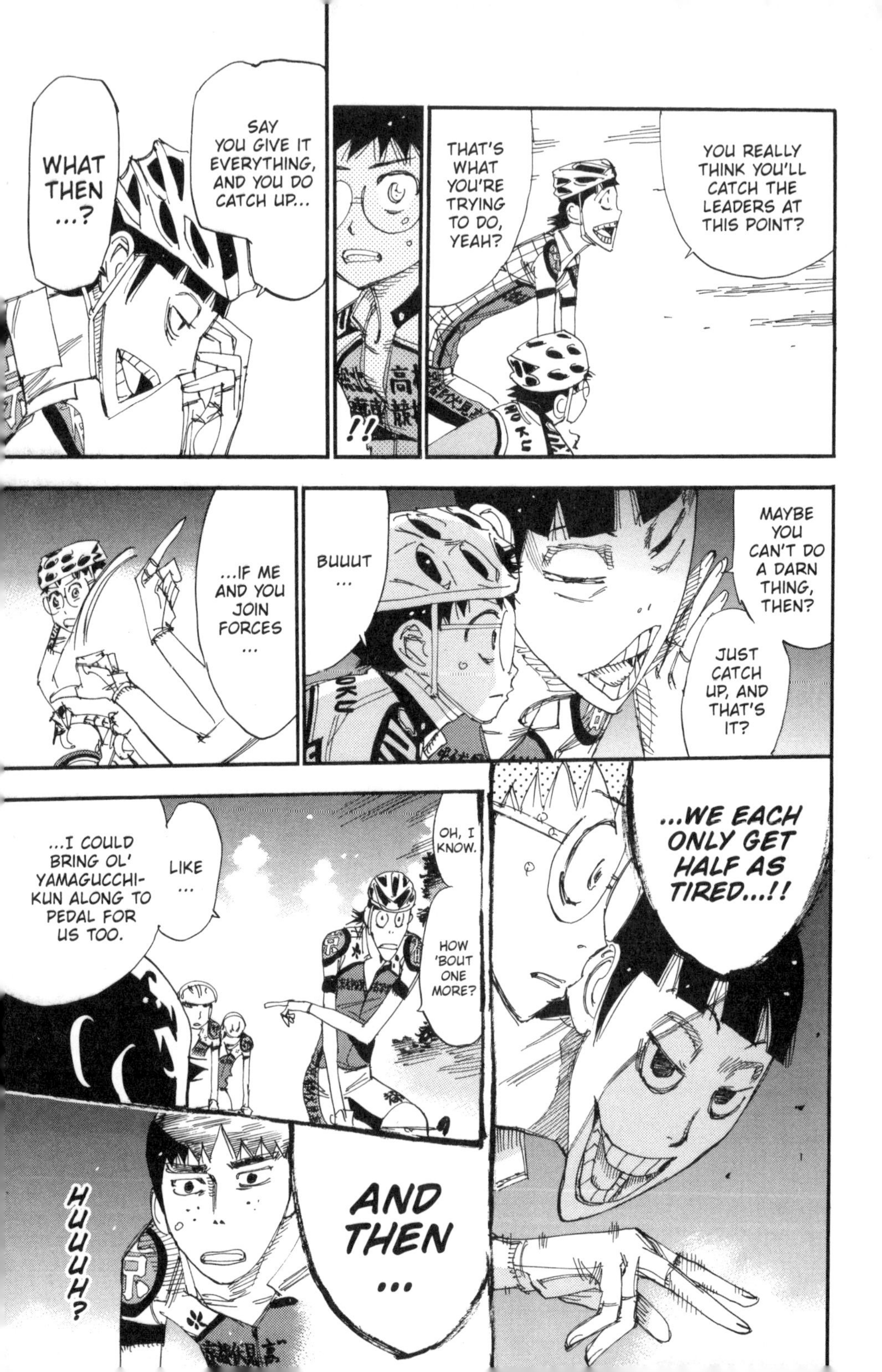
YOU REALLY THINK YOU'LL CATCH THE LEADERS AT THIS POINT?
THAT'S WHAT YOU'RE TRYING TO DO, YEAH?
!!
SAY YOU GIVE IT EVERYTHING, AND YOU DO CATCH UP...
WHAT THEN ...?
MAYBE YOU CAN'T DO A DARN THING, THEN?
JUST EACH CATCH UP, AND THAT'S IT?
BUUUT ...
...IF ME AND YOU JOIN FORCES ...
...WE EACH ONLY GET HALF AS TIRED...!!
OH, I KNOW.
HOW 'BOUT ONE MORE?
LIKE ...
...I COULD BRING OL' YAMAGUCCHI-KUN ALONG TO PEDAL FOR US TOO.
AND THEN ...
HUUUH?

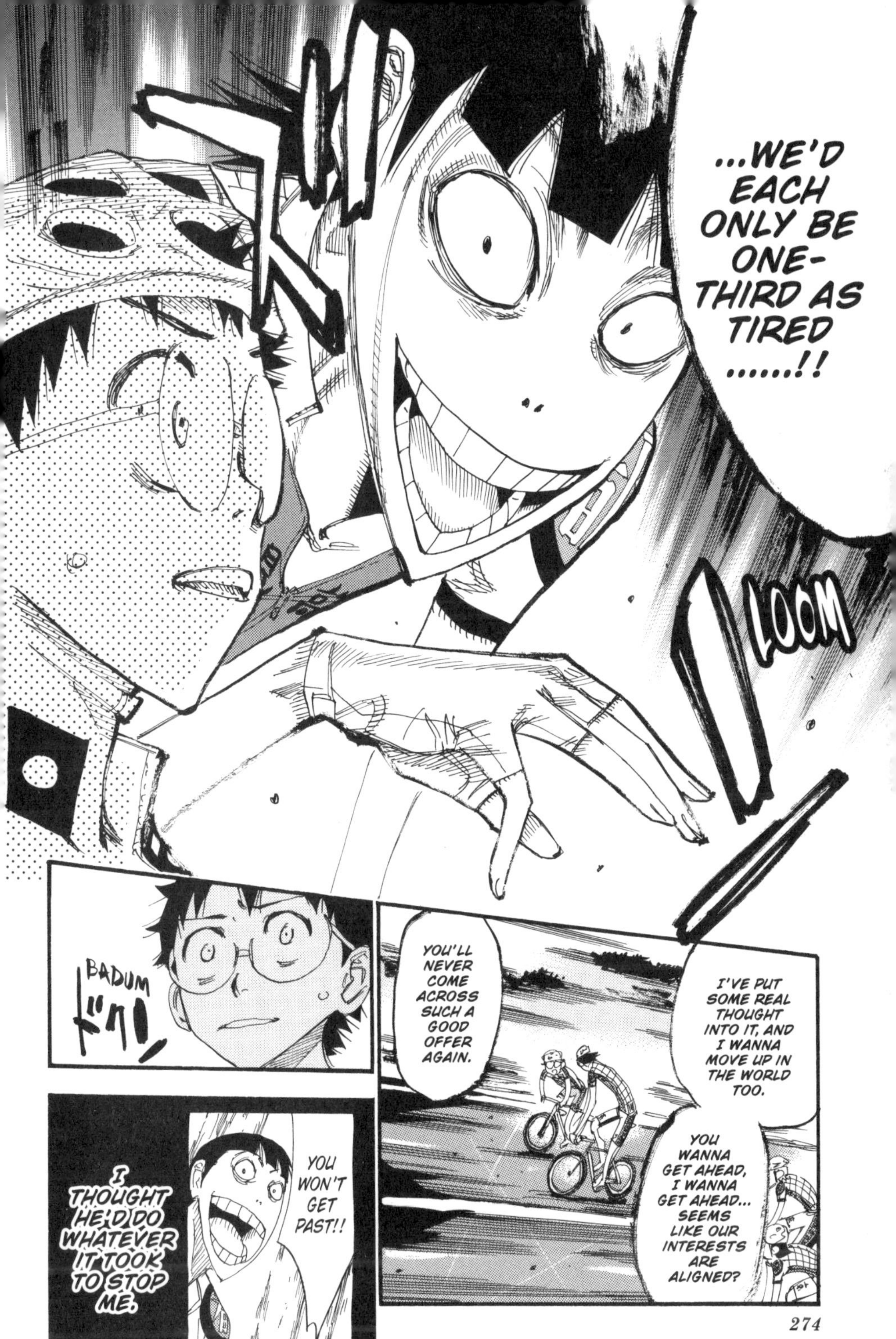
...WE'D EACH ONLY BE ONE-THIRD AS TIRED ......!!
LOOM
I'VE PUT SOME REAL THOUGHT INTO IT, AND I WANNA MOVE UP IN THE WORLD TOO.
YOU WANNA GET AHEAD, I WANNA GET AHEAD... SEEMS LIKE OUR INTERESTS ARE ALIGNED?
YOU'LL NEVER COME ACROSS SUCH A GOOD OFFER AGAIN.
BADUM
YOU WON'T GET PAST!!
I THOUGHT HE'D DO WHATEVER IT TOOK TO STOP ME.

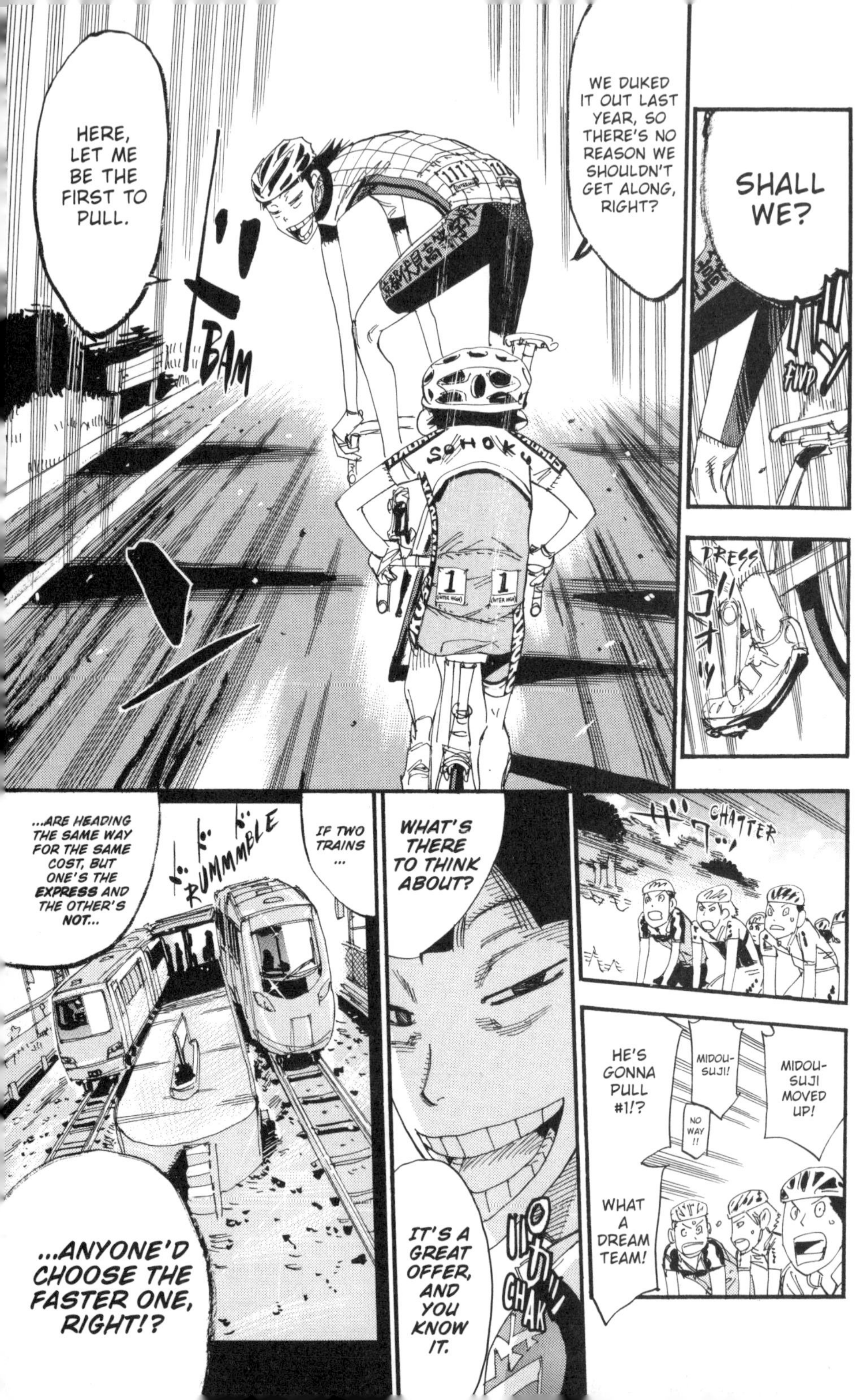
WE DUKED IT OUT LAST YEAR, SO THERE'S NO REASON WE SHOULDN'T GET ALONG, RIGHT?
SHALL WE?
FWP
PRESS
HERE, LET ME BE THE FIRST TO PULL.
BAM
CHATTER
MIDOU-SUJI MOVED UP!
MIDOU-SUJI!
HE'S GONNA PULL #1!?
NO WAY!!
WHAT A DREAM TEAM!
WHAT'S THERE TO THINK ABOUT?
IT'S A GREAT OFFER, AND YOU KNOW IT.
CHAK
IF TWO TRAINS...
...ARE HEADING THE SAME WAY FOR THE SAME COST, BUT ONE'S THE EXPRESS AND THE OTHER'S NOT...
RUMMMBLE
...ANYONE'D CHOOSE THE FASTER ONE, RIGHT!?

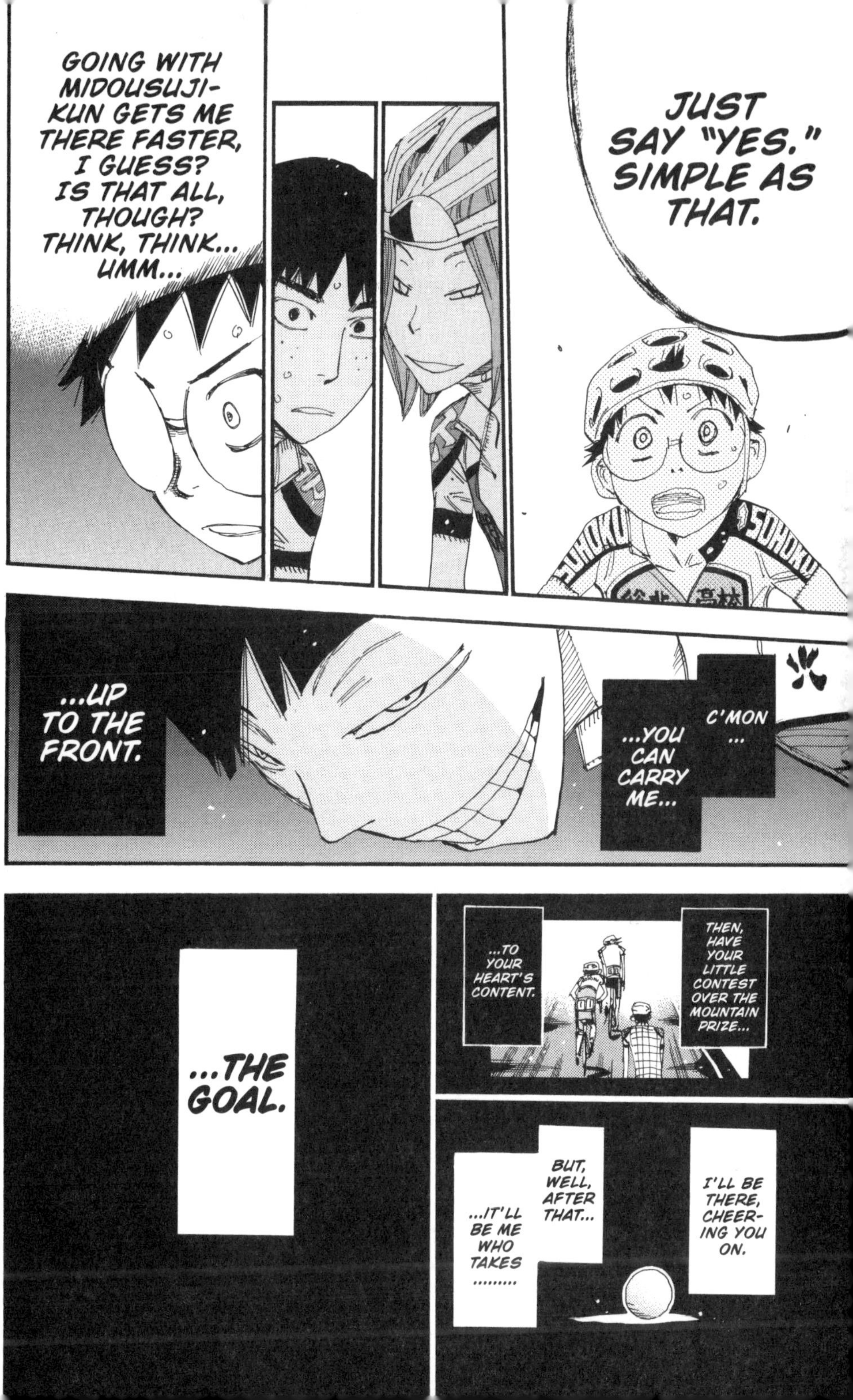
JUST SAY "YES." SIMPLE AS THAT.
GOING WITH MIDOUSUJI-KUN GETS ME THERE FASTER, I GUESS? IS THAT ALL, THOUGH? THINK, THINK... UMM...
C'MON...
...YOU CAN CARRY ME...
...UP TO THE FRONT.
THEN, HAVE YOUR LITTLE CONTEST OVER THE MOUNTAIN PRIZE...
...TO YOUR HEART'S CONTENT.
I'LL BE THERE, CHEERING YOU ON.
BUT, WELL, AFTER THAT...
...IT'LL BE ME WHO TAKES ....
...THE GOAL.

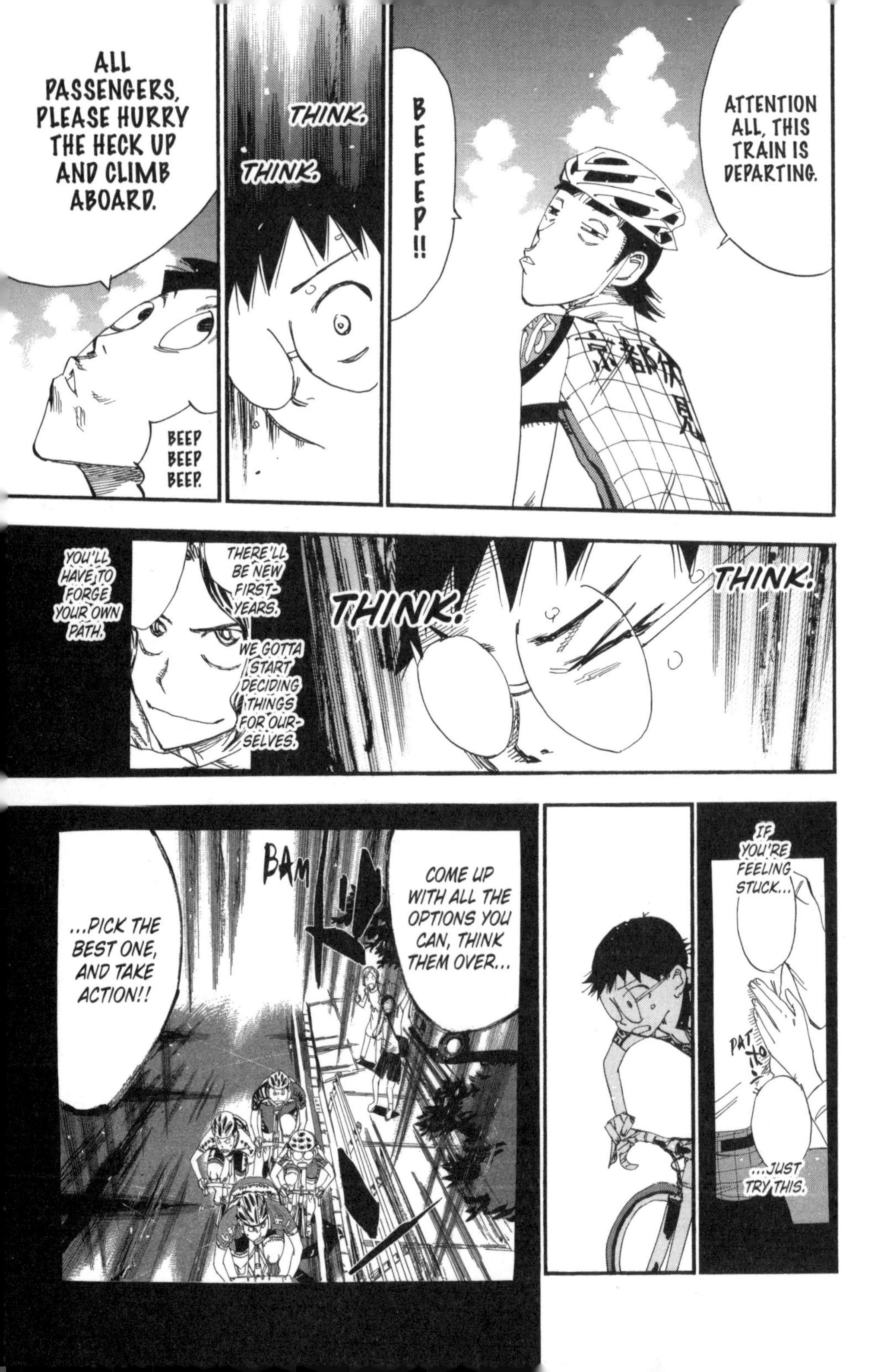
ATTENTION ALL, THIS TRAIN IS DEPARTING.
京都伏見
BEEEEP!!
THINK.
THINK.
ALL PASSENGERS, PLEASE HURRY THE HECK UP AND CLIMB ABOARD.
BEEP BEEP BEEP.
THINK.
THINK!
THERE'LL BE NEW FIRST-YEARS.
WE GOTTA START DECIDING THINGS FOR OURSELVES.
YOU'LL HAVE TO FORGE YOUR OWN PATH.
IF YOU'RE FEELING STUCK...
PAT
...JUST TRY THIS.
COME UP WITH ALL THE OPTIONS YOU CAN, THINK THEM OVER...
BAM
...PICK THE BEST ONE, AND TAKE ACTION!!

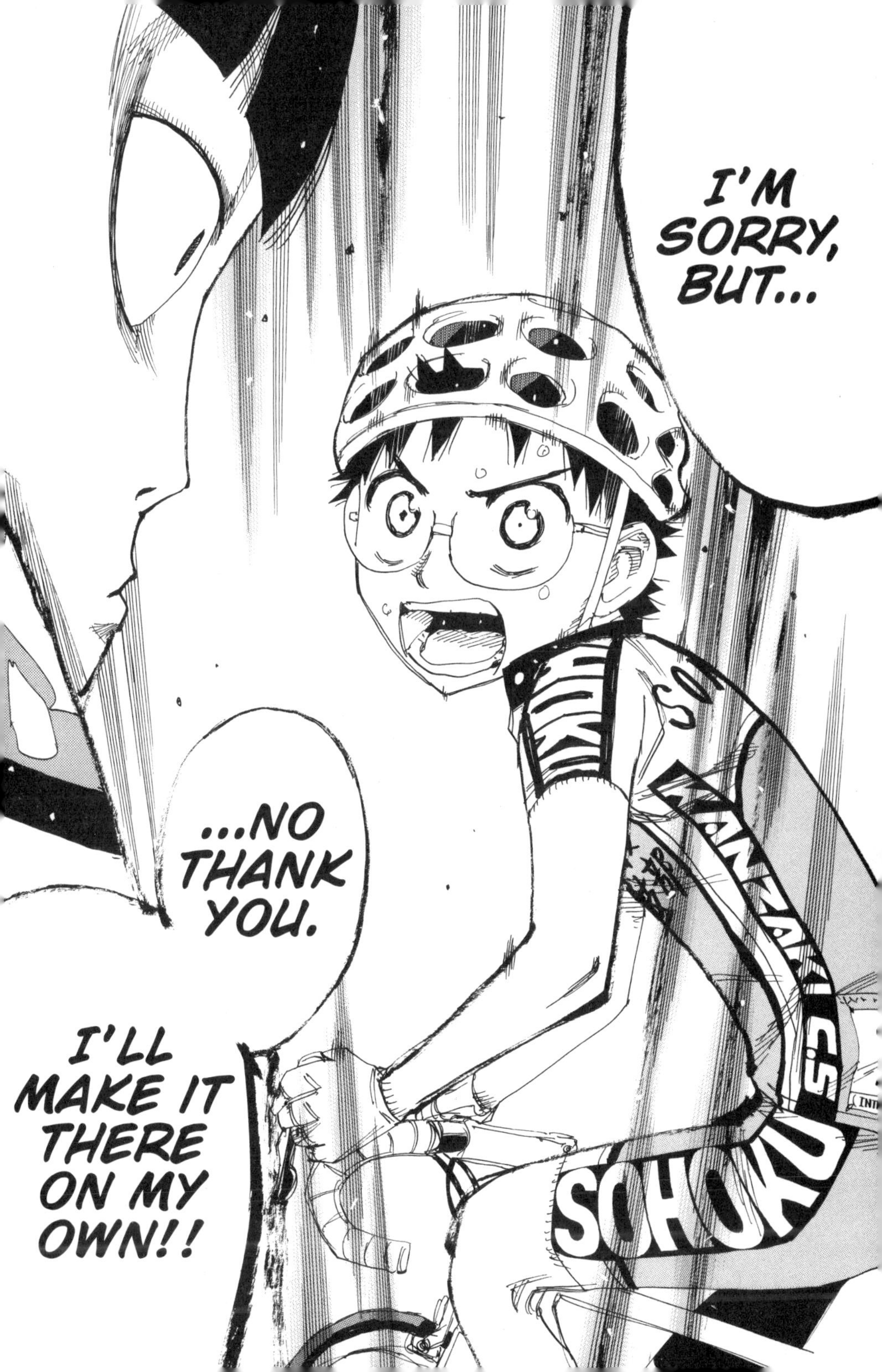
I'M SORRY, BUT...
...NO THANK YOU.
I'LL MAKE IT THERE ON MY OWN!!
SOHOKU

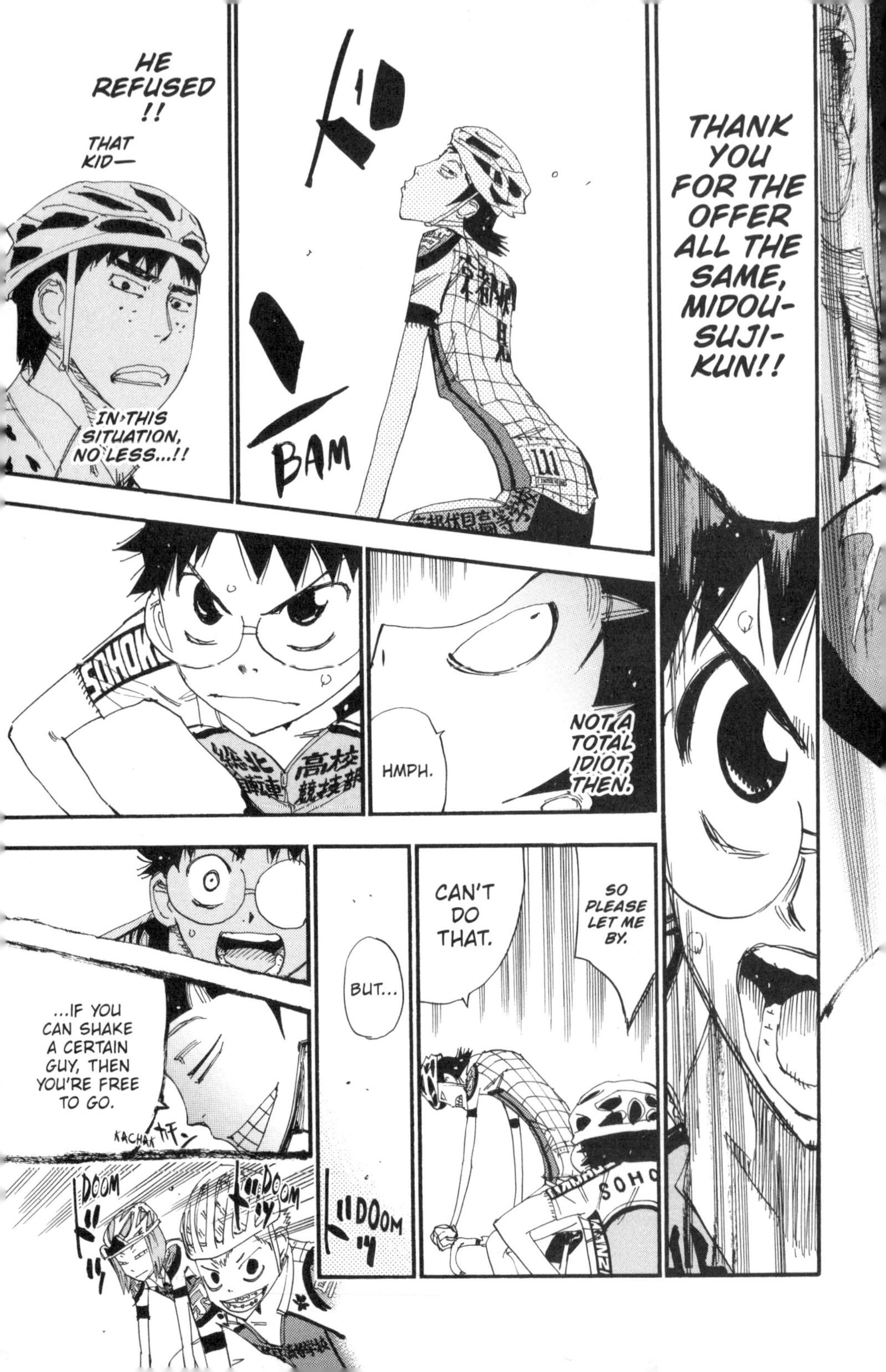
THANK YOU FOR THE OFFER ALL THE SAME, MIDOU-SUJI-KUN!!
BAM
HE REFUSED!!
THAT KID—
IN THIS SITUATION, NO LESS...!!
NOT A TOTAL IDIOT, THEN.
HMPH.
SO PLEASE LET ME BY.
CAN'T DO THAT.
BUT...
DOOM
...IF YOU CAN SHAKE A CERTAIN GUY, THEN YOU'RE FREE TO GO.
KACHAK
DOOM
DOOM

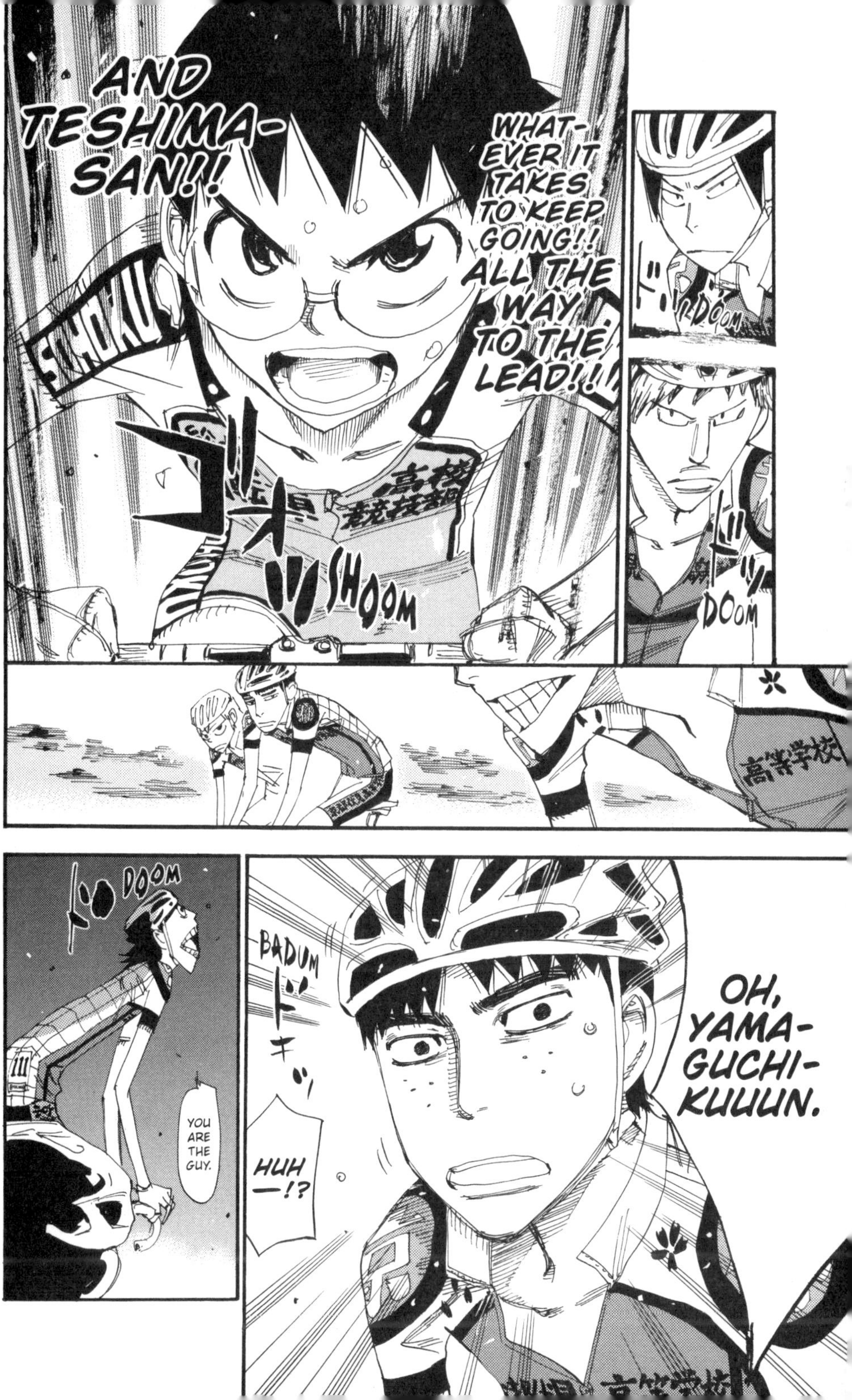
DOOM
DOOM
AND TESHIMA-SAN!!
WHAT-EVER IT TAKES TO KEEP GOING!! ALL THE WAY TO THE LEAD!!!
SHOOM
OH, YAMA-GUCHI-KUUUN.
BADUM
HUH—!?
DOOM
YOU ARE THE GUY.

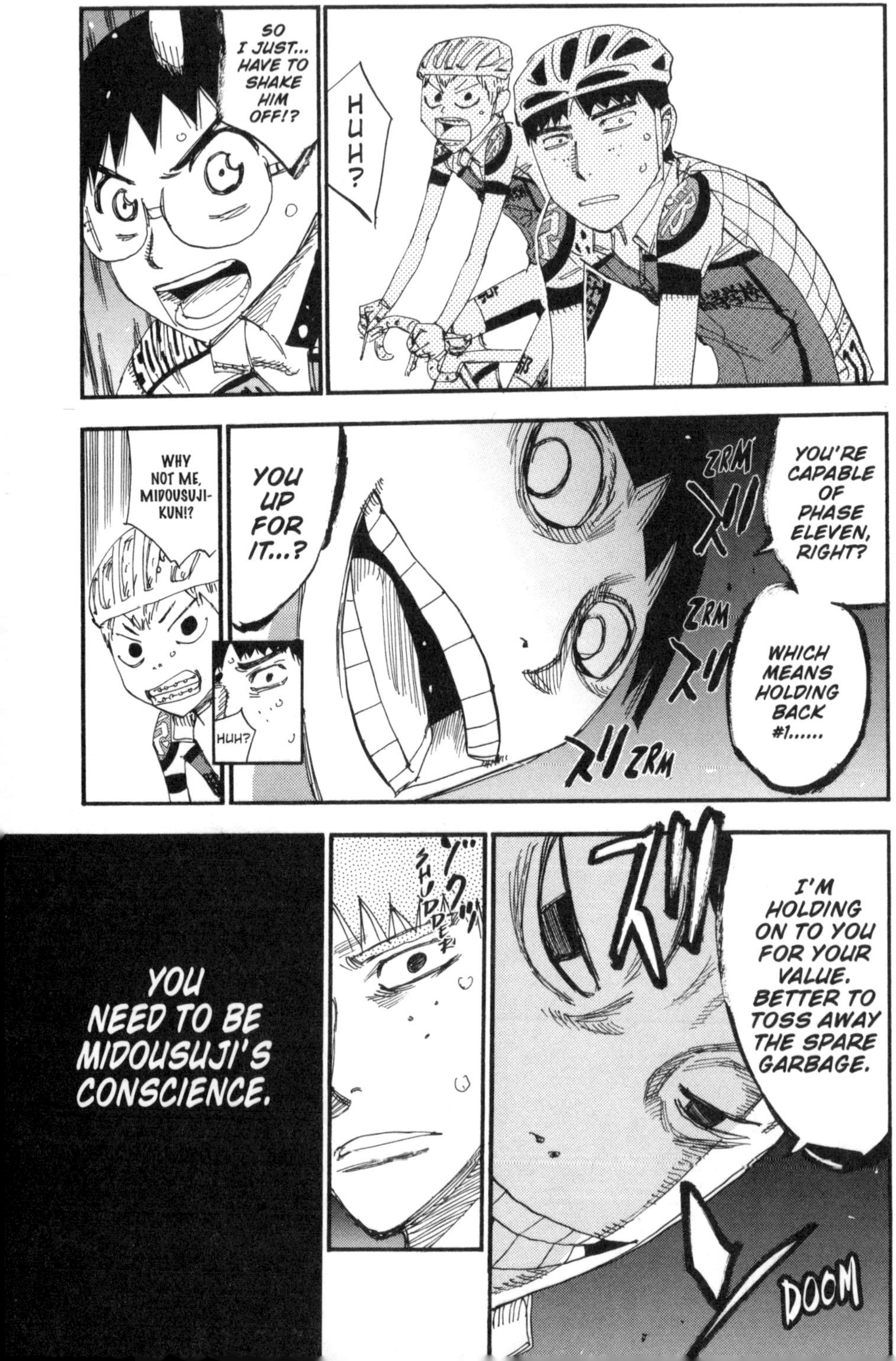
HUH?
SO I JUST... HAVE TO SHAKE HIM OFF!?
YOU'RE CAPABLE OF PHASE ELEVEN, RIGHT?
ZRM
ZRM
WHICH MEANS HOLDING BACK #1......
ZRM
YOU UP FOR IT...?
WHY NOT ME, MIDOUSUJI-KUN!?
HUH?
I'M HOLDING ON TO YOU FOR YOUR VALUE. BETTER TO TOSS AWAY THE SPARE GARBAGE.
DOOM
SHUDDER
YOU NEED TO BE MIDOUSUJI'S CONSCIENCE.

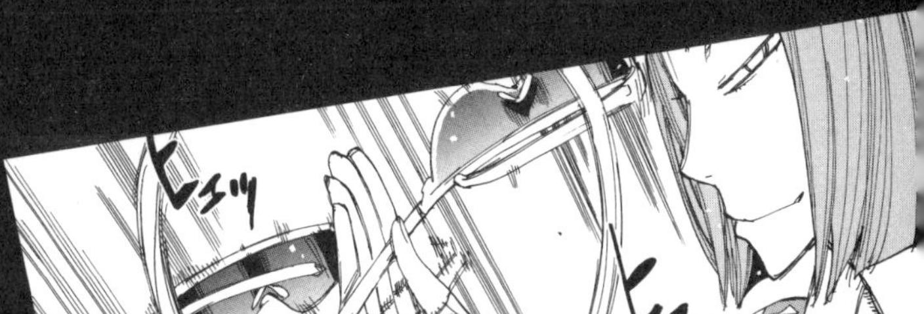
ヒョッ
ヒョッ

KOMARI

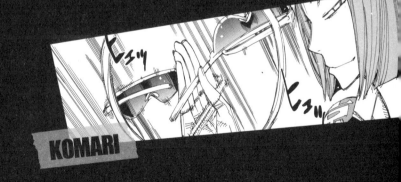

RIDE.324 MANAMI'S "WINGS"

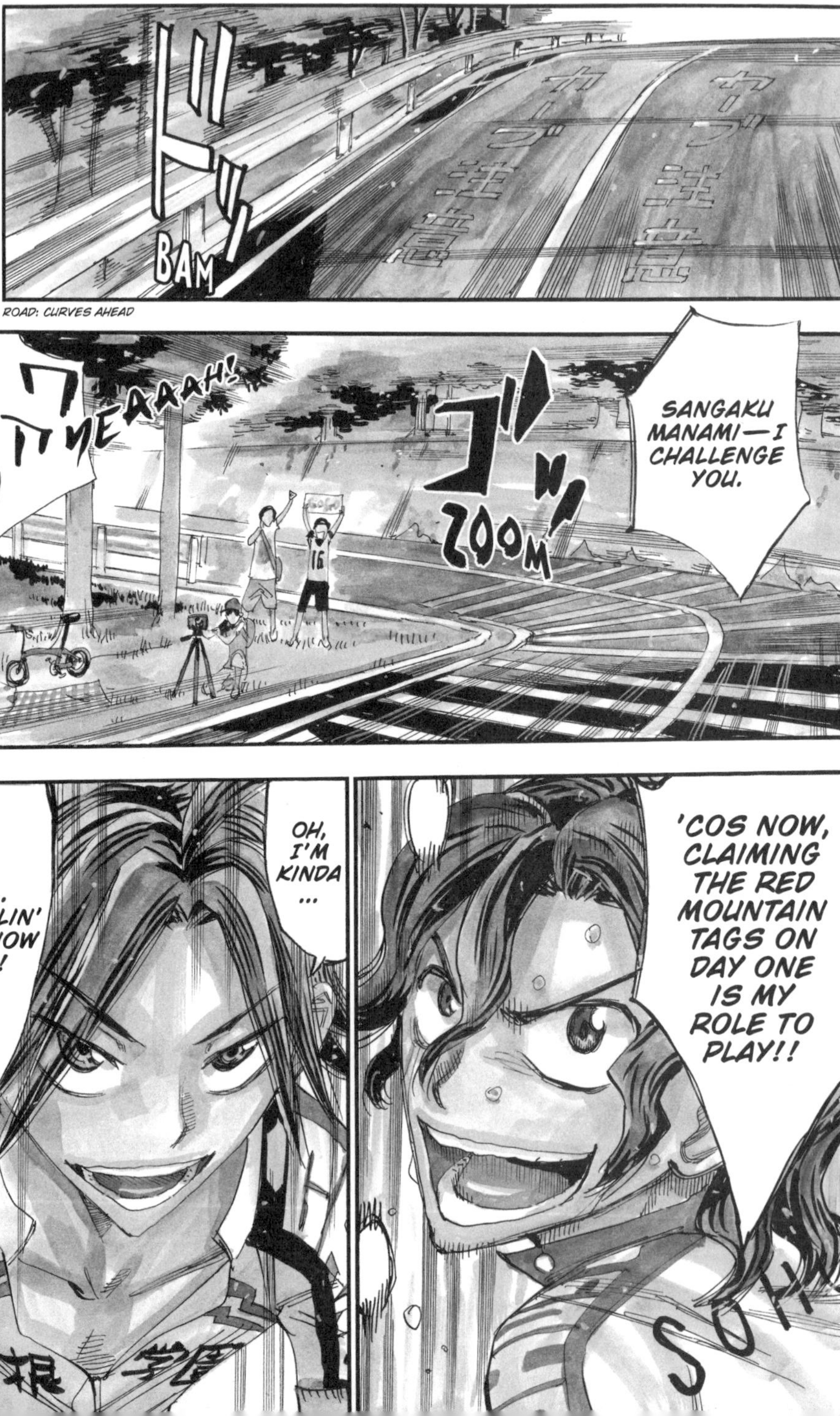
BAM
ROAD: CURVES AHEAD
SANGAKU MANAMI—I CHALLENGE YOU.
ZOOM
YEAAAAH!
'COS NOW, CLAIMING THE RED MOUNTAIN TAGS ON DAY ONE IS MY ROLE TO PLAY!!
SOH
OH, I'M KINDA ...
... FEELIN' IT NOW !!

RIDE.324 MANAMI'S "WINGS"

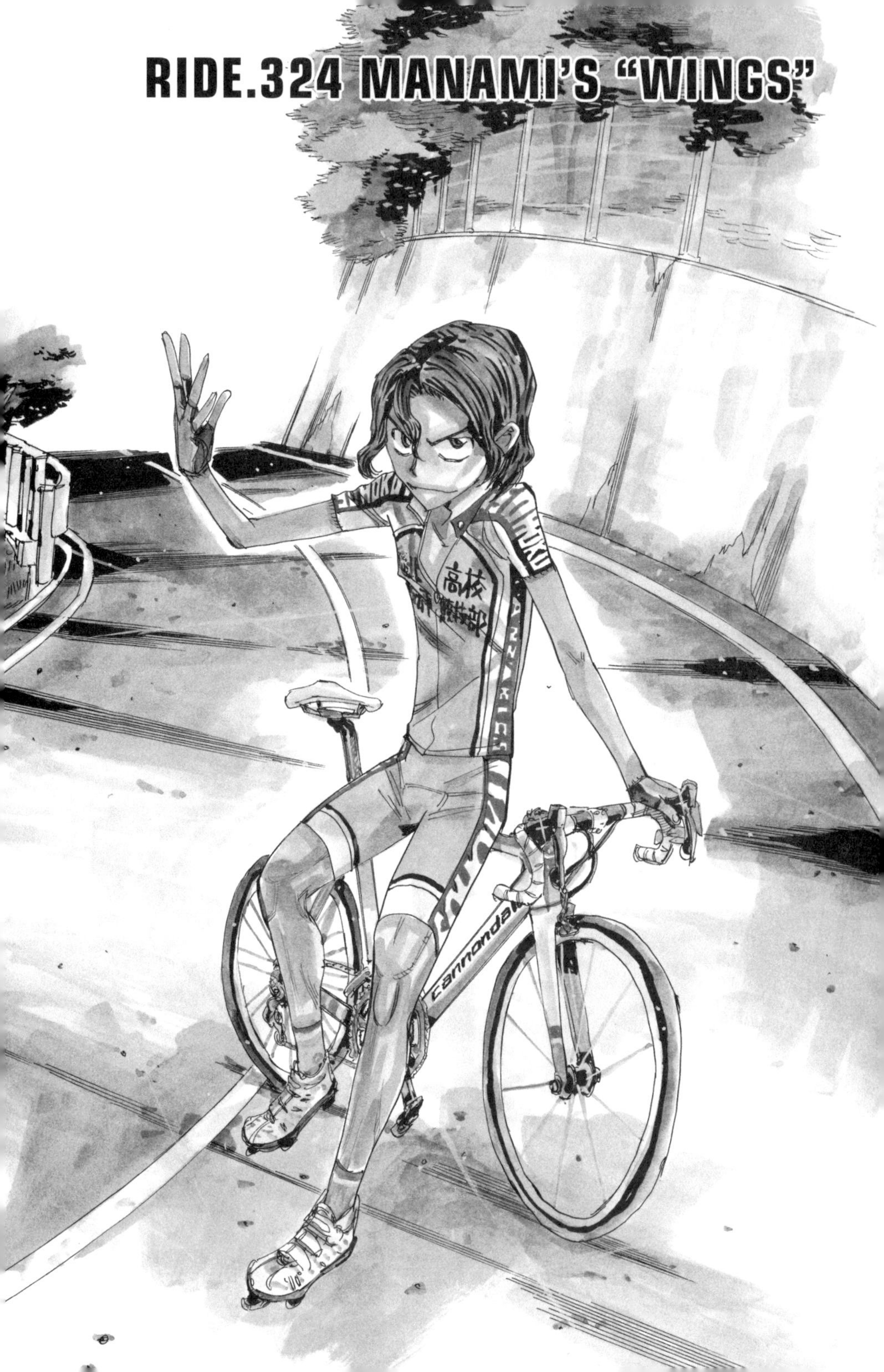

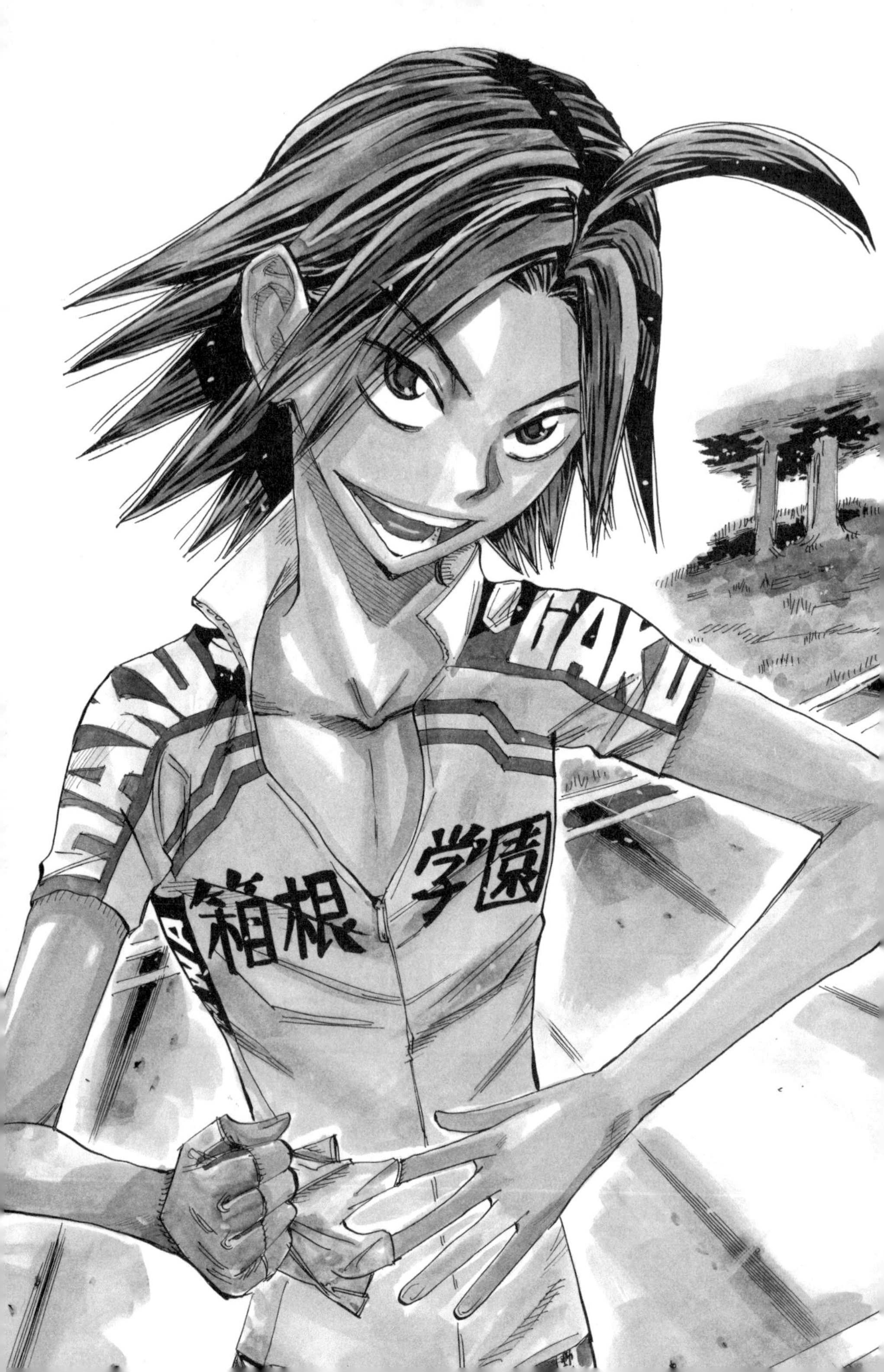

GAKU
箱根
学園

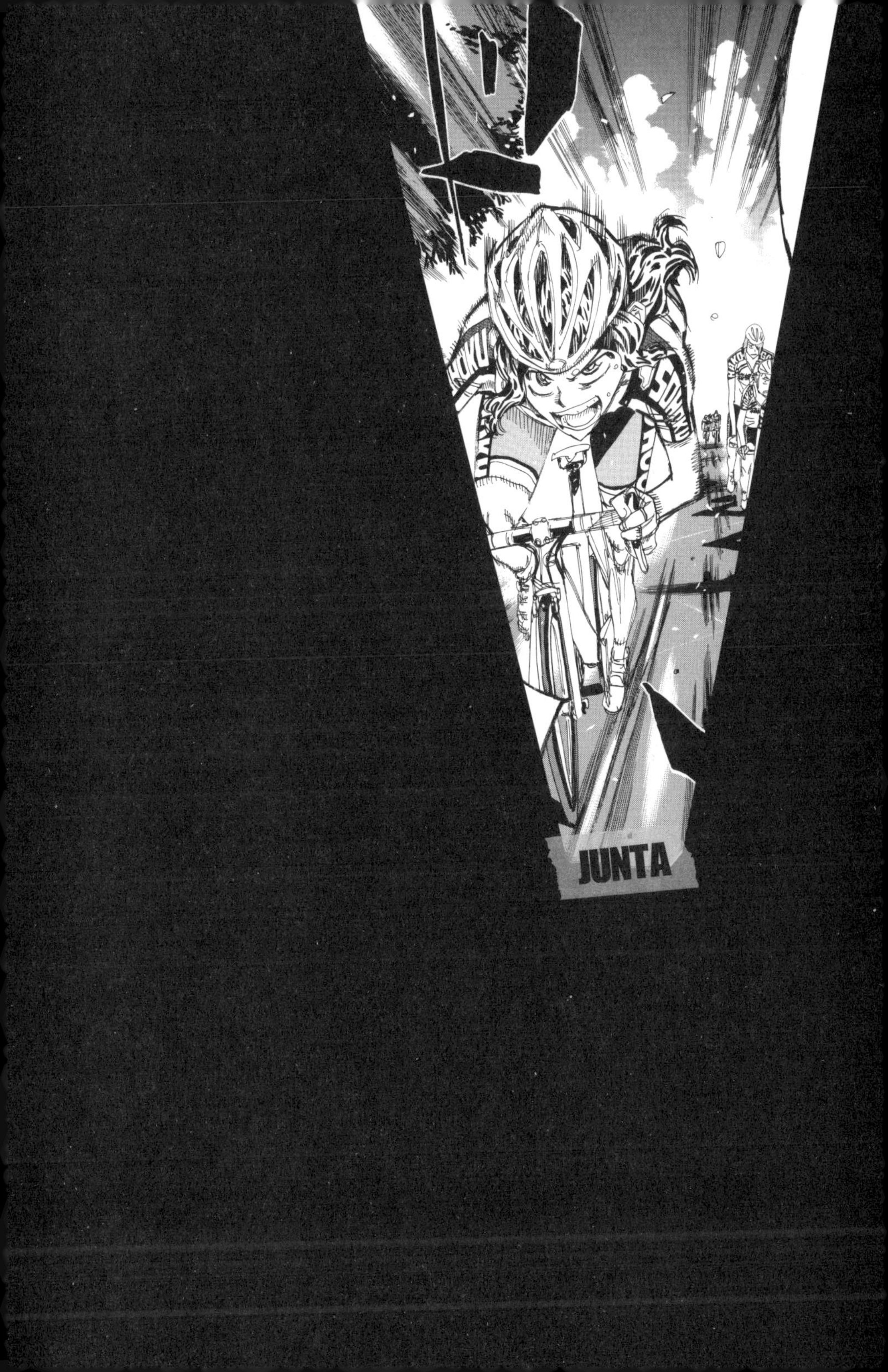
JUNTA

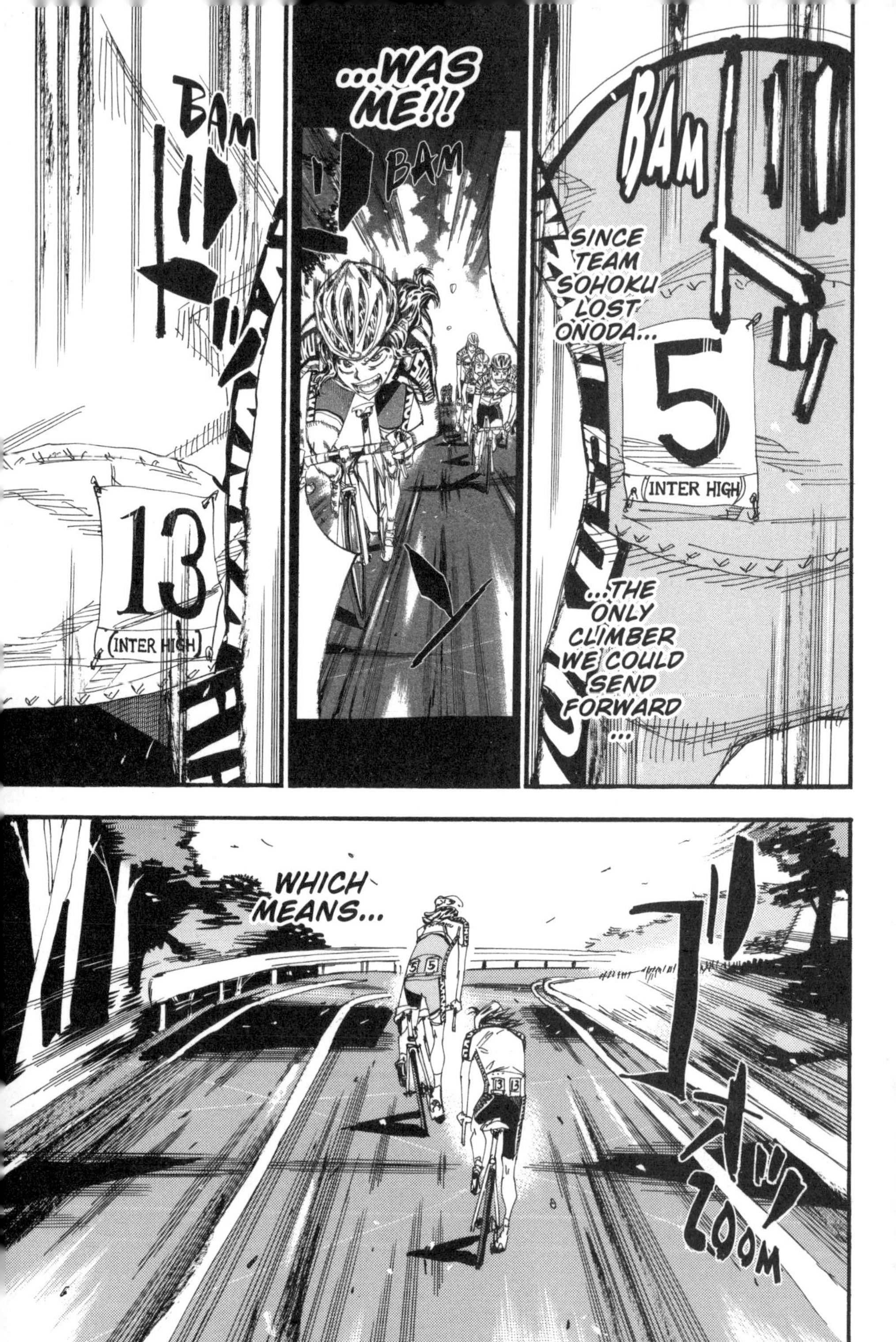
BAM
SINCE TEAM SOHOKU LOST ONODA...
5
INTER HIGH
...THE ONLY CLIMBER WE COULD SEND FORWARD...
...WAS ME!!
BAM
BAM
13
INTER HIGH
WHICH MEANS...
ZOOM

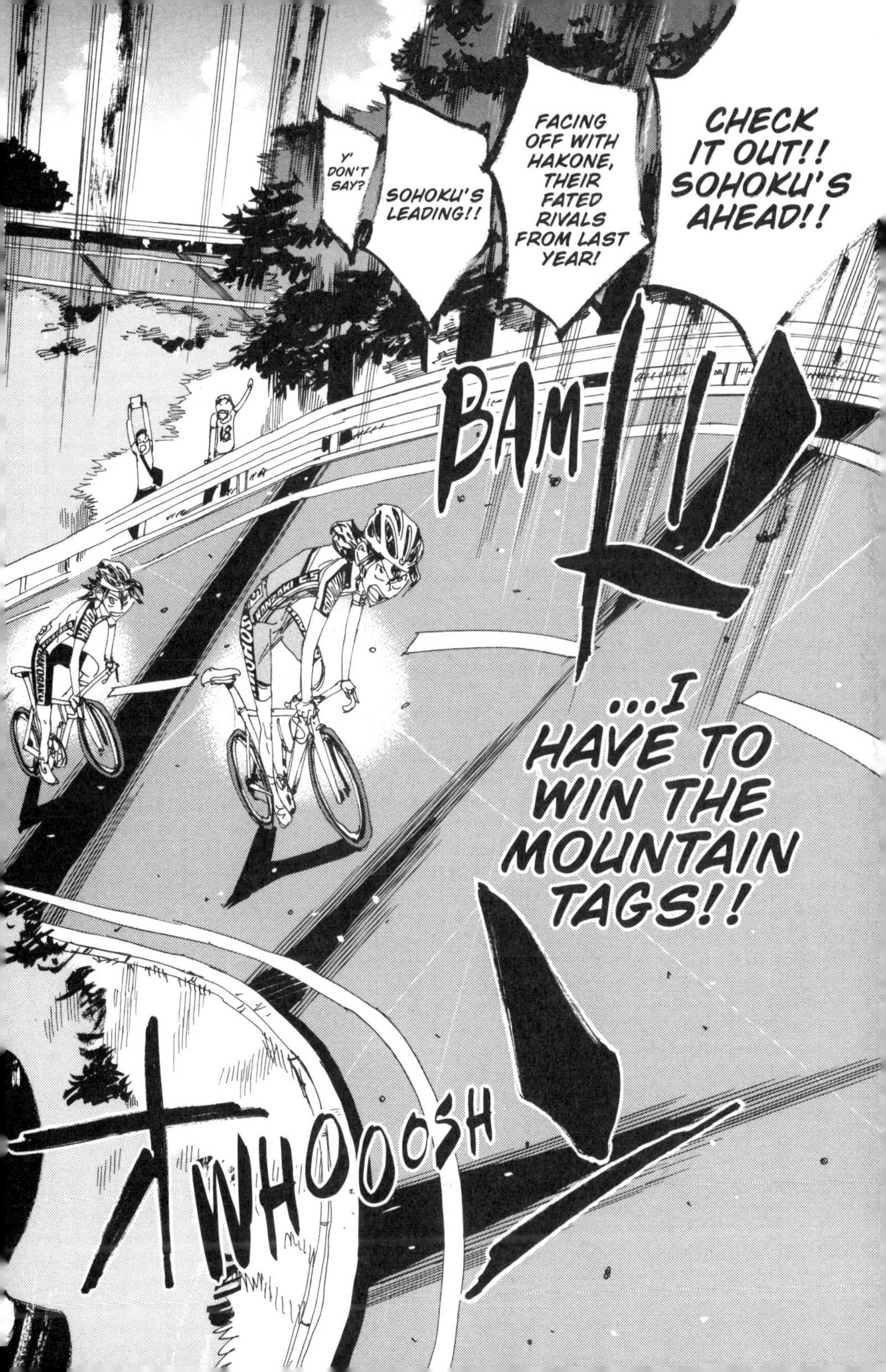
CHECK IT OUT!! SOHOKU'S AHEAD!!
FACING OFF WITH HAKONE, THEIR FATED RIVALS FROM LAST YEAR!
SOHOKU'S LEADING!!
Y' DON'T SAY?
BAM
...I HAVE TO WIN THE MOUNTAIN TAGS!!
WHOOOSH

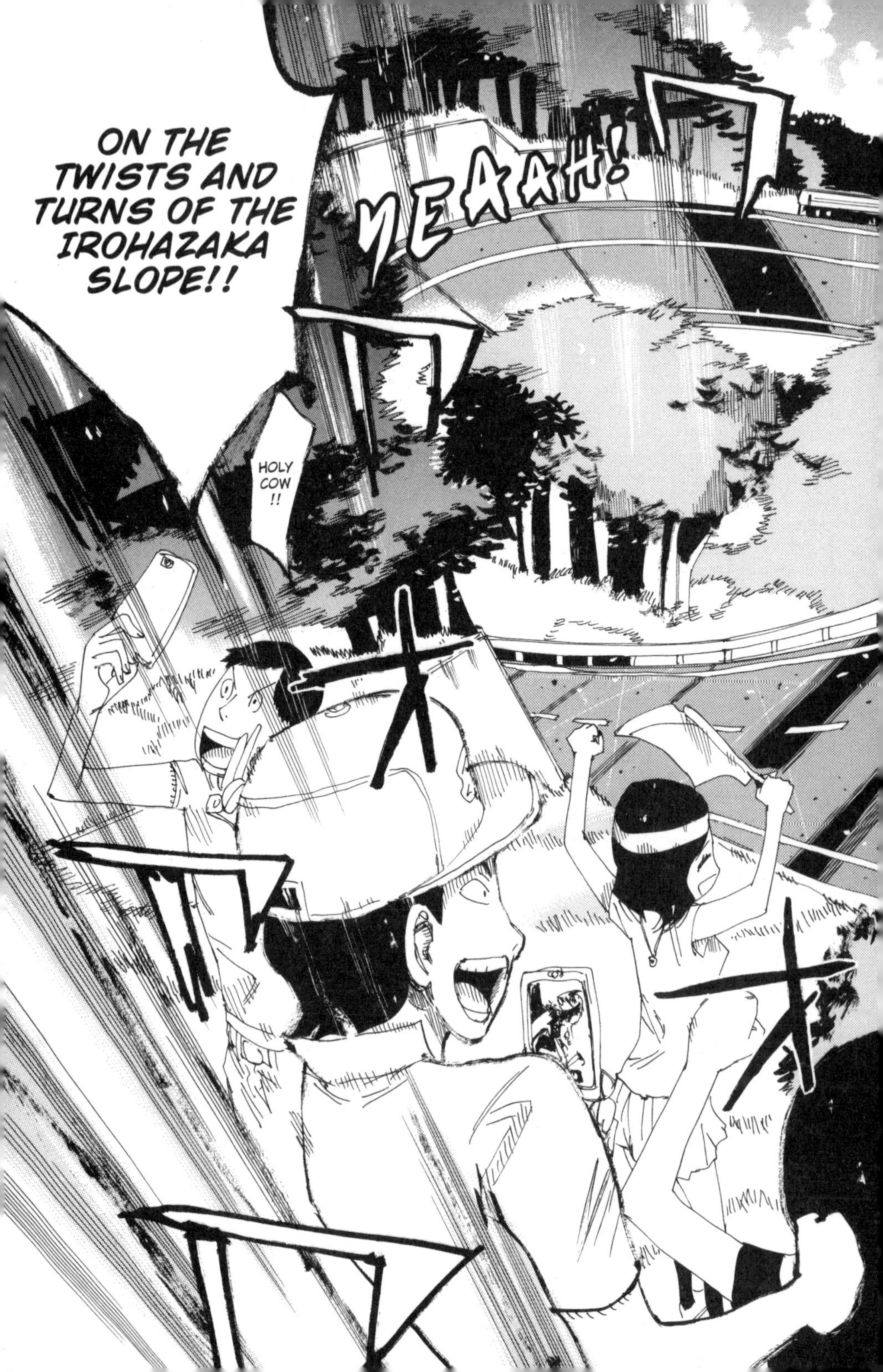
YEAAH!
ON THE TWISTS AND TURNS OF THE IROHAZAKA SLOPE!!
HOLY COW!!

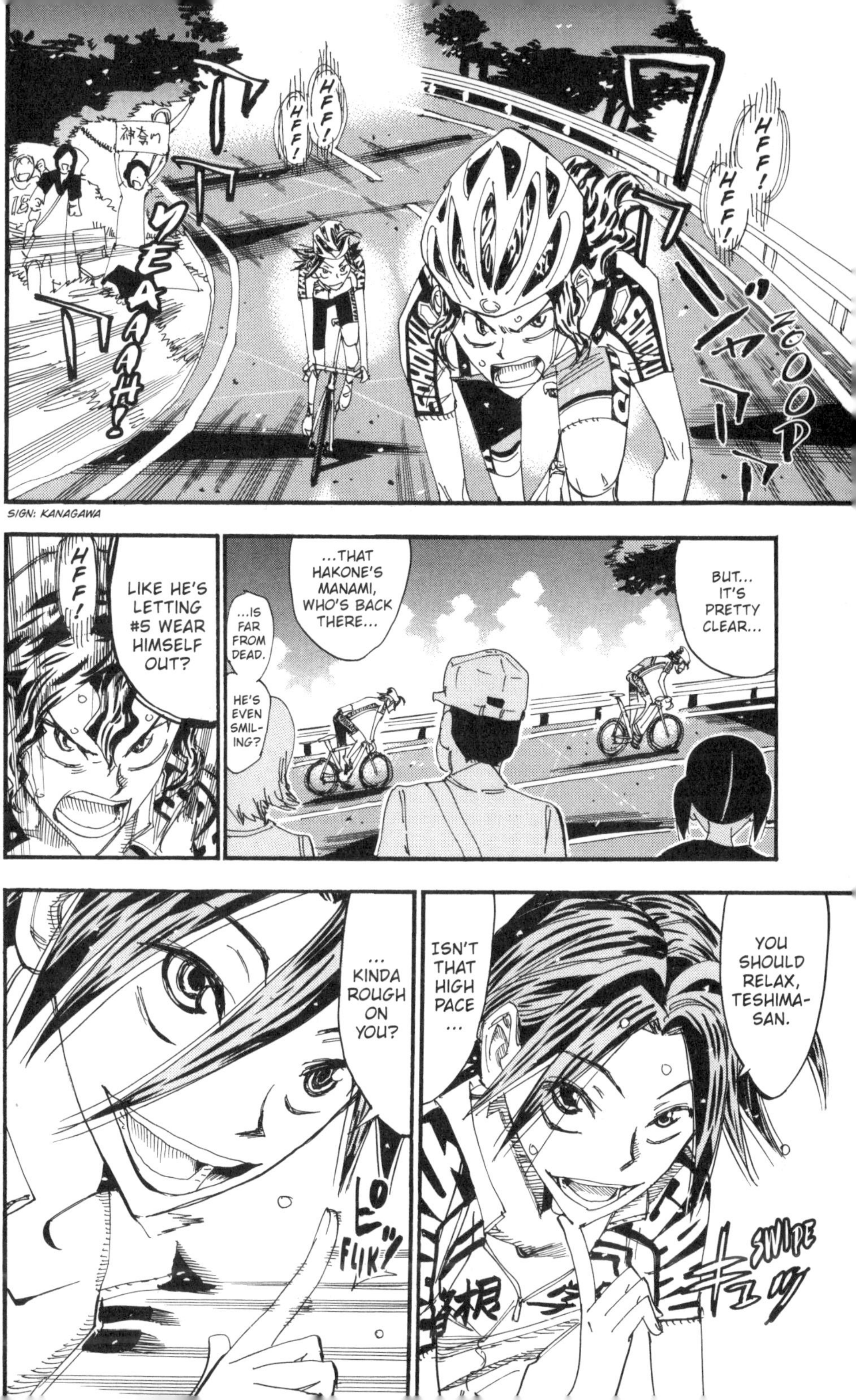
HFF! HFF!
ZOOOOP
HFF! HFF!
YEAAAAH!
神奈川
SIGN: KANAGAWA
BUT... IT'S PRETTY CLEAR...
...THAT HAKONE'S MANAMI, WHO'S BACK THERE...
...IS FAR FROM DEAD.
HE'S EVEN SMILING?
HFF!
LIKE HE'S LETTING #5 WEAR HIMSELF OUT?
YOU SHOULD RELAX, TESHIMA-SAN.
ISN'T THAT HIGH PACE...
SWIPE
... KINDA ROUGH ON YOU?
FLIK!

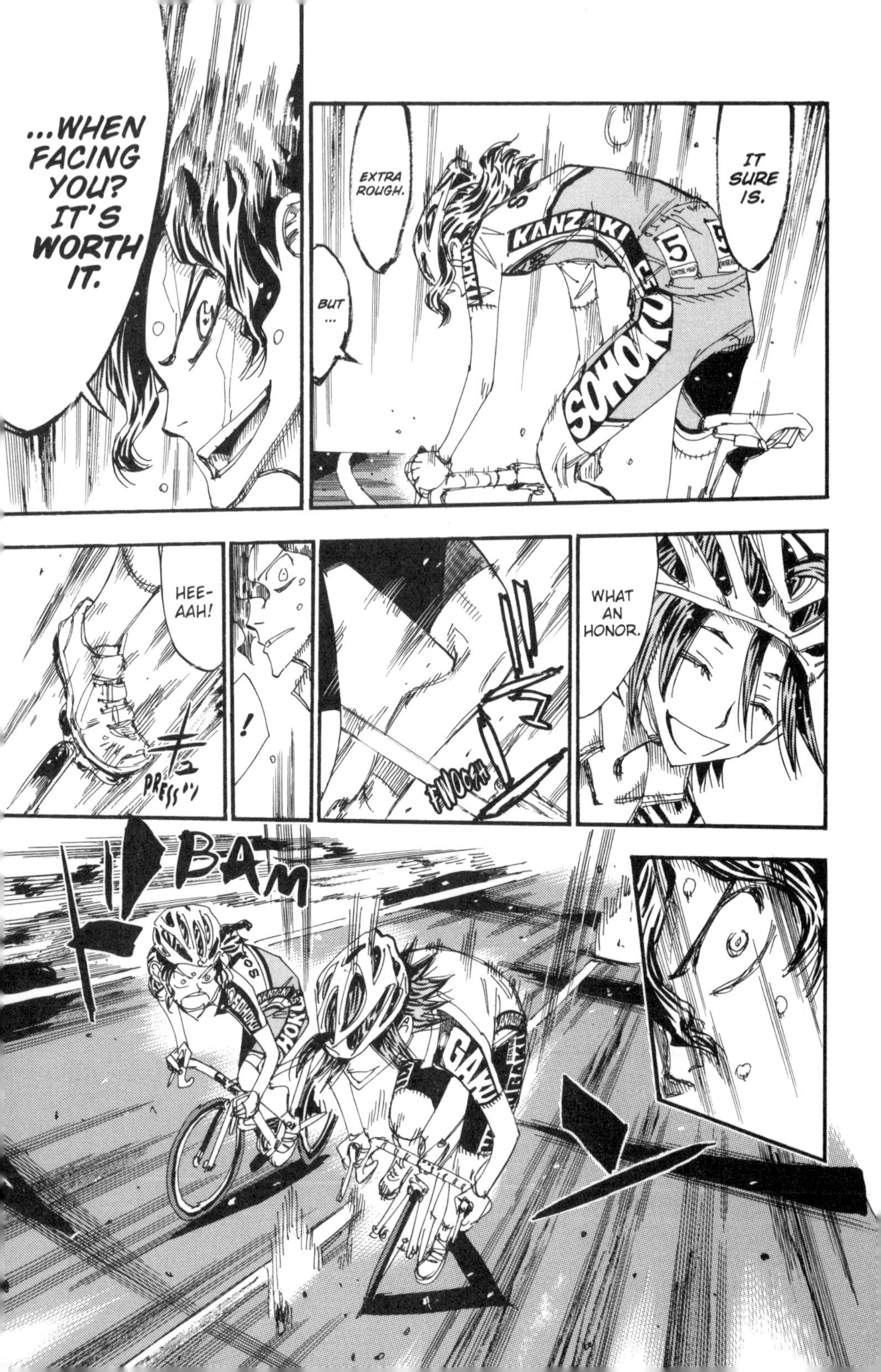
IT SURE IS.
EXTRA ROUGH.
BUT ...
...WHEN FACING YOU? IT'S WORTH IT.
WHAT AN HONOR.
FWOOSH
!
HEE-AAH!
PRESS
BAM

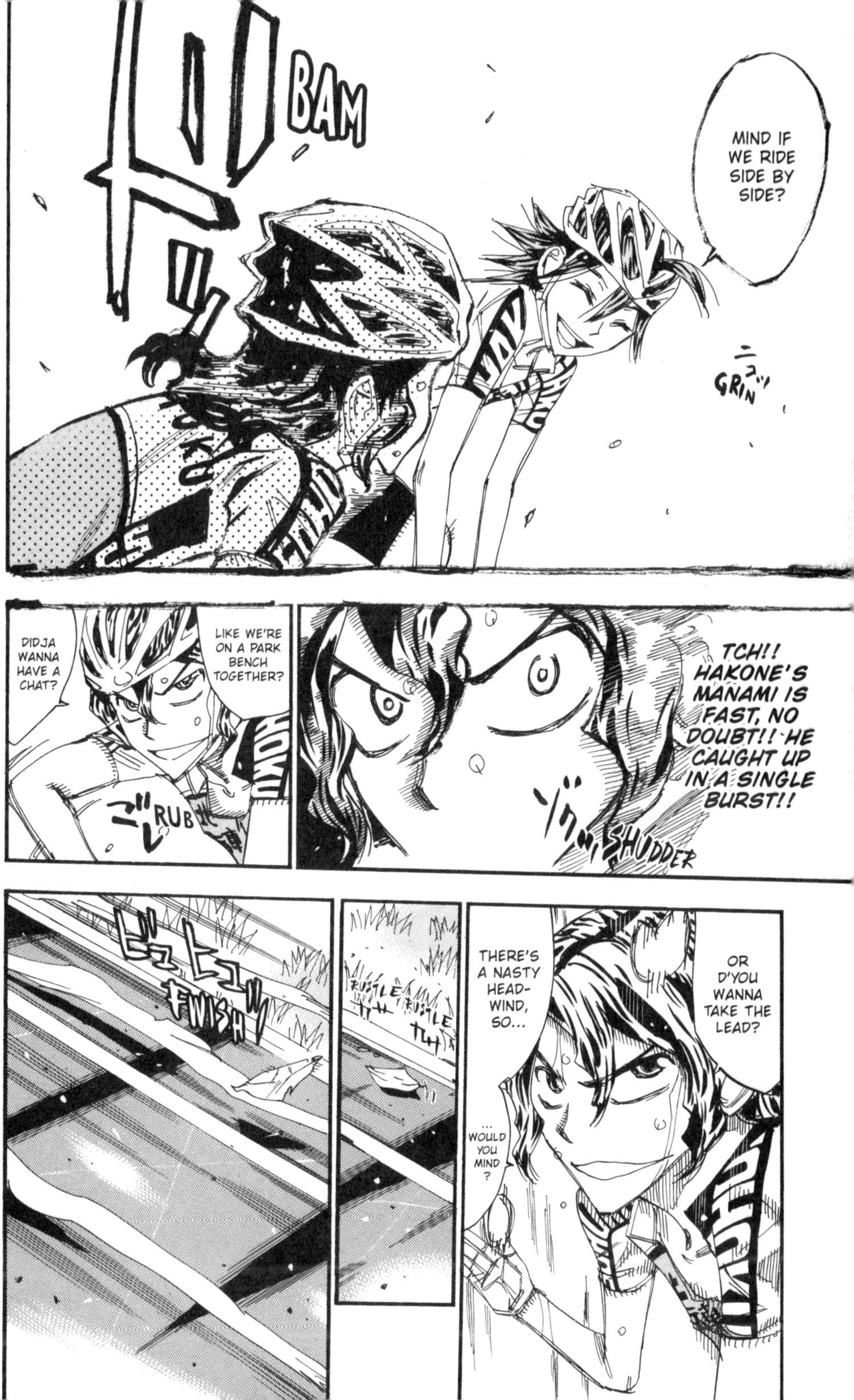
BAM
MIND IF WE RIDE SIDE BY SIDE?
GRIN
TCH!! HAKONE'S MANAMI IS FAST, NO DOUBT!! HE CAUGHT UP IN A SINGLE BURST!!
SHUDDER
LIKE WE'RE ON A PARK BENCH TOGETHER?
DIDJA WANNA HAVE A CHAT?
RUB
OR D'YOU WANNA TAKE THE LEAD?
THERE'S A NASTY HEAD-WIND, SO...
...WOULD YOU MIND?
RUSTLE RUSTLE
FWISH

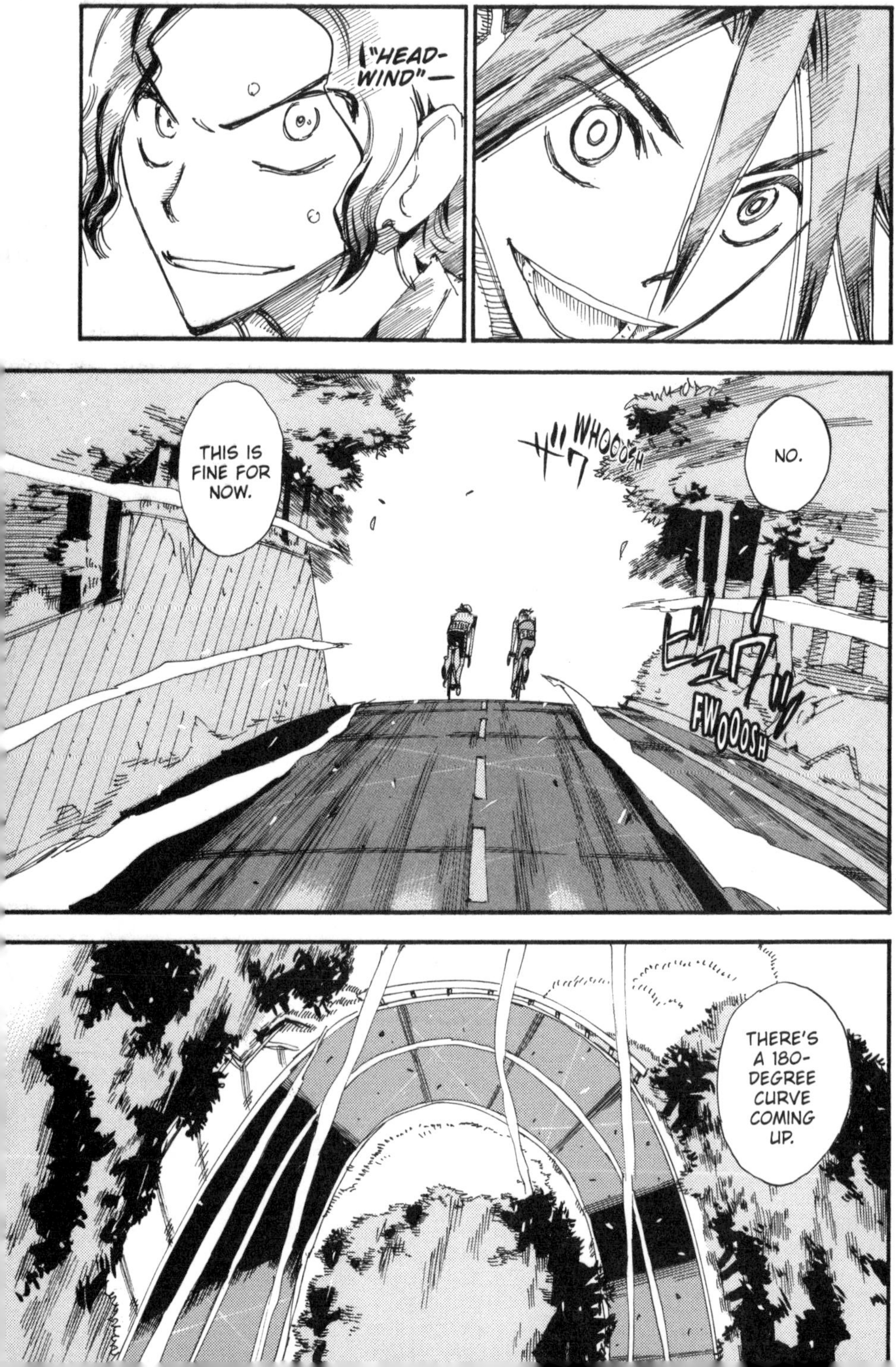
"HEAD-WIND"—
NO.
WHOOOSH
THIS IS FINE FOR NOW.
FWOOOSH
THERE'S A 180-DEGREE CURVE COMING UP.

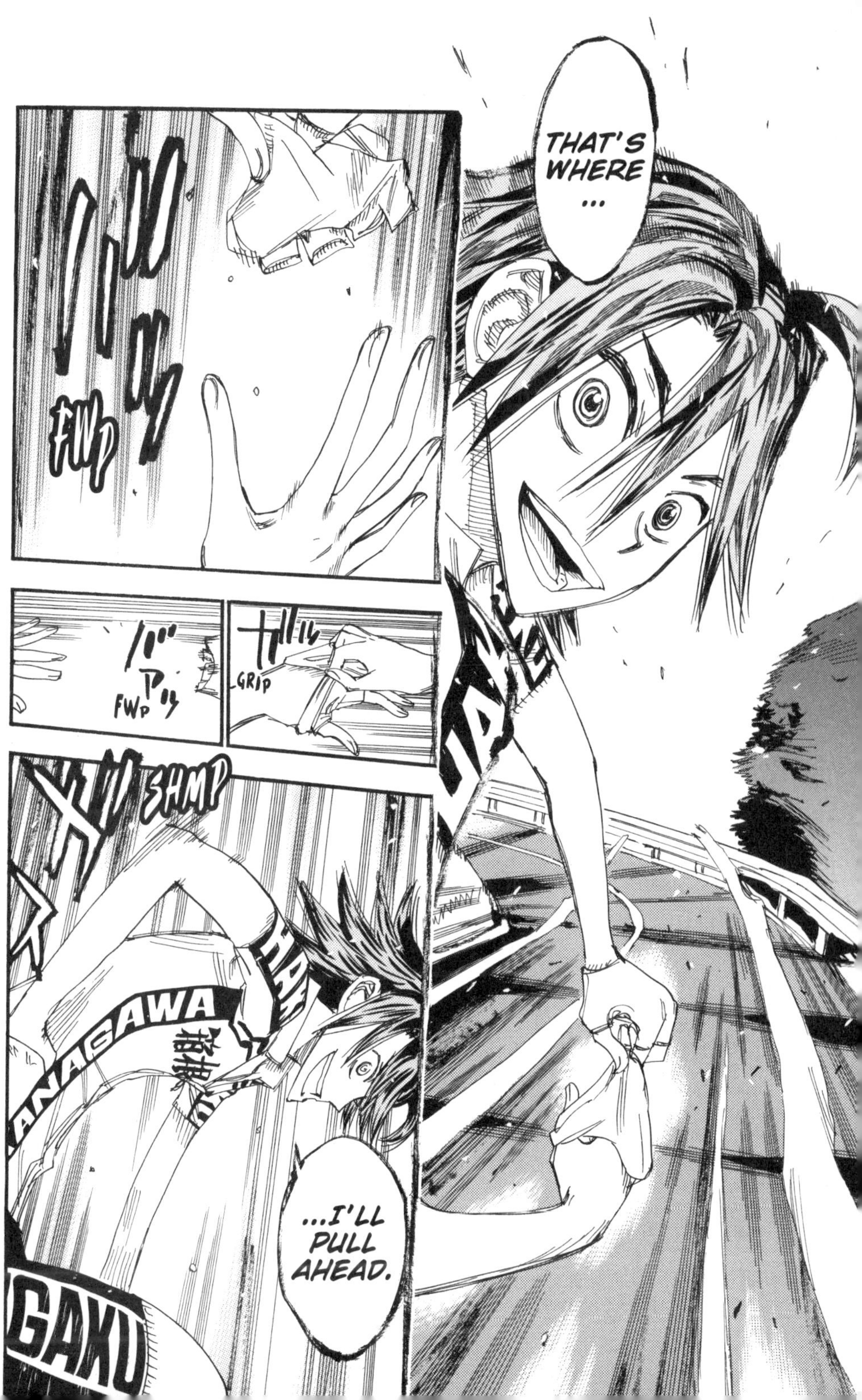
THAT'S WHERE ...
...I'LL PULL AHEAD.
FWP
GRIP
FWP
SHMP

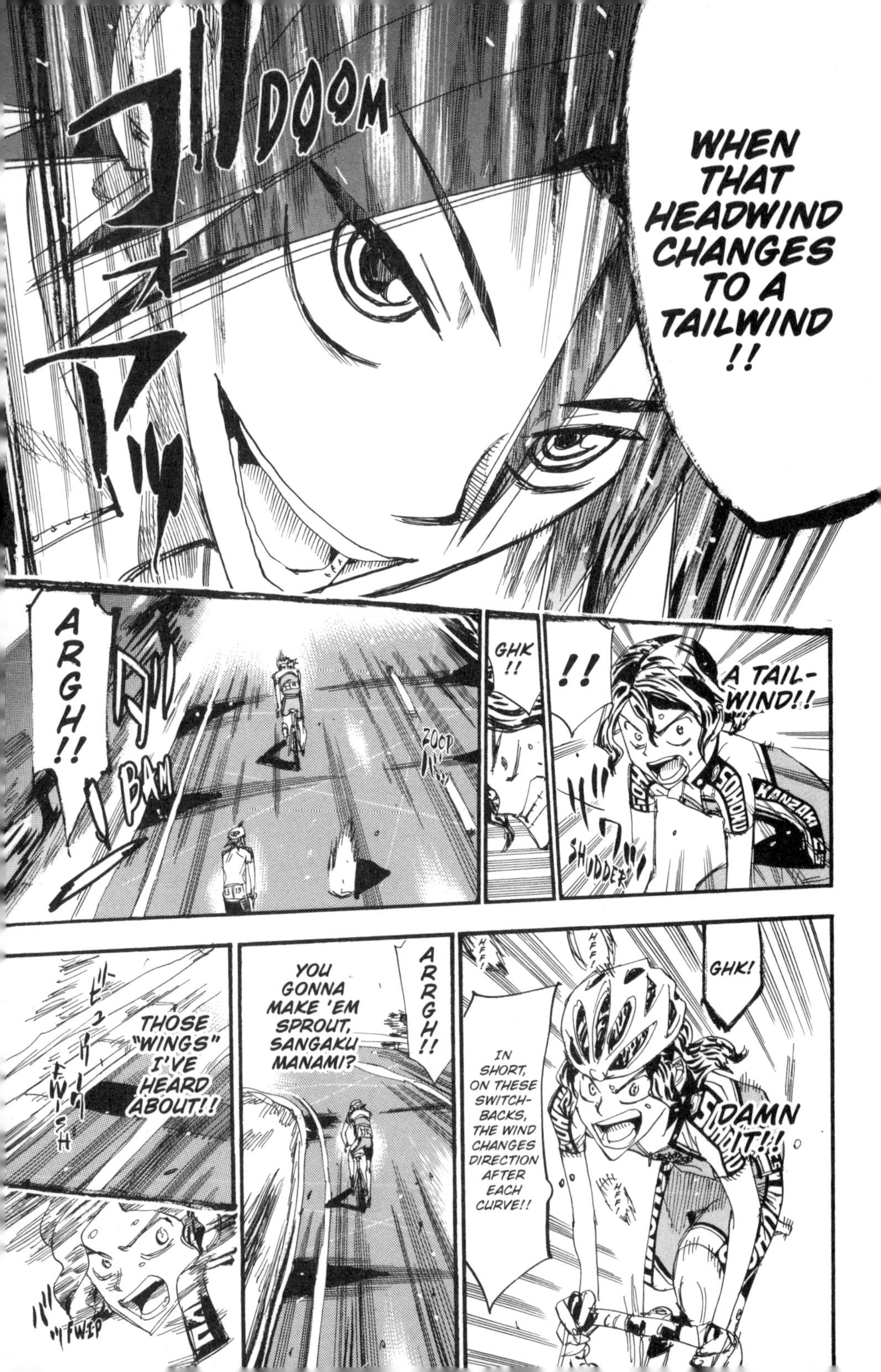
WHEN THAT HEADWIND CHANGES TO A TAILWIND!!
DOOM
!!
A TAIL-WIND!!
SHUDDER
GHK!!
ARGH!!
ZOOP
BAM
GHK!
IN SHORT, ON THESE SWITCH-BACKS, THE WIND CHANGES DIRECTION AFTER EACH CURVE!!
DAMN IT!!
HFF
ARRGH!!
YOU GONNA MAKE 'EM SPROUT, SANGAKU MANAMI?
THOSE "WINGS" I'VE HEARD ABOUT!!
FWISH
FWIP

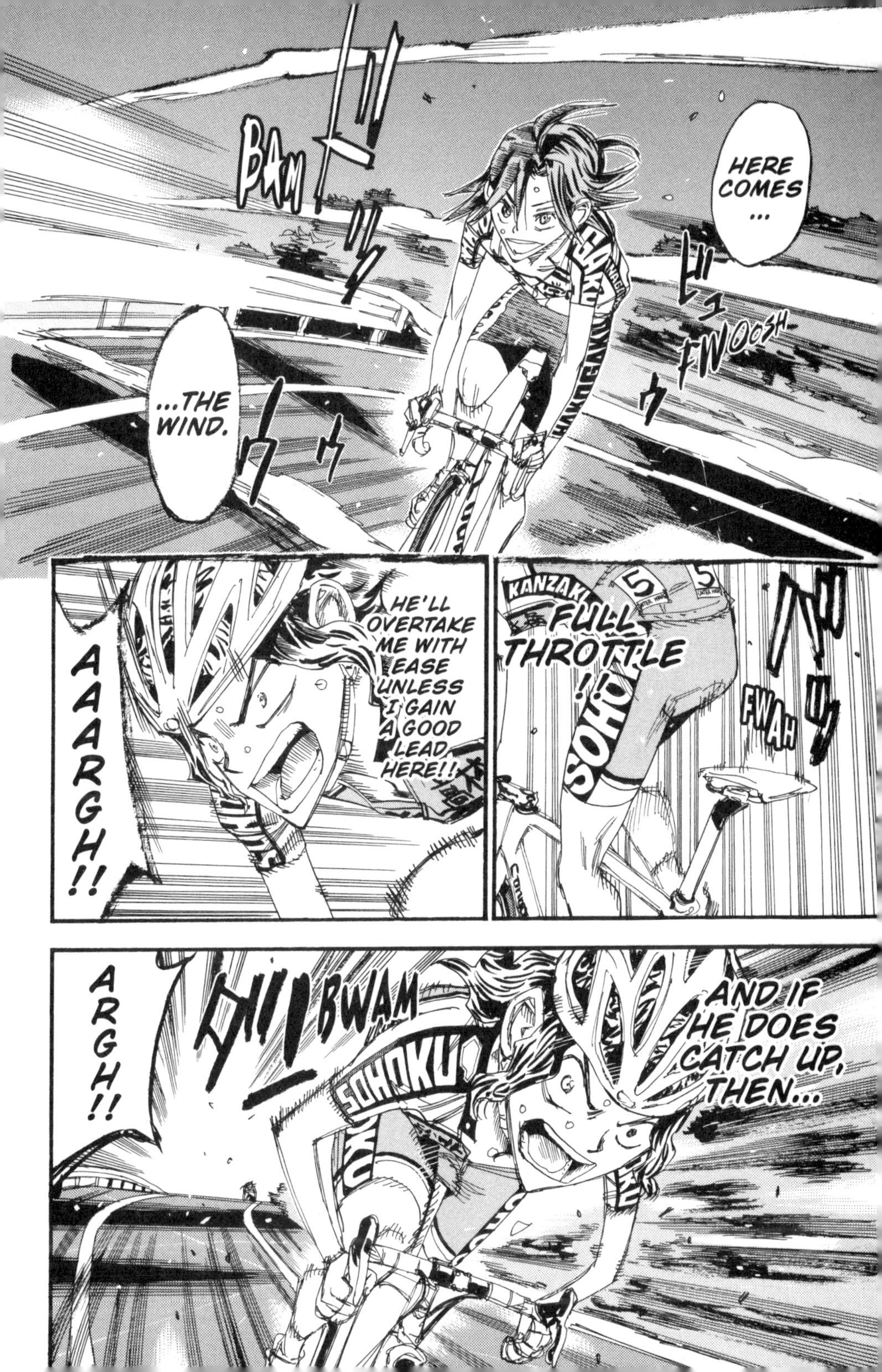
HERE COMES...
BAM
FWOOSH
...THE WIND.
FULL THROTTLE!!
FWAH
HE'LL OVERTAKE ME WITH EASE UNLESS I GAIN A GOOD LEAD HERE!!
AAAARGH!!
AND IF HE DOES CATCH UP, THEN...
BWAM
ARGH!!

KA-CHAK-KA-CHAK
FWAAH
WELL...

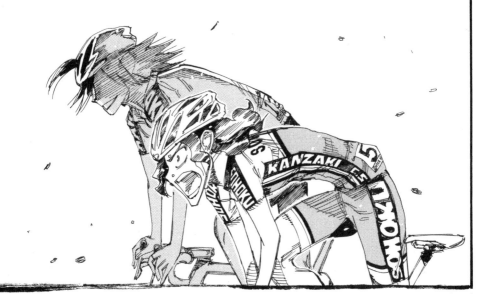

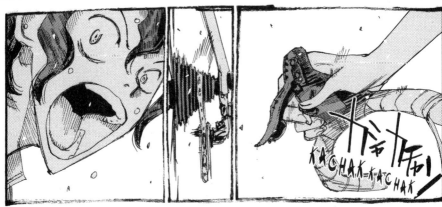

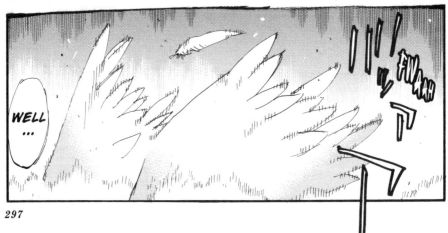

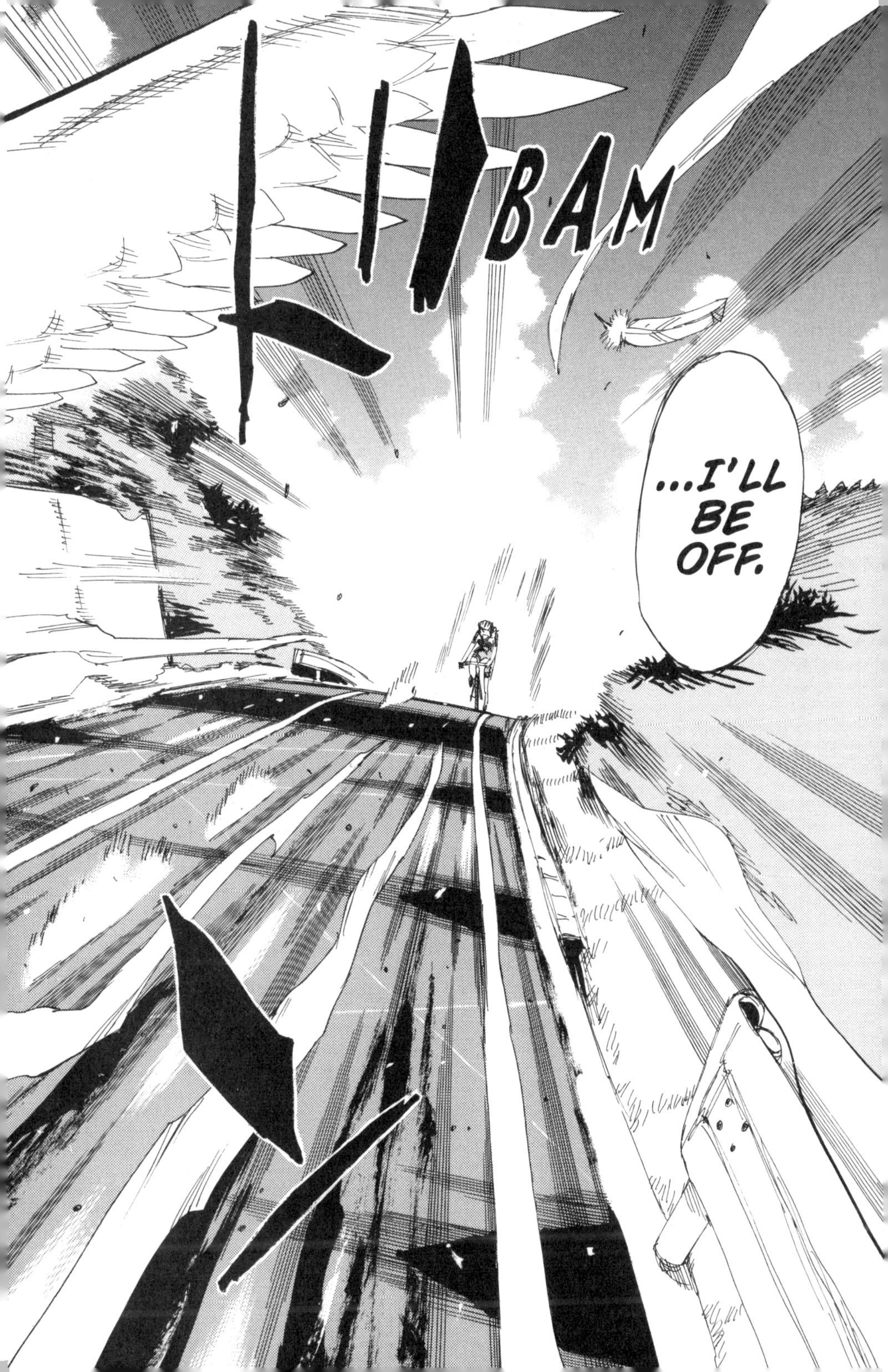
BAM
...I'LL BE OFF.

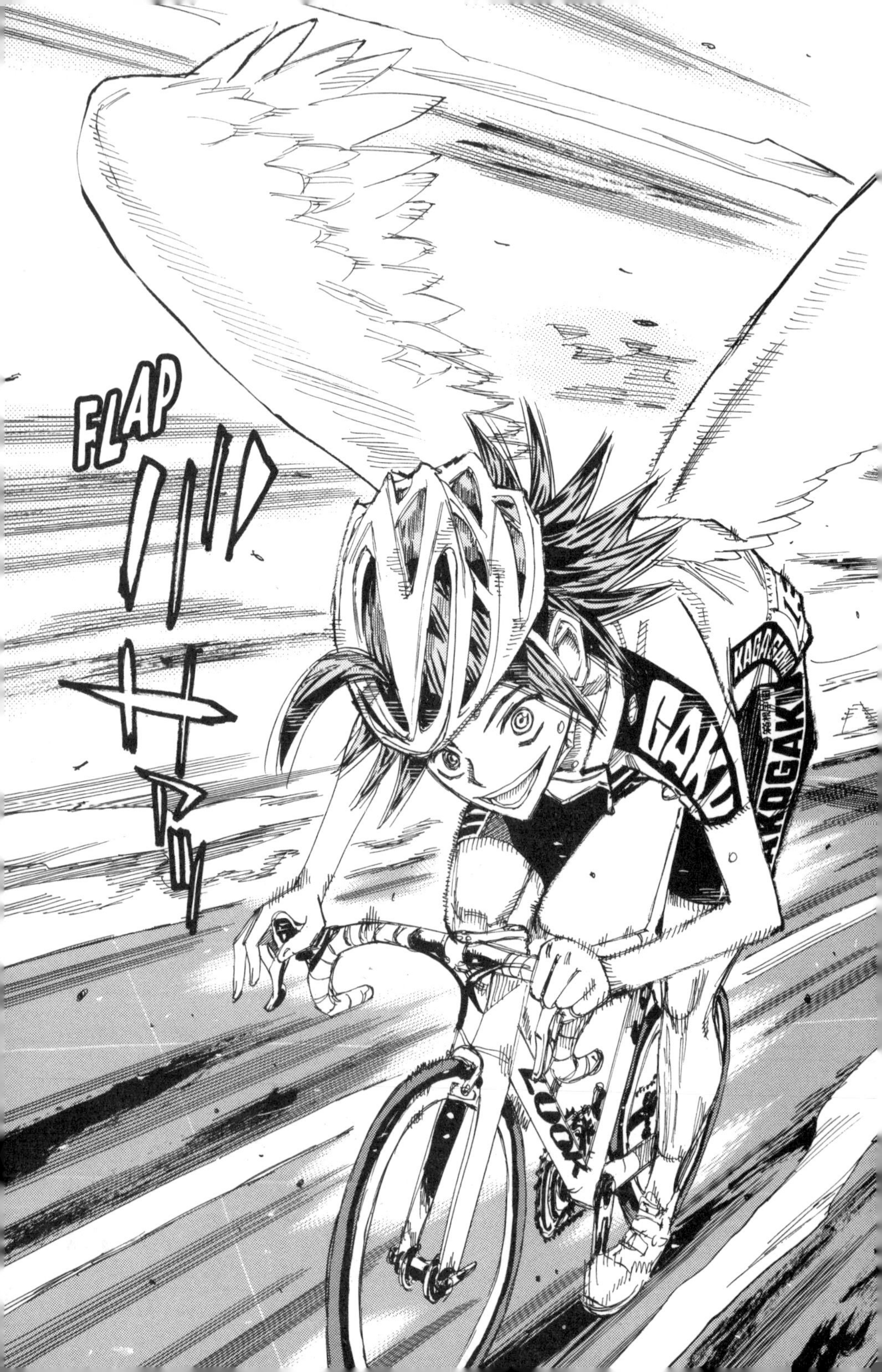
FLAP

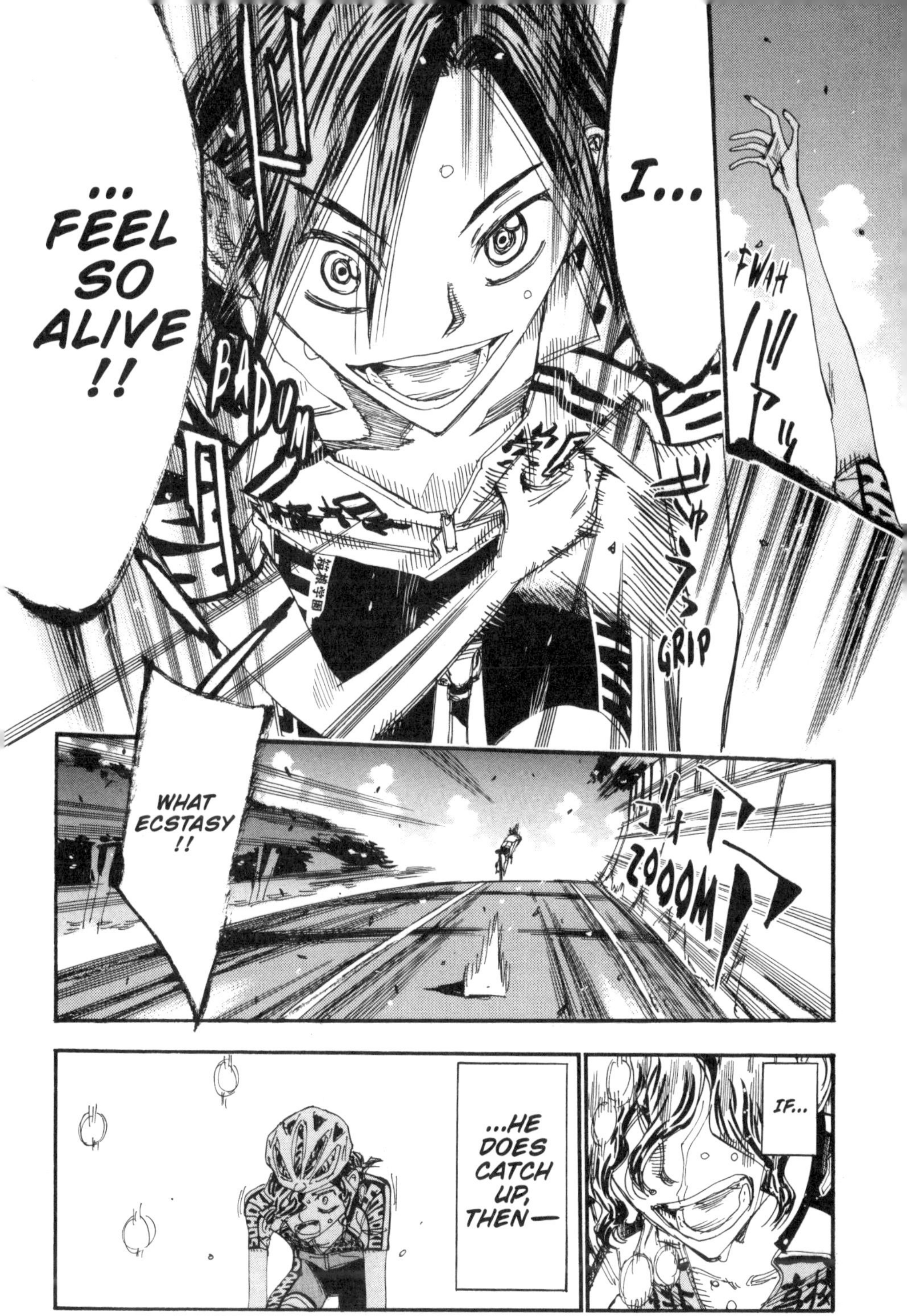
I...
FWAH
...FEEL SO ALIVE!!
BADOM
GRIP
WHAT ECSTASY!!
ZOOOM
IF...
...HE DOES CATCH UP, THEN—

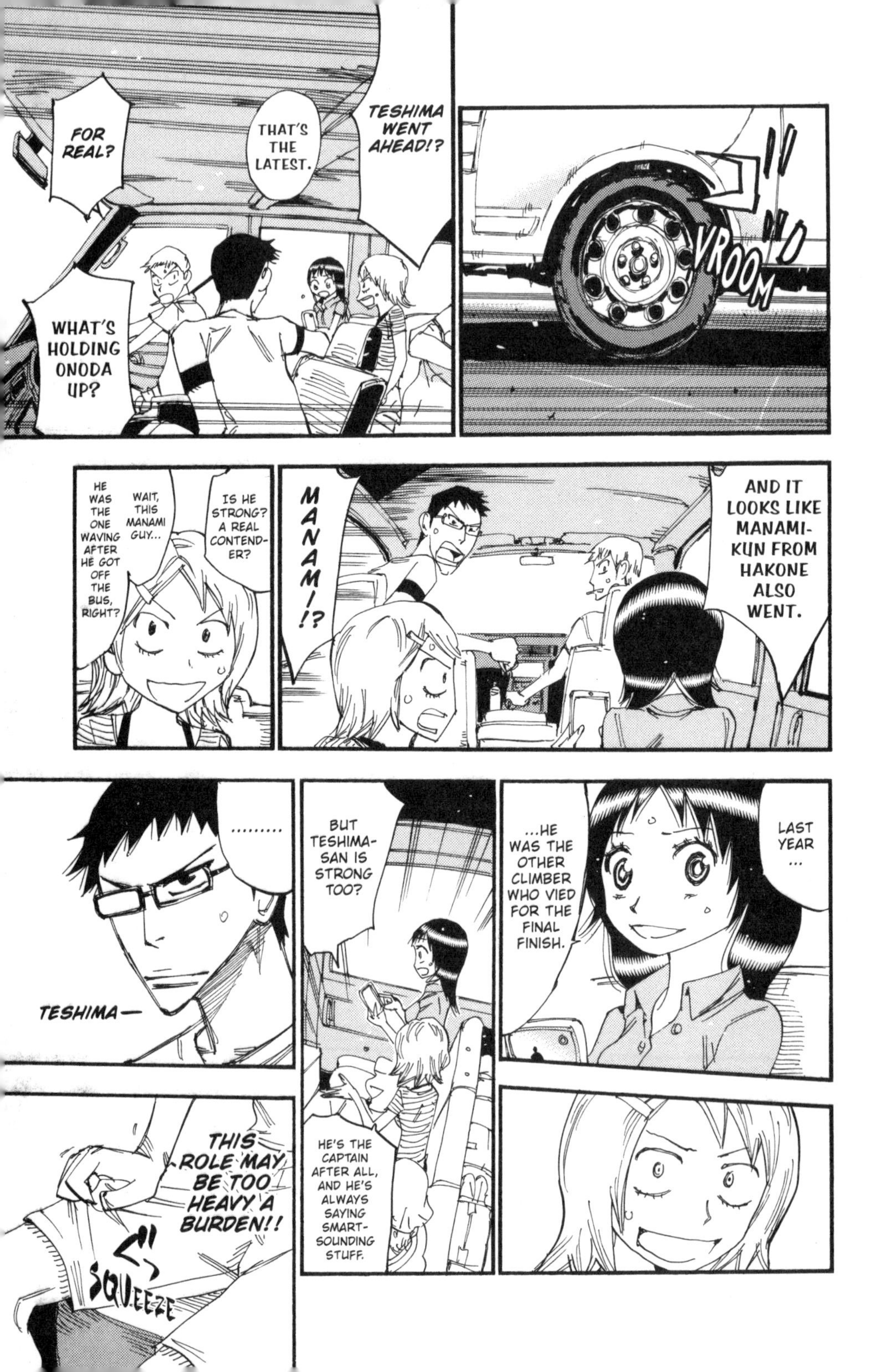
VROOM
TESHIMA WENT AHEAD!?
THAT'S THE LATEST.
FOR REAL?
WHAT'S HOLDING ONODA UP?
AND IT LOOKS LIKE MANAMI-KUN FROM HAKONE ALSO WENT.
MANAMI!?
IS HE STRONG? A REAL CONTENDER?
WAIT, THIS MANAMI GUY...
HE WAS THE ONE WAVING AFTER HE GOT OFF THE BUS, RIGHT?
LAST YEAR ...
...HE WAS THE OTHER CLIMBER WHO VIED FOR THE FINAL FINISH.
BUT TESHIMA-SAN IS STRONG TOO?
HE'S THE CAPTAIN AFTER ALL, AND HE'S ALWAYS SAYING SMART-SOUNDING STUFF.
....
TESHIMA—
THIS ROLE MAY BE TOO HEAVY A BURDEN!!
SQUEEZE

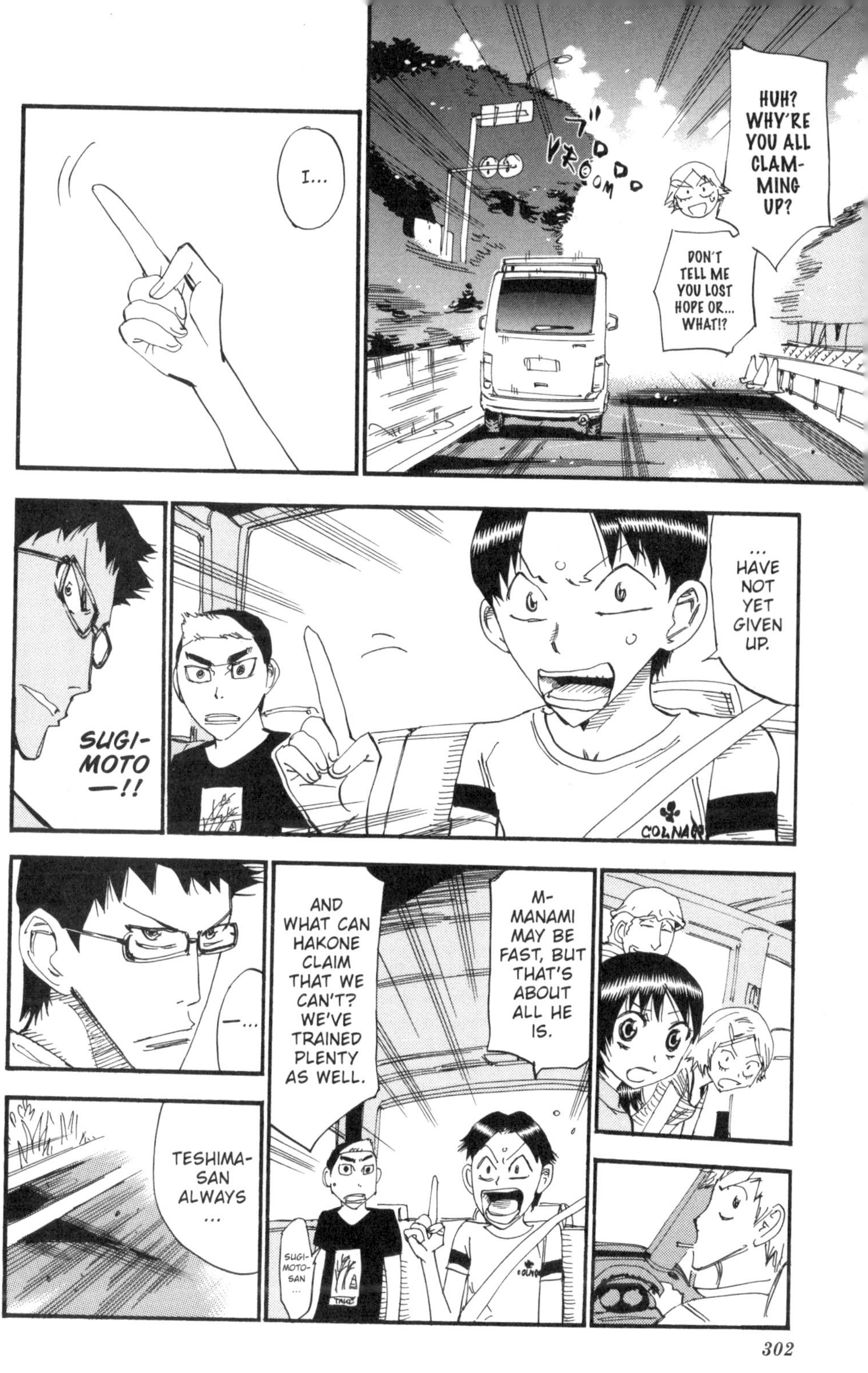
HUH? WHY'RE YOU ALL CLAMMING UP?
VROOOOM
DON'T TELL ME YOU LOST HOPE OR... WHAT!?
I...
...HAVE NOT YET GIVEN UP.
SUGIMOTO—!!
M-MANAMI MAY BE FAST, BUT THAT'S ABOUT ALL HE IS.
AND WHAT CAN HAKONE CLAIM THAT WE CAN'T? WE'VE TRAINED PLENTY AS WELL.
SUGIMOTO-SAN...
—...
TESHIMA-SAN ALWAYS...

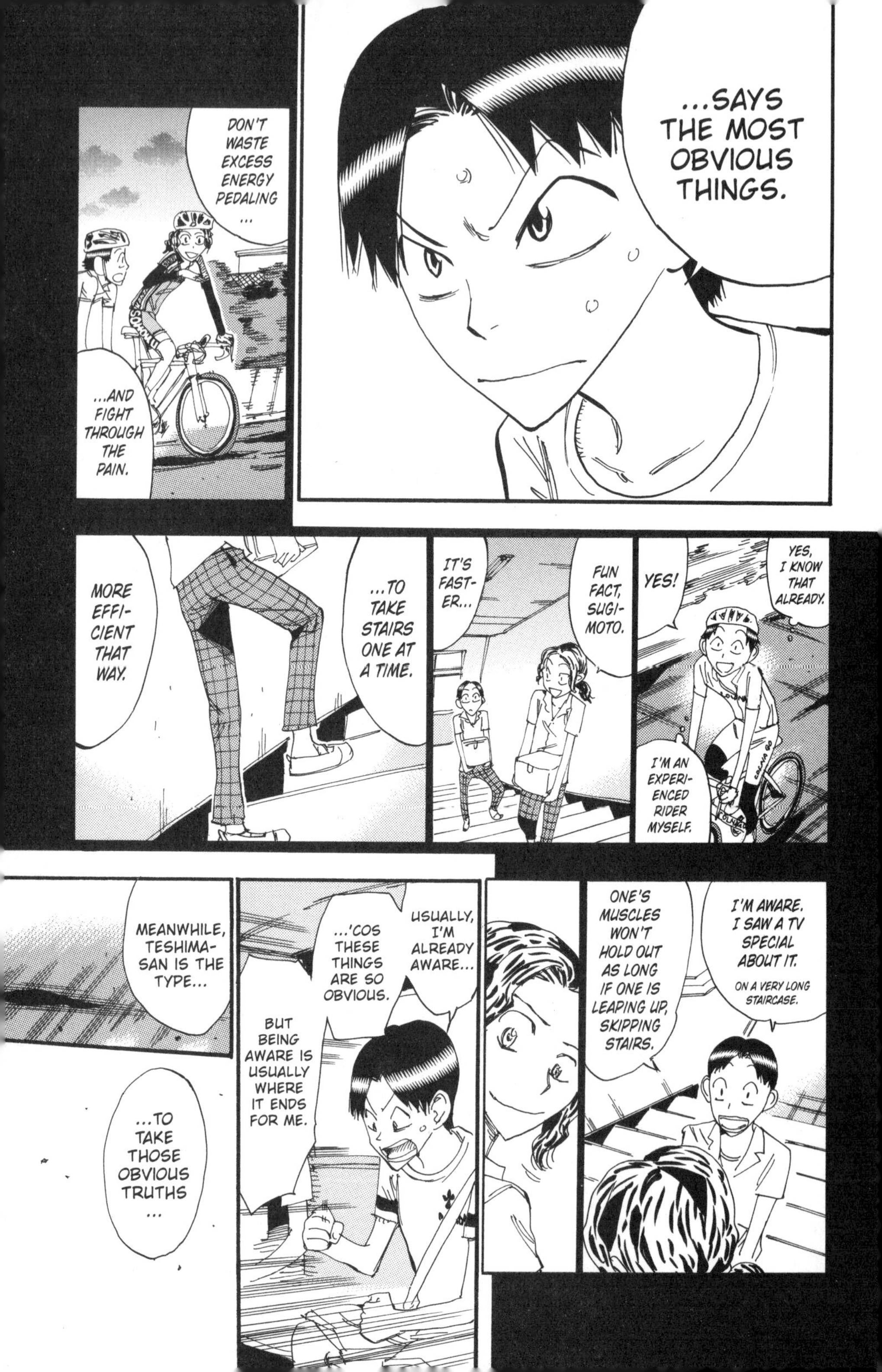
...SAYS THE MOST OBVIOUS THINGS.
DON'T WASTE EXCESS ENERGY PEDALING ...
...AND FIGHT THROUGH THE PAIN.
YES, I KNOW THAT ALREADY.
YES!
I'M AN EXPERI-ENCED RIDER MYSELF.
FUN FACT, SUGI-MOTO.
IT'S FAST-ER...
...TO TAKE STAIRS ONE AT A TIME.
MORE EFFI-CIENT THAT WAY.
I'M AWARE. I SAW A TV SPECIAL ABOUT IT.
ON A VERY LONG STAIRCASE.
ONE'S MUSCLES WON'T HOLD OUT AS LONG IF ONE IS LEAPING UP, SKIPPING STAIRS.
USUALLY, I'M ALREADY AWARE...
...'COS THESE THINGS ARE SO OBVIOUS.
BUT BEING AWARE IS USUALLY WHERE IT ENDS FOR ME.
MEANWHILE, TESHIMA-SAN IS THE TYPE...
...TO TAKE THOSE OBVIOUS TRUTHS ...

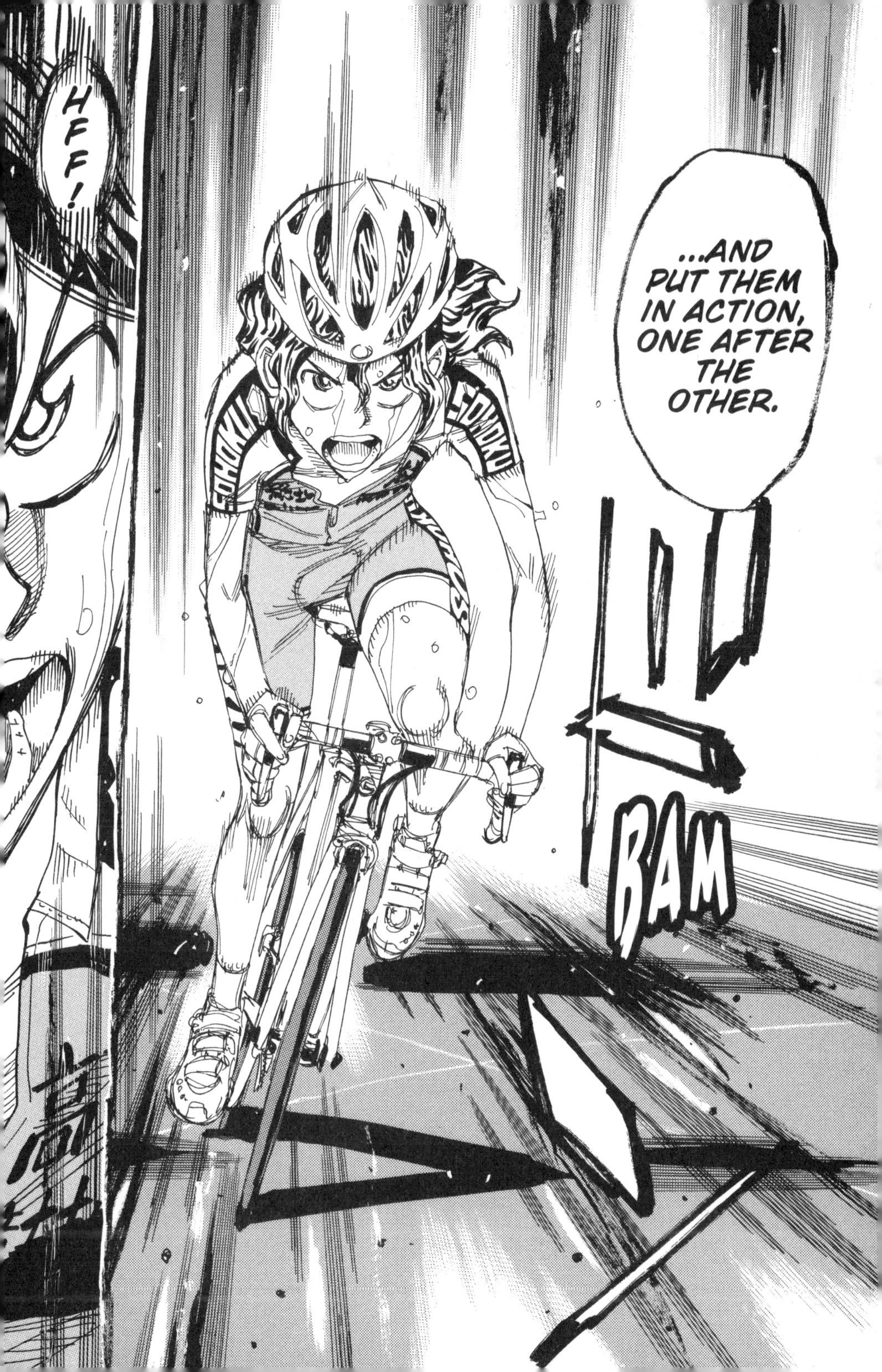
...AND PUT THEM IN ACTION, ONE AFTER THE OTHER.
BAM
HFF!

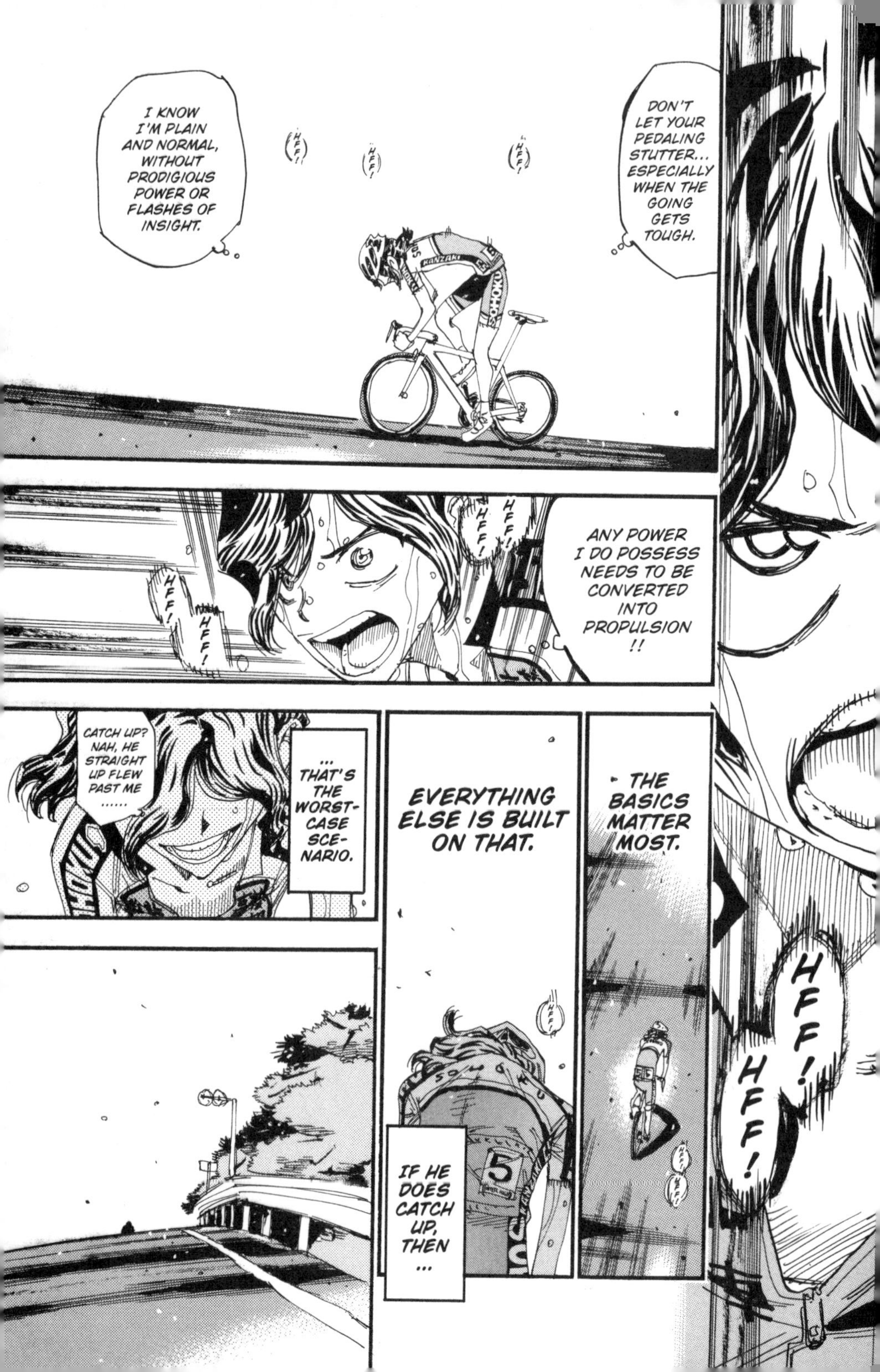
HFF!
HFF!
DON'T LET YOUR PEDALING STUTTER... ESPECIALLY WHEN THE GOING GETS TOUGH.
HFF!
HFF!
HFF!
I KNOW I'M PLAIN AND NORMAL, WITHOUT PRODIGIOUS POWER OR FLASHES OF INSIGHT.
ANY POWER I DO POSSESS NEEDS TO BE CONVERTED INTO PROPULSION !!
HFF!
HFF!
HFF!
HFF!
THE BASICS MATTER MOST.
EVERYTHING ELSE IS BUILT ON THAT.
IF HE DOES CATCH UP, THEN ...
... THAT'S THE WORST-CASE SCE-NARIO.
CATCH UP? NAH, HE STRAIGHT UP FLEW PAST ME ......

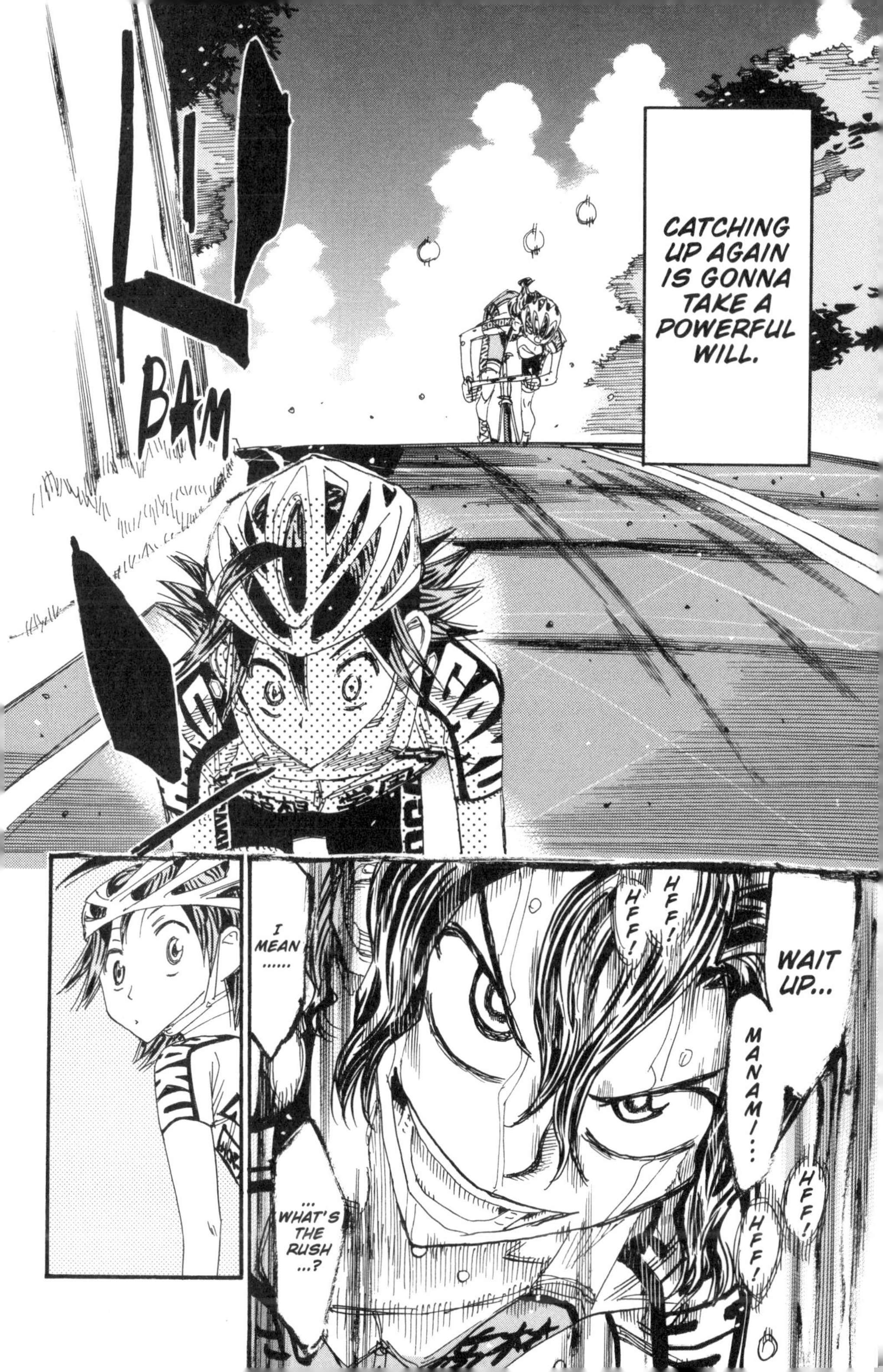
CATCHING UP AGAIN IS GONNA TAKE A POWERFUL WILL.
BAM
HFF!
HFF!
WAIT UP...
MANAMI!...
HFF!
HFF!
I MEAN......
...WHAT'S THE RUSH...?

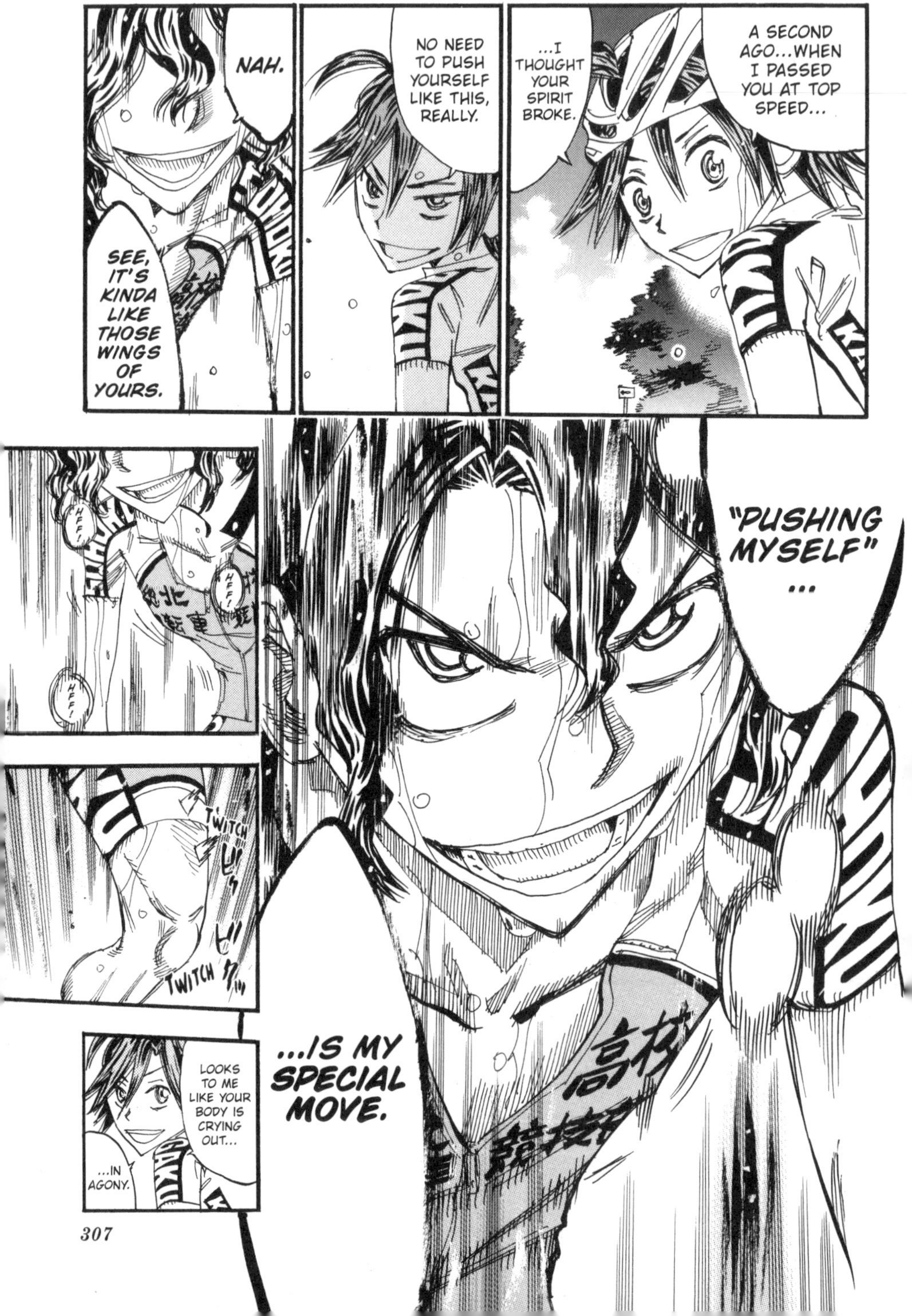
A SECOND AGO...WHEN I PASSED YOU AT TOP SPEED...
...I THOUGHT YOUR SPIRIT BROKE.
NO NEED TO PUSH YOURSELF LIKE THIS, REALLY.
NAH.
SEE, IT'S KINDA LIKE THOSE WINGS OF YOURS.
"PUSHING MYSELF"...
...IS MY SPECIAL MOVE.
HFF!
HFF!
HFF!
TWITCH
TWITCH
LOOKS TO ME LIKE YOUR BODY IS CRYING OUT...
...IN AGONY.

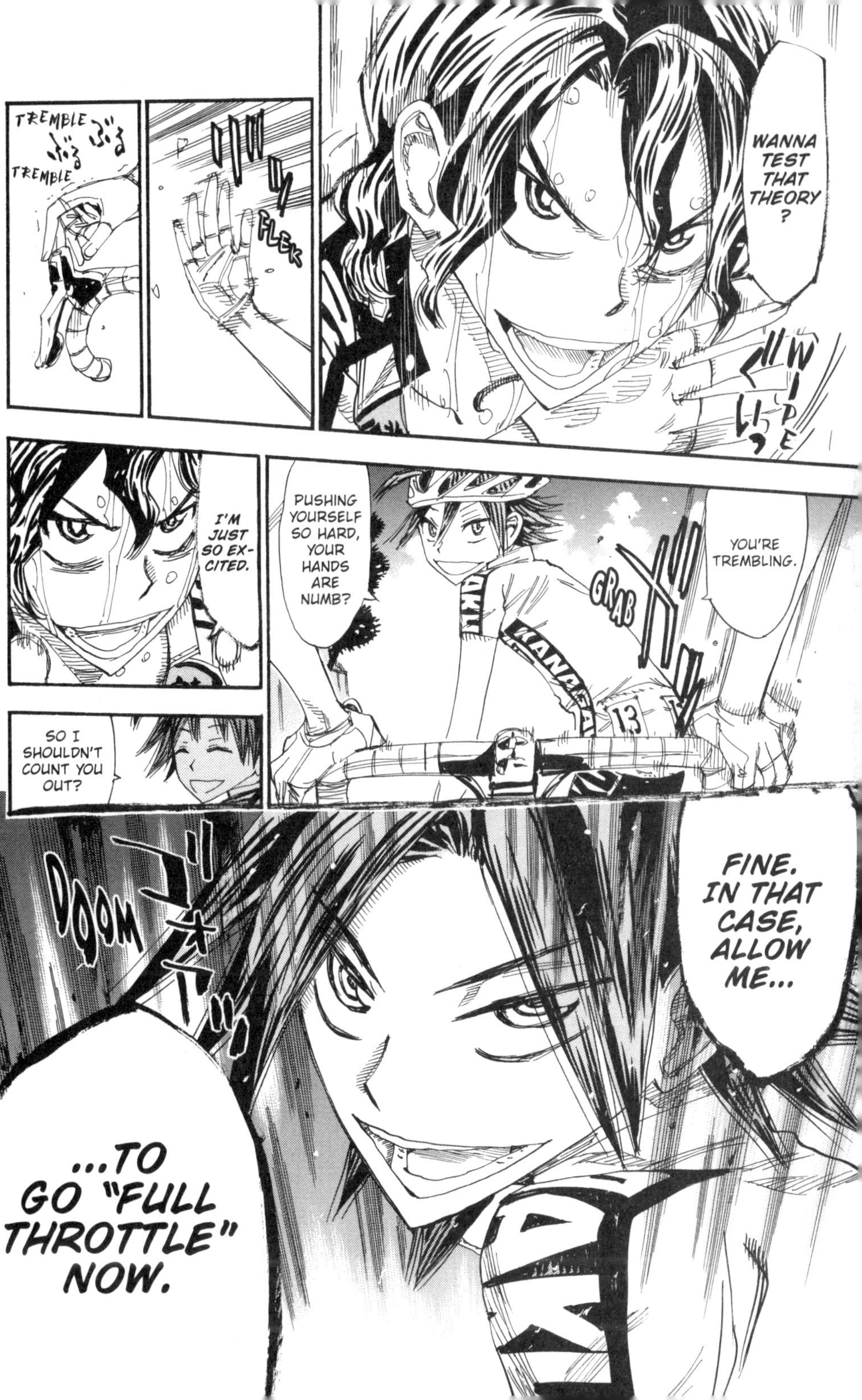
WANNA TEST THAT THEORY?
WIPE
FLEK
TREMBLE ぶる ぶる TREMBLE
YOU'RE TREMBLING.
GRAB
PUSHING YOURSELF SO HARD, YOUR HANDS ARE NUMB?
I'M JUST SO EX-CITED.
SO I SHOULDN'T COUNT YOU OUT?
FINE. IN THAT CASE, ALLOW ME...
DOOM
...TO GO "FULL THROTTLE" NOW.

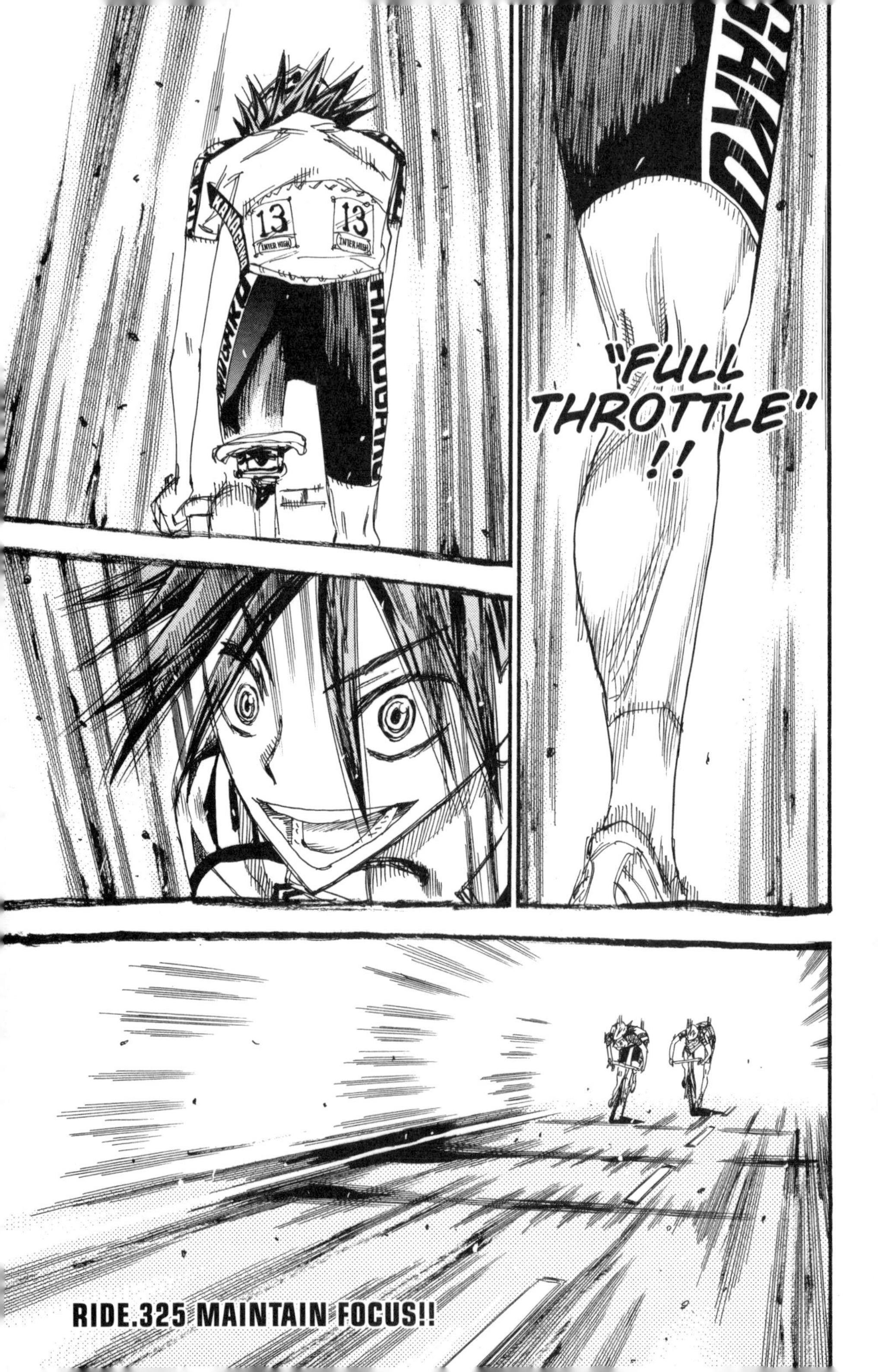
"FULL THROTTLE" !!
RIDE.325 MAINTAIN FOCUS!!

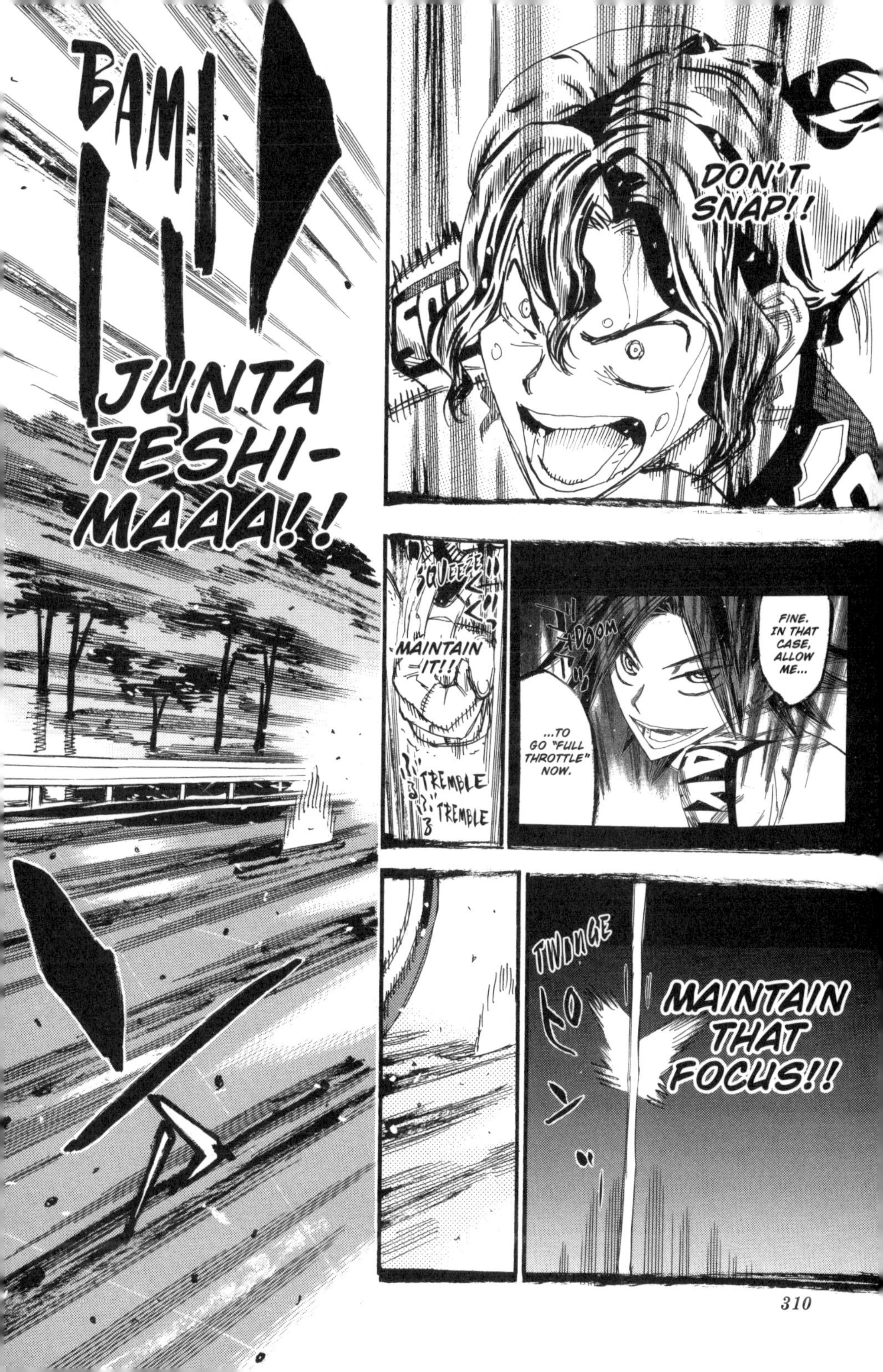
DON'T SNAP!!
DOOM
FINE. IN THAT CASE, ALLOW ME...
...TO GO "FULL THROTTLE" NOW.
SQUEEZE
MAINTAIN IT!!
TREMBLE
TREMBLE
TWINGE
MAINTAIN THAT FOCUS!!
BAM
JUNTA TESHIMAAAA!!

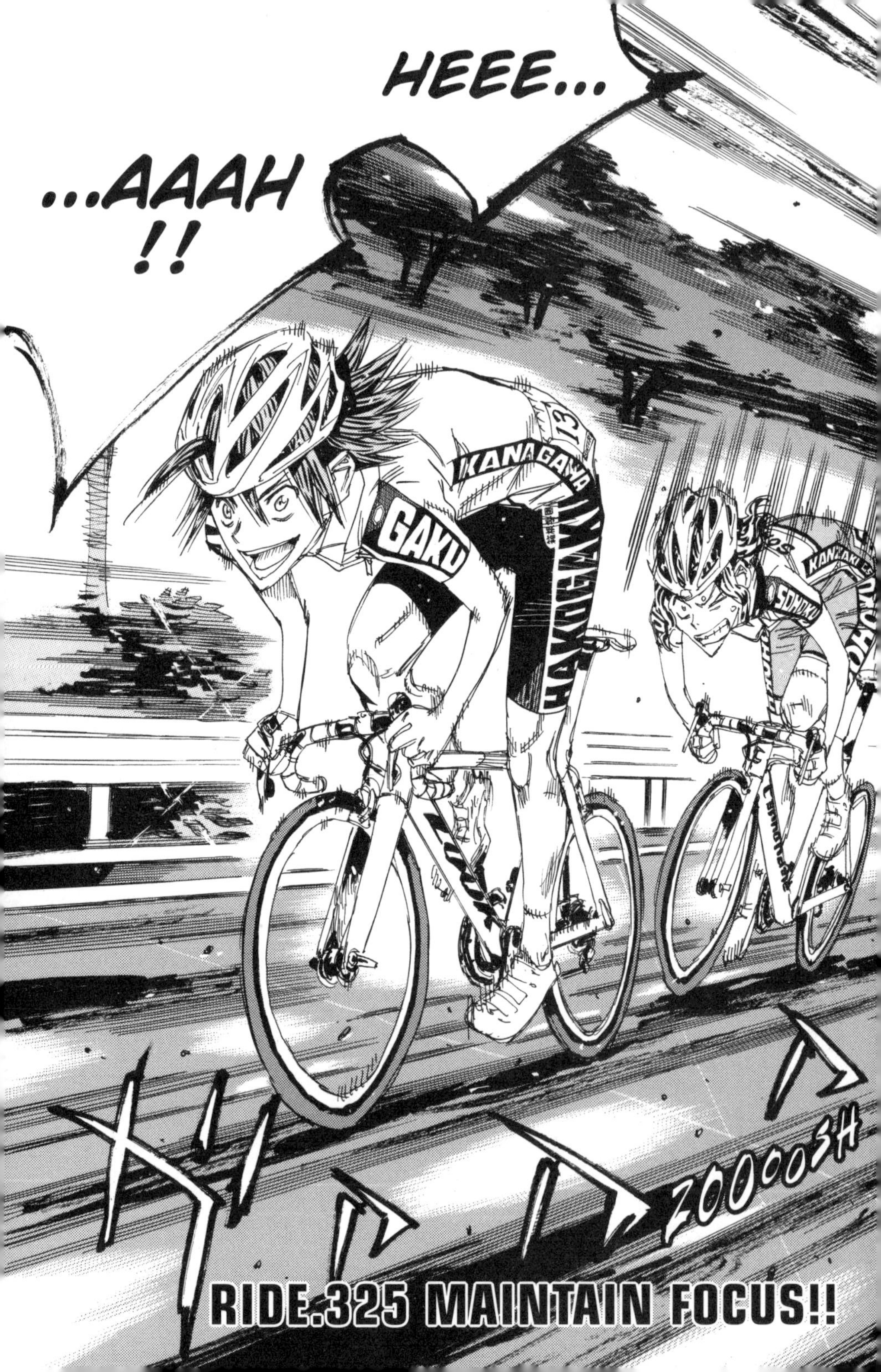
HEEEE...
...AAAH !!
KANAGAWA
GAKU
HAKOGAKU
SOHOKU
ZOOOOSH
RIDE.325 MAINTAIN FOCUS!!

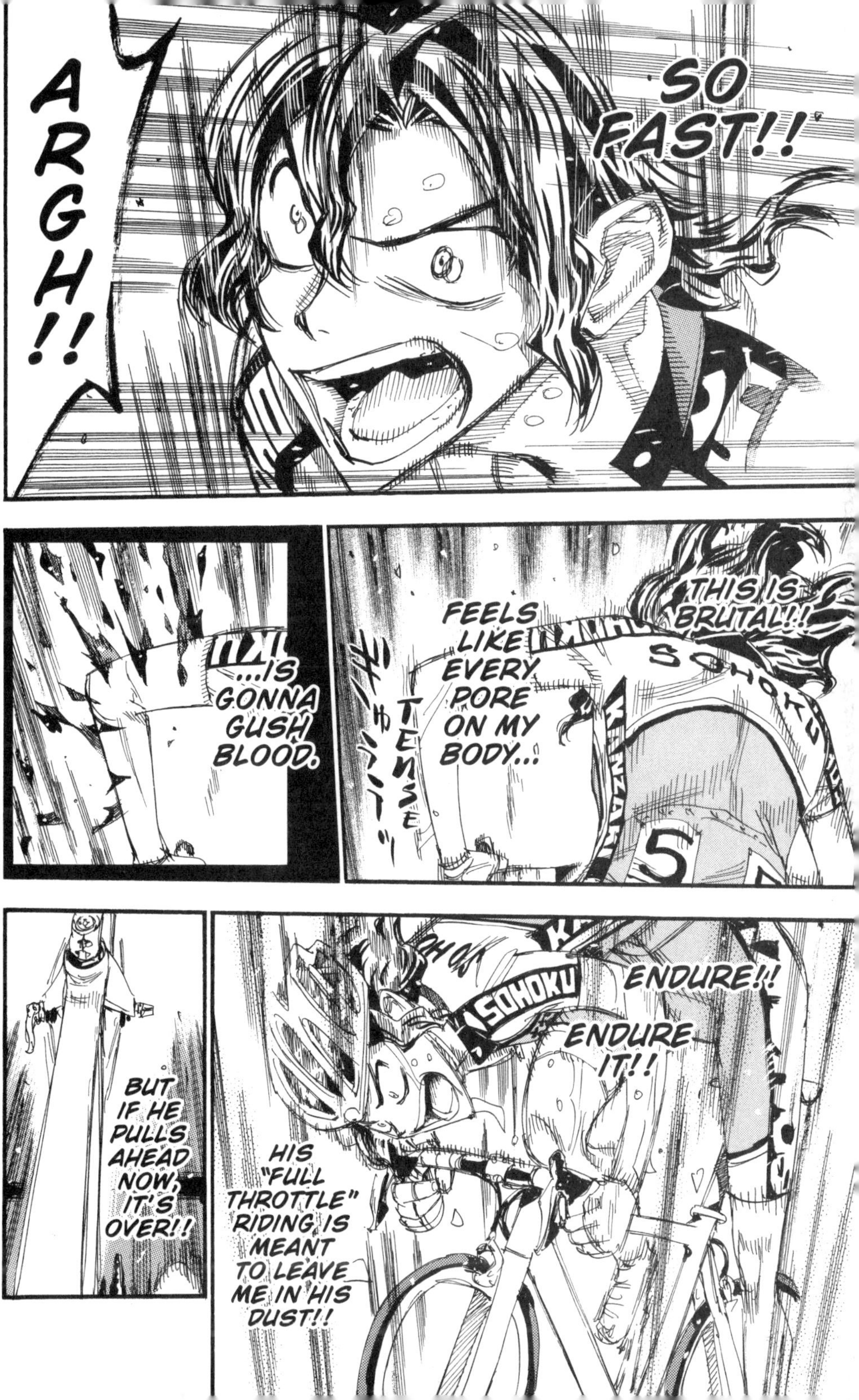
SO FAST!!
ARGH!!
THIS IS BRUTAL!!
FEELS LIKE EVERY PORE ON MY BODY...
TENSE
...IS GONNA GUSH BLOOD.
ENDURE!!
ENDURE IT!!
HIS "FULL THROTTLE" RIDING IS MEANT TO LEAVE ME IN HIS DUST!!
BUT IF HE PULLS AHEAD NOW, IT'S OVER!!

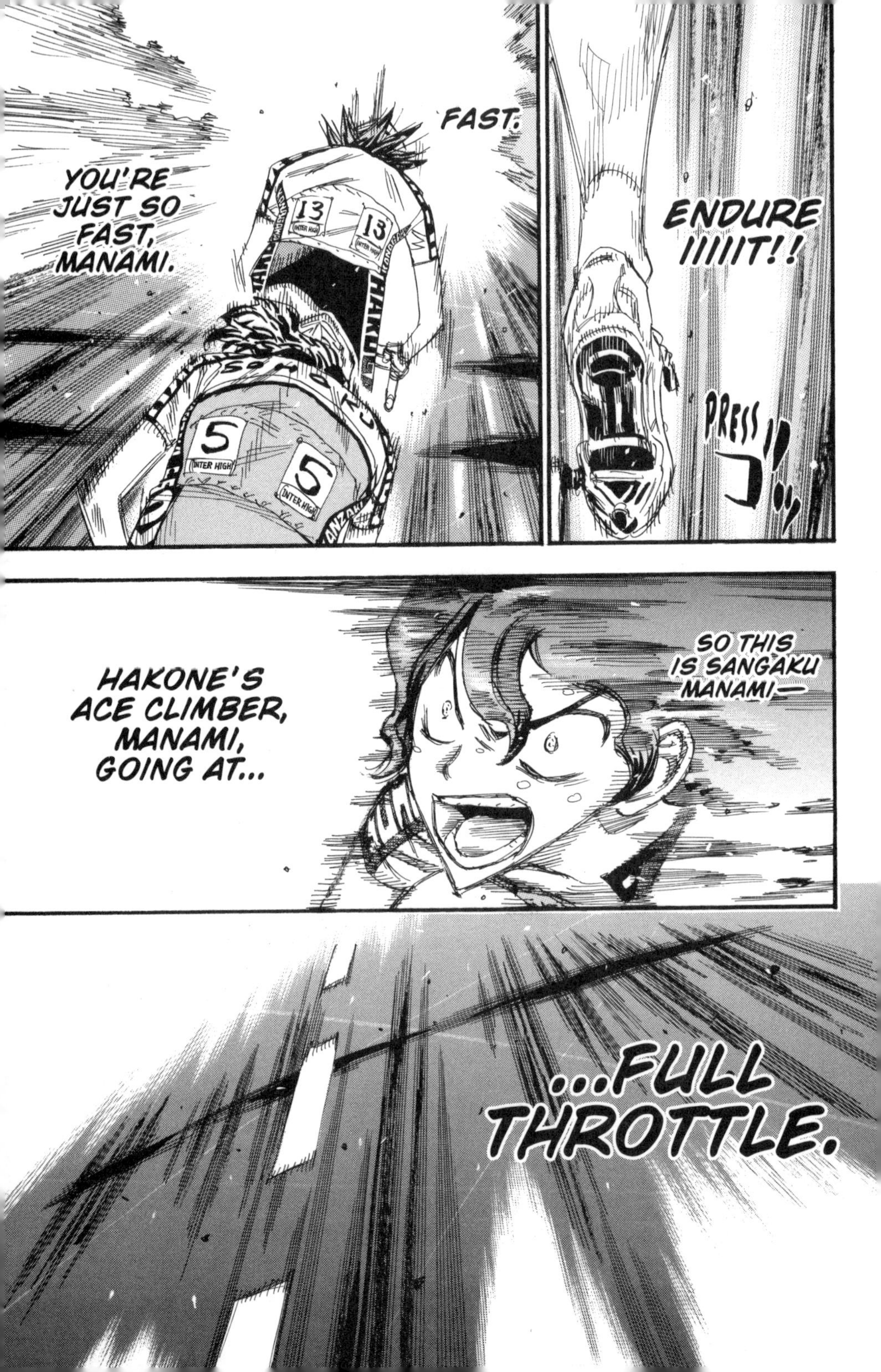
ENDURE
IIIIIT!!
PRESS
ゴ!!
FAST.
YOU'RE JUST SO FAST, MANAMI.
SO THIS IS SANGAKU MANAMI—
HAKONE'S ACE CLIMBER, MANAMI, GOING AT...
...FULL THROTTLE.

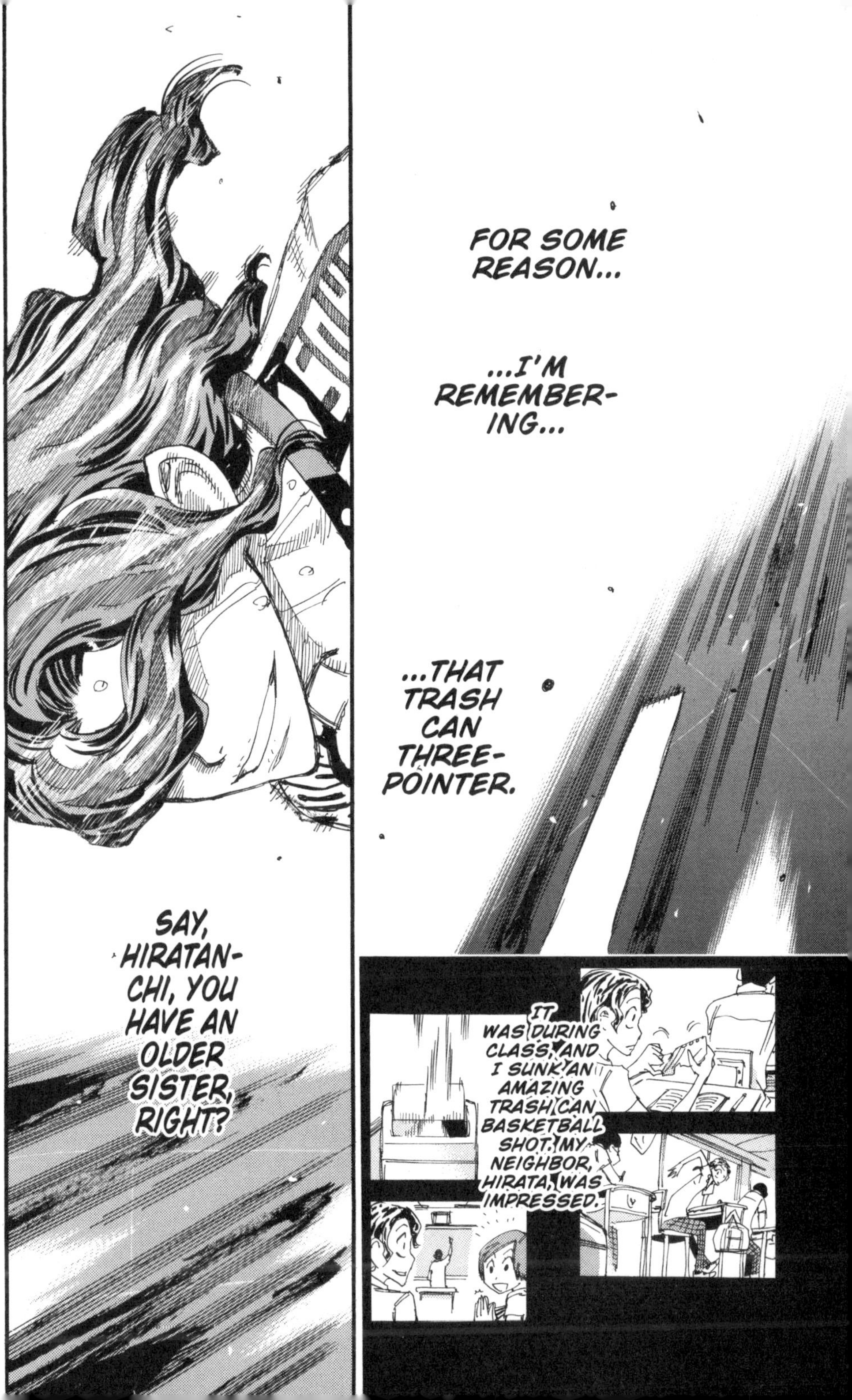
FOR SOME REASON...
...I'M REMEMBERING...
...THAT TRASH CAN THREE-POINTER.
IT WAS DURING CLASS, AND I SUNK AN AMAZING TRASH CAN BASKETBALL SHOT. MY NEIGHBOR, HIRATA, WAS IMPRESSED.
SAY, HIRATAN-CHI, YOU HAVE AN OLDER SISTER, RIGHT?

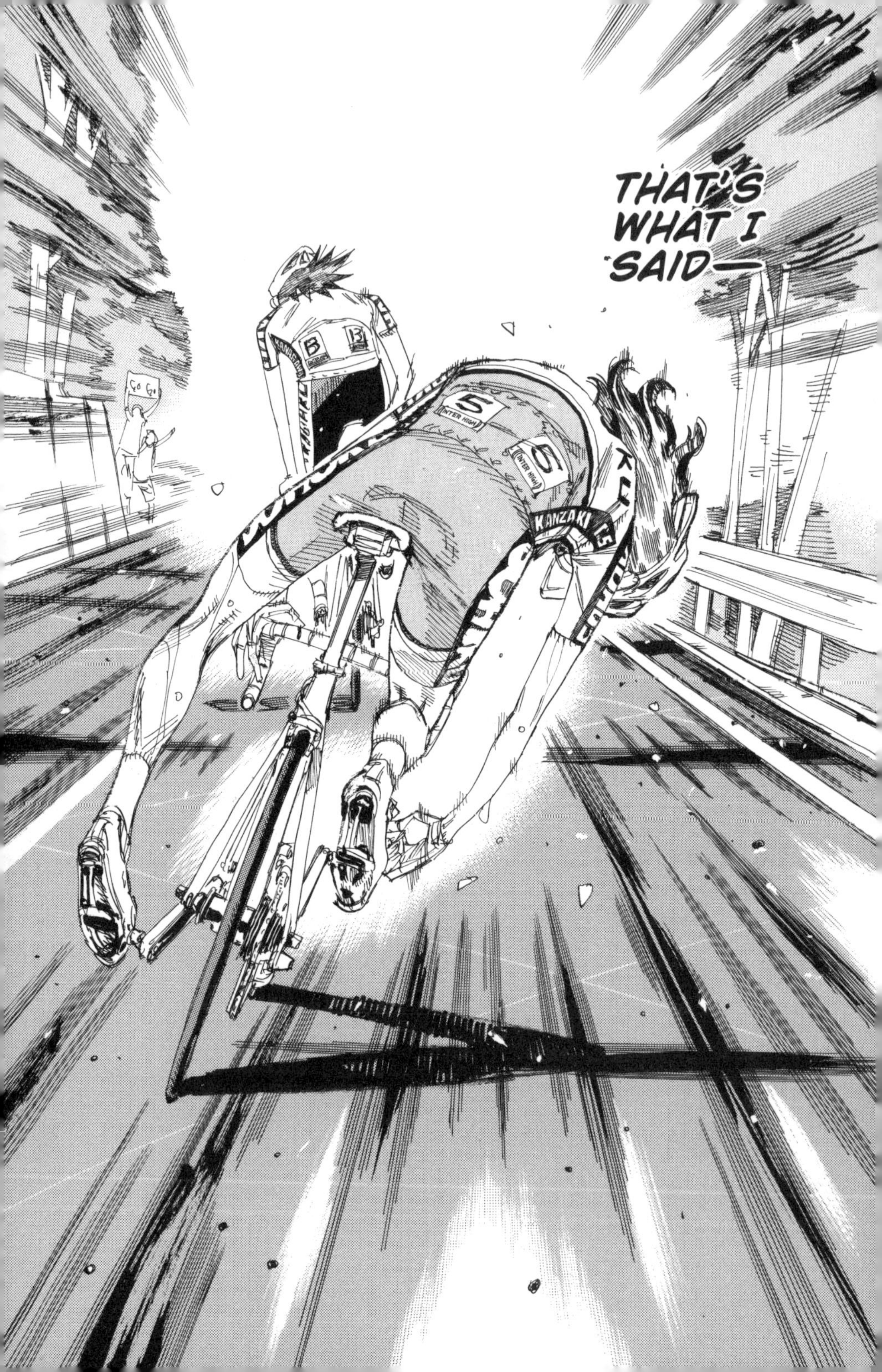
THAT'S WHAT I SAID—

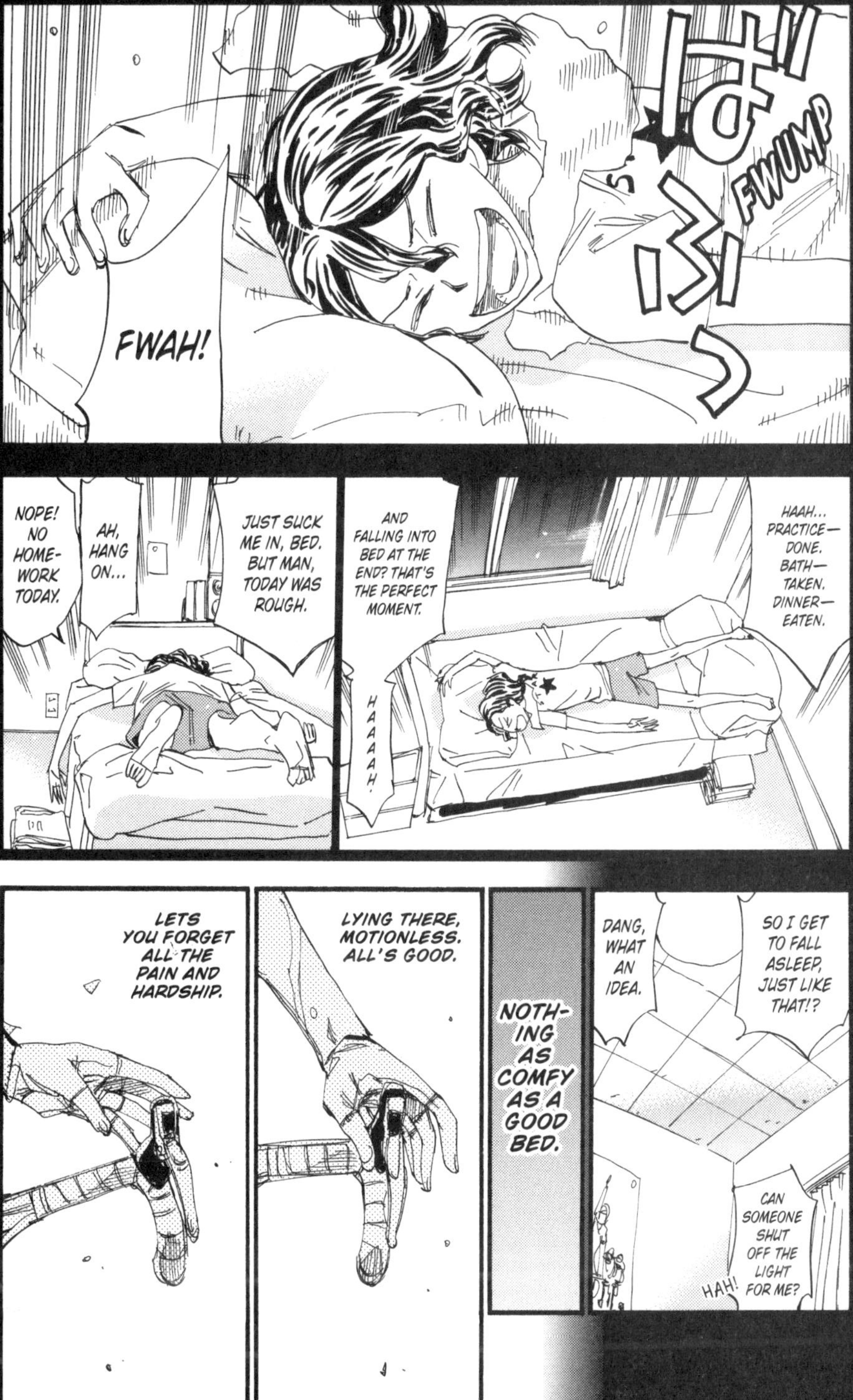
ばふっ
FWUMP
FWAH!
HAAH... PRACTICE—DONE. BATH—TAKEN. DINNER—EATEN.
AND FALLING INTO BED AT THE END? THAT'S THE PERFECT MOMENT.
HAAAAAH!
JUST SUCK ME IN, BED. BUT MAN, TODAY WAS ROUGH.
AH, HANG ON...
NOPE! NO HOMEWORK TODAY.
SO I GET TO FALL ASLEEP, JUST LIKE THAT!?
DANG, WHAT AN IDEA.
CAN SOMEONE SHUT OFF THE LIGHT FOR ME?
HAH!
NOTHING AS COMFY AS A GOOD BED.
LYING THERE, MOTIONLESS. ALL'S GOOD.
LETS YOU FORGET ALL THE PAIN AND HARDSHIP.

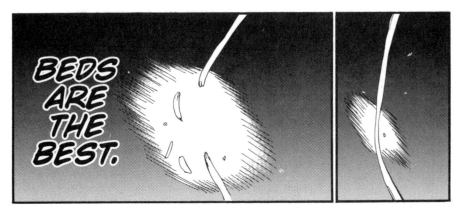

BEDS
ARE
THE
BEST.

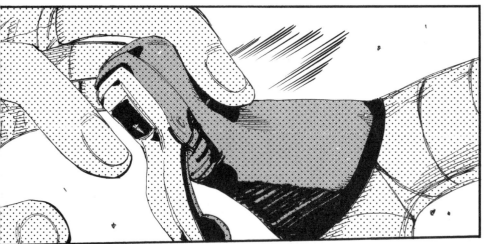

OOPS.

SQUEEZE

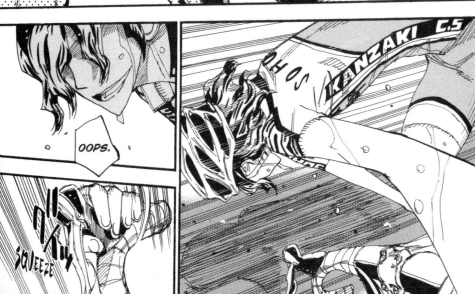

KANZAKI C.5

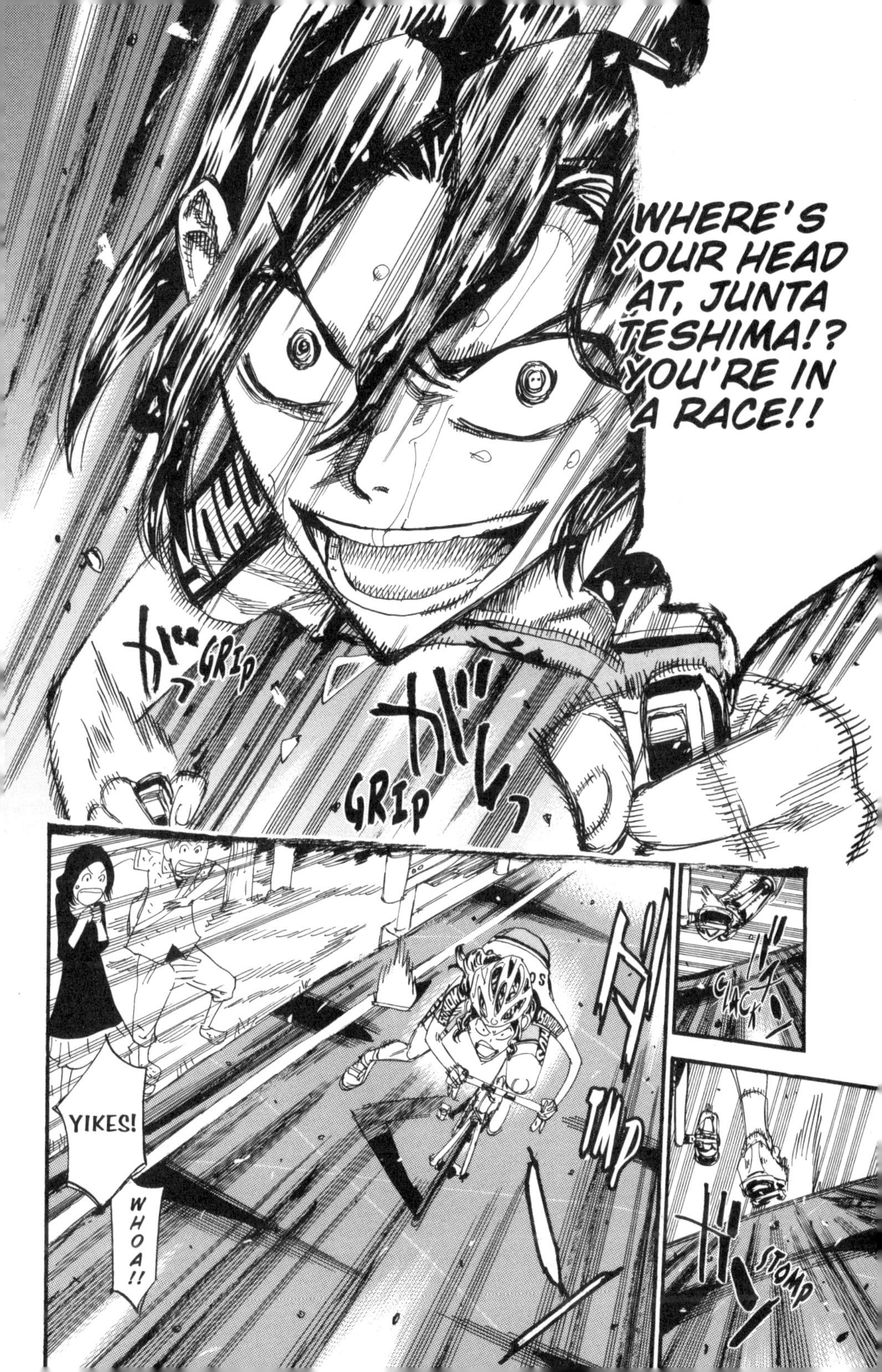
WHERE'S YOUR HEAD AT, JUNTA TESHIMA!? YOU'RE IN A RACE!!
GRIP
GRIP
CLACK
STOMP
TMP
YIKES!
WHOA!!

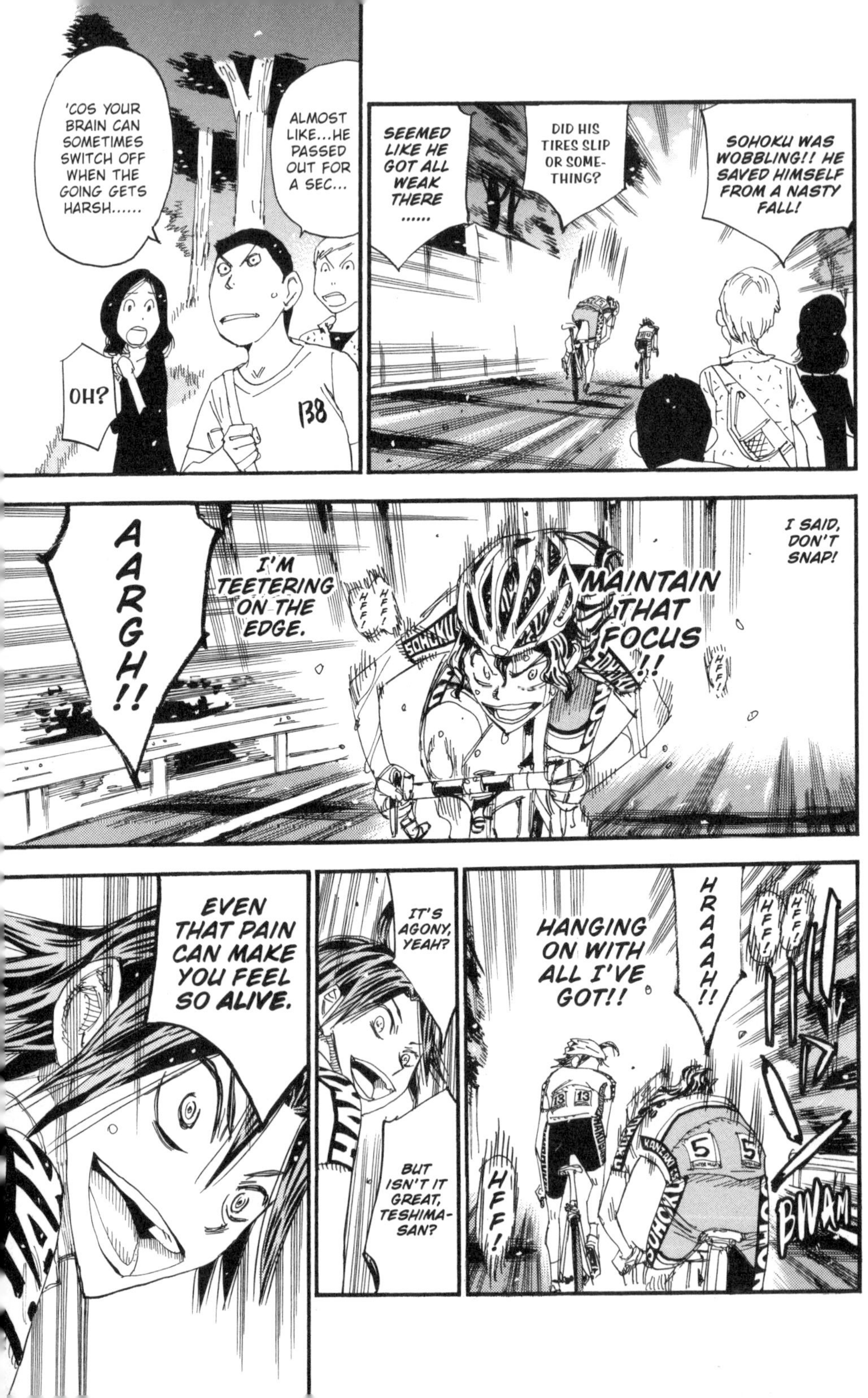
SOHOKU WAS WOBBLING!! HE SAVED HIMSELF FROM A NASTY FALL!
DID HIS TIRES SLIP OR SOME-THING?
SEEMED LIKE HE GOT ALL WEAK THERE ......
ALMOST LIKE...HE PASSED OUT FOR A SEC...
'COS YOUR BRAIN CAN SOMETIMES SWITCH OFF WHEN THE GOING GETS HARSH......
OH?
I SAID, DON'T SNAP!
HFF!
MAINTAIN THAT FOCUS!!
HFF! HFF!
I'M TEETERING ON THE EDGE.
AARGH!!
HFF! HFF!
HRAAAAH!!
HANGING ON WITH ALL I'VE GOT!!
BWAM
HFF!
IT'S AGONY, YEAH?
BUT ISN'T IT GREAT, TESHIMA-SAN?
EVEN THAT PAIN CAN MAKE YOU FEEL SO ALIVE.

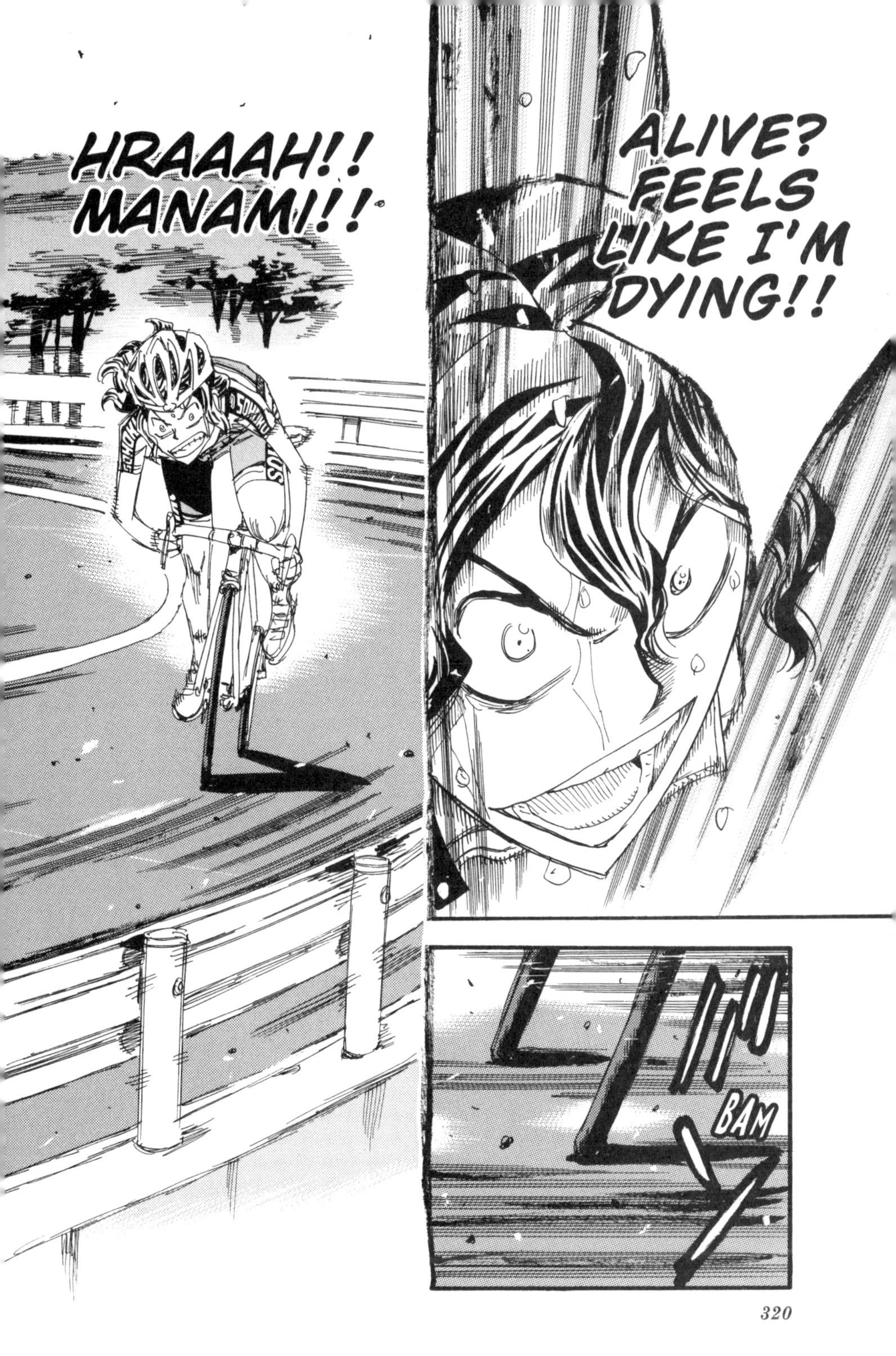
ALIVE? FEELS LIKE I'M DYING!!
BAM
HRAAAH!! MANAMI!!

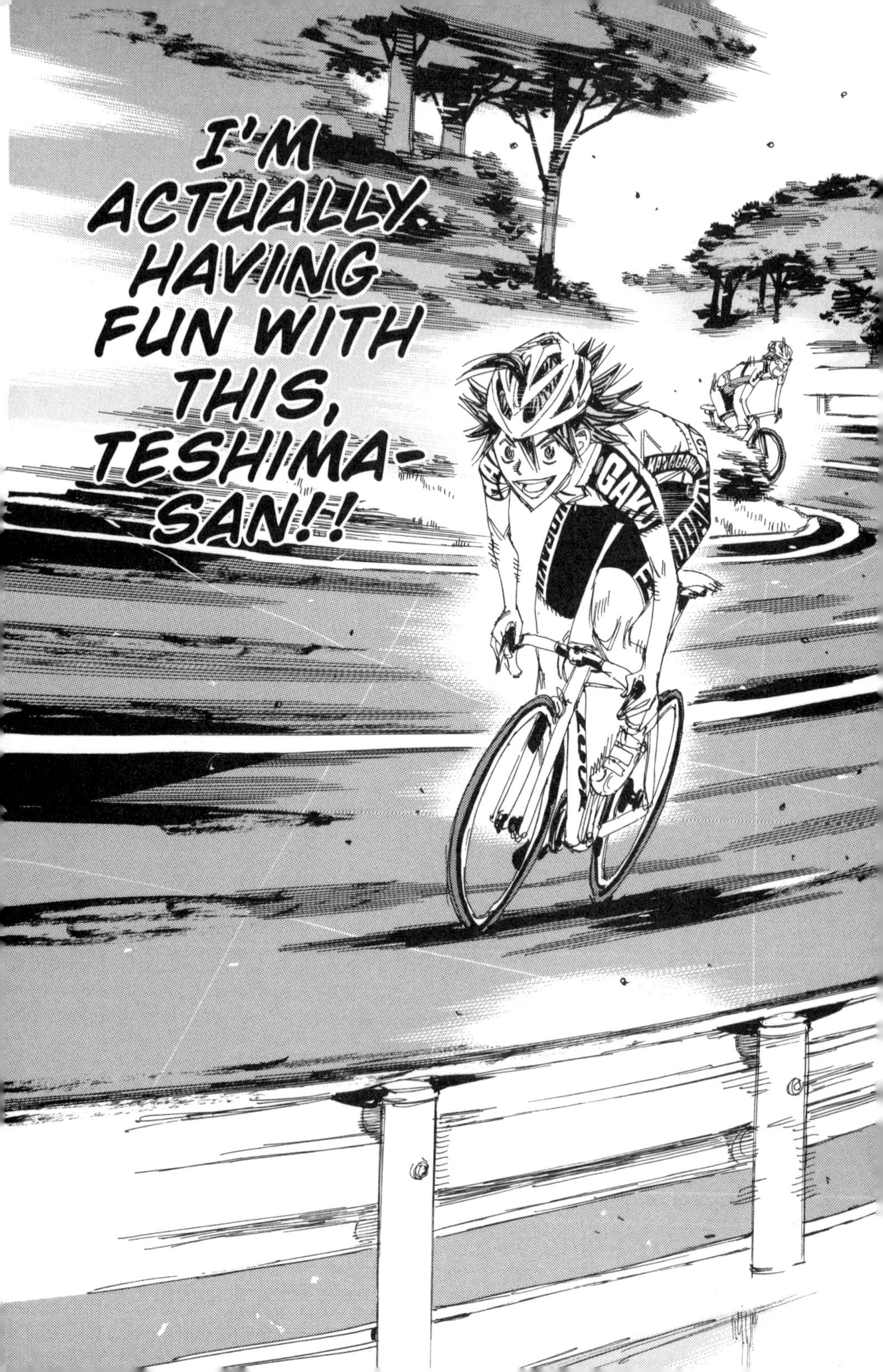
I'M ACTUALLY HAVING FUN WITH THIS, TESHIMA-SAN!!

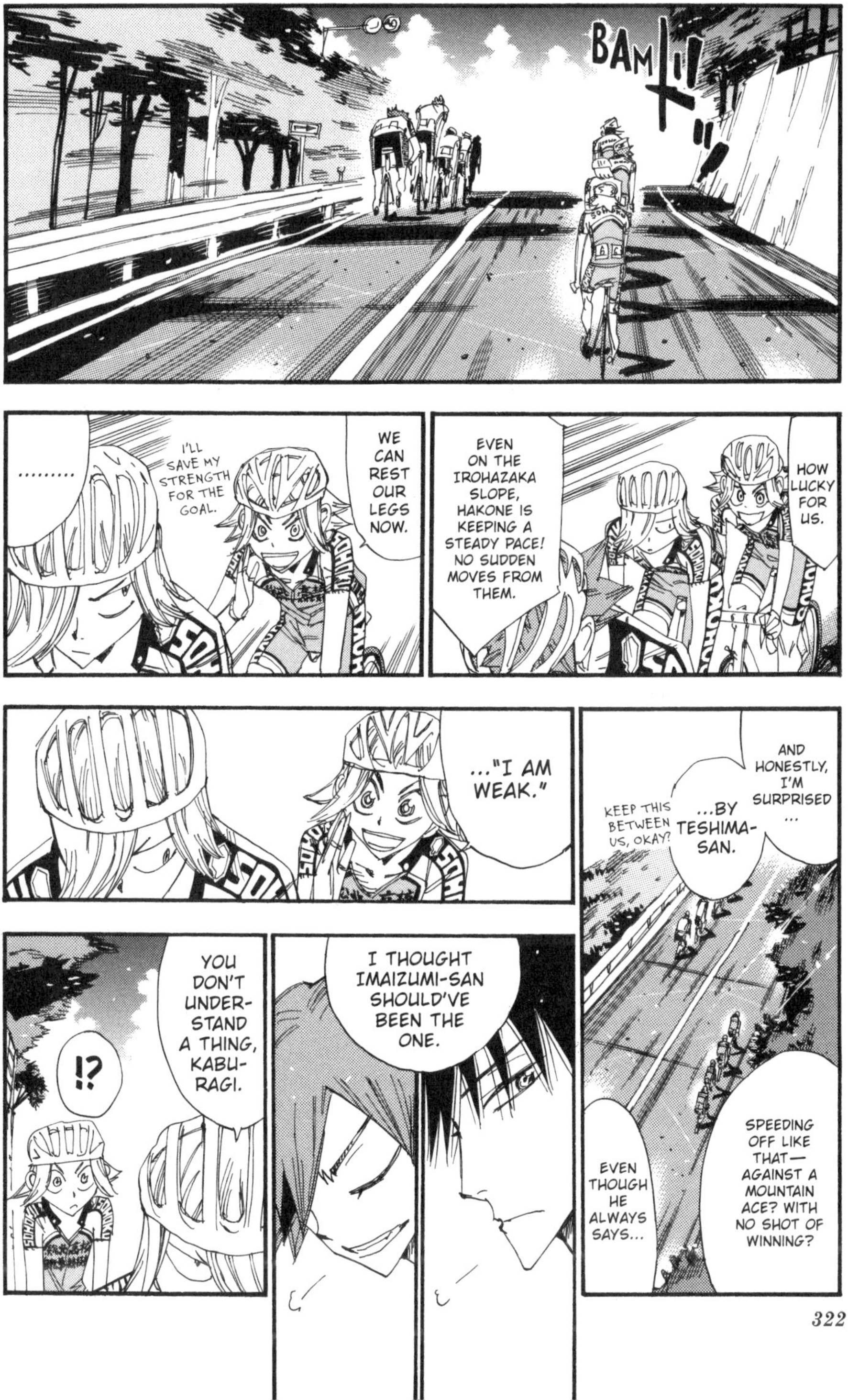
BAM!!
HOW LUCKY FOR US.
EVEN ON THE IROHAZAKA SLOPE, HAKONE IS KEEPING A STEADY PACE! NO SUDDEN MOVES FROM THEM.
WE CAN REST OUR LEGS NOW.
I'LL SAVE MY STRENGTH FOR THE GOAL.
....
AND HONESTLY, I'M SURPRISED...
...BY TESHIMA-SAN.
KEEP THIS BETWEEN US, OKAY?
SPEEDING OFF LIKE THAT—AGAINST A MOUNTAIN ACE? WITH NO SHOT OF WINNING?
EVEN THOUGH HE ALWAYS SAYS...
..."I AM WEAK."
I THOUGHT IMAIZUMI-SAN SHOULD'VE BEEN THE ONE.
YOU DON'T UNDER-STAND A THING, KABURAGI.
!?

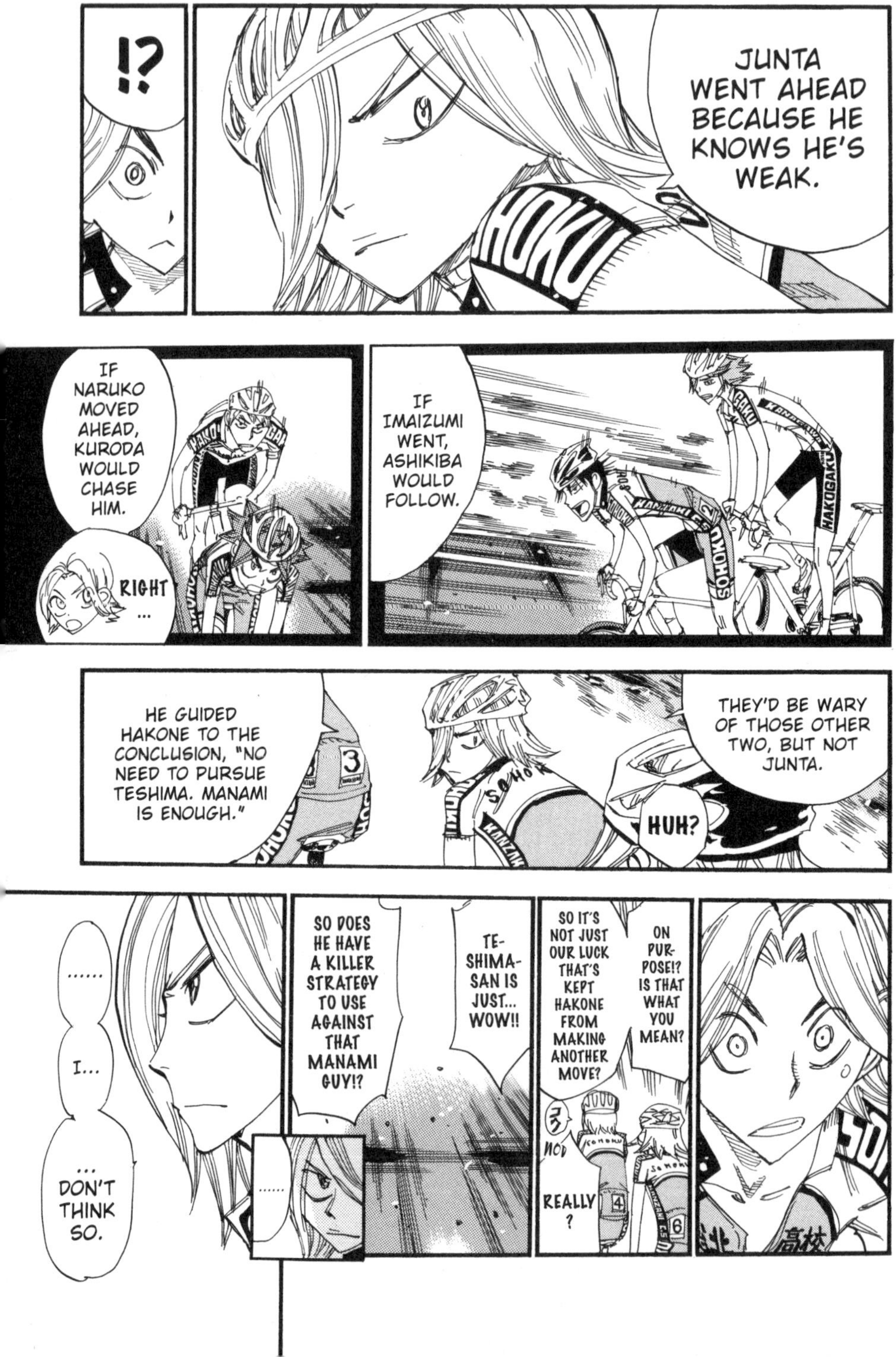
JUNTA WENT AHEAD BECAUSE HE KNOWS HE'S WEAK.
!?
IF IMAIZUMI WENT, ASHIKIBA WOULD FOLLOW.
IF NARUKO MOVED AHEAD, KURODA WOULD CHASE HIM.
RIGHT...
THEY'D BE WARY OF THOSE OTHER TWO, BUT NOT JUNTA.
HUH?
HE GUIDED HAKONE TO THE CONCLUSION, "NO NEED TO PURSUE TESHIMA. MANAMI IS ENOUGH."
ON PURPOSE!? IS THAT WHAT YOU MEAN?
SO IT'S NOT JUST OUR LUCK THAT'S KEPT HAKONE FROM MAKING ANOTHER MOVE?
NOD
REALLY?
TE-SHIMA-SAN IS JUST... WOW!!
SO DOES HE HAVE A KILLER STRATEGY TO USE AGAINST THAT MANAMI GUY!?
......
......
I...
...DON'T THINK SO.

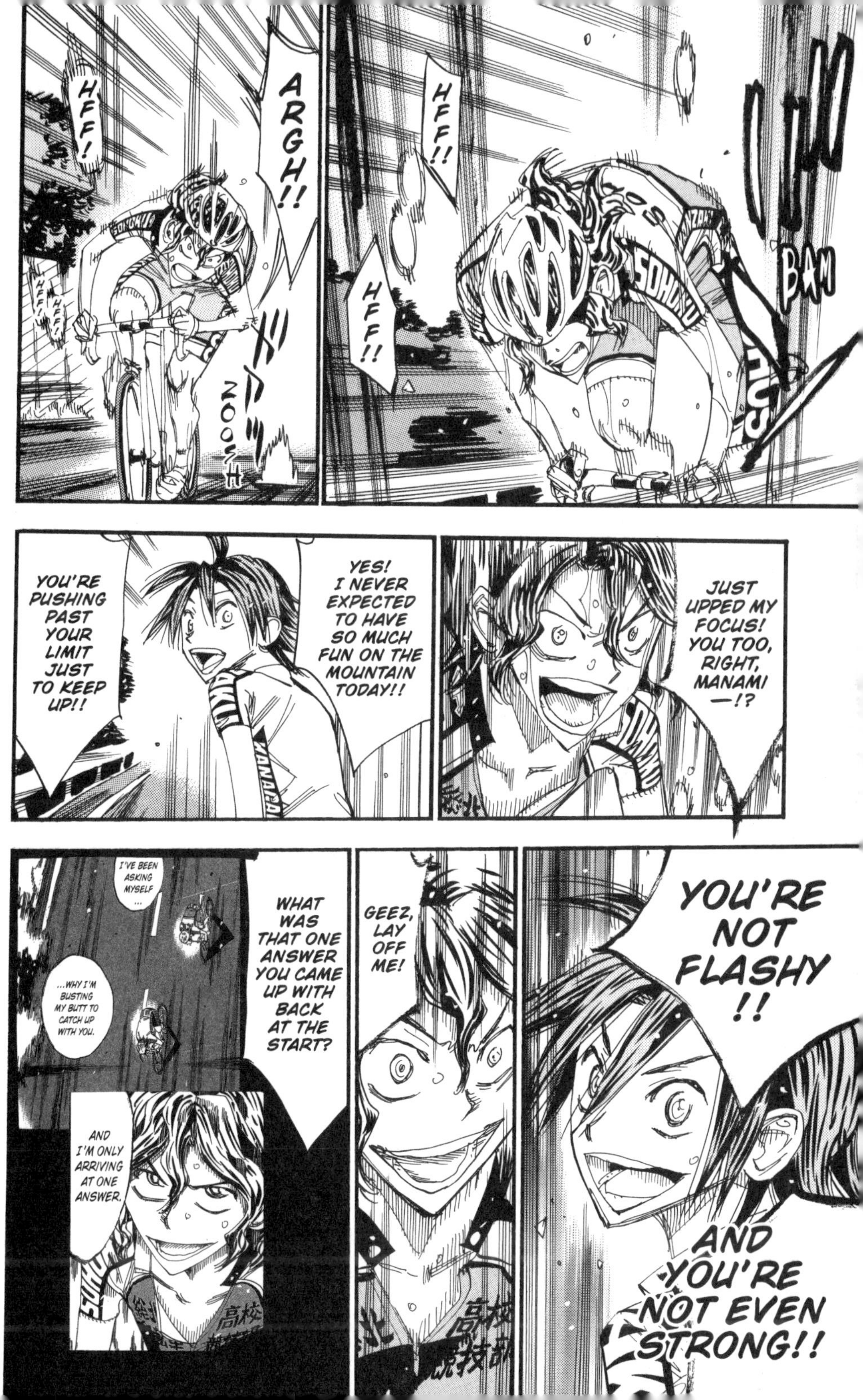
BAM
HFF!!
HFF!!
ARGH!!
HFF!
ZOOOSH
JUST UPPED MY FOCUS! YOU TOO, RIGHT, MANAMI—!?
YES! I NEVER EXPECTED TO HAVE SO MUCH FUN ON THE MOUNTAIN TODAY!!
YOU'RE PUSHING PAST YOUR LIMIT JUST TO KEEP UP!!
YOU'RE NOT FLASHY!!
AND YOU'RE NOT EVEN STRONG!!
GEEZ, LAY OFF ME!
WHAT WAS THAT ONE ANSWER YOU CAME UP WITH BACK AT THE START?
I'VE BEEN ASKING MYSELF...
...WHY I'M BUSTING MY BUTT TO CATCH UP WITH YOU.
AND I'M ONLY ARRIVING AT ONE ANSWER.

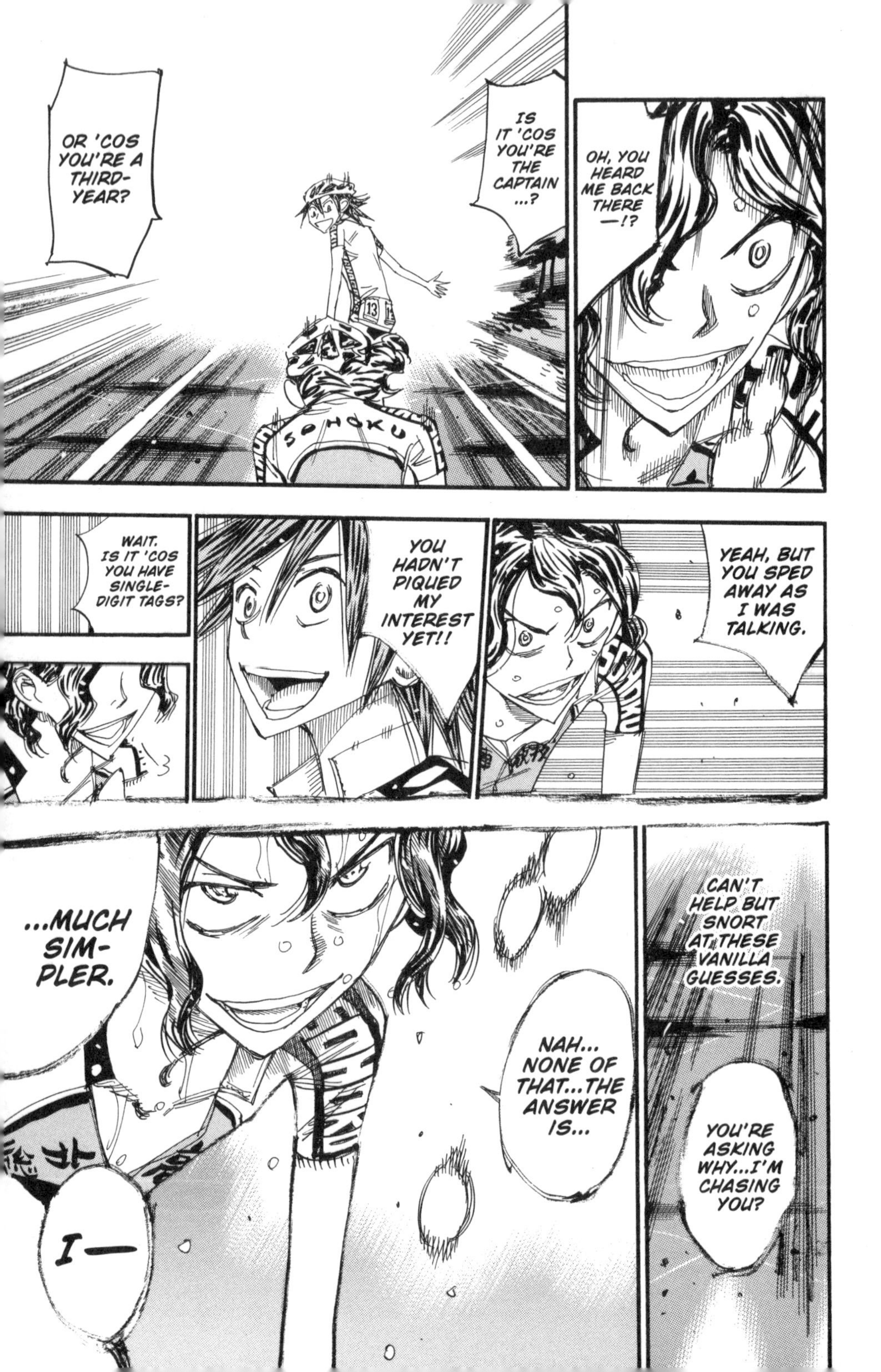
OH, YOU HEARD ME BACK THERE—!?
IS IT 'COS YOU'RE THE CAPTAIN...?
OR 'COS YOU'RE A THIRD-YEAR?
YEAH, BUT YOU SPED AWAY AS I WAS TALKING.
YOU HADN'T PIQUED MY INTEREST YET!!
WAIT. IS IT 'COS YOU HAVE SINGLE-DIGIT TAGS?
CAN'T HELP BUT SNORT AT THESE VANILLA GUESSES.
YOU'RE ASKING WHY...I'M CHASING YOU?
NAH... NONE OF THAT...THE ANSWER IS...
...MUCH SIMPLER.
I—

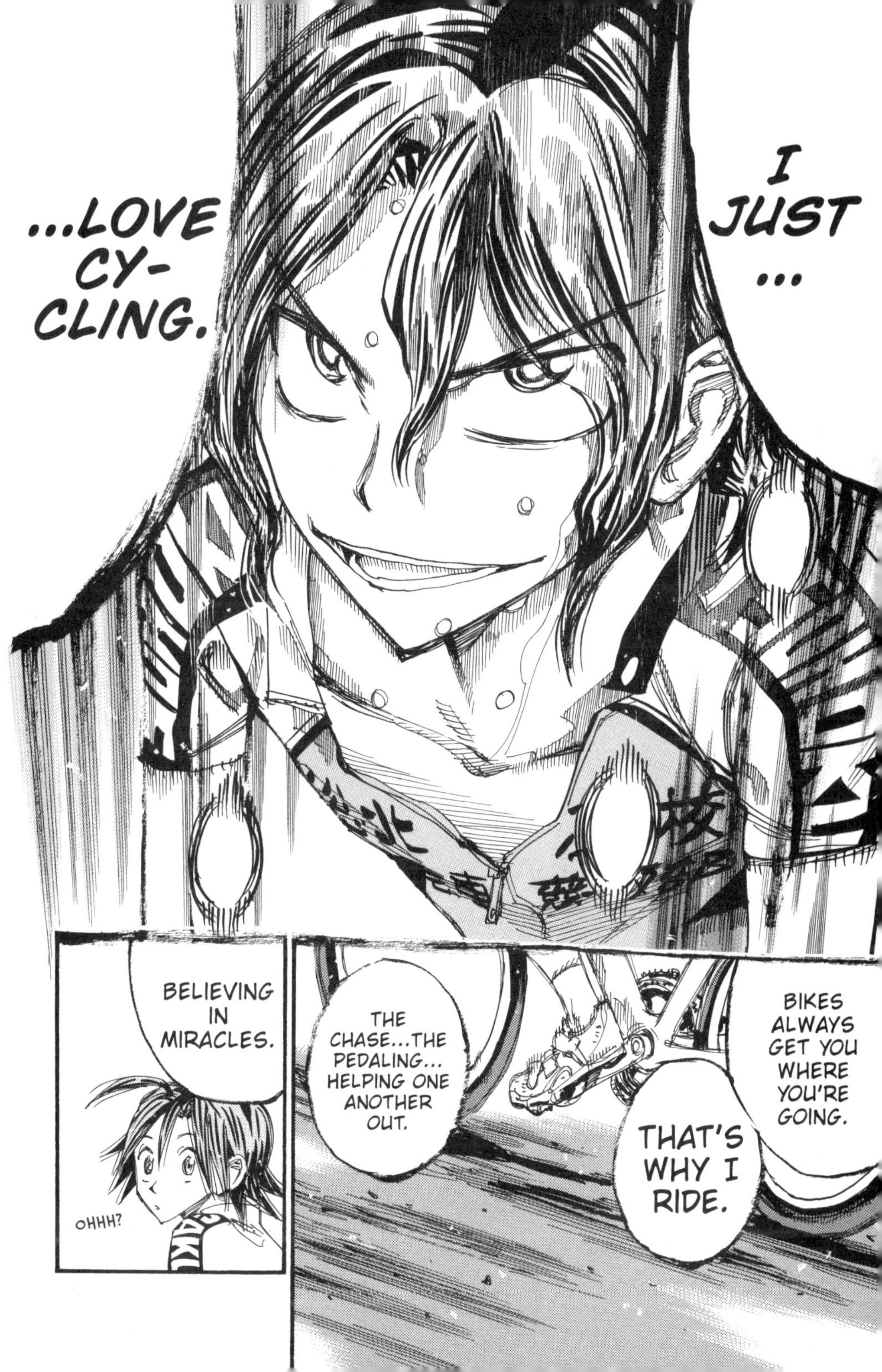
I JUST...
...LOVE CY-CLING.
BIKES ALWAYS GET YOU WHERE YOU'RE GOING.
THE CHASE...THE PEDALING... HELPING ONE ANOTHER OUT.
THAT'S WHY I RIDE.
BELIEVING IN MIRACLES.
OHHH?

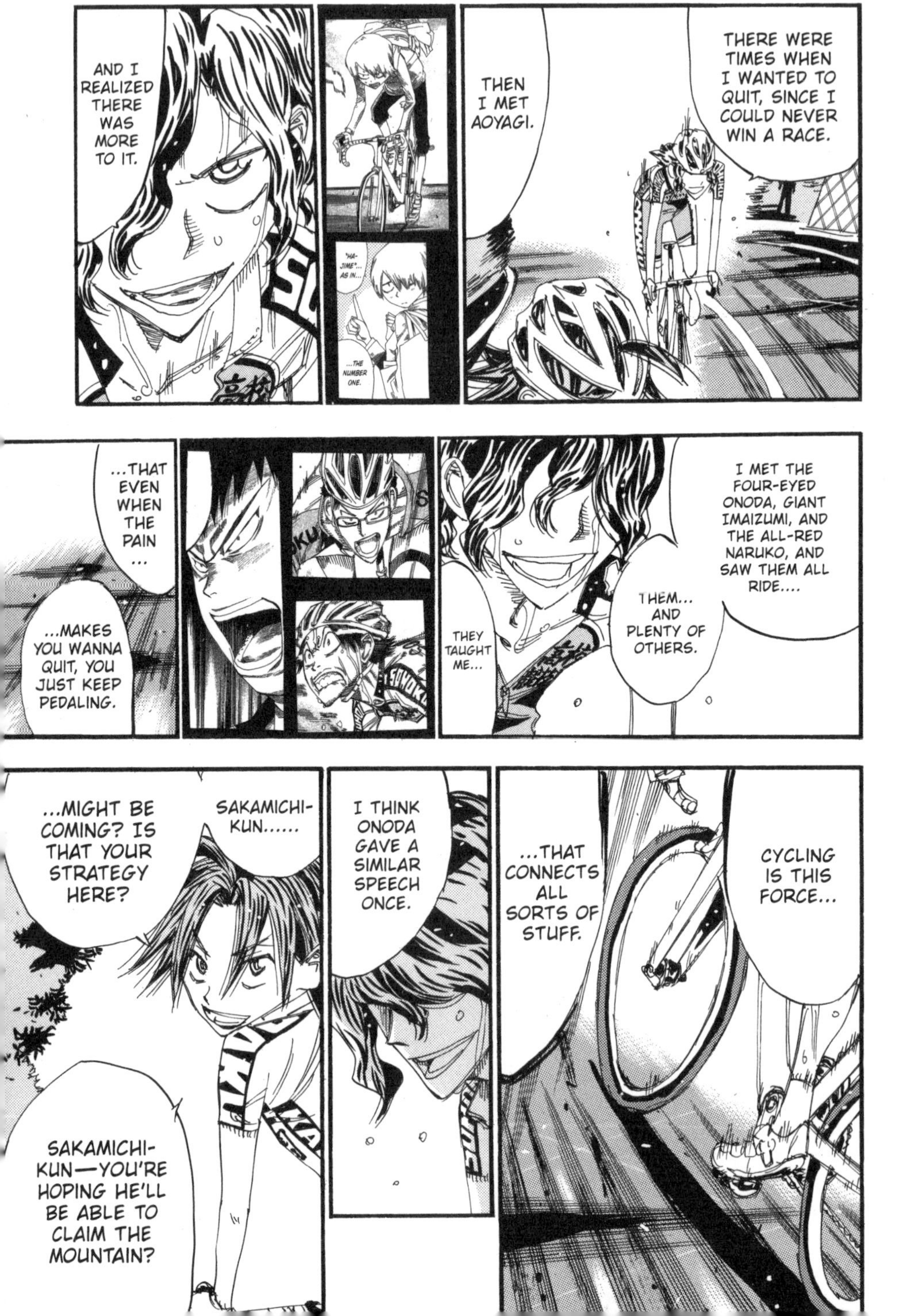
THERE WERE TIMES WHEN I WANTED TO QUIT, SINCE I COULD NEVER WIN A RACE.
THEN I MET AOYAGI.
"HA-JIME"... AS IN...
...THE NUMBER ONE.
AND I REALIZED THERE WAS MORE TO IT.
I MET THE FOUR-EYED ONODA, GIANT IMAIZUMI, AND THE ALL-RED NARUKO, AND SAW THEM ALL RIDE....
THEM... AND PLENTY OF OTHERS.
THEY TAUGHT ME...
...THAT EVEN WHEN THE PAIN ...
...MAKES YOU WANNA QUIT, YOU JUST KEEP PEDALING.
CYCLING IS THIS FORCE...
...THAT CONNECTS ALL SORTS OF STUFF.
I THINK ONODA GAVE A SIMILAR SPEECH ONCE.
SAKAMICHI-KUN......
...MIGHT BE COMING? IS THAT YOUR STRATEGY HERE?
SAKAMICHI-KUN—YOU'RE HOPING HE'LL BE ABLE TO CLAIM THE MOUNTAIN?

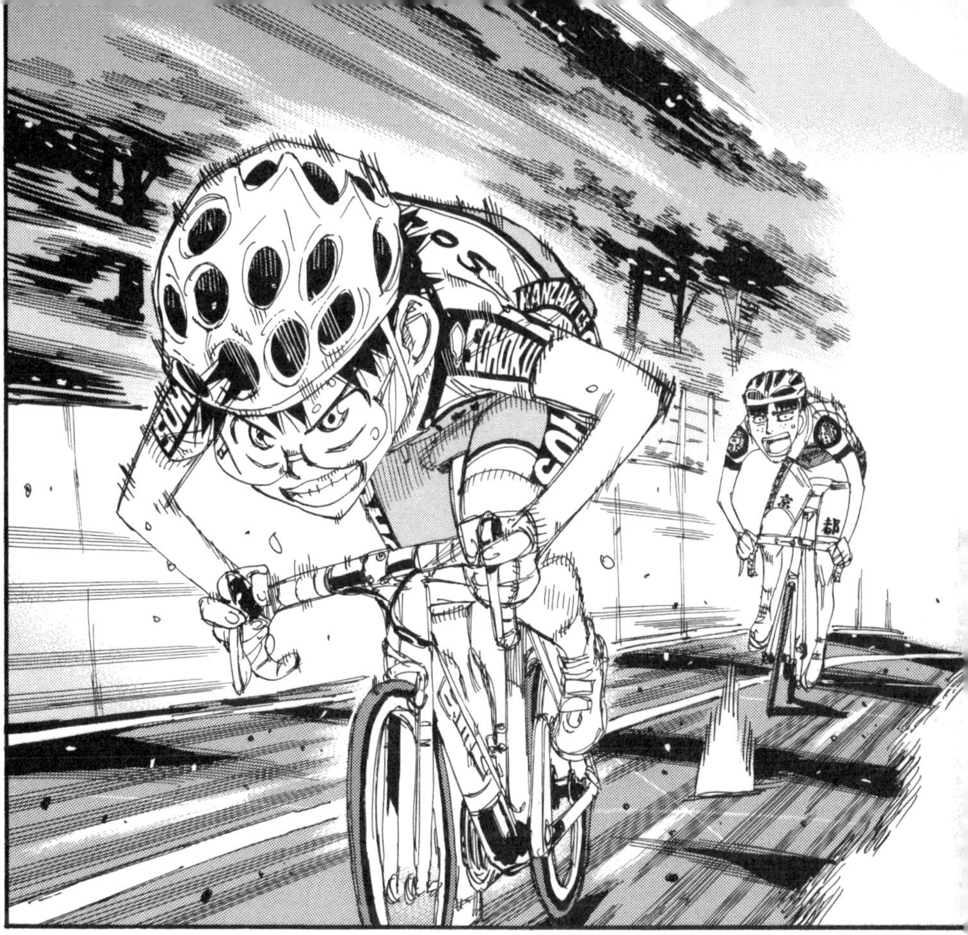
KANZAKI

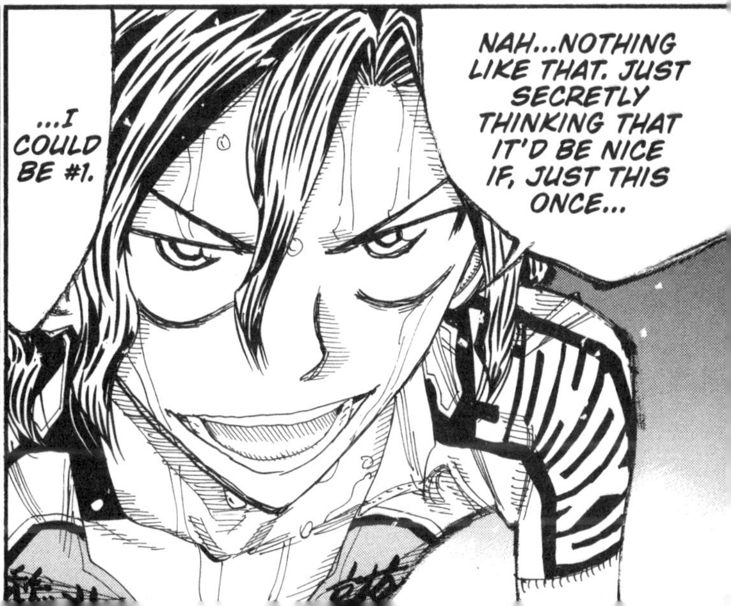
NAH...NOTHING LIKE THAT. JUST SECRETLY THINKING THAT IT'D BE NICE IF, JUST THIS ONCE...
...I COULD BE #1.

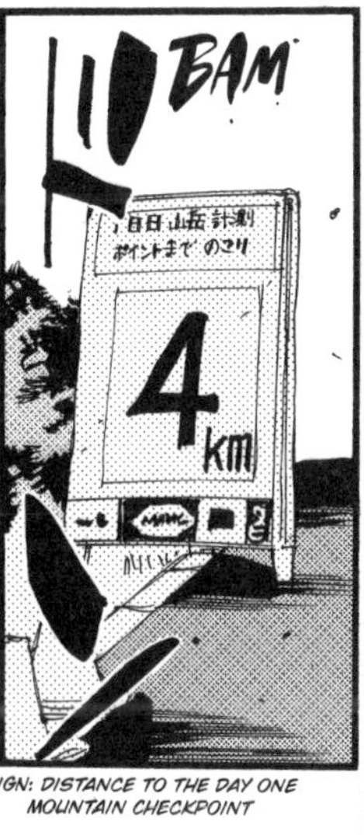
BAM
4 km

SIGN: DISTANCE TO THE DAY ONE MOUNTAIN CHECKPOINT

RIDE.326 SAKAMICHI VS. KYOTO-FUSHIMI'S YAMAGUCHI

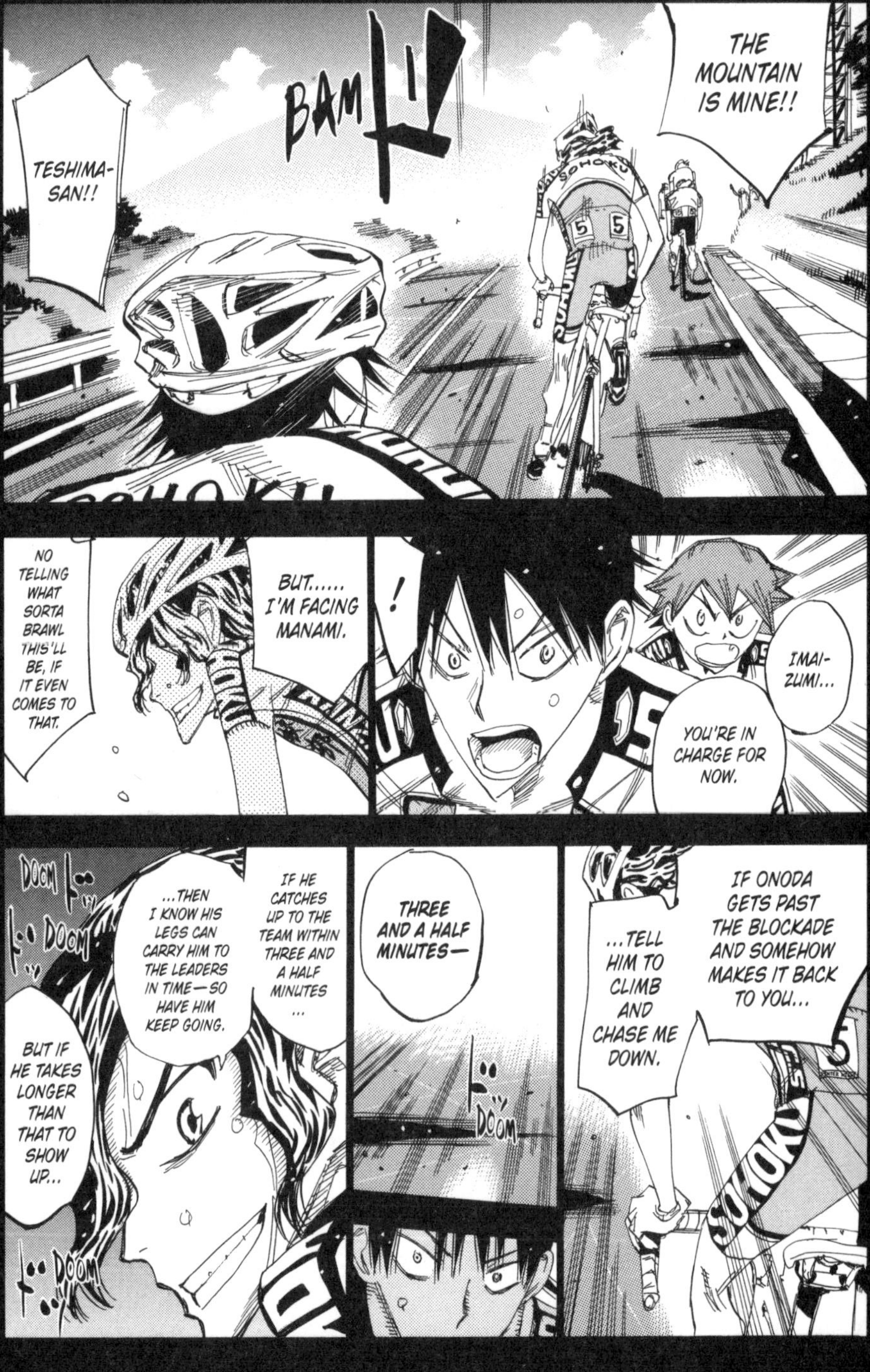
THE MOUNTAIN IS MINE!!
BAM
TESHIMA-SAN!!
!
IMAI-ZUMI...
YOU'RE IN CHARGE FOR NOW.
BUT...... I'M FACING MANAMI.
NO TELLING WHAT SORTA BRAWL THIS'LL BE, IF IT EVEN COMES TO THAT.
IF ONODA GETS PAST THE BLOCKADE AND SOMEHOW MAKES IT BACK TO YOU...
...TELL HIM TO CLIMB AND CHASE ME DOWN.
THREE AND A HALF MINUTES—
DOOM
IF HE CATCHES UP TO THE TEAM WITHIN THREE AND A HALF MINUTES...
...THEN I KNOW HIS LEGS CAN CARRY HIM TO THE LEADERS IN TIME—SO HAVE HIM KEEP GOING.
DOOM
DOOM
BUT IF HE TAKES LONGER THAN THAT TO SHOW UP...
DOOM

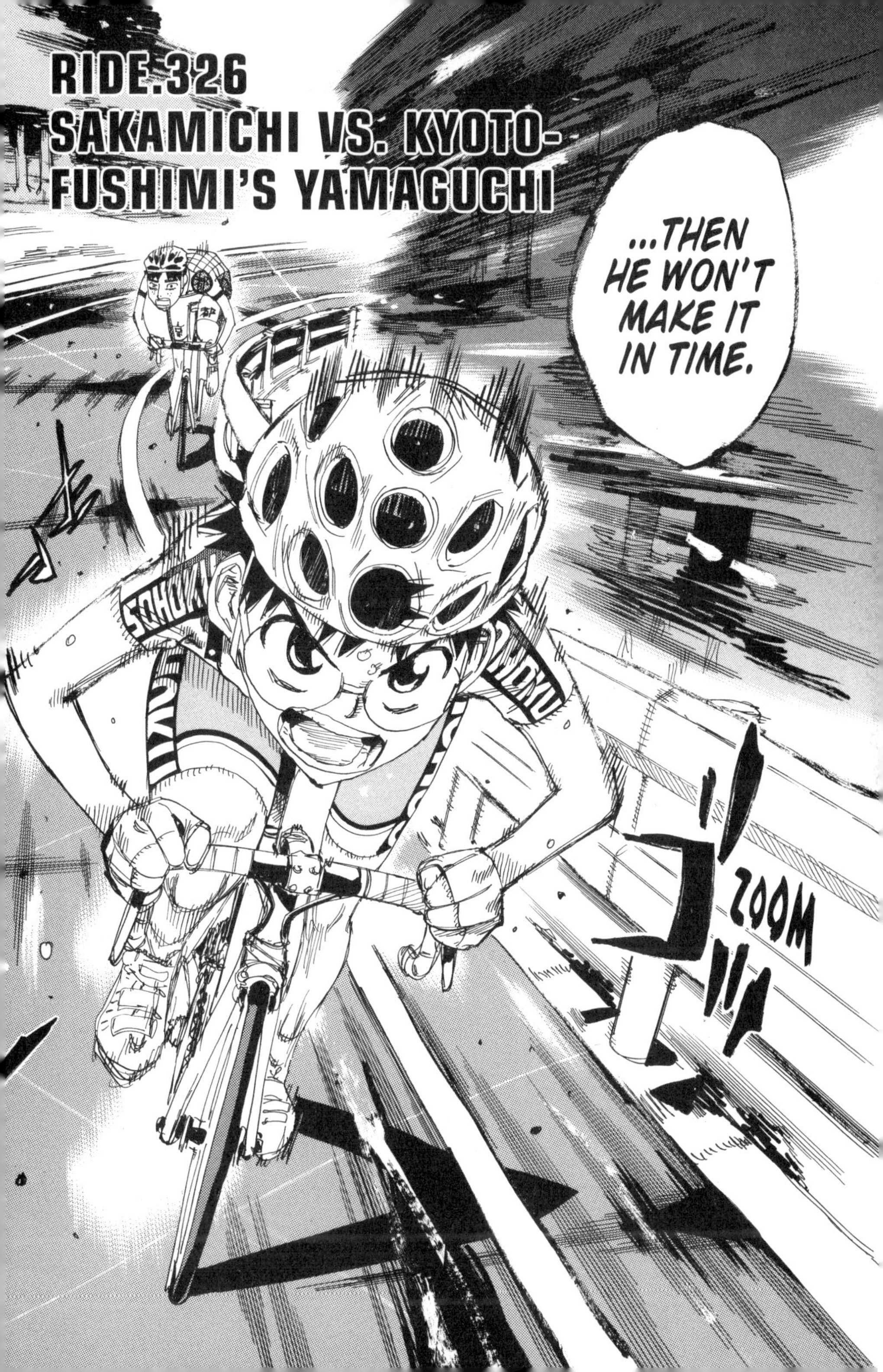
RIDE.326
SAKAMICHI VS. KYOTO-FUSHIMI'S YAMAGUCHI
...THEN HE WON'T MAKE IT IN TIME.
ZOOM

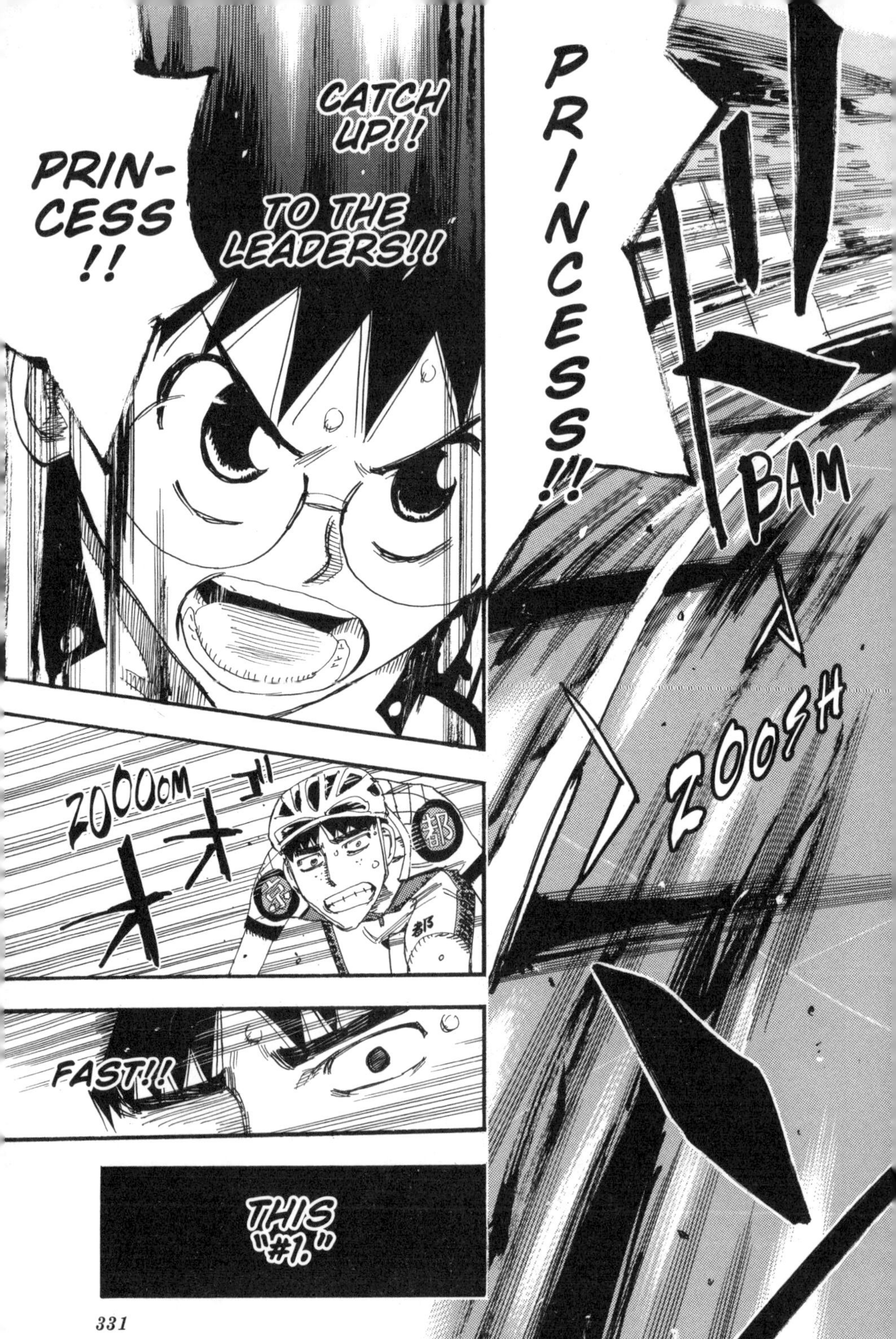
PRINCESS!!!
BAM
ZOOSH
CATCH UP!!
TO THE LEADERS!!
PRIN-CESS!!
ZOOOOM
FAST!!
THIS "#1."

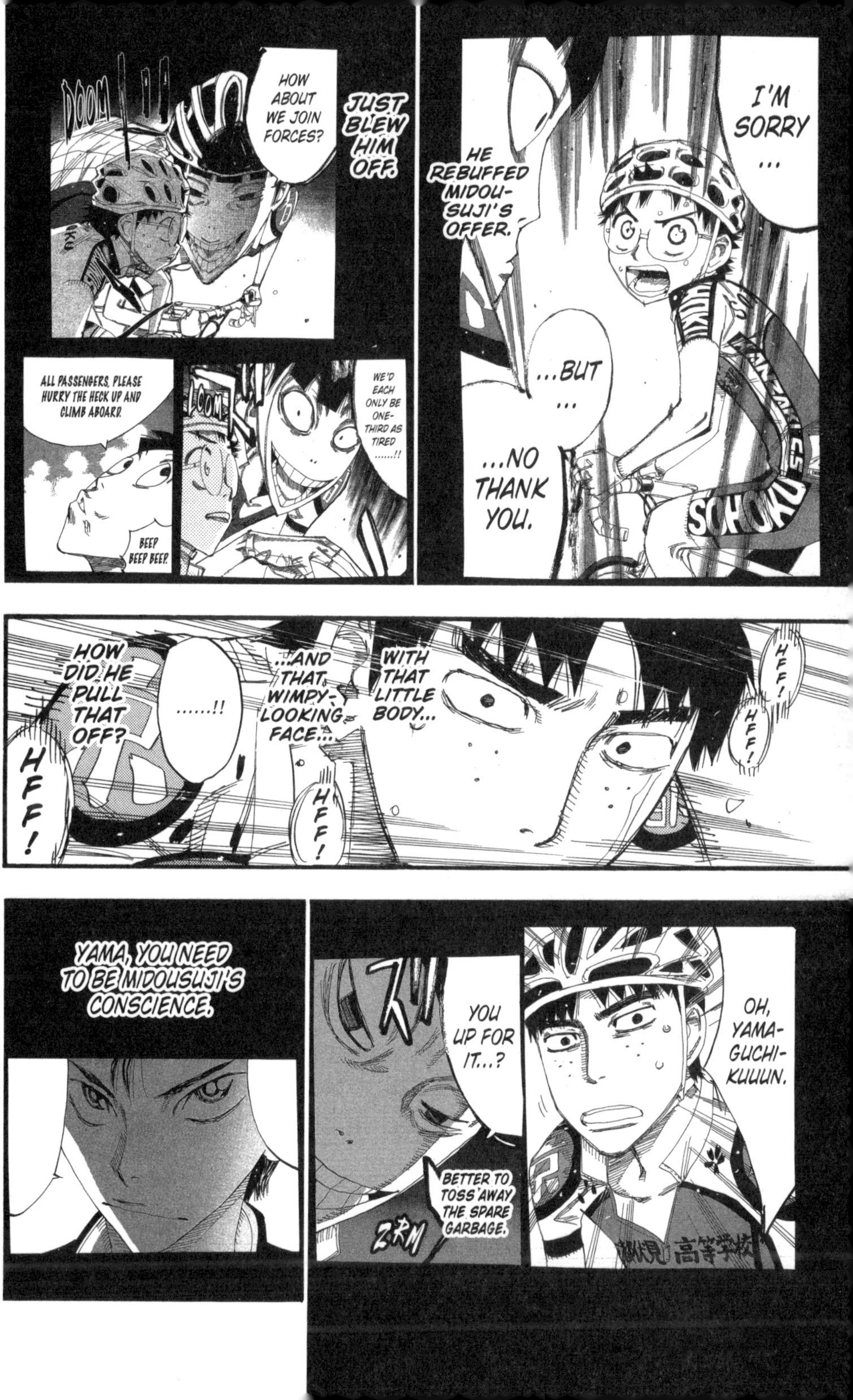
I'M SORRY ...
HE REBUFFED MIDOUSUJI'S OFFER.
...BUT ...
...NO THANK YOU.
SOHOKU
HOW ABOUT WE JOIN FORCES?
JUST BLEW HIM OFF.
DOOM
WE'D EACH ONLY BE ONE-THIRD AS TIRED ......!!
DOOM
ALL PASSENGERS, PLEASE HURRY THE HECK UP AND CLIMB ABOARD.
BEEP BEEP BEEP.
HFF! HFF! HFF!
WITH THAT LITTLE BODY...
...AND THAT WIMPY-LOOKING FACE...
......!!
HOW DID HE PULL THAT OFF?
HFF!
HFF!
OH, YAMAGUCHI-KUUUN.
YOU UP FOR IT...?
BETTER TO TOSS AWAY THE SPARE GARBAGE.
ZRM
YAMA, YOU NEED TO BE MIDOUSUJI'S CONSCIENCE.

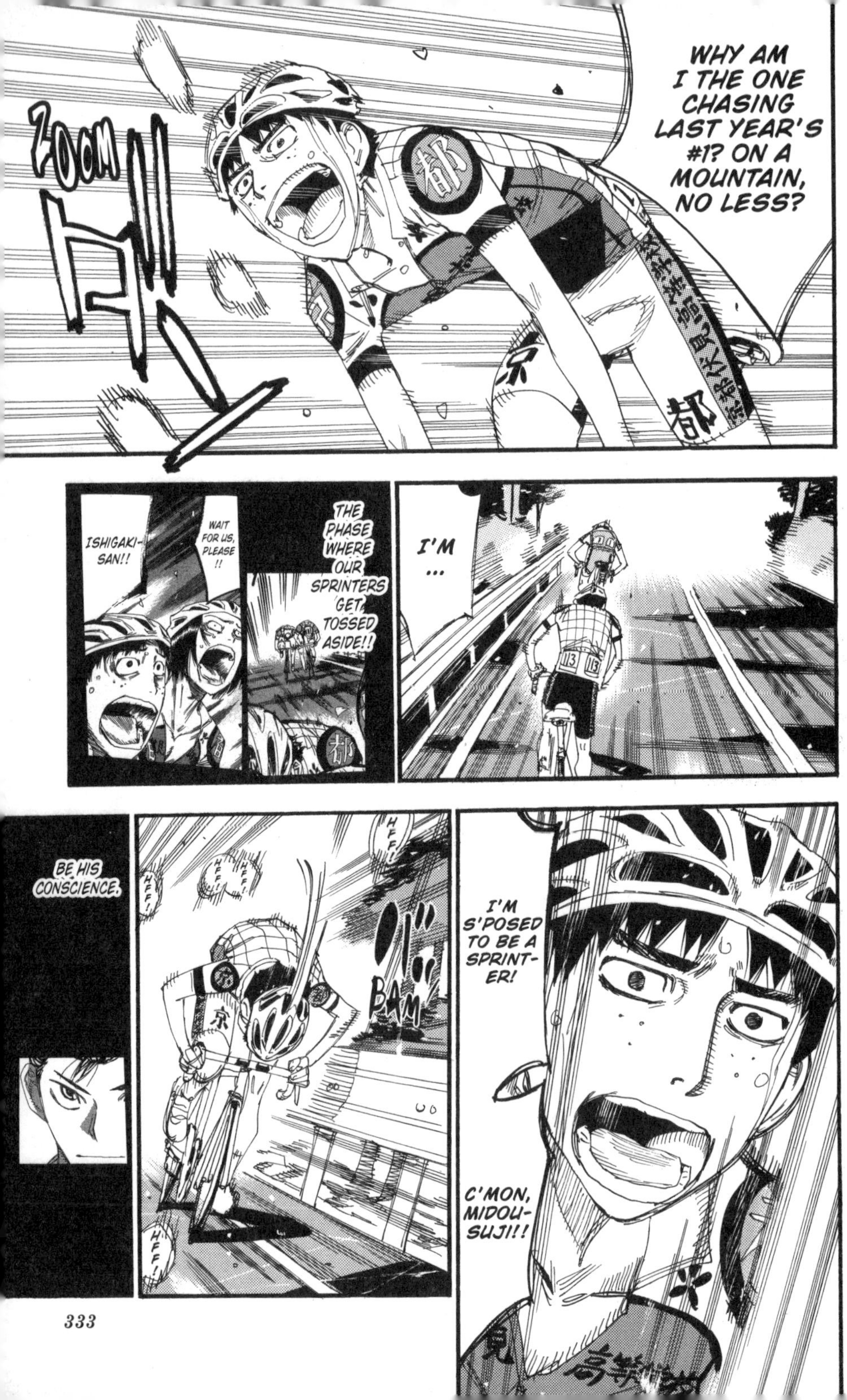
ZOOM
WHY AM I THE ONE CHASING LAST YEAR'S #1? ON A MOUNTAIN, NO LESS?
I'M ...
THE PHASE WHERE OUR SPRINTERS GET TOSSED ASIDE!!
WAIT FOR US, PLEASE!!
ISHIGAKI-SAN!!
I'M S'POSED TO BE A SPRINTER!
C'MON, MIDOUSUJI!!
HFF!
BAM
HFF!
HFF!
HFF!
BE HIS CONSCIENCE.

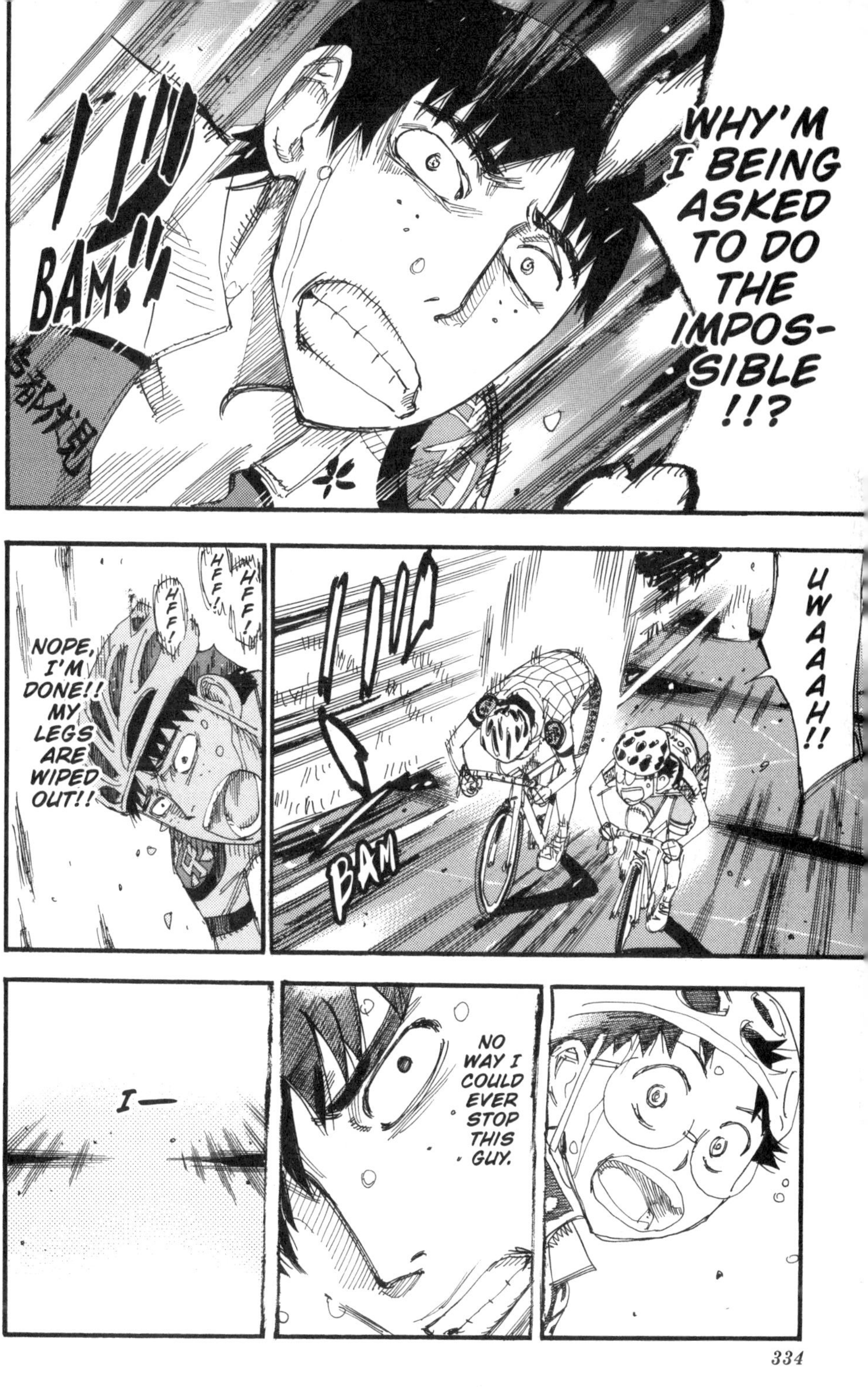
BAM!!
WHY'M I BEING ASKED TO DO THE IMPOSSIBLE!!?
UWAAAAH!!
BAM
HFF! HFF! HFF!
NOPE, I'M DONE!! MY LEGS ARE WIPED OUT!!
NO WAY I COULD EVER STOP THIS GUY.
I—

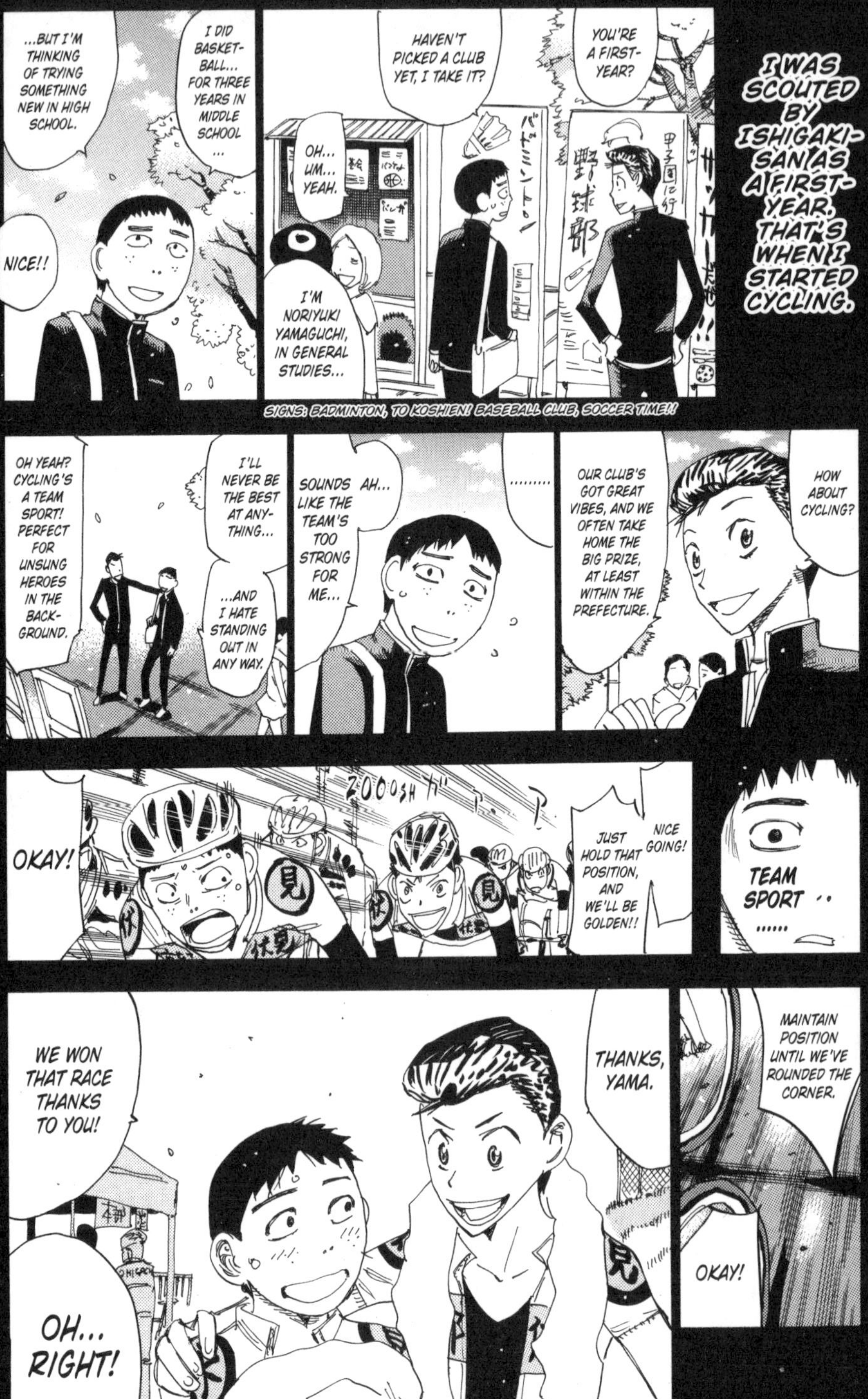
I WAS SCOUTED BY ISHIGAKI-SAN AS A FIRST-YEAR. THAT'S WHEN I STARTED CYCLING.
YOU'RE A FIRST-YEAR?
HAVEN'T PICKED A CLUB YET, I TAKE IT?
OH... UM... YEAH.
I'M NORIYUKI YAMAGUCHI, IN GENERAL STUDIES...
I DID BASKETBALL... FOR THREE YEARS IN MIDDLE SCHOOL...
...BUT I'M THINKING OF TRYING SOMETHING NEW IN HIGH SCHOOL.
NICE!!
SIGNS: BADMINTON, TO KOSHIEN! BASEBALL CLUB, SOCCER TIME!!
HOW ABOUT CYCLING?
OUR CLUB'S GOT GREAT VIBES, AND WE OFTEN TAKE HOME THE BIG PRIZE, AT LEAST WITHIN THE PREFECTURE.
....
AH...
SOUNDS LIKE THE TEAM'S TOO STRONG FOR ME...
I'LL NEVER BE THE BEST AT ANYTHING...
...AND I HATE STANDING OUT IN ANY WAY.
OH YEAH? CYCLING'S A TEAM SPORT! PERFECT FOR UNSUNG HEROES IN THE BACKGROUND.
TEAM SPORT ......
NICE GOING!
JUST HOLD THAT POSITION, AND WE'LL BE GOLDEN!!
ZOOOSH
OKAY!
MAINTAIN POSITION UNTIL WE'VE ROUNDED THE CORNER.
OKAY!
THANKS, YAMA.
WE WON THAT RACE THANKS TO YOU!
OH... RIGHT!

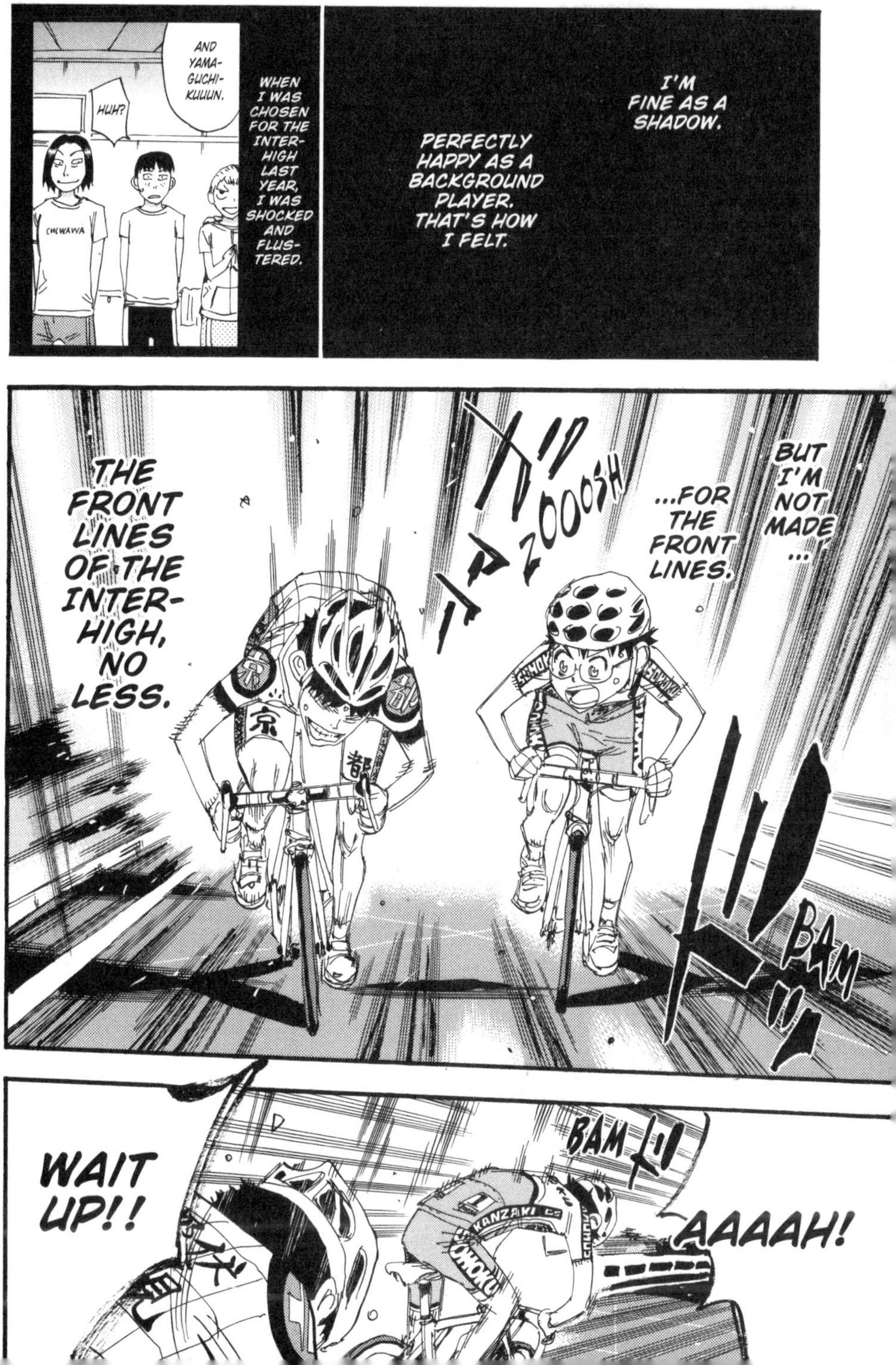
I'M FINE AS A SHADOW.
PERFECTLY HAPPY AS A BACKGROUND PLAYER. THAT'S HOW I FELT.
WHEN I WAS CHOSEN FOR THE INTER-HIGH LAST YEAR, I WAS SHOCKED AND FLUSTERED.
AND YAMA-GUCHI-KUUUN.
HUH?
CHIWAWA
BUT I'M NOT MADE...
...FOR THE FRONT LINES.
ZOOOSH
THE FRONT LINES OF THE INTER-HIGH, NO LESS.
BAM
BAM
AAAAH!
WAIT UP!!

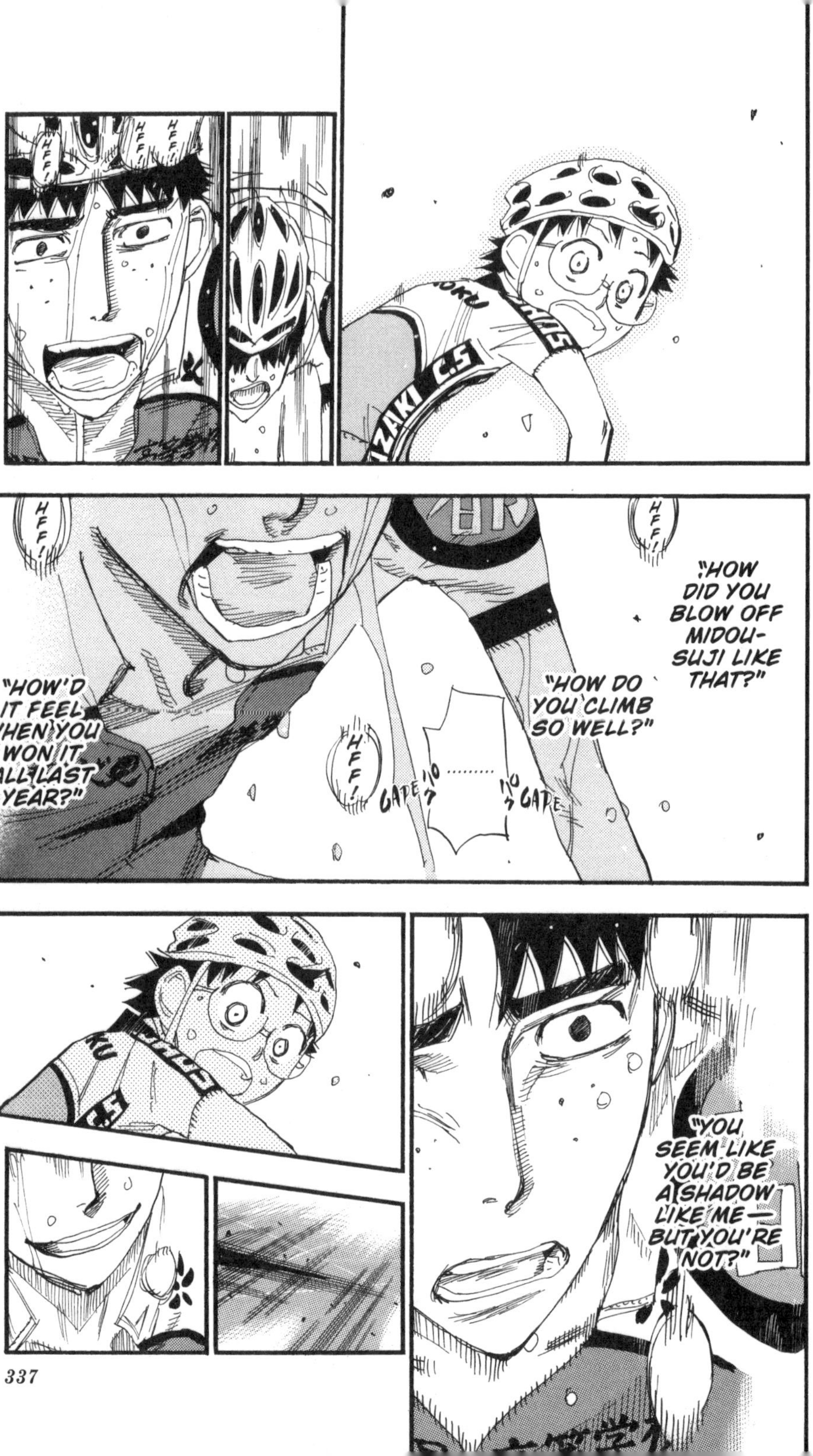
HFF!
HFF!
HFF!
HFF!
"HOW DID YOU BLOW OFF MIDOU-SUJI LIKE THAT?"
"HOW DO YOU CLIMB SO WELL?"
HFF!
GAPE
GAPE
"HOW'D IT FEEL WHEN YOU WON IT ALL LAST YEAR?"
HFF!
"YOU SEEM LIKE YOU'D BE A SHADOW LIKE ME—BUT YOU'RE NOT?"

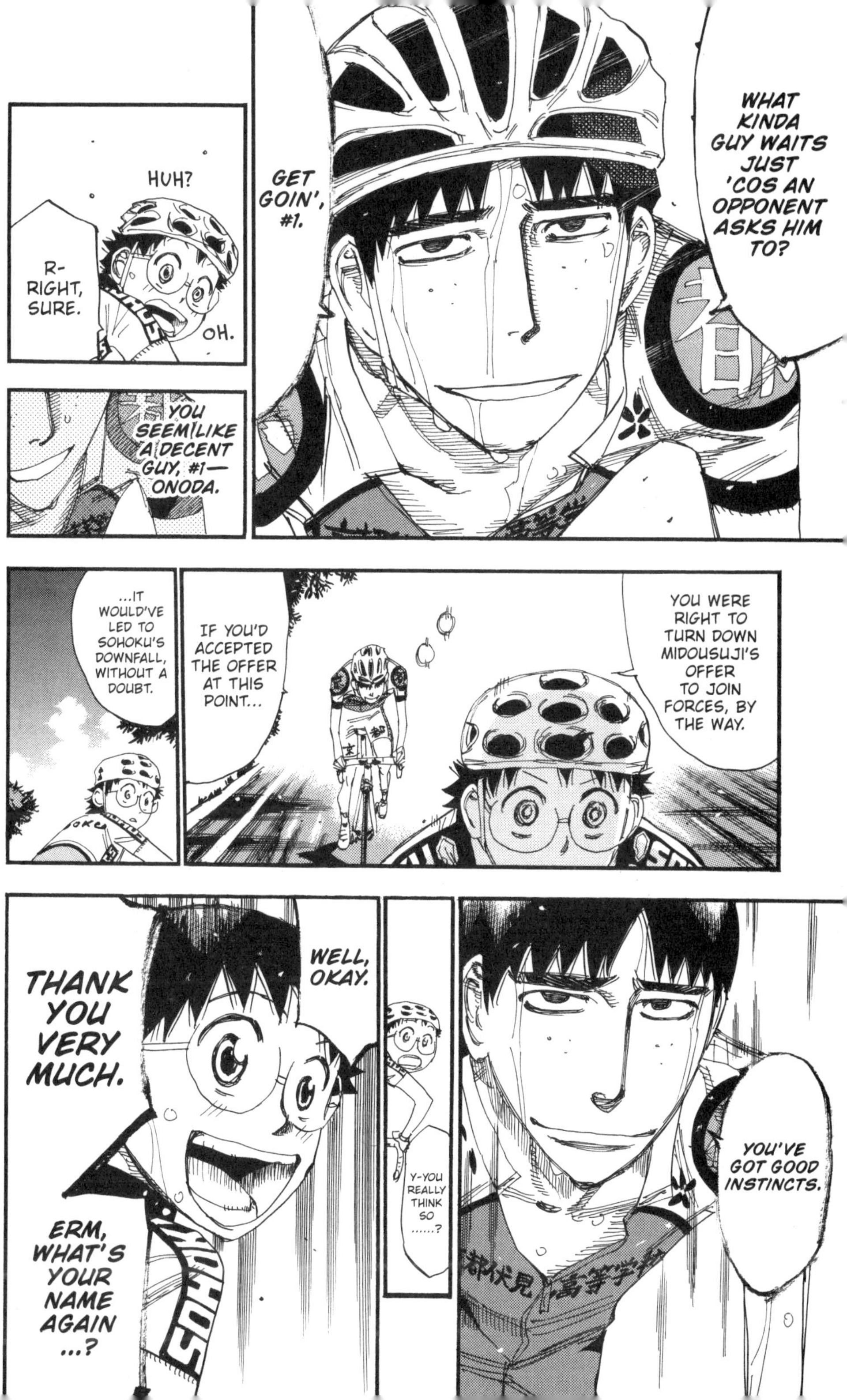
WHAT KINDA GUY WAITS JUST 'COS AN OPPONENT ASKS HIM TO?
GET GOIN', #1.
HUH?
R-RIGHT, SURE.
OH.
YOU SEEM LIKE A DECENT GUY, #1—ONODA.
YOU WERE RIGHT TO TURN DOWN MIDOUSUJI'S OFFER TO JOIN FORCES, BY THE WAY.
IF YOU'D ACCEPTED THE OFFER AT THIS POINT...
...IT WOULD'VE LED TO SOHOKU'S DOWNFALL, WITHOUT A DOUBT.
YOU'VE GOT GOOD INSTINCTS.
Y-YOU REALLY THINK SO ......?
WELL, OKAY.
THANK YOU VERY MUCH.
ERM, WHAT'S YOUR NAME AGAIN ...?

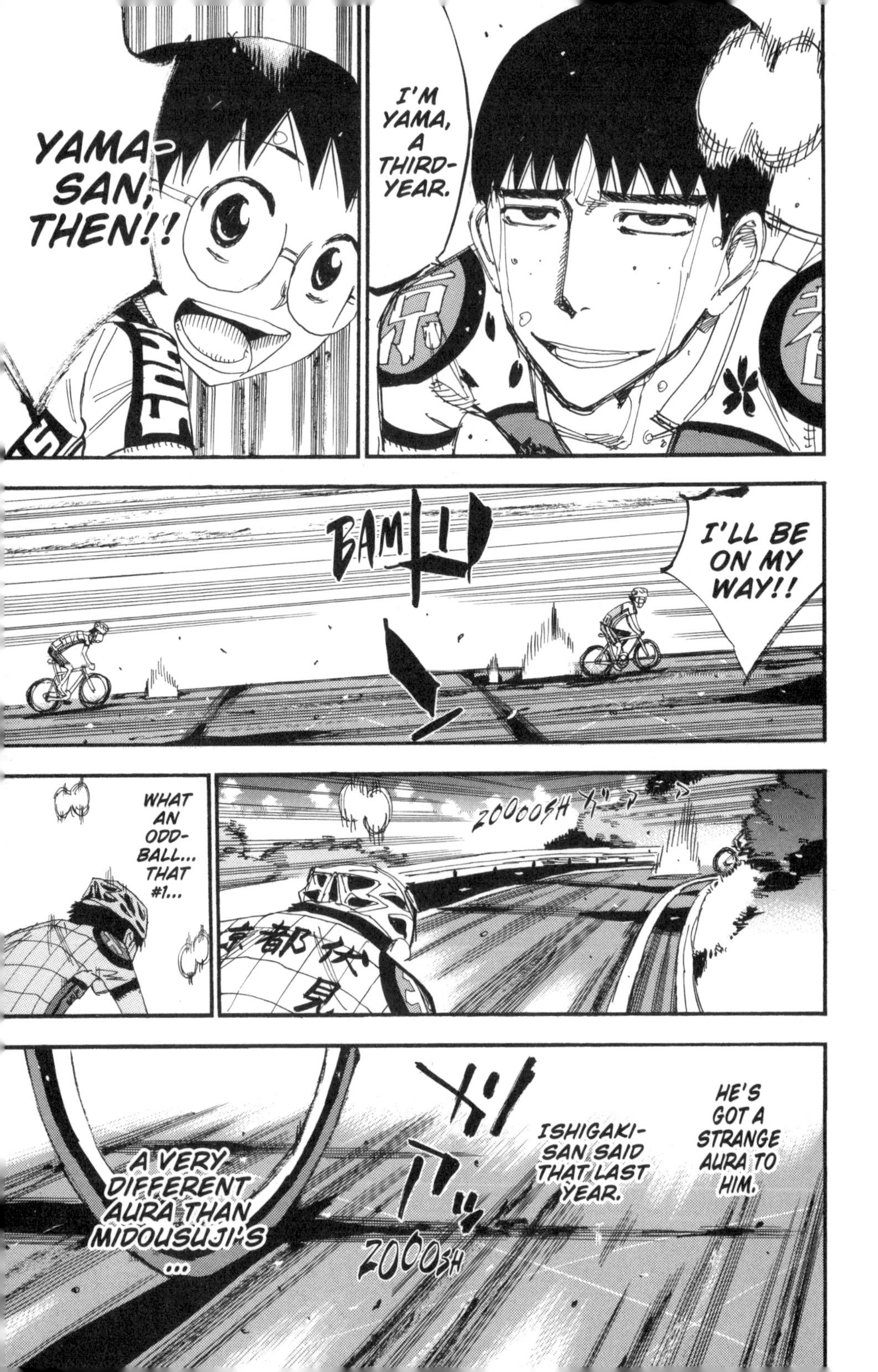
I'M YAMA, A THIRD-YEAR.
YAMA-SAN, THEN!!
I'LL BE ON MY WAY!!
BAM
ZOOOOSH
WHAT AN ODD-BALL... THAT #1...
HE'S GOT A STRANGE AURA TO HIM.
ISHIGAKI-SAN SAID THAT LAST YEAR.
ZOOOSH
A VERY DIFFERENT AURA THAN MIDOUSUJI'S ...

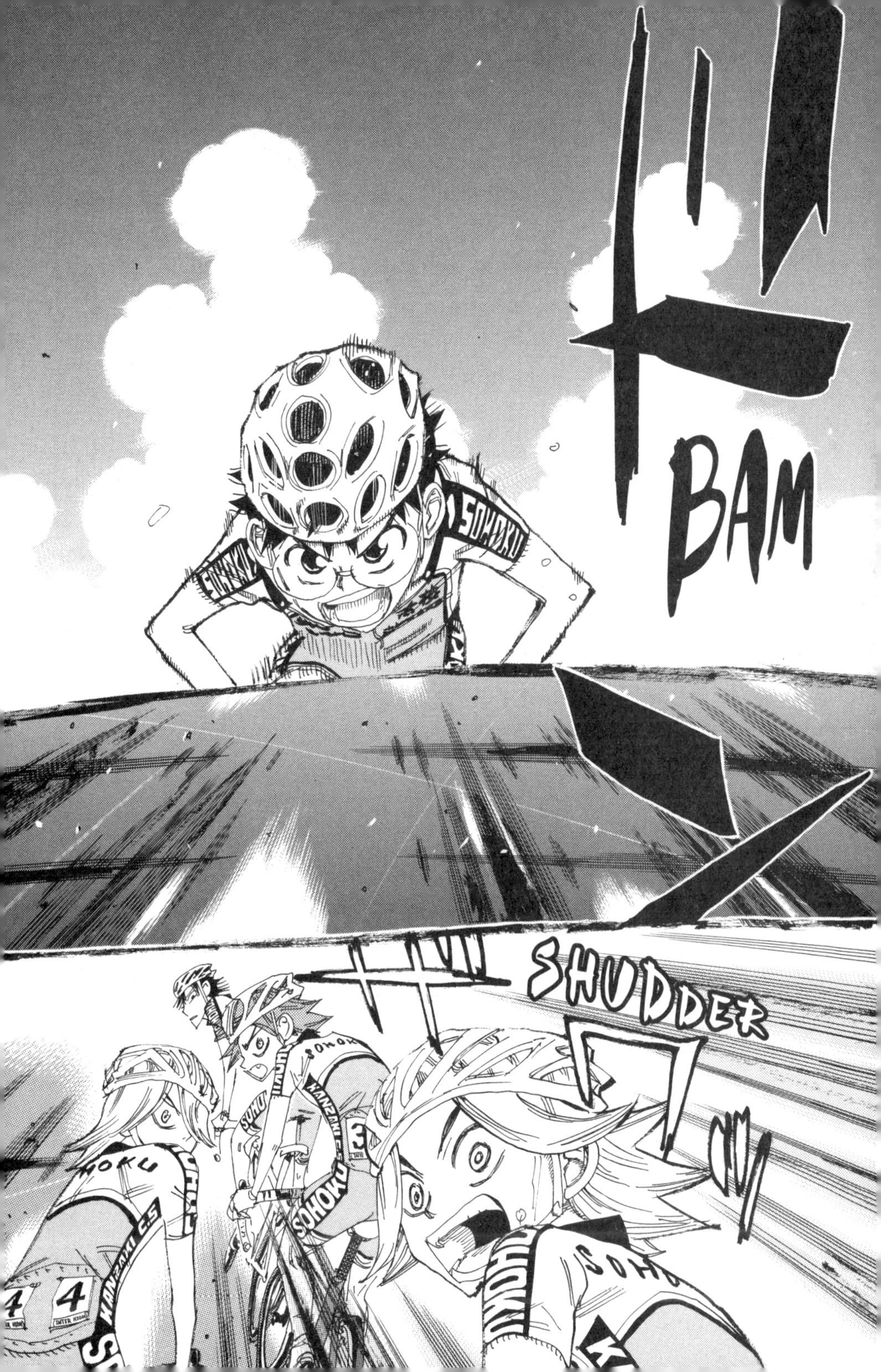
BAM
SHUDDER

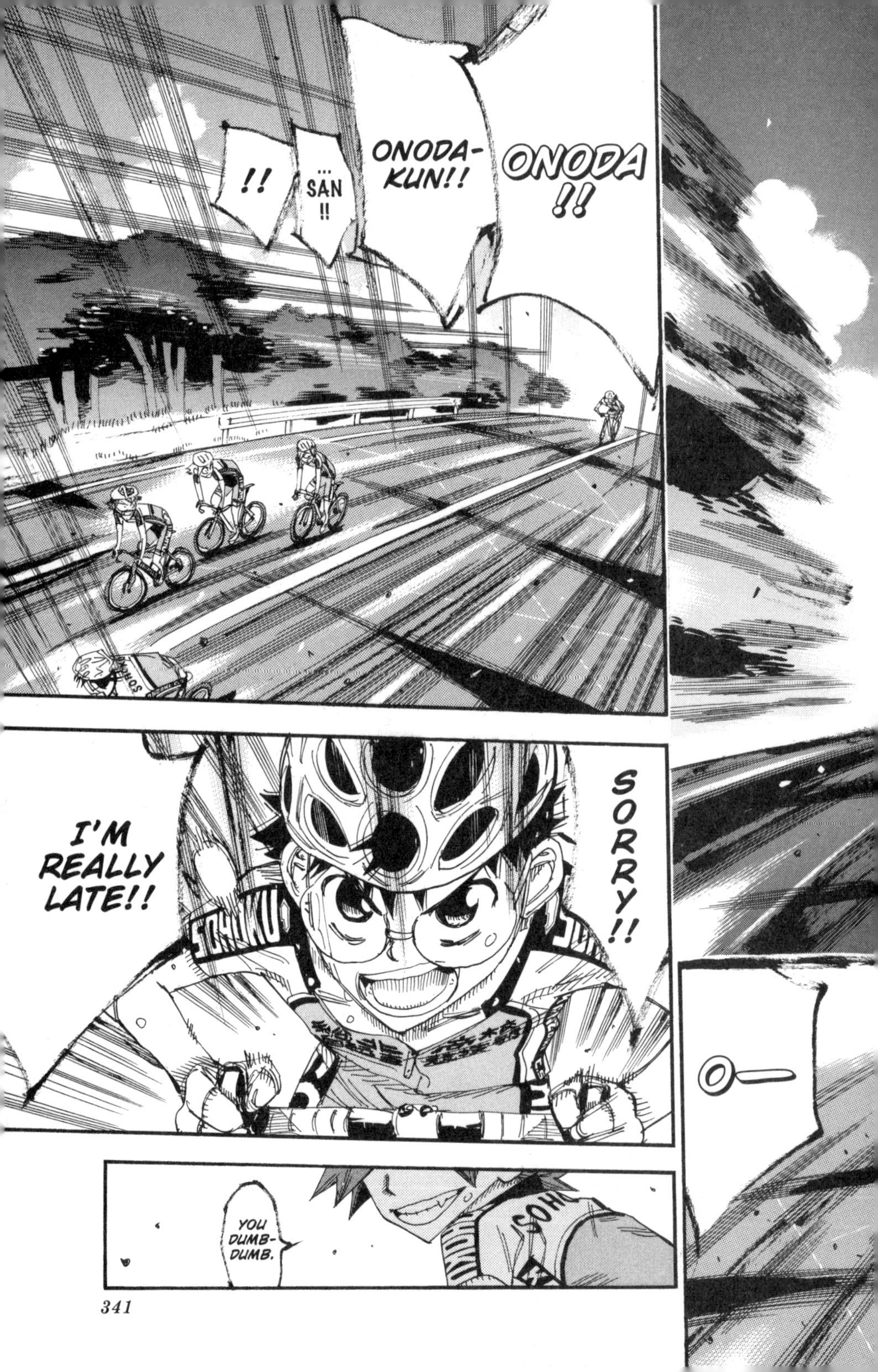
ONODA!!
ONODA-KUN!!
...SAN!!
!!
SORRY!!
I'M REALLY LATE!!
O—
YOU DUMB-DUMB.

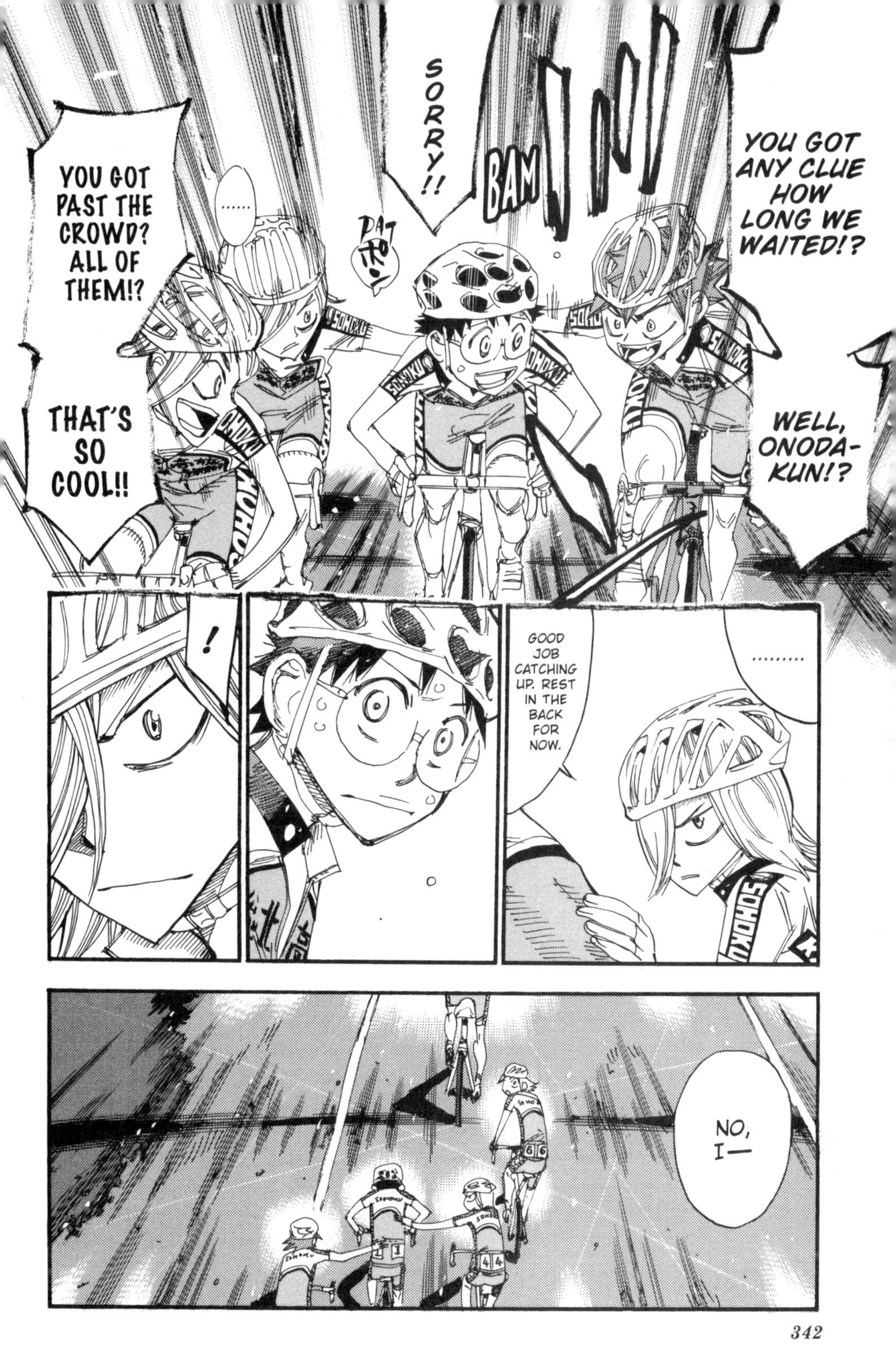
YOU GOT ANY CLUE HOW LONG WE WAITED!?
WELL, ONODA-KUN!?
BAM
SORRY!!
......
YOU GOT PAST THE CROWD? ALL OF THEM!?
THAT'S SO COOL!!
....
GOOD JOB CATCHING UP. REST IN THE BACK FOR NOW.
!
NO, I—

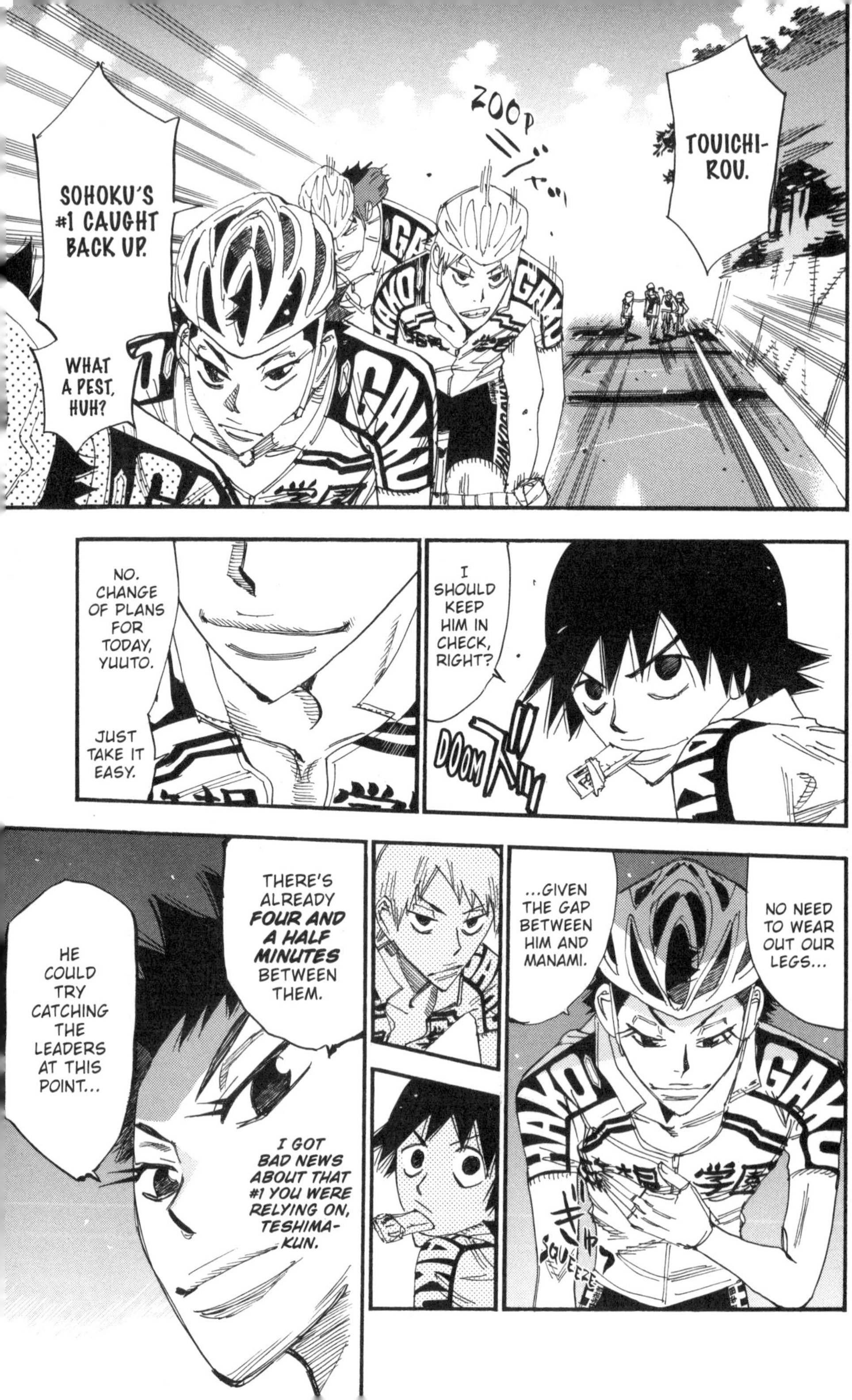
TOUICHI-ROU.
ZOOP
SOHOKU'S #1 CAUGHT BACK UP.
WHAT A PEST, HUH?
I SHOULD KEEP HIM IN CHECK, RIGHT?
DOOM
NO. CHANGE OF PLANS FOR TODAY, YUUTO.
JUST TAKE IT EASY.
NO NEED TO WEAR OUT OUR LEGS...
...GIVEN THE GAP BETWEEN HIM AND MANAMI.
SQUEEZE
HE COULD TRY CATCHING THE LEADERS AT THIS POINT...
THERE'S ALREADY FOUR AND A HALF MINUTES BETWEEN THEM.
I GOT BAD NEWS ABOUT THAT #1 YOU WERE RELYING ON, TESHIMA-KUN.

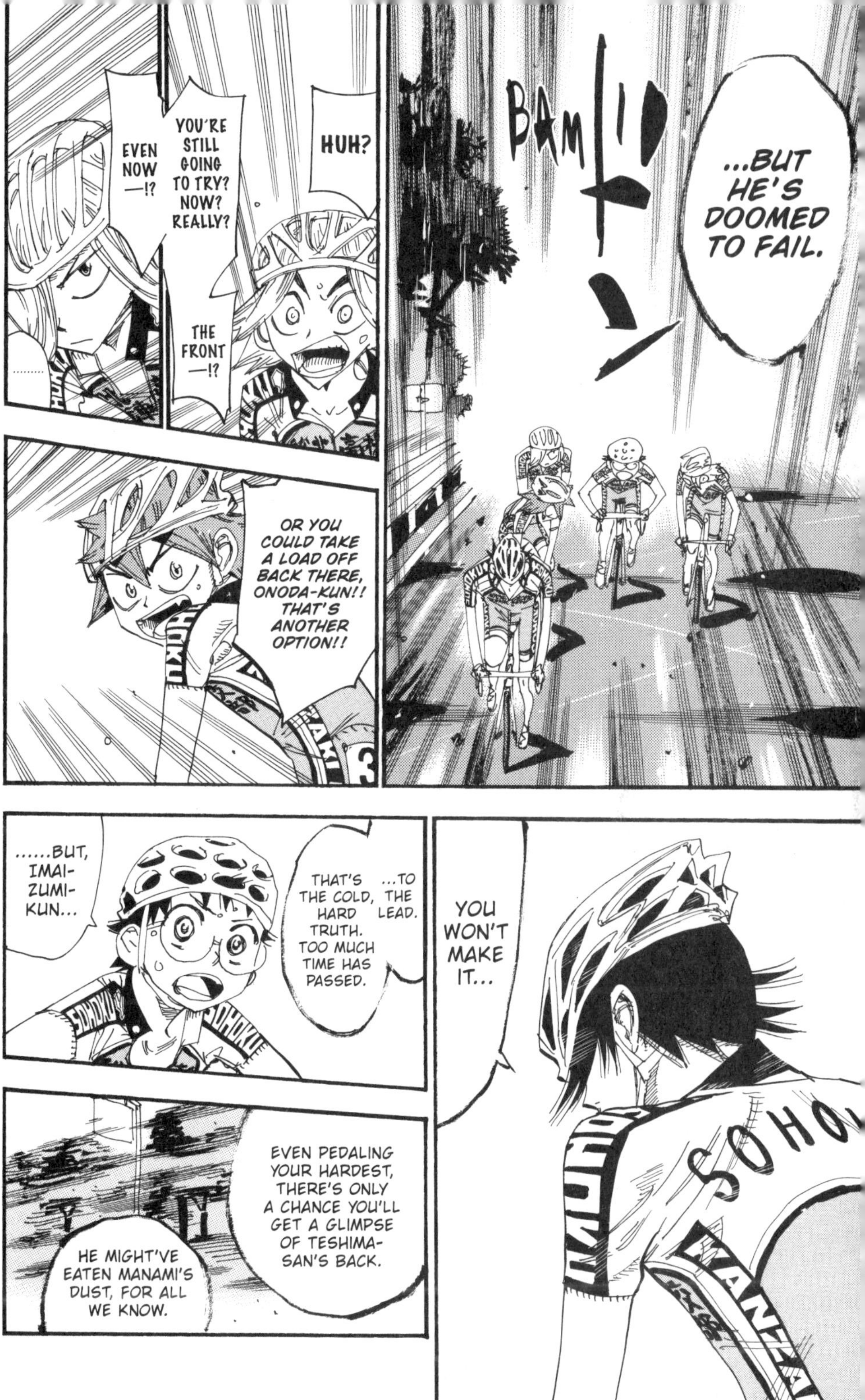
BAM
...BUT HE'S DOOMED TO FAIL.
HUH?
YOU'RE STILL GOING TO TRY? NOW? REALLY?
THE FRONT—!?
EVEN NOW—!?
....
OR YOU COULD TAKE A LOAD OFF BACK THERE, ONODA-KUN!! THAT'S ANOTHER OPTION!!
YOU WON'T MAKE IT...
...TO THE LEAD.
THAT'S THE COLD, HARD TRUTH. TOO MUCH TIME HAS PASSED.
......BUT, IMAIZUMI-KUN...
EVEN PEDALING YOUR HARDEST, THERE'S ONLY A CHANCE YOU'LL GET A GLIMPSE OF TESHIMA-SAN'S BACK.
HE MIGHT'VE EATEN MANAMI'S DUST, FOR ALL WE KNOW.

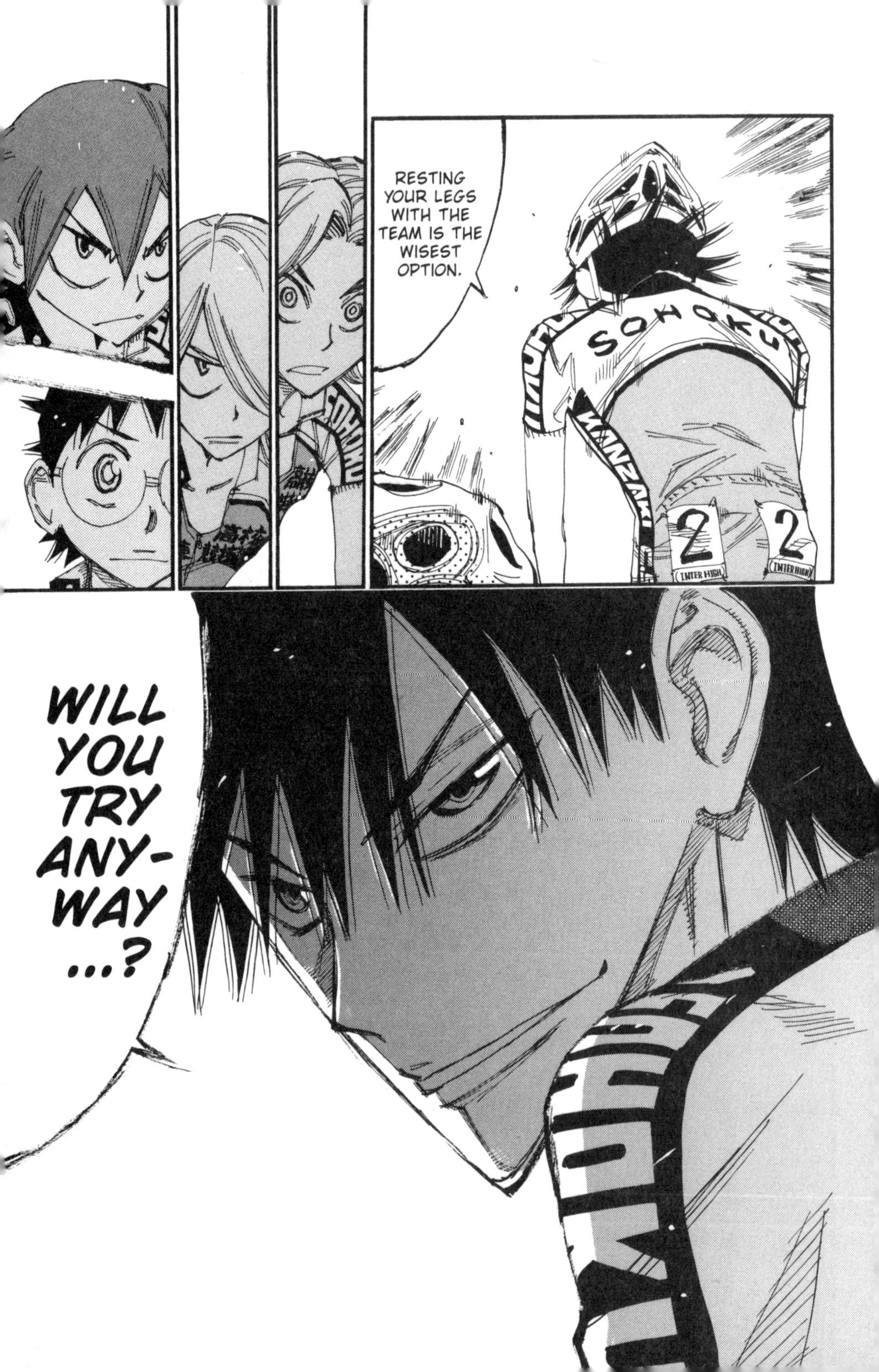
RESTING YOUR LEGS WITH THE TEAM IS THE WISEST OPTION.
SOHOKU
KANZAKI
2
INTER HIGH
2
INTER HIGH
WILL YOU TRY ANYWAY ...?

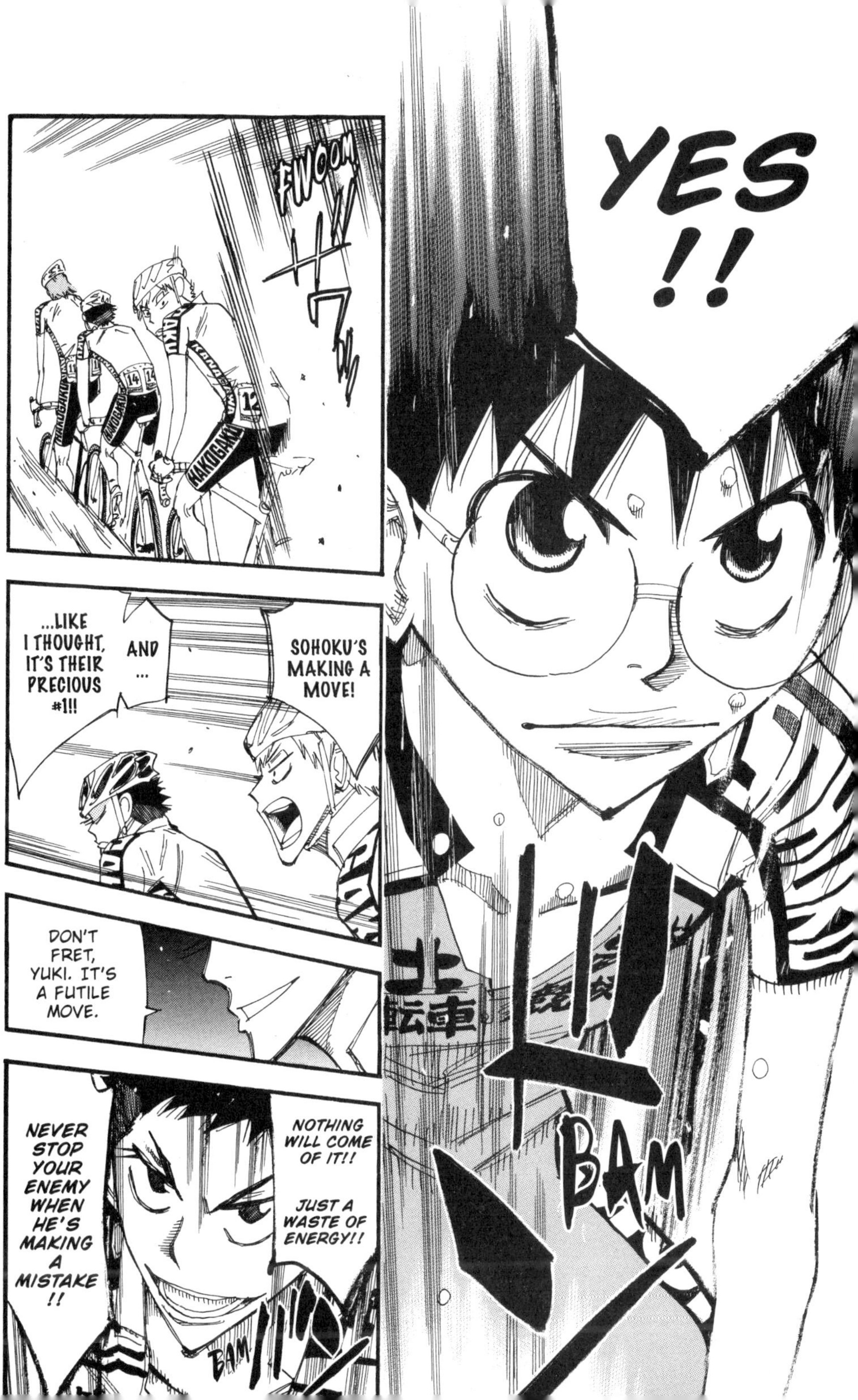
YES!!
BAM
FWOOM
SOHOKU'S MAKING A MOVE!
AND ...
...LIKE I THOUGHT, IT'S THEIR PRECIOUS #1!!
DON'T FRET, YUKI. IT'S A FUTILE MOVE.
NOTHING WILL COME OF IT!!
JUST A WASTE OF ENERGY!!
NEVER STOP YOUR ENEMY WHEN HE'S MAKING A MISTAKE!!
BAM

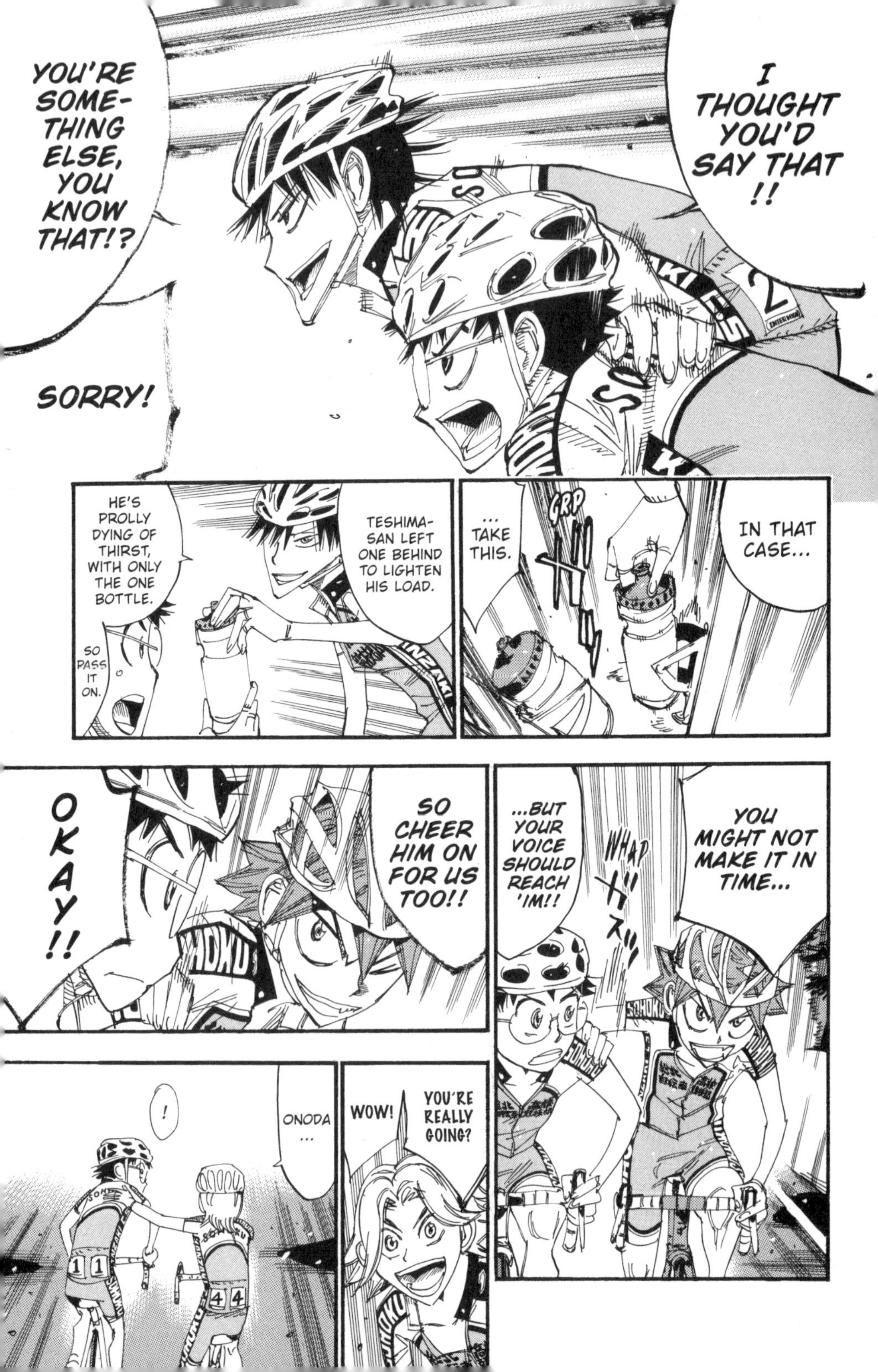
I THOUGHT YOU'D SAY THAT!!
YOU'RE SOMETHING ELSE, YOU KNOW THAT!?
SORRY!
IN THAT CASE...
GRP
...TAKE THIS.
TESHIMA-SAN LEFT ONE BEHIND TO LIGHTEN HIS LOAD.
HE'S PROLLY DYING OF THIRST, WITH ONLY THE ONE BOTTLE.
SO PASS IT ON.
YOU MIGHT NOT MAKE IT IN TIME...
WHAP
...BUT YOUR VOICE SHOULD REACH 'IM!!
SO CHEER HIM ON FOR US TOO!!
OKAY!!
YOU'RE REALLY GOING?
WOW!
ONODA...
!

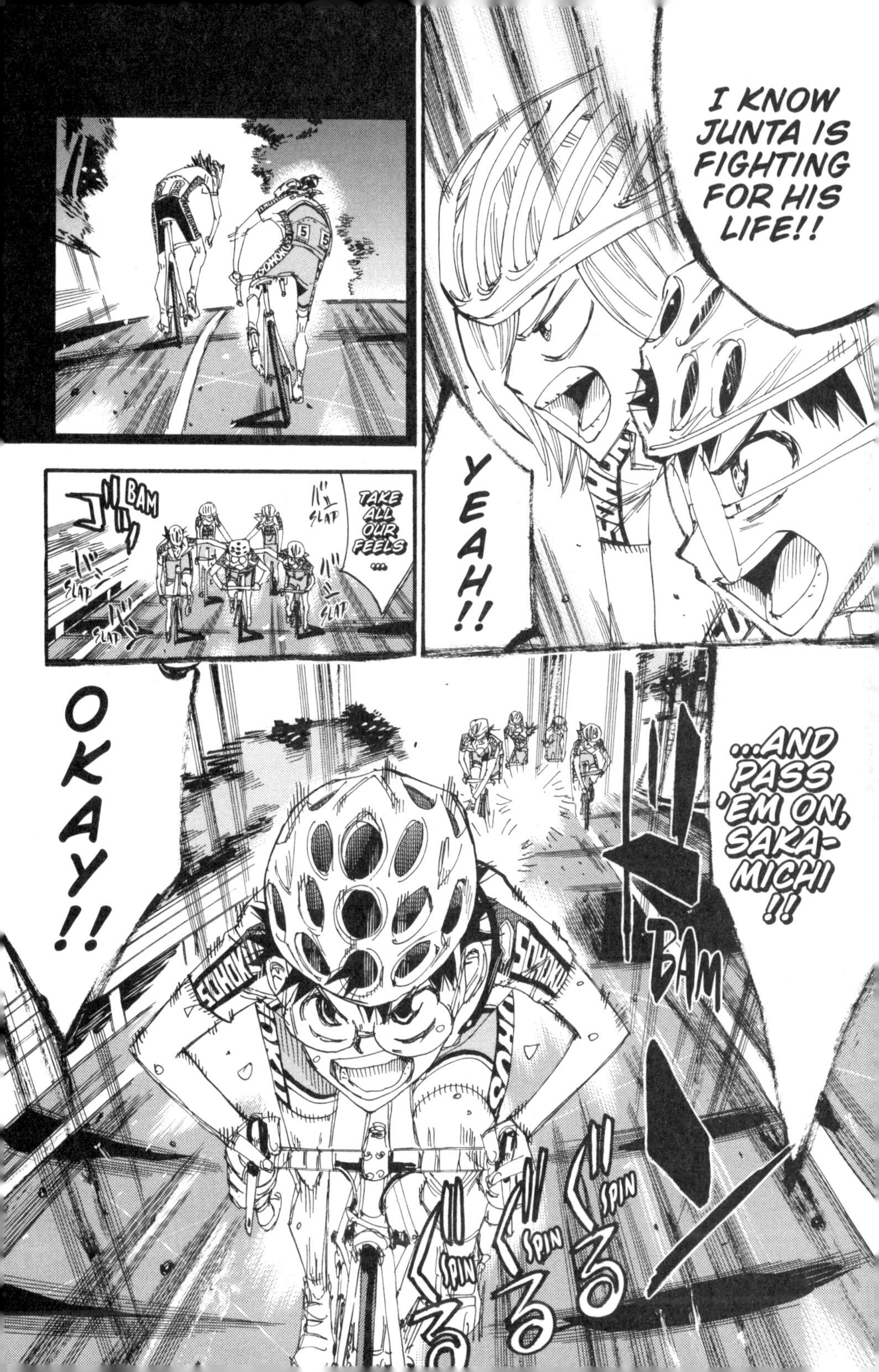
I KNOW JUNTA IS FIGHTING FOR HIS LIFE!!
YEAH!!
BAM
SLAP
SLAP
SLAP
SLAP
TAKE ALL OUR FEELS...
...AND PASS 'EM ON, SAKAMICHI!!
OKAY!!
BAM
SPIN
SPIN
SPIN

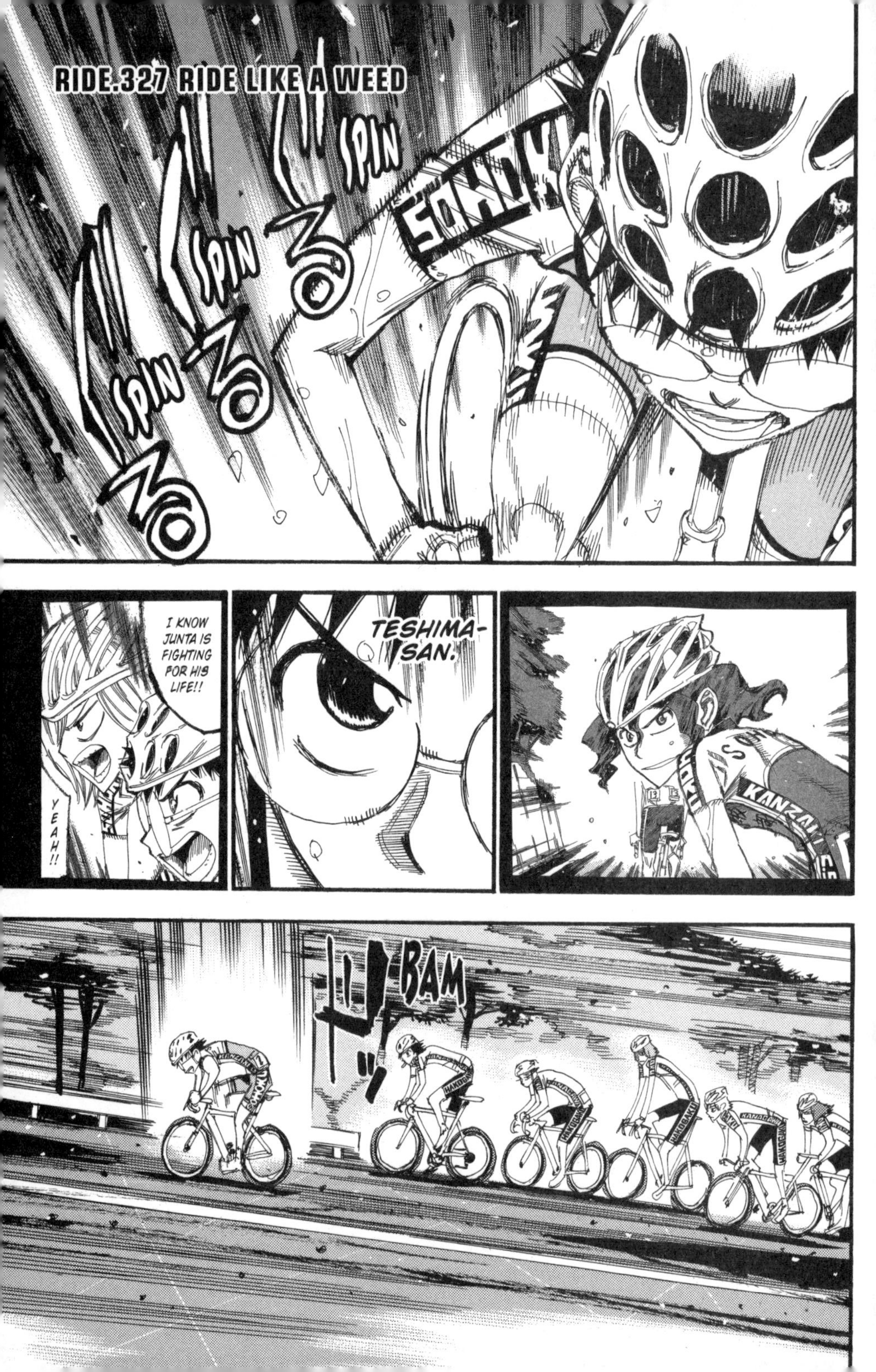
RIDE.327 RIDE LIKE A WEED
SPIN
SPIN
SPIN
TESHIMA-SAN.
I KNOW JUNTA IS FIGHTING FOR HIS LIFE!!
YEAH!!
BAM

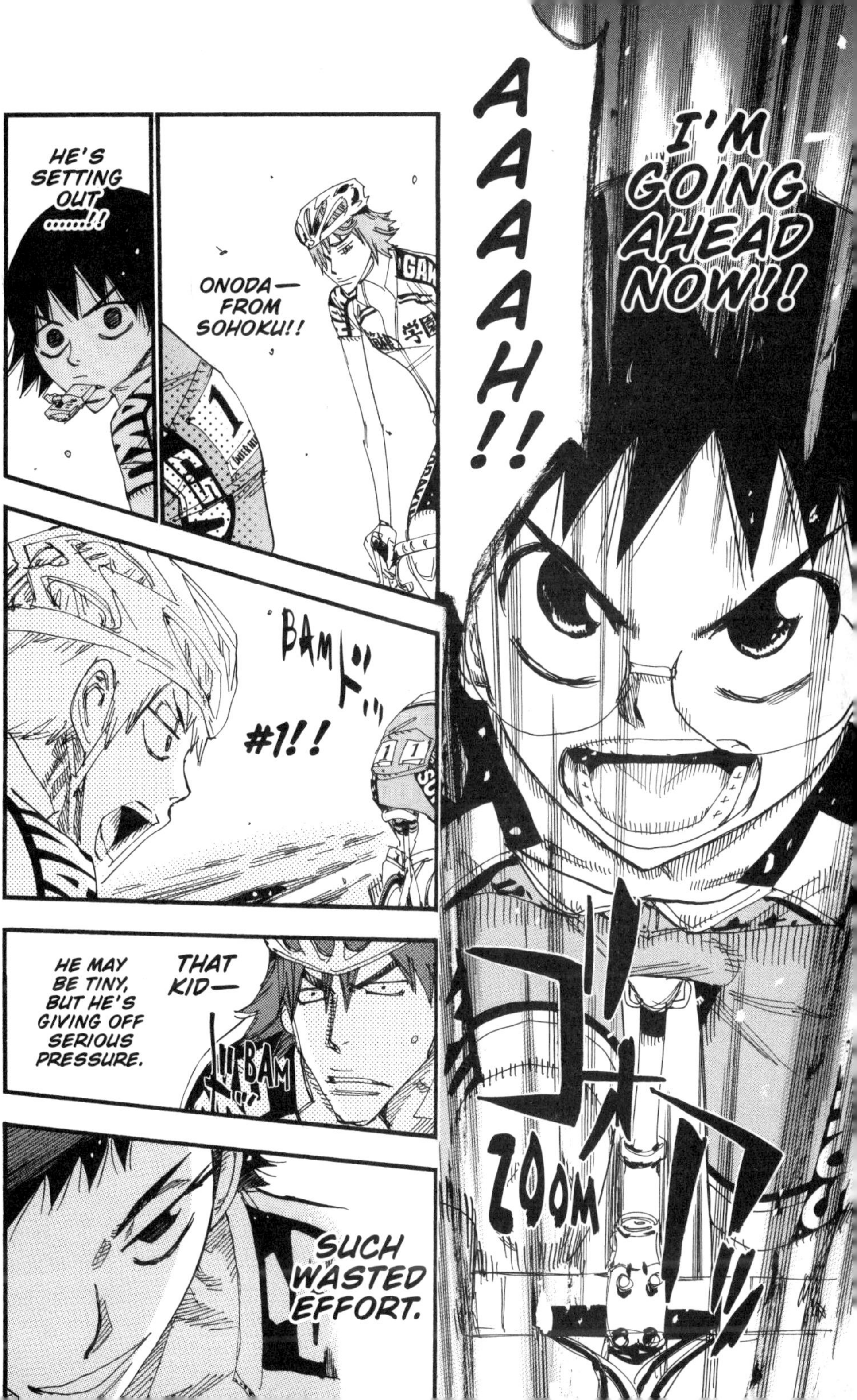
I'M GOING AHEAD NOW!!
AAAAAH!!
ZOOM
ONODA— FROM SOHOKU!!
HE'S SETTING OUT......!!
BAM
#1!!
THAT KID—
HE MAY BE TINY, BUT HE'S GIVING OFF SERIOUS PRESSURE.
BAM
SUCH WASTED EFFORT.

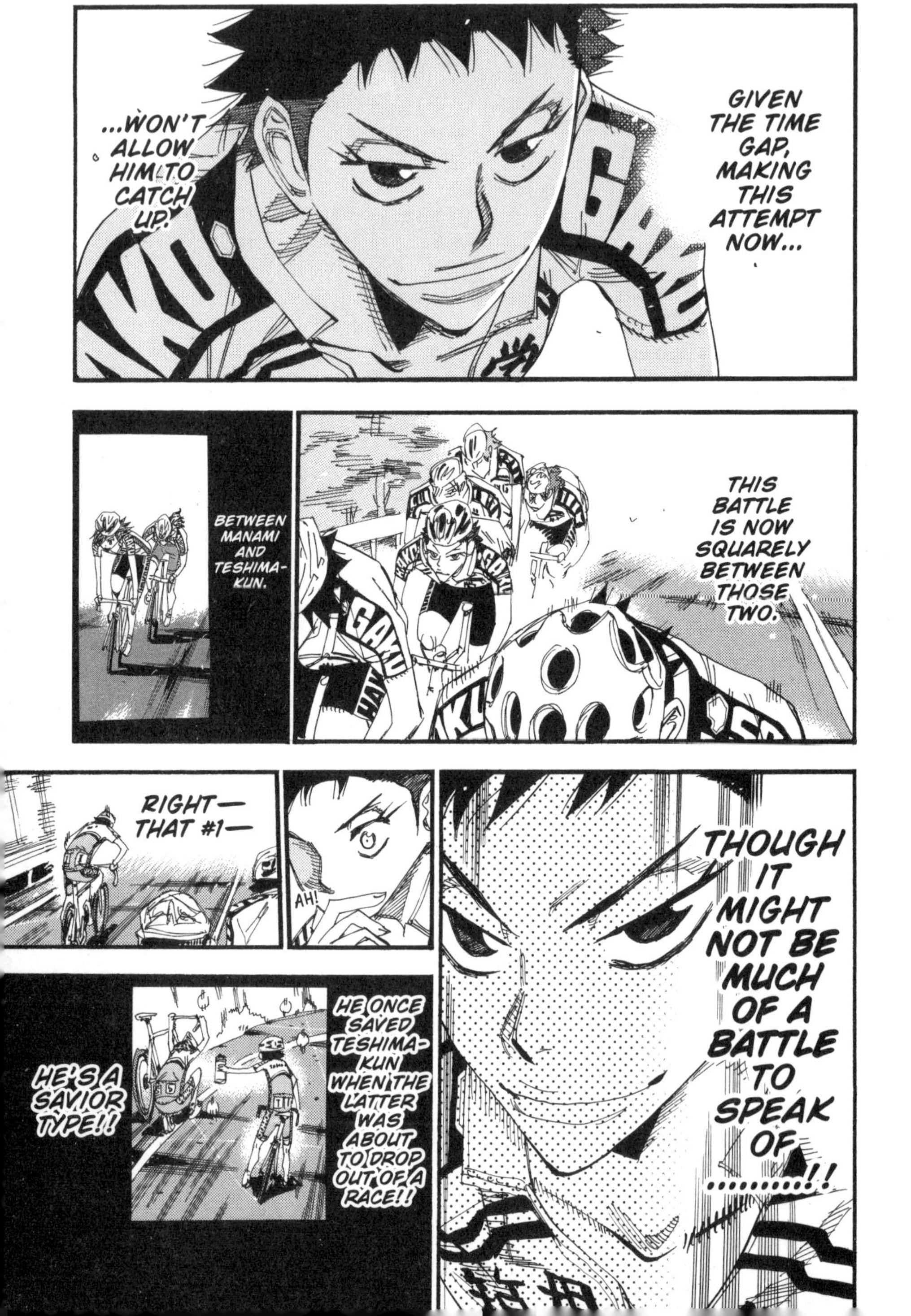
GIVEN THE TIME GAP, MAKING THIS ATTEMPT NOW...
...WON'T ALLOW HIM TO CATCH UP.
THIS BATTLE IS NOW SQUARELY BETWEEN THOSE TWO.
BETWEEN MANAMI AND TESHIMA-KUN.
THOUGH IT MIGHT NOT BE MUCH OF A BATTLE TO SPEAK OF..........!!
AH!
RIGHT— THAT #1—
HE ONCE SAVED TESHIMA-KUN WHEN THE LATTER WAS ABOUT TO DROP OUT OF A RACE!!
HE'S A SAVIOR TYPE!!

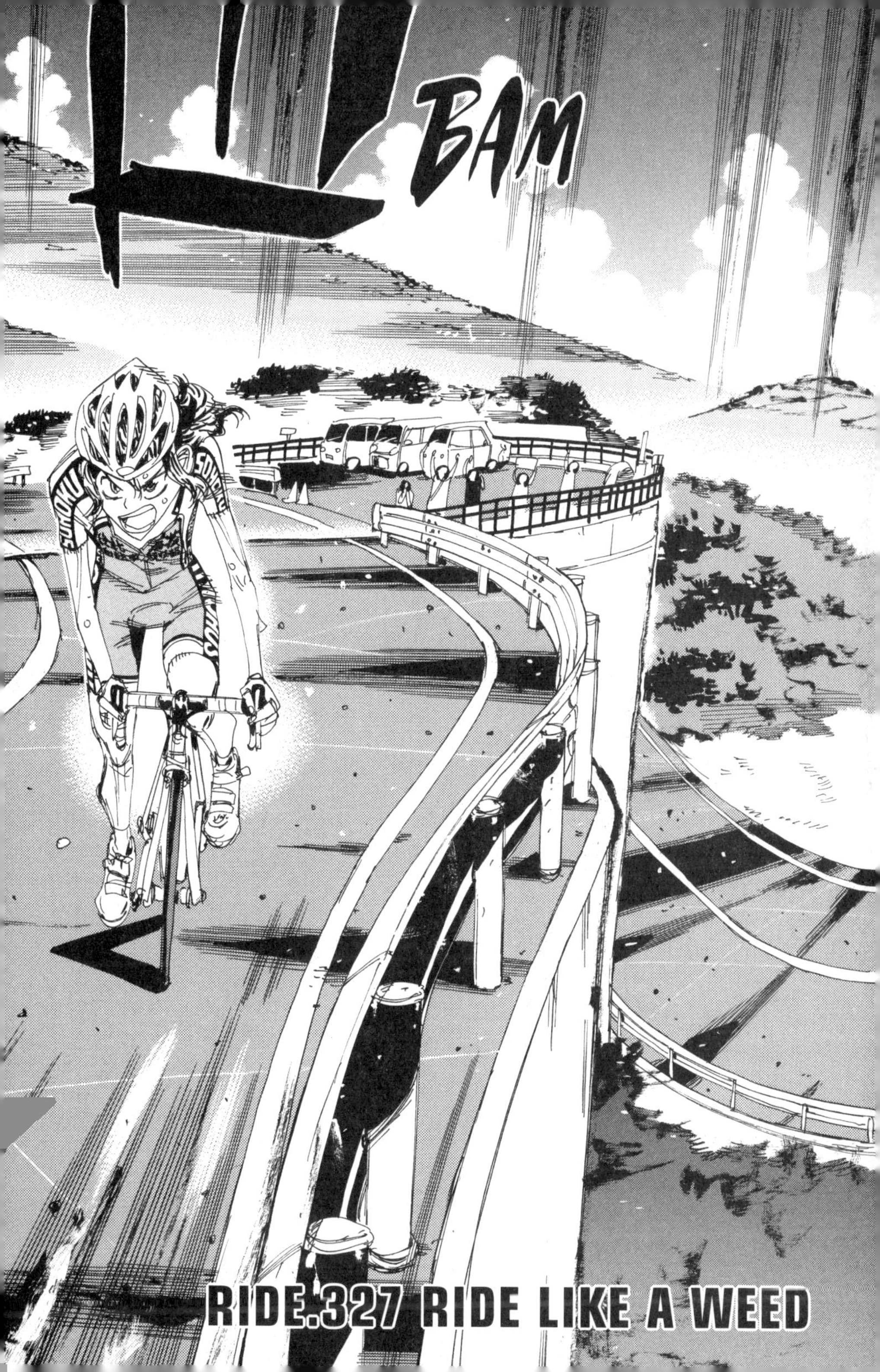
BAM
RIDE.327 RIDE LIKE A WEED

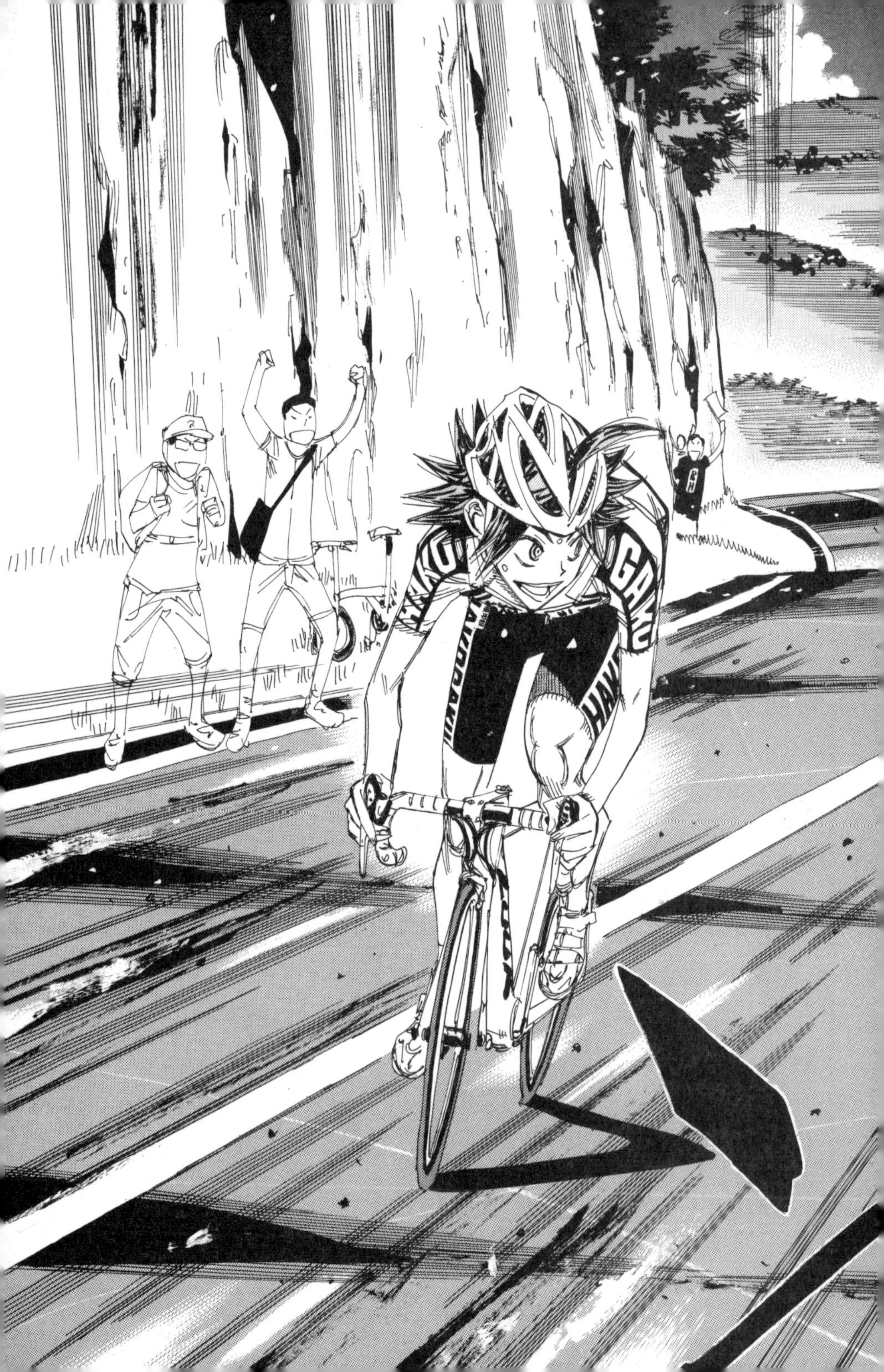

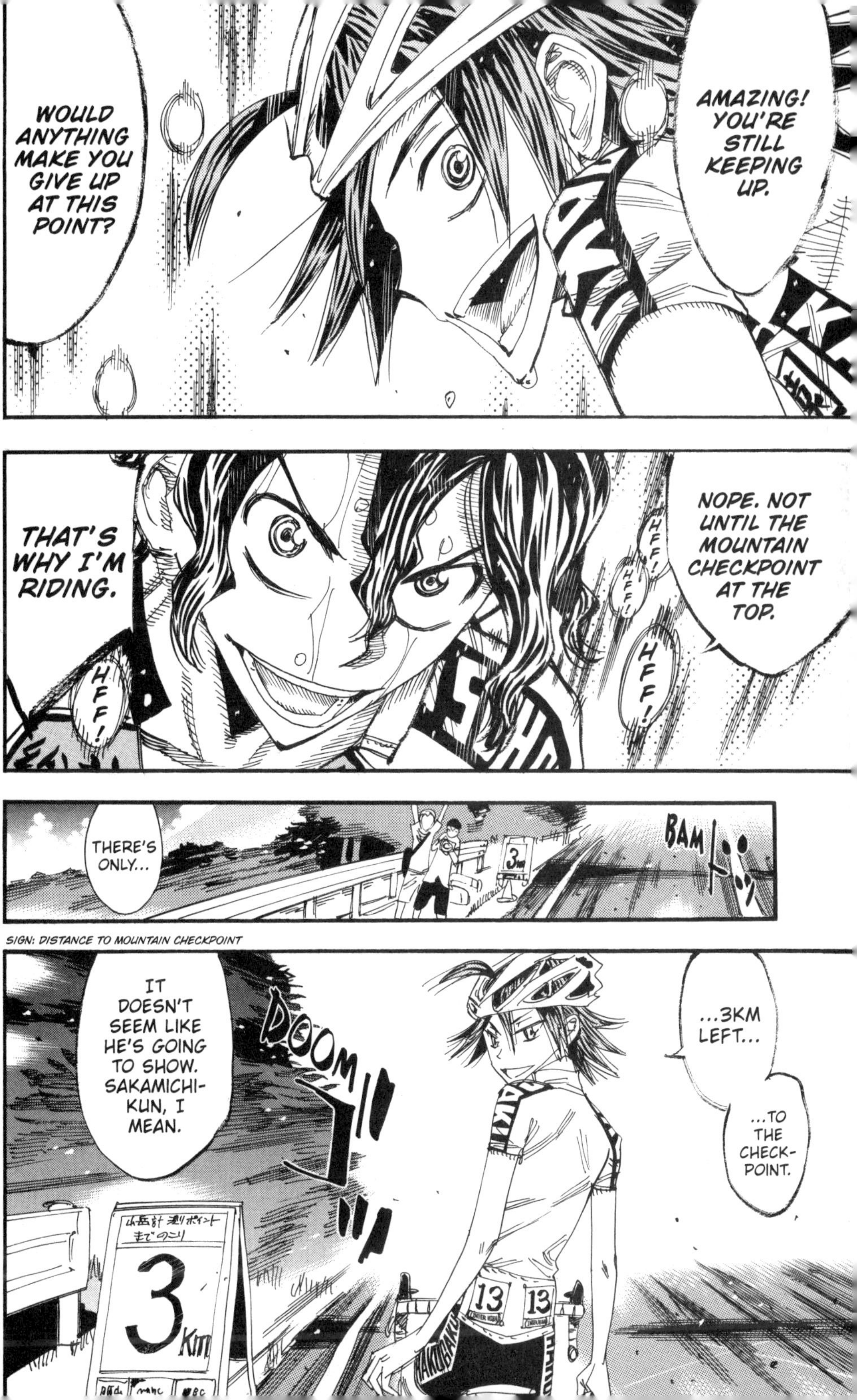
AMAZING! YOU'RE STILL KEEPING UP.
WOULD ANYTHING MAKE YOU GIVE UP AT THIS POINT?
NOPE. NOT UNTIL THE MOUNTAIN CHECKPOINT AT THE TOP.
HFF!
HFF!
HFF!
THAT'S WHY I'M RIDING.
HFF!
BAM
3 km
THERE'S ONLY...
SIGN: DISTANCE TO MOUNTAIN CHECKPOINT
...3KM LEFT...
...TO THE CHECK-POINT.
DOOM
IT DOESN'T SEEM LIKE HE'S GOING TO SHOW. SAKAMICHI-KUN, I MEAN.
3 Km
13
13

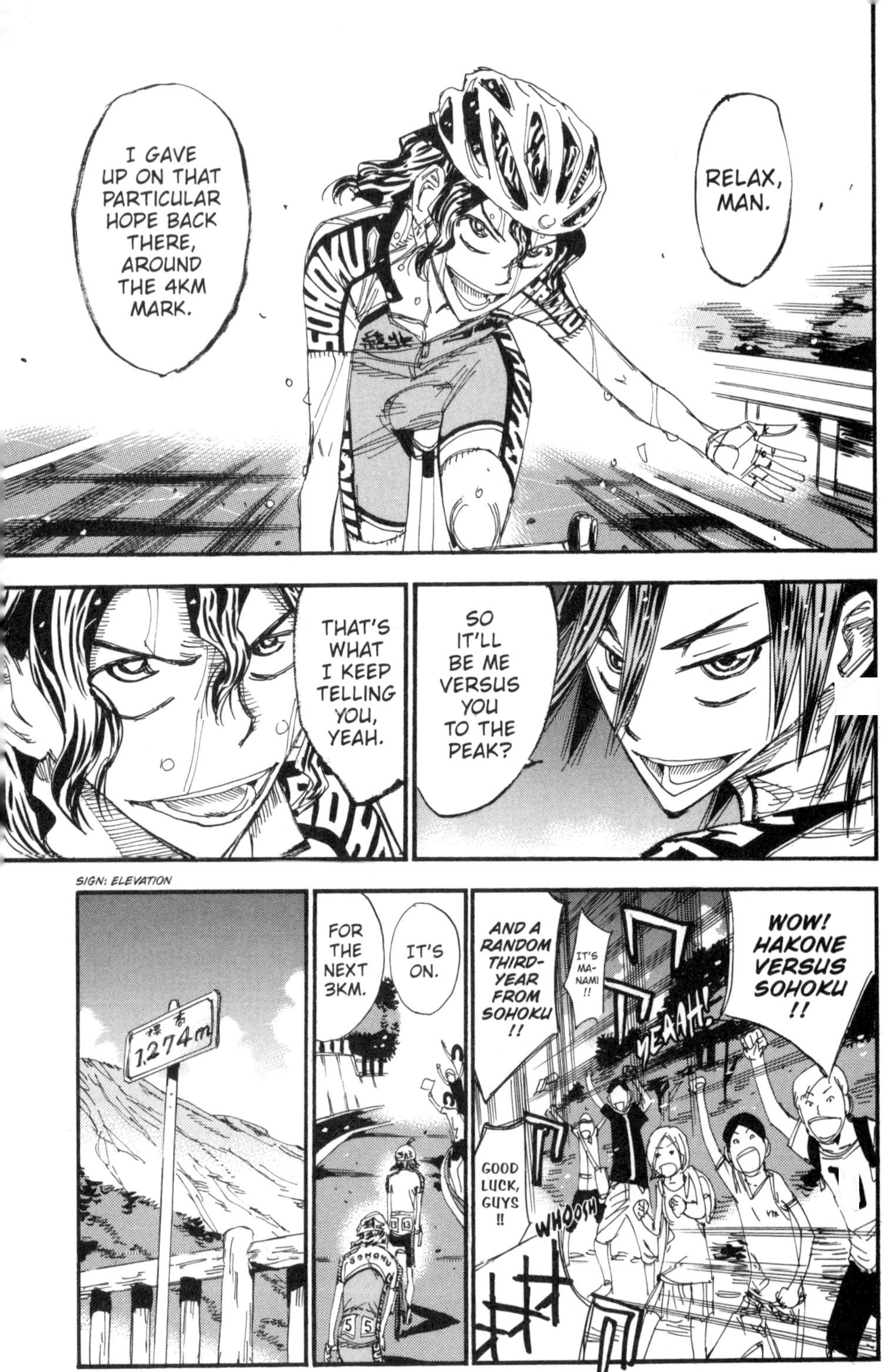
RELAX, MAN.
I GAVE UP ON THAT PARTICULAR HOPE BACK THERE, AROUND THE 4KM MARK.
SO IT'LL BE ME VERSUS YOU TO THE PEAK?
THAT'S WHAT I KEEP TELLING YOU, YEAH.
WOW! HAKONE VERSUS SOHOKU!!
AND A RANDOM THIRD-YEAR FROM SOHOKU!!
IT'S MA-NAMI!!
YEAAH!
GOOD LUCK, GUYS!!
WHOOSH
IT'S ON.
FOR THE NEXT 3KM.
SIGN: ELEVATION
標高 1,274m

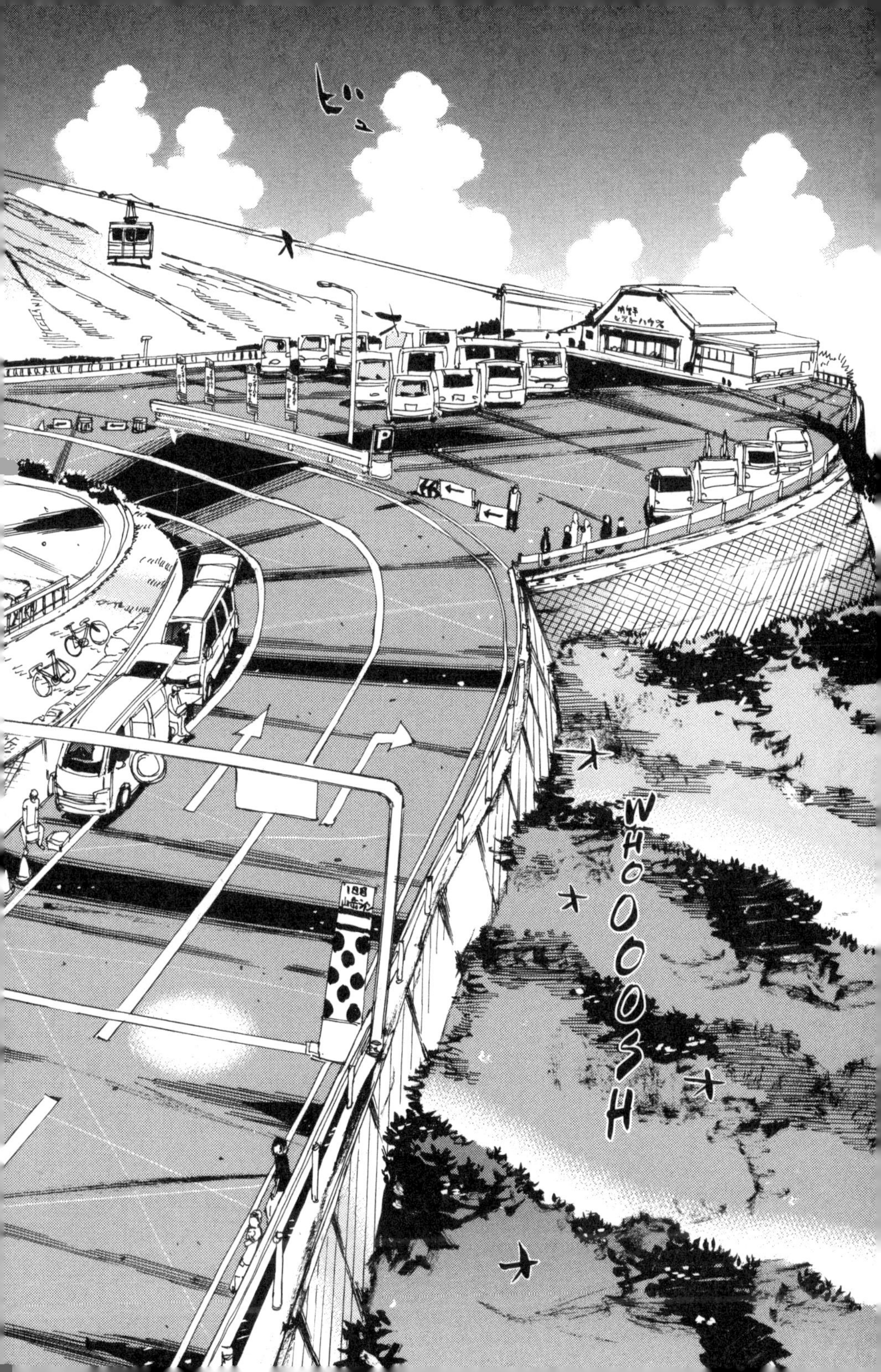
ビュ
WHOOOOSH
P

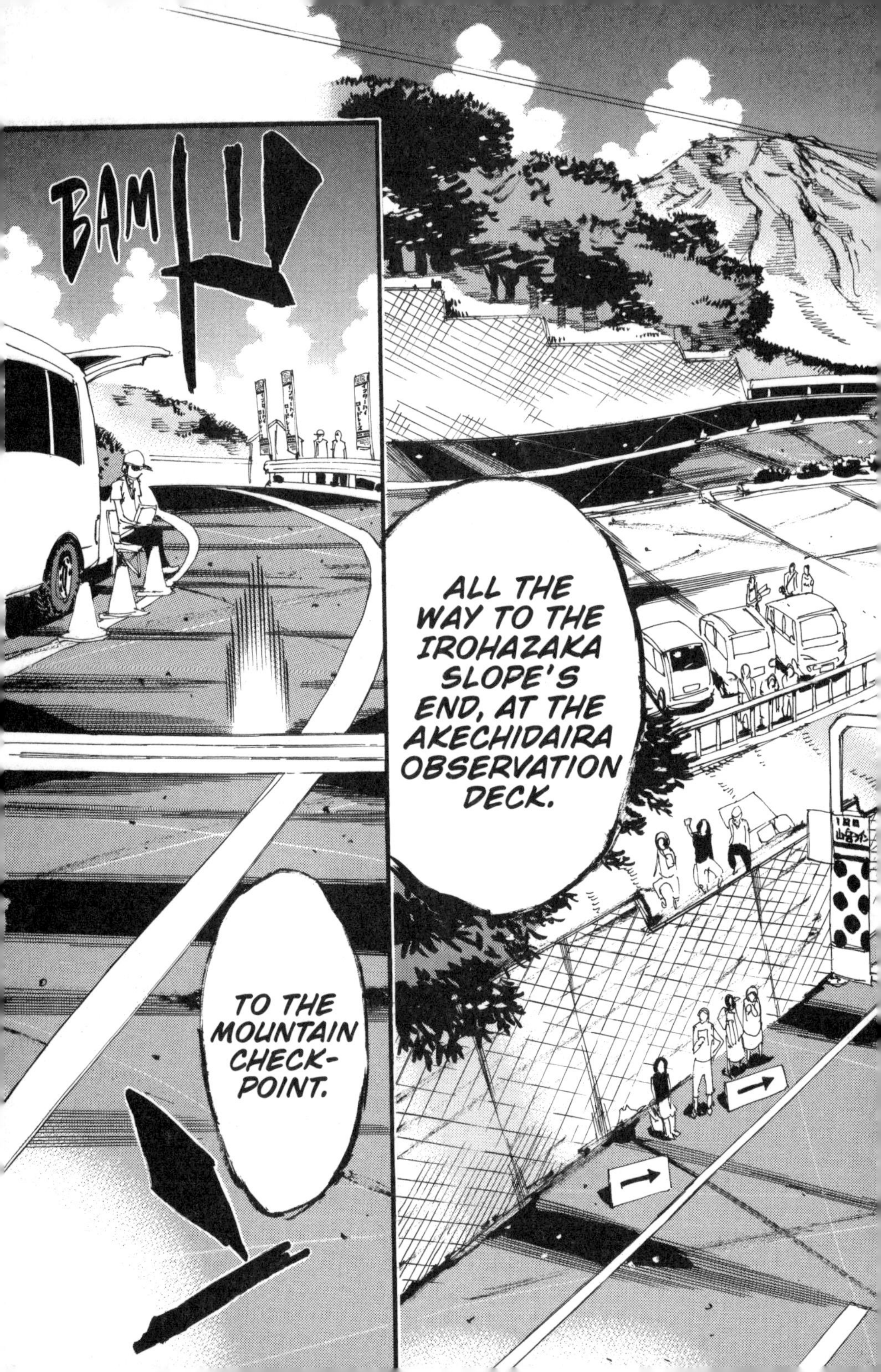
ALL THE WAY TO THE IROHAZAKA SLOPE'S END, AT THE AKECHIDAIRA OBSERVATION DECK.
BAM
TO THE MOUNTAIN CHECK-POINT.

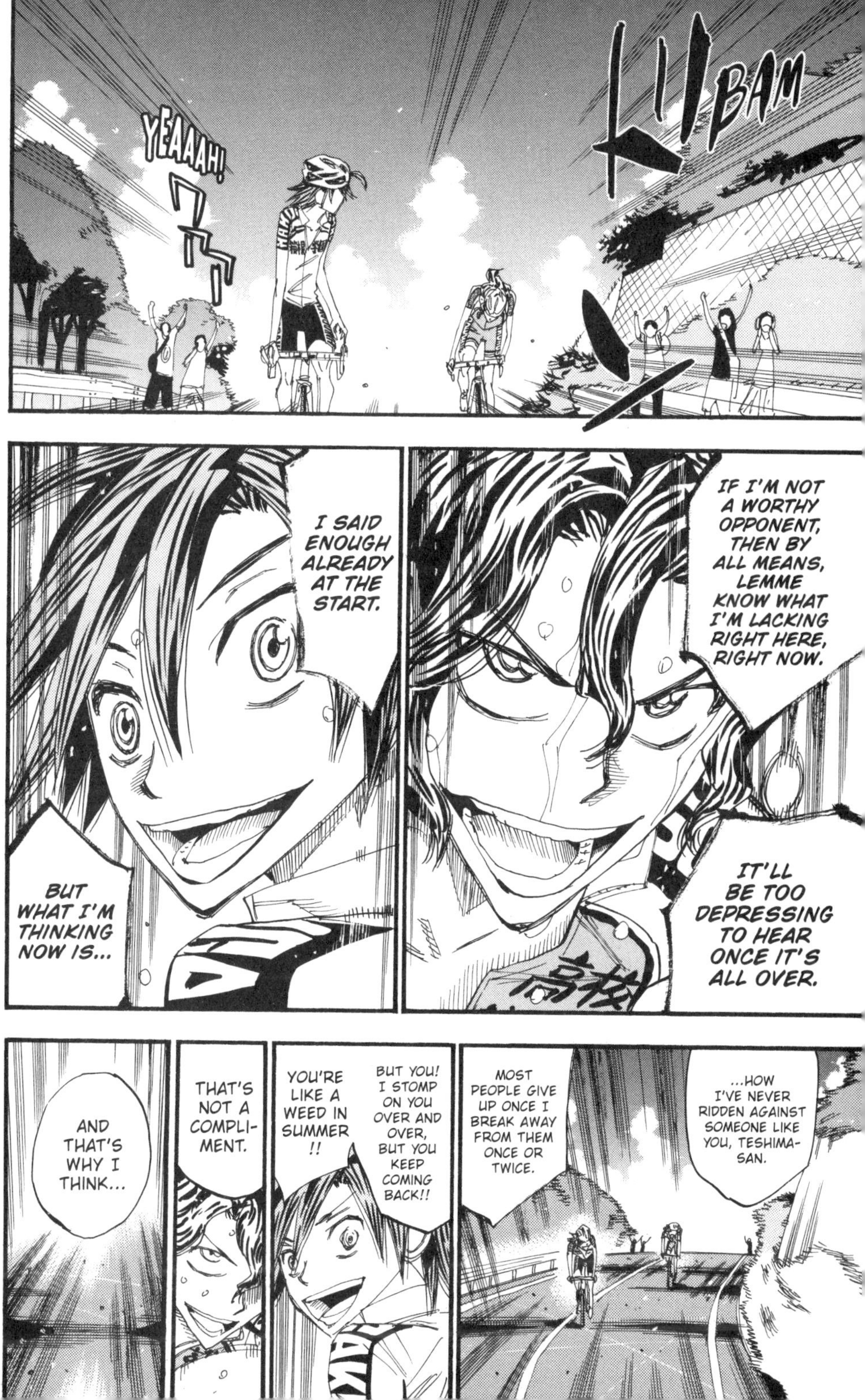

BAM
YEAAAH!
IF I'M NOT A WORTHY OPPONENT, THEN BY ALL MEANS, LEMME KNOW WHAT I'M LACKING RIGHT HERE, RIGHT NOW.
IT'LL BE TOO DEPRESSING TO HEAR ONCE IT'S ALL OVER.
I SAID ENOUGH ALREADY AT THE START.
BUT WHAT I'M THINKING NOW IS...
...HOW I'VE NEVER RIDDEN AGAINST SOMEONE LIKE YOU, TESHIMA-SAN.
MOST PEOPLE GIVE UP ONCE I BREAK AWAY FROM THEM ONCE OR TWICE.
BUT YOU! I STOMP ON YOU OVER AND OVER, BUT YOU KEEP COMING BACK!!
YOU'RE LIKE A WEED IN SUMMER !!
THAT'S NOT A COMPLIMENT.
AND THAT'S WHY I THINK...

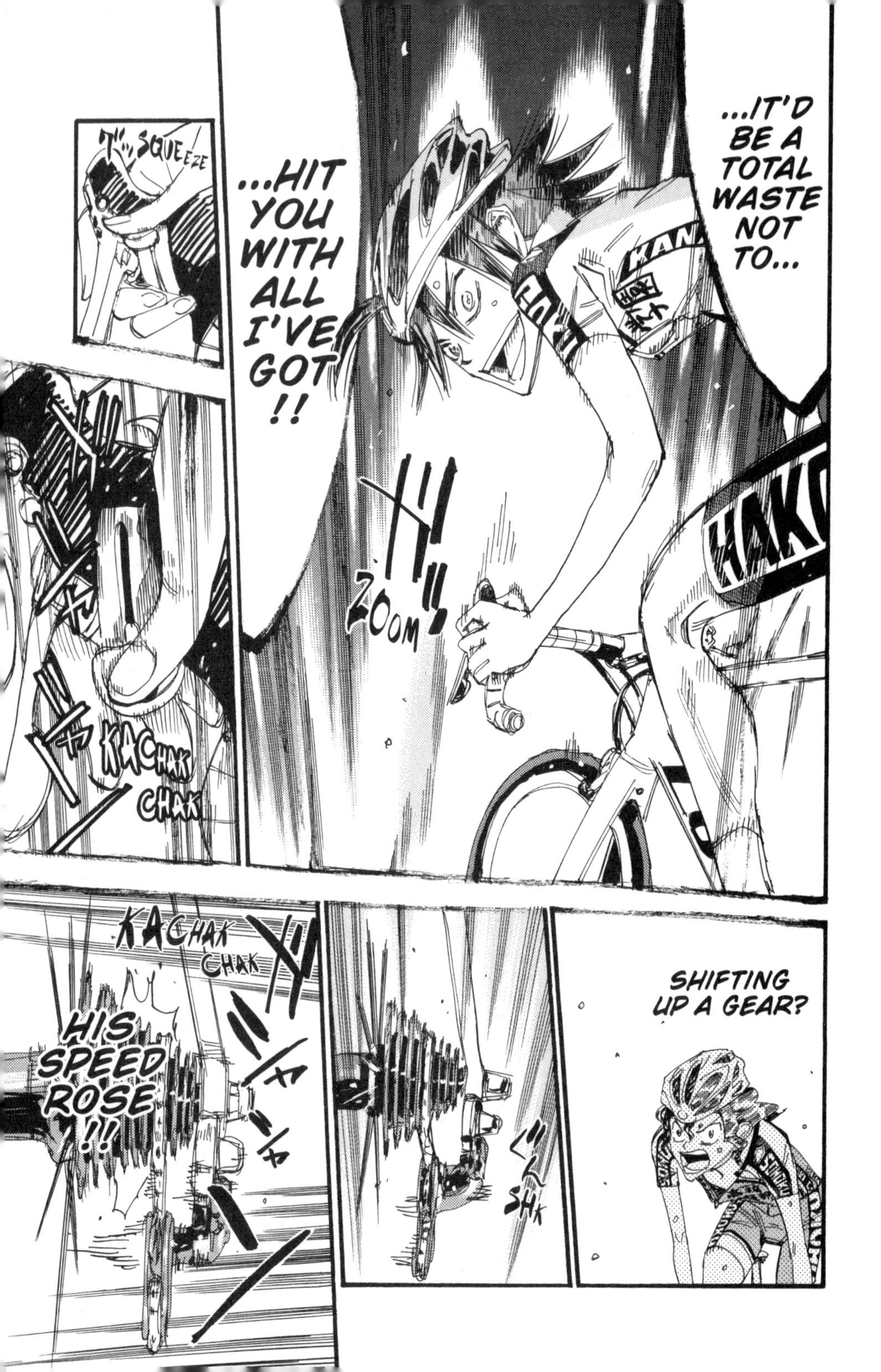
...IT'D BE A TOTAL WASTE NOT TO...
...HIT YOU WITH ALL I'VE GOT!!
ZOOM
SQUEEZE
KACHAK CHAK
SHIFTING UP A GEAR?
SHK
KACHAK CHAK
HIS SPEED ROSE!!

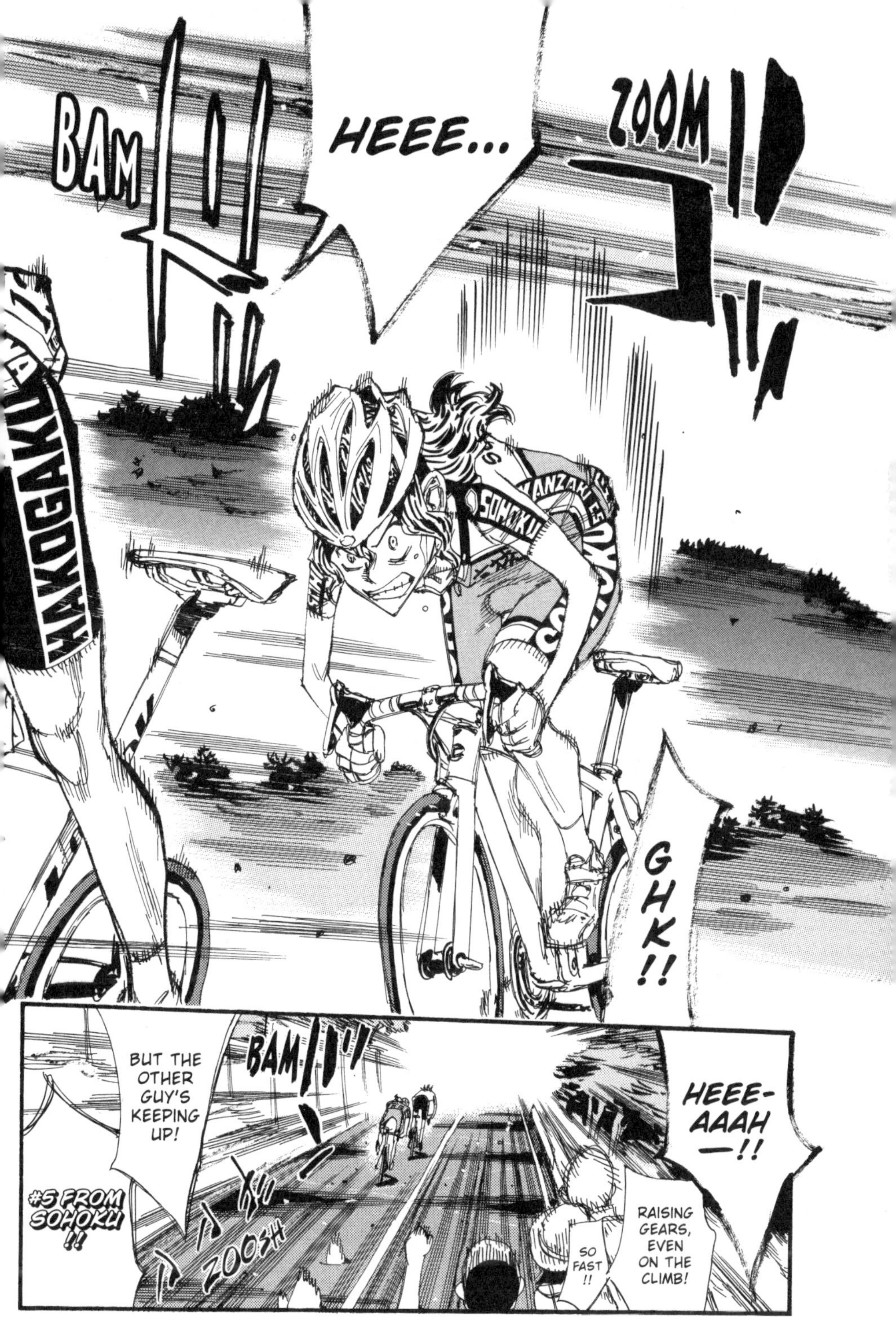
ZOOM!!
HEEE...
BAM!!
GHK!!
HEEE-AAAH—!!
RAISING GEARS, EVEN ON THE CLIMB!
SO FAST!!
BAM!!
ZOOSH
BUT THE OTHER GUY'S KEEPING UP!
#5 FROM SOHOKU!!

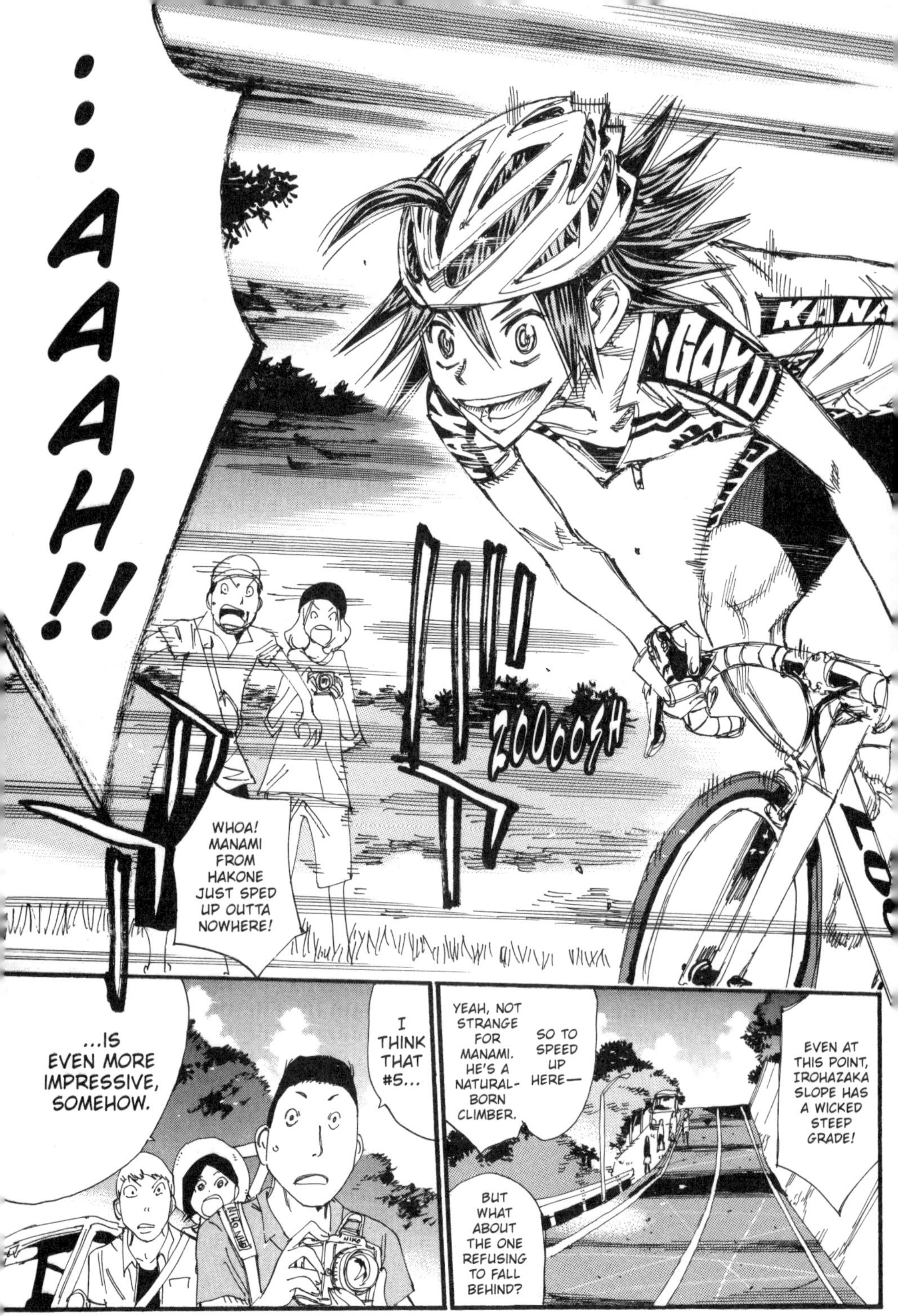
...AAAH!!
ZOOOOSH
WHOA! MANAMI FROM HAKONE JUST SPED UP OUTTA NOWHERE!
EVEN AT THIS POINT, IROHAZAKA SLOPE HAS A WICKED STEEP GRADE!
SO TO SPEED UP HERE—
YEAH, NOT STRANGE FOR MANAMI. HE'S A NATURAL-BORN CLIMBER.
BUT WHAT ABOUT THE ONE REFUSING TO FALL BEHIND?
I THINK THAT #5...
...IS EVEN MORE IMPRESSIVE, SOMEHOW.

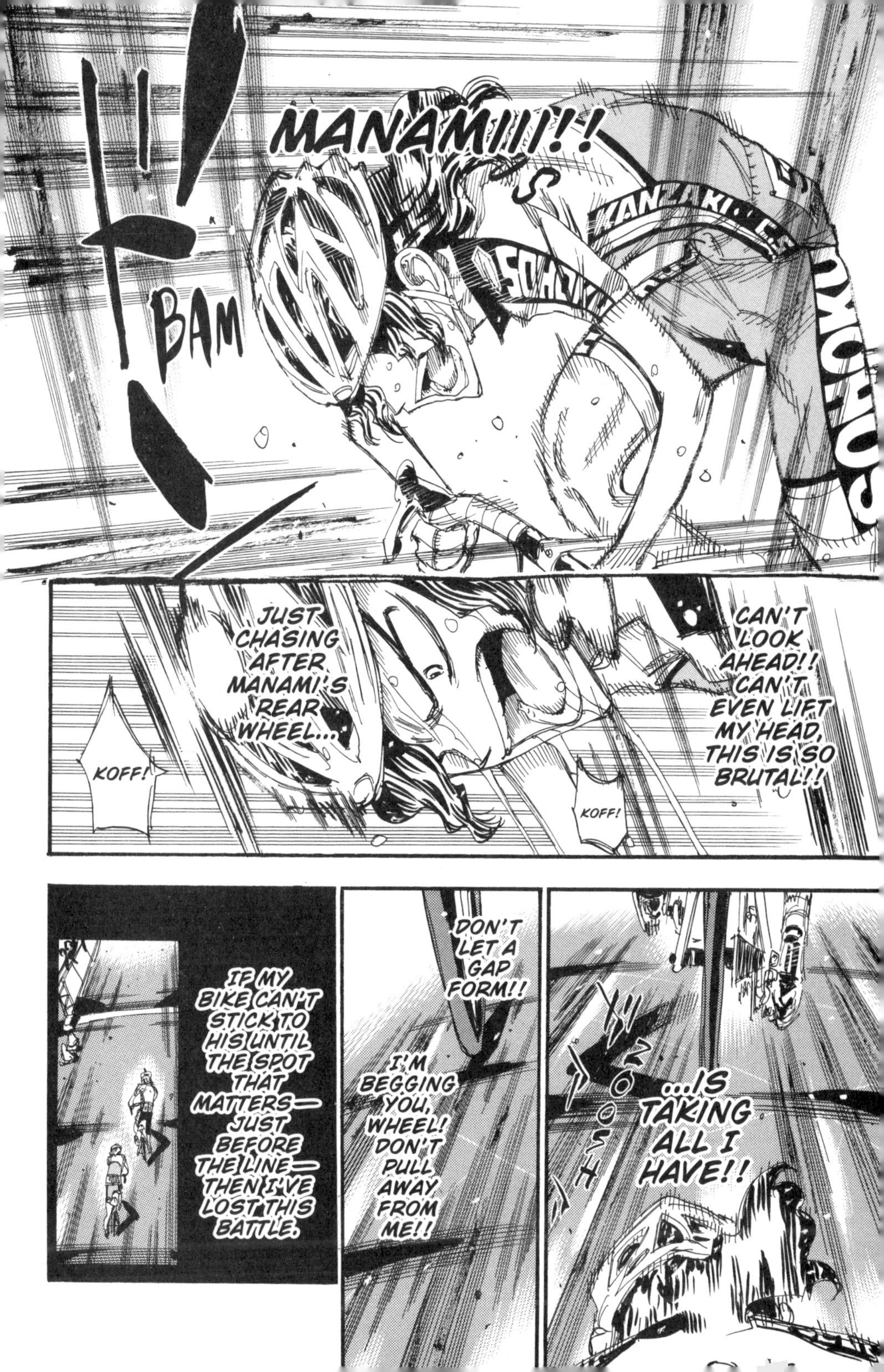
MANAMIIII!!
BAM
CAN'T LOOK AHEAD!! CAN'T EVEN LIFT MY HEAD, THIS IS SO BRUTAL!!
KOFF!
JUST CHASING AFTER MANAMI'S REAR WHEEL...
KOFF!
WHOOSH
...IS TAKING ALL I HAVE!!
DON'T LET A GAP FORM!!
I'M BEGGING YOU, WHEEL! DON'T PULL AWAY FROM ME!!
IF MY BIKE CAN'T STICK TO HIS UNTIL THE SPOT THAT MATTERS—JUST BEFORE THE LINE—THEN I'VE LOST THIS BATTLE.

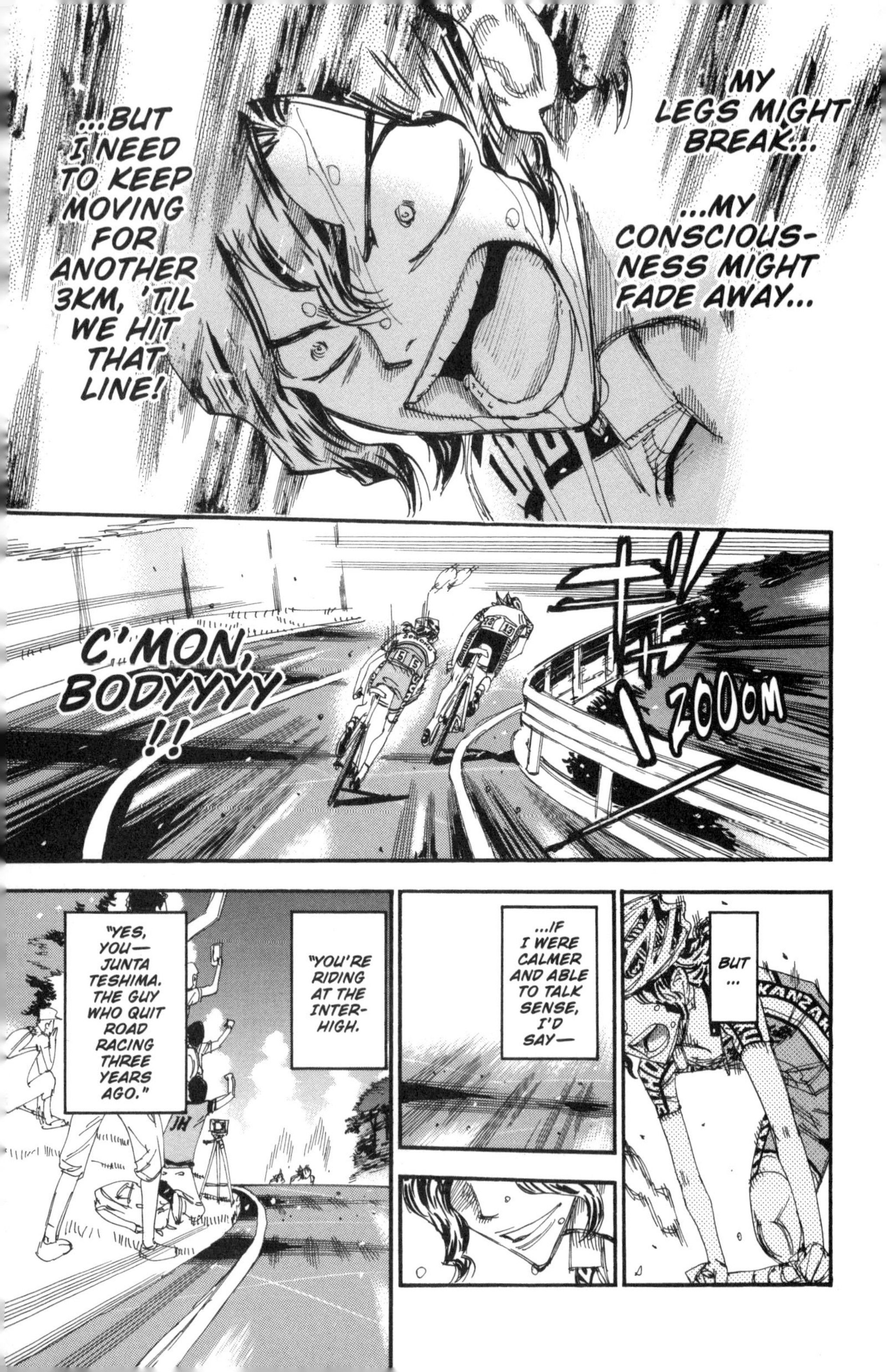
MY LEGS MIGHT BREAK...
...MY CONSCIOUSNESS MIGHT FADE AWAY...
...BUT I NEED TO KEEP MOVING FOR ANOTHER 3KM, 'TIL WE HIT THAT LINE!
ZOOOM
C'MON, BODYYYY!!
BUT ...
...IF I WERE CALMER AND ABLE TO TALK SENSE, I'D SAY—
"YOU'RE RIDING AT THE INTER-HIGH.
"YES, YOU—JUNTA TESHIMA. THE GUY WHO QUIT ROAD RACING THREE YEARS AGO."

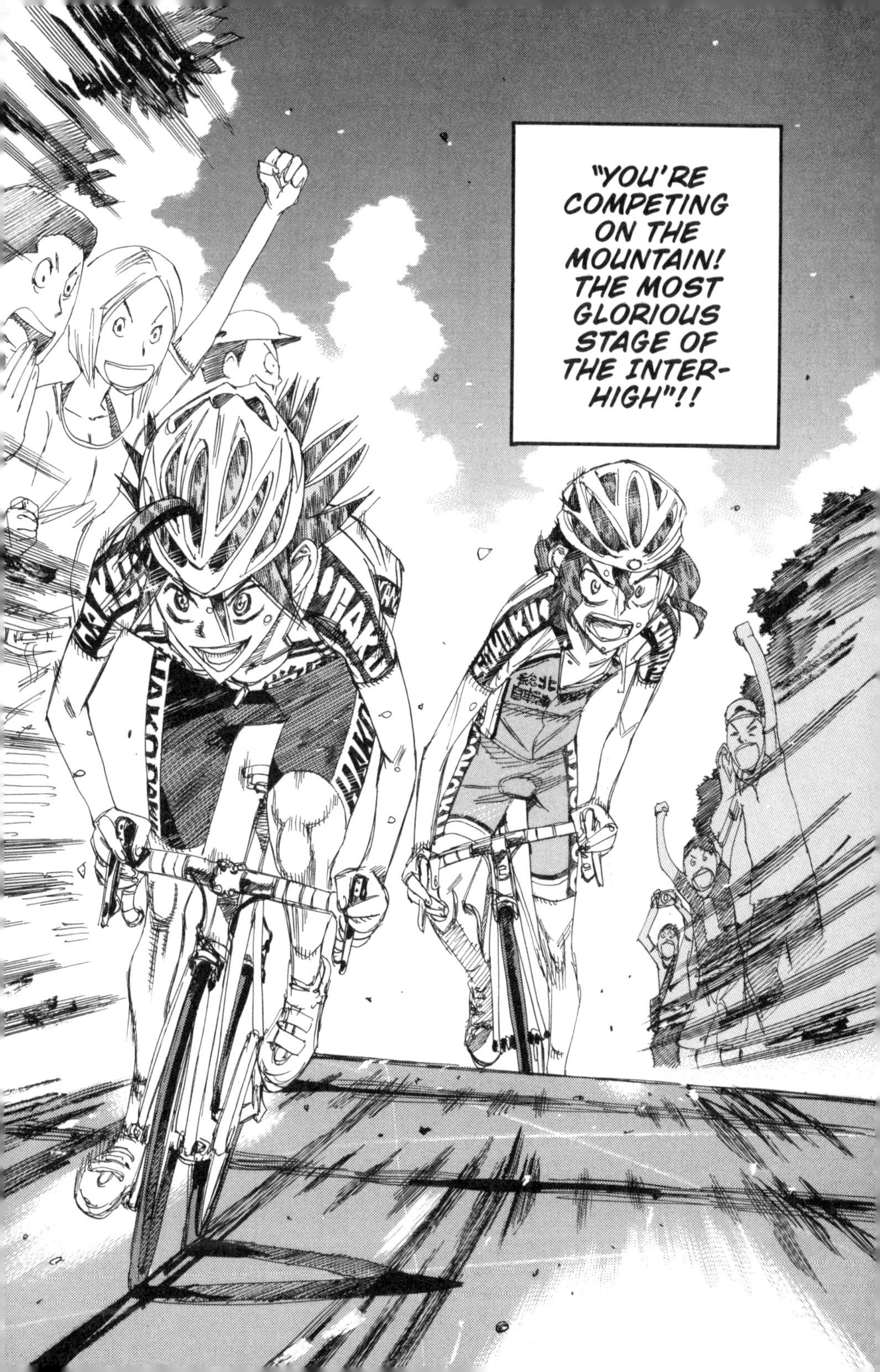
"YOU'RE COMPETING ON THE MOUNTAIN! THE MOST GLORIOUS STAGE OF THE INTER-HIGH"!!

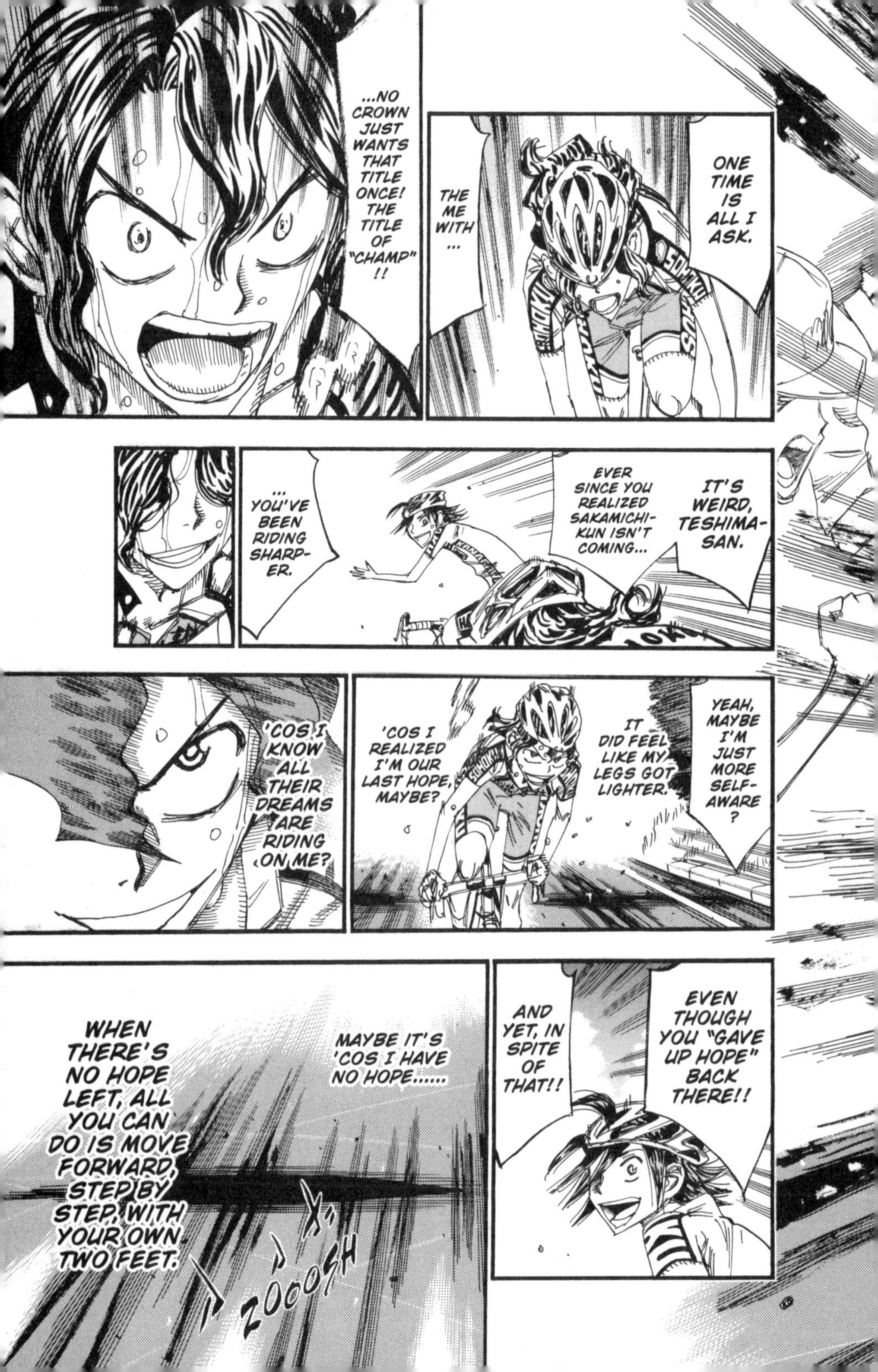
ONE TIME IS ALL I ASK.
THE ME WITH ...
...NO CROWN JUST WANTS THAT TITLE ONCE! THE TITLE OF "CHAMP"!!
IT'S WEIRD, TESHIMA-SAN.
EVER SINCE YOU REALIZED SAKAMICHI-KUN ISN'T COMING...
...YOU'VE BEEN RIDING SHARPER.
YEAH, MAYBE I'M JUST MORE SELF-AWARE?
IT DID FEEL LIKE MY LEGS GOT LIGHTER.
'COS I REALIZED I'M OUR LAST HOPE, MAYBE?
'COS I KNOW ALL THEIR DREAMS ARE RIDING ON ME?
EVEN THOUGH YOU "GAVE UP HOPE" BACK THERE!!
AND YET, IN SPITE OF THAT!!
MAYBE IT'S 'COS I HAVE NO HOPE......
WHEN THERE'S NO HOPE LEFT, ALL YOU CAN DO IS MOVE FORWARD, STEP BY STEP, WITH YOUR OWN TWO FEET.
ZOOOSH

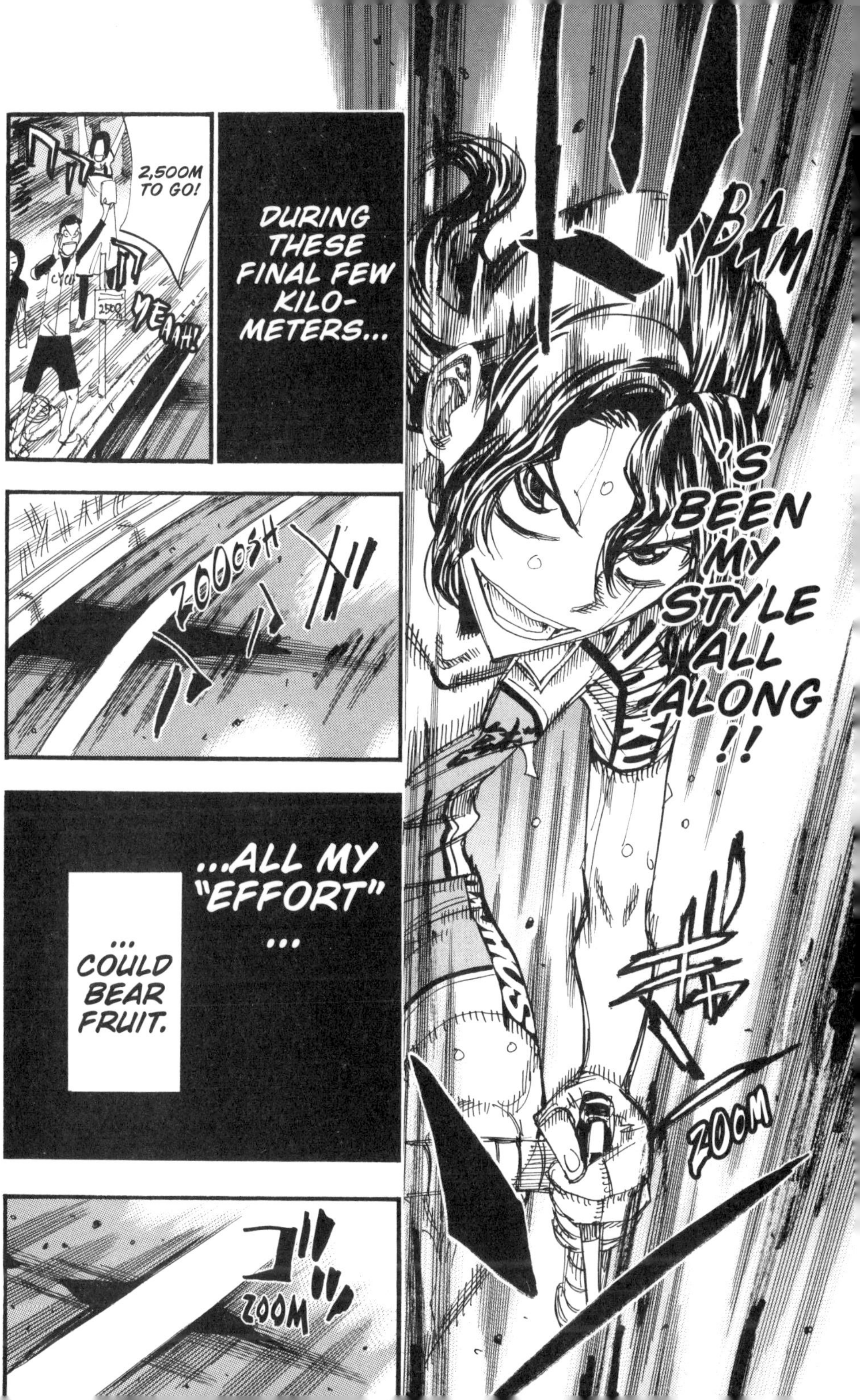
BAM
'S BEEN MY STYLE ALL ALONG!!
ZOOM
DURING THESE FINAL FEW KILO-METERS...
2,500M TO GO!
YEAAH!
ZOOOSH
...ALL MY "EFFORT"...
...COULD BEAR FRUIT.
ZOOM

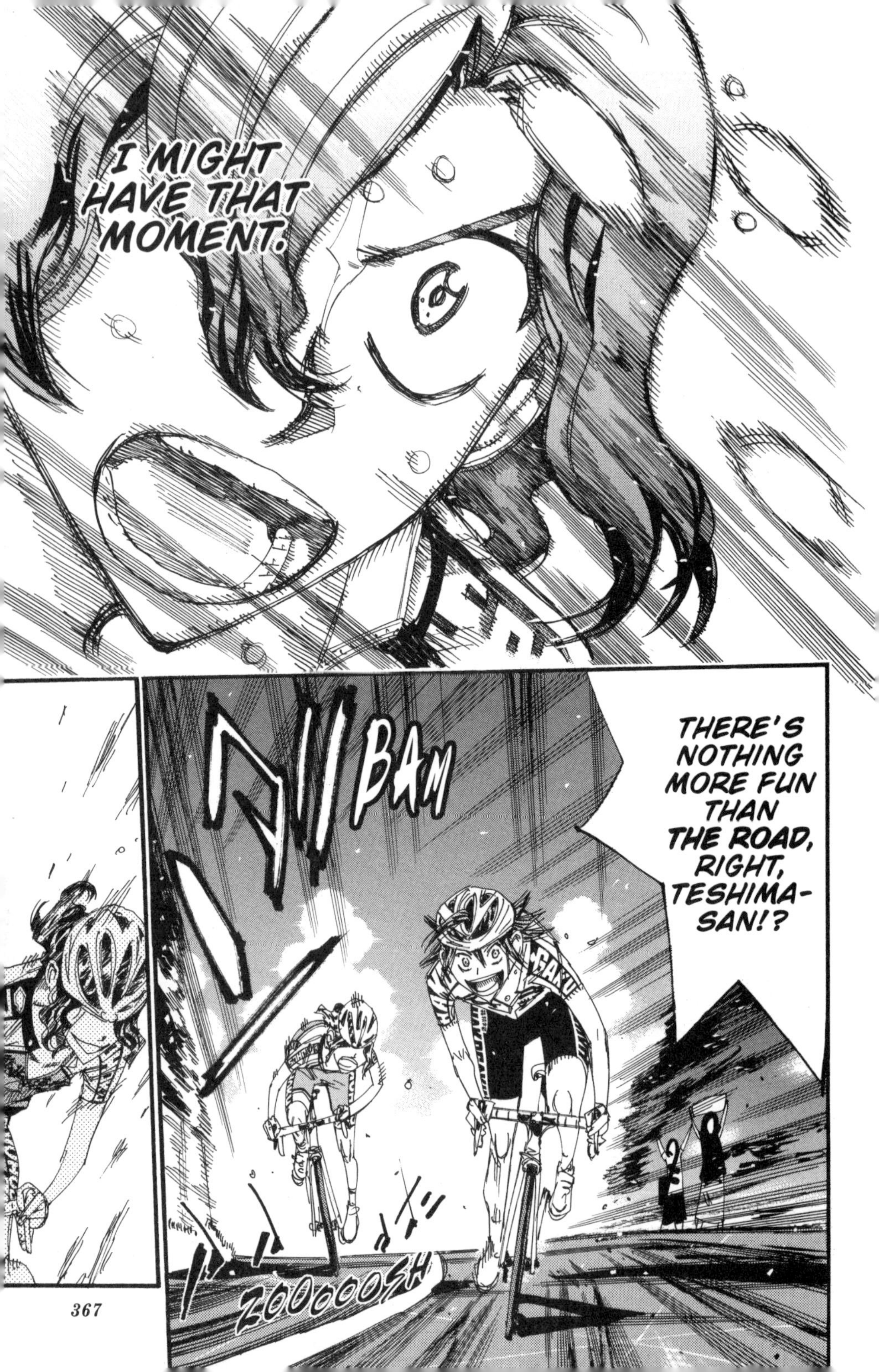
I MIGHT HAVE THAT MOMENT.
THERE'S NOTHING MORE FUN THAN THE ROAD, RIGHT, TESHIMA-SAN!?
BAM
ZOOOOOSH

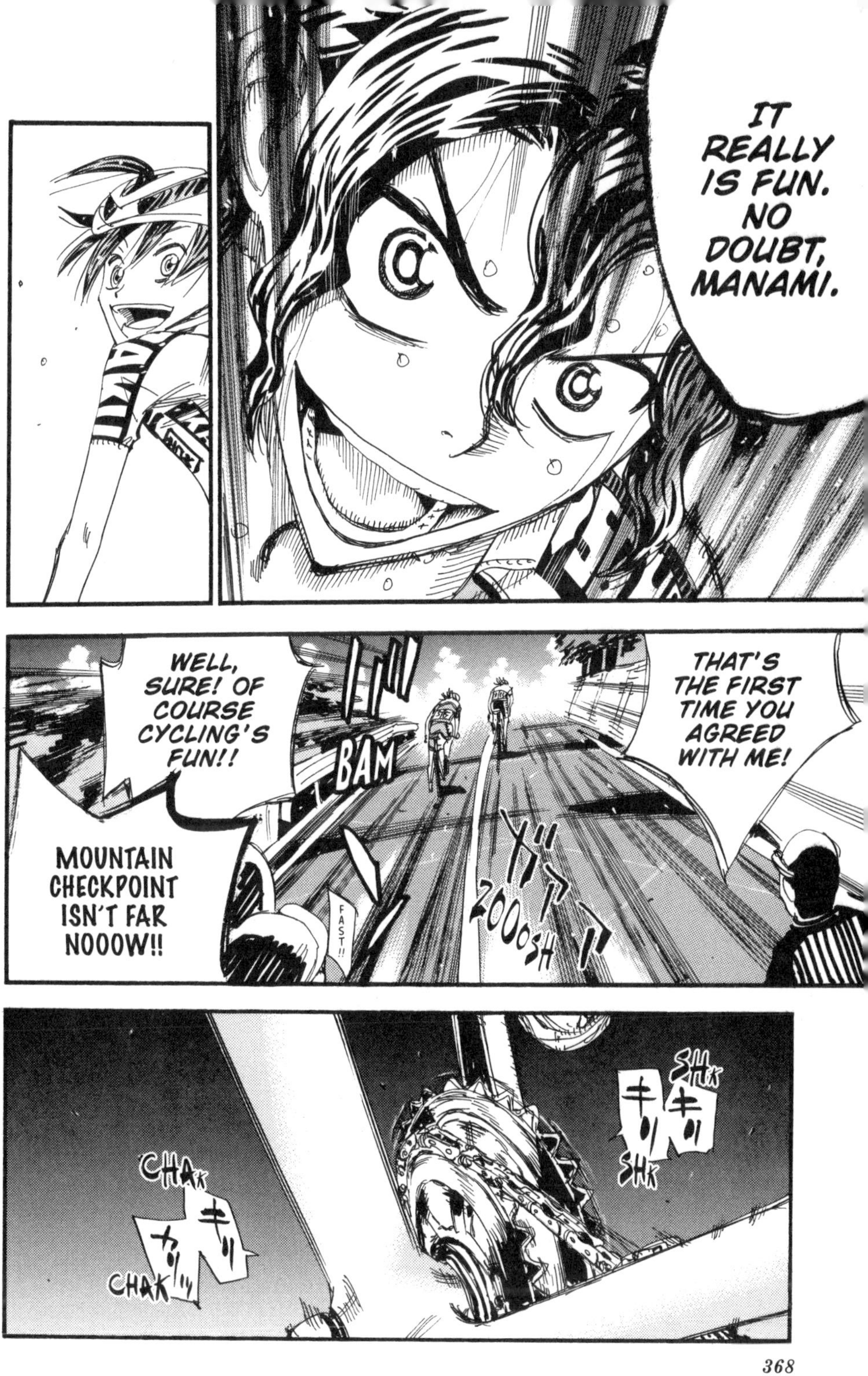
IT REALLY IS FUN. NO DOUBT, MANAMI.
THAT'S THE FIRST TIME YOU AGREED WITH ME!
WELL, SURE! OF COURSE CYCLING'S FUN!!
BAM
ZOOOSH
FAST!!
MOUNTAIN CHECKPOINT ISN'T FAR NOOOW!!
SHK
SHK
CHAK
CHAK

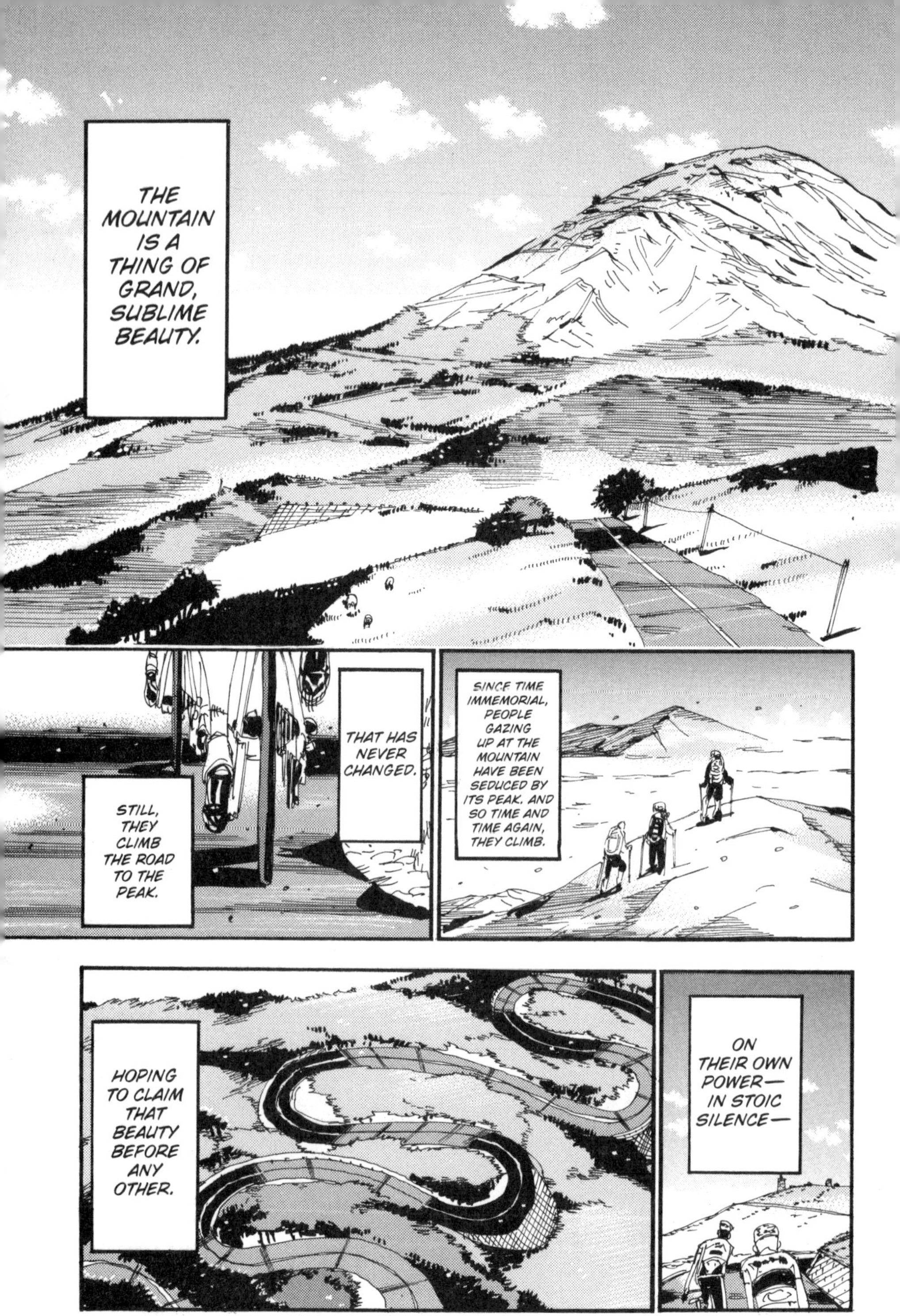
THE MOUNTAIN IS A THING OF GRAND, SUBLIME BEAUTY.
SINCE TIME IMMEMORIAL, PEOPLE GAZING UP AT THE MOUNTAIN HAVE BEEN SEDUCED BY ITS PEAK. AND SO TIME AND TIME AGAIN, THEY CLIMB.
THAT HAS NEVER CHANGED.
STILL, THEY CLIMB THE ROAD TO THE PEAK.
ON THEIR OWN POWER— IN STOIC SILENCE—
HOPING TO CLAIM THAT BEAUTY BEFORE ANY OTHER.

RIDE.328 SEARCH FOR AN OPENING!!

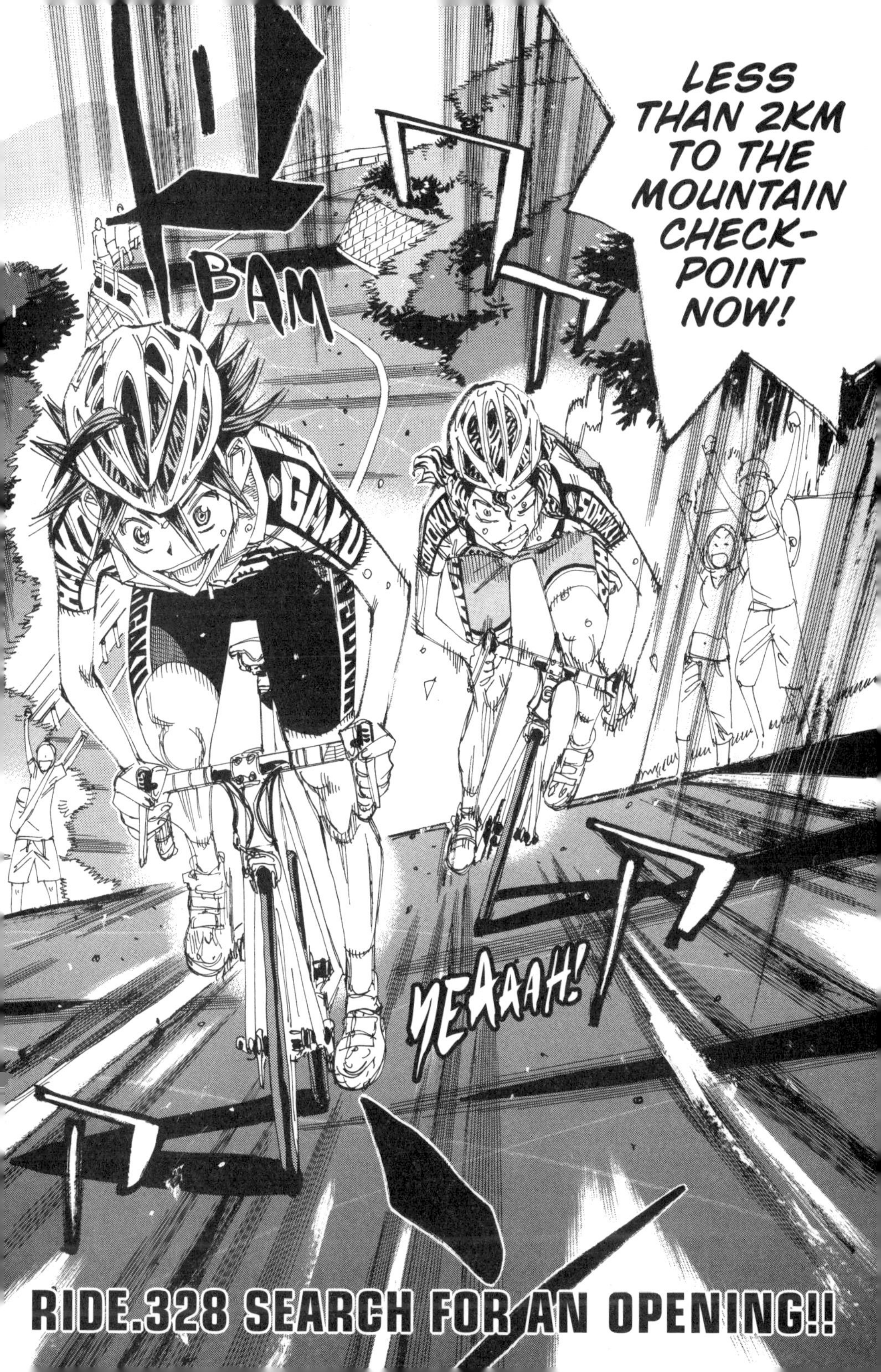
LESS THAN 2KM TO THE MOUNTAIN CHECK-POINT NOW!
BAM
YEAAAH!

RIDE.328 SEARCH FOR AN OPENING!!

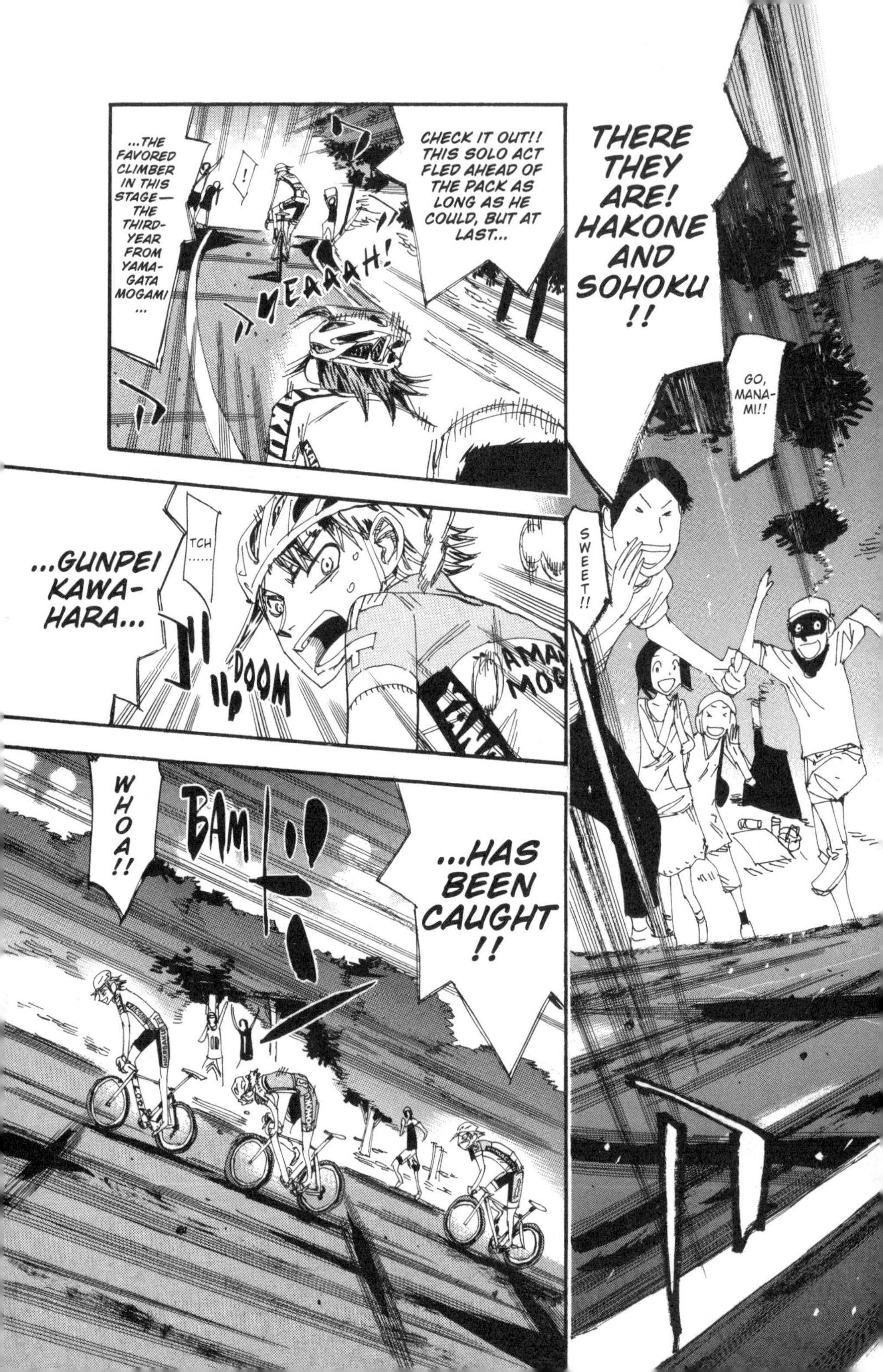
THERE THEY ARE! HAKONE AND SOHOKU!!
GO, MANAMI!!
SWEET!!
CHECK IT OUT!! THIS SOLO ACT FLED AHEAD OF THE PACK AS LONG AS HE COULD, BUT AT LAST...
...THE FAVORED CLIMBER IN THIS STAGE—THE THIRD-YEAR FROM YAMAGATA MOGAMI...
!
WEAAAH!
TCH......
...GUNPEI KAWAHARA...
DOOM
...HAS BEEN CAUGHT!!
BAM
WHOA!!

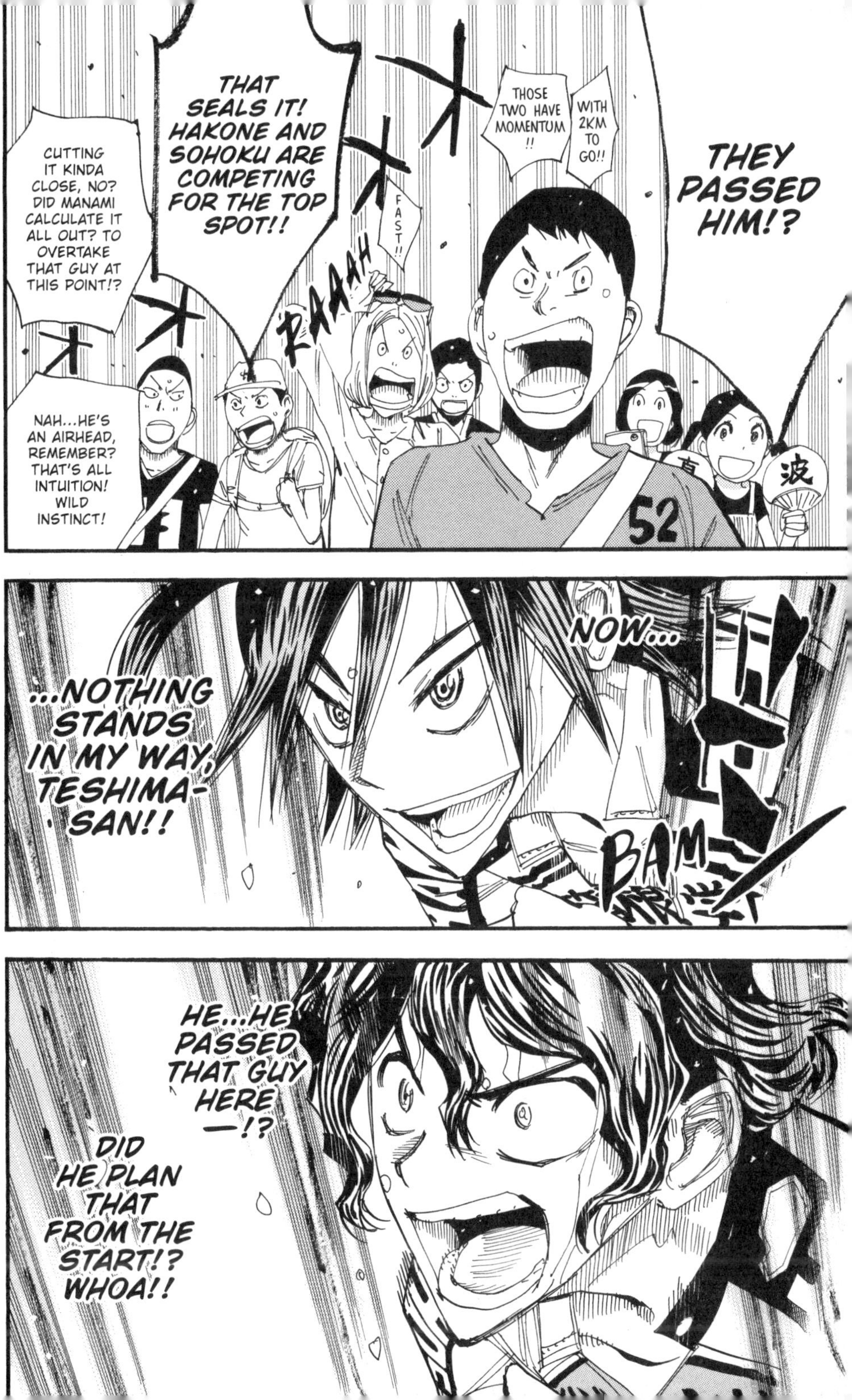
THEY PASSED HIM!?
WITH 2KM TO GO!!
THOSE TWO HAVE MOMENTUM!!
FAST!!
RAAAH
THAT SEALS IT! HAKONE AND SOHOKU ARE COMPETING FOR THE TOP SPOT!!
CUTTING IT KINDA CLOSE, NO? DID MANAMI CALCULATE IT ALL OUT? TO OVERTAKE THAT GUY AT THIS POINT!?
NAH...HE'S AN AIRHEAD, REMEMBER? THAT'S ALL INTUITION! WILD INSTINCT!
NOW...
...NOTHING STANDS IN MY WAY, TESHIMA-SAN!!
BAM
HE...HE PASSED THAT GUY HERE—!?
DID HE PLAN THAT FROM THE START!? WHOA!!

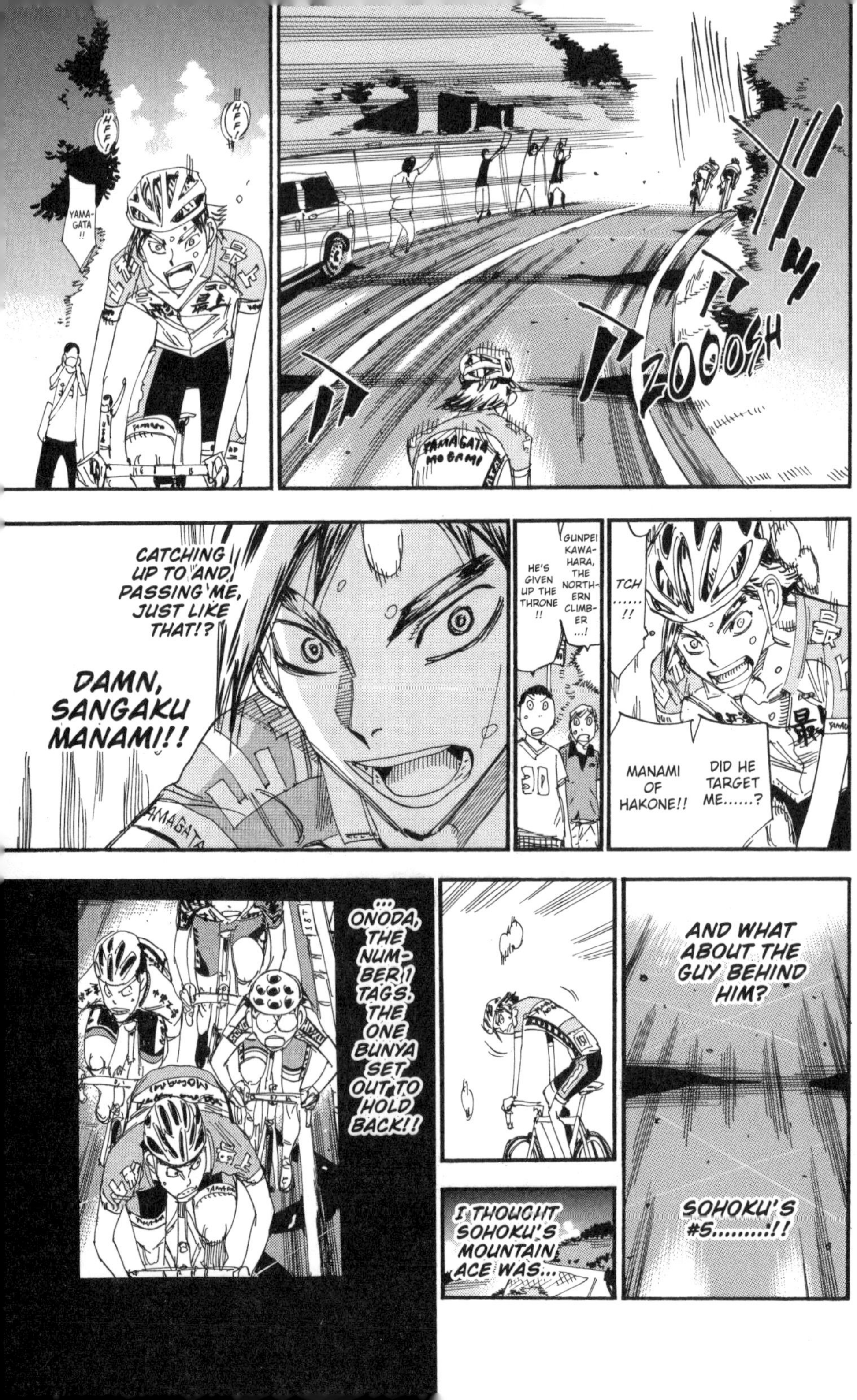
ZOOOSH
HFF!
HFF!
YAMAGATA!!
TCH......!!
DID HE TARGET ME......?
MANAMI OF HAKONE!!
GUNPEI KAWAHARA, THE NORTHERN CLIMBER...!
HE'S GIVEN UP THE THRONE!!
CATCHING UP TO AND PASSING ME, JUST LIKE THAT!?
DAMN, SANGAKU MANAMI!!
AND WHAT ABOUT THE GUY BEHIND HIM?
SOHOKU'S #5........!!
I THOUGHT SOHOKU'S MOUNTAIN ACE WAS...
...ONODA, THE NUMBER 1 TAGS. THE ONE BUNYA SET OUT TO HOLD BACK!!

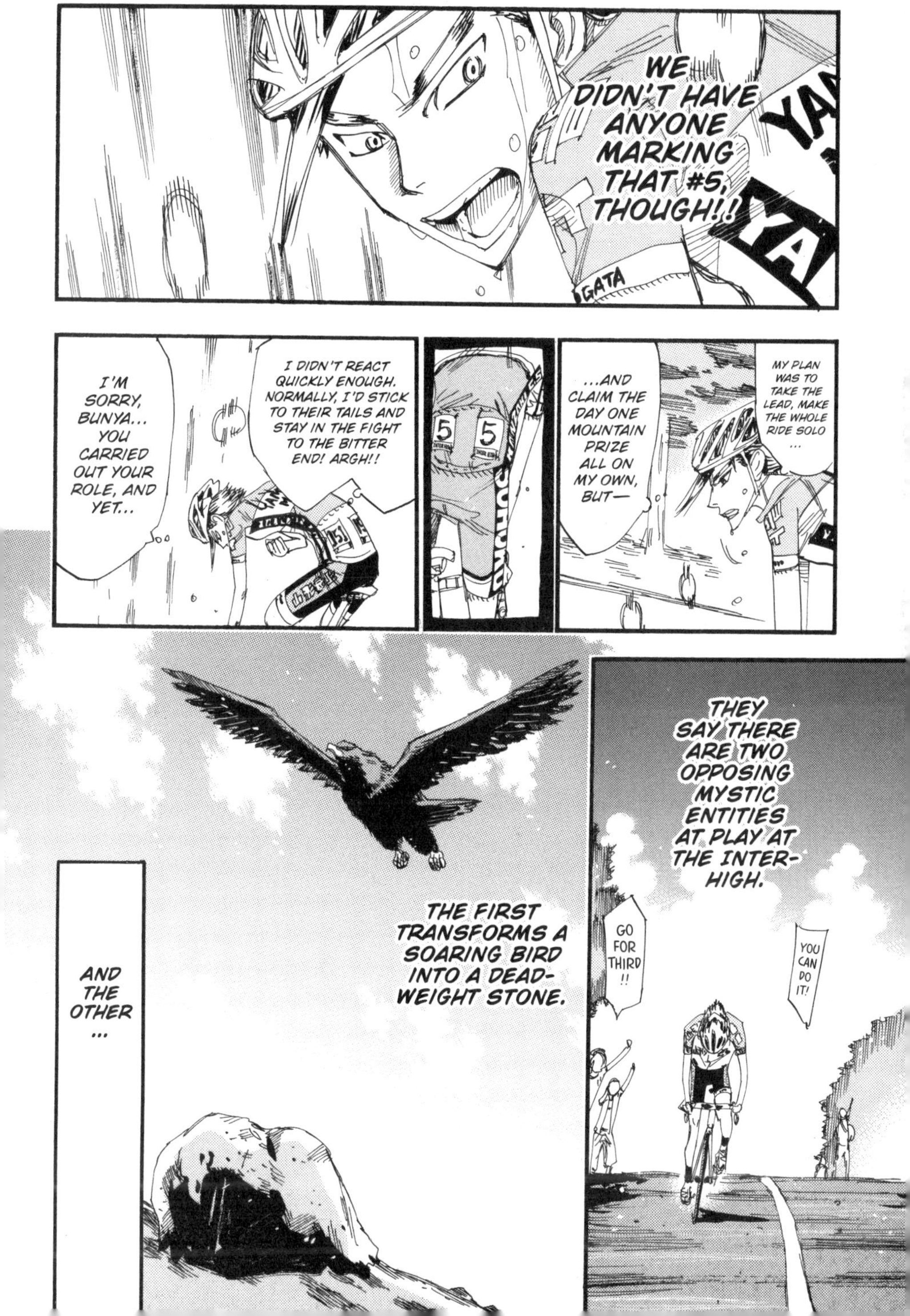
WE DIDN'T HAVE ANYONE MARKING THAT #5, THOUGH!!
MY PLAN WAS TO TAKE THE LEAD, MAKE THE WHOLE RIDE SOLO ...
...AND CLAIM THE DAY ONE MOUNTAIN PRIZE ALL ON MY OWN, BUT—
I DIDN'T REACT QUICKLY ENOUGH. NORMALLY, I'D STICK TO THEIR TAILS AND STAY IN THE FIGHT TO THE BITTER END! ARGH!!
I'M SORRY, BUNYA... YOU CARRIED OUT YOUR ROLE, AND YET...
THEY SAY THERE ARE TWO OPPOSING MYSTIC ENTITIES AT PLAY AT THE INTER-HIGH.
YOU CAN DO IT!
GO FOR THIRD!!
THE FIRST TRANSFORMS A SOARING BIRD INTO A DEAD-WEIGHT STONE.
AND THE OTHER ...

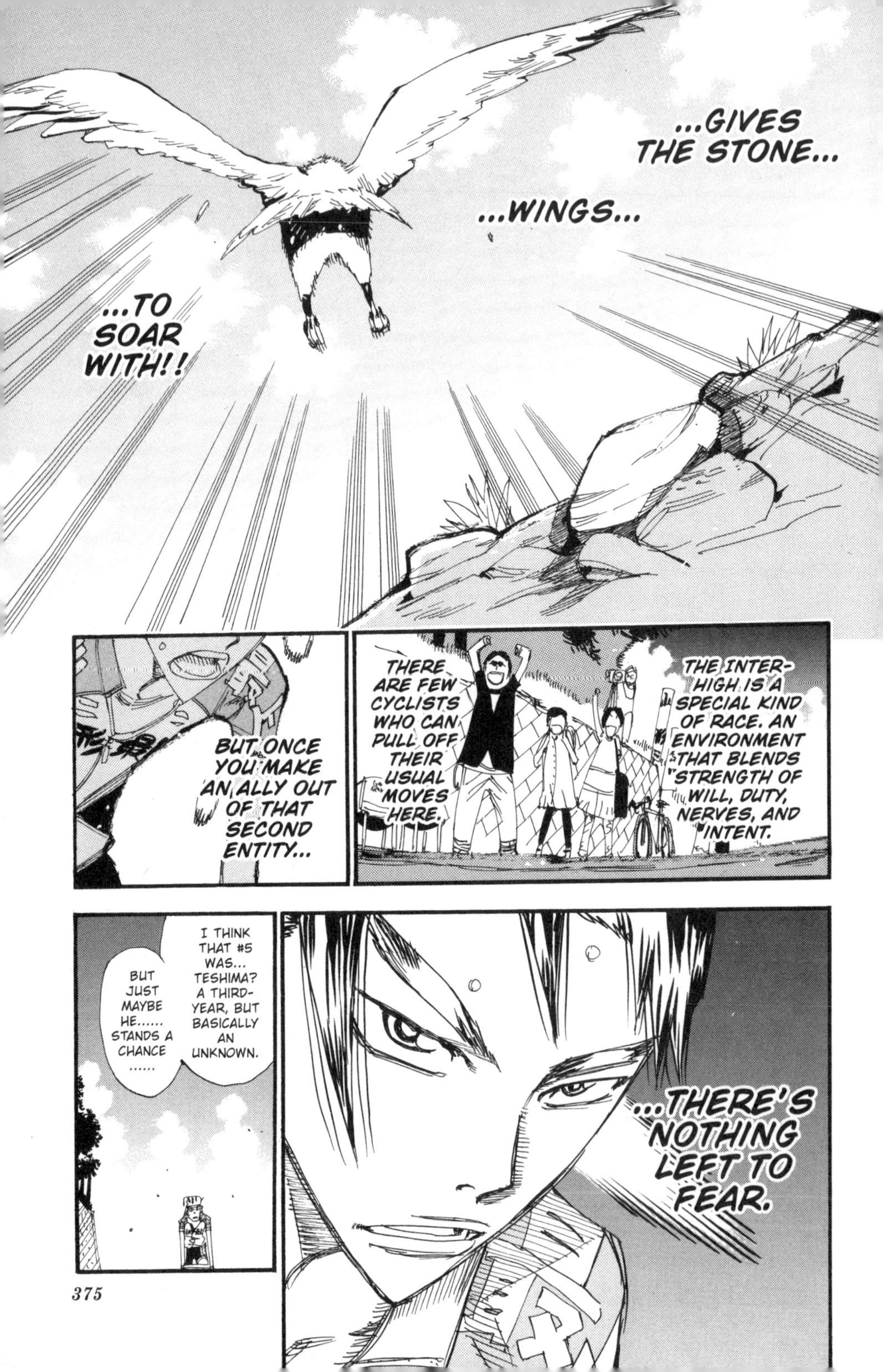
...GIVES THE STONE...
...WINGS...
...TO SOAR WITH!!
THE INTER-HIGH IS A SPECIAL KIND OF RACE. AN ENVIRONMENT THAT BLENDS STRENGTH OF WILL, DUTY, NERVES, AND INTENT.
THERE ARE FEW CYCLISTS WHO CAN PULL OFF THEIR USUAL MOVES HERE.
BUT ONCE YOU MAKE AN ALLY OUT OF THAT SECOND ENTITY...
...THERE'S NOTHING LEFT TO FEAR.
I THINK THAT #5 WAS... TESHIMA? A THIRD-YEAR, BUT BASICALLY AN UNKNOWN.
BUT JUST MAYBE HE...... STANDS A CHANCE ......

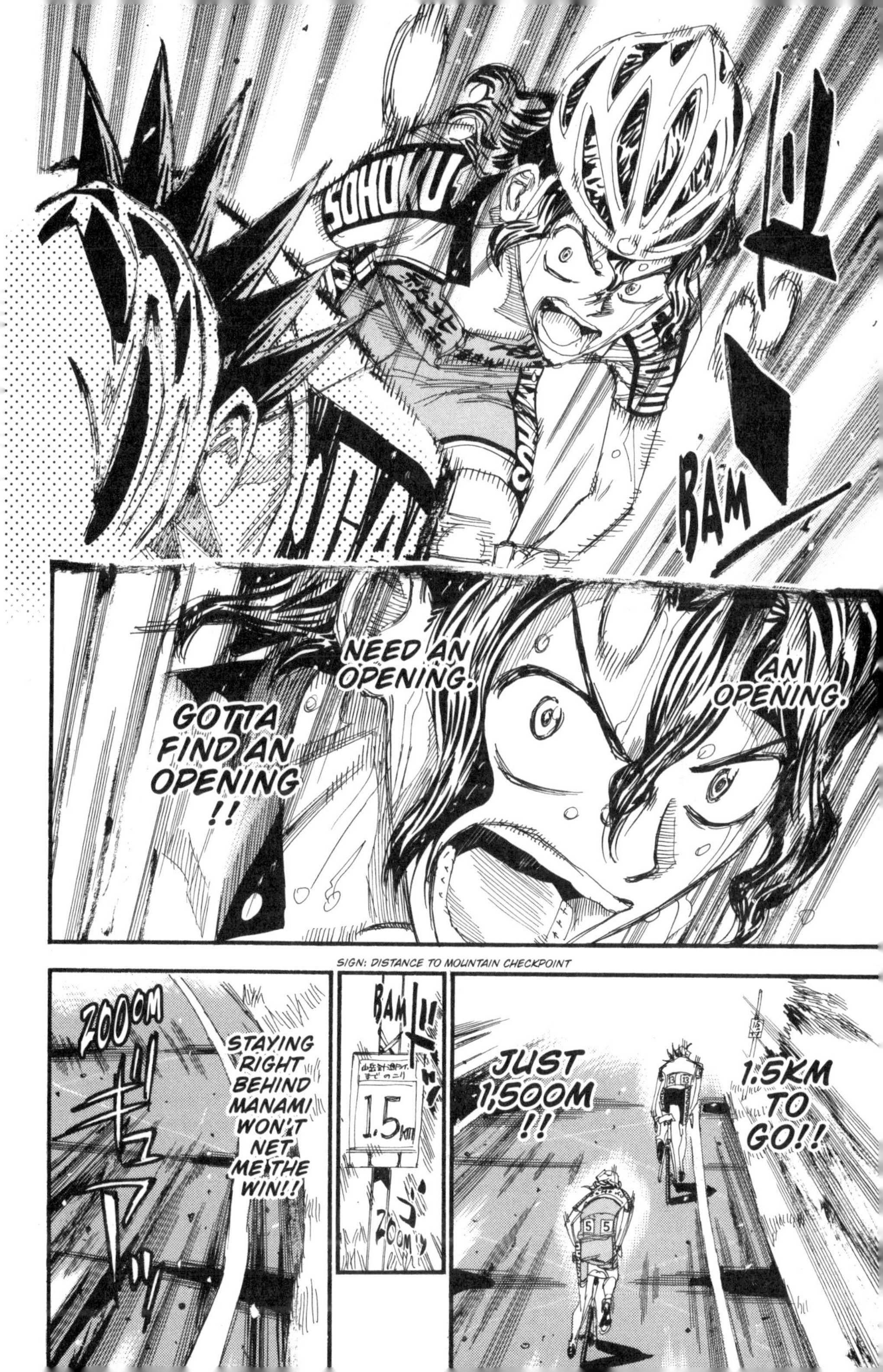
SOHOKU
BAM
AN OPENING.
NEED AN OPENING.
GOTTA FIND AN OPENING!!
SIGN: DISTANCE TO MOUNTAIN CHECKPOINT
1.5KM TO GO!!
JUST 1,500M!!
BAM
1.5km
ZOOM
ZOOM
STAYING RIGHT BEHIND MANAMI WON'T NET ME THE WIN!!

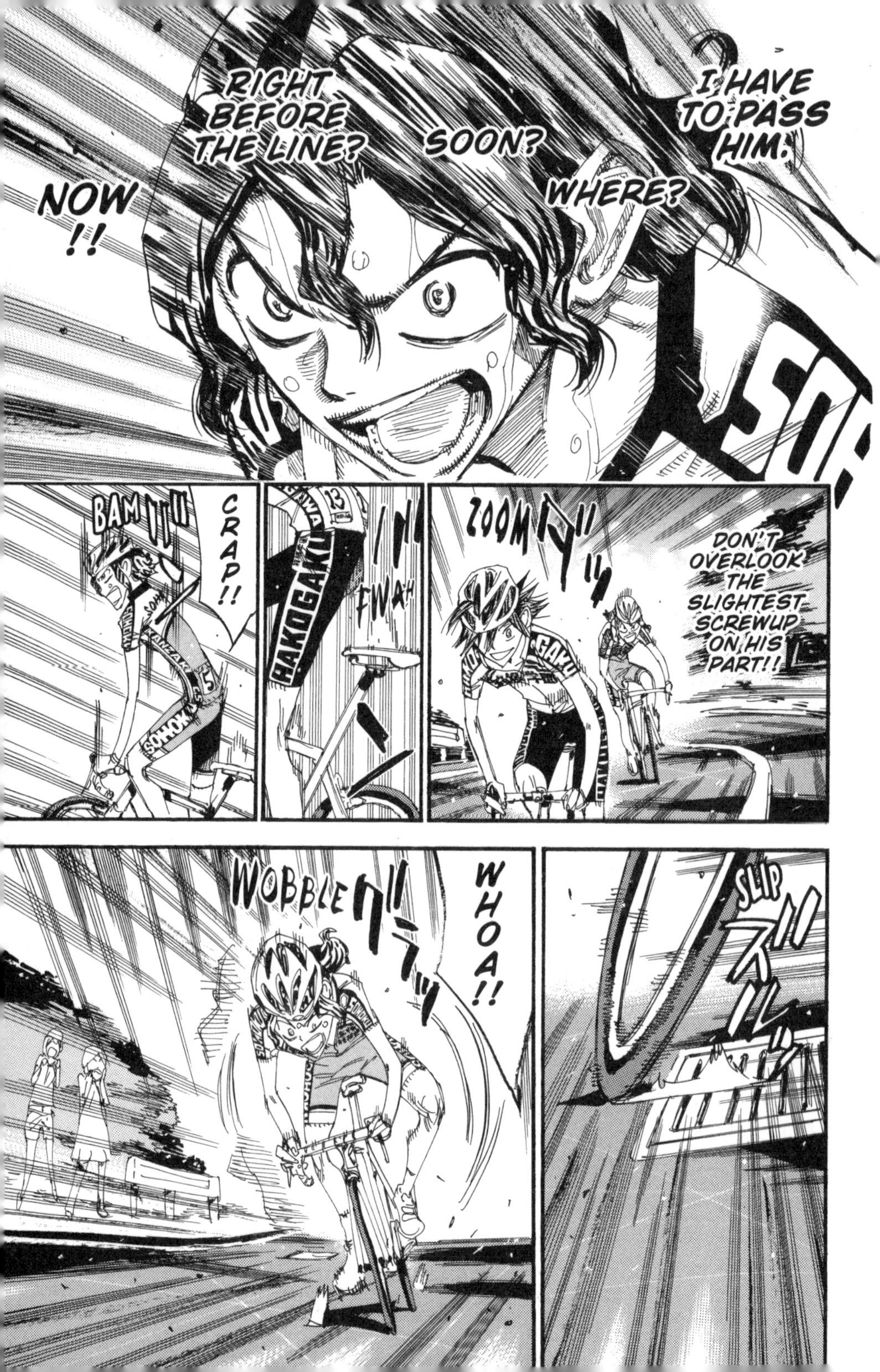
I HAVE TO PASS HIM.
WHERE?
SOON?
RIGHT BEFORE THE LINE?
NOW!!
ZOOM
DON'T OVERLOOK THE SLIGHTEST SCREWUP ON HIS PART!!
FWAH
CRAP!!
BAM
SLIP
WHOA!!
WOBBLE

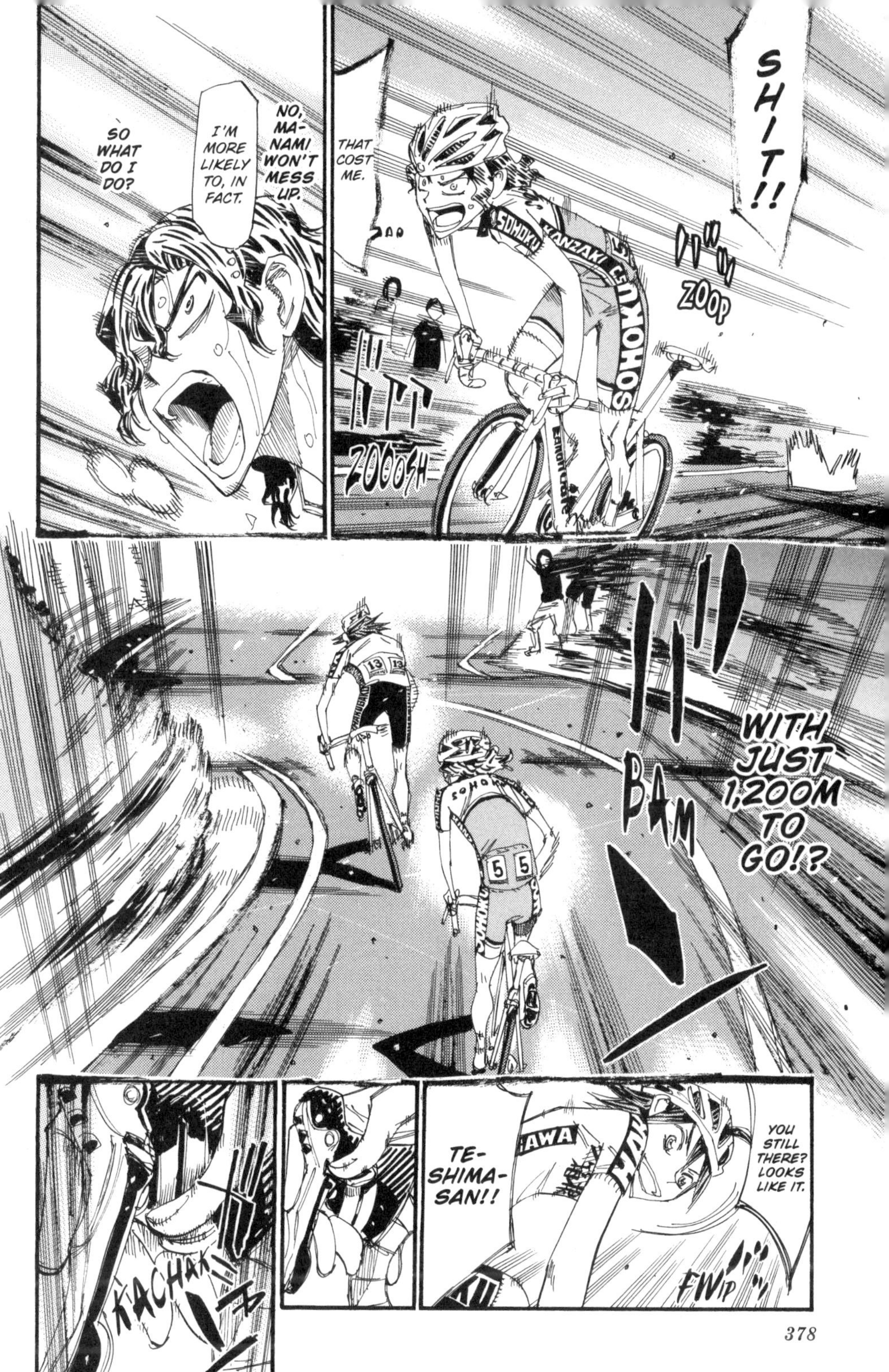
SHIT!!
ZOOP
THAT COST ME.
ZOOOSH
NO, MA-NAMI WON'T MESS UP.
I'M MORE LIKELY TO, IN FACT.
SO WHAT DO I DO?
BAM
WITH JUST 1,200M TO GO!?
YOU STILL THERE? LOOKS LIKE IT.
FWIP
TE-SHIMA-SAN!!
KACHAK

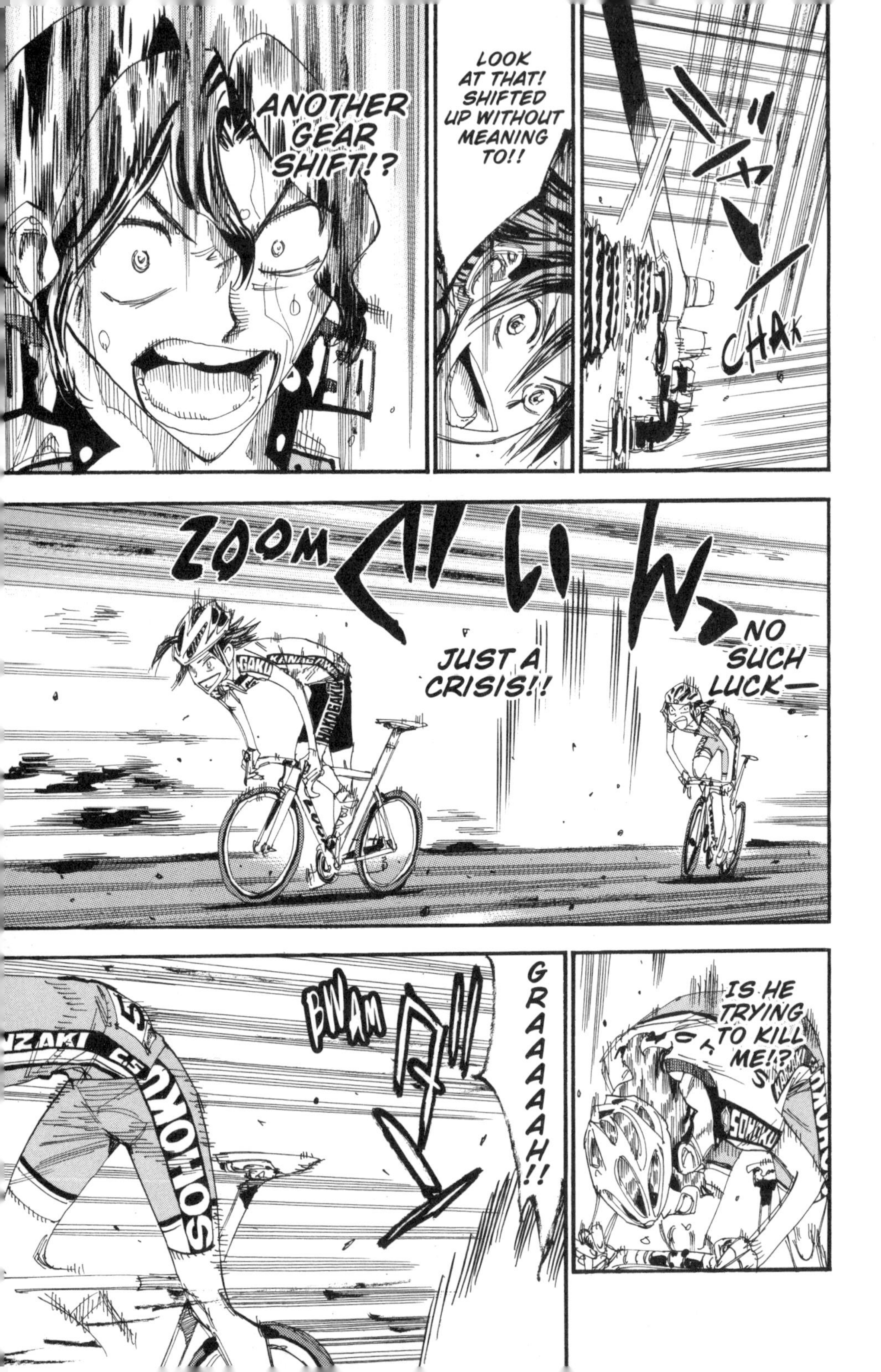
CHAK
LOOK AT THAT! SHIFTED UP WITHOUT MEANING TO!!
ANOTHER GEAR SHIFT!?
ZOOM
NO SUCH LUCK—
JUST A CRISIS!!
IS HE TRYING TO KILL ME!?
GRAAAAAAH!!
BWAM

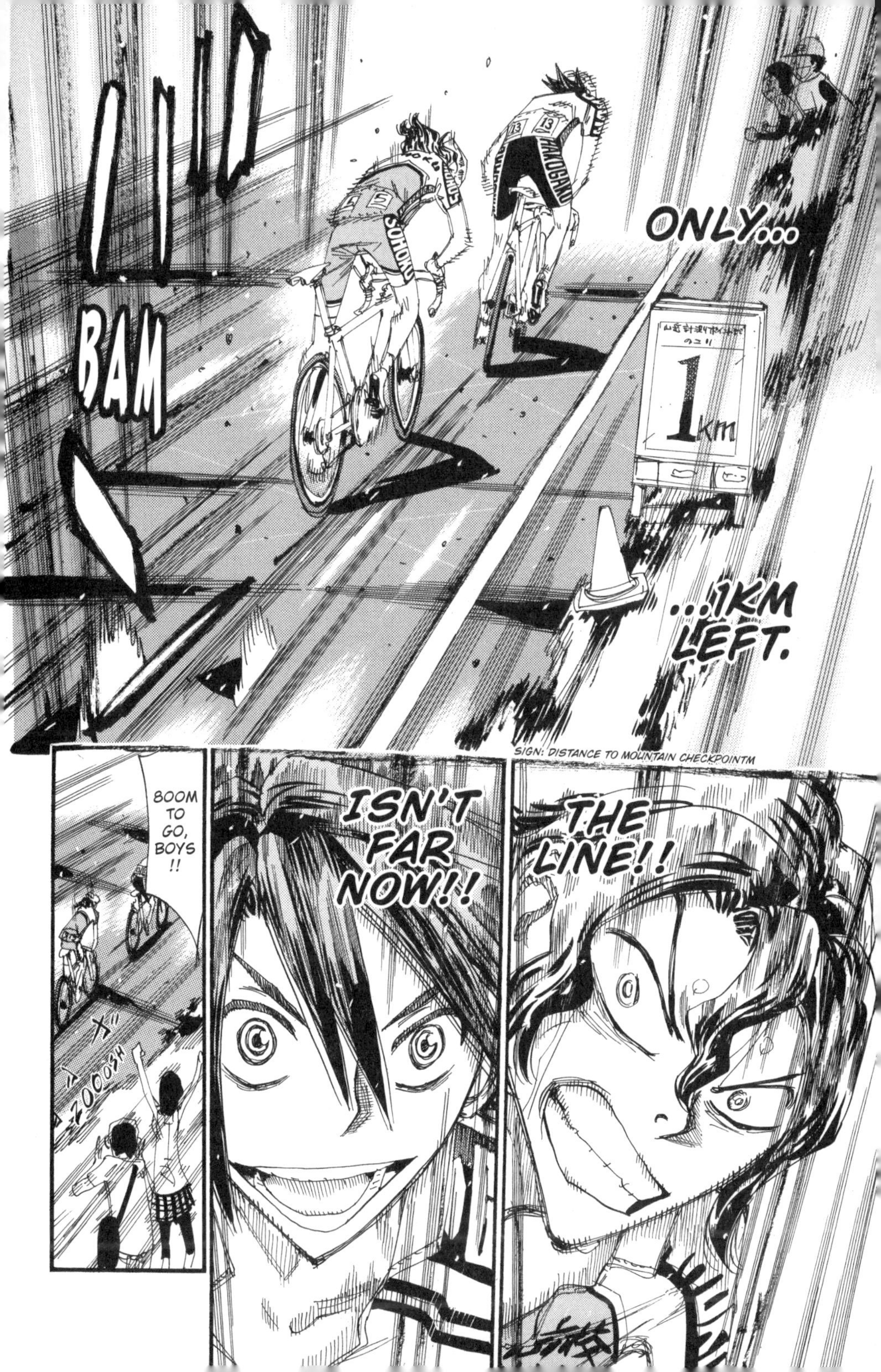

ONLY...
BAM
1km
...1KM LEFT.
SIGN: DISTANCE TO MOUNTAIN CHECKPOINTM
THE LINE!!
ISN'T FAR NOW!!
800M TO GO, BOYS!!
ZOOOSH

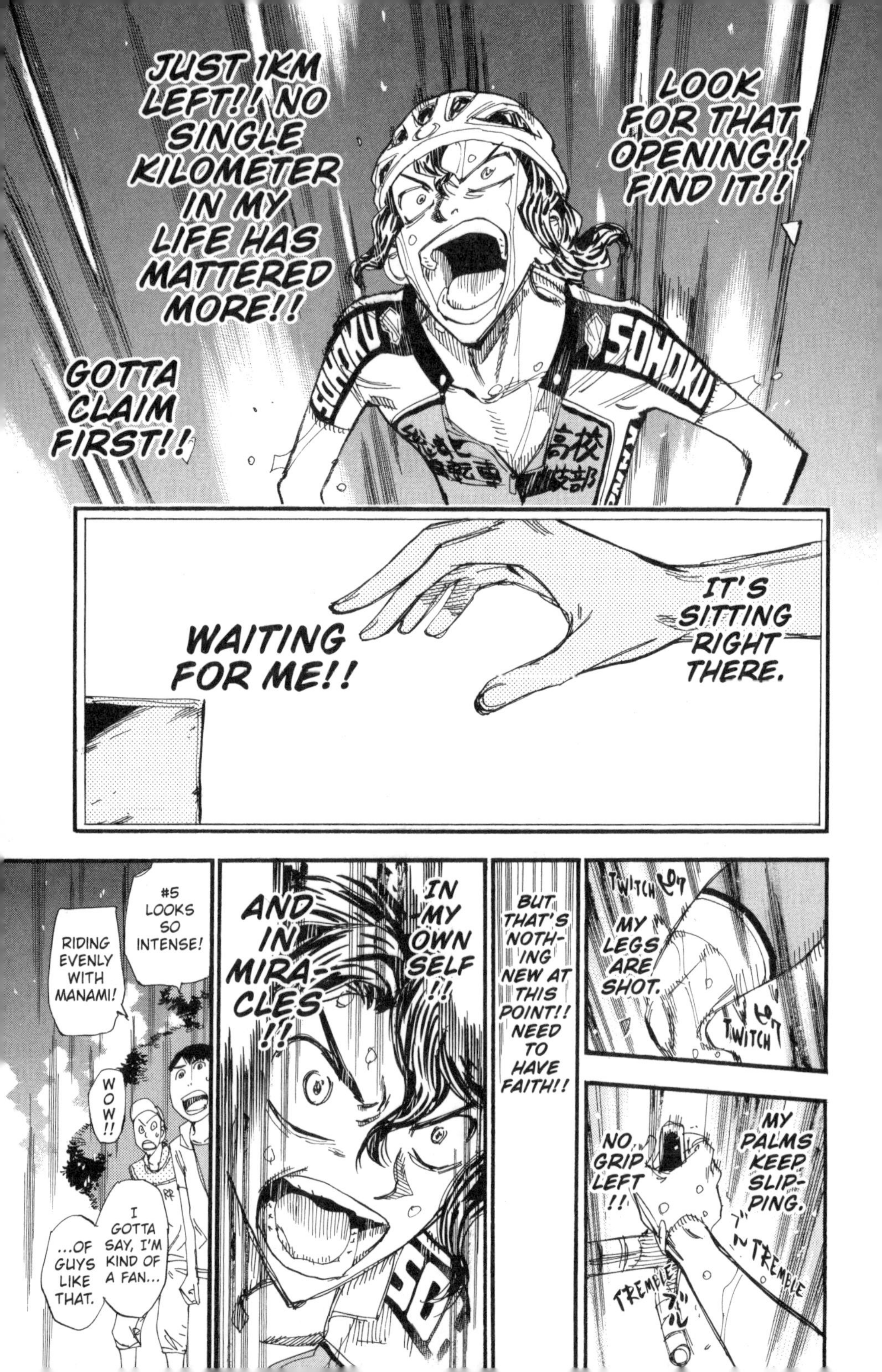
LOOK FOR THAT OPENING!! FIND IT!!
JUST 1KM LEFT!! NO SINGLE KILOMETER IN MY LIFE HAS MATTERED MORE!!
GOTTA CLAIM FIRST!!
IT'S SITTING RIGHT THERE.
WAITING FOR ME!!
TWITCH
MY LEGS ARE SHOT.
TWITCH
MY PALMS KEEP SLIPPING.
NO GRIP LEFT!!
TREMBLE
TREMBLE
BUT THAT'S NOTHING NEW AT THIS POINT!! NEED TO HAVE FAITH!!
IN MY OWN SELF!!
AND IN MIRACLES!!
#5 LOOKS SO INTENSE!
RIDING EVENLY WITH MANAMI!
WOW!!
I GOTTA SAY, I'M KIND OF A FAN...
...OF GUYS LIKE THAT.

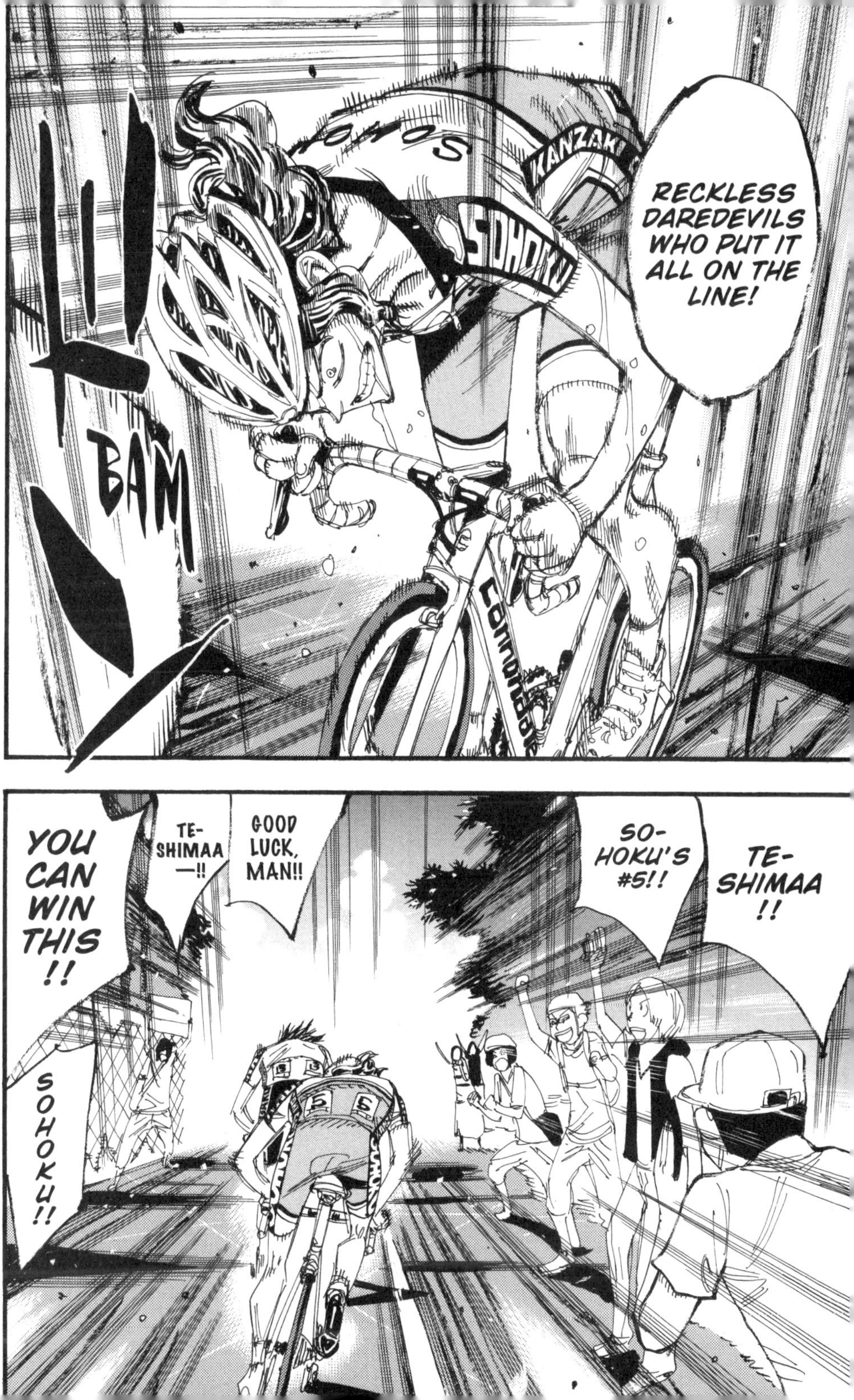
RECKLESS DAREDEVILS WHO PUT IT ALL ON THE LINE!
BAM
TE-SHIMAA!!
SO-HOKU'S #5!!
GOOD LUCK, MAN!!
TE-SHIMAA—!!
YOU CAN WIN THIS!!
SOHOKU!!

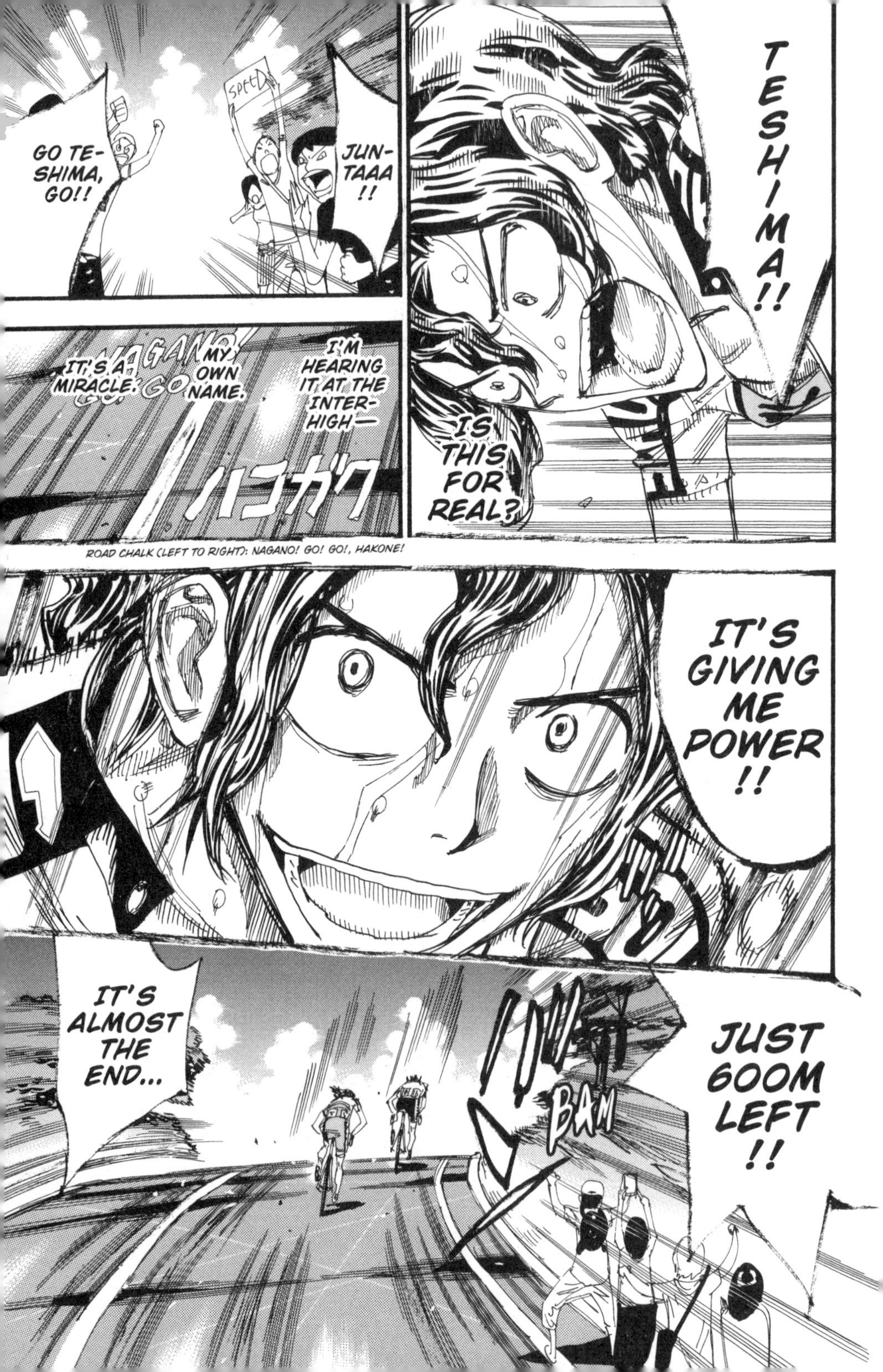
TESHIMA!!
IS THIS FOR REAL?
JUN-TAAA!!
GO TE-SHIMA, GO!!
I'M HEARING IT AT THE INTER-HIGH—
MY OWN NAME.
IT'S A MIRACLE.
ハコガク
ROAD CHALK (LEFT TO RIGHT): NAGANO! GO! GO!, HAKONE!
IT'S GIVING ME POWER!!
JUST 600M LEFT!!
BAM
IT'S ALMOST THE END...

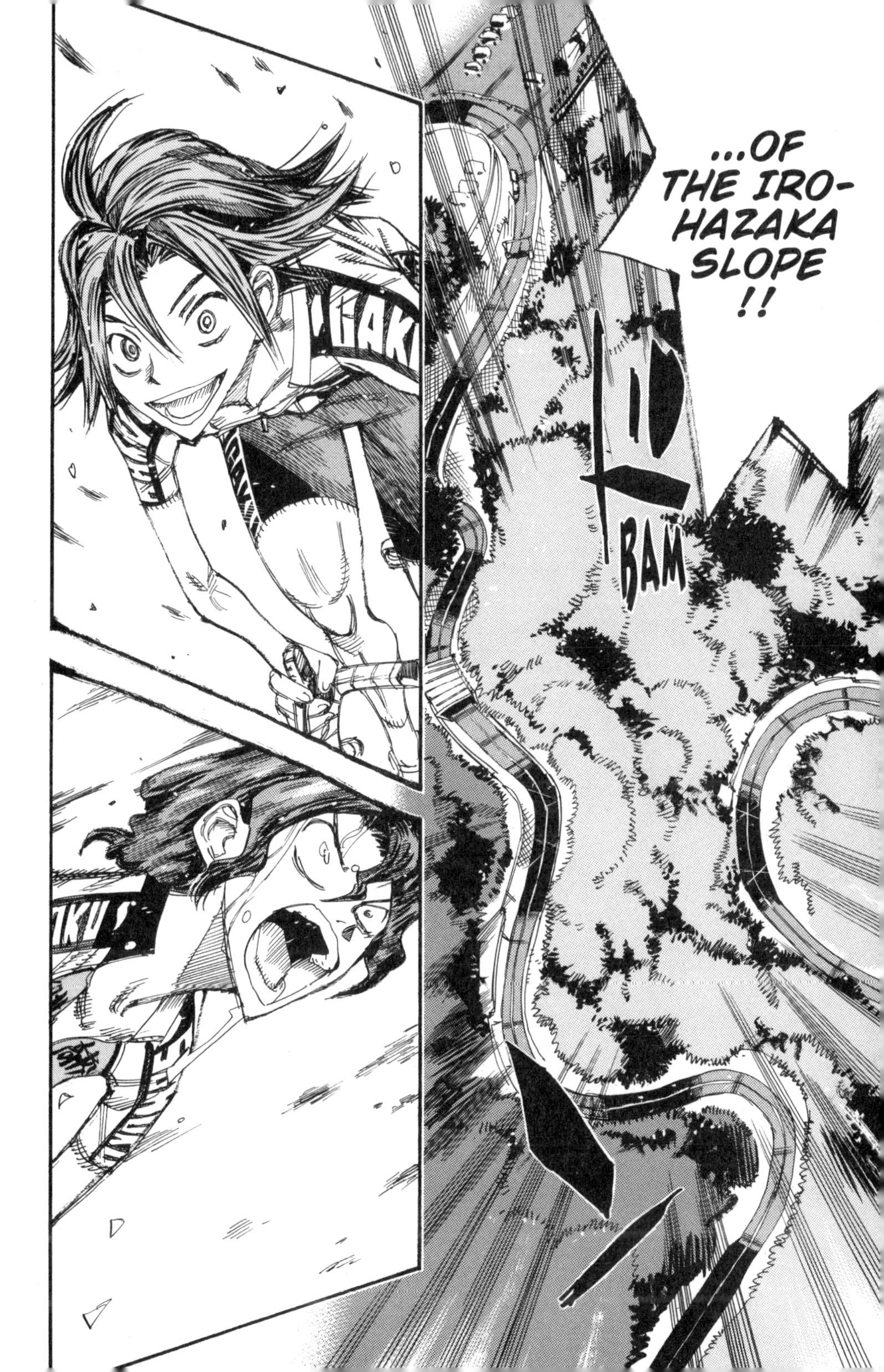
...OF THE IRO-HAZAKA SLOPE !!
BAM

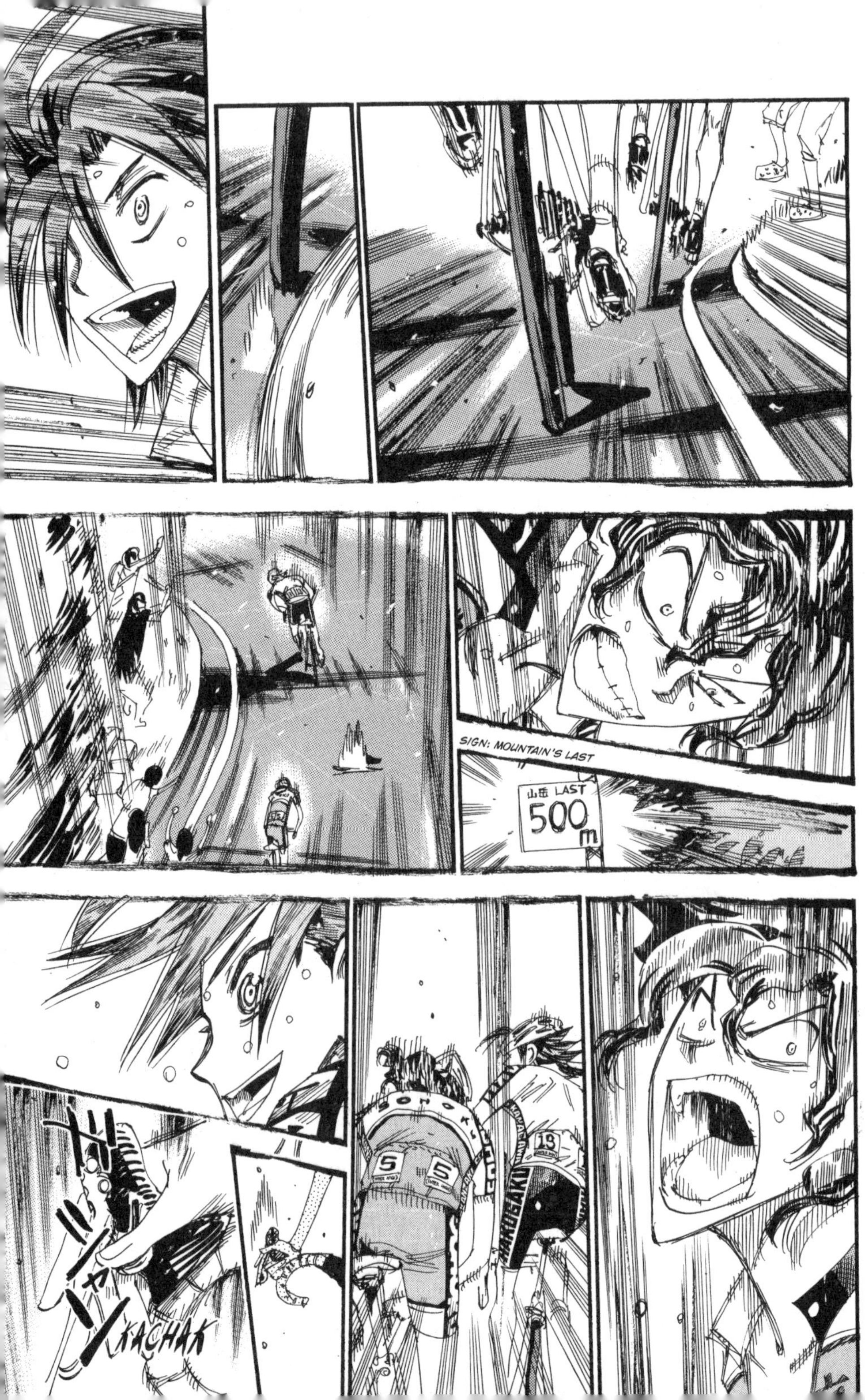
SIGN: MOUNTAIN'S LAST
山岳 LAST
500m
SOHOKU
HAKOGAKU
KACHAK

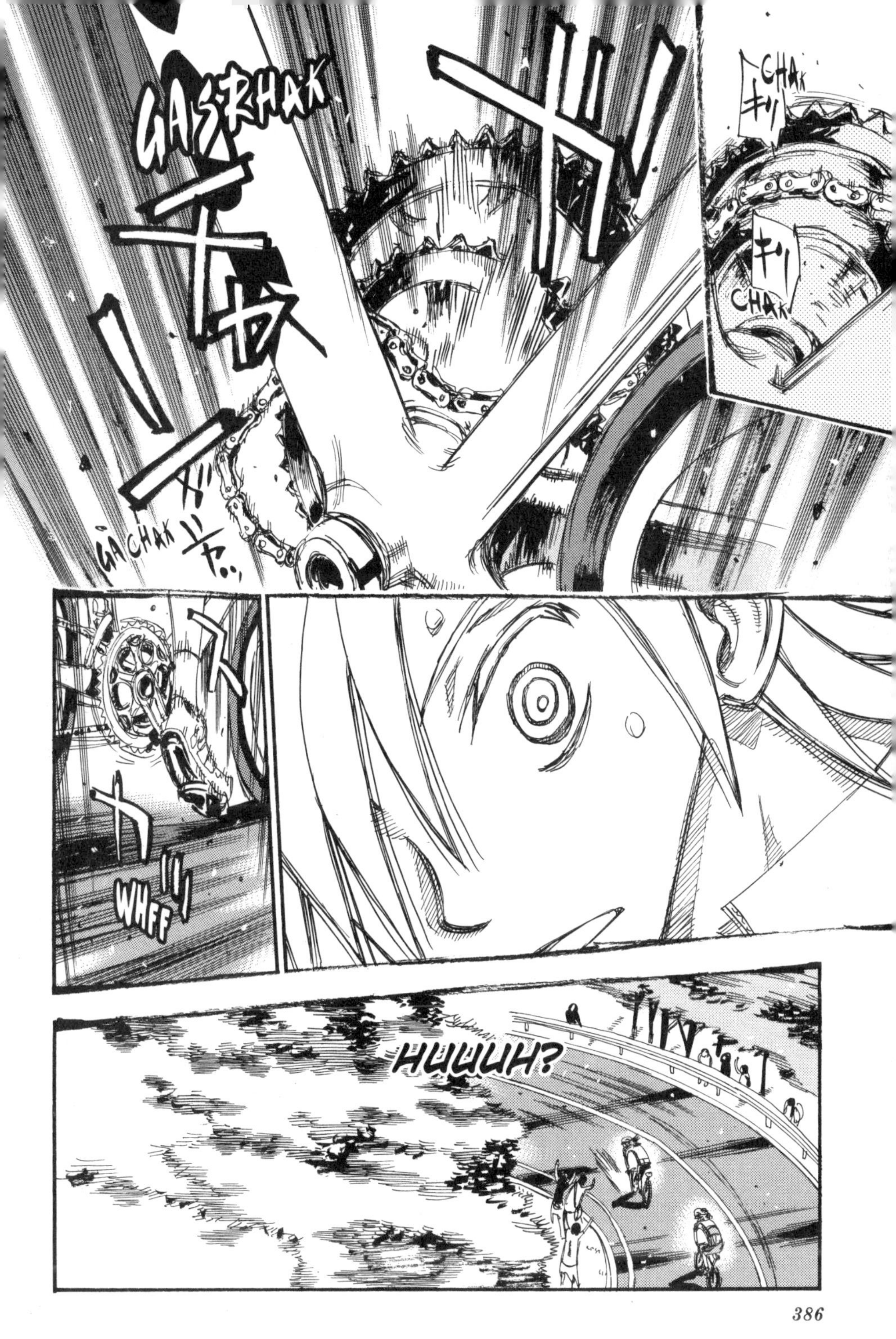
CHAK
CHAK
GASRHAK
GACHAK
WHFF
HUUUH?

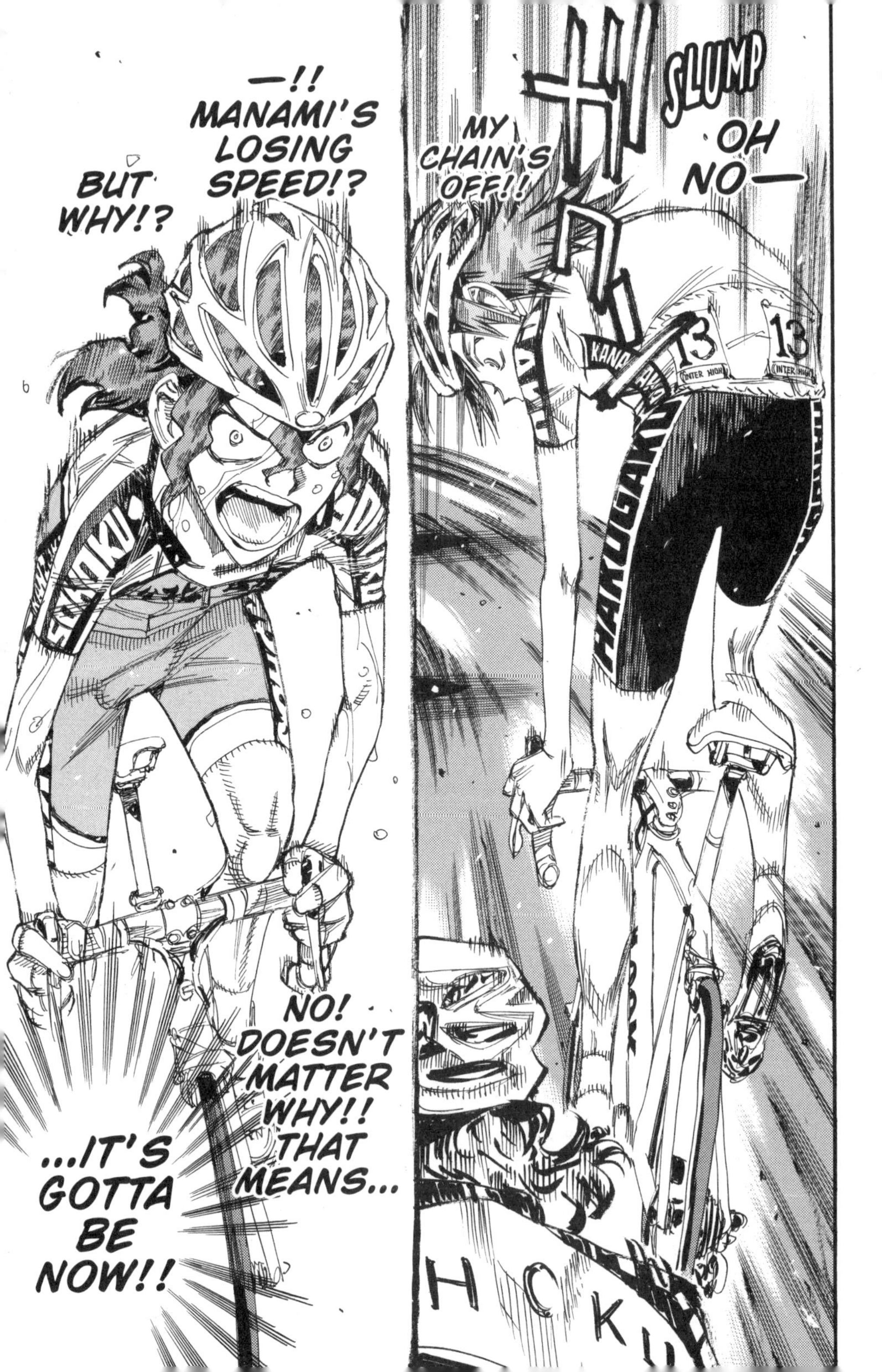
SLUMP
OH NO—
MY CHAIN'S OFF!!
—!! MANAMI'S LOSING SPEED!?
BUT WHY!?
NO! DOESN'T MATTER WHY!! THAT MEANS...
...IT'S GOTTA BE NOW!!

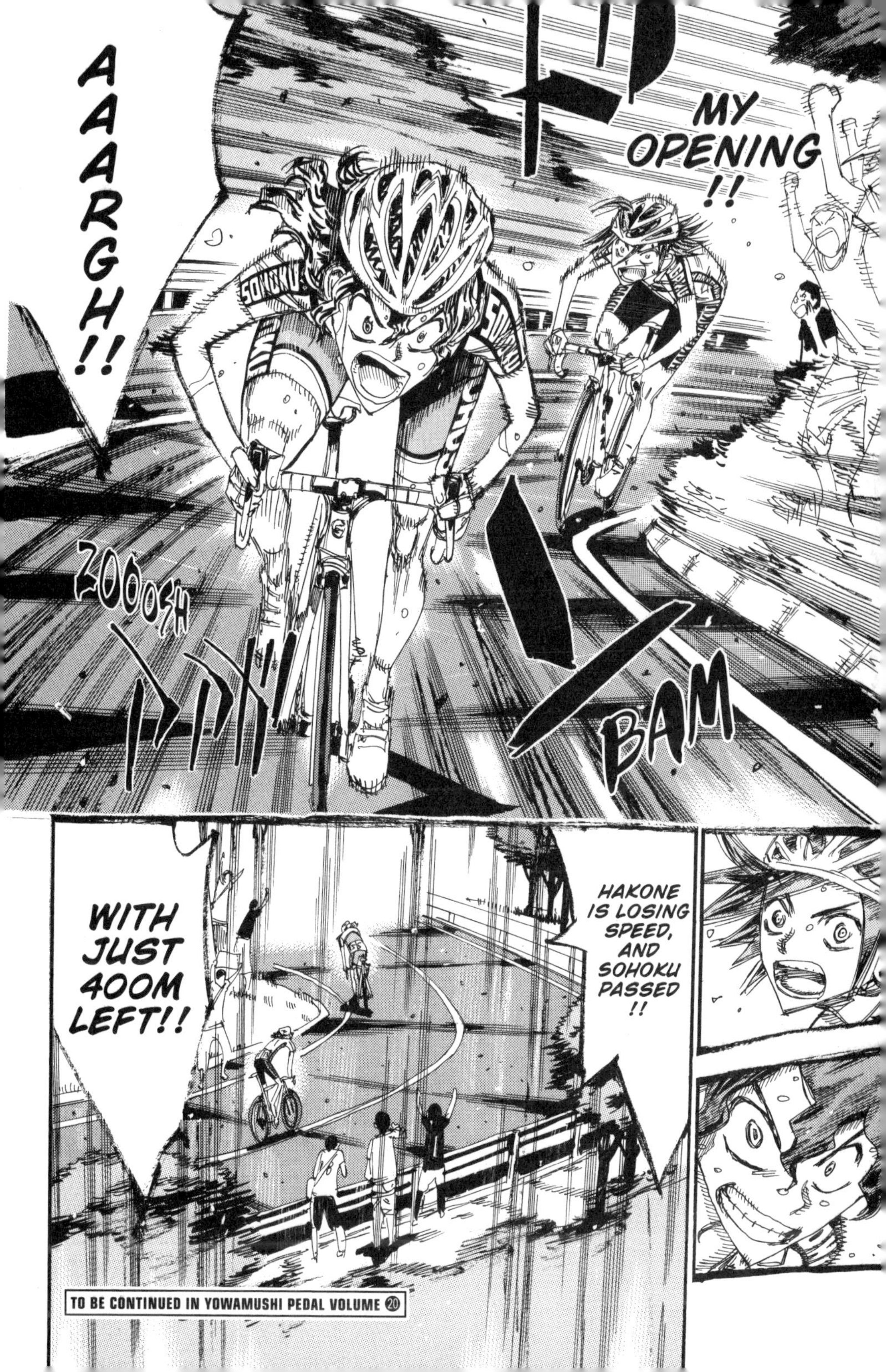
MY OPENING!!
AAAARGH!!
BAM
ZOOOSH
HAKONE IS LOSING SPEED, AND SOHOKU PASSED!!
WITH JUST 400M LEFT!!
TO BE CONTINUED IN YOWAMUSHI PEDAL VOLUME 20

CHECK OUT THE PHOTO AT THE END OF THIS SECTION!

I MADE A CYCLO-CROSS TEAM

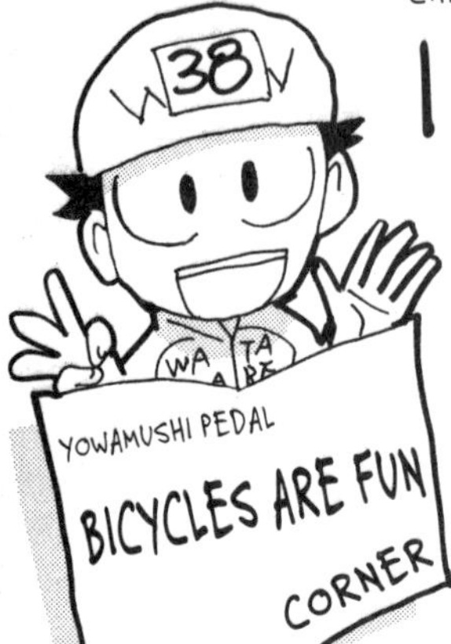
38
WA TA
YOWAMUSHI PEDAL
BICYCLES ARE FUN
CORNER

I TOUCHED ON THIS IN OMNIBUS 17, BUT CYCLO-CROSS IS A **WINTER CYCLING COMPETITION!!** IT'S A CROSS BETWEEN MOUNTAIN BIKING AND ROAD RACES, AND ITS GROWING POPULARITY MEANS THE NUMBER OF PARTICIPANTS IS INCREASING EVERY YEAR.

CYCLO-CROSS RACES ALSO GIVE SPECTATORS AN UP CLOSE AND PERSONAL LOOK AT THE ACTION. IT'S SO SIMPLE TO WATCH A COMPETITION AND CHEER FOR THE RACERS EACH TIME THEY ZIP AROUND THE COURSE.

IT'S EASY ENOUGH TO JOIN THE RACE, BUT THE COMPETITION IN...

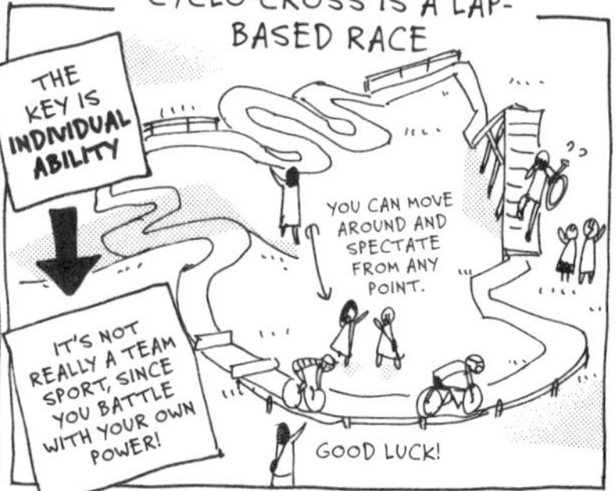
CYCLO-CROSS IS A LAP-BASED RACE
THE KEY IS INDIVIDUAL ABILITY
IT'S NOT REALLY A TEAM SPORT, SINCE YOU BATTLE WITH YOUR OWN POWER!
YOU CAN MOVE AROUND AND SPECTATE FROM ANY POINT.
GOOD LUCK!

...THE TOP...

DIVIDED INTO THREE CATEGORIES:

C1: TOP CATEGORY
C2: INTERMEDIATE
C3: BEGINNERS

THE TOP TWO COMPETITORS MOVE UP A CATEGORY

LOWEST TO HIGHEST LEVEL

...CATEGORY IS THE REAL DEAL!! AFTER ALL, YOU'VE GOT PROFESSIONAL MOUNTAIN BIKERS AND ROAD RACERS JOINING IN THE HIGH-LEVEL ACTION!! BEGINNERS AND TOP-CATEGORY RACERS USE THE EXACT SAME COURSE. HOWEVER, **CATEGORY C3 ONLY LASTS 30 MINUTES, C2 IS 40 MINUTES, AND C1 IS AN ENTIRE HOUR.** YOU'LL SEE A DIFFERENCE IN OVERALL SPEED AND TECHNIQUES! EVEN BEING A SPECTATOR IS LOTS OF FUN, SO I WANT EVERYONE TO KNOW ABOUT THIS SPORT!

SPECTATING FEELS LIKE BEING AT A FESTIVAL! YOU CAN CHEER ON THE RACERS WHILE EATING AND DRINKING! YOU CAN EVEN SHOW YOUR SUPPORT BY RINGING A COWBELL!

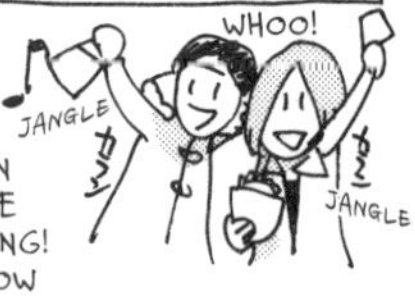
WHOO!
JANGLE
JANGLE

AND ON THAT NOTE—

I MADE MY OWN CYCLO-CROSS TEAM!

WE PARTICIPATED IN THE 2014-2015 CYCLO-CROSS SERIES AND OUR TEAM NAME WAS (HAD TO KEEP IT SIMPLE AND DIRECT! HA-HA!)...

...THE YOWAMUSHI PEDAL CYCLO-CROSS TEAM!!

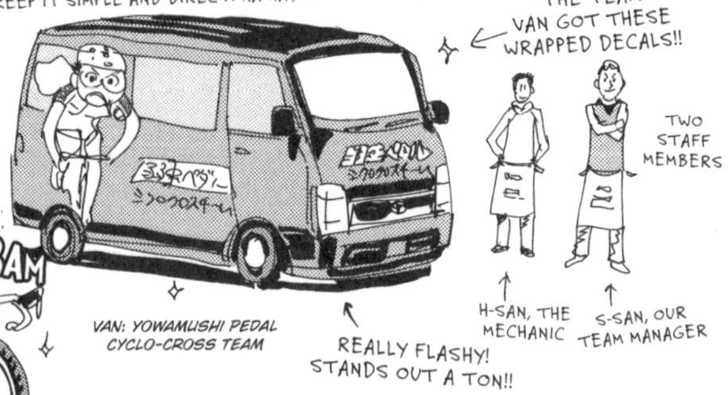
THE TEAM VAN GOT THESE WRAPPED DECALS!!
TWO STAFF MEMBERS
H-SAN, THE MECHANIC
S-SAN, OUR TEAM MANAGER
VAN: YOWAMUSHI PEDAL CYCLO-CROSS TEAM
REALLY FLASHY! STANDS OUT A TON!!

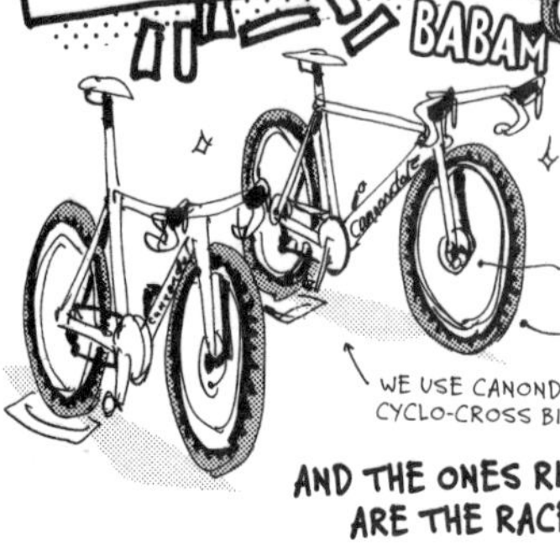
BABAM
DISC BRAKES
CYCLO-CROSS TIRES ARE EXTRA THICK
WE USE CANONDALE CYCLO-CROSS BIKES

AND THE ONES RIDING THESE BIKES... ARE THE RACERS, OF COURSE!!

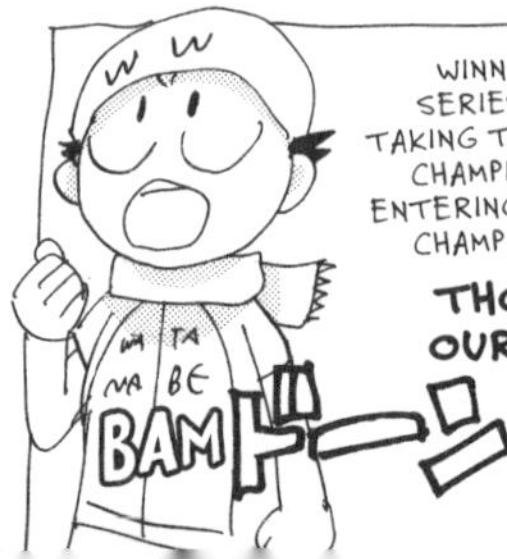
WA TA NA BE
BAM

WINNING THE SERIES TITLE... TAKING THE ALL-JAPAN CHAMPIONSHIPS... ENTERING THE WORLD CHAMPIONSHIPS...

THOSE ARE OUR GOALS!!

AIMING HIGH!!

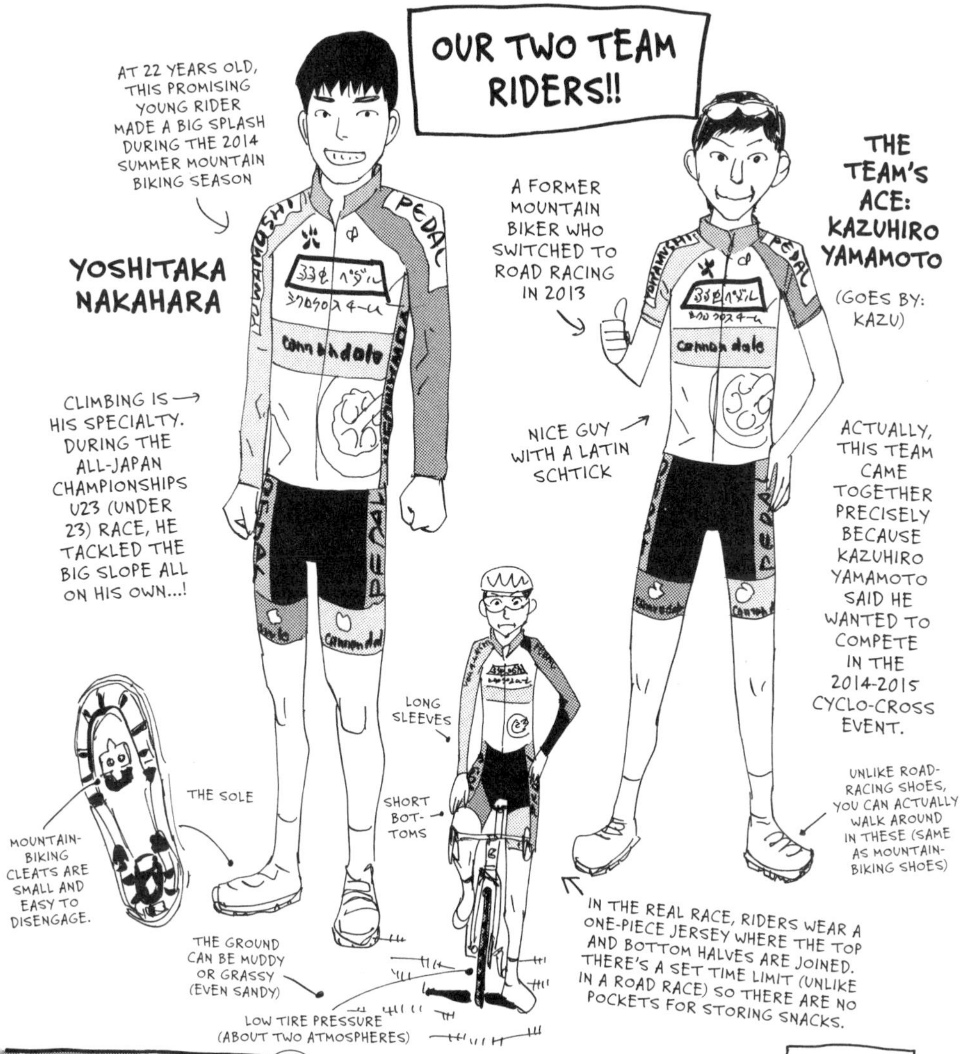
OUR TWO TEAM RIDERS!!
THE TEAM'S ACE: KAZUHIRO YAMAMOTO
(GOES BY: KAZU)
A FORMER MOUNTAIN BIKER WHO SWITCHED TO ROAD RACING IN 2013
NICE GUY WITH A LATIN SCHTICK
ACTUALLY, THIS TEAM CAME TOGETHER PRECISELY BECAUSE KAZUHIRO YAMAMOTO SAID HE WANTED TO COMPETE IN THE 2014-2015 CYCLO-CROSS EVENT.
UNLIKE ROAD-RACING SHOES, YOU CAN ACTUALLY WALK AROUND IN THESE (SAME AS MOUNTAIN-BIKING SHOES)
YOSHITAKA NAKAHARA
AT 22 YEARS OLD, THIS PROMISING YOUNG RIDER MADE A BIG SPLASH DURING THE 2014 SUMMER MOUNTAIN BIKING SEASON
CLIMBING IS HIS SPECIALTY. DURING THE ALL-JAPAN CHAMPIONSHIPS U23 (UNDER 23) RACE, HE TACKLED THE BIG SLOPE ALL ON HIS OWN...!
THE SOLE
MOUNTAIN-BIKING CLEATS ARE SMALL AND EASY TO DISENGAGE.
LONG SLEEVES
SHORT BOT-TOMS
IN THE REAL RACE, RIDERS WEAR A ONE-PIECE JERSEY WHERE THE TOP AND BOTTOM HALVES ARE JOINED. THERE'S A SET TIME LIMIT (UNLIKE IN A ROAD RACE) SO THERE ARE NO POCKETS FOR STORING SNACKS.
THE GROUND CAN BE MUDDY OR GRASSY (EVEN SANDY)
LOW TIRE PRESSURE (ABOUT TWO ATMOSPHERES)

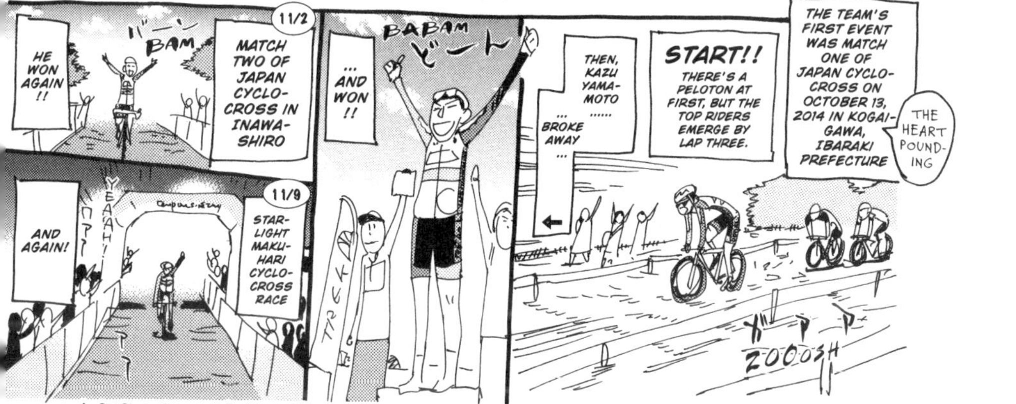
THE TEAM'S FIRST EVENT WAS MATCH ONE OF JAPAN CYCLO-CROSS ON OCTOBER 13, 2014 IN KOGAI-GAWA, IBARAKI PREFECTURE
THE HEART POUNDING
START!!
THERE'S A PELOTON AT FIRST, BUT THE TOP RIDERS EMERGE BY LAP THREE.
THEN, KAZU YAMAMOTO ......
... BROKE AWAY ...
ZOOOSH
BABAM
... AND WON !!
11/2
MATCH TWO OF JAPAN CYCLO-CROSS IN INAWASHIRO
BAM
HE WON AGAIN !!
11/9
STAR-LIGHT MAKU-HARI CYCLO-CROSS RACE
YEAAAH!
AND AGAIN!

↑ A CYCLO-CROSS EVENT HELD AT NIGHT

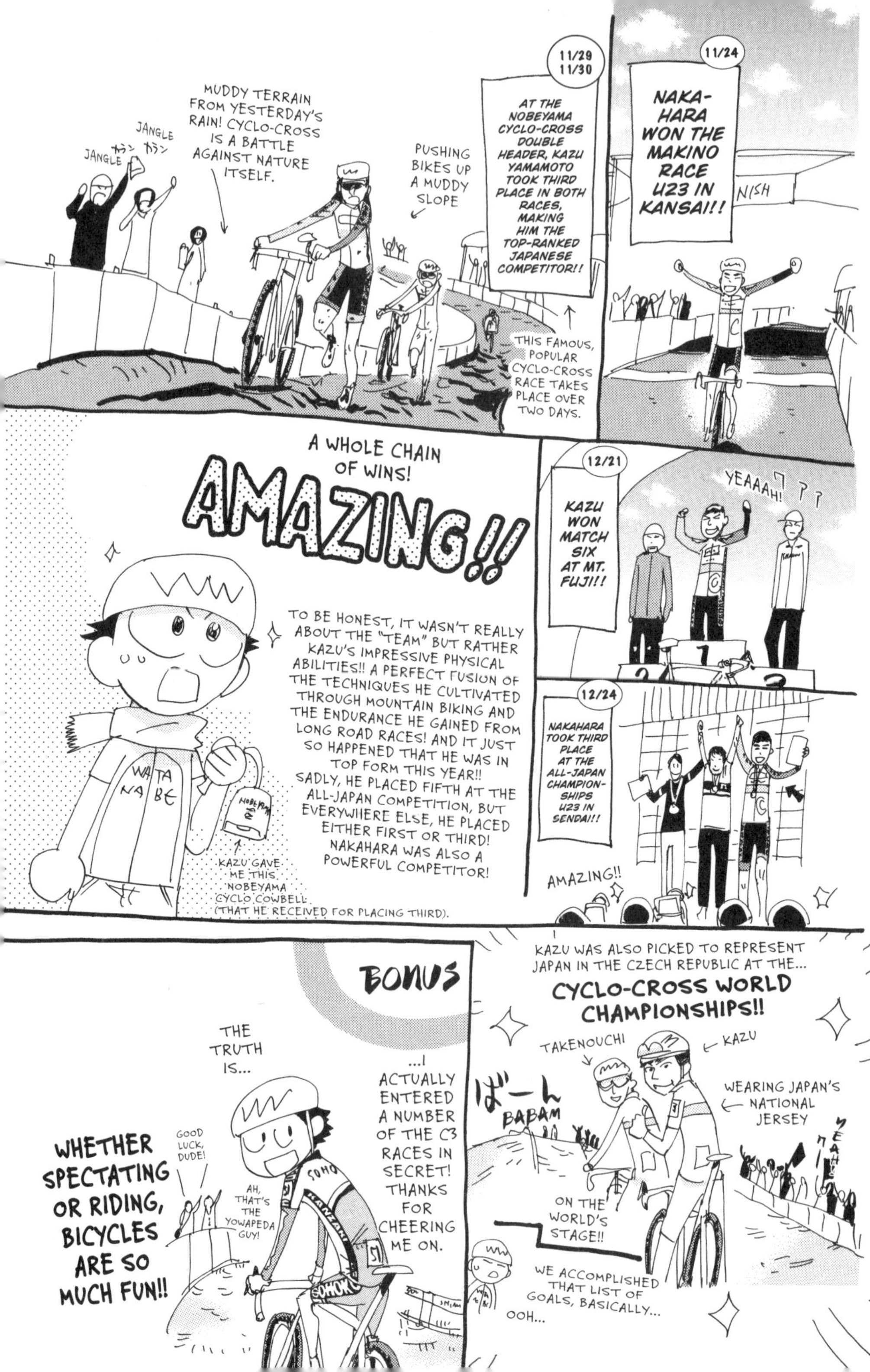

11/24
NAKAHARA WON THE MAKINO RACE U23 IN KANSAI!!
NISH
11/29 11/30
AT THE NOBEYAMA CYCLO-CROSS DOUBLE HEADER, KAZU YAMAMOTO TOOK THIRD PLACE IN BOTH RACES, MAKING HIM THE TOP-RANKED JAPANESE COMPETITOR!!
THIS FAMOUS, POPULAR CYCLO-CROSS RACE TAKES PLACE OVER TWO DAYS.
PUSHING BIKES UP A MUDDY SLOPE
MUDDY TERRAIN FROM YESTERDAY'S RAIN! CYCLO-CROSS IS A BATTLE AGAINST NATURE ITSELF.
JANGLE カラン
JANGLE カラン
12/21
KAZU WON MATCH SIX AT MT. FUJI!!
YEAAAH!
12/24
NAKAHARA TOOK THIRD PLACE AT THE ALL-JAPAN CHAMPIONSHIPS U23 IN SENDAI!!
AMAZING!!
A WHOLE CHAIN OF WINS!
AMAZING!!
TO BE HONEST, IT WASN'T REALLY ABOUT THE "TEAM" BUT RATHER KAZU'S IMPRESSIVE PHYSICAL ABILITIES!! A PERFECT FUSION OF THE TECHNIQUES HE CULTIVATED THROUGH MOUNTAIN BIKING AND THE ENDURANCE HE GAINED FROM LONG ROAD RACES! AND IT JUST SO HAPPENED THAT HE WAS IN TOP FORM THIS YEAR!! SADLY, HE PLACED FIFTH AT THE ALL-JAPAN COMPETITION, BUT EVERYWHERE ELSE, HE PLACED EITHER FIRST OR THIRD! NAKAHARA WAS ALSO A POWERFUL COMPETITOR!
WATANABE
KAZU GAVE ME THIS NOBEYAMA CYCLO COWBELL (THAT HE RECEIVED FOR PLACING THIRD).
KAZU WAS ALSO PICKED TO REPRESENT JAPAN IN THE CZECH REPUBLIC AT THE...
CYCLO-CROSS WORLD CHAMPIONSHIPS!!
ばーん
BABAM
TAKENOUCHI
KAZU
WEARING JAPAN'S NATIONAL JERSEY
YEAH!
ON THE WORLD'S STAGE!!
WE ACCOMPLISHED THAT LIST OF GOALS, BASICALLY...
OOH...
BONUS
THE TRUTH IS...
...I ACTUALLY ENTERED A NUMBER OF THE C3 RACES IN SECRET! THANKS FOR CHEERING ME ON.
GOOD LUCK, DUDE!
AH, THAT'S THE YOWAPEDA GUY!
SOHOKU
WHETHER SPECTATING OR RIDING, BICYCLES ARE SO MUCH FUN!!

National Route 299, Koumi, Minamisaku, Nagano Prefecture

WATARU WATANABE

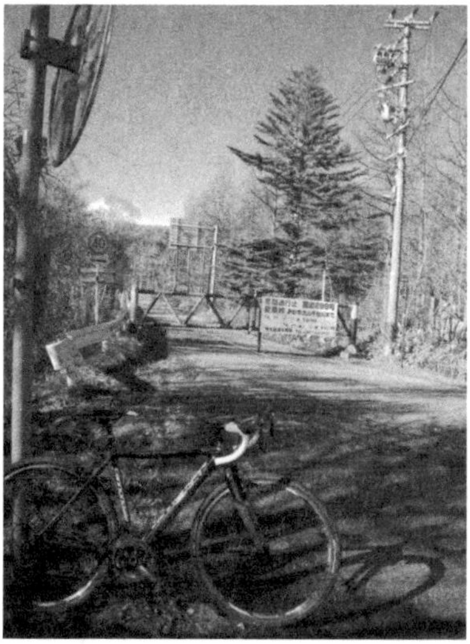

I set out to climb Mt. Nobeyama and reach Mugikusa Pass—the highest point of Route 299, at an elevation of 2,127m. All while making a pit stop for some Cyclo-Cross.

However! At the 1,706m point, the road was closed (for winter). Too bad!

I'll make the full climb next year!

The photo to the right shows the official jersey for the Yowamushi Pedal Cyclo-Cross Team. Flip to the section before this one for more details!

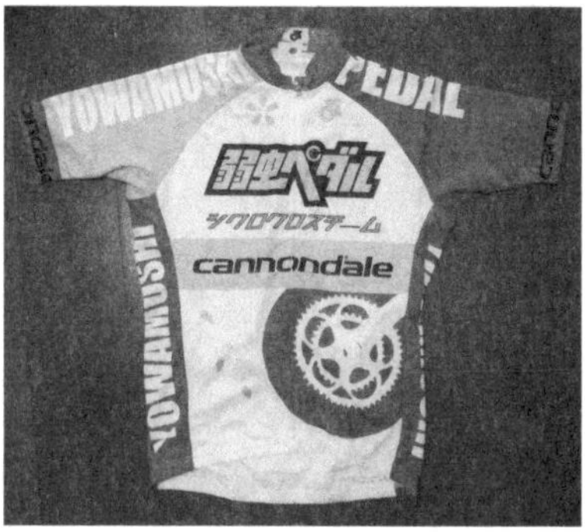
PEDAL
弱虫ペダル
シクロクロスチーム
cannondale
YOWAMUSHI

WATARU WATANABE

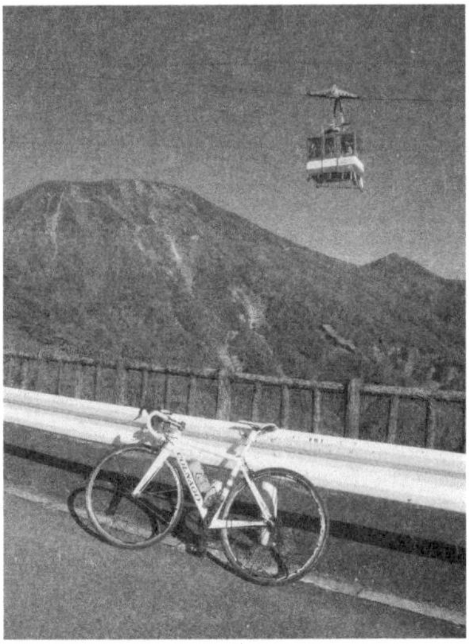

National Route 120, Nikko's Irohazaka Slope, Nikko City, Tochigi Prefecture

Nikko's Irohazaka Slope in Tochigi Prefecture is featured as a part of this Inter-High race.

On one sunny October morning, I did a climb up the slope myself. Higher up on the slope, the leaves were just starting to turn, making for some gorgeous views!

Going by bike allows one to bathe in the crisp, cool, autumn air—which feels amazing!

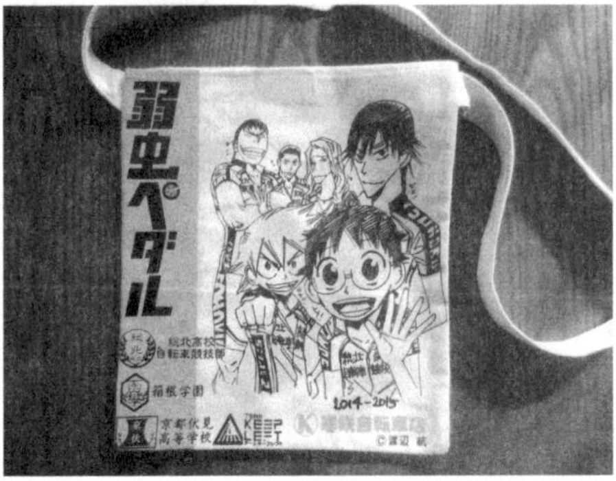
弱虫ペダル
2014-2015

To the left is a photo of this year's annual charity *sacoche*.

Translation Notes

Common Honorifics
-*san*: The Japanese equivalent of Mr./Mrs./Miss. If a situation calls for politeness, this is the fail-safe honorific.
-*kun*: Used most often when referring to boys, this indicates affection or familiarity. Occasionally used by older men among their peers, but it may also be used by anyone referring to a person of lower standing.
-*chan*: An affectionate honorific indicating familiarity used mostly in reference to girls; also used in reference to cute persons or animals of either gender.
-*senpai*: A suffix used to address upperclassmen or more experienced co-workers.
-*shi*: A more formal version of *san* common to written Japanese, it's the default honorific used in newspapers.
no honorific: Indicates familiarity or closeness; if used without permission or reason, addressing someone in this manner would constitute an insult.

A kilometer is approximately 0.6 of a mile.

PAGE 18
I'm in the right: Japanese names are written with characters called *kanji*, which are ideograms that can be pronounced in several different ways. Masakiyo Doubashi's first name is written with a *kanji* character meaning "right," "correct," or "just." So when he says, "I'm in the right," he literally is, because the "right" is in his name.

PAGE 44
Peloton: A cycling term for the "pack," or the main group of riders in a race.

PAGE 117
Domestique: The ace's helper on a cycling team.

PAGE 205
Toshogu Shrine World Heritage Site: The shrines and temples at Nikko form a single complex composed of 103 religious buildings. The complex is located in Tochigi Prefecture in the northern part of the Kanto region (north of Tokyo). The first buildings were constructed in the Nikko mountains in the eighth century by a Buddhist monk.

PAGE 207
Sacoche: A cycling term for a type of saddlebag that can be attached to a bike.

PAGE 266
Goofs: Midousuji primarily uses the term *zaku* in the Japanese version, which means "assorted vegetables for sukiyaki hot pot" but is also the name of the common enemy robot in the anime *Mobile Suit Gundam*. The former meaning refers to the rest of Kyoto-Fushimi being there to serve Midousuji, while the latter refers to how Midousuji treats his teammates as generic and interchangeable.

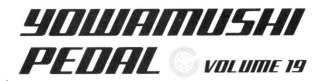

YOWAMUSHI PEDAL VOLUME 19

Read on for a sneak
peek of Volume 20!

YOWAMUSHI
PEDAL

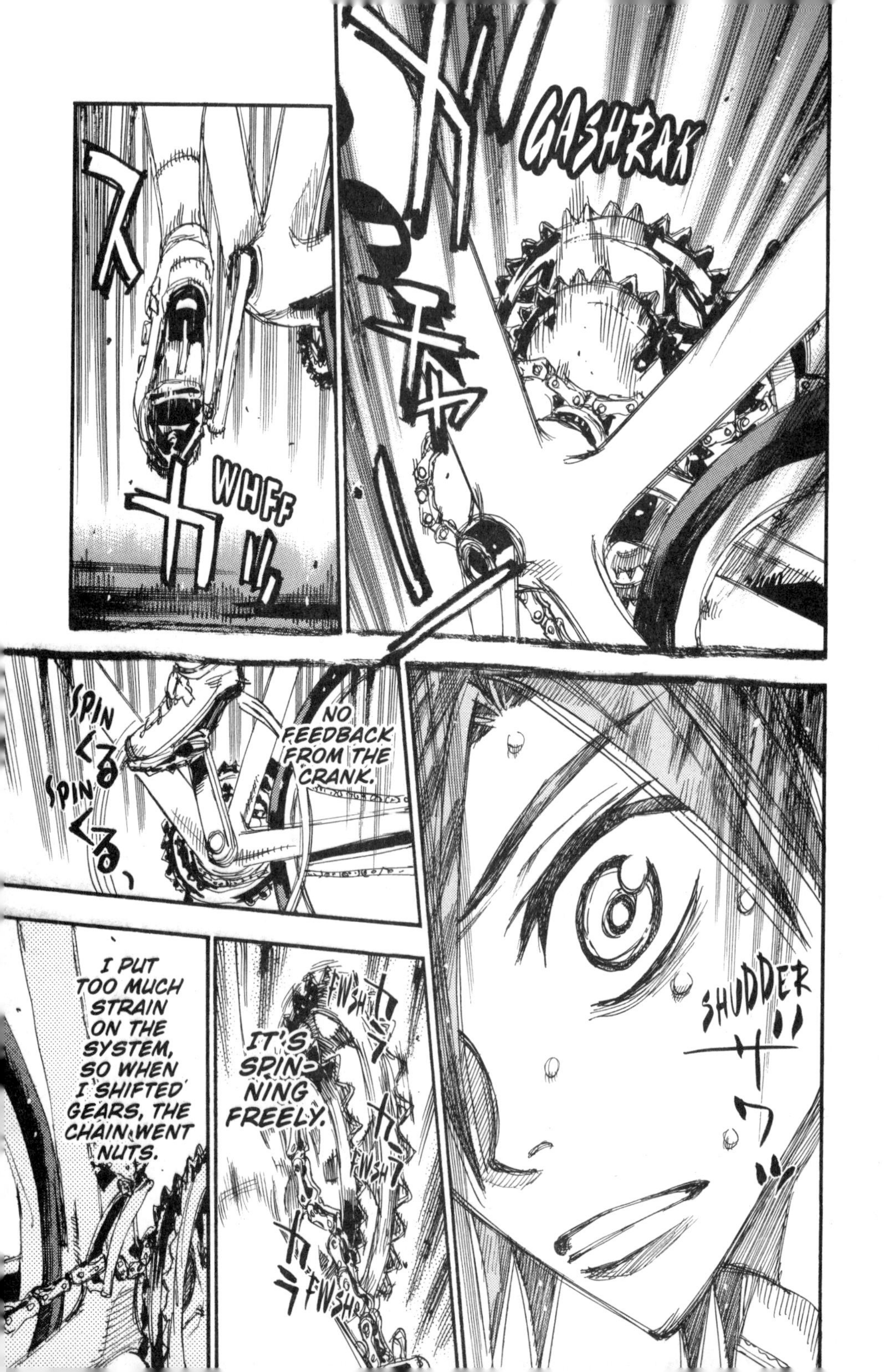
GASHRAK
WHFF
SHUDDER
NO FEEDBACK FROM THE CRANK.
SPIN
くる
SPIN
くる、
IT'S SPIN-NING FREELY.
FWSH
FWSH
FWSH
I PUT TOO MUCH STRAIN ON THE SYSTEM, SO WHEN I SHIFTED GEARS, THE CHAIN WENT NUTS.

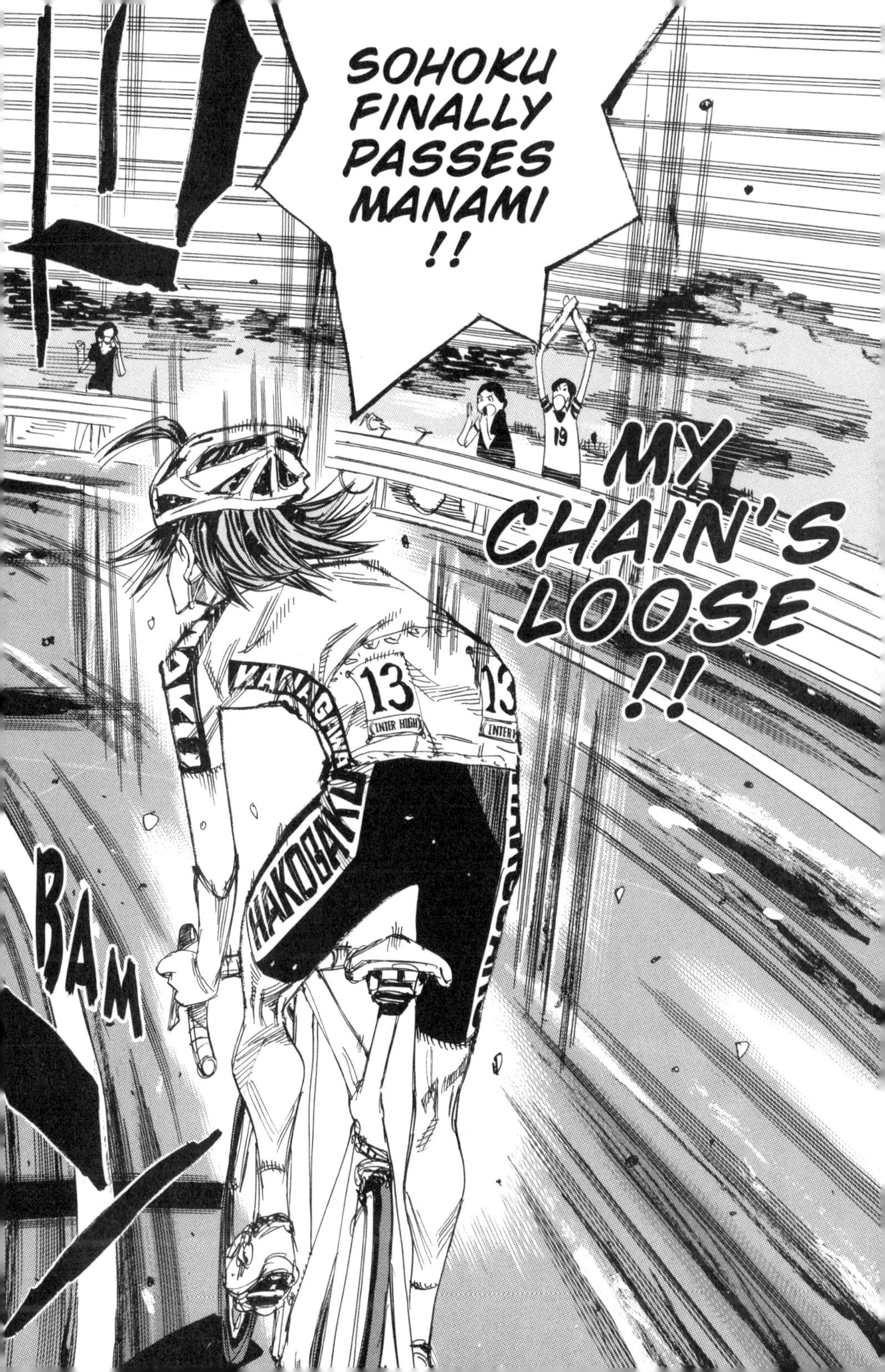
SOHOKU FINALLY PASSES MANAMI !!
MY CHAIN'S LOOSE !!
BAM

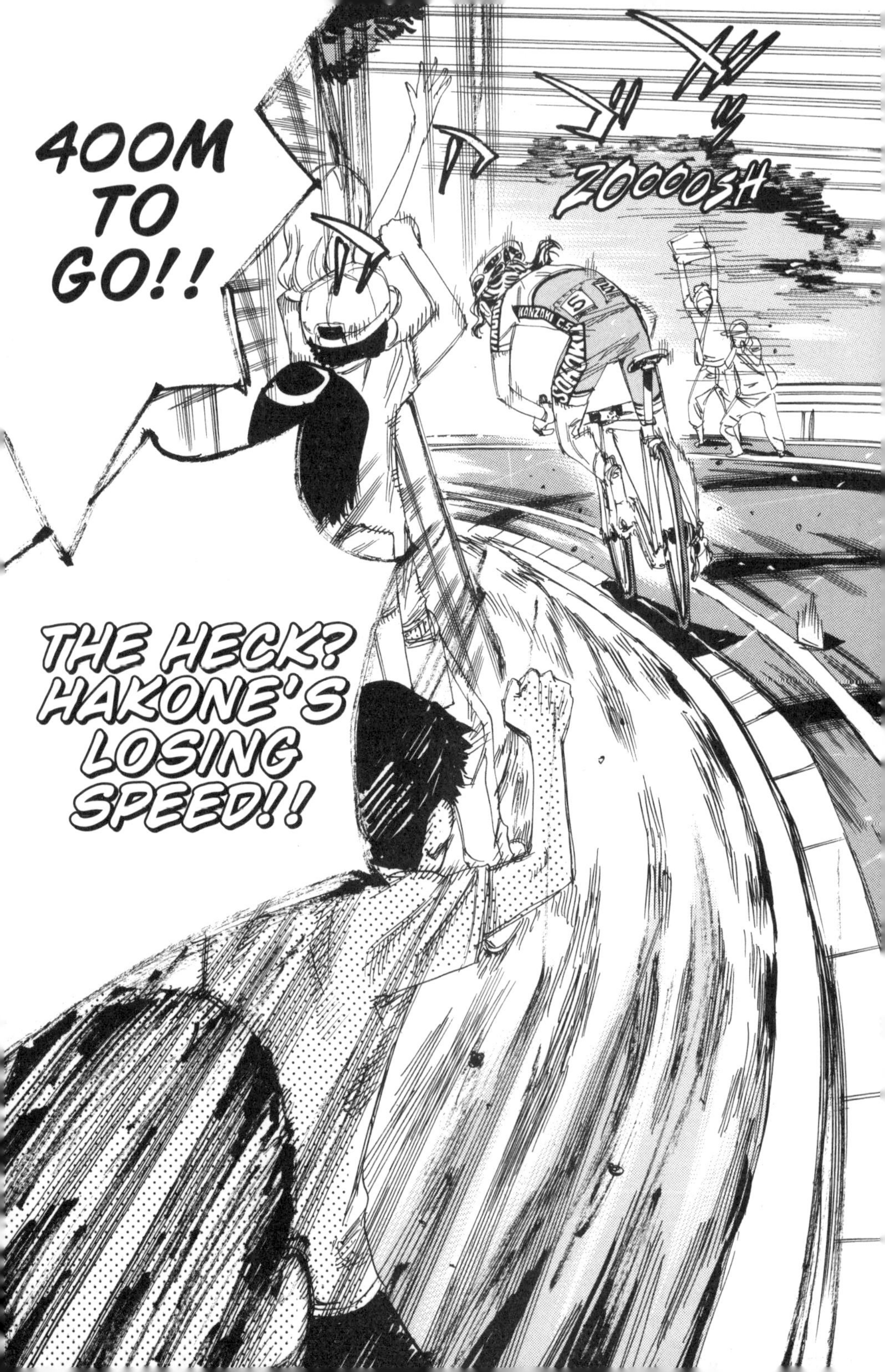
ZOOOOOSH
400M TO GO!!
THE HECK? HAKONE'S LOSING SPEED!!

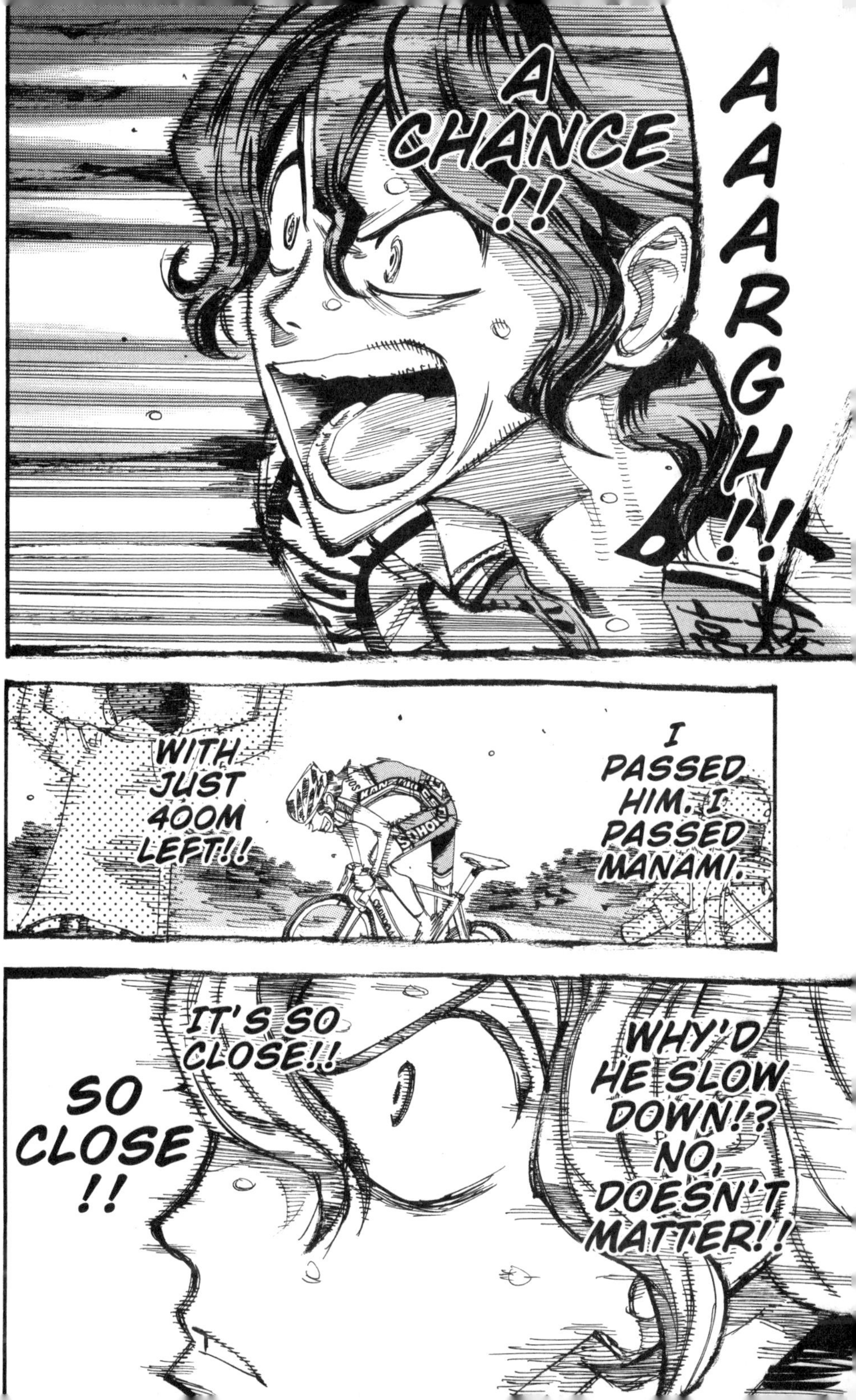
AAAARGH!!
A CHANCE!!
I PASSED HIM. I PASSED MANAMI.
WITH JUST 400M LEFT!!
WHY'D HE SLOW DOWN!? NO, DOESN'T MATTER!!
IT'S SO CLOSE!!
SO CLOSE!!

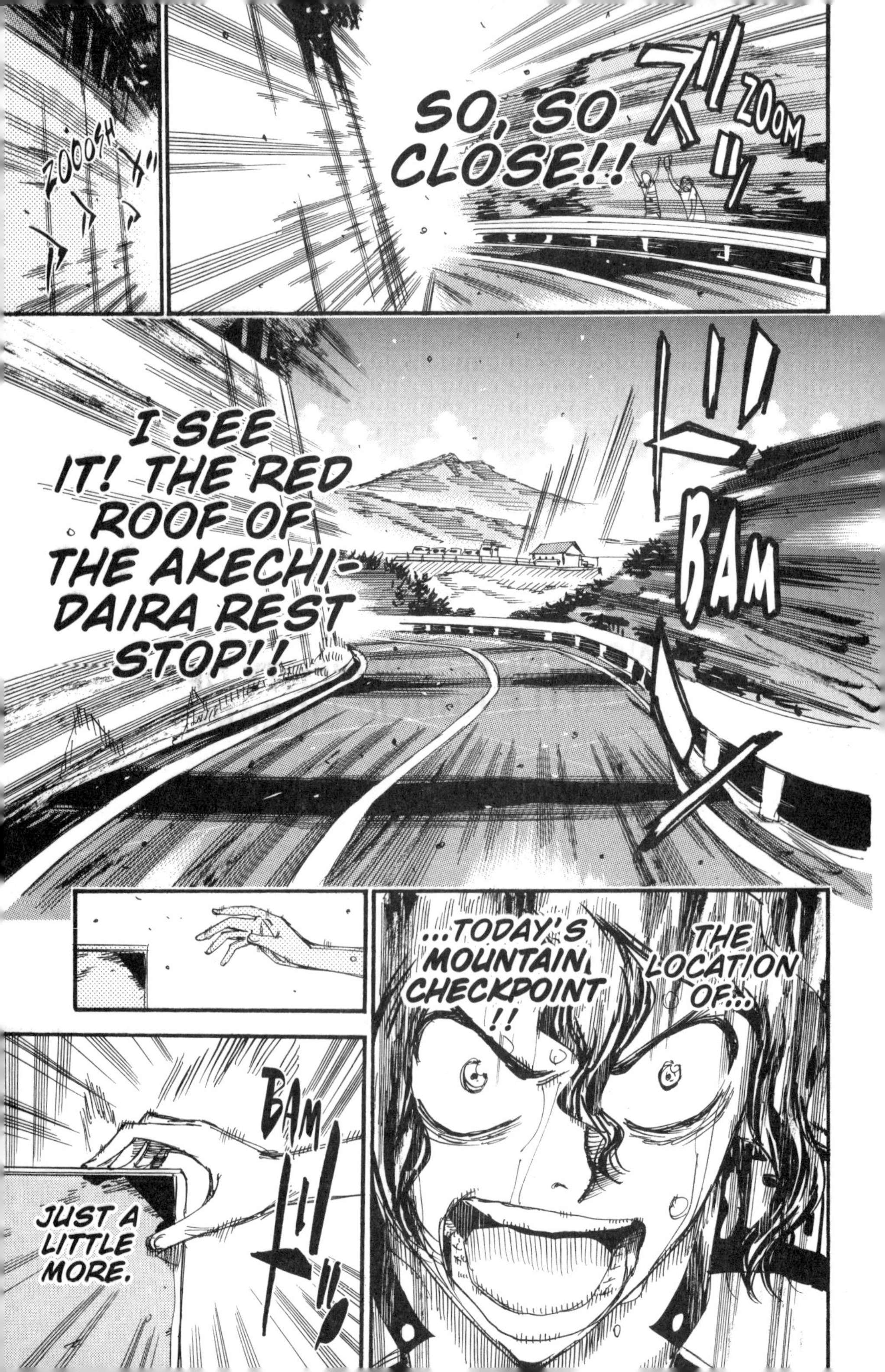
SO, SO CLOSE!!
ZOOM
ZOOOSH
I SEE IT! THE RED ROOF OF THE AKECHI-DAIRA REST STOP!!
BAM
THE LOCATION OF...
...TODAY'S MOUNTAIN CHECKPOINT!!
BAM
JUST A LITTLE MORE.

YOWAMUSHI PEDAL ⑲

WATARU WATANABE

Translation: Caleb D. Cook

Lettering: Rachel J. Pierce

This book is a work of fiction. Names, characters, places, and incidents are the product of the author's imagination or are used fictitiously. Any resemblance to actual events, locales, or persons, living or dead, is coincidental.

YOWAMUSHI PEDAL Volume 37, 38
© 2014, 2015 Wataru Watanabe
All rights reserved.
First published in Japan in 2014, 2015 by Akita Publishing Co., Ltd., Tokyo.
English translation rights arranged with Akita Publishing Co., Ltd. through Tuttle-Mori Agency, Inc., Tokyo.

English translation © 2022 by Yen Press, LLC

Yen Press
150 West 30th Street, 19th Floor
New York, NY 10001

Visit us at yenpress.com
facebook.com/yenpress
twitter.com/yenpress
yenpress.tumblr.com

First Yen Press Edition: January 2022

Yen Press is an imprint of Yen Press, LLC.
The Yen Press name and logo are trademarks of Yen Press, LLC.

The publisher is not responsible for websites (or their content) that are not owned by the publisher.

Library of Congress Control Number: 2015960124

ISBNs: 978-1-9753-3751-3 (paperback)
       978-1-9753-3752-0 (ebook)

10 9 8 7 6 5 4 3 2 1

WOR

Printed in the United States of America